THE HISTORY
OF THE
LEWIS AND CLARK
EXPEDITION

THE HISTORY
OF THE
LEWIS AND CLARK
EXPEDITION

BY
MERIWETHER LEWIS
AND
WILLIAM CLARK

EDITED BY
Elliott Coues

IN THREE VOLUMES
Volume II

DOVER PUBLICATIONS, INC.
NEW YORK

Published in Canada by General Publishing Company,
Ltd., 30 Lesmill Road, Don Mills, Toronto, Ontario.
Published in the United Kingdom by Constable and
Company, Ltd.

This Dover edition is an unabridged republication of
the four-volume edition published by Francis P. Harper
in 1893. The fourth volume of the Harper edition
consisted of illustrations and the Index; in this Dover
edition five illustrations and the Index are appended to
Volume III, and the remaining illustrations are arranged
on large plates inserted at the end of Volumes I and II.

International Standard Book Number: 0-486-21269-6
Library of Congress Catalog Card Number: 64-15500

Manufactured in the United States of America
Dover Publications, Inc.
180 Varick Street
New York, N.Y. 10014

CONTENTS

OF

THE SECOND VOLUME.

HISTORY OF THE EXPEDITION.

CHAPTER XVII.

CHAPTER XVIII.

CHAPTER XIX.

CHAPTER XX.

CHAPTER XXI.

CHAPTER XXII.

CHAPTER XXIII.

CHAPTER XXIV.

HISTORY OF THE EXPEDITION

under the command of

LEWIS AND CLARK

CHAPTER X.

THE MISSOURI FROM MARIA'S RIVER TO THE GREAT FALLS.

Captain Lewis names the north fork he explored Maria's river, being persuaded it is not the Missouri, and returns to the camp of the main party—Captain Clark's exploration of the south fork—J. Field treed by a bear—Tansy river named and described—Consultation on the route to be pursued—Doubts—Decision that the south fork is the Missouri—Determination to ascend it—Construction of a cache—Captain Lewis sets out with four men up the south fork—Is taken sick—Fishes caught—A fine prospect of the Rocky mountains—A different kind of cottonwood—Vast numbers of buffalo—Discovery of the Great Falls of the Missouri, June 13th, 1805—The Falls described—A man sent back to inform Captain Clark of the discovery—Further account of the Falls—The lone eagle's nest—A bear chases Captain Lewis into the river—He examines a river supposed to be Medicine river—Encounters a strange animal—Is charged by buffalo bulls—Sleeps with a rattlesnake—His messenger returns from the main party, having communicated the discovery of the Falls—Captain Clark ascends the south fork to join Captain Lewis—Shields' river—Consultation over a portage—Making carriages—Sacajawea sick—A sulphur spring—Portage creek—Captain Clark with five men explores for a portage—Cache on Portage creek—Hunting parties sent out—Captain Clark returns, having determined the portage—Medicine river—White Bear islands.

SATURDAY, June 8th, 1805. It continued to rain moderately all night, and the morning was cloudy till about ten o'clock, when it cleared off and became a fine day. They breakfasted about sunrise and then proceeded down the river in the same way as they had done yesterday, except that the traveling was somewhat better, as they had not so often to wade, though they passed some very dangerous bluffs. The only timber to be found is in the low grounds which are occasionally on the river, and these are the haunts of innumerable birds, which, when the sun began to shine, sang very delightfully. Among these birds they distinguished the brown thrush, robin, turtle-dove, linnet, goldfinch, large and small blackbird, wren, and some others. As they came along, the whole party were of opinion that this river was the true Missouri; but Captain Lewis, being fully persuaded that it was neither the main stream, nor that which it would be advisable to ascend, gave it the name of Maria's river.[1] After traveling all day they reached camp about five o'clock in the afternoon, and found Captain Clark and the party very anxious for their safety. As they had stayed two days longer than had been expected, and as Captain Clark had returned at the appointed time, it was feared that they had met with some accident.

(*p. 252*)[2] Captain Clark, on setting out with five men on the 4*th*, went seven miles on a course S. 25° W. to a spring; thence he went S. 20.° W. for eight miles to the river, where was an island, from which he proceeded in a course N. 45° W., and approached the river at the distances of 3, 5, and 13 miles,[3] at which place they

[1] So Lewis E 49, and Clark's map, in the possessive case, with *z* sound of the *s*, though in this country everyone calls the river *Marias*, with soft *c* sound of the *s*, a rhyme to *Josias*, and it is so on most maps. The river is named in the following passage, of extreme interest : " I deturmined to give it a name and in honour of Miss Maria W—d. called it Maria's River. it is true that the hue of the waters of this turbulent and troubled stream but illy comport with the pure celestial virtues and amiable qualifications of that lovely fair one ; but on the other hand it is a noble river ; one destined to become in my opinion an object of contention between the two great powers of America and Great Britin, with rispect to the adjustment of the North westwardly boundary of the former ; and that it will become one of the most interesting brances [branches] of the Missouri," etc., Lewis E 48, 49. The Ulyssean young captain is not successful in concealing the name of " that lovely fair one " ; for " W—d." spells " Wood " without any vowels. This lady was Miss Maria Wood, a cousin of his, afterward Mrs. M. Clarkson. There were a number of intermarriages between the Virginian Meriwethers, Lewises, and Woods ; but one such, the prospect of which Captain Lewis may have cherished in his heart of hearts, was destined never to be.

[2] Here the narrative goes back to June 4th, and takes up Captain Clark's exploration of the " south fork," *i. e.*, the Missouri itself, to June 8th inclusive. The codex continues in Lewis' hand, but is copied by him from a journal of Clark's, who writes in the first person singular. The five men with Captain Clark were Sergeant Gass, Privates R. and J. Fields and Shannon, and his servant York.

[3] Not clear, being too much condensed from the codex, which has nearly a page for this sentence. Captain Clark proceeds, from the point of junction of Maria's river with the Missouri, up the latter, but across country, on the courses said. He strikes the Missouri at 3, 5, 9, and 13 miles, and camps near the site of Fort Benton, which is now 12 miles by the trail, and 18 by water, above the mouth of Maria's river. The spring mentioned is Grog spring, at the Cracon

camped in an old Indian lodge made of sticks and bark.   In crossing the plains they observed several herds of buffalo, some mule-deer, antelopes, and wolves.   The river is rapid and closely hemmed in by high bluffs, crowded with bars of gravel, with little timber on the low grounds, and none on the highlands.   Near the camp this evening a white bear attacked one of the men [J. Fields], whose gun, happening to be wet, would not go off; he instantly made toward a tree, but was so closely pursued that as he ascended the tree he struck the bear with his foot.   The bear, not being able to climb, waited till he should be forced to come down; and as the rest of the party were separated from him by a perpendicular cliff of rocks, which they could not descend, it was not in their power to give him any assistance.   Fortunately, however, at last the bear became frightened at their cries and firing, and released the man.   In the afternoon it rained, and during the night there fell both rain and snow.

In the morning, *June 5th*, the hills to the S.E. were covered with snow, and the rain continued.   They proceeded in a course N.[4] 20° W., near the river, for several miles, till at the distance of 11 miles they reached a ridge, from the top of which, on the north side, they could plainly discern a mountain to the S. and W., at a great distance, covered with snow; a high ridge, projecting from the mountains to the

du Nez.   Between this point and Benton he discovers Shonkin creek (see Snow river, beyond), as duly noted in the codex.   Fort Benton is historic, long famous as the assumed head of steamboat navigation of the Missouri—not that boats could not steam a little further, but that there was then no place to go to.   It is supposed to be by water 339 miles above Milk river, 500 above the Yellowstone, and 805 above Bismarck; by the trail to Buford 378 miles, to Fort Shaw (on Medicine or Sun river) 63 miles.   The fort was built on the north or left bank of the Missouri, and just above it once stood Fort Campbell, near the spot where Captain Clark camps to-night.

[4] Read S. 20° W., though the text agrees with the codex.   This correction is confirmed by Lewis E 51, lower down on same page, where we read: " As this river [Missouri] continued it's width debth and rappidity, and the course West of *South*, going up further would be useless; I [Clark] therefore determined to return and accordingly set out on a course through the plain N. 30° E., and struck the little Tanzey [Teton] river at 20 mls.," etc.   N. 20° W. would have taken Captain Clark nearly at a right angle from the Missouri.

southeast, approached the river on the southeast side, forming some cliffs of a dark hard stone.   They also saw that
the river ran for a great distance west of south, with a rapid
current; from which, as well as from its continuing of the
same width and depth, Captain Clark thought it useless to
advance any further.   He there- (*p. 253*) fore returned across
the level plain in a direction N. 30° E., and reached, at the
distance of 20 miles, the little river [Teton] which is already
mentioned as falling into the north fork [Maria's], and to
which they gave the name of Tansy[5] river, from the great
quantity of that herb growing on its banks.   Here they
dined, and then proceeded a few miles, by a place where
the Tansy breaks through a high ridge on its north side,
and camped.

The next day, *June 6th*, the weather was cold, raw, and
cloudy, with a high northeast wind.   They set out early,
down the Tansy, whose low grounds resemble precisely,
except as to extent, those of the Missouri before it
branches, containing a great proportion of a species of cottonwood [*Populus angustifolia*], with a leaf like that of the
wild cherry.   After halting at twelve o'clock for dinner,
they ascended the plain, and at five o'clock reached the
camp through the rain, which had fallen without intermis-

[5] Tansy, Tansey, Tanzy, or Tanzey of the codices ; on the return trip next
year noted as Tansy or Rose river.   This is the Teton, now usually so called,
but not the Teton of L. and C.; also Breast river, and sometimes charted by a
Blackfoot name, Mone-e-kis or Monekis.   It is thus designated from the
Woman's Breast, or Teton Butte, a remarkably conspicuous landmark on its
upper reaches, some 200 feet high, and 125 miles by the trail from Fort Benton.
The word *Teton* is the French *téton*, breast, teat, nipple, and has nothing to do
with Teton, Titon, or Titonwan, aboriginal name of certain Sioux tribes, for
whom L. and C. named *their* Teton river.   It is applied to a number of conical
hills in various parts of the West.   The Teton heads in the Continental Divide
by numerous affluents which join in two main forks, and these in one stream,
which from about 112° W. long. winds in course slightly N. of E. to its entrance
into Maria's river.   On two of the most important and generally reliable maps
before me, the Teton is represented as having ruptured the narrow isthmus
of the Cracon du Nez, and fallen into the Missouri instead of into Maria's
river ; but I have satisfied myself, by advices direct from the spot, that this
is an error.

sion since noon. During his [Captain Clark's] absence the [main] party had been occupied in dressing skins; and, being able to rest themselves, were nearly freed from their lameness and swollen feet. All this night and the whole of the following day, *June 7th*, it rained, the wind being from the southwest, off the mountains; yet the rivers are falling, and the thermometer is 40° above zero. The rain continued till the next day, *June 8th*, at ten o'clock, when it cleared off and the weather became fine, the wind high from the southwest. The rivers at the point have now fallen six inches since our arrival, and this morning the water of the south fork became of a reddish-brown color, while the north branch continued of its usual whitish appearance. The mountains to the south are covered with snow.

June 9th.[6] We now consulted upon the course to be pursued. On comparing our observations, we were more than ever convinced of what we had already suspected, that Mr. Arrowsmith is incorrect in laying down, in the chain of Rocky mountains, one remarkable mountain called Tooth[7] mountain, nearly as far south as 45°—said to be so marked from (*p. 254*) the discoveries of a Mr. Fidler. We are now within 100 miles of the Rocky mountains, and in latitude 47° 24' 12.8".[8] Therefore it is highly improbable that the Missouri should make such a bend to the south, before it reaches the Rocky mountains, as to have suffered Mr. Fidler to come as low as 45° along the eastern borders, without touching that river. Yet the general course of

[6] The joint narrative here resumes. Captain Lewis' return was noted on the 8th.

[7] Arrowsmith's is a well-known old atlas. This Tooth mountain Clark located conjecturally on Lewis' map of 1806 at about 47° 30' N. lat., and little west of 112° W. long.—under the circumstances a wonderfully close approximation to the exact position of Teton Butte. The Mr. Fidler named was a surveyor in the employ of the Hudson's Bay Company, some of whose determinations of latitude proved very close—as, for example, those on the Red river for the parallel of 49° N.

[8] The mouth of Maria's river is nearly up to 48° N. lat., and scarcely east of 110° 31' W. long. Lewis' E 59, 60, gives his observations in detail.

Maria's river from this place, for 59 miles, as far as Captain Lewis ascended, was N. 69° W., and the south branch, or what we [now] consider to be the Missouri, which Captain Clark had examined as far as 45 miles in a straight line, ran in a course S. 29° W., and as far as it could be seen went considerably west of south; whence we conclude that the Missouri itself enters the Rocky mountains to the north of 45° [nearer 47° in fact].

In [9] writing to the President from our winter-quarters, we had already taken the liberty of advancing the southern extremity of Mr. Fidler's discoveries about a degree to the northward, from Indian information as to the bearing of the point at which the Missouri enters the mountains; but we think actual observation will place it one degree still further to the northward. This information of Mr. Fidler's, however, incorrect as it is, affords an additional reason for not pursuing Maria's river; for if he came as low even as 47° and saw only small streams coming down from the mountains, it is to be presumed that these rivulets do not penetrate the Rocky mountains so far as to approach any navigable branch of the Columbia; and they are most probably the remote waters of some northern branch of the Missouri. In short, being already in latitude 47° 24' [nearly 48°], we cannot reasonably hope by going further to the northward to find between this place and the Saskashawan any stream which can, as the Indians assure us the Missouri does, possess a navigable current for some distance

---

[9] To appreciate the following and preceding paragraphs, we must view them in historical perspective. It is one thing to look at the country from a Pullman car; it was another to sight it from camp in 1805—one thing to sit down in an easy-chair in front of a good map in 1893, and another to confront the Continental Divide in order to make a map, feeling that the success or failure of the Expedition, perhaps the life or death of the party, depended upon choosing one of two rivers which offered such a dilemma. Before the invincible explorers lay a thousand miles never trodden by the foot of white man; behind them, two thousand miles of water-course through a howling wilderness; but there was that within them which rendered a correct decision at the mouth of Maria's river.

in the Rocky mountains. The Indians assure us also that the water of the Missouri is nearly transparent at the Falls—this is the case with the southern branch; that the Falls lie a little to the (*p. 255*) south of sunset from them—this too is in favor of the southern fork, for it bears considerably south of this place, which is only a few minutes to the northward of Fort Mandan; and that the Falls are below the Rocky mountains, and near the northern termination of one range of those mountains. Now there is a ridge of mountains, which appear behind the South mountains and terminate to the southwest of us, at a sufficient distance from the unbroken chain of the Rocky mountains to allow space for several falls—indeed we fear for too many of them. If, too, the Indians had ever passed any stream as large as this southern fork, on their way up the Missouri, they would have mentioned it; so that their silence also seems to prove that this branch must be the Missouri. The body of water, also, which it discharges, must have been acquired from a considerable distance in the mountains; for it could not have been collected in the parched plains between the Yellowstone and the Rocky mountains; since that country could not supply nourishment for the dry channels which we passed on the south, and the travels of Mr. Fidler forbid us to believe that it could have been obtained from the mountains toward the northwest.

These observations, which satisfied our minds completely, we communicated to the party; but every one of them was of a contrary opinion. Much of their belief depended on Crusatte, an experienced waterman on the Missouri, who gave it as his decided judgment that the north fork was the genuine Missouri. The men, therefore, mentioned that, although they would most cheerfully follow us wherever we should direct, yet they were afraid that the south fork would soon terminate in the Rocky mountains, and leave us at a great distance from the Columbia. In order that nothing might be omitted which could prevent our falling into an error, it was agreed that one of us [10] should ascend the southern branch by land, until we reached either the falls or the mountains.   In the meantime, in order to lighten (*p. 256*) our burdens as much as possible, we determined to deposit here one of the periogues, and all the heavy baggage which we could possibly spare, as well as some provision, salt, powder, and tools.   This would at once lighten the other boats, and give them the crew which had been employed on board the periogue.

June 10*th.*   The weather being fair and pleasant we dried all our baggage and merchandise, and made our deposit. These holes, or caches as they are called by the Missouri traders, are very common, particularly among those who deal with the Sioux, as the skins and merchandise will keep perfectly sound for years; and be protected from robbery. Our cache is built in this manner: In the high plain on the north side of the Missouri, and 40 yards from a steep bluff, we chose a dry situation; then describing a small circle of about 20 inches' diameter, we removed the sod as gently and carefully as possible.   The hole is then sunk perpendicularly for a foot deep, or more if the ground be not firm. It is now worked gradually wider as we descend, till at length it becomes six or seven feet deep, shaped nearly like a kettle or the lower part of a large still, with the bottom somewhat sunk at the center.   As the earth is dug, it is handed up in a vessel and carefully laid on a skin or cloth, in which it is carried away, and usually thrown into the river, or concealed so as to leave no trace of it.   A floor of three or four inches in thickness is then made of dry sticks, on which is thrown hay, or a hide perfectly dry.   The goods being well aired and dried, are laid on this floor, and prevented from touching the wall by other dried sticks, in proportion as the merchandise is stowed away.   When the hole is nearly full, a skin is laid over the goods, and on this earth is thrown and beaten

---

[10] One of the two captains, with some of the men. " I preferred undertaking " this reconnoissance, Lewis E 57 ; and " accordingly gave orders to Drewyer, Joseph Fields, Gibson and Goodrich to hold themselves in readiness to accompany me," *ibid.* 61.

down until, with the addition of the sod first removed, the whole is on a level with the ground, and there remains not the slightest appearance of an excavation. In addition to this we made another of smaller dimensions, (*p. 257*) in which we placed all the baggage, some powder, and our blacksmith's tools, having previously repaired such of the tools we carry with us as require mending.[11] To guard against accident we hid two parcels of lead and powder in the two distinct places.

The red periogue was drawn up on the middle of a small island, at the entrance of Maria's river, and secured, by being fastened to the trees, from the effect of any floods. In the evening there was a high wind from the southwest, accompanied with thunder and rain. We now made another observation of the meridian altitude of the sun, and found that the mean latitude of the entrance of Maria's river, as deduced from three observations, is 47° 25′ 17.2″ north. We saw a small bird,[12] like the blue thrush or catbird, which we had not before met, and also observed that the bee-martin or kingbird[13] is common to this country, although there are no bees here ; in fact we have not met with the honey-bee since leaving the Osage river.

June 11*th.* This morning Captain Lewis with four men set out on their expedition up the south branch [*i. e.,* the

[11] Lewis E 60 pays a high tribute to John Shields : "We have been much indebted to the ingenuity of this man on many occasions ; without having served any regular apprenticeship to any trade, he makes his own tools principally, and works extremely well in either wood or metal, and in this way has been extreemly serviceable to us, as well as being a good hunter and an excellent water-man." I kept my eye on the Mandan Codex, to discover who was the blacksmith that did so well to supply the party with corn, without finding him named ; but we may be satisfied now that it was Shields.

[12] The Rocky Mountain bluebird, *Sialia arctica*, as no doubt any ornithologist would surmise. In fact, it was the white-rumped shrike, *Lanius excubitoroides* of Swainson, as I see from the good description of the bird, and its nest and eggs, Lewis E 61, 62.

[13] Both the common kingbird of the Atlantic States, *Tyrannus carolinensis*, and a related species, Say's flycatcher, *Tyrannus verticalis*, are found in this region. The Codex does not describe, but no doubt the text is right, as Lewis knew the kingbird well in Virginia, where it is commonly called bee-martin.

Missouri]. They soon reached the point [Cracon du Nez] where Tansy river approaches the Missouri, and observing a large herd of elk before them, descended and killed several, which they hung up along the river, so that the party in the boats might see them as they came along. They then halted for dinner; but Captain Lewis, who had been for some days afflicted with dysentery, was now attacked with violent pains, attended by a high fever, and was unable to go on. He therefore camped for the night under some willow-boughs. Having brought no medicine, he determined to try an experiment with the small twigs of the choke-cherry, which being stripped of their leaves and cut into pieces about two inches long, were boiled in pure water, till they produced a strong black decoction of an astringent bitter taste; a pint of this he took at sunset, and repeated the dose an hour afterward. By ten o'clock he was perfectly relieved from pain, a gentle (*p. 258*) perspiration ensued, his fever abated, and in the morning he was quite recovered.

One of the men [14] caught several dozen fish of two species. The first is about nine inches long, of a white color, round in shape; the mouth is beset both above and below with a rim of fine sharp teeth, the eye moderately large, the pupil dark, the iris narrow, and of a yellowish-brown color. In form and size it resembles the white chub of the Potomac, though its head is proportionally smaller. These readily bite at meat or grasshoppers; the flesh, though soft and of a fine white color, is not highly flavored. The second species is precisely of the form and about the size of the fish known by the name of the hickory-shad or old-wife, though it differs from it in having the outer edge of both the upper and lower jaw set with a rim of teeth, and the tongue and palate

---

[14] " Goodrich, who is remarkably fond of fishing," Lewis E 63. The first of these species is a percoid fish, *Stizostedion canadense*, a kind of pike-perch, of elongate form, with subconic head, and sharp canines as well as villiform teeth. The second is one of the Missouri herrings, *Hyodon alosoides*, a well-known clupeoid fish. *H. tergisus* is another species of this genus, also found in Missouri waters.

also defended by long sharp teeth bending inward ; the eye is very large, the iris wide, and of a silvery color.   These do not inhabit muddy water, and the flavor is much superior to that of the former species.   Of the first kind we had seen a few before we reached Maria's river ; but had found none of the last before we caught them in the Missouri above its junction .with that river.   The white cat [-fish, *Ictalurus punctatus*] continues as high as Maria's river, but they are scarce in this part of the Missouri, nor have we caught any of them since leaving the Mandans which weighed more than six pounds.

Of other game they saw a great abundance, even in their short march of nine miles.

June 12*th.*   This morning Captain Lewis left the bank of the river, in order to avoid the steep ravines, which generally run from the shore to the distance of one or two miles in the plain.   Having reached the open country he went for twelve miles in a course a little to the W. of S.W.; when, the sun becoming warm by nine o'clock, he returned to the river in quest of water, and to kill something for breakfast ; there being no water in the plain, and the buffalo, discovering them before they came within gunshot, took (*p. 259*) to flight.   They reached the banks in a handsome open low ground with cottonwood, after three miles' walk.   Here they saw two large brown bears, and killed them both at the first fire—a circumstance which has never before occurred since we have seen that animal.   Having made a meal of a part, and hung the remainder on a tree, with a note for Captain Clark, they again ascended the bluffs into the open plains.   Here they saw great numbers of the burrowing-squirrel, also some wolves, antelopes, mule-deer, and vast herds of buffalo.   They soon crossed a ridge considerably higher than the surrounding plains, and from its top had a beautiful view[15] of the Rocky

[15] For a general view of the main chain of the Rocky mountains, marking positions of Dearborn's river, Cadotte's Pass, and the Pass of Maria's river, see P. R. R. Rep. XII. pt. i., 1860, pl. lii.   This is substantially what Lewis has in sight at this moment : "an august spectacle and still rendered more formidable by the recollection that we had them to pass," Lewis E 65.

mountains, which are now completely covered with snow. Their general course is from S.E. to N. of N.W., and they seem to consist of several ranges which successively rise above each other, till the most distant mingles with the clouds. After traveling twelve miles they again met the river, where there was a handsome plain of cottonwood ; though it was not sunset, and they had only come 27 miles, yet Captain Lewis felt weak from his late disorder, and therefore determined to go no further that night.[16]

In the course of the day they killed a quantity of game and saw some signs of otter as well as beaver, and many tracks of the brown bear ; they also caught great quantities of the white fish mentioned yesterday. With the broad-leaved cottonwood [*Populus monilifera*], which has formed the principal timber of the Missouri, is here mixed another species [*P. angustifolia*], differing from the first only in the narrowness of its leaf and the greater thickness of its bark. The leaf is long, oval, acutely pointed, about 2½ or three inches long and from three-quarters of an inch to an inch in width ; it is smooth and thick, sometimes slightly grooved or channeled, with the margin a little serrate, the upper disk of a common, the lower of a whitish green. This species seems to be preferred by the beaver to the broad-leaved, probably because the former affords a deeper and softer bark.

(*p. 260*) *June 13th.* They left camp at sunrise, and ascending the river-hills went for six miles in a course generally southwest, over a country which, though more waving than that of yesterday, may still be considered level. At the extremity of this course they overlooked a most beautiful plain, where were infinitely more buffalo than we had ever before seen at a single view. To the southwest arose from the plain two mountains of a singular

---

[16] " This evening I ate very heartily, and after pening the transactions of the day amused myself catching those white fish mentioned yesterday ; . . . I caught upward of a dozen in a few minutes ; they bit most freely at the melt of a deer which goodrich had brought with him for the purpose of fishing," Lewis E 65.

appearance, more like ramparts of high fortifications than works of nature. They are square figures [17] with sides rising perpendicularly to the height of 250 feet, formed of yellow clay, and the tops seemed to be level plains. Finding that the river here bore considerably to the south, and fearful of passing the falls before reaching the Rocky mountains, they now changed their course to the south, and leaving those insulated hills to the right, proceeded across the plain.

In this direction Captain Lewis had gone about two miles, when his ears were saluted with the agreeable sound of a fall of water, and as he advanced a spray, which seemed driven by the high southwest wind, arose above the plain like a column of smoke, and vanished in an instant. Toward this point he directed his steps; the noise increased as he approached, and soon became too tremendous to be mistaken for anything but the Great Falls of the Missouri. Having traveled seven miles after first hearing the sound, he reached the falls about twelve o'clock. The hills as he approached were difficult of access and 200 feet high. Down these he hurried with impatience; and, seating himself on some rocks under the center of the falls, enjoyed the sublime spectacle of this stupendous object, which since the creation had been lavishing its magnificence upon the desert, unknown to civilization.

The river immediately at this cascade is 300 yards wide, and is pressed in by a perpendicular cliff on the left, which rises to about 100 feet and extends up the stream for a mile; on the right the bluff is also perpendi- (*p. 261*) cular for 300 yards above the falls. For 90 or 100 yards from the left cliff, the water falls in one smooth, even sheet, over a precipice of at least 80 feet. The remaining part of the river precipitates itself with a more rapid current, but being received as it falls by the irregular and somewhat projecting rocks below, forms a splendid prospect of perfectly white foam, 200 yards in length and 80 in perpendic-

[17] Elevations which answer this description, both in figure and direction, are now called Square Butte and Crown Butte. See note [27], p. 413.

ular elevation. This spray is dissipated into a thousand shapes, sometimes flying up in columns of 15 or 20 feet, which are then oppressed by larger masses of the white foam, on all which the sun impresses the brightest colors of the rainbow. As it rises from the fall it beats with fury against a ledge of rocks which extend across the river at 150 yards from the precipice. From the perpendicular cliff on the north, to the distance of 120 yards, the rocks rise only a few feet above the water; when the river is high the stream finds a channel across them 40 yards wide and near the higher parts of the ledge, which then rise about 20 feet and terminate abruptly within 80 or 90 yards of the southern side. Between them and the perpendicular cliff on the south the whole body of water runs with great swiftness. A few small cedars grow near this ridge of rocks, which serves as a barrier to defend a small plain of about three acres, shaded with cottonwood, at the lower extremity of which is a grove of the same tree, where are several Indian cabins of sticks; below the point of them the river is divided by a large rock, several feet above the surface of the water, and extending down the stream for 20 yards. At the distance of 300 yards from the same ridge is a second abutment of solid perpendicular rock about 60 feet high, projecting at right angles from the small plain on the north for 134 yards into the river. After leaving this, the Missouri again spreads itself to its usual distance of 300 yards, though with more than its ordinary rapidity.[18]

[18] " After wrighting this imperfect description I again viewed the falls and was so much disgusted with the imperfect idea which it conveyed of the scene that I determined to draw my pen across it and begin agin, but then reflected that I could not perhaps succeed better than pening the first impressions of the mind ; I wished for the pencil of Salvator Rosa ["a Titian" interlined] or the pen of Thompson [James Thomson, author of the "Seasons"], that I might be enabled to give to the enlightened world some just idea of this truly magnificent and sublimely grand object, which has from the commencement of time been concealed from the view of civilized man ; but this was fruitless and vain. I most sincerely regreted that I had not brought a crimeeobscura [sic] with me by the assistance of which I could have hoped to have done better but alas this was also out of my reach ; I therefore with the assistance of my pen only indeavoured

(*p. 262*) The hunters who had been sent out now returned loaded with buffalo-meat, and Captain Lewis camped for the night under a tree near the falls. The men were again dispatched to hunt for food against the arrival of the party, and Captain Lewis walked down the river to discover, if possible, some place where the canoes might be safely drawn on shore, in order to be transported beyond the falls. He returned, however, without discovering any such spot, the river for three miles below being one continued succession of rapids and cascades, overhung with perpendicular bluffs from 150 to 200 feet high ; in short, it seems to have worn itself a channel through the solid rock. In the afternoon they[19] caught in the falls some of both kinds of the white fish, and half a dozen trout[20] from 16 to 23 inches long, precisely resembling, in form and in the position of the fins, the mountain or speckled trout of the United States, except that the specks of the former are of a deep black, while those of the latter are of a red or gold color. They have long sharp teeth on the palate and tongue, and generally a small speck of red on each side,

to trace some of the stronger features of this seen by the assistance of which and my recollection aided by some able pencil I hope still to give to the world some faint idea of an object which at this moment fills me with such pleasure and astonishment," etc. Lewis E 70. Lewis elsewhere speaks of sketching the falls, and a view of them (scenery, not the map) embellishes at least one of the later editions of the History. But I have never found, anywhere in the Clark-Biddle correspondence, the slightest reference to such a picture as the Dublin edition presents, nor is there anything of the sort in the codices. It is therefore a late embellishment, from the imagination probably, and a copy of the Philadelphia ed. of 1814 is " perfect " without any such plate. I speak beyond of the map of the falls, which is an entirely different plate. A tinted view of the falls is given in the P. R. R. Rep. XII. pt. i. pl. lx., 1860 ; and modern pictures are of course abundant and easily accessible.

[19] That is to say, Goodrich did. " My fare is really sumptuous this evening ; buffaloe's humps, tongues, and marrowbones, fine trout, parched meal, pepper and salt, and a good appetite," Lewis E 72.

[20] The identical fish named *Salar lewisi* by Girard, Proc. Philada. Acad., 1856, p. 210, the types of his species being taken by Dr. Geo. Suckley at the Falls : see P. R. R. Rep. XII. pt. ii., 1860, p. 348, pl. lxxii. It is not, however, specifically distinct from *Salmo purpuratus.* For the white fish, see note [11], p. 362.

behind the front ventral fins; the flesh is of a pale yel-
lowish-red, or when in good order of a rose-colored
red.

June 14th. This morning one of the men [J. Fields] was
sent to Captain Clark with an account of the discovery of
the falls, and after employing the rest in preserving the meat
which had been killed yesterday, Captain Lewis proceeded
to examine the rapids above. From the falls he directed
his course southwest up the river. After passing one continued rapid, and three small cascades, each three or four
feet high, he reached at the distance of five miles a second
fall. The river is about 400 yards wide, and for the distance of 300 yards throws itself over to the depth of 19 feet,
so irregularly that he gave it the name of the Crooked falls.
From the southern shore it extends obliquely upward
about 150 yards, and then forms an acute angle downward
nearly to the commence- (*p. 263*) ment of four small islands
close to the northern side. From the perpendicular pitch
to these islands, a distance of more than 100 yards, the
water glides down a sloping rock, with a velocity almost
equal to that of its fall. Above this fall the river bends
suddenly to the northward.

While viewing this place Captain Lewis heard a loud
roar above him, and crossing the point of a hill for a few
hundred yards, he saw one of the most beautiful objects in
nature.

The whole of the Missouri is suddenly stopped by one
shelving rock, which, without a single niche, and with an
edge as straight and regular as if formed by art, stretches
itself from one side of the river to the other for at least a
quarter of a mile. Over this the water precipitates itself
in an even, uninterrupted sheet, to the perpendicular depth
of 50 feet, whence dashing against the rocky bottom it
rushes rapidly down, leaving behind it a spray of the
purest foam across the river. The scene which it presented
was indeed singularly beautiful, since, without any of the
wild, irregular sublimity of the lower falls, it combined all

the regular elegances which the fancy of a painter would select to form a beautiful waterfall. The eye had scarcely been regaled with this charming prospect, when at the distance of half a mile, Captain Lewis observed another of a similar kind. To this he immediately hastened, and found a cascade stretching across the whole river for a quarter of a mile, with a descent of 14 feet, though the perpendicular pitch was only six feet. This too, in any other neighborhood, would have been an object of great magnificence; but after what he had just seen, it became of secondary interest. His curiosity being, however, awakened, he determined to go on, even should night overtake him, to the head of the falls.

He therefore pursued the southwest course of the river, which was one constant succession of rapids and small cascades, at every one of which the bluffs grew lower, or the bed of the river became more on a level with the plains. At the distance of 2½ miles he arrived at another cata-(*p. 264*) ract, of 26 feet. The river is here 600 yards wide, but the descent is not immediately perpendicular, though the river falls generally with a regular and smooth sheet; for about one-third of the descent a rock protrudes to a small distance, receives the water in its passage, and gives it a curve. On the south side is a beautiful plain, a few feet above the level of the falls; on the north, the country is more broken, and there is a hill not far from the river. Just below the falls is a little island in the middle of the river, well covered with timber. Here on a cottonwood tree an eagle had fixed her nest, and seemed the undisputed mistress of a spot, to contest whose dominion neither man nor beast would venture across the gulfs that surround it, and which is further secured by the mist rising from the falls. This solitary bird could not escape the observation of the Indians, who made the eagle's nest a part of their description of the falls, which now proves to be correct in almost every particular, except that they did not do justice to the height. Just above this is a cascade of about five

feet, beyond which, as far as could be discerned, the velocity of the water seemed to abate.

Captain Lewis now ascended the hill which was behind
him, and saw from its top a delightful plain, extending from
the river to the base of the Snow [Rocky] [21] mountains, to
the south and southwest. Along this wide level country the
Missouri pursued its winding course, filled with water to
its even and grassy banks, while, about four miles above,
it was joined by a large [Medicine or Sun] river, flowing
from the northwest through a valley three miles in width,
and distinguished by the timber which adorned its shores.
The Missouri itself stretches to the south in one unruffled
stream of water, as if unconscious of the roughness it must
soon encounter, and bearing on its bosom vast flocks of
geese; while numerous herds of buffalo are feeding on the
plains which surround it.

Captain Lewis then descended the hill, and directed his
course toward the river falling in from the west. He soon
(*p. 265*) met a herd of at least 1,000 buffalo, and being
desirous of providing for supper, shot one of them. The
animal immediately began to bleed, and Captain Lewis,
who had forgotten to reload his rifle, was intently watching
to see him fall, when he beheld a large brown bear which
was stealing on him unperceived, and was already within
20 steps. In the first moment of surprise he lifted his rifle,
but remembering instantly that it was not charged, and
that he had no time to reload, he felt that there was no
safety but in flight. It was in the open level plain—not
a bush nor a tree within 300 yards, the bank of the
river sloping and not more than three feet high, so that
there was no possible mode of concealment. Captain
Lewis therefore thought of retreating in a quick walk, as
fast as the bear advanced, toward the nearest tree; but as
soon as he turned, the bear ran open-mouthed and at full

[21] The Rocky mountains have at various times been designated as the Shining
mountains, Snow or Snowey mountains, Stone or Stoney mountains, Rock mountains, and by several equivalents in other languages.

speed upon him.   Captain Lewis ran about 80 yards, but
finding that the animal gained on him fast, it flashed on his
mind that, by getting into the water to such a depth that
the bear would be obliged to attack him swimming, there
was still some chance of his life ; he therefore turned short,
plunged into the river about waist-deep, and facing about
presented the point of his espontoon.   The bear arrived at
the water's edge within 20 feet of him ; but as soon as he
put himself in this posture of defense, the bear seemed
frightened, and wheeling about, retreated with as much
precipitation as he had pursued.   Very glad to be released
from this danger, Captain Lewis returned to the shore,
and observed him run with great speed, sometimes looking
back as if he expected to be pursued, till he reached the
woods.   He could not conceive the cause of the sudden
alarm of the bear, but congratulated himself on his escape
when he saw his own track torn to pieces by the furious
animal, and learned from the whole adventure never to
suffer his rifle to be a moment unloaded.

He now resumed his progress in the direction which the
bear had taken, toward the western [Sun] river, and found it
a hand-(*p. 266*) some stream about 200 yards wide, apparently
deep, with a gentle current ; its waters clear, and its banks,
which were formed principally of dark brown and blue clay,
about the same height as those of the Missouri—that is,
from three to five feet.   What is singular is, that the river
does not seem to overflow its banks at any season, while it
might be presumed, from its vicinity to the mountains,
that the torrents arising from the melting of the snows
would sometimes cause it to swell beyond its limits.   The
contrary fact would induce a belief that the Rocky mountains yield their snows very reluctantly and equably to the
sun, and are not often drenched by very heavy rains.   This
river is no doubt that which the Indians call Medicine
river,[22] which they mentioned as emptying into the Missouri just above the falls.

<hr>

[22] " Midison R. or Mah-pah-pah, ahz-hah," Clark C 249 ; now Sun river.

After examining Medicine river, Captain Lewis set out
at half after six o'clock in the evening, on his return to the
camp, which he estimated to be at the distance of twelve
miles. In going through the low grounds on Medicine
river, he met an animal which at a distance he thought was a
wolf ; but on coming within 60 paces, it proved to be some
brownish-yellow animal standing near its burrow, which,
when he came nigh, crouched and seemed as if about to
spring on him. Captain Lewis fired, and the beast disappeared in its burrow. From the track and the general
appearance of the animal he supposed it to be of the tiger
kind.[23] He then went on ;[24] but, as if the beasts of the
forests had conspired against him, three buffalo bulls,
which were feeding with a large herd at the distance of
half a mile, left their companions and ran at full speed
toward him. He turned round, and unwilling to give up
the field, advanced toward them. When they came within
100 yards they stopped, looked at him for some time,
and then retreated as they came. He now pursued his
route in the dark, reflecting on the strange adventures
and sights of the day, which crowded on his mind so
rapidly that he would have been inclined to believe it all
enchantment, if the thorns of the prickly-pear, piercing his
feet, had not (*p. 267*) dispelled at every moment the illu-
sion. He at last reached the party, who had been very
anxious for his safety, and who had already decided on the
route which each should take in the morning to look for

[23] Probably the wolverene or carcajou, *Gulo luscus.*

[24] " It now seemed to me that all the beasts of the neighbourhood had made a
league to destroy me, or that dame fortune was disposed to amuse herself at my
expence, for I had not proceeded more than 300 yards from the burrow of this
tyger cat, before three bull buffaloe, which wer feeding with a large herd about
half a mile on my left, seperated from the herd and ran full speed towards me. . .
I . . . did not think it prudent to remain all night at this place which really from
the succession of curious adventures wore the impression on my mind of inchant-
ment ; at sometimes for a moment I thought it might be a dream ; but the
prickley pears which pierced my feet very severely once in a while, particularly
after it grew dark, convinced me that I was really awake," Lewis E 80.

him. Being much fatigued, he supped and slept well during the night.

June 15*th.* The men were again sent out, to bring in the game [Drewyer] killed yesterday and to procure more. They also obtained a number of fine trout, and several small catfish, weighing about four pounds and differing from the white catfish lower down the Missouri. On awaking this morning Captain Lewis found a large rattlesnake coiled on the trunk of a tree under which he had been sleeping. He killed it and found it like those we had seen before, differing from those of the Atlantic States, not in its colors, but in the form and arrangement of them ; it had 176 scuta on the abdomen, and 17 half-formed [25] scuta on the tail. There is a heavy dew on the grass about camp every morning, which no doubt proceeds from the mist of the falls, as it takes place nowhere in the plains or on the river, except here. The messenger [Joseph Fields] sent to Captain Clark returned with information of his having arrived five miles below at a rapid, which he did not think it prudent to ascend, where he would wait till Captain Lewis and his party rejoined him.

On *Tuesday,*[26] the 11*th*, the day when Captain Lewis left us, we remained at the entrance of Maria's river and completed the deposit of all the articles with which we could dispense. The morning had been fair, with a high wind from the southwest, which shifted in the evening to northwest, when the weather became cold and the wind high. The next morning,

Wednesday, 12*th*, we left camp with a fair day and a

[25] That is, the subcaudal scuta or urosteges were in two rows, those of one row alternating with those of the other, and none extending across the tail. This species is *Crotalus confluentus ;* the common one of the Atlantic States is *C. horridus.*

[26] Here the narrative returns to the main party, which is about to go up the Missouri from Maria's river ; Captain Lewis' party being already above, at the Falls. It is contained in Codex E 84–92, in Lewis' hand, but copied from a Clark journal, as written by the latter in the first person singular.

southwest wind. The river was now so crowded with islands that within the distance of 10½ miles we passed 11 of different dimensions, before reaching a high black bluff in a bend on the left, where we saw a great number of swallows [*Petrochelidon lunifrons*]. Within 1½ miles further we (*p. 268*) passed four small islands, two on each side, and at 15 miles from camp reached a spring, which the men called Grog spring. It is on the northern shore, at the [Cracon du Nez, a] point where Tansy river approaches within 100 yards of the Missouri.

From this place we proceeded three miles to a low bluff on the north, opposite an island, and spent the night in an old Indian camp. The bluffs under which we passed were composed of a blackish clay and coal for about 80 feet, above which for 30 or 40 feet is a brownish-yellow earth. The river is very rapid, and obstructed by bars of gravel and stone of different shapes and sizes, so that three of our canoes were in great danger in the course of the day. We had a few drops of rain about two o'clock in the afternoon. The only animals we killed were elk and deer ; but we saw great numbers of rattlesnakes.

Thursday, 13*th*. The morning was fair, and there was some dew on the ground. After passing two islands we reached, at the distance of a mile and a half, a small, rapid stream 50 yards wide, emptying on the south, rising in a mountain to the southeast, 12 or 15 miles distant, and at this time covered with snow. As it is the channel for the melted snow of that mountain, we called it Snow [27] river. Opposite its entrance is another island ; at 1¾ miles, a black bluff of slate on the south ; nine miles beyond which, after passing ten islands, we came-to on the southern shore, near an old Indian fortified camp, opposite the lower point of an island, having made 13 miles. The number of islands and shoals, the rapidity of the river, and the quantity of large stones,

---

[27] Now Shonkin or Shankin river, one of several streams which drain the Highwood mountains. It runs about north into the Missouri, immediately below Fort Benton.

render the navigation very disagreeable. Along the banks we distinguished several low bluffs or cliffs of slate. There were great numbers of geese and goslings ; the geese were not able to fly at this season. Gooseberries are ripe and in great abundance ; the yellow currant is also common, but not yet ripe. Our game consisted of buffalo and goats.[28]

(*p. 269*) *Friday, 14th.* Again the day is fine. We made two miles to a small island in the southern bend, after passing several bad rapids. The current becomes indeed swifter as we ascend, and the canoes frequently receive water as we drag them with difficulty along. At the distance of six miles, we reached Captain Clark's camp of June 4th, which is on the north side and opposite a large gravelly bar. Here the man [J. Fields] sent by Captain Lewis joined us, with the pleasing intelligence that he [Lewis] had discovered the falls, and was convinced that the course we were pursuing was that of the true Missouri. At 1½ miles we reached the upper point of an island, three-quarters of a mile beyond which we camped on the south, after making only 10¼ miles. Along the river was but little timber, but much hard slate in the bluffs.

Saturday, 15th. The morning being warm and fair, we set out at the usual hour, but proceeded with great difficulty, in consequence of the increased rapidity of the current. The channel is constantly obstructed by rocks and dangerous rapids. During the whole progress, the men are in the water hauling the canoes, and walking on sharp rocks and round stones, which cut their feet or cause them to fall. Rattlesnakes are so numerous that the men are constantly on their guard against being bitten by them ; yet they bear the fatigues with the most undiminished cheerfulness. We hear the roar of the falls very distinctly this morning. At 3¾ miles we came to a rock in a bend to the south, resembling a tower. At 6¾ miles we reached a large creek on the south, which, after one of our men, we called Shields'[29] river. It is

---

[28] " Killed a Goat, and Frazier 2 Buffaloe," Clark in Lewis E 87.

[29] Now known as Highwood creek or river, from the mountains of the same

rapid in its course, about 30 yards wide, and on sending a person five miles up it proved to have a fall of 15 feet, and some timber on its low ground. Above this river the bluffs of the Missouri are of red earth, mixed with strata of black stone; below it we passed some white clay in the banks, which mixes with water in every respect like (*p. 270*) flour. At 3¾ miles we reached a point on the north, opposite an island and a bluff; 1¼ miles further, after passing some red bluffs, we came-to on the north side, having made twelve miles. Here we found a rapid so difficult that we did not think proper to attempt the passage this evening, and therefore sent to Captain Lewis to apprise him of our arrival. We saw a number of geese, ducks, crows, and black-birds to-day, the two former with their young. The river rose a little this evening, but the timber is still so scarce that we could not procure enough for our use during the night.

June 16*th.* Some rain fell last night; this morning the weather was cloudy, and the wind high from the southwest. We passed the rapid [30] by doubly manning the periogue and canoes, and halted at the distance of 1¼ miles to examine the rapids above, which we found to be a continued succession of cascades as far as the view extended, which was about two miles. About a mile above where we halted was a large [Portage] creek, falling in on the south, opposite which is a large sulphur spring,[31] falling over the rocks on the north. Captain Lewis arrived [32] at two o'clock from the falls, about

name, which this stream drains to the northwest. See Clark's map, where the stream is charted, though without any name, between Snow river and Portage creek. It must not be confounded with a certain branch of the Yellowstone which Clark also named for John Shields, the ingenious artificer of the Expedition.

[30] This rapid is shown on the map of the falls, below Portage creek, marked "8 feet fall." On passing it, a halt is made on the "south," *i. e.*, larboard or left hand going up river, but then the river is crossed to make camp.

[31] This spring is shown on the map of the falls: see the plate, where "Sulphur spring" is lettered.

[32] " Found the Indian woman extreemly ill and much reduced by her indisposition. this gave me some concern, as well for the poor object herself, then with

five miles above us, and after consulting upon the subject of the portage, we crossed the river and formed a camp on the north, having come three-quarters of a mile to-day.

From our own observation we had deemed the south side to be the most favorable for a portage; but two men sent out for the purpose of examining it reported that the creek and the ravines intersected the plains so deeply that it was impossible to cross it. Captain Clark therefore resolved to examine more minutely what was the best route. The four canoes were unloaded at the camp, and then sent across the river, where, by means of strong cords, they were hauled over the first rapid, whence they may be easily drawn into the creek. Finding that the portage would be at all events too long to enable us to carry the boats on our shoulders, six men were set to work to make wheels for car- (*p. 271*) riages to transport them. Since leaving Maria's river the wife of Chaboneau, our interpreter, has been dangerously ill, but she now found great relief from the mineral water of the sulphur spring. It is situated about 200 yards from the Missouri, into which it empties over a precipice of rock about 25 feet high. The water is perfectly transparent, strongly impregnated with sulphur, and we suspect iron also, as the color of the hills and bluffs in the neighborhood indicates the presence of that metal. In short, the water to all appearance is precisely similar to that of Bowyer's sulphur spring in Virginia.

June 17th. Captain Clark set out, with five men, to explore the country; the rest were employed in hunting, making wheels, and in drawing the five canoes and all the baggage [" about a mile and a half," Gass] up the creek, which we now call Portage creek.[33] From this creek there is a gradual

a young child in her arms, as from the consideration of her being our only dependence for a friendly negociation with the Snake Indians, upon whom we depend for horses to assist us in our portage from the Missouri to the columbia river," Lewis E 82.

[33] So named in this work, as the base of the operations for making the long portage of the Great Falls. It is now known as Belt Mountain creek, from the mountains which it drains northwestwardly. A north branch of it also drains

ascent to the top of the high plain, while the bluffs of the creek lower down, and of the Missouri both above and below its entrance, were so steep as to render it almost impracticable to drag them up from the Missouri. We found great difficulty and some danger in even ascending the creek thus far, in consequence of the rapids and rocks of the channel of the creek, which just above where we brought the canoes has a fall of five feet, with high steep bluffs beyond it. We were very fortunate in finding, just below Portage creek, a cottonwood tree about 22 inches in diameter, large enough to make the carriage-wheels. It was, perhaps, the only one of the same size within 20 miles ; and the cottonwood which we are obliged to employ in the other parts of the work is extremely soft and brittle. The mast of the white periogue, which we mean to leave behind, supplied us with two axle-trees.

There are vast quantities of buffalo feeding on the plains or watering in the river, which is also strewed with the floating carcasses and limbs of these animals. They go in large herds to water about the falls, and as all the passages to the river near that place are nar- (*p. 272*) row and steep, the foremost are pressed into the river by the impatience of those behind. In this way we have seen ten or a dozen disappear over the falls in a few minutes. They afford excellent food for the wolves, bears, and birds of prey ; which circumstance may account for the reluctance of the bears to yield their dominion over the neighborhood.

June 18*th.* The periogue was drawn up a little below our camp, and secured in a thick copse of willow-bushes. We now began to form a cache or place of deposit,[34] and

from south slopes of the Highwood mountains, and the united streams come out through the gap between the latter and Little Belt mountains. It is called by mistake Bear creek on one map before me. Portage creek is the last point named in the Summary Statement of places on the Missouri, up to the Great Falls. For here the Statement proceeds with the itinerary of what was regarded as the shortest and most practicable route from Missourian to Columbian waters, being nearly that taken by Captain Lewis in returning, in 1806, from certain waters (Big Blackfoot river) of the Columbia to the Falls direct.

[34] Shown on the map of the falls, below Portage creek, at the spot marked

to dry our goods and other articles which required inspection. The wagons are completed. Our hunters brought us ten deer, and we shot two out of a herd of buffalo that came to water at Sulphur spring. There is a species of gooseberry [probably *Ribes oxyacanthoides*], growing abundantly among the rocks on the sides of the cliffs. It is now ripe, of a pale red color, about the size of the common gooseberry, and like it is an ovate pericarp of soft pulp enveloping a number of small whitish seeds, and consisting of a yellowish, slimy, mucilaginous substance, with a sweet taste; the surface of the berry is covered with a glutinous, adhesive matter, and its fruit, though ripe, retains its withered corolla. The shrub itself seldom rises more than two feet high, is much branched, and has no thorns. The leaves resemble those of the common gooseberry, except in being smaller, and the berry is supported by separate peduncles or foot-stalks half an inch long. There are also immense quantities of grasshoppers [*Caloptenus spretus*], of a brown color, on the plains; they, no doubt, contribute to the lowness of the grass, which is not generally more than three inches high, though it is soft, narrow-leaved, and affords a fine pasture for the buffalo.

June 19*th.* The wind blew violently to-day, as it did yesterday, and as it does frequently in this open country, where there is not a tree to break or oppose its force. Some men were sent for the meat killed yesterday, which, fortunately, had not been discovered by the wolves. Another party [Drewyer, Shannon, R. Fields] went to Medicine river [above the falls] in quest of elk, which we hope may be (*p. 273*) induced to resort there, from there being more wood in that neighborhood than on the Missouri. All the rest were occupied in packing the baggage and mending their moccasins, in order to prepare for the portage. We caught a number of the white fish, but no catfish or trout. Our poor Indian woman, who had recovered so far as to

" Deposit." Camp is still on the north, by Sulphur spring, but meanwhile the canoes and baggage have been taken across the Missouri to a point on Portage creek.

walk out, imprudently ate a quantity of the white-apple [*Psoralea esculenta*], which, with some dried fish, occasioned a return of her fever.[35]

The meridian altitude of the sun's lower limb, as observed with the octant by back observation, was 53° 15', giving as the latitude of our camp 47° 8' 59.5''[36]

June 20th. As we were desirous of getting meat enough to last us during the portage, so that the men might not be diverted from their labor to look for food, we sent out four hunters to-day; they killed 11 buffalo. This was indeed an easy labor, for there are vast herds coming constantly to the opposite bank of the river to water; they seem also to make much use of the mineral water of Sulphur spring, but whether from choice, or because it is more convenient than the river, we cannot determine, as they sometimes pass near the spring and go on to the river. Besides this spring, brackish water, or that of a dark color impregnated with mineral salts, such as we have frequently met on the Missouri, may be found in small quantities, in some of the steep ravines on the north side of the river, opposite us and at the falls.

Captain Clark returned this evening, having examined the whole course of the river, and fixed the route most practicable for the portage. The first day, the 17th, he was occupied in measuring the heights and distances along the banks of the river, and slept near a ravine at the foot of the Crooked falls, having very narrowly escaped falling into the river, where he would have perished inevitably, in descend-

---

[35] " I rebuked Sharbono severely for suffering her to indulge herself in such food, he being privy to it and having been previously told what she must only eat," Lewis E 96. Whatever the case may have been, Sacajawea was certainly a very sick woman. She was delirious at times, and excited the gravest apprehensions on the part of both the officers, who were unremitting in their attentions. The codex gives her symptoms and treatment day by day—and the latter was of the heroic order, like everything else those great men did. Forgetting perhaps the tender age of her infant, they diagnosed her case as " suppression of the mensis," and undertook to regulate her courses with the same precision with which they attended to those of the Missouri river.

[36] It is about 47° 36' N.; the longitude a little more than 111° W.

ing the cliffs near the grand cataract. The next day, the 18*th*,[37] he continued the same occupation, and arrived in the afternoon at the junction of Medicine and Missouri rivers; up the lat- (*p. 274*) ter he ascended and passed, at the distance of a mile, an island and a little timber in an eastward bend of the river. One mile beyond this, he came to the lower point of a large island; another small island is in the middle of the river, and one is near the left [-hand going up] shore, opposite the head of which he camped, near the mouth of a creek[38] [Flattery run], which appeared to rise in the South mountains. These three islands are opposite each other; he gave them the name of the Whitebear islands, from observing some of those animals on them. He killed a beaver, an elk, and eight buffalo. One of the men [Willard], who was sent a short distance from the camp to bring home some meat, was attacked by a white bear, closely pursued within 40 paces of the camp, and narrowly escaped being caught. Captain Clark immediately went with three men in quest of the bear, which he was afraid might surprise another of the hunters [Colter], who was out collecting the game. The bear was, however, too quick, for before Captain Clark could reach the man, the bear had attacked him and compelled him to take refuge in the water. He now ran off as they approached, and it being late they deferred pursuing him till the next morning.

[37] To-day discovering the famous fountain : "the largest fountain I ever saw, and doubt if it is not the largest in America," Clark in Lewis E 100 : see next chapter.

[38] This creek, like several others which fall into the Missouri from the S. or S.E., above and below the Great Falls, comes from the Little Belt mountains. It is now called Sand coulée, and there is a town on it of the same name, lettered Sand Coulle by the ingenious engraver of a certain military map. A railroad from Great Falls goes by, to points in the Highwood and Little Belt mountains.

CHAPTER XI.

THE GREAT FALLS AND THE PORTAGE OF THE MISSOURI.

Course of the portage determined upon—Description of the cascades and rapids from Medicine
river, above the falls, down to Portage creek, below the falls—A great fountain—A fishing-
duck—The portage begun and a camp set opposite White Bear islands—Missing hunters—
Shannon still absent—A skin-boat fitted up—J. Fields' encounter with a bear—Bears very
troublesome—Cache completed at Portage creek—Progress of the portage—Violent storm of
rain and hail—Narrow escape of Captain Clark and some of the party who return to camp
at Willow run—Men much bruised by hailstones—A remarkable fountain—Buffalo very
numerous—A heavy dew—The portage passed at last—Details of its length and course—A
bear-hunt—The Rocky Mountain rat—The building of the boat—Meteorological observations—A natural phenomenon—Observance of the Fourth of July—Heavy hailstorm—The
kit fox—A buffalo-hunt—The boat proves a failure, and is abandoned—Captain Clark, with
ten men, goes up river to find wood for canoes—The boat taken to pieces and cached—
Sergeant Ordway, with four canoes and eight men, goes up river to join Captain Clark—
Mosquitoes and gnats very troublesome—Sergeant Pryor dislocates his shoulder—Captain
Lewis sends the canoes and baggage up to Captain Clark's camp, and goes to this camp by
land—The party are there engaged in boat-building—Very large Indian lodge passed—
Flattery run—The new boats launched—Distances and bearings of mountain chains—Fort
mountain.

ON the 19*th*, Captain Clark, not being able to find the bear
mentioned in the last chapter, spent the day in examining the country both above and below the Whitebear
islands, and concluded that the place of his camp would be
the best point for the [upper] extremity of the portage.
The men were therefore occupied in drying the meat to be
left there. Immense numbers of buffalo were everywhere
around, and the men saw a summer-duck [*Aix sponsa*], which
is now sitting. Next morning, the 20*th*, he crossed the level
plain, fixing stakes to mark the route of the portage, till he
reached a large ravine, which would oblige us to make the
portage farther from the river. After this, there being no
other obstacle, he went to the [Missouri] river where [oppo-
site mouth of Medicine river] he had first struck it, and took
its courses and distances down to the [Portage creek] camp.
From this draught and survey of Captain Clark's, we had now

a clear and connected view of the falls, cascades, and rapids of the Missouri.[1]

This river is 300 yards wide at the point where it receives the waters of Medicine [Sun] river, which is 137 yards in width. The united current continues 328 poles to a (*p. 276*) small rapid on the north side, from which it gradually widens to 1,400 yards, and at the distance of 548 poles reaches the head of the rapids, narrowing as it approaches them. Here the hills on the north, which had withdrawn from the bank, closely border the river, which, for the space of 320 poles, makes its way over the rocks, with a descent of 30 feet. In this course the current is contracted to 580 yards, and after throwing itself over a small pitch of five feet, forms a beautiful cascade of 26 feet 5 inches ; this does not, however, fall immediately or perpendicularly, being stopped by a part of the rock, which projects at about one-third of the distance. After descending this fall, and passing the cottonwood island on which the eagle has fixed her nest, the river goes on for 532 poles over rapids and little falls, the estimated descent of which is 13½ feet, till it is

[1] The following paragraph should be read with reference to the map facing p. 261 of the 1814 edition, which we reproduce in facsimile. The original of this is a beautifully executed colored sketch, by Clark, with the lettering in his hand. This occupies pp. 132, 133 of Codex E. It is drawn on a scale of 600 poles to the inch, continuously on two facing pages of the codex, which, when laid out flat together, measure 14½ inches long by 4⅞ broad ; of which length only 10⅛ inches were engraved, and these reduced to 6⅞ inches. The original takes in the Missouri beyond Smith's river, with Fort mountain in the extreme S.W. corner of the chart. The engraver's work was faithfully and clearly done as far as it went, though he abbreviated the lettering of the original—a draught upon which no geographer or engineer could now look unmoved.

What means of mensuration the explorers had at their command does not appear from the published narrative. But we now know it was simply a spirit-level. Clark, in Lewis E 99, says : " Took the hight with as much accuracy as possible with a sperit level." These measurements were all Clark's. One of them, " 87 feet and ¾ of an inch " reads curiously. I fully expected to find in the codex that it was 87¾ feet, with an " in " belonging to a phrase " *in* pitch " or " *in* fall," and mistaken for *inch*. But Clark, in Lewis E 99, reads clearly " pitching over a rock of 87 F. ¾ of an Inch in hight." On the colored map, too, which occupies pp. 132, 133 of Codex E, it is written "87 feet ¾ of an

joined by a large fountain, boiling up underneath the rocks near the edge of the river, into which it falls with a cascade of eight feet. This is of the most perfect clearness, and rather of a bluish cast; even after falling into the Missouri, it preserves its color for half a mile. From this fountain the river descends with increased rapidity for the distance of 214 poles, during which the estimated descent is five feet. From this, for a distance of 135 poles, the river descends 14 feet 7 inches, including a perpendicular fall of 6 feet 7 inches. The river has now become pressed into a space of 473 yards, and here forms a grand cataract, by falling over a plain rock the whole distance across the river, to the depth of 47 feet 8 inches. After recovering itself, the Missouri proceeds with an estimated descent of three feet; till, at the distance of 102 poles, it is again precipitated down the Crooked falls of 19 feet perpendicular. Below this, at the mouth of a deep ravine, (*p. 277*) is a fall of five feet; after which, for the distance of 970 poles, the descent is much more gradual, not being more than ten feet. Then succeeds a handsome level plain, for the space of 178 poles, with a computed descent of three feet, making a bend

inch Pitch," in Clark's hand, where the engraver makes the phrase ''87 feet ¾ in pitch." That the actual survey and draught of the falls were entirely Captain Clark's work, is generously acknowledged by Captain Lewis : " Capt. Clark now furnished me with the field notes of the survey which he had made of the Missouri and it's Cataracts, cascades, &c.," Lewis E 103. The text of this report occupies E 103–106, with courses and distances in poles, widths in yards, pitches in feet and inches, all in due tabular form. Modern science confirms the extraordinary faithfulness of the description of the Great Falls as a whole, and the minute accuracy of the measurements in detail. The best contemporary skill in engineering, for the construction of the Black Eagle Falls dam for manufacturing purposes—a matter necessarily of prime pecuniary importance—verifies and confirms Lewis and Clark's figures, to a degree of minuteness which must be regarded as little short of marvelous. Thus, a paper by Mr. Maurice S. Parker, M. Am. Soc. C. E., on " Black Eagle Falls Dam, Great Falls, Montana," published in Trans. Amer. Soc. Civil Engrs., Vol. XXVIII. No. 1, for July, 1892, pp. 56–68, reproduces Lewis and Clark's published plate in facsimile, together with many new illustrations of the construction of this important work, and opens with the following reference to Lewis and Clark's work :
" The Falls of the Missouri River were first made known to the geographical

toward the north. Thence it descends during 480 poles, about 18½ feet, when it makes a perpendicular fall of two feet, which is 90 poles beyond [above] the great cataract, in approaching which it descends 13 feet within 200 yards. Now gathering strength from its confined channel, which is only 280 yards wide, the river rushes over the [Great] fall to the depth of 87 feet and three-quarters of an inch. After raging among the rocks and losing itself in foam, it is compressed immediately into a bed of 93 yards in width. It continues for 340 poles, to the entrance of a run or deep ravine, where there is a fall of three feet; which, joined to the decline of the river during that course, make the descent six feet. As it goes on, the descent within the next 240 poles is only four feet. From this, passing a run, or deep ravine, the descent for 400 poles is 13 feet; within 240 poles is a second descent of 18 feet; thence 160 poles is a descent of six feet; after which to the mouth of Portage creek, a distance of 280 poles, the descent is ten feet. From this survey and estimate it results that the river experiences a descent of 352 feet in the course of 2¾ miles, from the commencement of the rapids to the mouth of

world [*i. e.*, were discovered] in the year 1805, by the explorers Lewis and Clarke, on their expedition of exploration to the headwaters of the Missouri. The map of the river at the Falls, which accompanies their report (see page 57 [facsimile there]) is remarkably accurate and is a monument to the faithful work of these early explorers. They did not indicate the actual fall of the river on their map, giving only the height of rapids and falls. The total fall of the river for a distance of 10 miles from the first rapid to the foot of the fall known as the 'Great Falls' (which has a sheer drop of 75.5 feet) is 412.5 feet.

"When in 1887 the Great Northern Railroad was built through the town of Great Falls, the value of this water-power became apparent to its projectors, and steps were at once taken to utilize a part of it for commercial purposes by constructing a dam at the first fall, known as Black Eagle; the result is that what only a few years ago was wild prairie is now the site of a thriving city of nearly 10,000 inhabitants, which bids fair to rival the well-known cities that have grown great through the influence of water-power."

My attention was called to this article, which otherwise I might have overlooked, by my friend Mr. F. Firmstone, President of the Iron and Coal Company of Cranberry, N. C., where my preliminary editorial work was done on these volumes in the summer of 1892.

Portage creek, exclusive of the almost impassable rapids which extend for a mile below its [Portage creek's] entrance.

The latitude of our camp, below the entrance of Portage creek was found to be 47° 7' 10.3", as deduced from a meridian altitude of the sun's lower limb, taken with the octant by back observation giving 53° 10'. [Actually about 47° 36'.]

(*p. 278*) *Friday, June 21st.*[2] Having made the necessary preparations for continuing our route, a part[3] of the baggage was carried across the creek into the high plain, three miles in advance, and placed on one of the carriages with truck-wheels. The rest of the party were employed in drying meat and dressing elk-skins. We killed several mule-deer and an elk, and observed, as usual, vast quantities of buffalo, which came to drink at the river. For the first time on the Missouri, we have seen near the falls a species of fishing-duck, the body of which is brown and white, the wings white, the upper part of the neck of a brick-red, and with a narrow beak; this seems to be of the same kind common in the Susquehanna, Potomac, and James rivers.[4] The little wood which this neighborhood affords consists of the broad- and narrow-leaved cottonwood, the box-elder, the narrow and broad-leaved willow, and the large or sweet ʟwillow, which was not common below Maria's river, but which here attains the same

---

[2] It is not easy to keep track of all the movements of the party from this date, when the portage began, to July 2d, when it was finished. The officers and men were separated, variously engaged, exploring, hunting, transporting baggage, boat-building, etc., passing to and from the three camps connected with the portage ; viz., one below, near Portage creek ; one above, opposite WhiteBear islands ; and another between, at Willow run. The portage measured 17¾ miles, inclusive of the short course below Portage creek, and occupied 11 days.

[3] " I caused the Iron frame of the boat and necessary tools my private baggage and Instruments to be taken as a part of this load, also the baggage of Joseph Fields, Sergt. Gass, and John shields, whom I had seelected to assist me in constructing the leather boat," Lewis E 107.

[4] The same—the red-breasted merganser, *Mergus serrator.* Some of the plants about to be mentioned are : narrow-leaved cottonwood, *Populus angustifolia* ; willows, *Salix* spp., the narrow-leaved being perhaps *S. Longifolia ;* box-elder, *Negundo aceroides ;* gooseberry, *Ribes oxyacanthoides ?* redwood, the bearberry, *Arctostaphylos uva-ursi*, a favorite sort of kinikinik.

size, and has the same appearance, as in the Atlantic States. The undergrowth consists of roses, gooseberries, currants, small honeysuckles, and the redwood, the inner bark of which the *engagés* or watermen are fond of smoking, mixed with tobacco.

June 22d. We[5] now set out to pass the portage, and halted for dinner at [about] eight miles' distance, near a little stream [Willow run]. The axle-trees of our carriage, which had been made of an old mast, and the cottonwood tongues, broke before we came there. But we renewed them with the timber of the sweet willow, which lasted till within half a mile of our intended camp, when the tongues gave way, and we were obliged to take as much baggage as we could carry on our backs down to the river, where we formed a camp in a small grove of timber, opposite the Whitebear islands.

Here the banks on both sides of the river are handsome, level, and extensive; that near our camp is not more than two feet above the surface of the water. The river is about 800 yards wide just above these islands, ten feet deep (*p. 279*) in most places, and with a very gentle current. The plains, however, on this part of the river, are not so fertile as those from the mouth of the Muscleshell and thence downward; there is much more stone on the sides of the hills and on the broken land than is to be found lower down. We saw on the plains vast quantities of buffalo, a number of small birds, and the large brown curlew, which is now sitting and lays its eggs, which are of a pale blue with black specks, on the ground without any nest. There is also a species of lark, much resembling the bird called the old-field lark, with a yellow breast and a black spot on the crop; though it differs from the latter in having its tail formed of feathers of an unequal length and pointed; the beak, too, is somewhat longer and more curved, and the note differs considerably.[6] The prickly-pear annoyed us very much to-day,

---

[5] " All the party except Sergt. Ordway, Sharbono, Goodrich, York, and the Indian woman," Lewis E 108.

[6] This last observation is correct, as attested by all who have heard the

by sticking through our moccasins. As soon as we had kindled our fires, we examined the meat which Captain Clark had left here, but found that the greater part had been taken by the wolves.

June 23d. After we had brought up the canoe and baggage, Captain Clark went down to the camp at Portage creek, where four of the men [Ordway, Goodrich, Chaboneau, and York] had been left with the Indian woman. Captain Lewis during the morning prepared the camp, and in the afternoon went [with J. Fields] down in a canoe to Medicine [Sun] river, to look after the three men [Drewyer, Shannon, and R. Fields] who had been sent thither to hunt on the 19th, and from whom nothing had been heard. He went up this river about half a mile, and then walked along on the right bank, hallooing as he went, till at the distance of five miles he found one of them [Shannon], who had fixed his camp on the opposite bank, where he had killed seven deer and dried about 600 pounds of buffalo-meat, but had killed no elk, the animal chiefly wanted. He knew nothing of his companions, except that on the day of their departure from camp he had left them at the falls and come on to Medicine river, not having seen them since. As it was too late to return, Captain Lewis passed (*p. 280*) over on a raft, which he made for the purpose, and spent the night at Shannon's camp. The next morning,

Monday, June 24th,[7] he sent J. Fields up the river, with orders to go four miles and return, whether he found the two absent hunters [Drewyer and R. Fields] or not. Then

---

notes of the Eastern (*Sturnella magna*) and Western (*S. neglecta*) field-larks, from Lewis and Clark to the present writer; but the comparison made of the tail and beak does not hold good. The curlew I suppose to be *Numenius longirostris*, which is common in that country, though the color of the eggs, as given, raises a doubt.

[7] Lewis E 110, this date, has: "As it will give a better view of the transactions of the party, I shall on each day give the occurrences of both camps during our separation." See note, June 21st. Parallel narratives, of operations about 18 miles apart, therefore continue to run till the portage is finished and all the party are again together, above the falls.

descending the southwest side of Medicine river, he crossed the Missouri in the canoe, and sent Shannon back to his camp [on Sun river] to join Fields, and bring the meat which they had killed. This they did, and arrived in the evening at the camp on Whitebear islands. A part of the men from Portage creek also arrived, with two canoes and baggage. [R. Fields came with them, and gave us an account of his and Drewyer's hunt.]

On going down yesterday Captain Clark cut off several angles of the former route, so as to shorten the Portage considerably, and marked it with stakes. He arrived there in time to have two of the canoes carried up in the high plain, about a mile in advance. Here they all repaired their moccasins, and put on double soles to protect them from the prickly-pear, and from the sharp points of earth which have been formed by the trampling of the buffalo during the late rains. This of itself is sufficient to render the portage disagreeable to one who has no burden; but as the men are loaded as heavily as their strength will permit, the crossing is really painful. Some are limping with the soreness of their feet; others are scarcely able to stand for more than a few minutes, from the heat and fatigue. They are all obliged to halt and rest frequently; at almost every stopping-place they fall, and many of them are asleep in an instant; yet no one complains, and they go on with great cheerfulness. At the camp [of these men, midway in the portage] Drewyer and [R.] Fields joined them; for, while Captain Lewis was looking for them [these two] at Medicine river, they [had] returned to report the absence of Shannon, about whom they had been very uneasy. They had killed several buffalo at the bend of the Missouri above the falls, dried about 800 pounds of meat, and got 100 pounds of tallow; they had also killed some deer, but had seen no elk. After getting the party in motion with the canoes, Captain Clark returned to his camp at Portage creek.

(*p. 281*) We were now occupied [at White Bear camp] in fitting up a boat of skins, the frame of which had been prepared for the purpose at Harper's ferry [in Virginia]. It was made of iron, 36 feet long, 4½ feet in the beam, and 26 inches wide in the bottom. Two men [Gass and Shields] had been sent this morning for timber to complete it, but they could find scarcely any even tolerably straight sticks 4½ feet long; and as the cottonwood is too soft and brittle, we were obliged to use willow and box-elder.

June 25th. The [main] party returned to the lower camp. Two men [Gass and Shields] were sent on the large [White Bear] islands to look for timber. [Frazier was dispatched in a canoe to Drewyer's camp, to fetch the meat which the hunters had procured.] J. Fields was sent up the Missouri to hunt elk; but he returned about noon, and informed us that a few miles above he saw two white bears near the river; that in attempting to fire at them, he came suddenly on a third, which being only a few steps off immediately attacked him; that in running to escape from the monster, he leaped down a steep bank of the river, where, falling on a bar of stone, he cut his hand and knee, and bent his gun; but fortunately for him, the bank concealed him from his antagonist, or he would most probably have been lost. The other two [Gass and Shields] returned with a small quantity of bark and timber, which was all they could find on the island; but they had killed two elk. These were valuable, for we were desirous of procuring the skins of that animal in order to cover the boat, as they are more strong and durable than those of the buffalo, and do not shrink so much in drying. [In the evening Drewyer and Frazier arrived at our upper camp with the meat and tallow mentioned yesterday.] The party that went to the lower camp had one canoe and the baggage carried into the high plain to be ready in the morning, and then all who could make use of their feet had a dance on the green to the music of the violin.[8]

---

[8] "Such as were able to shake a foot amused themselves in dancing on the green to the music of the violin which Cruzatte plays extreemly well. Capt. C. somewhat unwell to-day; he made Charbono kook for the party," Lewis E 113, 114.

We have been unsuccessful in our attempt to catch fish, nor does there seem to be any in this part of the river. We observe a number of water-terrapins [doubtless *Emys elegans* of Maximilian]. There are great quantities of young black-birds [*Scolecophagus cyanocephalus*] on these islands, just beginning to fly. Among the vegetable productions we observe a species of wild rye [*Elymus sitanion*] which is now heading. It rises (*p. 282*) to the height of 18 or 20 inches, the beard remarkably fine and soft; the culen [culm] is jointed, and in every respect, except in height, it resembles the wild rye. Great quantities of mint [*Mentha canadensis*], like the peppermint, are also found here.

The winds are sometimes violent on these plains. The men informed us that as they were bringing one of the canoes along on truck-wheels, they hoisted the sail, and the wind carried her along for some distance.

June 26th. Two men [Gass and Shields] were sent on the opposite side of the river for bark and timber, of which they procured some, but by no means enough for our purposes. The bark of the cottonwood is too soft, and our only depend-ence is on the sweet willow, which has a tough, strong bark. The two hunters [Drewyer, J. Fields] killed seven buffalo. [Frazier was set to sewing skins to cover the new boat. Captain Lewis assigned to himself the duty of cooking, and made a suet dumpling for every man.] A party arrived from below with two canoes and baggage; the wind being from the southeast, they had made considerable progress with the sails. On their arrival one of the men [White-house] who had been considerably heated and fatigued, swallowed a very hearty draught of water, and was immedi-ately taken ill. Captain Lewis bled him with a penknife, having no other instrument at hand, and succeeded in restor-ing him to health the next day. Captain Clark[9] formed a

---

[9] "Captain Clark also selected the articles to be deposited in the cash, con-sisting of my desk which I had left for that purpose and in which I had left some books, my specimens of plants minerals &c. collected from Fort Mandan to that place, . . . and some other small articles belonging to the party which

second cache or deposit near the [lower] camp, and placed the swivel under the rocks near the river.

Antelopes are still scattered through the plains; the females with their young, which are generally two in number, and the males by themselves.

June 27th. The [main party left for the lower camp to bring up the remaining canoe and baggage. Whitehouse, being still unwell, was set to work with Frazier sewing skins for the new boat. The rest of the] party were employed in preparing timber for the boat, except two [Drewyer and J. Fields] who were sent to hunt. About one in the afternoon a cloud arose from the southwest, and brought with it violent thunder, lightning, and hail. Soon after it passed, the hunters came in, from about four miles above us. They had killed nine elk and three bears. As they were hunting on the river they saw a low ground covered with thick brushwood, where from the tracks along shore they thought a bear had probably taken refuge. They therefore landed, without making a noise, and climbed (*p. 283*) a tree about 20 feet above the ground. Having fixed themselves securely, they raised a loud shout, and a bear instantly rushed toward them. These animals never climb, and therefore when he came to the tree and stopped to look at them, Drewyer shot him in the head. He proved to be the largest we had yet seen; his noise [nose] appeared to be like that of a common ox; his fore feet measured nine inches across; the hind feet were 7 inches wide and 11¾ long, exclusive of the talons. One of these animals came within 30 yards of the camp last night, and carried off some buffalo-meat which we had placed on a pole.

In the evening after the storm, the water on this side of the river became of a deep crimson color, probably caused

could be dispensed with," Lewis E 115. The next page of the codex gives the detailed courses and distances of the portage, footing up 17¾ miles (not 18 as lettered roundly in the engraving, and also by Clark in his original draught). The courses are here reversed from those published, *i. e.*, "N. 42° E. 4 miles" etc., for "S. 42° W. 4 miles," etc., as they read in the opposite direction.

by some stream above washing down a kind of soft red stone, which we observe in the neighboring bluffs and gullies. At the camp below, the men who left us this morning were busy in preparing their loads for to-morrow, which were impeded by the rain, hail, and the hard wind from the northwest.

June 28th. The party were all occupied in making the boat.[10] They obtained a sufficient quantity of willow-bark to line her ; over these [pieces of bark] were placed the elk-skins ; and when these failed, we were obliged to use the buffalo-hides. The white bears have now become exceedingly troublesome ; they constantly infest our camp during the night, and though they have not attacked us, as our dog which patrols all night gives us notice of their approach, yet we are obliged to sleep with our arms by our sides for fear of accident, and we cannot send one man alone to any distance, particularly if he has to pass through brushwood. We saw two of them to-day on the large island opposite us ; but as we are all so much occupied now, we mean to reserve ourselves for some leisure moment, and then make a party to drive them from the islands. The river has risen nine inches since our arrival here.

(*p. 284*) At Portage creek, Captain Clark completed the cache, in which we deposited whatever we could spare from our baggage ; some ammunition, provisions, books, the specimens of plants and minerals, and a draught of the [Missouri] river from its entrance [into the Mississippi] to Fort Mandan. After closing it, he broke up the camp, and took all the remaining baggage to the high plain, about three miles. Portage creek has risen considerably in consequence of the rain ; the water has become of a deep crimson color, and ill tasted. On overtaking the canoe[11] he

---

[10] " Set Drewyer to shaving the Elk skins, Fields to make the cross stays for the boat, Frazier and Whitehouse continue their operations with the skins, Shields and gass finish the horizontal bars of the sections ; after which I sent them in surch of willow bark," Lewis E 118.

[11] Which had been hauled on trucks to a certain point in the portage, " he found

found that there was more baggage than could be carried on the two carriages; he therefore left some of the heavy articles which could not be injured, and proceeded to Willow run,[12] where he camped for the night. Here the party made a supper on two buffalo which they killed on the way; but passed the night in the rain, with a high wind from the southwest. In the morning,

Saturday, June 29th, finding it impossible to reach the upper end of the portage with the present load, in consequence of the state of the road after the rain, he sent back nearly all his party to bring on the articles which had been left yesterday. Having lost some notes and remarks which he had made on first ascending the river, he determined to go up to the Whitebear islands along its banks, in order to supply the deficiency. He there left one man to guard the baggage, and went on to the falls, accompanied by his servant York, Chaboneau, and his wife with her young child.

On his arrival there he observed a very dark cloud rising in the west, which threatened rain, and looked around for some shelter; but could find no place where the party would be secure from being blown into the river, if the wind should prove as violent as it sometimes does in the plains. At length, about a quarter of a mile above the falls, he found a deep ravine, where there were some shelving rocks, under which he took refuge. They were on the upper side of the ravine near the river, perfectly safe from the rain, and therefore laid down their guns, compass, and other articles which (*p. 285*) they carried with them. The shower was at first moderate; it then increased to a heavy rain, the effects of which they did not feel; but soon after, a torrent of rain and hail descended. The rain seemed to fall in a solid mass, and instantly, collecting in the ravine, came rolling down in a dreadful current, carrying the mud, rocks, and every-

there was more baggage than he could possibly take at one load on the two sets of trucks and therefore left some barrels of pork and flour and a few heavy boxes of amunition," Lewis E 119.

[12] A small creek on the south, in the course of the portage; now Box-elder.

thing that opposed it.[13] Captain Clark fortunately saw it a moment before it reached them, and springing up with his gun and shot-pouch in his left hand, with his right clambered up the steep bluff, pushing on the Indian woman with her child in her arms; her husband too had seized her hand and was pulling her up the hill, but he was so terrified at the danger that [he remained frequently motionless; and] but for Captain Clark, himself and his wife and child would have been lost. So instantaneous was the rise of the water that, before Captain Clark had reached his gun and begun to ascend the bank, the water was up to his waist, and he could scarcely get up faster than it rose, till it reached the height of 15 feet, with a furious current which, had they waited a moment longer, would have swept them into the river just above the Great Falls, down which they must inevitably have been precipitated. They reached the plain in safety and found York, who had separated from them just before the storm to hunt some buffalo, and was now returning to find his master. They had been obliged to escape so rapidly that Captain Clark lost his compass [i. e., circumferentor] and umbrella, Chaboneau left his gun, [with Captain Lewis' wiping-rod], shot-pouch, and tomahawk, and the Indian woman had just time to grasp her child, before the net[14] in which it lay at her feet was carried down the current.

[13] Such a storm is called a cloud-burst in the West, where it is no rare occurrence. Its suddenness and volume can hardly be exaggerated, and often cause loss of life. On this occasion Captain Clark and his companions had not a moment to spare. I remember a case in Arizona, when a six-mule team and driver were swept away and drowned by the torrent of water which flooded what had a few moments before been the dry bed of a coulée, used for years as a road. The town of Prescott, until lately the capital of Arizona, will probably suffer in this way, sooner or later.

[14] "The bier in which the woman carries her child and all it's cloaths were swept away as they lay at her feet," Lewis E 123. This is an interesting use of the old word *bier*, which we found early in this work employed for a covering for the head to keep off mosquitoes (whence our mosquito-*bar*); but it is now archaic, except in connection with funerals. The "net" of the text therefore is simply the child's cradle, made light and portable, something like a basket.

He had relinquished his intention of going up the river, and returned to the camp at Willow run. Here he found that the party sent this morning for the baggage had all returned to camp in great confusion,[15] leaving their loads on the plain. On account of the heat they generally go nearly naked, and with no covering on their heads. The hail was so large, and driven so furiously against them by the high wind, that it knocked several of them down. One of them particularly was (*p. 286*) thrown to the ground three times; most of them were bleeding freely, and complained of being much bruised. Willow run had risen six feet since the rain; and as the plains were so wet that they could not proceed, they passed the night at their camp.

At Whitebear camp, also, we had not been insensible to the hailstorm, though less exposed. In the morning there had been a heavy shower of rain, after which it became fair. After assigning to the men their respective employments, Captain Lewis took one of them [Drewyer], and went to see the large fountain near the falls. For about six miles he passed through a beautiful level plain, and then, on reaching the break of the river hills, was overtaken by the gust of wind from the southwest, attended by lightning, thunder, and rain. Fearing a renewal of the scene of the 27th, they took shelter in a little gully, where there were some broad stones with which they meant to protect themselves against the hail. Fortunately there was not much, and that of a small size; so that they felt no inconvenience, except that of being exposed without shelter for an hour, and being drenched by the rain. After it was over they proceeded to the fountain, which is perhaps the largest in America. It is situated in a pleasant level plain, about 25 yards from the river, into which it falls over some steep irregular rocks,

---

[15] Lewis E 122 has " consternation," the concrete sense of which was literally true, for several of the men had been knocked down together. Our use of the word is in its abstract sense. He says also that the men were " sorely mawled," and that " Capt. C. gave the party a dram to console them in some measure for their general defeat."

with a sudden ascent of about six feet in one part of its course. The water boils up from among the rocks and with such force, near the center, that the surface seems higher there than the earth on the sides of the fountain, which is a handsome turf of fine green grass. The water is extremely pure, cold, and pleasant to the taste, not being impregnated with lime or any foreign substance. It is perfectly transparent and continues its bluish cast for half a mile down the Missouri, notwithstanding the rapidity of the river. After examining it for some time, Captain Lewis returned to the camp.

(*p. 287*) *June* 30*th*. In the morning Captain Clark sent [two men to kill buffalo, two others to the falls to search for the articles lost yesterday, and kept one man to cook; he then dispatched the rest of] the men to bring up the baggage left on the plains yesterday. On their return the axle-trees and carriages were repaired, and the baggage was conveyed on the shoulders of the party across Willow run, which had fallen as low as three feet. The carriages being then taken over, a load of baggage was carried to the six-mile stake, deposited there, and the carriages brought back. Such is the state of the plains that this operation consumed the day. Two men were sent to the falls to look for the articles lost yesterday; but they found nothing but the compass, covered with mud and sand, at the mouth of the ravine; the place at which Captain Clark had been caught by the storm was filled with large rocks. The men complain much of the bruises received yesterday from the hail. A more than usual number of buffalo appeared about the camp to-day, and furnished plenty of meat. Captain Clark thought that at one view he must have seen at least 10,000. In the course of the day there was a heavy gust of wind from the southwest, after which the evening was fair.

At Whitebear camp we had a heavy dew this morning, which is quite a remarkable occurrence. The party continues to be occupied with the boat, the cross-bars for which are now finished, and there remain only the strips to complete the wood-work. The skins necessary to cover it have already been prepared; they amount to 28 elk-skins and four buffalo-skins. Among our game were two beaver, which we have had occasion to observe are found wherever there is timber. We also killed a large bull-bat or goatsucker [*Chordeiles henryi*] of which there are many in this neighborhood, resembling in every respect those of the same species in the United States. We have not seen the leather-winged bat [16] for some time, nor are there any of the small goatsucker [*Phalænoptilus nuttalli*] in this part of the Missouri. We have not seen that species of goatsucker called the whippoorwill [*Antrostomus vociferus*], which is commonly confounded (*p. 288*) in the United States with the large goatsucker which we observe here. This last prepares no nest, but lays its eggs on the open plains; they generally begin to sit on two eggs, and we believe raise only one brood in a season; at the present moment they are just hatching their young.

Monday, July 1st, 1805. After a severe day's work Captain Clark reached our camp in the evening, accompanied by his party, and all the baggage except that left at the six-mile stake, for which they were too much fatigued to return. The route, from the lower camp on Portage creek to that near Whitebear island, having been now measured and examined by Captain Clark, is as follows:

From our camp opposite the last considerable rapid to the entrance of Portage creek S. 9° E. for three-quarters of a mile; thence on a course S. 10° E. for two miles (though for the canoes the best route is to the left of this course, and strikes Portage 1¾ miles from its entrance, avoiding in

---

[16] This was written at a time when bats were birds and whales were fishes, for most persons. The codex gives no clew to the species; we may conjecture *Lasiurus pruinosus.* The bird commonly called bull-bat is the long-winged goatsucker or nighthawk, a light Western variety of which the text has in view.

At next date, July 1st, a new codex comes into the narrative. This is Clark G, running to Oct. 10th (parallel with Lewis E and F to Aug. 22d). But the Biddle text continues to follow E and F, mainly.

this way a very steep hill which lies above Portage creek);
from this S. 18° W. for four miles, passing the head of a
drain or ravine which falls into the Missouri below the Great
Falls, and thence to Willow run, which has always a plentiful
supply of good water and some timber; here the course
turns to S. 45° W. for four miles further; then S. 66° W.
for three miles, crossing at the beginning of this course the
head of a drain which falls into the Missouri at the Crooked
Falls, and reaching an elevated point of the plain; from
which S. 42° W.   On approaching the river on this course
there is a long and gentle descent from the high plain, after
which the road turns a little to the right of the course up
the river to our camp.   The whole portage is 17¾ miles.

At Whitebear camp we were occupied with the boat, and
digging a pit for the purpose of making some tar.   The
day has been warm, and the mosquitoes troublesome.   We
were fortunate enough to observe equal altitudes of the
(*p. 289*) sun with the sextant, which since our arrival here
we have been prevented from doing by flying clouds and
storms in the evening.

July 2d.   A shower of rain fell very early this morning.
We then dispatched some men for the baggage left behind
yesterday, and the rest were engaged in putting the boat
together.   This was accomplished in about three hours, and
then we began to sew on the leather over the cross-bars of
iron on the inner side of the boat which form the ends of
the sections.   By two o'clock the last of the baggage
arrived, to the great delight of the party, who were anxious
to proceed.   The mosquitoes we find very troublesome.

Having completed our celestial observations, we went
over to the large island to make an attack upon its inhabitants, the bears, which have annoyed us very much of late,
and were prowling about our camp all last night.   We
found that the part of the island frequented by the bears
forms an almost impenetrable thicket of the broad-leaved
willow.   Into this we forced our way in parties of three;
but could see only one bear, which instantly attacked

Drewyer. Fortunately, as he was rushing on, the hunter shot him through the heart within 20 paces and he fell, which enabled Drewyer to get out of his way. We then followed him 100 yards, and found that the wound had been mortal.

Not being able to discover any more of these animals, we returned to camp. Here, in turning over some of the baggage, we caught a rat [17] somewhat larger than the common European rat, and of a lighter color ; the body and outer parts of the legs and head of a light lead-color; the inner side of the legs, as well as the belly, feet, and ears, white ; the ears are not covered with hair, and are much larger than those of the common rat ; the toes also are longer ; the eyes are black and prominent, the whiskers very long and full ; the tail is rather longer than the body, and covered with fine fur and hair of the same size with that on the back, which (*p. 290*) is very close, short, and silky in its texture. This was the first we had met, although its nests are very frequent in the cliffs of rocks and hollow trees, where we also found large quantities of the shells and seed of the prickly-pear, on which we conclude the rats chiefly subsist.

[17] *Neotoma cinerea*, the Rocky Mountain pack-rat, now well known, then new to science, and not technically named till 1815 (Ord, Guthrie's Geogr., 2d. Am. ed. II. p. 292). See note [86], p. 40, and cf. my Monograph of the *Muridæ*, 1878, pp. 24-29. Lewis E 129 has an excellent description, deleted and marked in red ink " copy for Dr. Barton "—like most of the other zoölogical and the botanical matter of the codices, which never saw the light. When about to bring out this work, after the death of Governor Lewis, General Clark made a contract with Benj. S. Barton, of Philadelphia, by the terms of which the latter was to produce a formal work on the natural history of the Expedition. In consesequence of which, Mr. Biddle, of course, passed over such points in the codices. Dr. Barton soon died, having done nothing—nothing whatever was to be discovered among his papers. This is the simple explanation of the meagerness of the History in scientific matters with which the codices are replete—to the keenest regret of all naturalists, and the great loss of credit which was justly due these foremost explorers of a country whose almost every animal and plant was then unknown to science. My notes may in some measure throw back upon them a reflection of what is their just due—but it can never be more than reflected glory, for in the meantime others have carried off the honors that belong by right to Lewis and Clark.

The mosquitoes are uncommonly troublesome. The wind was again high from the southwest.

These winds are in fact always the coldest and most violent which we experience, and the hypothesis which we have formed on that subject is, that the air, coming in contact with the Snowy [18] mountains, immediately becomes chilled and condensed, and being thus rendered heavier than the air below, it descends into the rarified air below, or into the vacuum formed by the constant action of the sun on the open unsheltered plains. The clouds rise suddenly near these mountains, and distribute their contents partially over the neighboring plains. The same cloud will discharge hail alone in one part, hail and rain in another, and rain only in a third, all within the space of a few miles ; while at the same time there is snow falling on the mountains to the southeast of us. There is at present no snow on those mountains ; that which covered them on our arrival, as well as that which has since fallen, having disappeared. The mountains to the north and northwest of us are still entirely covered with snow ; indeed, there has been no perceptible diminution of it since we first saw them, which induces a belief either that the clouds prevailing at this season do not reach their summits or that they deposit their snow only. They glisten with great beauty when the sun shines on them in a particular direction, and most probably from this glittering appearance have derived the name of the Shining mountains.

July 3*d*. Nearly the whole party were employed in different labors connected with the boat, which is now almost completed. But we have not as yet been able to obtain tar from our kiln, a circumstance that will occasion us not a little embarrassment. Having been told (*p. 291*) by the Indians that on leaving the falls we should soon pass the buffalo country, we have before us the prospect of fasting

---

[18] Our authors so call those snow-capped ranges of the Rockies which they have already sighted. The mountains now specified as Snowy are to the southeast of the party (south of the Judith mountains).

occasionally.   But in order to provide a supply we sent out the hunters, who killed only a buffalo and two antelopes ; which, added to six beaver and two otter, have been all our game for two or three days.   At ten in the morning we had a slight shower, which scarcely wet the grass.

Thursday, July 4th, 1805.   The boat was now completed, except what is in fact the most difficult part, the making her seams secure.   We had intended to dispatch a canoe with part of our men to the United States early this spring ; but not having yet seen the Snake Indians, or knowing whether to calculate on their friendship or enmity, we have decided not to weaken our party, which is already scarcely sufficient to repel any hostility.   We were afraid too that such a measure might dishearten those who remain ; as we have never suggested it to them, they are all perfectly and enthusiastically attached to the enterprise, and willing to encounter any danger to insure its success.[19]   We had a heavy dew this morning.

Since our arrival at the falls, we have repeatedly heard a strange noise [20] coming from the mountains in a direction a little to the north of west.   It is heard at different periods of the day and night, sometimes when the air is perfectly still and without a cloud, and consists of one stroke only, or of five or six discharges in quick succession.   It is loud, and resembles precisely the sound of a six-pound piece of ordnance at the distance of three miles.   The Minnetarees fre-

[19] " All appear perfectly to have made up their minds to suceed in the expedition or purish in the attempt.   we all believe that we are now about to enter on the most perilous and difficult part of our voyage, yet I see no one repining ; all appear ready to met those difficulties which await us with resolution and becoming fortitude," Lewis E 131.

[20] " Witnessed a nois," Lewis E 134, curiously.   Perhaps no passage in the History has been more hardly handled than this one.   Some learned dunces denied it, and suspected romancing ; some who were wise enough to believe it were at a loss to explain it.   Let it be understood, once for all, that Lewis and Clark never embellished.   If they are witnesses to the fact of a certain noise, that noise was heard, and it was exactly such a noise as they say it was.   The fact is, every old miner and mountaineer in Montana and Idaho has heard just such noises.

quently mentioned this noise like thunder, which they said
the mountains made; but we had paid no attention to it,
believing it to have been some superstition or perhaps a
falsehood. The watermen also of the party say that the
Pawnees and Ricaras give the same account of a noise heard
in the Black mountains to the westward of them. The
solution of the mystery given by the philosophy (*p. 292*)
of the watermen is, that it is occasioned by the bursting of
the rich mines of silver confined within the bosom of the
mountain.

An elk and a beaver are all that were killed to-day; the
buffalo seem to have withdrawn from our neighborhood,
though several of the men, who went to-day to visit the falls
for the first time, mention that they are still abundant at
that place. We contrived, however, to spread not a very
sumptuous but a comfortable table in honor of the day,
and in the evening gave the men a drink of spirits, which
was the last of our stock. Some of them appeared sensible
to the effects of even so small a quantity; and as is usual
among them on all festivals, the fiddle was produced and a
dance begun, which lasted till nine o'clock, when it was
interrupted by a heavy shower of rain. They continued
their merriment, however, till a late hour.[21]

July 5th. The boat was brought up into a high situation,
and fires were kindled under her, in order to dry her
more expeditiously. Despairing now of procuring any tar,
we formed a composition of powdered charcoal with bees-
wax and buffalo-tallow to supply its place; should this
resource fail us it will be very unfortunate, as in every
other respect the boat answers our purposes completely.
Although not quite dry, she can be carried with ease by five

---

[21] " We drank the last of our spirits in celebrating the day, and amused ourselves
with dancing till 9 o'clock at night, when a shower of rain fell and we retired
to rest," Gass, p. 106. They had not a drop for more than a year afterward.
Lewis E 135 gives the menu as "bacon, beans, suit dumplings and buffaloe
beaf &c. in short we had no just cause to covet the sumptuous feasts of our
countrymen on this day."

men; her form is as complete as could be wished; she is very strong, and will carry at least 8,000 pounds, with her complement of hands. Besides our want of tar, we have been unlucky in sewing the skins with a needle which had sharp edges instead of a point merely. Although a large thong was used in order to fill the holes, yet it shrinks in drying and leaves them open, so that we fear the boat will leak.

A large herd of buffalo came near us and we procured three of them; besides which we killed two wolves and three antelopes. In the course of the day other herds of buffalo came near our camp on their way down the river. These herds move with great method and regularity. (*p. 293*) Although ten or twelve herds are seen scattered from each other over a space of many miles, yet if they are undisturbed by pursuit they will be uniformly traveling in the same direction.

July 6th. Last night there were several showers of rain and hail, attended with thunder and lightning. About day-break a heavy storm came on from the southwest, with one continued roar of thunder, and rain and hail. The hail, which was as large as musket-balls, covered the ground completely; on collecting some of it, it lasted during the day and served to cool the water. The red and yellow currant is abundant and now ripe, although still a little acid. We have seen in this neighborhood what we have not met before, a remarkably small fox [*Vulpes velox*], which associates in bands and burrows in the prairie, like the small wolf [coyote], but have not yet been able to obtain any of them, as they are extremely vigilant and betake themselves on the slightest alarm to their burrows, which are very deep.

July 7th. The weather is warm but cloudy, so that the moisture retained by the bark after the rain leaves it slowly, though we have small fires constantly under the boat. We have no tents, and therefore are obliged to use the sails to keep off the bad weather. Our buffalo-skins are scarcely sufficient to cover our baggage, but the men are now dress-ing others to replace their present leather clothing, which soon rots by being so constantly exposed to water. In the evening the hunters returned with the skins of only three buffalo, two antelope, four deer, and three wolves, and reported that the buffalo had gone further down the river; two other hunters, who left us this morning, could find noth-ing except one elk; in addition to this we caught a beaver. The mosquitoes still disturb us very much, and the blowing-flies [blowflies] swarm in vast numbers round the boat. At four in the afternoon we had a light shower of rain, attended with some thunder and lightning.[22]

(*p. 294*) *July 8th.* In order more fully to replace the notes of the river which he had lost, and which he was prevented from supplying by the storm of the 29th ult., Captain Clark set out after breakfast, taking with him nearly the whole party, with a view of shooting buffalo if there should be any near the falls. After getting some distance on the plains the men were divided into squads, and he with two others struck the Missouri at the entrance of Medicine river, whence they proceeded down to the great cataract. He found that the immense herds of buffalo had entirely disappeared, and he thought had gone below the falls. Having made the necessary measurements, he returned through the plains, and reached camp late in the evening; the whole party had killed only three buffalo, three antelopes, and a deer; they had also shot a small fox, and brought in a living ground-squirrel,[23] somewhat larger than those of the United States [*Tamias striatus*].

---

[22] "Captain Clark's black man york is veiy unwell to-day and he gave him a doze of tartar emettic which operated very well and he was much better in the evening. this is a discription of medicine that I never have recourse to in my practice except in cases of intermittent fever," Lewis E 138.

[23] A find of remarkable interest, which nobody has noticed all these years, because the text gives no clew. Clark P 52 has at date of July 6th, 1805: " The men brought me a liveing Grown [ground] squirrel which is something larger than those of the U. S. . . . this is a much handsomer animal, its principle colour is a redish brown but [it] is marked Longitudinally with a much greater

The day was warm and fair, but a slight rain fell in the afternoon. The boat having now become sufficiently dry, we gave her a coat of the composition, which after a proper interval was repeated, and the next morning,

Tuesday, July 9th, she was launched into the water, and swam perfectly well. The seats were then fixed and the oars fitted; but after we had loaded her, as well as the canoes, and were on the point of setting out, a violent wind caused the waves to wet the baggage, so that we were forced to unload the boats. The wind continued high until evening, when to our great disappointment we discovered that nearly all the composition had separated from the skins and left the seams perfectly exposed; so that the boat now leaked very much. To repair this misfortune without pitch is impossible, and as none of that article is to be procured, we therefore, however reluctantly, are obliged to abandon her, after having had so much labor in the construction.[24] We now saw that the section of the boat cov-

number of black or dark brown stripes [than a chipmunk is marked with]. . . the spaces between which is marked by ranges of pure white circular spots." Now this is clearly the pale striped spermophile, *Spermophilus tridecemlineatus pallidus,* first technically named by J. A. Allen, in 1874 (Proc. Bost. Soc. Nat. Hist. XVI. p. 291), and carefully distinguished from the common federation squirrel or 13-lined spermophile by him, in our Monographs of the *Rodentia,* 1877, p. 873. The curious point is that here we have the pale Western variety described before the stock species to which it belongs had a name ; for Dr. S. L. Mitchill did not describe his federation squirrel till June, 1821 (Med. Repos. XXI. p. 248). After L. and C., Mr. Thomas Nuttall, who was with Hunt and Stuart, of the overland Astorian party, in 1811-12, was the next to notice *pallidus,* as he did at the Mandans ; and he is said by Say (Long's Exp. R. Mts. II. p. 174) to have sent specimens to London in 1814. In 1874 I found this animal abundant in Montanan localities not far from the very spot where Captain Clark penned the above notice.

[24] "We called her the Experiment, and expect she will answer our purpose," Gass, p. 106, July 8th. But the "Experiment" proved a melancholy failure, and the more's the pity, as the iron frame had been packed all the way from Virginia. It was a pet scheme of Captain Lewis', and he felt very sore about it. The boat was not water-tight, and could not be made so, which was enough to condemn her ; although, as Lewis E 136 remarks naïvely, "the boat in every other rispect completely answers my most sanguine expectations." Codex E has page after page about this boat, with all of her captain's hopes and fears—the

ered with buffalo-skins on which hair had been left answered better than the elk-skins, and leaked but little; while that part which was covered with (*p. 295*) hair about one-eighth of an inch retained the composition perfectly, and remained sound and dry. From this we perceived that had we employed buffalo instead of elk skins, not singed them so closely as we did, and carefully avoided cutting the leather in sewing, the boat would have been sufficient even with the present composition; or had we singed instead of shaving the elk-skins, we might have succeeded. But we discovered our error too late; the buffalo had deserted us, and the traveling season was so fast advancing that we had no time to spare for experiments; therefore, finding that she could be no longer useful, she was sunk in the water, so as to soften the skins, and enable us the more easily to take her to pieces.

It now became necessary to provide other means for transporting the baggage which we had intended to stow in her. For this purpose we shall want two [more] canoes; but for many miles—from below the mouth of the Muscleshell river to this place—we have not seen a single tree fit to be used in that way. The hunters, however, who have hitherto been sent after timber, mention that there is a low ground on the opposite side of the river, about eight miles above us by land, and more than twice [being thrice] that distance by water, in which we may probably find trees large enough for our purposes. Captain Clark therefore deter-

while that Captain Clark maintains a discreet silence on the subject, and attends imperturbably to his portage, till Captain Lewis should get tired of his toy; when he intended to hunt for cottonwoods to make canoes. Lewis E 142 has: "I bid a dieu to my boat and her expected services."

A letter before me, from Mr. Biddle to General Clark, dated Philadelphia, July 7th, 1810, gives an interesting glimpse of the author's progress in writing this History: "Ever since my return to Philadelphia [from Fincastle, early the previous spring], I have been engaged seven or eight or even more hours a day on our work. . . To-day I have sent you and ten men up into a bottom to look for wood to make canoes, after the unhappy failure of your iron boat. So you see how far I am." This was penned five years to a day after the events to which it refers.

mined to set out by land for that place, with ten of the best
workmen, who would be occupied in building the canoes till
the rest of the party, after taking the boat to pieces and
making the necessary deposits, should transport the baggage, and join them with the other six canoes.

July 10*th.* He accordingly passed over to the opposite
side of the river with his party, and proceeded eight miles
by land, the distance by water being 23¾ miles. Here he
found two cottonwood trees, but on cutting them down, one
proved to be hollow, split at the top in falling, and both
were much damaged at the bottom. He searched the
neighborhood, but could find none which would suit better,
and therefore was obliged to make use of those (*p. 296*)
which he had felled, shortening them in order to avoid the
cracks, and supplying the deficiency by making them as wide
as possible. They were equally at a loss for wood of which
they might make handles for their axes; the eyes of which
not being round, they were obliged to split the timber in
such a manner that 13 of the handles broke in the course
of the day, though made of the best wood they could find
for the purpose, which was the choke-cherry.

The rest of the party took the frame of the boat to pieces,
deposited it in a cache or hole, with a draught of the country from Fort Mandan to this place, and also some other
papers and small articles of less importance. After this we
amused ourselves with fishing; and though we had thought
on our arrival that there were no fish in this part of the
river, we caught below the falls some of a species of white
chub, but few in number and small in size.

Sergeant Ordway, with four canoes and eight men, had set
sail in the morning, with part of the baggage, to the place
where Captain Clark had fixed his camp [later called Canoe
camp]; but the wind was so high that he only reached
within three miles of that place, and camped for the night.

July 11*th.* In the morning one of the canoes joined
Captain Clark. The other three, having on board more
valuable articles, which would have been injured by the

water, went on more cautiously, and did not reach camp till evening. Captain Clark then had the canoes unloaded and sent back, but the high wind prevented their floating down nearer than about eight miles above us. His party were busily engaged with the canoes, and their hunters supplied them with three fat deer and a buffalo, in addition to two deer and an antelope killed yesterday. The few men who were with Captain Lewis were occupied in hunting, but with not much success, having killed only one buffalo. They heard about sunset two discharges of the tremendous mountain artillery. They also saw several very large gray eagles, much larger than those of the United (*p. 297*) States, and most probably a distinct species,[25] though the bald eagle of this country is not quite so large as that of the United States. The men have been much afflicted with painful whitlows, and one of them [Bratton] is disabled from working by this complaint in his hand.

July 12*th.* In consequence of the wind the canoes did not reach the lower camp till late in the afternoon, before which time Captain Lewis sent all the men he could spare up the river [about seven miles], to assist in building the boats, and the day was too far advanced to reload and send them up before morning. The mosquitoes are very troublesome, and they have a companion not less so, a large black gnat, which does not sting, but attacks the eyes in swarms [and is probably the buffalo-gnat, a species of *Simulium*].

The party with Captain Clark are employed on the canoes. In the course of the work Sergeant Pryor dislocated his shoulder yesterday, but it was replaced immediately, and though painful does not threaten much injury. The hunters brought in three deer and two otter [*Lutra canadensis*]. This last animal has been numerous since the water has become sufficiently clear for them to take fish. The blue-crested fisher, or, as it is sometimes called, the kingfisher

---

[25] Not so ; the large gray eagle is *Aquila chrysaëtos*, of the same species as elsewhere in the United States ; and the bald eagles are of the same size as elsewhere.

[*Ceryle alcyon*], is an inhabitant of this part of the river; it is a bird rare on the Missouri; indeed we did not see more than three or four of them from its entrance to Maria's river, and even those did not seem to reside on the Missouri, but on some of the clearer streams which empty into it, as they were seen near the mouths of those streams.

July 13*th*. The morning being fair and calm, Captain Lewis had all the remaining baggage embarked on board the six canoes, which sailed with two men in each for the upper camp. Then, with a sick man [Lepage] and the Indian woman, he left camp, and crossing over the river went on by land to join Captain Clark. From the head of the White-bear islands he proceeded in a southwest direction, to the distance of three miles, till he struck the Missouri, which he then followed [up, for about four miles], till he reached the place where all the party were occupied in boat-building.

On his way he passed a ve- (*p. 298*) ry large Indian lodge, which was probably designed as a great council-house; but it differed in its construction from all that we had seen, lower down the Missouri or elsewhere. The form of it was a circle 216 feet in circumference at the base; it was composed of 16 large cottonwood poles about 50 feet long, and at their thicker ends, which touched the ground, about the size of a man's body. They were distributed at equal distances, except that one was omitted to the east, probably for the entrance. From the circumference of this circle the poles converged toward the center, where they were united and secured by large withes of willow-brush. There was no covering over this fabric, in the center of which were the remains of a large fire, and around it the marks of about 80 leathern lodges. He also saw a number of turtle-doves [*Zenaidura carolinensis*], and some pigeons, of which he shot one, differing in no respect from the wild pigeon [*Ectopistes migratorius*] of the United States.

The country exhibits its usual appearances; the timber being confined to the river, and the country on both sides,

as far as the eye can reach, being entirely destitute of trees
or brush.   In the low ground in which we are building the
canoes, the timber is larger and more abundant than we
have seen it on the Missouri for several hundred miles.
The soil too is good, for the grass and weeds reach about two
feet high, being the tallest we have observed this season ;
though on the high plains and prairies the grass is at no
season above three inches in height.   Among these weeds
are the sand-rush [*Equisetum* sp.?] and nettle [probably
Urtica gracilis] in small quantities.   The plains are still
infested by great numbers of the small birds already mentioned, among which is the brown curlew [*Numenius longirostris.*]   The current of the river is here extremely
gentle.   The buffalo have not yet quite gone, for the
hunters brought in three, in very good order.   It requires
some diligence to supply us plentifully, for as we reserve
our parched meal for the Rocky mountains, where we do
not expect to find much game, our principal article of food
is meat, and the consumption of the whole 32 persons
belonging to the party amounts (*p. 299*) to four deer, an
elk and a deer, or one buffalo, every 24 hours.   The mosquitoes and gnats persecute us as violently as below, so
that we can get no sleep unless defended by biers, with
which we are all provided.   We here found several plants
hitherto unknown to us, of which we preserved specimens.

Sergeant Ordway proceeded with the six canoes five
miles up the river, but the wind becoming so high as to wet
the baggage, he was obliged to unload and dry it.   The
wind abated at five o'clock in the evening, when he again
proceeded eight miles and camped.   The next day,

Sunday, July 14*th,* he joined us about noon.   On leaving
Whitebear camp, he passed at a short distance a little
creek or run coming in on the left.   This had been already
examined and called Flattery run [now known as Sand
coulée] ; it contains back-water only, with very extensive
low grounds, which, rising into large plains, reach the
mountains on the east.   He then passed a willow-island on

the left, within one mile and a half, and reached two miles further a cliff of rocks, in a bend on the same side. In the course of another mile and a half, he passed two islands covered with cottonwood, box-elder, sweet-willow, and the usual undergrowth, like that of the Whitebear islands. At 13¾ miles he came to the mouth of a small creek [26] on the left; within the following nine miles he passed three timbered islands, and after making 23¼ miles from the lower camp, arrived at the point of woodland on the north where the canoes were constructed.

The day was fair and warm ; the men worked very industriously, and were enabled by the evening to launch the boats, which now want only seats and oars to be complete. One of them is 25, the other 33 feet in length, and 3 feet wide. Captain Lewis walked out between three and four miles over the rocky bluffs to a high situation, two miles from the river, a little below Fort Mountain creek [for which see beyond]. The country which he saw was in most parts (*p. 300*) level, occasionally varied by gentle rises and descents, but with no timber except along the water. From this position, the point at which the Missouri enters [*i. e.*, leaves] the first chain of the Rocky mountains bore S. 28° W., about 25 miles, according to our estimate.

To the northern extremity of that chain, N. 73° W., at the distance of 80 miles.

To the same extremity of the second chain, N. 65° W., 150 miles.

To the most remote point of a third and continued chain of these mountains, N. 50° W., about 200 miles.

The direction of the first chain was from S. 20° E. to N. 20° W.; of the second, from S. 45° E. to N. 45° W.; but the eye could not reach their southern extremities, which most probably may be traced to Mexico. In a course S.

[26] This will be found on some maps as Kamas or Camas creek, for which I can find no name in the codices. It is marked Kamas R. on Stevens' map. The name has in at least one instance been carried on to Smith's river by mistake.

75° W., and at the distance of eight miles, is a mountain, which from its appearance we call Fort mountain.[27] It is situated in the level plain and forms nearly a square, each side of which is a mile in extent. These sides, which are composed of a yellow clay with no mixture of rock or stone whatever, rise perpendicularly to the height of 300 feet, where the top becomes a level plain covered, as Captain Lewis now observed, with a tolerably fertile mold two feet thick, on which was a coat of grass similar to that of the plain below. It has the appearance of being perfectly inaccessible, and although the mounds near the falls somewhat resemble it, yet none of them are so large.

[27] See note-[17], p. 365. Any doubt which may have existed regarding the identification of Fort mountain can be done away with by the data given here and elsewhere. On p. 1078 this elevation is mentioned again, as being " about 20 miles in a northeastern direction " from Lewis and Clark's Pass. On p. 1260 it is given as in the plain between Medicine river and the Missouri, 15 miles from the mouth of the former. Though these indications are not exact, there is no question that Fort mountain is that entirely isolated mesa-like formation which rises to the height of about 4,600 feet, a short distance south of Fort Shaw, and is now generally called Square Butte, from its figure. Two or three miles west of Square Butte, and only about the same distance from Fort Shaw, is a second somewhat similar elevation, of about the same height, but larger and more irregular in figure. Two of the points of this elevation are known as Crown Butte and Nipple Butte. When Captain Lewis first sighted these elevations from about the Great Falls (p. 365), they were separate to his line of vision, and accordingly he alludes to them both. In the present place, where one of them is named Fort mountain, Crown Butte is behind and hidden by Square Butte ; the latter is also nearest the Missouri. These points confirm the identification of Fort mountain. My friend, General John Gibbon, U. S. A., who was stationed at Fort Shaw, and was very familiar with the country thereabouts, tells me that he once started from the fort to go through Lewis and Clark's Pass, but was not sure he was in this Pass till he sighted and recognized Square Butte, in the exact direction and at the apparent distance given by Captain Lewis. The isolation of the Square, Crown, and Nipple in the plains renders them conspicuous landmarks for many miles in every direction. The prominence known as Bird-tail Rock is much further south, in much more broken country, and not to be considered for a moment in the present connection.

CHAPTER XII.

THE MISSOURI FROM THE GREAT FALLS TO THE THREE FORKS.

Fort Mountain creek—Smith's river—Prickly-pear and other plants—Shoshone or Snake Indian lodges—Captain Lewis reconnoiters—Difficult navigation of rapids—Pine island—Sunflowers, currants, service-berries, etc.—Bighorns—Dearborn's river—Captain Clark reconnoiters—Ordway's creek—Flax of two kinds—Indian lodges—Buffalo-chips—Snow-capped mountains sighted—The Gates of the Rocky Mountains—Potts' creek—Indians fire the prairie—Lewis' woodpecker—Old Indian road—Whiteearth creek—Pryor's creek—A beautiful prairie—Grouse, swan, geese, and cranes—Onion island—Sacajawea recognizes her country, on approaching the Three Forks—Birds and plants—Whitehouse's creek—Ten islands—Broad island—Beaver and other animals—Indian horse seen—Captain Clark discovers the Three Forks, July 25th—Gass' creek, formed from five mountain streams—A second mountain chain—Howard's creek—New species of prickly-pear—Exploration of the Forks by different parties—Site for a fort noted—The southeast Fork named Gallatin's river—Illness of Captain Clark—Anxiety to reach the Snake Indians.

ONDAY, July 15th, 1805. We rose early, embarked all our baggage on board the canoes, which, though light in number, are still heavily loaded, and at ten o'clock set out on our journey.[1] At the distance of three miles we passed an island, just above which is a small creek coming in from the left, which we called Fort Mountain creek,[2] the channel of which is ten yards wide, but now perfectly dry. At six miles we came to an island, opposite a bend toward the north side ; and reached at 7½ mile the lower point of a woodland, at the entrance of a beautiful river, which in honor of [Robert Smith] the Secretary of the Navy, we called Smith's river. This stream falls into a bend on the south side of the Missouri, and is 80 yards wide. As far as we could discern its course, it wound through a charming

[1] Gass calls the place left to-day Canoe camp. This is where the two new canoes were built, at a point 23¼ miles above Whitebear Islands and 7½ below Smith's river.

[2] An insignificant run, now called by another name, but seldom charted. It would hardly have been noticed, had not Fort mountain been observed from an eminence near its mouth.

valley toward the southeast, in which many herds of buffalo were feeding, till at the distance of 25 miles it entered the Rocky mountains, and was lost from our view.[3] After dining near this place, we proceeded 4¾ miles to the head of an island; 4¼ miles beyond which is a second island, on the left; 3¼ miles further, in a bend of the river toward the north,[4] is a wood where we camped for the night [3¾ miles below Little Muddy creek], after making 19¾ miles.

(*p. 302*) We find the prickly-pear, one of the greatest beauties as well as the greatest inconveniences of the plains, now in full bloom. The sunflower, a plant common on every part of the Missouri from its entrance to this place, is very abundant, and in bloom. The lamb's-quarter [*Chenopodium album*], wild cucumber, sand-rush [*Equisetum arvense ?*], and narrow-dock [*Rumex salicifolius*], are also common. Two elk, a deer, and an otter were our game to-day.

The river has now become so much more crooked than below, that we omit taking all its short meanders, but note only its general course, and lay down the small bends on our daily chart by the eye. The general width is from 100 to 150 yards. Along the banks are large beds of sand, raised above the plains; and as they always appear on the

---

[3] Smith's river later acquired the name of Deep river, and is marked on some maps Deep or Smith's river. A popular encyclopedic map before me has Camas or Smith river; but Camas or Kamas is a name which belongs to a small stream lower down the Missouri, on the same side, next above Flattery run. The name of Robert Smith still obtains with most geographers, as that of one of the "Cabinet" group, with those of Dearborn, Gallatin, and Madison; all four of these persons having held portfolios under President Jefferson. Smith's river heads in Meagher Co., about White Sulphur Springs, in the vicinity of some sources of the Musselshell, and runs N.N.W., between the Big Belt and Little Belt mountains, to the Missouri.

[4] The great river is now flowing approximately north from the Three Forks, to bend eastward in the region about the Great Falls and thence through Montana. The Expedition is ascending the river, thus going approximately south. Independently of minor bends, therefore, the left bank of the river, on the right hand, is west, and conversely; so the "north" of the text is west, and the "south" is east. The codices invariably continue to use "starboard" and "larboard." Compare the reverse case, note [117], p. 52.

sides of the river opposite the southwest exposure, they seem obviously brought there from the channel of the river by the incessant winds from that quarter. We find also more timber than for a great distance below the falls.[5]

July 16th. There was a heavy dew last night. We soon passed about 40 little booths, formed of willow-bushes as a shelter against the sun. These seemed to have been deserted about ten days, and as we supposed by the Snake Indians or Shoshonees, whom we hope soon to meet, as they appeared from their tracks to have a number of horses with them. At 3¾ miles we passed a creek or run in a bend on the left [read right] side ; and four miles further, another run or small rivulet, on the right [read left].[6]

After breakfasting on a buffalo shot by one of the hunters, Captain Lewis resolved to go on ahead of the party to the point where the river enters the Rocky mountains, and make the necessary observations before our arrival. He therefore set out with Drewyer, and two of the sick men [Lepage and Potts] to whom he supposed the walk would be useful. He traveled on the north [-west] side of the river through a handsome level plain, which continued on the opposite side also, and at the (*p. 303*) distance of eight miles passed a small stream on which he observed a considerable quantity of the aspen tree [*Populus tremuloides*]. A little before twelve o'clock he halted, on a bend to the north, in a low ground well covered with timber, about 4½ miles below the mountains, and obtained a meridian altitude, by which he found the latitude was N. 46° 46′ 50″ 2‴ [actually N. of 47°]. His route then lay through a high waving plain to a rapid [the Half-breed],

---

[5] The Missouri, here above the mouth of Smith's river, is about to leave the vast sheet of the cretaceous it has traversed, and enter upon a paleozoic (permo-carboniferous) formation, with, however, an exposure of the tertiary along its immediate banks to above the Three Forks. Its continuation (the Jefferson) soon after that strikes archæan rocks.

[6] The first of these small streams is Little Muddy creek, on the right or west; second, Bird creek, on the left. No names in the codex. Camp is to be above St. Clair and Cascade, past Knapp creek, and about opposite Chestnut.

where the Missouri first leaves the Rocky mountains; and here he camped[7] for the night [near the present town of Hardy].

In the meantime we [the main party] had proceeded, after breakfast, one mile to a bend on the left, opposite which was the frame of a large lodge situated on the prairie, constructed like that already mentioned above the Whitebear islands, but only 60 feet in diameter; round it were the remains of about 80 leathern lodges, all of which seemed to have been built during the last autumn. Within the next 15¾ miles we passed ten islands, on the last of which we camped near the right [-hand] shore, having made 23 miles. The next morning,

Wednesday, July 17*th*, we set out early; at four miles' distance joined Captain Lewis at the foot of the [Half-breed] rapids, and after breakfast began the passage of them. Some of the articles most likely to be injured by the water were carried around. We then double-manned the canoes, and with the aid of the towing-line got them up without accident. For several miles below the rapids, the current of the Missouri becomes stronger as you approach, and the spurs of the mountains advance toward the river, which is deep, and not more than 70 yards wide. At the rapids, the river is closely hemmed in on both sides by the hills, and foams for half a mile over the rocks which obstruct its channel. The low grounds are now not more than a few yards in width, but they furnish room for an Indian road, which winds under the hills on the north [-west] side of the river. The general range of these hills is from S.E. to N.W.; the cliffs themselves are about 800 feet above (*p. 304*) the water, formed almost entirely of a hard black granite, on which are scattered a few dwarf pine and cedar trees. Immediately in the gap is a large rock, 400 feet high, which on one side is washed

---

[7] The mosquitoes must have been very troublesome: "I had left my bier, of course suffered considerably, and promised in my wrath that I never will be guilty of a similar piece of negligence while on this voyage," Lewis E 157. With which good resolution the codex ends. The narrative continues directly with Codex F, July 17th–Aug. 22d, 1805 ; this is also a Lewis.

by the Missouri, while on its other side a handsome little plain separates it from the neighboring mountains. It may be ascended with some difficulty nearly to its summit, and affords a beautiful prospect of the plains below, in which we could observe large herds of buffalo. After ascending the rapids for half a mile, we came to a small island at the head of them, which we called Pine island, from a large pine-tree at the lower end of it, the first we have seen near the river for a great distance. A mile beyond Captain Lewis' camp we had a meridian altitude, which gave us the latitude of 46° 42' 14" 7'''. As the canoes were still heavily loaded, all those not employed in working them walked on shore [Pine island still there, at mouth of Sheep creek, east; below the rapids is Hardy creek, west.]

The navigation is now very laborious. The river is deep, but with little current, and from 70 to 100 yards wide; the low grounds are very narrow, with but little timber, and that chiefly the aspen tree. The cliffs are steep, and hang over the river so much that often we could not cross them, but were obliged to pass and repass from one side of the river to the other, in order to make our way. In some places the banks are formed of dark black granite rising perpendicularly to a great height, through which the river seems, in the progress of time, to have worn its channel. On these mountains we see more pine than usual, but it is still in small quantities. Along the bottoms, which have a covering of high grass, we observed the sunflower blooming in great abundance. The Indians of the Missouri, more especially those who do not cultivate maize, make great use of the seed of this plant for bread, or in thickening their soup. They first parch and then pound it between two stones, until it is reduced to a fine meal. Sometimes they add a portion of water, and drink it thus diluted; at other times they add a sufficient proportion of marrow-grease to (*b. 305*) reduce it to the consistency of common dough, and eat it in that manner. This last composition we preferred to all the rest, and thought it at that time a very palatable dish.

There is little of the broad-leaved cottonwood on this side of the falls, much of the greater part of what we see being of the narrow-leaved species. There are great quantities of red or purple, yellow, and black currants. These currants are very pleasant to the taste, and much preferable to those of our common gardens. The bush rises to the height of six or eight feet; the stem is simple, branching, and erect. These shrubs associate in corps [copses], either in upper or timbered lands near the water-courses. The leaf is petiolate, of a pale green, and in form resembles that of the red currant so common in our gardens. The perianth of the fruit is one-leaved, five-cleft, abbreviated and tubular [i. e., the berry is crowned with the coherent five-lobed calyx]. The corolla [i. e., colored calyx] is monopetalous, funnel-shaped, very long, and of a fine orange color. There are five stamens and one pistillum of the first [species, red or purple, *Ribes hudsonianum*]; the filaments are capillar, inserted on the corolla, equal and converging; the anthers ovate and incumbent. The germ [germen, ovary] of the second species [yellow, the buffalo currant, *Ribes aureum* of Pursh] is round, smooth, inferior, and pediceled; the style long and thicker than the stamens, simple, cylindrical, smooth, and erect; it remains with the corolla [calyx] until the fruit is ripe; the stamen is simple and obtuse, and the fruit much the size and shape of our common garden currants, growing like them in clusters, supported by a compound footstalk. The peduncles are longer in this species, and the berries are more scattered. The fruit is not so acid as the common currant, and has a more agreeable flavor. The other species [black, *Ribes viscosissimum*] differs in no respect from the yellow currant, except in the color and flavor of the berries.

The service-berry [*Amelanchier alnifolia*] differs in some points from that of the United States [*A. canadensis*]. The bushes are small, sometimes not more than two feet high, and rarely exceeding eight inches [more]. They are proportionately small in their stems, growing very thickly, associated in clumps. The fruit is of the same form, but for (*p. 306*) the most part larger and of a very dark purple. They are now ripe and in great perfection. There are two species of gooseberry [*Ribes rotundifolium ? R. oxyacanthoides ?*] here, but neither of them is yet ripe; nor is the choke-cherry [*Prunus demissa*], though in great quantities. There are also the box-elder [*Negundo aceroides*], red-willow [*Cornus stolonifera*], and a species of sumach [*Rhus aromatica* var. *trilobata*]. In the evening we saw some mountain rams or big-horned animals [*Ovis montana*], but no other game of any sort.

After leaving Pine island we passed a small run [Sheep creek] on the left, which is formed by a large spring rising at the distance of half a mile under the mountain. One mile and a half above that island is another, and two miles further a third island, the river making small bends constantly to the north [right]. From this last island to a point of rocks on the south [left] side the low grounds become rather wider, and three-quarters of a mile beyond these rocks, in a bend on the north [right], we camped[8] opposite a very high cliff, having made during the day 11½ miles.

July 18*th*. This morning early, before our departure, we saw a large herd of the big-horned animals, which were bounding among the rocks on the opposite cliff with great agility. These inaccessible spots secure them from all their enemies, and their only danger is in wandering among these precipices, where we would suppose it scarcely possible for any animal to stand; a single false step would precipitate them at least 500 feet into the water.

At 1¼ miles we passed another single cliff on the left;

[8] This camp was very near a place on the Mont. Cent. Ry. now called Mid Cañon (Canon if the engraver is Teutonic, or the printer is out of sorts, and Canyon in the local vernacular), seven miles by rail and nearly twice as far by boat below Craig. The place is several river-miles above the tunnel and Smith's creek, and three of the same below the mouth of Dearborn's river. No doubt a person living at Mid Cañon would recognize from this paragraph the "small run," the "point of rocks," and the "high cliff," opposite which latter he could point to the precise spot where camp was pitched.

at the same distance beyond which is the mouth of a large river[9] emptying from the north. It is a handsome, bold, and clear stream, 80 yards wide—that is, nearly as broad as the Missouri—with a rapid current, over a bed of small smooth stones of various figures. The water is extremely transparent; the low grounds are narrow, but possess as much wood as those of the Missouri. The river has every appearance of being navigable, though to what distance we cannot ascertain, as the country which it waters is broken and mountainous. In honor of the Se- (*p. 307*) cretary at War we called it Dearborn's river.

Being now very anxious to meet with the Shoshonees or Snake Indians, for the purpose of obtaining the necessary information of our route, as well as to procure horses, it was thought best for one of us to go forward with a small party and endeavor to discover them, before the daily discharge of our guns, which is necessary for our subsistence, should give them notice of our approach. If by an accident they hear us, they will most probably retreat to the mountains, mistaking us for their enemies, who usually attack them on this side.

Accordingly Captain Clark set out with three men [J. Fields, Potts, and York], and followed the course of the river on the north [west] side; but the hills were so steep at first that he was not able to go much faster than our-

[9] The most notable of all the smaller rivers named by the Expedition—not for its length, but for its heading in and about that gap of the Rocky mountains which the Expedition will discover next year on the return journey, and which is thereafter to become famous as Lewis and Clark's Pass. The then Secretary of War was General Henry Dearborn, for whom was later named Fort Dearborn, when the present city of Chicago consisted of that fort and some log cabins—say about 1811; and one of the principal business streets still bears the name. Gass calls this river the Clear-water. Clark never saw Lewis and Clark's Pass; he was never again so near it as he was to-day. But I hold a certain unpublished map which actually dots a trail from the mouth of Dearborn's river to the head of its middle fork, *i. e.*, to *Cadotte's* Pass, and so over the Continental Divide to the Big Blackfoot river. This map was made by one of the greatest geographical geniuses this country ever produced—I mean William Clark. The case will come up again, toward the close of this work.

selves. In the evening, however, he cut off many miles of the circuitous course of the river by crossing a mountain, over which he found a wide Indian road, which in many places seemed to have been cut or dug down in the earth. He passed also two branches of a stream which he called Ordway's[10] creek, where he saw a number of beaver-dams extending in close succession toward the mountains, as far as he could distinguish. On the cliffs were many of the big-horned animals. After crossing this mountain he camped near a small stream of running water, having traveled 20 miles.

On leaving Dearborn's river we [the main party] passed at 3½ miles a small creek [larboard, now called Stickney creek], and at six beyond this, an island on the north side of the river, which makes within that distance many small bends [thus passing Dog creek and Craig, right, and Wegner creek and Stickney, left]. At 2½ miles further is another island; three-quarters of a mile beyond this is a small [now Rock] creek on the north side. At 1½ miles above this creek is a much larger stream, 30 yards wide, discharging with a bold current on the north side; the banks are low, and the bed is formed of stones altogether. To this stream we gave [above] the name of Ordway's creek, after Sergeant John Ordway. At two miles beyond this the valley widens. We passed several bends of the river, and (*p. 308*) camped in the center of one on the south, having made 21 miles.

Here we found a small grove of the narrow-leaved cottonwood, there being none of the broad-leaved kind since we entered the mountains. The water of these rivulets which come down from the mountains is very cold, pure,

---

[10] Now Little Prickly-pear creek. The Montana Central meanders this creek, on the way to Silver City and so to Helena. Some of its ties are laid in the very foot-prints of the great pioneer. The two "branches" of the creek which Clark then crossed, and now the railroad passes, are, first, Rock (a separate stream); second, Wolf. A principal tributary of the Little Prickly-pear is Cañon, Canon, or Canyon creek, heading in the Continental Divide, west of Marysville, and thus connecting with Pacific waters by tributaries of the Blackfoot river.

and well-tasted. Along their banks, as well as on the Missouri, the aspen [*Populus tremuloides*] is very common, but of a small kind. The river is somewhat wider than we found it yesterday; the hills are more distant from the river and not so high; there are some pines on the mountains, but they are principally confined to the upper regions of them; the low grounds are still narrower, and have little or no timber. The soil near the river is good, and produces a luxuriant growth of grass and weeds; among these productions the sunflower holds a very distinguished place.

For several days past we have discovered a species of flax [*Linum perenne*] in the low grounds, the leaf-stem and pericarp of which resemble those of the flax [*L. usitatissimum*] commonly cultivated in the United States; the stem rises to the height of 2½ or 3 feet, and springs, to the number of eight or ten, from the same root, with a strong thick bark apparently well calculated for use; the root seems to be perennial, and it is probable that the cutting of the stems may not at all injure it; for though the seeds are not yet ripe, there are young suckers shooting up from the root, whence we may infer that the stems, which are fully grown and in the proper stage of vegetation to produce the best flax, are not essential to the preservation or support of the root—a circumstance which would render it a most valuable plant. To-day we have met with a second species of flax [*Campanula rotundifolia*], smaller than the first, as it seldom obtains a greater height than nine or twelve inches; the leaf and stem resemble those of the species just mentioned, except that the latter is rarely branched, and bears a single monopetalous bell-shaped blue flower, suspended with its limb downward.

We saw several herds of the bighorn, but they were in the cliffs beyond our reach. We killed an elk (*p. 309*) this morning, and found part of a deer which had been left for us by Captain Clark. He pursued his route,

Friday, July 19*th*, early in the morning, and soon passed the remains of several Indian camps formed of willow-brush, which seemed to have been deserted this spring. At the same time he observed that the pine-trees had been stripped of their bark about the same season, which our Indian woman says her countrymen do in order to obtain the sap and the soft parts of the wood and bark for food. About eleven o'clock he met a herd of elk and killed two of them ; but such was the want of wood in the neighborhood that he was unable to procure enough to make a fire, and was therefore obliged to substitute the dung of the buffalo,[11] with which he cooked his breakfast. They then resumed their course along an old Indian road. In the afternoon they reached a handsome valley, watered by a large creek,[12] both of which extended a considerable distance into the mountain. This they crossed, and during the evening traveled over a mountainous country covered with sharp fragments of flint rock ; these bruised and cut their feet very much, but were scarcely less troublesome than the prickly-pear of the open plains, which have now become so abundant that it is impossible to avoid them, and the thorns are so strong that they pierce a double sole of dressed deer-skin ; the best resource against them is a sole of buffalo-hide in parchment [i. e., hard-dried]. At night they reached the river much fatigued, having passed two mountains in the course of the day, and traveled 30 miles. Captain Clark's first employment, on lighting a fire, was to extract from his feet the briars [thorns], which he found 17 in number.

In the meantime we proceeded very well, though the

[11] This was the usual fuel of the treeless regions before the buffalo were exterminated. I have traveled for weeks with no other fuel. The pieces of dried dung are commonly called buffalo-chips, sometimes " bodewash "—the latter word a corruption of the French name *bois de vache*.

[12] Below named Potts' creek ; now the Great or Big Prickly-pear creek. Clark, we must remember, is off west of the Missouri ; he has followed up Ordway's creek some distance, and then swung over toward the Missouri. I have not his courses and distances in detail, but judge that he struck Potts' creek below the entrance of its tributary, Silver creek, and was thus already near his camp on the Missouri.

water appears to increase in rapidity as we advance. The current has indeed been strong during the day, and obstructed by some rapids, which are not, however, much broken by rocks, and are perfectly safe. The river is deep; its general width is from 100 to 150 (*p. 310*) yards. For more than 13 miles we went along the numerous bends of the river, and then reached two small islands; 3¾ miles beyond which is a small [now Cottonwood] creek in a bend[13] to the left, above a small island on the right side of the river. We were regaled about 10 p. m. with a thunder-storm of rain and hail, which lasted for an hour. During the day, in this confined valley through which we are pass-ing, the heat is almost insupportable; yet, whenever we obtain a glimpse of the lofty tops of the mountains, we are tantalized with a view of the snow. These mountains have their sides and summits partially varied with little copses of pine, cedar, and balsam-fir [*Abies subalpina*].

A mile and a half beyond this creek, the rocks approach the river on both sides, forming a most sublime and extra-ordinary spectacle. For 5¾ miles these rocks rise perpen-dicularly from the water's edge, to the height of nearly 1,200 feet. They are composed of a black granite near the base, but from their lighter color above, and from the fragments, we suppose the upper part to be flint, of a yellowish-brown and cream color. Nothing can be imagined more tremen-dous than the frowning darkness of these rocks, which pro-ject over the river and menace us with destruction. The river, of 150 yards in width, seems to have forced its channel down this solid mass; but so reluctantly has the rock given way that, during the whole distance, the water is very deep even at the edges, and for the first three miles there is not

---

[13] This is Ox-bow bend, and the "small creek" is "left" there yet, at a place called Ming's Bar. The remarkable cañon of the Missouri about to be described results from the confinement of the river by a spur of the Big Belt mountains. The grim sentinel at the "Gates of the Rockies" is a remarkable elevation called the Bear's Teeth, from several pillars of rock which form its crest. A colored view of the Bear's bare teeth, from a point where the Missouri bursts its gates, is given on plate li. of Stevens' report (P.R.R. Rep. XII. pt. i, 1860).

a spot, except one of a few yards, in which a man could stand between the water and the towering perpendicular of the mountain. The convulsion of the passage must have been terrible, since at its outlet are vast columns of rock, torn from the mountain, which are strewn on both sides of the river—the trophies, as it were, of a victory. Several fine springs burst out from the chasms of the rock, and contribute to increase the river, which has now a strong current; but very fortunately we are able to overcome it with our oars, since (*p. 311*) it would be impossible to use either the cord or the pole. We were obliged to go on some time after dark, not being able to find a spot large enough to camp on; but at length, about two miles above a small island in the middle of the river, we met with a spot on the left side, where we procured plenty of light wood and pitch-pine. This extraordinary range of rocks we called the Gates of the Rocky mountains.

We had made 22 miles; and 4¼ miles from the entrance of the Gates. The mountains are higher to-day than they were yesterday. We saw some bighorns, a few antelopes and beaver, but since entering the mountains have found no buffalo; the otter are, however, in great plenty; the mosquitoes have become less troublesome than they were.

July 20th. By employing the towrope whenever the banks permitted the use of it, the river being too deep for the pole, we were enabled to overcome the current, which is still strong. At the distance of half a mile we came to a high rock in a bend to the left in the Gates. Here the perpendicular rocks cease, the hills retire from the river, and the valleys suddenly widen to a greater extent than they have done since we entered the mountains. At this place was some scattered timber, consisting of narrow-leaved cottonwood, aspen, and pine. There are also vast quantities of gooseberries, service-berries, and several species of currant, among which is one of a black color, the flavor of which is preferable to that of the yellow, and would be deemed superior to that of any currant in the United States.

We here killed an elk, which was a pleasant addition to our stock of food. At a mile from the Gates a large creek [14] comes down from the mountains and empties behind an island in the middle of a bend to the north [west]. To this stream, which is 15 yards wide, we gave the name of Potts' creek, after John Potts, one of our men.

Up this valley about seven miles we discovered a great smoke, as if the whole country had been set on fire ; but were at a loss (*p. 312*) to decide whether it had been done accidentally by Captain Clark's party, or by the Indians as a signal on their observing us. We afterward learned that this last was the fact ; for they had heard a gun fired by one of Captain Clark's men, and believing that their enemies were approaching had fled into the mountains, first setting fire to the plains as a warning to their countrymen.

We continued our course along several islands [passed Beaver creek, on the left, at five miles from the Gates], and having made in the course of the day 15 miles, camped just above an island, at a spring on a high bank, on the left side of the river. In the latter part of the evening we had

---

[14] " Smoke creek," Lewis F 13, erased and " Potts's" interlined; " Potts's Vally creek," Clark I 4 ; charted by Clark, 1814, nameless, between Ordway's and Pryor's creeks ; thus corresponding to *Big Prickly-pear creek* of present maps. This identification is necessary, because no other is possible. Lewis F 15 says that at one mile from the Gates "a large creek falls in behind some islands on Stard. side. The Indians set the plains on fire up this Creek. call it Potts's Creek.'' The assigned position is about the place now called American Bar, where there is now no such creek. Big Prickly-pear creek now comes in 10 or 12 miles higher up, nearly opposite El Dorado, and is much more than 15 yards wide; had it been there then, L. and C. would never have missed it. As they give nothing whatever for Big Prickly-pear, except Potts', we may be sure that what Potts' was in 1805 is now Big Prickly-pear. The case is by no means singular ; these waters were meandering an alluvial plain, and even some beaver-dams might easily turn a Potts' creek into another channel, and alter its tributary streams so as to swell its volume. The codex gives good collateral security for this identification. By Lewis F 15 a small creek from the left (east) falls in at five miles above the alleged mouth of Potts'. This is just right for a certain Beaver creek there now (not noticed in the Biddle text). Then, by the codex, 8½ miles above this Beaver creek is camp, on the left, at a spring—near present site of El Dorado, about opposite which Big Prickly-pear creek now falls in, some twelve miles N.E. of Helena.

passed through a low range of mountains, and the country became more open, though still unbroken and without timber, and the lowlands not very extensive. Just above our camp the river is again closed in by the mountains. We found on the banks an elk which Captain Clark had left us, with a note mentioning that he should pass the mountains just above us, and await our arrival at some convenient place. We saw, but could not procure, some red-headed ducks and sand-hill cranes [*Grus canadensis*] along the sides of the river, and a woodpecker [15] about the size of the lark-woodpecker [*Colaptes auratus*], which seems to be a distinct species. It is as black as a crow, with a long tail, and flies like a jay-bird. The whole country is so infested by the prickly-pear that we could scarcely find room to lie down at our camp.

Captain Clark, on setting out this morning, had gone through the valley about six miles to the right of the river. He soon fell into an old Indian road, which he pursued till he reached the Missouri, at the distance of 18 miles from his last camp, just above the entrance of a large creek, which we afterward [July 22d] called Whiteearth creek. Here he found his party so much cut and pierced with the sharp flint and the prickly-pear that he proceeded only a small distance further, and then halted to wait for us. Along his track he had taken the precaution to strew signals, such as pieces of cloth, paper and linen, to prove to the Indians, if by (*p. 313*) accident they met his track, that we were white men. But he observed a smoke some distance ahead, and concluded that the whole country had now taken the alarm.

Sunday, July 21st. On leaving our camp we passed an island at half a mile, and reached at one mile a bad rapid, at the place where the river leaves the mountain. Here the cliffs are high and covered with fragments of broken

---

[15] This is the remarkable woodpecker later named Lewis' in honor of Captain Lewis; *Picus torquatus* of Wilson, Am. Orn. III., 1811, p. 31, pl. 20, fig. 3, now *Asyndesmus torquatus* of Coues, Proc. Philada. Acad., 1866, p. 56.

rocks ; the current is also strong ; but although more rapid
the river is wider and shallower, so that we are able to use
the pole occasionally, though we principally depend on the
towline.   On leaving the rapid, which is about half a mile
in extent, the country opens on each side ; the hills become
lower ; at one mile is a large island on the left side, 4½
beyond which is a large and bold creek, 28 yards wide,
coming in from the north, where it waters a handsome
valley.   We called it Pryor's[16] creek, after one of the
sergeants, John [read Nathaniel] Pryor.   At a mile above
this creek, on the left side of the Missouri, we obtained a
meridian altitude, which gave 46° 10' 32" 9''' as the latitude
of the place.

For the following four miles, the country, like that
through which we passed during the rest of the day, is
as rough and mountainous as we found it yesterday ; but
at the distance of twelve miles we came toward evening
into a beautiful plain, ten or twelve miles wide, extending
as far as the eye could reach.   This plain or rather valley
is bounded by two nearly parallel ranges of high mountains, whose summits are partially covered with snow,
below which the pine is scattered along the sides down to
the plain in some places, though the greater part of their
surface has no timber, and exhibits only a barren soil with
no covering except dry parched grass or black rugged
rocks.   On entering the valley the river assumes a totally
different aspect.   It spreads to more than a mile in width,
and though more rapid than before, is shallow enough in

[16] " John " Pryor was written, and left in the codex, Lewis F 18, later deleted
in red ink ; but as no " Nathaniel " was interlined, " John " was printed.   Pryor's
is now Mitchell's creek of various nameless and unauthoritative cartographers, who
had no right to meddle with L. and C.'s nomenclature—which, however, they
very likely never heard of.   A branch of it is Spokane creek : town of same name
on it.   The " bad rapid " above mentioned is next above a place now called
Trout Ferry, from a creek there called Trout creek, from the east, on which is
a town of York, or New York ; below which, and next above El Dorado, is
another stream called Soup creek, also from the east.   But L. and C. have neither
soup nor trout in the account of to-day.

almost every part for the use of the pole, while its bed is formed of smooth stones and some large rocks, as it has been indeed since we entered (*p. 314*) the mountains.   It is also divided by a number of islands, some of which are large near the northern shore.   The soil of the valley is a rich black loam, apparently very fertile, and covered with a fine green grass about 18 inches or two feet in height ; while that of the high grounds is perfectly dry, and seems scorched by the sun.   The timber, though still scarce, is in greater quantities in this valley than we have seen it since entering the mountains, and seems to prefer the borders of the small creeks to the banks of the river itself.   We advanced 3½ miles in this valley and camped [17] on the left [hand] side, having made in all 15½ miles.

Our only large game to-day was one deer.   We saw, however, two pheasants [18] of a dark brown color, much larger than the same species of bird in the United States.   In the morning we also saw three swans which, like the geese, have not yet recovered the feathers of the wings, and are unable to fly.   We killed two of them, and the third escaped by diving and passing down the current.   These

[17] In Meagher Co., about site of Cañon Ferry, which town is on right bank of the Missouri, between two little creeks from the east—the upper, Magpie, the lower, Cave—neither of which does the text or codex mention.   The latitude above given for a mile above Pryor's creek is too low ; that point is about 46° 36′—certainly N. of Helena by a few miles.

The next move will take the Expedition past a point on the Missouri due east of Helena.   Since leaving Dearborn's river they have come almost south, up the Missouri, between the Big Belt mountains on the east and the main divide of the Rockies on the west ; Meagher Co. on the left hand or right bank, Lewis and Clark Co. on the right hand or left bank.   Before Cascade Co. was delimited (in 1887) to include some country (3,050 square miles) about the Great Falls, Lewis and Clark Co. was a great tract in the shape of a wineglass—bounded by the Missouri east, the Rockies west, Medicine or Sun river across the brim, and the parallel of Helena part way across the foot—rest of the foot a broken line. On crossing this parallel, early to-morrow, the Expedition will still have Meagher Co. on the east or left, but will pass from Lewis and Clark into Jefferson Co., on the west or right hand—the latter county extending up the Missouri to the Three Forks, and thence up Jefferson river for some distance.

[18] The dusky grouse, *Dendragapus obscurus richardsoni;* had these "pheas-

are the first we have seen on the river for a great distance, and as they had no young with them, we presume that they do not breed in this neighborhood. Of the geese we daily see great numbers, with their young perfectly feathered except on the wings, where both young and old are deficient ; the first are very fine food, but the old ones are poor and unfit for use. Several of the large brown or sandhill crane [*Grus canadensis*] are feeding in the low grounds on the grass, which forms their principal food. The young cranes cannot fly at this season; they are as large as a turkey, and of a bright reddish-bay color. Since the river has become shallow we have caught a number of trout [*Salmo purpuratus*], and a fish [*Hyodon alosoides*], white on the belly and sides, but of a bluish cast on the back, with a long pointed mouth opening somewhat like that of the shad.

This morning Captain Clark, wishing to hunt but fearful of alarming the Indians, went up the river for three miles; when, finding neither any of them nor of their recent (*p. 315*) tracks, he returned, and then his little party separated to look for game. They killed two bucks and a doe, and a young curlew nearly feathered. In the evening they found the mosquitoes as troublesome as we did. These insects attack us as soon as the labors and fatigues of the day require some rest, and annoy us till several hours after dark, when the coldness of the air obliges them to disappear; but such is their persecution that were it not for our biers we should obtain no repose.[19]

ants " been any variety of the ruffed grouse, they could not have been correctly described as so large.

[19] Clark in Lewis F 18 describes these " biers " as " made of check or gauze, like a trunk to get under." Many have thought that Lewis and Clark make too much of these insects, for such brave men as they were. But such critics as these know nothing of mosquitoes—not even if they have been born and bred in New Jersey. My first lesson in mosquitoes was learned in Labrador in 1860 ; it was retaught me in 1873 on the Red River of the North—where horses, cattle, and caribou are sometimes killed by breathing mosquitoes till their nasal passages are plugged solid—where, in walking across a piece of prairie, colored gray with a veil of the insects settled on the herbage, one leaves a trail of bright green grass, over which a gray cloud hangs in the air.

July 22d. We set out at an early hour. The river being divided into so many channels, by both large and small islands, that it was impossible to lay it down accurately by following in a canoe any single channel, Captain Lewis walked on shore, took the general courses of the river, and from the rising grounds laid down the situation of the islands and channels, which he was enabled to do with perfect accuracy, the view not being obstructed by much timber. At 1¼ miles we passed an island somewhat larger than the rest, and four miles further reached the upper end of another, on which we breakfasted. This is a large island, forming in the middle of a bend to the north a level fertile plain, ten feet above the surface of the water and never overflowed. Here we found great quantities of a small onion [*Allium cernuum*] about the size of a musketball, though some were larger; it is white, crisp, and as well flavored as any of our garden onions [*A. cepa*]; the seed is just ripening, and as the plant bears a large quantity to the square foot, and stands the rigors of the climate, it will no doubt be an acquisition to the settlers. From this production we called it Onion island.

During the next 7¼ miles we passed several long circular bends, and a number of large and small islands which divide the river into many channels, and then reached the mouth of a creek on the north side [right hand, left bank]. It is composed of three creeks, which unite in a handsome valley about four miles before they discharge into the Missouri, where it is about (*p. 316*) 15 feet wide and eight feet deep, with clear, transparent water. Here we halted for dinner, but as the canoes took different channels in ascending, it was some time before they all joined.

We were delighted to find that the Indian woman recognizes the country; she tells us that to this creek her countrymen make excursions to procure white paint on its banks, and we therefore call it Whiteearth creek.[20] She

[20] So Lewis F 22; elsewhere White-earth and White Earth in the codices; "white paint Creek," Lewis F 14; now Beaver creek of some obscure map-

says also that the Three Forks of the Missouri are at no great distance—a piece of intelligence which has cheered the spirits of us all, as we hope soon to reach the head of that river. This is the warmest day, except one, we have experienced this summer. In the shade the mercury stood at 80°, which is the second time it has reached that height during this season. We camped on an island, after making 19¾ miles.

In the course of the day we saw many geese, cranes, small birds common to the plains, and a few pheasants. We also observed a small plover or curlew of a brown color, about the size of a yellow-legged plover or jack-curlew, but of a different species.[21] It first appeared near the mouth of Smith's river, but is so shy and vigilant that we were unable to shoot it. Both the broad- and narrow-leaved willow continue, though the sweet willow has become very scarce. The rosebush, small honeysuckle, pulpy-leaved thorn, southernwood, sage, box-elder, narrow-leaved cottonwood, redwood, and a species of sumach, are all abundant. So, too, are the red and black gooseberries, service-berry, choke-cherry, and the black, yellow, red, and purple currants, which last seems to be a favorite food of the bear. Before camping we landed and took on board Captain Clark, with the meat he had collected during this day's hunt, which consisted of one deer and an elk; we had,

maker, who, if he ever heard of Lewis and Clark, presumed to tamper with their names. A place called Placer is on it, at its forks above described, where the railroad from Gallatin City to Helena crosses it. At this point the Expedition has left Lewis and Clark Co. behind, on the right, and now has Jefferson Co. on the same side. Three small creeks from the left, in Meagher Co., are Hellgate, Avalanche, and White Gulch, unnoticed in the text.

[21] Apparently Bartram's sandpiper, *Bartramia longicauda*, which I found common in various parts of Montana—but the codex has no more satisfactory description than the text. I have been expecting for some weeks to find recognizable mention of the mountain plover (*Charadrius montanus* of Townsend, 1839, now *Podasocys montanus* of Coues, 1866). This may be the bird Lewis actually had in view, but I cannot make the identification. See my B.N.W., 1874, p. 456. The plants about to be mentioned have been already identified, as far as possible. See back.

ourselves, shot a deer and an antelope. The mosquitoes and gnats were unusually fierce this evening.

July 23d. Captain Clark proceeded with four men along the right bank. During the whole day the (*p. 317*) river is divided by a number of islands, which spread it out sometimes to the distance of three miles; the current is very rapid and has many ripples; the bed is formed of gravel and smooth stones. The banks along the low grounds are of a rich loam, followed occasionally by low bluffs of yellow and red clay, with a hard red slatestone intermixed. The low grounds are wide, and have very little timber; but there is a thick underbrush of willow, rose, and currant bushes. These are succeeded by high plains extending on each side to the base of the mountains, which lie parallel to the river, eight to twelve miles apart, and are high and rocky, with some small pine and cedar interspersed on them. At the distance of seven miles a creek 20 yards wide, after meandering through a beautiful low ground on the left for several miles parallel to the river, empties near a cluster of small islands. The stream we called Whitehouse's [22] creek, after Joseph Whitehouse, one of the party, and the islands, from their number, received the name of the Ten islands.

About ten o'clock we came up with Drewyer, who had gone out to hunt yesterday, and not being able to find our camp had stayed out all night; he supplied us with five deer. At 3¼ miles beyond Whitehouse's creek we came to the lower point of an island, where the river is 300 yards wide, continued along it for 1¼ miles, and then passed a second island just above it. We halted rather early for dinner, in order to dry some part of the baggage which had been wet in the canoes. We then proceeded, and at 5½

[22] So Lewis F 23, 24: White House creek, Clark I 4. This is the stream now called Duck creek, which receives that from Confederate gulch, and falls into the Missouri a short distance below Magnolia. Two others passed to-day are North (on which is Canton) and South creek; these are all in Meagher Co., and part of the long series of short streams which fall down from the Big Belt range that the Missouri skirts for many miles.

miles had passed two small islands. Within the next three miles we came to a large island, which from its figure we called Broad island. From that place we made 3½ miles, and camped on an island to the left, opposite a much larger one on the right. Our journey to-day was 22¼ miles, the greater part of which was made by means of our poles and cords, the use of which the banks much favored. During the whole time (*p. 318*), we had small flags hoisted in the canoes to apprise the Indians, if there were any in the neighborhood, of our being white men and their friends ; but we were not so fortunate as to discover any of them.

Along the shores we saw great quantities of the common thistle [of this region, *Cnicus drummondi*], and procured a further supply of wild onions [*Allium cernuum*] and a species of garlic [*Allium geyeri ?*] growing on the highlands, which is now green and in bloom ; it has a flat leaf, and is strong, tough, and disagreeable. There was also much of the wild flax, of which we now obtained some ripe seed, as well as some bulrush [*Juncus* or *Scirpus* sp.] and cattail flag [*Typha latifolia*]. Among the animals we met with a black snake [23] about two feet long, with the belly as dark as any other part of the body, which was perfectly black, and which had 128 scuta on the belly and 63 on the tail. We also saw antelopes, crane, geese, ducks, beaver, and otter ; and took up four deer which had been left on the water-side by Captain Clark. He had pursued all day an Indian road on the right side of the river, and camped late in the evening, at the distance of 25 miles [24] from our camp of last night. In the course of his walk he met besides deer a number of antelopes and a herd of elk, but

[23] Not a member of the genus *Bascanion*, but of *Heterodon*. This is the dark variety of so-called spreading adder or blowing viper, which Baird and Girard called *Heterodon niger*, Cat. Serpents N.A., 1853, p. 55 (after Troost). See Coues and Yarrow, Bull. U. S. Geol. Surv., IV. 1878, p. 271, under head of *Heterodon simus nasicus*. Cope makes it a subspecies of *H. platyrhinus*.

[24] Broad island not now identifiable ; main camp below Bedford. Captain Clark's camp should be somewhat past Townsend, in Meagher Co., and at or near mouth of Deep creek, on which is town of Deepdale.

all the tracks of Indians, though numerous, were of an old date.

July 24th. We proceeded for 4¼ miles along several islands to a small run, just above which the low bluffs touch the river. Within 3½ miles further we came to a small island on the north, and a remarkable bluff, composed of earth of a crimson color, intermixed with strata of slate, either black or of a red resembling brick. The following 6¾ miles brought us to an assemblage of islands, having passed four at different distances; within the next five miles we met the same number of islands, and camped on the north, after making 19½ miles.[25]

The current of the river was strong, and obstructed, as indeed it has been for some days, by small rapids or ripples which descend from one to three feet in the course of 150 (*b. 319*) yards; but we are rarely incommoded by any fixed rocks, and therefore, though the water is rapid, the passage is not attended with danger. The valley through which the river passes is like that of yesterday; the nearest hills generally conceal the most distant from us; but when we obtain a view of them, they present themselves in an amphitheater, rising above each other as they recede from the river, till the most remote are covered with snow.

We saw many otter and beaver to-day. The latter seem to contribute very much to the number of islands and the widening of the river. They begin by damming up the small channels of about 20 yards between the islands; this obliges the river to seek another outlet, and as soon as this is effected the channel stopped by the beaver becomes filled with mud and sand. The industrious animal is then

[25] This is many miles of navigation for little actual advance—mostly poling the boats through sluices between uncounted islands. Lewis F 27 says that he has learned to "push a tolerable good pole" himself; he speaks of the excessive fatigue of all the party, and remarks: "our trio of pests still invade and obstruct us on all occasions, these are the musquetoes eye knats and prickley pears, equal to any three curses that ever poor Egypt laiboured under, except the *mahometant* yoke." Camp is past Greyson's creek, left, and I suppose near a small (Dry) creek. Gass' creek is not yet reached. The "small run" is Indian creek, on the right.

driven to another channel, which soon shares the same fate, till the river spreads on all sides, and cuts the projecting points of the land into islands. We killed a deer, and saw great numbers of antelopes, cranes, some geese, and a few red-headed ducks. The small birds of the plains and the curlew are still abundant; we saw but could not come within gunshot of a large bear. There is much of the track of elk, but none of the animals themselves; and from the appearance of bones and old excrement, we suppose that buffalo have sometimes strayed into the valley, though we have seen no recent sign of them. Along the water are a number of snakes, some of a uniform brown color, others black, and a third speckled on the abdomen, and striped with black and brownish-yellow on the back and sides. The first [*Pityophis sayi?*], which is the largest, is about four feet long; the second [*Heterodon niger*] is of the kind mentioned yesterday; the third [*Eutænia vagrans*] resembles in size and appearance the garter-snake [*E. sirtalis*] of the United States. On examining the teeth of all these several kinds we found them free from poison; they are fond of the water, in which they take shelter on being pursued. The mosquitoes, gnats, and prickly-pear, our three persecutors, still continue with (*p. 320*) us, and, joined with the labor of working the canoes, have fatigued us all excessively.

Captain Clark continued along the Indian road, which led him up a creek. About ten o'clock he saw, at the distance of six miles, a horse feeding in the plains. He went toward him, but the animal was so wild that he could not get within several hundred paces of him. He then turned obliquely to the river, where he killed a deer and dined, having passed in this valley five handsome streams, only one of which had any timber; another had some willows, and was very much dammed up by the beaver. After dinner he continued his route along the river, and camped at the distance of 30 miles. As he went along he saw many tracks of Indians, but none of recent date. The next morning,

Thursday, July 25th, at the distance of a few miles, he arrived at the Three Forks of the Missouri.[26] Here he found that the plains had been recently burnt on the north side, and saw the track of a horse which seemed to have passed about four or five days since. After breakfast he examined the rivers, and finding that the north [*i. e.*, right-hand] branch [the Jefferson], though not larger, contained more water than the middle branch [the Madison], and bore more to the westward, he determined to ascend it. He therefore left a note informing Captain Lewis of his intention, and then went up that stream on the north [his right, its left] side for àbout 25 miles. Here Chaboneau was unable to proceed any further, and the party therefore camped, all of them much fatigued, their feet blistered and wounded by the prickly-pear.

In the meantime we left our camp, and proceeded very well, though the water is still rapid and has some occasional ripples. The country is much like that of yesterday; there are, however, fewer islands, for we passed only two. Behind one of them is a large creek, 25 yards wide, to which we gave the name of Gass'[27] creek, from one of our sergeants, Patrick Gass. It is formed by the union of five streams, which descend from the mountains and join in (*p. 321*) the plain near the river. On this island we saw a large brown bear, but he retreated to the shore and ran off before we could approach him. These animals seem more shy than they were below the mountains. The antelopes have again collected in small herds, composed of several females with

[26] " Three forks of Missouri at Jeferson Madderson & Gallitin's rivers," Clark I 4—with remark : " W. C. return to party very sick." Captain Clark had over-worked himself afoot for several days, and he was not the most robust in body of the party. His feet were blistered badly, besides being pierced with *Opuntia* thorns ; he must have been in great distress. But he discovered three great rivers all at once to-day, and might well be satisfied to return to the main party.

[27] " Gasses Vally Creek Std. 25 [yards wide]," Clark I 4, where it is made 14 miles above " York's 8 islands," 37 above Whitehouse's creek, 11 below Howard's, and 32 below the three Forks. It is now called Hot or Warm Springs creek. Main fork is Crow creek ; on this are Crow Creek City and Radersburg.

their young, attended by one or two males, though some of
the males are still solitary or wander in parties of two over
the plains, which the antelope invariably prefers to the
woodlands, and to which it always retreats if by accident it
is found straggling in the hills, confiding, no doubt, in its
wonderful fleetness. We also killed a few young geese;
but as this game is small, and very incompetent to the
subsistence of the party, we have forbidden the men any
longer to waste their ammunition on them.

About 4½ miles above Gass' creek the valley in which
we have been traveling ceases; the high craggy cliffs again
approach the river, which now enters or rather leaves what
appears to be a second great chain of the Rocky mountains.[28]
About a mile after entering these hills or low mountains we
passed a number of fine bold springs, which burst out near
the edge of the river under the cliffs on the left, and furnish
fine freestone water. Near these we met with two of the
worst rapids we have seen since entering the mountains;
a ridge of sharp pointed rocks stretching across the river,
leaving but small and dangerous channels for navigation.
The cliffs are of a lighter color than those we have already
passed; in the bed of the river is some limestone, which is
small, worn smooth, and seems to have been brought down
by the current. We went about a mile further and camped
under a high bluff on the right, opposite a cliff of rocks,
having made 16 miles.

All these cliffs appeared to have been undermined by the
water at some period, and fallen down from the hills on
their sides, the strata of rock sometimes lying with their
edges upward, while others not detached from the hills are
(*p. 322*) depressed obliquely on the side next the river, as

[28] This formation is called the " Little Gate of the Mountains," Clark I 4.
The Missouri is still skirted on the east by the Big Belt or Girdle mountains,
the main Rockies being further off, on the west. What the text means by the
" second great chain " which the river " enters or rather leaves," is the southern
end of the Big Belt mountains, which stretches east and west, somewhat like the
foot of an L, and is cut off from the main stem by a gap in which Howard's
creek runs to the Missouri. See on.

if they had sunk to fill up the cavity formed by the washing of the river. In the open places among the rocky cliffs are two kinds of gooseberries, one yellow and the other red. The former species was observed for the first time near the falls; the latter differs from it in no respect except in color and in being of a larger size; both have a sweet flavor, and are rather indifferent fruit.

July 26th. We again found the current strong and the ripples frequent. These we were obliged to overcome by means of the cord and the pole, the oar being scarcely ever used except in crossing to take advantage of the shore. Within 3¾ miles we passed seven small islands, and reached the mouth of a large creek, which empties itself in the center of a bend on the left side. It is a bold running stream, 15 yards wide, and received the name of Howard's creek, after John [*sic* 29] P. Howard, one of the party. One mile beyond it is a small run, which falls in on the same side, just above a rocky cliff. Here the mountains recede from the river, and the valley widens to the extent of several miles. The river now becomes crowded with islands, of which we passed ten in the next 13¾ miles; then, at the distance of 18 miles, we camped on the left shore near a rock in the center of a bend toward the left, opposite two more islands.

This valley has wide low grounds covered with high grass, and in many places with a fine turf of greensward. The soil of the highlands is thin and meager, without any covering except a low sedge, and a dry kind of grass which is almost as inconvenient as the prickly-pear. The seeds of it are armed with a long, twisted, hard beard at their upper

---

29 Read Thomas P. Howard, as Lewis F 31, correctly. Now called Green creek; also Sixteen-mile creek. This heads about Black butte, Three buttes, and other eminent points in the Crazy mountains of Meagher Co., south of White Sulphur Springs, and flows E.S.E. through the gap that separates the foot from the stem of the Big Belt mountains. It is a singular place—for here are some sources of the Musselshell, whose mouth we passed so long ago, and other mountain brooks whose waters find their way into the Yellowstone by way of Shields' river. At the mouth of Howard's creek is the town of Painted Rock, 18 miles by rail north of Gallatin City.

extremity, while the lower part is a sharp, firm point, beset at its base with little stiff bristles, with the points in a direction contrary to the subulate point, to which they answer as a barb. We see also another species of prickly-pear [*Mamillaria missouriensis*]. It is of a globular form, composed of an assemblage of little conic leaves (*p. 323*), springing from a common root to which their small points are attached as to a common center ; the base of the cone forms the apex of the leaf, which is garnished with a circular range of sharp thorns like the cochineal-plant, quite as stiff as, and even more keen than, those of the common flat-leaved species.

Between the hills the river had been confined within 150 or 200 yards ; but in the valley it widens to 200 or 250 yards, and sometimes is spread by its numerous islands to the distance of three-quarters of a mile. The banks are low, but the river never overflows them. On entering the valley we again saw the snow-clad mountains before us, but the appearance of the hills, as well as of the timber near us, is much as heretofore.

Finding Chaboneau unable to proceed, Captain Clark left him with one [J. Fields] of the men, and accompanied by the other went up the [Jefferson] river about twelve miles, to the top of a mountain. Here he had an extensive view of the river-valley upward, and saw a large creek [Philosophy river] which flowed in on the right side. He however discovered no fresh sign of Indians, and therefore determined to examine the middle branch [Madison river] and join us by the time we reached the forks. He descended the mountain by an Indian path which wound through a deep valley, and at length reached a fine cold spring. The day had been very warm ; the path was unshaded by timber, and his thirst was excessive ; he was therefore tempted to drink. But although he took the precaution of previously wetting his head, feet, and hands, he soon found himself very unwell. He continued his route, and after resting with Chaboneau at his camp, resumed his march across the north [*i. e.*, right-hand] fork [Jefferson river] near a large island. The first part was knee-deep; but on the other side of the island the water came to their waists, and was so rapid that Chaboneau was on the point of being swept away; and not being able to swim, would have perished if Captain Clark had not rescued him.[30] While crossing the island they killed two brown bears and saw (*p. 324*) great quantities of beaver. He then went on to a small river, which falls into the north fork some miles above its junction with the two others. Here, finding himself grow more unwell, he halted for the night at the distance of four miles from his last encampment.

July 27th. We proceeded but slowly, the current being still so rapid as to require the utmost exertions of us all to advance, and the men losing their strength fast in consequence of their constant efforts. At half a mile we passed an island, and 1¼ miles further again entered a ridge of hills, which now approach the river with cliffs apparently sinking, like those of yesterday. They are composed of a solid limestone of a light lead-color when exposed to the air, though when freshly broken it is of a deep blue, and of excellent quality and very fine grain. On these cliffs were numbers of the bighorn. At 2½ miles we reached the center of a bend toward the south, passing a small island; and at 1¼ miles beyond this reached, about nine in the morning, the mouth of a river [the Gallatin] 70 yards wide, which falls in from the southeast. Here the country suddenly opens into extensive and beautiful meadows and plains, surrounded on every side with distant and lofty mountains.

Captain Lewis went up this stream for about half a mile, where, from the height of a limestone cliff, he could observe its course about seven miles, and see the Three Forks of the

---

[30] On most occasions Captain Clark showed himself possessed of rare judgment and fortitude. To-day, however, he was not up to the mark, and the cowardly wife-beating tenderfoot still lived. The latter may serve to remind one regretfully of the boy's definition of "amphibious," as something that could not live on land and died in the water.

Missouri, of which this river is one.   Its extreme point
bore S. 65° E.   During the seven miles it passes through a
green extensive meadow of fine grass, dividing itself into
several streams, the largest passing near the ridge of hills
on which he stood.   On the right side of the Missouri a
high, wide, and extensive plain succeeds to this low meadow,
which reaches the hills.   In the meadow a large spring rises
about a quarter of a mile from this southeast fork, into
which it discharges on the right side, about 400 paces from
where he stood.   Between the southeast [Gallatin] and middle [Madison] forks a distant range (*p. 325*) of snow-topped
mountains [the Madison range] spreads from east to south,
above the irregular broken hills nearer to this spot.   The
middle [Madison] and southwest [Jefferson] forks unite at
half a mile above the entrance of the southeast [Gallatin]
fork.   The extreme point at which the former can be seen
bears S. 15° E. to the distance of 14 miles, where it turns
to the right around the point of a high plain and disappears from view.   Its low grounds are several miles in
width, forming a smooth and beautiful green meadow ;
and, like the southeast fork, it divides into several streams.

Between these two forks, and near their junction with
that from the southwest, is a position admirably well calculated for a fort.[31]   It is a limestone rock of an oblong form,
rising from the plain perpendicularly to the height of 25 feet
on three of its sides ; the fourth, toward the middle fork,
being a gradual ascent covered with a fine greensward, as
is also the top, which is level and contains about two acres.

An extensive plain lies between the middle and southwest forks, the last of which, after watering a country like
that of the other two branches, disappears about twelve
miles off, at a point bearing S. 30° W.   It is also more
divided and serpentine in its course than the other two, and

[31] Perhaps the identical spot where Manuel Lisa built his fort in 1808.   It was
afterward burned by the Blackfeet.   Mr. Peter Koch, of Bozeman, informs me
that he saw the charred remains of the stockade in 1871.   I understand the
place has since been washed away by the Madison.

possesses more timber in its meadows. This timber consists
almost exclusively of the narrow-leaved cottonwood, with
an intermixture of box-elder and sweet-willow, the underbrush being thick, like that of the Missouri lower down.
A range of high mountains, partially covered with snow, is
seen at a considerable distance running from south to west,
and nearly all around us are broken ridges of country, like
that below, through which those united streams appear to
have forced their passage. After observing the country,
Captain Lewis descended to breakfast.

We then left the mouth of the southeast fork, which in
honor of [Albert Gallatin] the Secretary of the Treasury, we
called Gallatin's river, and at the distance of half a mile
reached the confluence of the southwest [Jefferson] and
middle [Madison] branch of the Missouri. Here we found
the letter (*p. 326*) from Captain Clark. And as we agreed
with him that the direction of the southwest fork gave it a
decided preference over the others, we ascended that branch
of the river for a mile, and camped in a level, handsome
plain on the left, having advanced only seven miles. Here
we resolved to await the return of Captain Clark, and in
the meantime make the necessary celestial observations,
as this seems an essential point in the geography of the
western world, and also to recruit the men and air the baggage. This was accordingly all unloaded, and stowed away
on shore.

Near the Three Forks we saw many collections of mud-
nests of the small martin [*Petrochelidon lunifrons*], attached
to the smooth faces of the limestone rock, where they
were sheltered by projections of the rock above it. In
the meadows were numbers of the duck or mallard [*Anas
boscas*] with their young, now nearly grown. The hunters
returned toward evening with six deer, three otter, and a
muskrat; they had seen great numbers of antelopes, and
much sign of the beaver and elk.

During all last night Captain Clark had a high fever
and chills, accompanied with great pain. He however pur-

sued his route eight miles to the middle branch ; where, not finding any fresh Indian track, he came down it and joined us about three o'clock, very much exhausted with fatigue and the violence of his fever.   Believing himself bilious, he took a dose of Rush's pills, which we have always found sovereign in such cases, with bathing the lower extremities in warm water.

We are now very anxious to see the Snake Indians. After advancing for several hundred miles into this wild and mountainous country, we may soon expect that the game will abandon us.   With no information of the route, we may be unable to find a passage across the mountains when we reach the head of the river—at least, such a pass as will lead us to the Columbia.   Even are we so fortunate as to find a branch of that river, the timber which we have hitherto seen in these mountains does not promise us any fit to make (*p. 327*) canoes, so that our chief dependence is on meeting some tribe from whom we may procure horses.   Our consolation is that this southwest branch can scarcely head with any other river than the Columbia ;[32] and that if any nation of Indians can live in the mountains we are able to endure as much as they can, and have even better means of procuring subsistence.

[32] Some of the western sources of the Jefferson or Missouri are in the Continental Divide with side sources of the Lemhi river, a branch of Salmon river, a branch of Snake river, a branch of the Columbia.   But the true source is Lake Red Rock, near the Yellowstone Park, fed by streams from a mountain, on the other side of which is Lake Henry, similarly the source of the Snake River or South Fork of the Columbia.   L. and C. never knew how exactly right they were.

CHAPTER XIII.

THE JEFFERSON, MADISON, AND GALLATIN RIVERS:
UP THE JEFFERSON TO ITS MAIN FORKS.

These three rivers determined, and the name Missouri discontinued—Their characters—Goose-berries—Sacajawea identifies a spot—Recovery of Captain Clark—Ascent of the Jefferson river—Philosophy river, a branch of the Jefferson—The Jefferson described—Captain Lewis with three men goes ahead to seek the Shoshones or Snake Indians—Dusky grouse—Blue crow—Frazier's creek—Fields' creek—No fresh Indian sign—Birth creek—Captain Clark meanwhile proceeds—Fresh Indian sign—Panther creek—Progress of the separated parties —Their respective routes—They meet at the three forks of Jefferson river—Shannon lost again—The middle fork the true continuation of the Jefferson—The northwest fork named Wisdom river—Turf creek—The southeast fork named Philanthropy river—Progress up the Jefferson—Beaver's-head sighted, and identified by Sacajawea—Shannon found again—He had gone upon Wisdom river unwisely—Captain Lewis with three men resolves to go on till they shall meet Indians—Meantime the main party proceed—Captain Lewis reaches Rattlesnake cliff by an Indian road—Road and river both fork, and neither fork of the river is navigable—He leaves a note for Captain Clark and party to await him here, and proceeds up the southwest (left) fork—Finds the road gives out, returns and takes the west (right) fork, leaving note for Captain Clark to that effect—Progress of Captain Clark and party.

UNDAY, July 28th, 1805. Captain Clark continued very unwell during the night, but was somewhat relieved this morning. On examining the two streams, it became difficult to decide which was the larger or the real [continuation of the] Missouri. They are each 90 yards wide, and so perfectly similar in character and appearance that they seem to have been formed in the same mold. We were therefore induced to discontinue the name of Missouri, and gave to the southwest branch the name of Jefferson, in honor of the President of the United States and the projector of the enterprise. We called the middle branch Madison, after James Madison, Secretary of State. These two, as well as Gallatin river, run with great velocity and throw out large bodies of water. Gallatin river is, however, the most rapid of the three; and though not quite as deep, is navigable for a considerable distance. Madison river, though much less rapid than the Gallatin, is somewhat

more so than the Jefferson.   The beds of all of them are
formed of smooth pebble and gravel, and the waters are
perfectly transparent.   The timber in the neigh- (*p. 329*)
borhood would be sufficient for the ordinary uses of an
establishment ; which, however, it would be advisable to
build of brick, as the earth appears calculated for that purpose, and along the shores are some bars of fine pure sand.

The greater part of the men, having yesterday put their
deer-skins in water, were this day engaged in dressing them
for the purpose of making clothing.   The weather was very
warm ; the thermometer in the afternoon was at 90°, and
the mosquitoes were more than usually inconvenient.   We
were, however, relieved from them by a high wind from the
southwest, which came on at four o'clock, bringing a storm
of thunder and lightning, attended by refreshing showers,
which continued till after dark.   In the evening the
hunters returned with eight deer and two elk ; and the
party who had been sent up the Gallatin reported that,
after passing the point where it escaped from Captain
Lewis' view yesterday, it turned more toward the east, as
far as they could discern the opening of the mountains
formed by the valley which bordered it.   The low grounds
were still wide, but not so extensive as near its mouth, and
though the stream is rapid and much divided by islands, it
is still sufficiently deep for navigation with canoes.   The
low grounds, though not more than eight or nine feet above
the water, seem never to be overflowed, except a part on
the west side of the middle fork, which is stony and seems
occasionally inundated ; they are furnished with great
quantities of small fruit, such as currants and gooseberries.

Among the last of these is a black species [*Ribes oxyacanthoides*], which we observe not only in the meadows but
along the mountain rivulets.   From the same root rise a
number of stems to the height of five or six feet, some of
them particularly branched and all reclining.   The berry is
attached by a long peduncle to the stem from which it
hangs ; it is of a smooth ovate form, as large as the common

garden gooseberry, and as black as jet, though the pulp is of a bright crimson color. It is extremely acid. The form of the leaf resembles that of the (*p. 330*) common gooseberry [*Ribes grossularia*], though larger. The stem is covered with very sharp thorns or briars. The grass is very luxuriant, and would yield fine hay in parcels of several acres. The sand-rush grows in many places as high as a man's breast, and as thick as stalks of wheat; this would supply the best food during the winter to cattle of any trading or military post.

Sacajawea, our Indian woman, informs us that we are camped on the precise spot where her countrymen, the Snake Indians, had their huts five years ago, when the Minnetarees of Knife river first came in sight of them, and from which they hastily retreated three miles up the Jefferson, and concealed themselves in the woods. The Minnetarees, however, pursued and attacked them, killed four men, as many women and a number of boys, and made prisoners of four other boys and all the females, of whom Sacajawea was one. She does not, however, show any distress at these recollections, or any joy at the prospect of being restored to her country; for she seems to possess the folly or the philosophy of not suffering her feelings to extend beyond the anxiety of having plenty to eat and a few trinkets to wear.

July 29th. This morning the hunters brought in some fat deer of the long-tailed red kind [*Cervus virginianus macrurus*] which are quite as large as those of the United States, and are the only kind we have found at this place. There are numbers of the sand-hill cranes [*Grus canadensis*] feeding in the meadows; we caught a young one, of the same color as the red deer, which though it had nearly attained its full growth, could not fly; it is very fierce, and strikes a severe blow with its beak. The kingfisher [*Ceryle alcyon*] has become quite common on this side of the falls; but we have seen none of the summerduck [*Aix sponsa*] since leaving that place. The mallard, which we saw for the first time on the 20th inst., with their young, are now abundant, though they do not breed on the Missouri below the mountains. The small birds already described are also abun- (*p. 331*) dant in the plains; here, too, are great quantities of grasshoppers or crickets; and among other animals, a large ant with a reddish-brown body and legs, and a black head and abdomen, which builds little cones of gravel, ten or twelve inches high, without any mixture of sticks, and but little earth. In the river we see a great abundance of fish, but we cannot tempt them to bite by anything on our hooks. The whole party have been engaged in dressing skins, and making them into moccasins and leggings. Captain Clark's fever has almost left him, but he remains very languid, and has a general soreness in his limbs. The latitude of our camp, as the mean of two observations of the meridian altitude of the sun's lower limb with octant by back observation, is N. 45° 24' 8" 5''' [it is more nearly 46°].

July 30*th*. Captain Clark was this morning much restored; and, therefore, having made all the observations necessary to fix the longitude, we reloaded our canoes and begun to ascend Jefferson river. The river now becomes very crooked and forms bends on each side; the current is rapid, and cut into a great number of channels and sometimes shoals, the beds of which consist of coarse gravel. The islands are unusually numerous. On the right are high plains, occasionally forming cliffs of rocks and hills; while the left is an extensive low ground and prairie, intersected by a number of bayous or channels falling into the river. Captain Lewis, who had walked through it with Chaboneau, his wife, and two invalids, joined us at dinner, a few miles above our camp. Here the Indian woman said was the place where she had been made prisoner. The men being too few to contend with the Minnetarees, mounted their horses and fled as soon as the attack began. The women and children dispersed, and Sacajawea, as she was crossing at a shoal place, was overtaken in the middle of the river by her pursuers. As we proceeded, the low grounds were covered with cottonwood and thick under-brush; on both sides of the river, except where the high hills pre- (*p. 332*) vented it, the ground was divided by bayous; and these were dammed up by the beaver, which are very numerous here. We made 12¼ miles, and camped on the north side.

Captain Lewis proceeded after dinner through an extensive low ground of timber and meadow-land intermixed; but the bayous were so obstructed by beaver-dams that, in order to avoid them, he directed his course toward the high plain on the right. This he gained with some difficulty, after wading up to his waist through the mud and water of a number of beaver-dams. When he desired to rejoin the canoes he found the underbrush so thick, and the river so crooked, that this, joined to the difficulty of passing the beaver-dams, induced him to go on and endeavor to intercept the river at some point where it might be more collected into one channel, and approach nearer the high plain. He arrived at the bank about sunset, having gone only six miles in a direct course from the canoes; but he saw no traces of the men, nor did he receive any answer to his shouts and the firing of his gun. It was now nearly dark; a duck lighted near him and he shot it. He then went on the head of a small island, where he found some driftwood, which enabled him to cook his duck for supper, and laid down to sleep on some willow-brush. The night was cool, but the driftwood gave him a good fire, and he suffered no inconvenience, except from the mosquitoes.

July 31*st*. This morning he waited till after seven o'clock, when he became uneasy lest we should have gone beyond his camp last evening, and determined to follow us. Just as he set out with this intention, he saw one of the party in advance of the canoes. Although our camp was only two miles below him, in a straight line, we could not reach him sooner, in consequence of the rapidity of the water and the circuitous course of the river. We halted for breakfast, after which Captain Lewis continued his route.

At the distance of one mile from camp we passed the principal entrance of a stream on the left [right-hand bank] which rises in (*p. 333*) the snowy mountains to the southwest, between Jefferson and Madison rivers, and discharges itself by seven mouths, five below, and one three miles above this, which is the largest, and about 30 yards wide ; we called it Philosophy[1] river. The water of it is abundant and perfectly clear ; and the bed, like that of the Jefferson, consists of pebble and gravel. There is some timber in the bottoms of the river, and vast numbers of otter and beaver, which build on its smaller mouths and the bayous of its neighborhood. The Jefferson continues as yesterday, shoaly and rapid ; but as the islands though numerous are small, it is more collected into one current than it was below, and is from 90 to 120 yards in width. The low ground has a fertile soil of rich black loam, and contains a considerable quantity of timber, with the bulrush and cat-tail flag very abundant in the moist parts ; while the drier situations are covered with fine grass, tansy, thistles, onions, and flax. The uplands are barren, and without timber ; the soil is a light yellow clay, intermixed with small smooth pebble and gravel ; the only produce is the prickly-pear, the sedge, and the bearded grass, which is as dry and inflammable as tinder.

As we proceeded the low grounds became narrower and the timber more scarce, till at the distance of ten miles the high hills approach and overhang the river on both sides, forming cliffs of a hard black granite, like almost all those below the limestone cliffs at the Three Forks of the Missouri. They so continue for 1¾ miles, where we came

---

[1] As an attribute of "that illustrious personage, Thomas Jefferson," Lewis F 40, a tribute to him, and a tributary of his river. Only the latter remains, as a plain every-day Willow creek, with a Willow City at its mouth, on a branch of the N. P. R. R. Clark G 40 has "Pholosiphy River." The "snowy mountains" of the text are the South Boulder range.

to a point of rock on the right side, at which place the hills again retire, and the valley widens to the distance of a mile and a half. Within the next five miles we passed four islands, and reached the foot of a mountain in a bend of the river to the left. From this place we went a mile and a quarter to the entrance of a small run [Antelope creek [2]] discharging on the left, and camped on an island just above it, after making 17¾ miles.

We observe some pines on the hills on both sides of our camp, which are very (*p. 334*) lofty. The only game we have seen are one bighorn, a few antelopes, deer, and one brown bear, which escaped from our pursuit. Nothing was, however, killed to-day, nor have we had any fresh meat except one beaver for the last two days; so that we are now reduced to an unusual situation, for we have hitherto always had a great abundance of flesh.[3]

Thursday, August 1st, 1805. We left early, and at the distance of a mile reached a point of rocks on the left side, where the river passes through perpendicular cliffs. At 2¾ miles further we halted for breakfast under a cedar-tree, in a bend to the right.

Here, as had been previously arranged, Captain Lewis left us, with Sergeant Gass, Chaboneau, and Drewyer, intending to go on in advance in search of the Shoshonees.[4] He began his route along the north side of the

[2] This creek discharges a short distance above Sapington, whence a branch of the N. P. R. R. runs down to Harrison, Pony, and Red Bluff.

[3] "When we have plenty of fresh meat I find it impossible to make the men take any care of it, or use it with the least frugallity. tho' I expect that necessity will shortly theach them this art," Lewis F 50, which continues: "We have a lame crew just now, two with tumers or bad boils on various parts of them, one with a bad stone bruise, one with his arm accidentally dislocated but fortunately well replaced, and a fifth has streigned his back by sliping and falling backwards on the gunwall of the canoe. The latter is Sergt. Gass."

[4] Note here that Captain Lewis and three men go ahead to scout for Indians, while Captain Clark and the main party follow after. Two threads of narrative are thus to be taken up in alternating paragraphs, the connection of which was not always clear at first sight, especially as the "he's," "we's," and "they's" were a little mixed. I take some slight liberties in adjusting the pronouns here and

river over a high range of mountains, as Captain Clark, who ascended them on the 26th, had observed from them a large valley spreading to the north of west, and concluded that on leaving the mountain the river took that direction ; but when he reached that valley, Captain Lewis found it to be the passage of a large creek [North Boulder], falling just above the mountain into the Jefferson, which bears to the southwest. On discovering his error, he bent his course toward that river, which he reached about two in the afternoon, very much exhausted with heat and thirst. The mountains were very bare of timber, and the route lay along the steep and narrow hollows of the mountain, exposed to the midday sun, without air, shade, or water. Just as he arrived there a herd of elk passed ; they killed two of them, on which they made their dinner, and left the rest on the shore for the party in the canoes. After dinner he resumed his march, and camped on the north side of the river [left bank of the Jefferson], after making 17 miles.

In crossing the mountains Captain Lewis saw a flock of the black or dark brown pheasant,[5] of which he killed one. This bird is one-third larger than the common pheasant [*Bonasa umbellus*] of the Atlantic States ; (*p. 335*) its form is much the same. The male has not, however, the tufts of long black feathers on the sides of the neck so conspicuous in the Atlantic pheasant, and both sexes are booted nearly to the toes. The color is a uniform dark brown [slate-gray], with a small mixture of yellow or yellowish-brown specks on some of the feathers, particularly those of the tail, though the extremities of these are perfectly black for about an inch. The eye is nearly black, and the iris has a small dash of yellowish-brown ; the feathers of the tail are somewhat longer than those of our pheasant,

---

there. The geography hence to the mountains is best followed in Captain Clark's wake, as Captain Lewis' trail is quite blind in the text, and really needs more annotation than I have given it. Captain Lewis rejoins the main party Aug. 6th.

[5] That is, the northern dusky grouse, *Dendragapus obscurus richardsoni*, then new to science, the following description of which is sufficiently pertinent.

but the same in number, 18, and nearly equal in size, except that those of the middle are somewhat the longest; the flesh is white and agreeably flavored.

He also saw among the scattered pines near the top of the mountain a blue bird[6] about the size of a robin, but in action and form something like a jay; it is constantly in motion, hopping from spray to spray, and its note, which is loud and frequent, is, as far as letters can represent it, *char ah! char ah! char ah!*

After breakfast we [Captain Clark and party] proceeded. At the distance of 2¼ miles the river enters a high mountain, which forms rugged cliffs of nearly perpendicular rocks. These are of a black granite at the lower part, and the upper consists of a light-colored freestone; they continue from the point of rocks close to the river for nine miles which we passed before breakfast, during which the current is very strong. At 9¼ miles we passed an island, and a rapid with a fall of six feet, and reached the entrance of a large [South Boulder] creek on the left side. In passing this place the towline of one of the canoes broke just at the shoot of the rapids; [the boat] swung on the rocks and nearly upset. To the creek as well as the rapid we gave the name of Frazier's, after Robert Frazier, one of the party.

Here the country opens into a beautiful valley from six to eight miles in width. The river then becomes crooked and crowded with islands; its low grounds wide and fertile; though covered with fine (*p. 336*) grass from nine inches to two feet high, they possess but a small proportion of timber, and that consists almost entirely of a few narrow-leaved cottonwoods distributed along the verge of the river. The soil of the plain is tolerably fertile, and consists of a black or dark yellow loam. It gradually ascends on each side to the bases of two ranges of high mountains, which lie parallel

[6] This is the so-called blue crow, or Cassin's or Maximilian's jay, here first discovered and described, but not for years afterward scientifically named *Gymnokitta cyanocephala* (first *Gymnorhinus cyanocephalus*, Maximilian, Reise in das Innere Nord Amer. II., 1841, p. 21 : see my B. N. W., 1874, p. 209).

to the river. The tops of them are yet in part covered with snow; while in the valley we are nearly suffocated with heat during the day, at night the air is so cold that two blankets are not more than sufficient covering. In passing through the hills we observed some large cedar trees, and some juniper also.

From Frazier's creek we went 3¾ miles, and camped on the [our] left side, having come 13 miles. Directly opposite our camp is a large [North Boulder] creek which we call Fields' creek, from Reuben Fields, one of our men. Soon after we halted two of the hunters [J. and R. Fields] went out and returned with five deer, on which we dined, with one bighorn we killed in coming through the mountain, and the elk left by Captain Lewis. We were again well supplied with fresh meat. In the course of the day we saw a brown bear, but were not able to shoot him.

August 2d. Captain Lewis, who slept in the valley a few miles above us, resumed his journey early, and after making five miles and finding that the river still bore to the south, determined to cross it, in hopes of shortening the route. For the first time, therefore, he waded across it [from west to east], though there are probably many places above the falls where it might be attempted with equal safety. The river was about 90 yards wide, the current rapid, and about waist deep; the bottom was formed of smooth pebble with a small mixture of coarse gravel. He then continued along the left [*i. e.,* east] bank of the river till sunset and camped, after traveling 24 miles. He met no fresh tracks of Indians. Throughout the valley are scattered the bones and excrement of the buffalo of an old date, but there seems to be no hope of meeting the animals themselves in the moun-
(*p. 337*) tains. He saw an abundance of deer and antelope, and many tracks of elk and bear. Having killed two deer, they feasted sumptuously, with a dessert of currants of different colors—two species red, others yellow, deep purple, and black; to these were added black gooseberries and deep purple service-berries, somewhat larger than ours, from

which they differ also in color, size, and the superior excellence of their flavor. In the low grounds of the river were many beaver-dams formed of willow-brush, mud, and gravel, so closely interwoven that they resist the water perfectly; some of them were five feet high, and overflowed [caused the river to overflow] several acres of land.

In the meantime we [Captain Clark and party] proceeded slowly, the current being so strong as to require the utmost exertions of the men to make any advance, even with the aid of the cord and pole, the wind being from the northwest. The river is full of large and small islands, and the plain is cut by great numbers of bayous or channels, in which are multitudes of beaver. In the course of the day we passed some villages of barking-squirrels; we saw several rattlesnakes on the plains; young ducks, both of the duckon-mallard [*sic*⁷] and red-headed fishing-duck species; some geese; also the black woodpecker [Lewis', *Asyndesmus torquatus*], and a large herd of elk. The channel, current, banks, and general appearance of the river are like those of yesterday. At 14¾ miles we reached a rapid creek or bayou [on our right], about 30 yards wide, to which we gave the name of Birth ⁸ creek. After making 17 miles we halted in a smooth plain in a bend toward the left.

August 3d. Captain Lewis continued his course along the [east bank of the] river through the valley, which continued much as it was yesterday, except that it now widens to nearly twelve miles. The plains are more broken, and have some scattered pine near the mountains, where they rise higher than hitherto. In the level parts of the plains and the river-

---

⁷ That is, duck-in-mallard or duckinmallard, old name of the mallard duck, *Anas boscas*. The fishing-duck is the red-breasted merganser, *Mergus serrator*, the female of which has a snuffy-brown head; the male's head is dark green.

⁸ The text has no location for right or left, and also omits a second creek, just above Birth creek, on the same side. "A creek on Stard. side which we called *birth* Creek," Lewis F 59. The name is confirmed, Clark G 43; and G 47 has it "rapid & 30 yds. wide." Three-quarters of a mile above Birth creek is the "mouth of a bayou in a Stard. bend;" and camp is 1½ miles beyond this last. Birth (noting Captain Clark's birth-day—b. Aug. 1st, 1770) creek is that now

bottoms there is no timber, except small cottonwood, near the margin, and an undergrowth of narrow-leaved willow, small honeysuckle, rosebush, currant, service-berry, goose-(*p. 338*) berry, and a little of a small species of birch [*Betula occidentalis*]. This has a finely indented oval [leaf] of small size and deep green color ; the stem is simple, ascending and branching, and seldom rises higher than ten or twelve feet. The mountains continue high on each side of the valley, but their only covering is a small species of pitch-pine [*Pinus flexilis*] with a short leaf, growing on the lower and middle regions, while for some distance below the snowy tops there is neither timber nor herbage of any kind.

About eleven o'clock Drewyer killed a doe, on which they breakfasted, and after resting two hours continued till night, when they reached the river near a low ground more extensive than usual. From the appearance of the timber Captain Lewis [wrongly] supposed that the river forked above him, and therefore camped [on east bank of the Jefferson, 1½ miles above its forks] with an intention of examining it more particularly in the morning. He had now made 23 miles, the latter part of which was for eight miles through a high plain covered with prickly-pears and bearded grass, which rendered the walking very inconvenient. But even this was better than the river-bottoms they crossed in the evening, which, though apparently level, were formed into deep holes as if they had been rooted up by hogs, and the holes were so covered with thick grass that they were in danger of falling at every step. Some parts of these low grounds, however, contain turf or peat of an excellent quality for many feet deep apparently, as well as the mineral salts which we have already mentioned on the Missouri. They saw many deer, antelopes, ducks, geese, some beaver and great traces of their work, and the small

called White Tail Deer, on which is a place called Whitehall (perhaps by improving on White Tail). The distance from Boulder or Fields' creek is quite right for this identification. A branch of the N. P. R. R. comes to Whitehall, thence to Pipestone, and goes up Pipestone creek, en route to Butte City, Silver Bow, etc.

birds and curlews as usual. The only fish which they observed in this part of the river were the trout [*Salmo purpuratus*], and a species of white fish with a remarkably long small mouth, which one of our men recognized as the fish called in the Eastern States the bottlenose.

On setting out with the canoes we [Captain Clark and party] found the river as usual much crowded with islands, and the current more rapid as well as shallower, so that in many places we were (*p. 339*) obliged to man the canoes double, and drag them over the stone and gravel of the channel. Soon after we set off Captain Clark, who was walking on shore, observed a fresh track, which he knew to be that of an Indian from the large toes being turned inward, and on following it found that it led to the point of a hill, from which our camp of last night could be seen. This circumstance strengthened the belief that some Indian had strayed hither, and had run off alarmed at the sight of us. At 2¼ miles is a small creek [Pipestone] in a bend toward the right, which runs down from the mountains at a little distance; we called it Panther[9] creek, from an animal of that kind [cougar, *Felis concolor*] killed by Reuben Fields at its mouth. It is precisely the same animal common to the western parts of the United States, and measured 7½ feet from the nose to the extremity of the tail. At 6¾ miles beyond this stream is another, on the left, formed by the drains which convey the melted snows from a mountain near it, under which the [Jefferson] river passes, leaving the low grounds on the right side, and making several bends in its course. On this [small] stream [from our left] are many large beaver-dams. One mile above it is a small run on the left, after leaving which begins a very bad rapid,

---

[9] Now Pipestone creek, draining from the northwest. The distance from Birth creek is satisfactory. (See last note.) The next two runs mentioned, on the left, drain from the South Boulder range. No more streams are named, from Panther creek to Wisdom river, though several are passed on each side. The principal of these is Fish creek, on the right, draining from the north side of Table mountain.

where the bed of the river is formed of solid rock; this we passed in the course of a mile, and camped on the lower point of an island. Our journey had been only 13 miles, but the badness of the river made it very laborious, as the men were compelled to be in the water during the greater part of the day. We saw only deer, antelopes, and the common birds of the country.

August 4th. This morning Captain Lewis proceeded early and, after going S.E. by E. for four miles, reached a bold running [Turf] creek, twelve yards wide, with clear cold water, furnished apparently by four drains from the snowy [South Boulder] mountains on the left [east]. After passing this creek he changed his direction to S.E.; and, leaving the valley in which he had traveled for the two last days, entered another which bore east. At the distance of three miles on this (*p. 340*) course he passed a handsome little river [Philanthropy], about 30 yards wide, which winds through the valley. The current is not rapid, nor is the water very clear; but the river affords a considerable quantity of water, and appears as if it might be navigable for some miles. The banks are low, and the bed is formed of stone and gravel. He now changed his route to S.W.; and, passing a high plain which separates the valleys, returned to the more southern, or that which he had left. In passing this he found a river [the Jefferson], about 45 yards wide, the water of which has a whitish-blue tinge, with a gentle current and a gravelly bottom. This he waded and found waist-deep. He then continued down it, till at the distance of three-quarters of a mile he saw the entrance of the small river [Philanthropy] he had just passed; as he went on two miles lower down, he found the mouth of the [Turf] creek he had seen in the morning. Proceeding further down three miles, he arrived at the junction of this [Jefferson] river with another [Wisdom], which rises from the S.W. and runs through the south valley about 12 miles before it forms its junction, where it is 50 yards wide. He now found that his camp of last night was about 1½ miles above the entrance of this large river on the right side [*i. e.*, his camp had been on east bank of the Jefferson, 1½ miles above entrance of Wisdom river on the opposite side].

This is [Wisdom river] a bold, rapid, clear stream, but its bed is so much obstructed by gravelly bars, and subdivided by islands, that navigation must be very insecure, if not impracticable. The other or middle stream [the Jefferson] has about two-thirds its quantity of water, is more gentle, and may be safely navigated. As far as it could be observed, its course was about southwest; but the opening of the valley induced him to believe that further above it turned more toward the west. Its water is more turbid and warmer than that of the other branch, whence it may be presumed to have its sources at a greater distance in the mountains, and to pass through a more open country. Under this impression he left a note recommending to Captain Clark the middle fork, and then continued his course along the right [*i. e.*, west] side of the other or more rapid (*p. 341*) branch. After traveling 23 miles [in all to-day], he arrived near a place where the river leaves the valley and enters the mountains. Here he camped for the night.

The country he passed is like that of the rest of this valley, though there is more timber in this part on the rapid fork than there has been on the river, in the same extent, since he entered it; for in some parts of the valley the Indians seem to have destroyed a great portion of the little timber there was, by setting fire to the bottoms. He saw some antelopes, deer, cranes, geese, and ducks of the two species common to this country; though the summer-duck has ceased to appear, nor does it seem to be an inhabitant of this part of the river.

We [Captain Clark and party] proceeded soon after sunrise. The first five miles we passed four bends on the left, and several bayous on both sides. At eight o'clock we stopped to breakfast, and found a note that Captain Lewis had written on the 2d instant. During the next four miles, we passed three small bends of the river to the right, two small islands, and two bayous on the same side. Here we reached a bluff on the left ; our next course was six miles to camp. In this course we met six circular bends on the right, and several small bayous, and halted for the night in a low ground of cottonwood on the right. Our day's journey, though only 15 miles in length, was very fatiguing.

The river is still rapid, and the water, though clear, is very much obstructed by shoals or ripples at every 200 or 300 yards. At all these places we are obliged to drag the canoes over the stones, as there is not a sufficient depth of water to float them, and in the other parts the current obliges us to have recourse to the cord. But as the brushwood on the banks will not permit us to walk on shore, we are under the necessity of wading through the river as we drag the boats. This soon makes our feet tender, and sometimes occasions severe falls over the slippery stones ; and the men, by being constantly wet, are becoming more feeble. In the course of the day (*p. 342*) the hunters killed two deer, some geese and ducks, and the party saw some antelopes, cranes, beaver, and otter.

August 5th. This morning Chaboneau complained of being unable to march far to-day. Captain Lewis therefore ordered him and Sergeant Gass to pass the rapid [cross Wisdom] river and proceed through the level low ground to a point of high timber on the middle fork, seven miles distant, and await his return. He then went along the north [up the west] side of the rapid river about four miles, where he waded it, and found it so rapid and shallow that it would be impossible to navigate it. He continued along the left [up the east] side for a mile and a half, when the mountains came close on the river and rose to a considerable height, with a partial covering of snow. From this place the course of the river was to the east of north. After ascending with some difficulty a high point of the mountain, he had a pleasing view of the valley he had passed, which continued for about 20 miles further on each side of the middle fork, then seemed to enter the mountains, and was lost to view. In that direction, however, the hills which terminate the valley are much lower than those along either of the other forks, particularly the rapid one, where they continue rising in ranges above each other as far as the eye could reach. The general course of the middle fork [the Jefferson], as well as that of the gap which it forms on entering the mountains, is considerably to the south of west [10]—circumstances which gave a decided preference to this branch as our future route.

Captain Lewis now descended the mountain,[11] crossed [a plain] over to the middle fork [Jefferson], about five miles distant, and found it still perfectly navigable. There is a very large and plain Indian road leading up it, but it has at present no tracks, except those of horses which seem to have used it last spring. The river here made a great bend to the S.E.; he therefore directed his course, as well as he could, down to the spot where he had ordered Chaboneau and Gass to repair, and struck the river about three miles above (*p. 343*) their camp. It was now dark, and he was therefore obliged to make his way through the thick brush of the pulpy-leaved thorn and the prickly-pear for two hours before he reached their camp.[12] Here he was fortunate enough to find the remains of some meat, which was his only food during the march of 25 miles to-day. He had seen no game of any sort except a few antelopes, which were very shy.

The soil of the plains is a meager clay, of a light yellow color, intermixed with a large proportion of gravel, and producing nothing but twisted or bearded grass, sedge, and prickly-pears. The drier parts of the low grounds are also more indifferent in point of soil than those further down the river; although they have but little grass, they are covered with southernwood [sage-brush, species of *Arte-*

[10] " Considerably to the west of south," Lewis F 67—that is, as he looks up the Jefferson (from an eminence on Wisdom river), it is coming from a gap in the mountians about 20 miles ahead of him, and flowing considerably to the east of north.

[11] " Here Drewyer missed his step and had a very dangerous fall ; he sprained one of his fingers, and hirt his leg very much," Lewis F 67.

[12] Gass, p. 116, this date, notes the movements of the separated parties, but in terms not readily intelligible without the above clew.

misia], pulpy-leaved thorn [*Sarcobatus vermiculatus*], and prickly-pears, while the moist parts are fertile and supplied with fine grass and sand-rushes.

We [Captain Clark and party] passed within the first 4¼ miles three small islands and the same number of bad rapids. At the distance of three-quarters of a mile is another rapid of difficult passage ; 3¾ miles beyond this are the forks of the river, in reaching which we had two islands and several bayous on different sides to pass. Here we had come 9¼ miles. The river was straighter and more rapid than yesterday, the labor of the navigation proportionally increased, and we therefore proceeded very slowly, as the feet of several of the men were swollen, and all were languid with fatigue. We arrived at the forks [of Jefferson and Wisdom rivers] about four o'clock; but unluckily Captain Lewis' note had been left on a green pole which the beaver had cut down and carried off with the note—an accident which deprived us of all information as to the character of the two branches of the river. Observing, therefore, that the northwest[13] fork [Wisdom river] was most in our direction, and contained as much water as the other, we ascended it. We found it extremely rapid, and its waters were scattered in such a manner that for a quarter of a mile we were forced to cut a passage (*b. 344*) through the willow-brush that leaned over the little channels and united at the top. After going up it for a mile we camped on an island which had been overflowed, and was still so wet that we were compelled to make beds of brush to keep ourselves out of the mud. Our provision consisted of two deer which had been killed [by J. and R. Fields] in the morning.

August 6th. We [Captain Clark and party] proceeded

[13] "Northwest" and "southwest" fork, are each said, in different places, of Wisdom (or Big Hole) river, in a manner perplexing at first sight. But we have only to remember that this river, viewed at large, is the northwest fork of the Jefferson, *i. e.*, flows southeast from the northwest ; and that then, when near the Jefferson, it loops up toward the northeast. *i. e.*, comes from the southwest to a person looking up it at its mouth.

up the northwest [Wisdom] fork, which we found still very rapid and divided by several islands, while the plains near it were intersected by bayous. After passing with much difficulty over stones and rapids, we reached a bluff on the right, at the distance of nine miles, our general course being S. 30° W., and halted for breakfast.

Here we were joined by Drewyer, who informed us of the state of the two rivers, and of Captain Lewis' note; so we immediately began to descend the [Wisdom] river in order to take the other branch [Jefferson]. On going down, one of the canoes upset and two others filled with water, by which all the baggage was wet and several articles were irrecoverably lost. As one of them swung round in a rapid current, Whitehouse was thrown out of her; while down, the canoe passed over him, and had the water been two inches shallower would have crushed him to pieces; but he escaped with a severe bruise of his leg. In order to repair these misfortunes we hastened [down] to the forks, where we were joined by Captain Lewis. We then passed over to the left [east] side, opposite the entrance of the rapid fork, and camped on a large gravelly bar, near which there was plenty of wood. Here we opened, and exposed to dry, all the articles which had suffered from the water; none of them were completely spoiled except a small keg of powder; the rest of the powder, which was distributed in the different canoes, was quite safe, although it had been under the water for upward of an hour. The air is indeed so pure and dry that any wood-work immediately shrinks, unless it is kept filled with water; but we had placed our powder in small canisters of lead, each containing powder enough for the canister when melted into bullets, (*p. 345*) and secured with cork and wax, which answered our purpose perfectly.

Captain Lewis had risen very early; having nothing to eat, he sent out Drewyer to the woodland on the [his] left in search of a deer, and directed Sergeant Gass to keep along the middle branch [down the Jefferson], to meet us if we were ascending it. He had then set off with Chaboneau [directly] toward the forks; but five miles above them, hearing us on the [his] left, he [changed his course] and struck the [Wisdom] river as we were descending [it], and came on board at the forks.

In the evening we [Captain Clark's party, had] killed three deer and four elk, which furnished us once more with a plentiful supply of meat. Shannon, the same man who had been lost for 15 days [Aug. 28th to Sept. 11th, 1804], was sent out this morning to hunt, up the northwest fork. When we decided on returning, Drewyer was directed to go in quest of him, but he returned with information that he had gone several miles up the [Wisdom] river without being able to find Shannon. We now had the trumpet sounded, and fired several guns; but he did not return, and we fear he is again lost.[14]

August 7th. We remained here this morning for the purpose of making some celestial observations, and also in order to refresh the men and complete the drying of the baggage. We obtained a meridian altitude, which gave the latitude of our camp as N. 45° 2' 43" 8''' [nearer 45°32']. We were now completely satisfied that the middle branch was the most navigable, and the true continuation of the Jefferson. The northwest fork seems to be the drain of the melting snows of the mountains; its course cannot be so long as the other branch, and although it contains now as great a quantity of water, yet the water has obviously overflowed the old bed, and spread into channels which leave the low grounds covered with young grass, resembling that of the adjoining lands, which are not inundated; whence we readily infer that the supply is more precarious than that of the other branch, the waters of which, though more

[14] This gentleman, one of the most intelligent of the party in other matters, seems to have lacked the faculty of orientation, and should hardly have been allowed to go out of sight of camp alone. He was always getting lost by himself and found by others. Almost every exploring party has at least one such man, whom they have to hunt for as they do wood, water, grass, or the right road itself. This time Shannon was only lost for three days, as he managed to find himself at camp on the 9th.

gentle, are more constant.   This northwest fork we called Wisdom river.[16]

(*p. 346*) As soon as the baggage was dried, it was reloaded on board the boats ; but we found it so much diminished that we would be able to proceed with one canoe less.   We therefore hauled up the superfluous one into a thicket of brush, where we secured her against being swept away by the high tide.   At one o'clock all set out, except Captain Lewis, who remained till the evening in order to complete the observation of equal altitudes.   We passed several bends of the river both to the right and left, as well as a number of bayous on both sides, and made seven miles by water, though the distance by land is only three.   We then camped on a creek which rises in a high [South Boulder] mountain to the N.E., and after passing through an open plain for several miles discharges itself on the left, where it is a bold running stream twelve yards wide.   We called it Turf creek, from the number of bogs and the quantity of turf on its waters.   In the course of the afternoon there fell a shower of rain attended with thunder and lightning, which lasted about forty minutes, and the weather remained so cloudy all night that we were unable to take any lunar observation.   Being uneasy about Shannon, we sent Reuben Fields in search of him this morning ; but we have as yet no intelligence of either of them.   Our only game to-day was one deer [which Drewyer had killed].

---

[16] Now called Big Hole river.   Valleys among mountains in various parts of the West were and are commonly called " holes."   This one is certainly deep enough to be considered a big hole, for in Silver Bow Co., on the one hand, the mountains rise to 8,000 feet or more, and on the other, in Beaver-head Co., to 9,000 or more.   The river is very crooked, in general like the character ∞, with a very large upper and much smaller lower loop, where it sweeps N.E. into the Jefferson.   It runs of course wholly east of the Continental Divide, in which it heads by many affluents, the southernmost of which are close by some sources of the Jefferson.   Across the Continental Divide, southerly, are the side-sources of the Lemhi and Salmon rivers, tributary to the Snake and so to the Columbia. Wisdom or Big Hole river is now followed for some distance by the railroad from Dillon to Silver Bow and Butte City.

August 8th.[16]   There was a heavy dew this morning.
Having left one of the canoes, there are now more men to
spare for the chase ; four were sent out at an early hour, after
which we proceeded.   We made five miles by water along
two islands and several bayous ; but as the river formed
seven different bends toward the left, the distance by land
was only two miles south of our camp.   At the end of that
course we reached the upper principal entrance of a stream
which we called Philanthropy river."   This river empties
into the Jefferson on the southeast side, by two channels a
short distance from each other ; from its size and its southeastern course we presume that it rises in the Rocky mountains near[18] the sources of the Madison.   It is 30 yards
(*p. 347*) wide at its entrance, has a very gentle current, and

---

[16] " ☞ The courses from the entrance of Wisdom river to the forks of
Jefferson river are taken directly to the objects mentioned and the distance set
dout [down] is that by land on a direct line between the points," Lewis F 75—
an important memorandum, as courses and distances have hitherto been river-
miles, sometimes 1½, 2, or even 3 times as far as straight land-miles from point
to point.

[17] Lewis F 73, Aug. 6th : "I called the bold rapid an clear stream *Wisdom*,
and the more mild and placid one which flows in from the S.E. Philanthrophy, in
commemoration of two of those cardinal virtues, which have so eminently
marked that deservedly selibrated character [Jefferson] through life "—another
such virtue having been already commemorated in Philosophy river.   To complete this system of geographical ethics, they should have discontinued the name
of Jefferson for the main stream, and called this *Paine* river, whose two main
forks should have been *Religion* and *Common Sense ;* for Thomas Paine's soul
flowed into Jefferson's, bearing a precious quality of spiritual reasonableness,
which informed and filled the mind of the greatest statesman America ever produced.   What we owe to Jefferson is history—what Jefferson owed to Paine is
the very mystery of godlikeness.   It is well to keep the reputed paternity of our
country before the common people by the name of Washington, and uphold
William Tell among the simple Swiss ; but Washington's intellect shrinks out
of sight before Jefferson's, and Jefferson's dwarfs in comparison with Paine's.
Washington whipped some average British soldiery ; Jefferson was more than a
match for Napoleon Bonaparte ; he gave us more than half of our country with
a stroke of the pen, without spilling a drop of blood ; and the whole of our
country has grown up on principles enunciated from the French jail where
Thomas Paine lay languishing, dreaming dreams that we have awakened to realize.

[18] Not very near—for the Madison heads in Yellowstone Park, and Philanthropy
river is a much shorter stream, now called Stinking Water, by a euphemism.

is navigable for some distance.   One mile above this river
we passed an island, a second at the distance of six miles
further, during which the river makes a considerable bend
to the east.   Reuben Fields returned about noon with
information that he had gone up Wisdom river to its
entrance into the mountains, but could find nothing of
Shannon.   We made seven miles beyond the last island,
and after passing some small bayous camped under a few
high trees on the left, at the distance of 14 miles above
Philanthropy river by water, though only six by land.

The river has in fact become so very crooked that
although by means of the pole, which we now use constantly, we make a considerable distance, yet being obliged
to follow its wanderings, at the end of the day we find ourselves very little advanced on our general course.   It forms
itself into small circular bends, which are so numerous
that within the last 14 miles we passed 35 of them, all
inclining toward the right; it is, however, much more gentle
and deep than below Wisdom river, and its general width
is from 35 to 45 yards.   The general appearance of the
surrounding country is that of a valley five or six miles
wide, inclosed between two high mountains.   The bottom
is rich, with some small timber on the islands and along
the river, consisting rather of underbrush, with a few cottonwoods, birches, and willows.   The high grounds have some
scattered pines, which just relieve the general nakedness of
the hills and the plain, where there is nothing except grass.
Along the bottoms we saw to-day a considerable quantity
of buffalo-clover, sunflower, flax, greensward, thistle, and
several species of rye grass, some of which rise to the
height of three or four feet.   There is also a grass with a
soft smooth leaf which rises about three feet high, and
bears its seed very much like timothy; but it does not grow
luxuriantly, nor would it apparently answer so well in our
meadows as that plant.   We preserved some of its seeds,
(*p. 348*) which are now ripe, in order to make the experiment.   Our game consisted of deer and antelope; we saw

a number of geese and ducks just beginning to fly, and some cranes. Among the inferior animals we have an abundance of the large biting or hare-fly, of which there are two species, one black, the other smaller and brown, except the head, which is green. The green or blowing-flies unite with them in swarms to attack us, and seem to have relieved the eye-gnats, which have now disappeared. The mosquitoes too are in large quantities, but not so troublesome as they were below. Through the valley are scattered bogs and some very good turf ; the earth of which the mud is composed is of a white or bluish-white color, and seems to be argillaceous. On all the three rivers, but particularly on the Philanthropy, are immense quantities of beaver, otter, and muskrat. At our camp there was an abundance of rosebushes and briars, but so little timber that we were obliged to use willow-brush for fuel. The night was again cloudy, which prevented the lunar observations.

On our right is the point of a high plain, which our Indian woman recognizes as the place called the Beaver's Head,[19] from a supposed resemblance to that object. This, she says, is not far from the summer retreat of her countrymen, which is on a river beyond the mountains, running to the west. She is therefore certain that we shall meet them either on this river, or on that immediately west of its source, which, judging from its present size, cannot be far distant. Persuaded of the absolute necessity of procuring horses to cross the mountains, it was determined that one of us should proceed in the morning to the

---

[19] The Beaver-head, Beaver's-head, or Beaver Head is a famous landmark on the river, about halfway between the forks below and the present county town of Dillon, giving name to the county, and with some geographers to the river itself above the forks. This conspicuous " Point of Rocks " marks the north end of the straight edge of Beaver-head county along its E. border, which boundary hence crosses obliquely over to Wisdom or Big Hole river and meanders the latter for a long distance N.W. Here the Expedition enters Beaver-head county, in which it will remain until the Continental Divide is crossed into Idaho. Here is also the place where the 5,000 foot contour-line *crosses* Jefferson river, whose valley has hitherto been lower than this.

head of the river, and penetrate the mountains till he found the Shoshonees, or some other nation, who could assist us in transporting our baggage, the greater part of which we should be compelled to leave, without the aid of horses.

August 9th.[20] The morning was fair and fine. We set off early and proceeded very well, though there were more (*p. 349*) rapids in the river than yesterday. At eight o'clock we halted for breakfast, part of which consisted of two fine geese killed before we stopped.

Here we were joined by Shannon, for whose safety we had been so uneasy. The day on which he left us on his way up Wisdom river, after hunting for some time and not seeing the party arrive, he returned to the place where he had left us. Not finding us there he supposed we had passed him, and he therefore marched up the river during all the next day, when he was convinced that we had not gone on, as the river was no longer navigable. He now followed the course of the river down to the forks, and then took the branch which we are pursuing. During the three days of his absence he had been much wearied by his march, but had lived plentifully, and brought the skins of three deer. As far as he had ascended Wisdom river it kept its course obliquely down toward the Jefferson.

Immediately after breakfast, Captain Lewis took Drewyer, Shields, and M'Neal, and slinging their knapsacks they set out with a resolution to meet some nation of Indians before they returned, however long they might be separated

[20] Though the Three Forks, and some of their branches, have been named in the narrative before it reaches this date, it seems from Gass' Journal that the names were not determined, or at least announced, till now. His entry of August 9th, p. 118, reads: "This morning our commanding officers thought proper that the Missouri should lose its name at the confluence of the three branches we had left on the 30th ultimo. The north branch, which we went up, they called JEFFERSON; the west or middle branch, MADISON; the south branch, about 2 miles up which a beautiful spring comes in, GALLATIN! and a small river above the forks they called *Philosophy*. Of the three branches we had just left, they called the north *Wisdom*, the south *Philanthropy*, and the west or middle fork, which we continued our voyage along, retained the name of JEFFERSON."

from the party.²¹   He directed his course across the low ground to the plain on the right, leaving the Beaver's Head about two miles to the left.   After walking eight miles to the river, which they waded, they went on to a commanding point, from which he saw the place at which it enters the mountain ; but as the distance would not permit his reaching it this evening, he descended toward the river, and, after traveling eight miles further, camped for the evening some miles below the mountain.   They passed, before reaching their camp, a handsome little stream [unnamed], formed by some large springs which rise in the wide bottom on the left side of the river.   In their way they killed two antelopes, and took with them enough of the meat for their supper and breakfast the next morning.

(*p. 350*) In the meantime we [Captain Clark ²² and main party] proceeded, and in the course of 11 miles from our last camp passed two small islands, 16 short round bends in the river, and halted in a bend toward the right, where we dined.   The river increases in rapidity as we advance, and is so crooked that the 11 miles, which have cost us so much labor, only bring us four miles in a direct line.   [We

²¹ Here again begins a double thread of narrative, continuing to the end of the chapter. See back, note at Aug. 1st, equally applicable now.

²² Captain Clark was sadly disappointed at not being able to take the lead in the trip upon which Captain Lewis started to-day : "Capt. Lewis and 3 men set out after brackft. to examine the river above, find a portage if possible, also the Snake Indians. I should have taken this trip had I have been able to march, from the rageing fury of a tumer on my anckle," Clark G 55.   He had been suffering since his first side-trip over flint rocks and prickly-pears.   Thus at July 22d, we read : "I opened the bruses and blisters of my feet which caused them to be painfull dispatched all the men to hunt in the Bottom for Deer, deturmined my self to lay by & nurs my feet. having nothing to eat but venison and currents, I find my self much weaker," Clark G 23.   Then he had taken a fever from wading in the cold water when overheated on a scorching march, for we read at July 27th : "I was very unwell all last night with a high fever and akeing in all my bones. my fever &c continus, deturmined to prosue my intended rout," Clark G 31.   Only his indomitable spirit kept him off his back.   To his sufferings is probably due some of the difficulty we have had in locating certain creeks and pitching certain camps, between the Three Forks of the Missouri and the Three Forks of the Jefferson.

made another course, S. 10° E., which advanced us only one mile further, though it was three miles by the river-bends (Lewis F 80 and Clark G 60).] The weather became overcast toward evening, and we experienced a slight shower, attended with thunder and lightning. The three hunters who were sent out killed only two antelopes, game of every kind being scarce.

August 10*th.* Captain Lewis continued his route at an early hour through the wide bottom along the left [hand or right] bank of the river. At about five miles he passed a large [Black-tailed Deer] creek, and then fell into an Indian road leading toward the point where the river entered the mountain. This he followed till he reached a high perpendicular cliff of rocks, where the river makes its passage through the hills, and which he called Rattlesnake cliff, from the number of that animal which he saw there. Here he kindled a fire and waited the return of Drewyer, who had been sent out on the way to kill a deer. He came back about noon, with the skin of three deer and the flesh of one of the best of them. After a hasty dinner they returned to the Indian road, which they had left for a short distance, to see the cliff. It led them sometimes over the hills, sometimes in the narrow bottoms of the river, till at the distance of 15 miles from Rattlesnake cliffs they reached a hand-some, open, and level valley, where the river divided into two nearly equal branches.[23]

[23] A western branch, on Captain Lewis' right, and a southeastern, on his left. It is important to fix this point in mind ; for here is the end of the navigation of the Jefferson by the Expedition. Here the canoes are to be left, to be picked up on Captain Clark's return next year. Here is the westernmost point in the course of the Jefferson ; for here the river begins to turn southeastwardly, and then sweeps eastwardly along the Atlantic base of the Great Divide to its heads about Red Rock lake, near the Yellowstone National Park. *This* branch is of course the main Jefferson or Missouri, though it was not so regarded by Lewis and Clark, who will follow up the western branch (Prairie creek) into Shoshone cove, and so to one of its sources on the main Divide, of which the text will speak as the "fountain-head" of the Missouri. The point where Captain Lewis stands at this moment may be called the Two Forks of the Jefferson (in distinction from the Three Forks, where Wisdom and Philanthropy rivers

The mountains over which they had passed were not very high, but rugged and close to the riverside. The river, which before it entered the mountain was rapid, rocky, very crooked, much divided by islands, and shallow, now becomes more direct in its course, as it is hemmed in by the hills, and has not so many bends or islands, but be-(*p. 351*) comes more rapid and rocky, and continues as shallow. On examining the two branches of the river it was evident that neither of them was navigable further. The road forked with the river; and Captain Lewis therefore sent a man up each of them for a short distance, in order that, by comparing their respective information, he might be able to take that which seemed to have been most used this spring. From their account he resolved to choose that which led along the southwest branch of the river, which was rather the smaller of the two. He accordingly wrote a note to Captain Clark informing him of the route, and recommending his staying with the party at these forks till he [Lewis] should return. This note he fixed on a dry willow-pole at the forks of the river, and then proceeded up the southwest branch; but after going a mile and a half the road became scarcely distinguishable, and the tracks of the horses which he had followed along the Jefferson were no longer seen. Captain Lewis therefore returned to examine the other road himself, and found that the horses had in fact passed along the western or right [hand] fork [now Prairie creek], which had the additional recommendation of being larger than the other.

come in near together). This is almost exactly on the parallel of 45° N., vicinity of present town of Grayling, Beaver-head Co., and here the Utah and Northern R. R. comes along the main fork and makes a crossing. The Expedition here strikes the Rocky mountains at perhaps the very worst point that could have been found for their journey beyond the Divide, since leaving Maria's river. They will make the Continental Pass easily enough, but at a point which has never yet been available for a through route, in consequence of the character of the country on the Pacific side. Had they taken the other fork, and kept it a little way, they would have struck the pass through which the railroad just named now comes from Snake river. But it is easy to be wise after the event.

This road he concluded to take. He therefore sent back Drewyer to the forks with a second letter to Captain Clark, apprising him of the change, and then proceeded. The valley of the west fork, through which he now passed, bears a little to the north of west, and is confined, within the space of about a mile in width, by rough mountains [6,000 feet and more] and steep cliffs of rock. At the distance of 4½ miles it opens into a beautiful and extensive plain about ten miles long and five or six in width. This is surrounded on all sides by higher rolling or waving country, intersected by several little rivulets from the mountains, each bordered by its wide meadows. The whole prospect is bounded by these mountains, which nearly surround it, so as to form a beautiful cove,[24] 16 or 18 miles in diameter. On entering this cove the river bends to the northwest, and bathes (*p. 352*) the foot of the hills to the right. At this place they halted for the night on the right [hand] side of the river, and having lighted a fire of dry willow-brush, the only fuel which the country affords, supped on a deer. They had traveled to-day 30 miles by estimate—that is, 10 to Rattlesnake cliff, 15 to forks of Jefferson river, and 5 to camp.

In this cove some parts of the low grounds are tolerably fertile, but much the greater portion is covered with prickly-pear, sedge, twisted grass, pulpy-leaved thorn, southernwood, and wild sage ; like the uplands, it has a very inferior soil. These last have little more than the prickly-pear and the twisted or bearded grass, nor are there in the whole cove more than three or four cottonwood trees, and these are small. At the apparent extremity of the bottom above,

---

[24] This cove is an important place in L. and C.'s itinerary, not only now on the outward journey, but next year, when Clark returns this way. They will call it Shoshonee or Shoshone cove. Its bottom is something over 5,000 feet above sea-level, and the mountains on both hands rise 1,000 feet or more higher. The cove is that one of the so-called "holes" in the mountains through which Prairie creek meanders. The plain has become known as Horse plains, or Horse prairie, a name also applied to the creek ; and on one of the upper southern branches of the creek is now a town called Horse Prairie. Just over the mountains to the north is Bannack or Bannock City, on Grasshopper (Willard's) creek.

and about ten miles to the westward, are two perpendicular cliffs rising to a considerable height on each side of the river [Prairie creek], at this distance seeming like a gate.

In the meantime we [Captain Clark and party] proceeded at sunrise, and found the river not so rapid as yesterday, though more narrow, still very crooked, and so shallow that we were obliged to drag the canoes over many ripples in the course of the day.   At 6½ miles we had passed eight bends on the north and two small bayous on the left, and came to what the Indians call the Beaver's Head,²⁵ a steep rocky cliff about 150 feet high, near the right side of the river.   Opposite to this, at 300 yards from the water, is a low cliff about 50 feet in height, which forms the extremity of a spur of the [Ruby] mountain, about four miles distant on the left.   At four o'clock we were overtaken by a heavy shower of rain, attended with thunder, lightning, and hail. The party were defended from the hail by covering themselves with willow-bushes, but they got completely wet, and in this situation, as soon as the rain ceased, continued till we camped.   This we did at a low bluff on the left, after passing, in the course of 6½ miles, four islands and 18 bends on the right, and a (*p. 353*) low bluff and several bayous on the same side.   We had now come 13 miles, yet were only four on our route toward the mountains.   The game seems to be declining; for our hunters procured only a single deer, though we found another for us [ourselves] that had been killed three days before by one of the hunters [J. Fields] during an excursion, and left for us on the river.

²⁵ As already intimated, the best known landmark in these parts, celebrated by the Indians from time immemorial, and still called by the English of the name they gave it.   Yesterday's camp of the main party was only a couple of miles direct below the Beaver's Head, though 6½ by water; it was just above a small stream on their left, unnamed then, now called McHesser's creek.   To-day, the 10th, they camp two miles direct, 6½ by water, above the Head, on the left hand or right bank of the river, passing unnamed a creek which makes in from the east near the Head.   Thus the main party is still a good way below Dillon, on the Jefferson; while Captain Lewis is camped in Shoshone cove, five miles up Prairie creek.   The itinerary for the day is in Lewis F 84, and Clark G 60, 61.

CHAPTER XIV.

THE JEFFERSON FROM THE BEAVER'S HEAD TO A SOURCE
OF THE MISSOURI IN THE ROCKY MOUNTAINS.

Captain Lewis continues in advance of the main party—Lone Indian horseman sighted and sig-
naled, but put to flight—Preparations to meet the expected Indians—Meanwhile Captain
Clark and party continue up the Jefferson to Three-thousand-mile island—Captain Lewis'
party separates to reconnoiter—Plain Indian road found—It leads to a fountain-head of
the Jefferson, and thus to a source of the Missouri in the Rockies—The river straddled and
God thanked—They stand on the Great Divide between Atlantic and Pacific waters, August 12th—They strike a source of the Columbia river within a mile, and taste its water—
Meanwhile Captain Clark's party proceeds—Captain Lewis soon meets Indians—Their
interview—A band of nearly sixty mounted warriors advances to meet him—Fraternal
embraces—Parley and ceremony—They conduct Captain Lewis and party to their camp—
They smoke in council—Indian information of the country—Fresh Columbia river
salmon—Previous alarm of the Indians, by the lone horseman, supposing Captain Lewis
party to have been hostile Indians—Music and dancing—Meanwhile Captain Clark's
party labors up the Jefferson—M'Neal's creek—Captain Lewis remains with the Shoshones—An antelope-hunt—Meanwhile Captain Clark's party proceeds—Captain Lewis
urges the Shoshone chief to go with him to meet the main party—Fearing treachery,
the Indians hesitate—The chief overcomes their doubts—Captain Lewis, the chief, and
many warriors set out—Meanwhile Captain Clark's party proceeds—Willard's creek—Captain Lewis keeps on with the Indians—Excitement over a deer killed by Drewyer—Indian
voracity—Renewed suspicions of the Indians at not meeting the expected party of
whites—The situation critical—A successful stratagem—Captain Clark's party almost
reaches Captain Lewis and the Indians.

SUNDAY, August 11th, 1805.[1] Captain Lewis again proceeded early, but had the mortification to find that the
track which he followed yesterday soon disappeared. He
determined therefore to go on [ten miles] to the narrow gate
or pass of the river which he had seen from the camp [his,
on Prairie creek], in hopes of being able to recover the
Indian path. For this purpose he waded across the river,
which was now about twelve yards wide, barred in several
places by the dams of the beaver, and then went straight
forward to the pass, sending one man along the river to his

[1] Throughout this chapter we continue to have the double narrative of Captain Lewis in advance, and Captain Clark bringing up the main party. It is
chiefly, however, devoted to the former.

left and another on the right,[2] with orders to search for the road, and if they found it to let him know by raising a hat on the muzzle of their guns.

In this order they went along for about five miles, when Captain Lewis perceived, with the greatest delight, a man on horseback, at the distance of two miles, coming down the plain toward them. On examining him with the glass Captain Lewis saw that he was of a different nation from any Indians we had hitherto met. He was armed with a bow (*p. 355*) and a quiver of arrows, and mounted on an elegant horse without a saddle ; a small string attached to the under jaw answered as a bridle.

Convinced that he was a Shoshonee,[3] and knowing how

---

[2] " I now sent Drewyer to keep near the creek to my right and Shields to my left, with orders," etc., Lewis F 85 ; *i. e.*, he had crossed Prairie creek from north to south, and the three men went abreast some distance apart, up the south side of the stream, which is therefore to the right of all three of them as they advance. The text reverses the actual relative positions of the creek, two of the men, and Captain Lewis. M'Neal walked with the latter.

[3] The Shoshonees, Shoshonis, Shoshones, etc., *or* Snake Indians, give name to the important Shoshonean family of Indians, several of whose tribes besides this one are familiar to us by name, as noted below. They also give name to the great southern branch of the Columbia river. I anticipate the very full account of these Indians which our authors will give, by introducing here a notice of the Shoshonean linguistic stock, representing the best results of modern research and criticism.

The Shoshonee or Snake tribe is named in 1836 by Gallatin, in his synopsis of the Indian Tribes in the Trans. and Coll. Amer. Antiq. Soc. II., pp. 120, 306. There he included only the one tribe, vaguely noted as living on the waters of the Columbia. On the strength of the vocabulary he possessed (Say's), he regarded this tribe as of a distinct linguistic stock, and his name is now adopted as designative of the Shoshonean family. (See also Gallatin, Trans. Amer. Ethn. Soc. II. 1848 ; and in Schoolcraft's Ind. Tribes, III. 1853, p. 402.)

The Shoshoni tribes of Hale, U. S. Expl. Exped. VI. 1846, pp. 199, 218, include, besides the Shoshonis themselves, the Wihinasht, Panasht, Yutas, Sampiches, and Comanches. (See also Latham, Trans. Philol. Soc., London, 1856, p. 73, and Opuscula, 1860, p. 340.) The Shoshonees of Turner, P. R. R. Rep. III. pt. iii, 1856, pp. 55, 71, 76, include the Comanches, the Chemehuevis, and Cahuillos. The Shoshones or Snakes are given in Pritchard, Phys. Hist. Mankind, V. 1847, p. 429, as inhabiting the Rocky mountains on both sides and the shores of the Missouri. The Shoshones of Keene, App. Stanford's Comp. Cent. and So. Amer., 1878, pp. 460, 477, are nearly as above, but include the

much our success depended on the friendly offices of that nation, Captain Lewis was full of anxiety to approach without alarming him, and endeavor to convince him that he [Lewis] was a white man.   He therefore proceeded toward the Indian at his usual pace.   When they were within a mile of each other the Indian suddenly stopped.   Captain Lewis immediately followed his example, took his blanket from his knapsack, and holding it with both hands at the two

Washoes, which are Indians of a different linguistic stock.   The term " Snake " is synonymous with the above, in their several acceptations, as used by Gallatin, Hale, Pritchard, Turner, Keene, and others.   The Shóshoni of Gatschet, Mag. Amer. Hist. 1877, p. 154, indicates the whole Shoshonean family, in the sense now understood.   We may further note that the name " Paduca," as used by Pritchard and Latham in various places, is inexactly synonymous with the above, as covering some of the Shoshonean tribes, but including some other tribes of different linguistic stock.

Lewis and Clark meet their Shoshonees at nearly the extreme northern point of the geographical distribution of the great Shoshonean family.   This family occupied a large area of the great interior basin of the United States. From this area the general boundary trended south and considerably eastward, nearly to the Gulf of Mexico.   The stocks successively bounding the area on this hand are the Siouan and Kiowan in what is now Wyoming, the Algonquian in Colorado, a corner of Caddoan (middle group) in Kansas, Siouan again in Kansas and the Indian Territory, then Caddoan (southern group) nearly to the Gulf, from which the Shoshonean were cut off by the Karankawan and Coahuiltecan families.   The southern boundary of Shoshonean area was, in a general way, the Colorado river, where Shoshonean tribes encountered Athapascan tribes (especially Apaches and Navajos) in Arizona and New Mexico, and Yuman tribes in Arizona and Southern California.   They had, however, an isolated outlying group in Arizona (the Chemehuevis).   They touched the Pacific for a little distance just north of Yuman tribes, but elsewhere were cut off from the ocean by that extraordinary agglomeration of diverse family stocks which were massed on the coast of California and Oregon.   On the northwest the Shoshoneans were bordered by Shahaptian and Salishan tribes, in Oregon and Washington.   The " hub " of this great area, of very irregular outline, may be located about Great Salt Lake ; and Shoshonean tribes, to speak roundly, occupied Utah, Nevada, most of Colorado, much of Oregon, southern Idaho, western Wyoming, part of southern California, with parts of Montana, Kansas, Indian Territory, Texas, and New Mexico, respectively, and a spot in Arizona.

The foregoing paragraph is drawn up from Powell's map.   The same authority indicates the principal Shoshonean tribes, at present, as follows :

    1. *Bannock*, Fort Hall Reservation, 514 ; Lemhi Reservation, 75.

    2. *Chemehuevi*, Colorado River Agency in Arizona, about 200.

corners, threw it above his head and unfolded it as he brought it to the ground, as if in the act of spreading it. This signal,[4] which originates in the practice of spreading a robe or skin, as a seat for guests to whom they wish to show distinguished kindness, is the universal sign of friendship among the Indians on the Missouri river and the Rocky mountains. As usual, Captain Lewis repeated this signal three times; still the Indian kept his position, and looked with an air of suspicion on Drewyer and Shields, who were now advancing on each side. Captain Lewis was afraid to make any signal for them to halt, lest he should increase the suspicions of the Indian, who began to be uneasy, and they were too distant to hear his voice. He therefore took from his pack some beads, a looking-glass, and a few trinkets, which he had brought for the purpose, and leaving his gun, advanced, unarmed, toward the Indian. He remained in the same position till Captain Lewis came within 200 yards of him, when he turned his horse and began to move off slowly. Captain Lewis then called out to him in as

3. *Comanche*, on the Kiowa, Comanche, and Wichita Reservation, Ind. Terr., 1,598.

4. *Gosiute*, in Utah at large, 256.

5. *Pai-ute* (Piute), about 2,300, scattered in S. E. Cala. and S. W. Nev.

6. *Paviotso*, about 3,000, scattered in W. Nev. and S. Oreg.

7. *Saidyuka*, Klamath Agency, 145.

8. *Shoshoni*, under Fort Hall Agency, 979, and at Lemhi Agency, Idaho, 249. *These* are they whom Lewis and Clark are about to meet. Lewis and Clark's account of them, as they were at the beginning of this century, will be forever the best.

9. *Tobikhar*, under Mission Agency, Cal., about 2,200.

10. *Tukuarika* ("Sheepeaters"), Lemhi Agency, 108.

11. *Tusayan* (*i. e.*, the Mokis, or Moquis), dwelling on their mesa of the same name, 1,996 by the census of 1890.

12. *Uta* or *Ute* Indians, with a total of 2,839; under Southern Ute Agency, Colo., 985; on Ourey Reservation, Utah, 1,021; on Uintah Reservation, Utah, 833.

[4] The signal is as well known and as much used now as then. I saw George Boyd use it, on Maria's river, with excellent results and to our immense relief, as we suspected a certain party of Indians so strongly that we halted and got ready to fight. It has been of late years extended to the purpose of calling together separated parties, in the same way that the dinner horn is blown to the hands on a farm.

loud a voice as he could, repeating the word "tabba bone!" which in the Shoshonee language means white man; but looking over his shoulder the Indian kept his eyes on Drewyer and Shields, who were still advancing, without recollecting the impropriety of doing so at such a moment, till Captain Lewis made a signal (*p. 356*) to them to halt. This Drewyer obeyed; but Shields did not observe it, and still went forward. Seeing Drewyer halt, the Indian turned his horse about as if to wait for Captain Lewis, who now reached within 150 paces, repeating the words "tabba bone," holding up the trinkets in his hand, and at the same time stripping up the sleeve of his shirt to show the color of his skin. The Indian suffered him to advance within 100 paces; then suddenly turning his horse, and giving him the whip, leaped across the creek and disappeared in an instant among the willow-bushes. With him vanished all the hopes, which the sight of him had inspired, of a friendly introduction to his countrymen.

Though sadly disappointed by the imprudence of his two men,[5] Captain Lewis determined to make the incident of some use. Therefore, calling the men to him, they all set off after the track of the horse, which they hoped might lead them to the camp of the Indian who had fled; or, if he had given the alarm to any small party, their track might conduct them to the body of the nation. They now fixed a small flag of the United States on a pole, which was carried by one of the men as a signal of their friendly intentions, should the Indians observe them as they were advancing. The route lay across an island formed by a nearly equal division of the creek in the bottom. After reaching the open grounds on the right[6] side of the creek, the track turned toward some high hills about three miles

---

[5] " I fet soarly chagrined at the conduct of the men—particularly Sheilds to whom I principally attributed this failure in obtaining an introduction to the natives. I now called the men to me and could not forbare abraiding them a little," etc., Lewis F 87.

[6] North side—the Indian had jumped the creek, from south to north, below

distant. Presuming that the Indian camp might be among these hills, and that by advancing hastily he might be seen and alarm them, Captain Lewis sought an elevated situation near the creek, had a fire made of willow-brush, and took breakfast. At the same time he prepared a small assortment of beads, trinkets, awls, some paint, and a looking-glass, and placed them on a pole near the fire, in order that if the Indians returned they might discover that the party were white men and friends. While making these preparations a very heavy shower of rain and hail (*p. 357*) came on, and wet them to the skin. In about 20 minutes it was over, and Captain Lewis then renewed his pursuit ; but as the rain had made the grass which the horse had trodden down rise again, his track could with difficulty be distinguished. As they went along they passed several places where the Indians seemed to have been digging roots to-day, and saw the fresh track of eight or ten horses ; but they had been wandering about in so confused a manner that he could not discern any particular path, and at last, after pursuing it about four miles along the valley, to the left [*i. e.*, westward], under the foot of the hills, he lost the track of the fugitive Indian. Near the head of the valley they had passed a large bog covered with moss and tall grass, among which were several springs of pure cold water. They now turned a little to the left along the foot of the high hills, and reached a small creek, where they camped for the night, having made about 20 miles, though not more than ten in a direct line from their camp of last evening.

The morning [*August* 11*th*] being rainy and wet, we [Captain Clark and party] did not set out with the canoes till after an early breakfast. During the first three miles we passed three small islands, six bayous on different sides of

the first main fork, and Captain Lewis was on his trail. " After passing [crossing] to the open ground on the N. side of the creek, we observed that the track made out toward the high hills about 3 m. distant in that direction," Lewis E 87. He was therefore heading north from Prairie creek when he stopped, etc., as per text, before turning to the left or west.

the river, and the same number of bends toward the right. Here we reached the lower point of a large island, which we called Three-thousand-mile [7] island, on account of its being at that distance from the mouth of the Missouri. It is 3½ miles in length, and as we coasted along it we passed several small bends of the river toward the left, and two bayous on the same side. After leaving the upper point of Three-thousand-mile island, we followed the main channel on the left side, which led us by three small islands, several small bayous, and 15 bends toward the right. Then, at the distance of 7½ miles, we camped on the upper end of a large island near the right. The river was shallow and rapid; so that we (*p. 358*) were obliged to be in the water during a great part of the day, dragging the canoes over the shoals and ripples. Its course was so crooked that, notwithstanding we had made 14 miles by water, we were only five miles from our camp of last night.

The country consists of a low ground on the river about five miles wide, succeeded on both sides by plains of the same extent, which reach to the base of the mountains. These low grounds are very much intersected by bayous, and in those on the left side is a large proportion of bog covered with tall grass, which would yield a fine turf. There are very few trees, and those small narrow-leaved cottonwoods ; the principal growth being the narrow-leaved willow and currant bushes, among which were some bunches of privy [privet, see note [53] p. 84] near the river. We saw a number of geese, ducks, beaver, otter, deer, and antelopes, of all which one beaver was killed with a pole from the boat, three otters with a tomahawk, and the hunters brought in three deer and an antelope.

August 12*th.* This morning, as soon as it was light, Captain Lewis sent Drewyer to reconnoiter, if possible, the route

---

[7] No such island now exists. To-day's camp is only seven miles direct above the Beaver's Head, and consequently only about halfway from that point to Dillon.

of the Indians. In about an hour and a half he returned, after following the tracks of the horse which we had lost yesterday to the mountains, where they ascended and were no longer visible. Captain Lewis now decided on making a circuit along the foot of the mountains which formed the cove, expecting by that means to find a road across them, and accordingly sent Drewyer on one side, and Shields on the other. In this way they crossed four small rivulets near each other, on which were some bowers or conical lodges of willow-brush, which seemed to have been made recently. From the manner in which the ground in the neighborhood was torn up, the Indians appeared to have been gathering roots ; but Captain Lewis could not discover what particular plant they were searching for, nor could he find any fresh track, till at the distance of four (*p. 359*) miles from his camp he met a large plain Indian road which came into the cove from the northeast, and wound along the foot of the mountains to the southwest, approaching obliquely the main stream he had left yesterday. Down this road he now went toward the southwest. At the distance of five miles it crossed a large run or [Painter[8]] creek, which is a principal branch of the main stream into which it falls, just above the high cliffs or gates observed yesterday, and which they now saw below them. Here they halted and breakfasted on the last of the deer, keeping a small piece of pork in reserve against accident.

They then continued through the low bottom, along the main stream, near the foot of the mountains on their right. For the first five miles, the valley continues toward the southwest, being from two to three miles in width ; then the main stream, which had received two small branches from the left in the valley, turned abruptly to the west through

[8] On the right hand, from the northwest. Next considerable branch of Prairie creek is one from the left or south, on which is now a place called Horse Prairie. Next, from the north, come two affluents (or one forked stream), Coyote and Bloody Dick. Above these the main stream is called Trail creek, flowing due east from the "fountain-head." This last rivulet leads up into the Pass.

a narrow bottom between the mountains. The road was still plain, and, as it led them directly on toward the mountain, the stream gradually became smaller, till, after going two miles, it had so greatly diminished in width that one of the men [M'Neal], in a fit of enthusiasm, with one foot on each side of the river, thanked God that he had lived to bestride the Missouri. As they went along their hopes of soon seeing the Columbia [*i. e.*, the Pacific watershed] arose almost to painful anxiety, when after four miles from the last abrupt turn of the river [which turn had been to the west], they reached a small gap formed by the high mountains, which recede on each side, leaving room for the Indian road. From the foot of one of the lowest of these mountains, which rises with a gentle ascent of about half a mile, issues the remotest water[9] of the Missouri.

They had now reached the hidden sources of that river, which had never yet been seen by civilized man. As they quenched their thirst at the chaste and icy fountain—as they sat down by the brink of that little rivulet, which yielded its distant and modest tribute to the parent ocean —they felt themselves rewarded for all their labors and all their difficulties.

They (*p. 360*) left reluctantly this interesting spot, and pursuing the Indian road through the interval of the hills,

[9] Which gives rise to that western fork of the Jefferson which Lewis thus traced up Shoshone cove ; but he would have had to be many miles eastward of this spring, at the highest fountain which feeds Red Rock lake, near the Yellowstone Park, in order to verify the text literally. However, we understand that point. Here Lewis F 91 must of course be transcribed, *ipsissimis verbis :* " At the distance of 4 miles further the road took us to the most distant fountain of the waters of the mighty Missouri in surch of which we have spent so many toilsome days and wristless nights. thus far I had accomplished one of those great objects on which my mind had been unalterably fixed for many years, judge then of the pleasure I felt in allying my thirst with this pure and ice-cold water which issues from the base of a low mountain or hill of a gentle ascent for ½ a mile. the mountains are high on either hand [but] leave this gap at the head of this rivulet through which the road passes. here I halted a few minutes and rested myself. two miles below Mc.Neal had exultingly stood with one foot on each side of this little rivulet and thanked his god that he had lived to bestride the mighty & heretofore deemed endless Missouri."

arrived at the top of a ridge, from which they saw high mountains, partially covered with snow, still to the west of them. The ridge on which they stood formed the dividing line between the waters of the Atlantic and Pacific oceans.[10]

They followed a descent much steeper than that on the eastern side, and at the distance of three-quarters of a mile reached a handsome, bold creek of cold, clear water, running to the westward. They stopped to taste for the first time the waters of the Columbia; and after a few minutes followed the road across steep hills and low hollows, till they reached a spring on the side of a mountain. Here they found a sufficient quantity of dry willow-brush for fuel, and therefore halted for the night. Having killed nothing in the course of the day, they supped on their last piece of pork, and trusted to fortune for some other food to mix with a little flour and parched meal, which was all that now remained of their provisions.

[10] The same is now the boundary line between Montana and Idaho. The opposite counties here are Beaver's-head in the former, and Lemhi in the latter.

How slight and little obvious may be a crossing of the Great Divide between the Atlantic and Pacific watersheds is well illustrated in the case of the mountains between North and Middle Park in Colorado. The North Platte river heads by numerous affluents in North Park, runs northward through Medicine Bow mountains in Wyoming, and then makes a great bend eastward to join the other Platte and seek the Missouri. North Park is therefore entirely in the Atlantic watershed. It is bounded on the east by the Medicine Bow range, and on the west by the Continental Divide, a range of mountains which comes south from Wyoming and here takes the name of Park Range. To inclose North Park on the south, Park Range curves eastward till it meets Medicine Bow Range. Consequently the Continental Divide, separating North from Middle Park, runs east-west instead of north-south. Middle Park contains the headwaters of Grand river, which unites with the Green to form the Colorado of the West, which seeks the Gulf of California; this Park is therefore wholly on the Pacific watershed. In the summer of 1877 I conducted an expedition of the U. S. Geological and Geographical Survey through North and Middle Park. We started from Cheyenne, Wyo., crossed Medicine Bow mountains, and entered North Park by an easy road from the north. Across the Park, to the southwest, is visible Rabbit-ears mountain, so-called from a pair of peaks it presents. We crossed to the foot of this mountain, where we

Before reaching the fountain of the Missouri they saw several large hawks nearly black,[11] and some heath-cocks [*Centrocercus urophasianus*] ; these last have a long pointed tail and are of a uniform dark brown color ; they are much larger than the common dunghill fowl, and similar in habits and mode of flying to the grouse or prairie-hen. Drewyer also wounded, at the distance of 130 yards, an animal which we had not yet seen, but which, after falling, recovered itself and escaped. It seemed to be of the fox kind, rather larger than the small wolf of the plains, with a skin in which black, reddish-brown, and yellow were curiously intermixed.[12]

On the creek of the Columbia [*i. e.*, of Lemhi river] they found a species of currant [*Ribes viscosissimum*], which does not grow as high as that of the Missouri, though it is more branching ; and its leaf, the under disk of which is covered with a hairy pubescence, is twice as large. The fruit is of the ordinary size and shape of the currant, and supported in the usual man- (*p. 361*) ner, but is of a deep purple color, acid, and of a very inferior flavor.

discovered that a way could be found or made into Middle Park, practicable for our wagons. One of the ultimate sources of the North Platte comes down from the Rabbit-ears ; but on skirting around the base of this mountain we found ourselves on a head of Muddy creek, one of the side-sources of Grand river. It was but a step from one to the other, and perfectly practicable for a wagon-road, though we had one upset from carelessness of the driver. There was, however, no sign of a road by the way we came for several miles, and probably no wagon had before passed over the ground there. The actual divide was imperceptible, and we only became aware that we had crossed it when we noticed a tiny streamlet running in the opposite direction from that taken by the rivulet on which we had broken camp at daylight. We crossed Middle Park by Hot Sulphur Springs, came out of Park Range (the continuation of Medicine Bow Range) by Boulder, and struck the open prairie north of Denver, whence we returned to Cheyenne. A small herd of buffalo, long isolated and since extinct, then ranged in the timber of the Rabbit-ears and neighboring mountains, and I believe that one of these, on the south border of North Park, has been named Buffalo Peak. Thus it is certain that the buffalo has ranged in Middle Park, and so on the Pacific watershed.

[11] Either *Buteo calurus* or the melanistic phase of *Buteo swainsoni*.

[12] Probably the wolverine or carcajou, *Gulo luscus*.

We [Captain Clark and party, *August 12th*] proceeded in the boats, but as the river was very shallow and rapid, navigation was extremely difficult. The men, who are almost constantly in the water, are getting feeble and sore, and so much worn down by fatigue that they are very anxious to commence traveling by land. We went along the main channel, which is on the right side, and after passing nine bends in that direction, three islands, and a number of bayous, reached at the distance of 5½ miles the upper point of a large island. At noon there was a storm of thunder which continued about half an hour; after which we proceeded; but, as it was necessary to drag the canoes over the shoals and rapids, we made but little progress. On leaving the island we passed a number of short bends, several bayous, and one run of water on the right side; and having gone by four small and two large islands, camped on a smooth plain to the left near a few cottonwood trees. Our journey by water was just twelve miles, and four in a direct line. The hunters supplied us with three deer and a fawn.

August 13th. Very early in the morning Captain Lewis resumed the Indian road, which led him in a western direction, through an open broken country. On the left was a deep valley at the foot of a high range of mountains running from southeast to northwest, with their sides better clad with timber than the hills to which we have been for some time accustomed, and their tops covered in part with snow. At five miles' distance, after following the long descent of another valley, he reached a creek [from the right, tributary to the Lemhi] about ten yards wide; and on rising [surmounting] the hill beyond it, had a view of a handsome little valley on the left, about a mile in width, through which he judged, from the appearance of the timber, that some stream of water most probably passed.

On the creek they had just left were some bushes of white maple [*Acer glabrum*], sumach of the small species

with the winged rib [*Rhus aromatica* var. *trilobata*], and a
species of honey- (*p. 362*) suckle [*Actea spicata* var. *arguta ?*]
resembling in its general appearance and the shape of its
leaf the small honey-suckle of the Missouri, except that it
is rather larger and bears a globular berry, about the size of
a garden-pea, of a white color and formed of a soft mucilaginous substance, in which are several small brown seeds,
irregularly scattered without any cell, but enveloped in a
smooth, thin pellicle.

They proceeded along a waving plain parallel to this valley for about four miles, when they discovered two women,
a man, and some dogs, on an eminence at the distance of a
mile before them.   The strangers first viewed them, apparently with much attention, for a few minutes, and then two
of them sat down as if to await Captain Lewis' arrival.   He
went on till he reached within about half a mile, then
ordered his party to stop, put down his knapsack and rifle,
and unfurling the flag advanced alone toward the Indians.
The females soon retreated behind the hill, but the man
remained till Captain Lewis came within 100 yards from
him, when he too went off, though Captain Lewis called
out "tabba bone!" loud enough to be heard distinctly.
He hastened to the top of the hill, but they had all disappeared.   The dogs, however, were less shy, and came
close to him ; he therefore thought of tying a handkerchief
with some beads round their necks, and then let [-ting] them
loose, to convince the fugitives of his friendly disposition ;
but they would not suffer him to take hold of them, and soon
left him.   He now made a signal to the men, who joined
him, and then all followed the track of the Indians, which
led along a continuation of the same road they had been
already traveling.   It was dusty, and seemed to have been
much used lately both by foot-passengers and horsemen.

They had not gone along it more than a mile, when on a
sudden they saw three female Indians, from whom they
had been concealed by the deep ravines which intersected
the road, till they were now within 30 paces of each other.

One of them, a young woman, immediately took to flight; the other two, an elderly woman and a (*p. 363*) little girl, seeing they were too near for them to escape, sat on the ground, and holding down their heads seemed as if reconciled to the death which they supposed awaited them. The same habit of holding down the head and inviting the enemy to strike, when all chance of escape is gone, is preserved in Egypt to this day.

Captain Lewis instantly put down his rifle, and advancing toward them, took the woman by the hand, raised her up, and repeated the words "tabba bone!" at the same time stripping up his shirt-sleeve to prove that he was a white man—for his hands and face had become by constant exposure quite as dark as their own. She appeared immediately relieved from her alarm; and Drewyer and Shields now coming up, Captain Lewis gave them some beads, a few awls, pewter mirrors, and a little paint, and told Drewyer to request the woman to recall her companion, who had escaped to some distance and, by alarming the Indians, might cause them to attack him without any time for explanation. She did as she was desired, and the young woman returned almost out of breath. Captain Lewis gave her an equal portion of trinkets, and painted the tawny cheeks of all three of them with vermilion, a ceremony which among the Shoshonees is emblematic of peace.

After they had become composed, he informed them by signs of his wishes to go to their camp, in order to see their chiefs and warriors; they readily obeyed, and conducted the party along the same road down the river. In this way they marched two miles, when they met a troop of nearly 60 warriors, mounted on excellent horses, riding at full speed toward them. As they advanced Captain Lewis put down his gun, and went with the flag about 50 paces in advance. The chief, who with two men was riding in front of the main body, spoke to the women, who now explained that the party was composed of white men, and showed exultingly the presents they had received. The three men immediately leaped from their horses, came up to Captain Lewis and embraced him with great cordiality, putting their left arm over his right (*p. 364*) shoulder and clasping his back, applying at the same time their left cheek to his, and frequently vociferating, "ah hi e ! ah hi e !—I am much pleased ! I am much rejoiced ! " The whole body of warriors now came forward, and our men received the caresses, with no small share of the grease and paint of their new friends. After this fraternal embrace, of which the motive was much more agreeable than the manner, Captain Lewis lighted a pipe and offered it to the Indians, who had now seated themselves in a circle around the party. But before they would receive this mark of friendship they pulled off their moccasins ; a custom, as we afterward learned, which indicates the sacred sincerity of their professions when they smoke with a stranger, and which imprecates on themselves the misery of going barefoot forever if they are faithless to their words—a penalty by no means light to those who rove the thorny plains of their country.

It is not unworthy to remark the analogy which some of the customs of these wild children of the wilderness bear to those recorded in Holy Writ. Moses[13] was admonished to pull off his shoes, for the place on which he stood was holy ground. Why this was enjoined as an act of peculiar reverence—whether it was from the circumstance that in the arid region in which the patriarch then resided, it was deemed a test of the sincerity of devotion to walk upon the burning sands barefooted, in some measure analogous to the pains inflicted by the prickly-pear, does not appear.

After smoking a few pipes, some trifling presents were distributed amongst the Indians, with which they seemed very much pleased, particularly with the blue beads and the vermilion. Captain Lewis then informed the chief that the object of his visit was friendly, and should be

[13] The analogy suggested might be deemed more pertinent had the incident narrated in the Jewish myth any foundation in fact.

explained as soon as he reached their camp; but that in the meantime, as the sun was oppressive and no water near, he wished to go there as soon as possible. They now put on their moccasins, and their chief, whose name was Cameahwait, made a short speech to the warriors. Captain Lewis then gave him the (*p. 365*) flag, which he informed him was among white men the emblem of peace, and now that he had received it was to be in future the bond of union between them. The chief then moved on, our party followed him, and the rest of the warriors in a squadron brought up the rear. After marching a mile they were halted by the chief, who made a second harangue; on which six or eight young men rode forward to their camp, and no further regularity was observed in the order of march. At the distance of four miles from where they had first met, they reached the Indian camp, which was in a handsome level meadow on the bank of the river.

Here they were introduced into an old leathern lodge, which the young men who had been sent from the party had fitted up for their reception. After being seated on green boughs and antelope-skins, one of the warriors pulled up the grass in the center of the lodge, so as to form a vacant circle of two feet in diameter, in which he kindled a fire. The chief then produced his pipe and tobacco, the warriors all pulled off their moccasins, and our party were requested to take off their own. This being done, the chief lighted his pipe at the fire within the magic circle, and then retreating from it began a speech several minutes long, at the end of which he pointed the stem toward the four cardinal points of the heavens, beginning with the east and concluding with the north. After this ceremony he presented the stem in the same way to Captain Lewis, who, supposing it an invitation to smoke, put out his hand to receive the pipe; but the chief drew it back, and continued to repeat the same offer three times, after which he pointed the stem first to the heavens, then to the center of the little circle, took three whiffs himself, and presented it again to

Captain Lewis. Finding that this last offer was in good earnest, he smoked a little ; the pipe was then held to each of the white men, and after they had taken a few whiffs was given to the warriors.

This pipe [14] was made of a dense transparent green stone, very highly polished, about 2½ inches long, and of an (*p. 366*) oval figure, the bowl being in the same situation with the stem. A small piece of burnt clay is placed in the bottom of the bowl to separate the tobacco from the end of the stem, and is of an irregular round figure, not fitting the tube perfectly close, in order that the smoke may pass with facility. The tobacco is of the same kind with that used by the Minnetarees, Mandans, and Ricaras of the Missouri. The Shoshones do not cultivate this plant, but obtain it from the Rocky Mountain Indians, and some of the bands of their own nation who live further south.

The ceremony of smoking being concluded, Captain Lewis explained to the chief the purposes of his visit ; and as by this time all the women and children of the camp had gathered around the lodge to indulge in a view of the first white men they had ever seen, he distributed among them the remainder of the small articles he had brought with him.

It was now late in the afternoon, and our party had tasted no food since the night before. On apprising the chief of this circumstance, he said that he had nothing but berries to eat, and presented some cakes made of service-berries and choke-cherries which had been dried in the sun. On these Captain Lewis made a hearty meal, and then walked down toward the [Lemhi] river. He found it a rapid clear stream 40 yards wide and three feet deep ; the banks were low and abrupt, like those of the upper part of the Missouri, and the bed was formed of loose stones and gravel. Its course, as far as they could observe it, was a little to the north of west, and was bounded on each side by a range of high mountains, of which those on the east are the lowest and most distant from the river.

[14] Lewis F 99 figures this pipe in pen-and-ink.

The chief informed him that this stream discharged, at the distance of half a day's march, into another [Salmon river] of twice its size, coming from the southwest ; but added, on further inquiry, that there was scarcely more timber below the junction of those rivers than in this neighborhood, and that the river was rocky, rapid, and so closely confined between high mountains that it was impossible to pass down (*p. 367*) it either by land or water to the great lake [Pacific ocean [15]], where, as he had understood, the white men lived.

This information was far from being satisfactory, for there was no timber here that would answer the purpose of building canoes—indeed not more than just sufficient for fuel ; and even that consisted of the narrow-leaved cotton-wood, the red and the narrow-leaved willow, choke-cherry, service-berry, and a few currant bushes, such as are common on the Missouri. The prospect of going on by land is more pleasant, for there are great numbers of horses feeding in every direction round the camp, which will enable us to transport our stores, if necessary, over the mountains. Captain Lewis returned from the river to his lodge ; on his way an Indian invited him into his bower, and gave him a small morsel of boiled antelope and a piece of fresh salmon roasted. This was the first salmon he had seen, and perfectly satisfied him that he was now on the waters of the Pacific. On reaching his lodge he resumed his conversation with the chief, after which he was entertained with a dance by the Indians.

It now proved, as our party had feared, that the men whom they had first met this morning had returned to the camp and spread the alarm that their enemies, the Minnetarees of Fort de Prairie, whom they call Pahkees, were advancing on them. The warriors instantly armed themselves, and were coming down in expectation of an attack, when they were agreeably surprised by meeting our party. The greater part of them were armed with bows and arrows and shields, but a few had small fusils, such as are furnished

[15] " The great or stinking lake as they call the Ocean," Lewis F 106.

by the Northwest Company's traders, and which they had obtained from the Indians on the Yellowstone, with whom they are now at peace. They had reason to dread the approach of the Pahkees, who had attacked them in the course of this spring and totally defeated them. On this occasion 20 of their warriors were either killed or made prisoners; they lost their whole camp, except the leathern lodge which they had fitted up for us, (*p. 368*) and were now obliged to live in huts of a conical figure, made with willow-brush. The music and dancing, which were in no respect different from those of the Missouri Indians, continued nearly all night; but Captain Lewis retired to rest about twelve o'clock, when the fatigues of the day enabled him to sleep, though he was awakened several times by the yells of the dancers.

Whilst all these things were occurring to Captain Lewis we [Captain Clark's party, *August 13th*] were slowly and laboriously ascending the river. For the first 2½ miles we went along the island opposite which we camped last evening, and soon reached a second island, behind which comes in a small creek on the left [hand] side of the river. It rises in the [Ruby] mountains to the east, and forms a handsome valley for some miles from its mouth, where it is a bold running stream about seven yards wide; we called it M'Neal's creek, after Hugh M'Neal, one of our party. Just above this stream, and at the distance of four miles from camp, is a point of limestone rock on the right, about 70 feet high, forming a cliff over the river. From the top of it the Beaver's Head bore N. 24° E., twelve miles distant; the course of Wisdom river—that is, the direction of its valley through the mountains—is N. 25° W.; while the gap through which the Jefferson enters the mountains is ten miles above us on a course S. 18° W. From this limestone rock we proceeded along several islands on both sides, and after making twelve[16]

[16] Distances to-day variant in text and both codices—a very rare thing. Lewis F 102 makes 16 miles by water, 5 miles by land (direct advance); Clark G 62

miles arrived at a cliff of high rocks on the right, opposite
which we camped in a smooth, level prairie, near a few
cottonwood trees, but were obliged to use the dry willow-
brush for fuel. The river is still very crooked ; the bends
are short and abrupt, and obstructed by so many shoals,
over which the canoes were to be dragged, that the men
were in the water three-fourths of the day. They saw
numbers of otter, some beaver, antelopes, ducks, geese, and
cranes, but they killed nothing except a single deer. However, they caught some very fine trout [*Salmo purpuratus*],
as they have (*p. 369*) done for several days past. The
weather had been cloudy and cool during the forepart of
the day, and at eight o'clock a shower of rain fell.

August 14th. In order to give time for the boats to reach
the forks of Jefferson river, Captain Lewis determined to
remain here and obtain all the information he could collect
with regard to the country. Having nothing to eat but a
little flour and parched meal, with the berries of the Indians,
he sent out Drewyer and Shields, who borrowed horses
from the natives, to hunt for a few hours. About the same
time the young warriors set out for the same purpose.

There are but few elk [*Cervus canadensis*] or black-tailed
deer [*Cariacus macrotis*] in this neighborhood, and as the
common red deer [*Cariacus virginianus macrurus*] secrete
themselves in the bushes when alarmed, they are soon safe
from arrows, which are but feeble weapons against any
animals which the huntsmen cannot previously run down
with their horses. The chief game of the Shoshonees,
therefore, is the antelope, which, when pursued, retreats to
the open plains, where the horses have full room for the
chase. But such is its extraordinary fleetness and wind
that a single horse has no possible chance of outrunning it

gives 10 miles by water, 4 by land ; text ostensibly follows F, but reduces river-
miles nearly to G. But however this may be, the main party has this afternoon
passed the site of Dillon ; and M'Neal's creek is certainly that now called Black-
tailed Deer on the east, from the Ruby mountains ; Dillon at its mouth.

or tiring it down ; the hunters are therefore obliged to resort to stratagem. About 20 Indians, mounted on fine horses, and armed with bows and arrows, left the camp ; in a short time they descried a herd of ten antelopes. They immediately separated into little squads of two or three, and formed a scattered circle round the herd for five or six miles, keeping at a wary distance, so as not to alarm the antelopes till they were perfectly inclosed, and usually selecting some commanding eminence as a stand. Having gained their positions, a small party rode toward the herd. With wonderful dexterity the huntsman preserved his seat and the horse his footing, as he ran at full speed over the hills, down the steep ravines, and along the borders of the precipices. They were soon outstripped by the antelopes, which, on gaining the other extremity of the circle, were dri- (*p. 370*) ven back and pursued by the fresh hunters. They turned and flew, rather than ran, in another direction ; but there, too, they found new enemies. In this way they were alternately pursued backward and forward, till at length, notwithstanding the skill of the hunters, they all escaped, and the party, after running for two hours, returned without having caught anything, their horses foaming with sweat. This chase, the greater part of which was seen from the camp, formed a beautiful scene ; but to the hunters it is exceedingly laborious, and so unproductive, even when they are able to worry the animal down and shoot him, that 40 or 50 hunters will sometimes be engaged for half a day without obtaining more than two or three antelopes.

Soon after they returned, our two huntsmen came in with no better success. Captain Lewis therefore made a little paste with the flour, and the addition of some berries formed a very palatable repast. Having now secured the good will of Cameahwait, Captain Lewis informed him of his wish that he would speak to the warriors, and endeavor to engage them to accompany him to the forks of Jefferson river ; where by this time another chief, with a large party of white men, was awaiting his [Lewis'] return ; that it would be necessary to take about 30 horses to transport the merchandise; that they should be well rewarded for their trouble; and that, when all the party should have reached the Shoshonee camp, they would remain some time among them to trade for horses, as well as concert plans for furnishing them in future with regular supplies of merchandise. He readily consented to do so, and after collecting the tribe together, he made a long harangue. In about an hour and a half he returned, and told Captain Lewis that they would be ready to accompany him in the morning.

As the early part of the day [*August* 14*th*[17]] was cold, and the men were stiff and sore from the fatigues of yesterday, we [Captain Clark's party] did not set out till seven o'clock. At the distance of a mile we passed a bold stream on the right, which comes from a snowy (*p. 371*) mountain to the north [-west], and at its entrance is four yards wide and three feet deep. We called it Track creek. At six miles further we reached another stream which heads in some springs at the foot of the mountains on the left. After passing a number of bayous and small islands on each side, we camped [on the east side] about half a mile by land below Rattlesnake cliffs. The river was cold, shallow, and, as it approached the mountains, formed one continued rapid, over which we were obliged to drag the boats with great labor and difficulty. By using constant exertions we succeeded in making 14 miles, but this distance did not carry us more than 6½ in a straight line.[18] Several of

[17] Chaboneau develops to-day as a wife-beater, exactly as was to have been expected of such an arrant coward. "I checked our interpreter for striking his woman at their Dinner," Clark G 58.

[18] Distances of the text may be almost disregarded in pitching camp to-day, and in identifying the two streams passed, for the text and both the codices are all three variant. Lewis F 110 has: "S. 14° W. 7 [miles by land advance] to the gap of the mountain at the rattlesnake Clifts where the river enters the mountains, the same being 16 miles by the meanders of the river." Clark G 62 has: "S. 14° W. 22 miles by water the river making a genl. [general] Bend to the

the men received wounds and lamed themselves in hauling the boats over the stones. The hunters [J. and R. Fields] supplied them with five deer and an antelope.

August 15th. Captain Lewis rose early, and having eaten nothing yesterday except his scanty meal of flour and berries, felt the inconveniences of extreme hunger. On inquiry [of M'Neal] he found that his whole stock of provisions consisted of two pounds of flour. This he ordered to be divided into two equal parts, and one-half of it to be boiled with the berries into a sort of pudding. After presenting a large share to the chief, he and his three men breakfasted on the remainder. Cameahwait was delighted at this new dish ; he took a little of the flour in his hand, tasted and examined it very narrowly,[19] and asked if it was made of roots. Captain Lewis explained the process of preparing it, and the chief said it was the best thing he had eaten for a long time.

This being finished, Captain Lewis now endeavored to hasten the departure of the Indians, who still hesitated and seemed reluctant to move, although the chief addressed

East (8 miles by land) to a place the river Passes a mountain high Clifts on either side, . . . Encamped 14th. of August at 20 miles on the Lar side, a high Clift on the Course 3 miles near the upper part of which the creek passes." Whatever the actual distances, Dillon was passed yesterday. Camp is identifiable by the topographical details to-day. Thus it is easy to adjust the creeks mentioned. " Track Cr." is the only stream charted by Clark on the west between Wisdom river and Willard's creek. It is that now called Rattlesnake creek. The " snowy mountain" in which it is said to head is a peak now called Bald mountain. "Another stream " of the text, from the left, unnamed, is the first one on the east above Black-tailed Deer creek. This latter is the largest stream on this side of the Jefferson since Philanthropy (Stinking-water) river has been passed ; at and near its mouth are Dillon and Glendale, from which points the U. and N. R. R. follows up the Jefferson. It is the only creek on the left charted by Clark, from Philanthropy river to the forks, as M'Neal's, which on his map corresponds well to Black-tailed Deer creek in position. See M'Neal's of the text, p. 494, and note there.

[19] " Taisted and examined very *scrutinously,*" Lewis F iii, using a good adverb, but one so rare that the Century Dictionary, in admitting it, cited the Imperial to support the word. Dr. C. P. G. Scott may like to have this reference for his new edition of Worcester.

them twice for the purpose of urging them.   On inquiring
the reason, Cameahwait told him that some foolish person
had suggested that he was in league with their enemies the
Pahkees, and had come only to draw them into ambus-
cade; but that he himself did not believe it.   Captain
Lewis felt (*p. 372*) uneasy at this insinuation; he knew
the suspicious temper of the Indians, accustomed from
their infancy to regard every stranger as an enemy, and
saw that if this suggestion were not instantly checked, it
might hazard the total failure of the enterprise.   Assuming,
therefore, a serious air, he told the chief that he was sorry
to find they placed so little confidence in him, but that he
pardoned their suspicions because they were ignorant of
the character of white men, among whom it was disgraceful
to lie, or entrap even an enemy by falsehood; that if they
continued to think thus meanly of us, they might be assured
no white man would ever come to supply them with arms
and merchandise; that there was at this moment a party
of white men waiting to trade with them at the forks of the
river; and that, if the greater part of the tribe entertained
any suspicion, he hoped there were still among them some
who were men, who would go and see with their own eyes
the truth of what he said, and who, even if there was any
danger, were not afraid to die.   To doubt the courage of
an Indian is to touch the tenderest string of his mind, and
the surest way to rouse him to any dangerous achievement.
Cameahwait instantly replied that he was not afraid to die,
and mounting his horse, for the third time harangued the
warriors.   He told them that he was resolved to go if he
went alone, or if he were sure of perishing; that he hoped
there were among those who heard him some who were not
afraid to die, and who would prove it by mounting their
horses and following him.   This harangue produced an
effect on six or eight only of the warriors, who now joined
their chief.   With these Captain Lewis smoked a pipe;
and then, fearful of some change in their capricious temper,
set out immediately.

It was about twelve o'clock when his small party left the camp, attended by Cameahwait and the eight warriors. Their departure seemed to spread a gloom over the village; those who would not venture to go were sullen and melancholy, and the women were crying and imploring the Great Spirit to protect their warriors, as (*p. 373*) if they were going to certain destruction. Yet such is the wavering inconsistency of these savages, that Captain Lewis' party had not gone far when they were joined by ten or twelve more warriors; and before reaching the creek which they had passed on the morning of the 13th, all the men of the nation and a number of women had overtaken them, having changed, from the surly ill-temper in which they were two hours ago, to the greatest cheerfulness and gayety. When they arrived at the spring on the side of the mountain, where the party had camped on the 12th, the chief insisted on halting to let the horses graze; to which Captain Lewis assented, and smoked with them. They are excessively fond of the pipe, in which, however, they are not able to indulge much, as they do not cultivate tobacco themselves, and their rugged country affords them but few articles to exchange for it. Here they remained for about an hour, and on setting out, by engaging to pay four of the party, Captain Lewis obtained permission for himself and each of his men to ride behind an Indian. But he soon found riding without stirrups was much more tiresome than walking, and therefore dismounted, making the Indian carry his pack. About sunset they reached the upper part of the level valley, in the cove through which he had passed, and which they now called Shoshonee cove. The grass being burnt on the north side of the river, they crossed over to the south, and camped about four miles above the narrow pass between the hills, noticed as they traversed the cove before. The river was here about six yards wide, and frequently dammed up by the beaver.

Drewyer had been sent forward to hunt; but he returned in the evening unsuccessful, and their only supper therefore was the remaining pound of flour, stirred in a little boiling water, and then divided between the four white men and two of the Indians.

In order not to exhaust the strength of the men, Captain Clark did not leave camp till after breakfast [*August 15th*]. Although he was scarcely half a mile below Rattlesnake cliffs, he (*p. 374*) was obliged to make a circuit of two miles by water before he reached them.   The river now passed between low and rugged mountains and cliffs, formed of a mixture of limestone and a hard black rock, with no covering except a few scattered pines.   At a distance of four miles is a bold little stream [Big Hill creek], which throws itself from the mountains down a steep precipice of rocks on the left.   One mile further are a second point of rocks and an island; about a mile beyond which is a creek on the right, ten yards wide and 3 feet 3 inches in depth, with a strong current.   We called it Willard's[20] creek, after one of our men, Alexander Willard.   Three miles beyond this creek, after passing a high cliff on the right, opposite a steep hill, we reached a small meadow on the left bank of the river. During its passage through these hills to Willard's creek, the river had been less tortuous than usual; so that, in the first six miles to Willard's creek, we had advanced four miles on our route.   We continued on for two miles,[21] till we reached in the evening a small bottom, covered with clover and a few cottonwood trees.   Here we passed the night, near the remains of some old Indian lodges of brush.

The river is, as it has been for some days, shallow and

[20] Grasshopper creek of late maps, after Charles Lumley, 1862 (see Cont. Mont. Hist. Soc. I. 1876, p. 100); the most considerable stream on this side above Rattlesnake (or Track) creek, and below what L. and C. call the forks of the Jefferson, *i. e.*, Prairie creek.   Clark's map charts it as "Willard Cr."   This is the stream on which is now the town of Bannack or Bannock.   It rises in the mountains by many affluents, some of which are in relation with certain sources of Wisdom (or Big Hole) river; thus Willard's creek becomes of note in connection with Captain Clark's return trip in 1806, and so with the location of "Clark's Pass" of the Rocky mountains.   I recur to this point in due course.

[21] "To the mouth of a small run on the Lard Side, passed several spring

rapid ; and our men, who are for hours together in the river, suffer not only from fatigue, but from the extreme coldness of the water, the temperature of which is as low as that of the freshest springs in our country. In walking along the side of the river, Captain Clark came very near being bitten twice by rattlesnakes, and the Indian woman narrowly escaped the same misfortune. We caught a number of fine trout [*Salmo purpuratus*] ; but the only game procured to-day was a buck, which had a peculiarly bitter taste, proceeding probably from its favorite food, the willow.

August 16*th*. As neither our party nor the Indians had anything to eat, Captain Lewis sent two of his hunters [Drewyer and Shields] ahead this morning to procure some provisions. At the same time he requested Cameahwait to prevent his young men (*p. 375*) from going out, lest by their noise they might alarm the game. But this measure immediately revived their suspicions. It now began to be believed that these men were sent forward in order to apprise the enemy of their coming ; and as Captain Lewis was fearful of exciting any further uneasiness, he made no objection on seeing a small party of Indians go on each side of the valley, under pretense of hunting, but in reality to watch the movements of our two men. But even this precaution did not quiet the alarms of the Indians, a considerable part of whom returned home, leaving only 28 men and three women.

After the hunters had been gone about an hour, Captain Lewis again mounted, with one of the Indians behind him, and the whole party set out. But just as they passed through the narrows, they saw one of the spies coming back at full speed across the plain. The chief stopped and seemed uneasy ; the whole band were moved with fresh suspicions, and Captain Lewis himself was much disconcerted, lest by

runs," Clark G 59. Two of these runs, on the left, are now known as Gallagher's and Henneury's, or Heanebury's creeks. Both are specified, Clark G 67. Camp is at the former. One more creek, on the left, and the Two Forks are reached.

some unfortunate accident some of their enemies might have perhaps straggled that way.   The young Indian had scarcely breath to say a few words as he came up, when the whole troop dashed forward as fast as their horses could carry them.   Captain Lewis, astonished at this movement, was borne along for nearly a mile before he learned, with great satisfaction, that it was all caused by the spy's having come to announce that one of the white men had killed a deer. Relieved from his anxiety, he now found the jolting very uncomfortable ; for the Indian behind him, being afraid of not getting his share of the feast, had lashed the horse at every step since they set off; he therefore reined him in, and ordered the Indian to stop beating him.   The fellow had no idea of losing time in disputing this point, and jumping off the horse ran for a mile at full speed.   Captain Lewis slackened his pace, and followed at a sufficient distance to observe them.   When they reached the place where Drewyer had thrown out the intestines, they all dismounted in confusion and ran tum- (*p. 376*) bling over each other like famished dogs.   Each tore away whatever part he could, and instantly began to eat it.   Some had the liver, some the kidneys—in short, no part on which we are accustomed to look with disgust escaped them.   One of them, who had seized about nine feet of the entrails, was chewing at one end, while with his hand he was diligently clearing his way by discharging the contents at the other.   It was indeed impossible to see these wretches ravenously feeding on the filth of animals, the blood streaming from their mouths, without deploring how nearly the condition of savages approaches that of the brute creation.   Yet, though suffering with hunger, they did not attempt, as they might have done, to take by force the whole deer, but contented themselves with what had been thrown away by the hunter. Captain Lewis now had the deer skinned, and after reserving a quarter of it gave the rest of the animal to the chief, to be divided among the Indians, who immediately devoured nearly the whole of it without cooking.   They now went toward the [Prairie] creek, where there was some brushwood to make a fire, and found Drewyer, who had killed a second deer. The same struggle for the entrails was renewed here, and on giving nearly the whole deer to the Indians, they devoured it even to the soft part of the hoofs. A fire being made, Captain Lewis had his breakfast, during which Drewyer brought in a third deer. This too, after reserving one-quarter, was given to the Indians, who now seemed completely satisfied and in good humor.

At this place they remained about two hours to let the horses graze; then continued their journey, and toward evening reached the lower part of the [Shoshone] cove, having on the way shot an antelope, the greater part of which was given to the Indians. As they were now approaching the place where they had been told by Captain Lewis they would see the white men, the chief insisted on halting. They therefore all dismounted, and Cameahwait, with great ceremony and as if for ornament, put tippets or skins round the necks of our (*p. 377*) party, similar to those worn by themselves. As this was obviously intended to disguise the white men, Captain Lewis, in order to inspire them with more confidence, put his cocked hat and feather on the head of the chief; and as his own over-shirt was in the Indian form, and his skin browned by the sun, he could not have been distinguished from an Indian. The men followed his example, and the change seemed to be very agreeable to the Indians.

In order to guard, however, against any disappointment, Captain Lewis again explained the possibility of our [the main party's] not having reached the forks, in consequence of the difficulty of the navigation; so that if they [the Indians] should not find us [the main party] at that spot, they might be assured of our not being far below. They again all mounted their horses and rode on rapidly, making one of the Indians carry their flag, so that we might recognize them as they approached us; but, to the mortification and disappointment of both parties, on coming within two miles of the forks no canoes were to be seen. Uneasy, lest at this moment he should be abandoned, and all his hopes of obtaining aid from the Indians be destroyed, Captain Lewis gave the chief his gun, telling him that, if the enemies of his nation were in the bushes, he might defend himself with it ; that for his own part he was not afraid to die, and that the chief might shoot him as soon as they discovered themselves betrayed. The other three men at the same time gave their guns to the Indians, who now seemed more easy, but still wavered in their resolutions. As they went on toward the point [forks], Captain Lewis, perceiving how critical his situation had become, resolved to attempt a stratagem, which his present difficulty seemed completely to justify. Recollecting the notes he had left at the point for us, he sent Drewyer for them with an Indian, who witnessed his taking them from the pole. When they were brought, Captain Lewis told Cameahwait that on leaving his brother chief [Clark] at the place where the river issues from the mountains, it was agreed that the boats should not be (*p. 378*) brought higher than the next forks we should meet ; but that, if the rapid water prevented the boats from coming on as fast as they expected, his brother chief was to send a note to the first forks above him to let him know where the boats were ; that this note had been left this morning at the forks, and mentioned that the canoes were just below the mountains, and coming slowly up in consequence of the current. Captain Lewis added that he would stay at the forks for his brother chief, but would send a man down the river ; and that if Cameahwait doubted what he said, one of their young men would go with him, whilst he and the other two remained at the forks. This story satisfied the chief and the greater part of the Indians ; but a few did not conceal their suspicions, observing that we told different stories, and complaining that the chief exposed them to danger by a mistaken confidence.

Captain Lewis now wrote, by the light of some willow-brush, a note to Captain Clark, which he gave to Drewyer, with an order [for Captain Clark] to use all possible expedition in ascending the river; and engaged an Indian to accompany him [Drewyer] by the promise of a knife and some beads. At bedtime the chief and five others slept round the fire of Captain Lewis, and the rest hid themselves in different parts of the willow-brush to avoid the enemy, who, they feared, would attack them in the night. Captain Lewis endeavored to assume a cheerfulness he did not feel, to prevent the despondency of the savages. After conversing gayly with them he retired to his mosquito-bier, by the side of which the chief now placed himself. He lay down, yet slept but little, being in fact scarcely less uneasy than his Indian companions. He was apprehensive that, finding the ascent of the river impracticable, Captain Clark might have stopped below Rattlesnake bluff, and the messenger would not meet him. The consequence of disappointing the Indians at this moment would most probably be that they would retire and secrete themselves in the mountains, so as to prevent our having an opportunity of recovering their confi- (*p. 379*) dence. They would also spread a panic through all the neighboring Indians, and cut us off from the supply of horses so useful and almost so essential to our success. He was at the same time consoled by remembering that his hopes of assistance rested on better foundations than their generosity—their avarice and their curiosity. He had promised liberal exchanges for their horses; but what was still more seductive, he had told them that one of their countrywomen, who had been taken with the Minnetarees, accompanied the party below; and one of the men had spread the report of our having with us a man [York] perfectly black, whose hair was short and curled. This last account had excited a great degree of curiosity, and they seemed more desirous of seeing this monster than of obtaining the most favorable barter for their horses.

In the meantime we [Captain Clark's party] set out after breakfast [*August* 16*th*]; although we proceeded with more ease than we did yesterday, the river was still so rapid and shallow as to oblige us to drag the large canoes during the greater part of the day. For the first seven miles the river formed a bend to the right so as to make our advance only three miles in a straight line. The stream is crooked, narrow, small, and shallow, with high lands occasionally on the banks, and strewed with islands, four of which are opposite each other. Near this place we left the valley, to which we gave the name of Service-berry valley, from the abundance of that fruit, now ripe, which is found in it. In the course of the four following miles we passed several more islands and bayous on each side of the river, and reached a high cliff on the right. At 2½ miles beyond this the cliffs approach on both sides, and form a very considerable rapid near the entrance of a bold, running stream on the left.[22] The water was now excessively cold, and the rapids had been frequent and troublesome. On ascending an eminence Captain Clark saw the forks of the river, and sent the hunters up. They must have left it only a short time before Captain Lewis' arrival, (*p. 380*) but fortunately had not seen the note which enabled him to induce the Indians to stay with him. From the top of this eminence he could discover only three trees through the whole country; nor was there, along the sides of the cliffs they had passed in the course of the day, any timber except a few small pines. The low grounds were supplied with willow, currant-bushes, and service-berries. After advancing half a mile further we came to the lower point of an island near the middle of the river, about the center of the valley. Here we halted for the night, only four miles by land, though ten by water, below the point where Captain Lewis lay. Although we had made only 14 miles, the labors of the men had fatigued and exhausted them very much. We therefore collected some small willow-brush for a fire, and lay down to sleep.

[22] Last creek before the forks are reached ; now called Clark's cañon ; town of Grayling at the mouth of it.

CHAPTER XV.

ACROSS THE GREAT DIVIDE TO COLUMBIAN WATERS.

Captain Clark brings up the main party—Affecting interview of Sacajawea with her long-lost brother, whom she recognizes in the Shoshone chief Cameahwait—Camp set and council held—Speeches and presents made—Consultation on the route to be taken—Horses to be procured—Captain Clark to reconnoiter in advance, with eleven men and some Indians—A recapitulation of some characteristics of the Missouri—Captain Lewis and party remain—Captain Clark and party proceed—He reaches the Indian camp, near where it was when Captain Lewis was in it—Council held, inquiries made, and guide engaged—Indian information of the route—The prospect dubious, and obstacles formidable—Captain Clark resolves to try the river first, and sets out—Description of fish-weirs—He names Lewis' river—Its difficulties not exaggerated by the Indians—Exploration pushed with unfavorable result—No practicable route by water from the present situation—Formidable snow-capped mountains in prospect—The intended route abandoned—A more northern route indicated by the Shoshone guide—A man sent back to inform Captain Lewis of the result of the reconnoissance—Captain Clark's repulse, after great hardships—He will rejoin Captain Lewis, Aug. 29th—Narrative of the main party resumed—Their occupations—Good behavior of the Indians—A cache made.

$\mathfrak{S}$ATURDAY, August 17th, 1805. Captain Lewis rose very early and dispatched Drewyer and the Indian down the river in quest of the boats. Shields was sent out at the same time to hunt, while M'Neal prepared a breakfast out of the remainder of the meat. Drewyer had been gone about two hours, and the Indians were all anxiously waiting for some news, when an Indian, who had straggled a short distance down the river, returned with a report that he had seen the white men, who were only a short distance below, and were coming on. The Indians were transported with joy, and the chief, in the warmth of his satisfaction, renewed his embrace to Captain Lewis, who was quite as much delighted as the Indians themselves. The report proved most agreeably true.[1]

[1] Gass, who was with the main party that Captain Clark brought up here, gives a more prosaic memorandum of the meeting: "*Saturday* 17*th.* A fine morning. We proceeded on about 2 miles, and discovered a number of the natives, of the Snake nation, coming along the bank on the South side. Captain Lewis had been as far as the waters of the Columbia river [watershed], and met them

On setting out at seven o'clock, Captain Clark, with Chaboneau and his wife, walked on shore; but they had not gone more than a mile before Captain Clark saw Sacajawea, who was with her husband 100 yards ahead, begin to dance and show every mark of the most extravagant joy, turning round to him and pointing to several Indians, whom he now saw advancing on horseback, sucking her fingers at the same time, to indicate that they were of her native tribe. As they (*p. 382*) advanced, Captain Clark discovered among them Drewyer dressed like an Indian, from whom he learned the situation of the party. While the boats were performing the circuit, he went toward the forks with the Indians, who, as they went along, sang aloud with the greatest appearance of delight.

We soon drew near the camp, and just as we approached it a woman made her way through the crowd toward Sacajawea; recognizing each other, they embraced with the most tender affection. The meeting of these two young women had in it something peculiarly touching, not only from the ardent manner in which their feelings were expressed, but also from the real interest of their situation. They had been companions in childhood; in the war with the Minnetarees they had both been taken prisoners in the same battle; they had shared and softened the rigors of their captivity till one

there. We continued on about 2 miles further to a place where the river forks, and there halted and encamped, after much fatigue and difficulty. The water is so shallow that we had to drag the canoes, one at a time, almost all the way. The distance across from this place to the waters of the Columbia river is about 40 miles, and the road or way said to be good. There were about 20 of the natives came over with Captain Lewis and had the same number of horses. Here we unloaded the canoes, and had a talk with the Indians; and agreed with them that they should lend us some of their horses to carry our baggage to the Columbia river."

Clark G 64–66 makes rather more of the meeting than was the blunt soldier's wont; but it is entirely to the same affect as Biddle gives from Lewis F 123–128, and may be passed, excepting one memorandum: "This nation call themselves Cho-shon-nê the cheif is named Too-et-te-con'l Black Gun is his War name Ka-me-ah-wah—or Come & Smoke." The latter is of course the "Cameahwait" of the text, and this name was bestowed on Captain Clark: "I was called by this name afd. by the Snake Inds.," *ibid.*

of them had escaped from the Minnetarees, with scarce a
hope of ever seeing her friend relieved from the hands of
her enemies.   While Sacajawea was renewing among the
women the friendships of former days, Captain Clark went
on, and was received by Captain Lewis and the chief, who,
after the first embraces and salutations were over, conducted
him to a sort of circular tent or shade of willows.   Here
he was seated on a white robe, and the chief immediately
tied in his hair six small shells resembling pearls, an ornament highly valued by these people, who procure them in
the course of trade from the sea-coast.   The moccasins of
the whole party were then taken off, and after much ceremony the smoking began.   After this the conference was to
be opened.   Glad of an opportunity of being able to converse more intelligibly, Sacajawea was sent for; she came
into the tent, sat down, and was beginning to interpret,
when, in the person of Cameahwait, she recognized her
brother.   She instantly jumped up, and ran and embraced
him, throwing over him her blanket, and weeping profusely.   The chief was himself moved, though not in the
same degree.   After some conversation between them
she resumed her seat and attempted to in- (*p. 383*) terpret
for us; but her new situation seemed to overpower her,
and she was frequently interrupted by her tears.   After
the council was finished the unfortunate woman learned
that all her family were dead except two brothers, one of
whom was absent, and a son of her eldest sister, a small
boy, who was immediately adopted by her.

The canoes arriving soon after, we formed a camp in a
meadow on the left-hand side, a little below the forks, took
out our baggage, and by means of our sails and willow poles
formed a canopy for our Indian visitors.   About four o'clock
the chiefs and warriors were collected and, after the customary ceremony of taking off the moccasins and smoking
a pipe, we explained to them in a long harangue the purposes of our visit, making themselves the one conspicuous
object of the good wishes of our government, on whose

strength, as well as friendly disposition, we expatiated. We told them of their dependence on the will of our government for all their future supplies of whatever was necessary either for their comfort or defense; that, as we were sent to discover the best route by which merchandise could be conveyed to them, and no trade would be begun before our return, it was mutually advantageous that we should proceed with as little delay as possible; that we were under the necessity of requesting them to furnish us with horses to transport our baggage across the mountains, and a guide to show us the route; but that they should be amply remunerated for their horses, as well as for every other service they should render us. In the meantime our first wish was, that they should immediately collect as many horses as were necessary to transport our baggage to their village, where at our leisure we would trade with them for as many horses as they could spare.

The speech made a favorable impression. The chief, in reply, thanked us for our expressions of friendship toward himself and his nation, and declared their willingness to render us every service. He lamented that it would be so long before they should be supplied with firearms, but that till (*p. 384*) then they could subsist as they had heretofore done. He concluded by saying that there were not horses enough here to transport our goods, but that he would return to the village to-morrow, bring all his own horses, and encourage his people to come over with theirs. The conference being ended to our satisfaction, we now inquired of Cameahwait what chiefs were among the party, and he pointed out two of them. We then distributed our presents: to Cameahwait we gave a medal of small size, with the likeness of President Jefferson, and on the reverse a figure of hands clasped with a pipe and tomahawk; to this was added an uniform coat, a shirt, a pair of scarlet leggings, a carrot of tobacco, and some small articles. Each of the other chiefs received a small medal struck during the presidency of General Washington, a shirt, handkerchief, leggings, knife, and some tobacco. Medals of the same sort were also presented to two young warriors, who, though not chiefs, were promising youths and very much respected in the tribe. These honorary gifts were followed by presents of paint, moccasins, awls, knives, beads, and looking-glasses. We also gave them all a plentiful meal of Indian corn, of which the hull is taken off by being boiled in lye; as this was the first they had ever tasted, they were very much pleased with it. They had, indeed, abundant sources of surprise in all they saw— the appearance of the men, their arms, their clothing, the canoes, the strange looks of the negro, and the sagacity of our dog, all in turn shared their admiration, which was raised to astonishment by a shot from the air-gun. This operation was instantly considered "great medicine," by which they, as well as the other Indians, mean something emanating directly from the Great Spirit, or produced by his invisible and incomprehensible agency. The display of all these riches had been intermixed with inquiries into the geographical situation of their country; for we had learned by experience that to keep savages in good temper their attention should not be wearied with too much business, but that (*p. 385*) serious affairs should be enlivened by a mixture of what is new and entertaining. Our hunters brought in, very seasonably, four deer and antelope, the last of which we gave to the Indians, who in a very short time devoured it.

After the council was over we consulted as to our future operations. The game does not promise to last here for a number of days, and this circumstance combined with many others to induce our going on as soon as possible. Our Indian information as to the state of the Columbia[2] is of a very alarming kind, and our first object is of course to ascertain the practicability of descending it, of which the Indians discourage our expectations. It was therefore agreed that Captain Clark should set off in the morning with 11 men

[2] Meaning of course Salmon river, upon a tributary of which (the Lemhi) Captain Lewis had been, and where was the Shoshone village.

furnished, besides their arms, with tools for making canoes; that he should take Chaboneau and his wife to the camp of the Shoshonees, where he was to leave them, in order to hasten the collection of horses; that he was then to lead his men down to the Columbia, and if he found it navigable, and the timber in sufficient quantity, begin to build canoes. As soon as he had decided as to the propriety of proceeding down the Columbia, or across the mountains, he was to send back one of the men with information of it to Captain Lewis, who by that time would have brought up the whole party and the rest of the baggage, as far as the Shoshonee village.

Preparations were accordingly made this evening for such an arrangement. The sun is excessively hot in the day time, but the nights very cold, and rendered still more unpleasant from the want of any fuel except willow-brush. The appearances of game for many days' subsistence are not very favorable.

Sunday, August 18*th.* [3] In order to relieve the men of Captain Clark's party from the heavy weight of their arms, provisions, and tools, we exposed a few articles to barter for horses, and soon obtained three very good ones, in exchange for which we gave a uniform coat, a pair of leggings, a few handkerchiefs, three knives, and some other small ar- (*p. 386*) ticles, the whole of which did not, in the United States, cost

[3] A sadly interesting passage is this, Lewis F 129, when we remember how near the young nobleman was to his tragic end: "This day I completed my thirty-first year, and conceived that I had in all human probability now existed about half the period which I am to remain in this sublunary world. I reflected that I had as yet done but little, very little indeed, to further the hapiness of the human race, or to advance the information of the succeeding generation. I viewed with regret the many hours I have spent in indolence, and now soarly feel the want of that information which those hours would have given me had they been judiciously expended. but since they are past and cannot be recalled, I dash from me the gloomy thought, and resolve in future to redouble my exertions and at least indeavour to promote those two primary objects of human existence, by giving them the aid of that portion of talents which nature and fortune have bestowed upon me; or in future, to live *for mankind*, as I have heretofore lived *for myself*."

more than $20 ; a fourth was purchased by the men for an old checkered shirt, a pair of old leggings, and a knife. The Indians seemed to be quite as well pleased as ourselves at the bargain they had made. We now found that the two inferior chiefs were somewhat displeased at not having received a present equal to that given to the great chief, who appeared in a dress so much finer than their own. To allay their discontent, we bestowed on them two old coats, and promised them if they were active in assisting us across the mountains they should have an additional present. This treatment completely reconciled them, and the whole Indian party, except two men and two women, set out in perfect good humor to return [to their] home with Captain Clark.

After going 15 miles through a wide, level valley, with no wood but willows and shrubs, he camped in the Shoshonee cove near the narrow pass where the highlands approach within 200 yards of each other, and the river is only ten yards wide.[4] The Indians went on further, except the three chiefs and two young men, who assisted in eating two deer brought in by the hunters.

After their departure everything was prepared for the transportation of the baggage, which was now exposed to the air and dried. Our game was one deer and a beaver, and we saw an abundance of trout [*Salmo purpuratus*] in the river, for which we fixed a net in the evening.

We have now reached the extreme navigable point of the Missouri, which our observation places in latitude 43° 30'

---

[4] Gass' account of this day's march, p. 121, is as follows : " *Sunday 18th.* A fine morning. We bought three horses of the Indians. Captain Clark and 11 more, with our interpreter and his wife and all the Indians set out at 11 o'clock to go over to the Columbia.—The Indians went for horses to carry our baggage, and we to search for timber to make canoes for descending the Columbia. We proceeded up the north [*i. e.*, west] branch which is [not] the largest and longest branch of the Jefferson, toward a handsome valley [Shoshone cove] about 5 miles wide. In this we found a number of springs and small branches, but no timber. There is plenty of grass and clover, and also some flax, all along it. The

43" N.[5] It is difficult to comprise in any general description the characteristics of a river so extensive, and fed by so
many streams, which have their sources in a great variety
of soils and climates.   But the Missouri is still sufficiently
powerful to give to all its waters something of a common
character, which is of course decided by the nature of the
country through which it passes.   The bed of the river is
chiefly composed of a blue mud, from which the wa- (*p. 387*)
ter itself derives a deep tinge.   From its junction here to
the place near which it leaves the mountains, its course is
embarrassed by rapids and rocks which the hills on each
side have thrown into its channel.   From that place its current, with the exception of the falls, is not difficult of navigation, nor is there much variation in its appearance to the
mouth of the Platte.   That powerful river throws out vast
quantities of coarse sand, which contribute to give a new
face to the Missouri, which is thence much more impeded by
islands.   The sand, as it is drifted down, adheres in time to
some of the projecting points from the shore, and forms a
barrier to the mud, which at length fills to the same height
with the sand-bar itself.   As soon as it has acquired a consistency, the willow grows there the first year, and by its roots
assists the solidity of the whole.   As the mud and sand
accumulate, the cottonwood next appears; till the gradual
excretion of soils raises the surface of the point above the
highest freshets.   Thus stopped in its course, the water seeks
a passage elsewhere ; and as the soil on each side is light
and yielding, what was only a peninsula becomes gradually

Indians all except 5 went on ahead.   We traveled 15 miles and encamped close
on the branch which is about 5 yards wide."   Clark I 4 makes it 15 miles too.
To-night's camp is there called " Three Forks in Snake Indian Valley," *i. e.*, the
point in Shoshone cove where Prairie creek receives two affluents, pretty nearly
but not exactly together ; it is 15 miles from the forks of the Jefferson.

    [5] This is very far out of the way.   I supposed " 43° " to be misprint for 44°.
As the observations are generally about one-half a degree too far south, 44° 30'
would mean about 45°, their actual station.   But in Clark G 68 the figures
stand as in the text.   It is therefore simply a mistaken observation.   A better
one, Lewis F 130, is 44° 37' 57 $\frac{4}{10}$", and thus less than 30' out of the way, or
about as usual.   A mean of three observations is 44° 35' 28$\frac{1}{10}$", Lewis F 149.

an island, and the river indemnifies itself for the usurpation by encroaching on the adjacent shore. In this way the Missouri, like the Mississippi, is constantly cutting off the projections of the shore, and leaving its ancient channel, which is then marked by the mud it has deposited, and a few stagnant ponds.

The general appearance of the country, as it presents itself on ascending, may be thus described : From its mouth to the two Charletons, a ridge of highlands borders the river at a small distance, leaving between them fine rich meadows. From the mouth of the two Charletons the hills recede from the river, giving greater extent to the low grounds; but they re-approach the river for a short distance near Grand river, and again at Snake creek. From that point they retire, nor do they come again to the neighborhood of the river till above the Sauk prairie, where they are com- (*p. 388*) paratively low and small. Thence they diverge and reappear at the Charaton Scarty, after which they are scarcely if at all discernible till they advance to the Missouri nearly opposite the Kansas.

The same ridge of hills extends on the south side in almost one unbroken chain from the mouth of the Missouri to the Kansas, though decreasing in height beyond the Osage. As they are nearer the river than the hills on the opposite sides, the intermediate low grounds are, of course, narrower, but the general character of the soil is common to both sides.

In the meadows and along the shore the tree most common is the cottonwood, which, with the willow, forms almost the exclusive growth of the Missouri. The hills, or rather high grounds, for they do not rise higher than from 150 to 200 feet, are composed of a good rich black soil, which is perfectly susceptible of cultivation, though it becomes richer on the hills beyond the Platte, and in general thinly covered with timber. Beyond these hills the country extends into high open plains, which are on both sides sufficiently fertile ; but the south has the advantage of better streams of water, and may, therefore, be considered as preferable for settlements.   The lands, however, become much better, and the timber more abundant, between the Osage and the Kansas.

From the Kansas to the Nadawa the hills continue at nearly an equal distance, varying from four to eight miles of each other, except that, from the Little Platte to nearly opposite the ancient Kansas village, the hills are more remote, and the meadows, of course, wider on the north side of the river.   From the Nadawa the northern hills disappear, except at occasional intervals, when they are seen at a distance, till they return about 27 miles above the Platte near the ancient village of the Ayoways.   On the south the hills continue close to the river from the ancient village of the Kansas up to Council bluff, 50 miles beyond the Platte, (*p. 389*) forming high prairie lands.   On both sides the lands are good; and perhaps this distance from the Osage to the Platte may be recommended as among the best districts on the Missouri for the purposes of settlers.

From the Ayoway village the northern hills again retire from the river, to which they do not return till 320 miles above, at Floyd's river.   The hills on the south also leave the river at Council bluffs, and reappear at the Mahar village, 200 miles up the Missouri.   The country thus abandoned by the hills is more open, and the timber in smaller quantities, than below the Platte; so that, though the plain is rich and covered with high grass, the want of wood renders it less calculated for cultivation than below that river.

The northern hills, after remaining near the Missouri for a few miles at Floyd's river, recede from it at the Sioux river, the course of which they follow; and though they again visit the Missouri at Whitestone river, where they are low, yet they do not return to it till beyond James river. The high lands on the south, after continuing near the river at the Mahar villages, again disappear, and do not approach it till the Cobalt[6] bluffs, about 44 miles from the villages. Then from those bluffs to the Yellowstone river, a distance of about 1,000 miles, they follow the banks of the river with scarcely any deviation.

From the James river the lower grounds are confined within a narrow space by the hills on both sides, which now continue near each other up to the mountains. The space between them, however, varies from one to three miles as high as the Muscleshell river, from which the hills approach so high as to leave scarcely any low grounds on the river, and near the falls reach the water's edge. Beyond the falls the hills are scattered and low to the first range of mountains.

The soil, during the whole length of the Missouri below the Platte, is, generally speaking, very fine, and though the (*p. 390*) timber is scarce, there is still sufficient for the pur- poses of settlers. But beyond that river, though the soil is still rich, yet the almost total absence of timber, and partic- ularly the want of good water, of which there is but a small quantity in the creeks, and even that brackish, oppose pow- erful obstacles to its settlement. The difficulty becomes still greater between the Muscleshell river and the falls, where, besides the great scarcity of timber, the country itself is less fertile.

The elevation of these highlands varies as they pass through this extensive tract of country. From Wood river they are about 150 feet above the water, and continue at that height till they rise near the Osage, from which place to the ancient fortification they again diminish in size. Thence they continue higher to the Mandan village, after which they are rather lower to the neighborhood of Mus- cleshell river, where they are met by the Northern hills, which have advanced at a more uniform height, varying from 150 to 200 or 300 feet. From this place to the moun-

[6] This is simply another name for the Mineral bluffs of p. 81, above the Big Sioux river.   In the Summary Statement they are spoken of as the "copperas, *cobalt*, pirites, and alum bluffs."

tains the height of both is nearly the same, from 300 to 500 feet, and the low grounds are so narrow that the traveler seems passing through a range of high country. From Maria's river to the falls the hills descend to the height of about 200 or 300 feet.

Monday, August 19th. The morning was cold, and the grass perfectly whitened by the frost. We[7] were engaged in preparing packs and saddles, to load the horses as soon as they should arrive. A beaver was caught in a trap, but we were disappointed in trying to catch trout in our net; we therefore made a seine of willow-brush, and by hauling it procured a number of fine trout, and a species of mullet which we had not seen before. It is about 16 inches long; the scales are small; the nose is long, obtusely pointed, and exceeding the under jaw; the mouth opens with folds at the sides; it has no teeth, and the tongue and palate are smooth. The (*p. 391*) color of its back and sides is a bluish brown, while the belly is white; it has the faggot-bones, whence we conclude it to be of the mullet species.[8] It is by no means so well flavored a fish as the trout, which are the same as those we first saw at the falls, larger than the speckled trout of the mountains in the Atlantic States, and equally well flavored. In the evening the hunters returned with two deer.

Captain Clark[9] in the meantime [*August 19th*] proceeded through a wide, level valley, in which the chief pointed out

[7] Captain Lewis and the main party, left at the forks of the Jefferson yesterday, when Captain Clark and a small party started up the west fork, or Prairie creek, through Shoshone cove.

[8] "Mullet" is a common local name of various cyprinoid fishes of the United States belonging to the family *Catostomidæ*, and more properly called suckers. The species here meant is doubtless *Catostomus longirostris* of Lesueur, now called *C. catostomus* (after Forster), in the curious tautological nomenclature affected by naturalists in such cases.

[9] From this point to the entry under date of Aug. 28th inclusive, the narrative continues solely with Captain Clark's reconnoissance to discover a practicable route. Then it returns to the main party at date of Aug. 20th. As it is not always easy to trace the movements of the Expedition among these moun-

a spot where many of his tribe were killed in battle a year ago. The Indians accompanied him during the day, and as they had nothing to eat he was obliged to feed them from his own stores, the hunters not being able to kill anything. Just as he was entering the mountains, he met an Indian with two mules and a Spanish saddle, who was so polite as to offer one of them to him to ride over the hills. Being on foot Captain Clark accepted his offer, and gave him a waistcoat as a reward for his civility. He camped for the night on a small stream [tributary of the Lemhi], and the next morning,

Tuesday, August 20th,[10] he set out at six o'clock. In passing through a continuation of the hilly, broken country he met several parties of Indians. On coming near the camp [Indian village], which had been removed since we [Lewis]

---

tains, I give Gass' parallel accounts day by day. He accompanied Captain Clark's reconnoissance.

Clark G 69 has for Aug. 19th: "We proceeded on up the main branch [of Prairie creek] with a gradual assent to the head and passed over a low mountain and Decended a steep Decent to a butifull stream, passed over a second hill of a verry steep assent & thro' a hilley countrey for 8 miles an[d] Encamped on a small stream." This is all that the great soldier and geographer has to say about crossing the Continental Divide; but Captain Lewis had been there just before him, and he wasted no words. Clark I 4 makes the "Head Spring of the Jefferson" 13 miles from his camp of Aug. 18th, thus 28 miles from the forks of the Jefferson. Thence it is made 8 miles to to-night's camp, on the small tributary of the Lemhi river; whence it is a couple of miles only to the Lemhi itself. Codex G makes the last two courses 6+4 miles, instead of 8+2; but the total of 10 miles is the same. The whole trip is 38 miles.

Gass' account of Aug. 19th, p. 122, may be transcribed: "We proceeded at 8 o'clock along the valley for six miles, when the hills come more close to the branch, which here divides into three parts or other small branches, and two miles further the principal branch again forks, where the mountains commence with a thick growth of small pines on our left, and large rocks on our right. At 1 o'clock we dined at the head spring of the Missouri and Jefferson river, about 25 [*i. e.*, 28] miles from the place where we had left the canoes, and from which the course is nearly west. . . At three o'clock we proceeded on, and at the foot of the dividing ridge, we met two Indians coming to meet us, and who appeared very glad to see us. It is not more than a mile from the head spring of the Missouri to the head of one of the branches of the Columbia. We proceeded on through the mountain, passed some fine springs, and camped about 36 miles from our camp, where the canoes are" [36 miles from the forks where the canoes had been left].

[10] Gass, p. 122, has: "*Tuesday 20th.* We set out early and traveled about 4

left it two miles higher up the river, Cameahwait requested that the party should halt. This was complied with. A number of Indians came out from the camp, and with great ceremony several pipes were smoked. This being over, Captain Clark was conducted to a large leathern lodge prepared for his party in the middle of the camp, the Indians having only shelters of willow-bushes. A few dried berries and one salmon, the only food the whole village could contribute, were then presented to him ; after which he proceeded to repeat in council what had been already told them, the purposes of his visit; urged them to take their horses over and assist in transporting our baggage, and expressed a wish to obtain a guide to examine the river. This was explained and enforced to the (*p. 392*) whole village by Cameahwait ; and an old man was pointed out who was said to know more of their geography to the north than any other person, and whom Captain Clark engaged to accompany him. After explaining his views, he distributed a few presents, the council was ended, and nearly half the village set out to hunt the antelope, but returned without success.

Captain Clark in the meantime made particular inquiries as to the situation of the country, and the possibility of soon reaching a navigable water. The chief began by drawing on the ground a delineation of the rivers, from which it appeared that his information was very limited. The [Lemhi] river on which the camp is, he divided into two branches just above us, which, as he indicated by the opening of the mountains, were in view. He next made it discharge into a

miles, to a village of the Indians on the bank of a branch of the Columbia river, about ten yards wide and very rapid. . . We had a long talk with them, and they gave us very unfavourable accounts with respect to the rivers. From which we understood that they are not navigable down, and expect to perform the rout by land. Here we procured a guide, and left our interpreters to go on with the natives, and assist Captain Lewis and his party to bring on the baggage. Captain Clarke and our party proceeded down the river with our guide, through a valley about 4 miles wide, of a rich soil, but almost without timber. There are high mountains on both sides, with some pine trees on them. We went about 8 miles, and camped on a fine spring."

larger [Salmon] river, ten [*i. e.*, 18] miles below, coming from the southwest; the joint stream continued one day's march to the northwest, and then inclined to the westward for two days' march further. At that place he put several heaps of sand, on each side, which, as he explained them, represented vast mountains of rock always covered with snow, in passing through which the river was so completely hemmed in by the high rocks that there was no possibility of traveling along the shore; that the bed of the river was obstructed by sharp-pointed rocks, and such was its rapidity that, as far as the eye could reach, it presented a perfect column of foam. The mountains, he said, were equally inaccessible, as neither man nor horse could cross them; that such being the state of the country, neither he nor any of his nation had ever attempted to go beyond the mountains. Cameahwait said also that he had been informed by the Chopunnish, or Pierced-nose [Nez-percé] Indians, who reside on this river west of the mountains, that it [Salmon river [11]] ran a great way toward the setting sun, and at length lost itself in a great lake of water [Pacific ocean], which was ill-tasted, and where the white men lived.

An Indian belonging to a band of Shoshonees who live to the southwest, and who happened to be at camp, was then brought in, and in- (*p. 393*) quiries were made of him as to the situation of the country in that direction. This he described in terms scarcely less terrible than those in which Cameahwait had represented the west. He said that his relations lived at the distance of 20 days' march from this place, on a course a little to the west of south and not far from the whites, with whom they traded for horses, mules, cloth, metal, beads, and the shells here worn as ornaments, which are those of a species of pearl-oyster [abalone, *Haliotis*]. In order to reach his country we should be obliged during the first seven days to climb over steep rocky mountains, where there was no game and we should find nothing but roots for subsistence. Even for these we should be obliged to contend

[11] Cameahwait was quite right, though very elliptical. Understand simply that Salmon river flows into the Snake, this into the Columbia, and this into the Pacific.

with a fierce, warlike people, whom he called the Broken Moccasins, or Moccasins with Holes, who lived like bears in holes,
and fed on roots and the flesh of such horses as they could
steal or plunder from those who passed through the mountains.   So rough indeed was the passage, that the feet of the
horses would be wounded in such a manner that many of them
would be unable to proceed.   The next part of the route
would be for ten days through a dry, parched desert of sand,
inhabited by no animal which would supply us with subsistence ; and as the sun had now scorched up the grass and
dried up the small pools of water which are sometimes
scattered through this desert in the spring, both ourselves
and our horses would perish for want of food and water.
About the middle of this plain a large river [the Snake]
passes from southeast to northwest, which, though navigable, afforded neither timber nor salmon.   Three or four
days' march beyond this plain his relations lived, in a
country tolerably fertile and partially covered with timber,
on another large river [Multnomah] running in the same
direction as the former; this last discharges into a third
large river [the Columbia] on which reside many numerous
nations, with whom his own were at war; but whether this
last emptied itself into the great or stinking lake, as they
called the [Pacific] ocean, he did not know; that from his
country to (*p. 394*) the stinking lake was a great distance,
and that the route to it, taken by such of his relations as
had visited it, was up the river on which they lived and over
to that on which the white people lived, which they knew
discharged itself into the ocean.   This route he advised us
to take, but added that we had better defer the journey till
spring, when he would himself conduct us.

   This account persuaded us that the streams of which
he spoke were southern branches of the Columbia, heading
[approximately] with the Rio des Apostolos and Rio
Colorado, and that the route which he mentioned was to
the Gulf of California.   Captain Clark therefore told him
that this road was too much toward the south for our pur-

pose, and then requested to know if there was no route on the left of the river where we now are, by which we might intercept it below the mountains. But he [the Indian] knew of none except that through the barren plains, which he said joined the mountains on that side, and through which it was impossible to pass at this season, even if we were fortunate enough to escape the Broken Moccasin Indians. Captain Clark recompensed the Indian by a present of a knife, with which he seemed much gratified, and now inquired of Cameahwait by what route the Pierced-nose Indians, who he said lived west of the [Bitter-root] mountains, crossed over to the Missouri. This[12] he said was toward the north, but that the road was a very bad one; that during the passage he had been told they suffered excessively from hunger, being obliged to subsist for many days on berries alone, there being no game in that part of the mountains, which were broken and rocky, and so thickly covered with timber that they could scarcely pass.

Surrounded by difficulties as all the other routes are, this seems to be the most practicable of all the passages by land; since, if the Indians can pass the mountains with their women and children, no difficulties which they could encounter could be formidable to us; and if the Indians below the [west of the Bitter-root] mountains are so numer-

[12] In fact there were two trails by which the Indians crossed the Bitter-root mountains, and which later became known to us as the Southern and Northern Nez-percé trails. Cameahwait had the latter of these in mind, and this is the one which the Expedition will take. They will have a hard road to travel for the first part of the way before they reach it; and then they will find it still harder. To have crossed the Rockies will prove to be nothing in comparison with what remains to be done by land, before they reach a navigable stream. The way now directly westward before them proves to be absolutely impracticable by any means in their power. They will have to make a long detour northward, of nearly two degrees of latitude, to a point nearly on a parallel with the Missourian Gates of the Rockies, before they can strike west for the Columbia. All these points will appear in due course as we proceed. The move on foot at the present moment is, that Captain Clark proposes to see for himself whether the Expedition can be led down Salmon river. He is repulsed, and returns, after a reconnoissance of 70 miles and back.

ous as they are represented to be, they must have some means of subsistence equally within (*p. 395*) our power. They tell us, indeed, that the nations to the westward subsist principally on fish and roots, and that their only game are elk, deer, and a few antelope, there being no buffalo west of the [Bitter-root] mountains. The first inquiry, however, was to ascertain the truth of their information relative to the difficulty of descending the [Salmon] river.

For this purpose Captain Clark set out at three o'clock in the afternoon, accompanied by the guide and all his men, except one [Cruzatte], whom he left with orders to purchase a horse and join him as soon as possible. At the distance of four miles he crossed the [Lemhi] river, and eight miles from the [Indian] camp halted for the night at a small stream. The road which he followed was a beaten path through a wide rich meadow, in which were several old lodges. On the route he met a number of men, women, and children, as well as horses, and one of the men, who appeared to possess some consideration, turned back with him, and observing a woman with three salmon, obtained them from her, and presented them to the party. Captain Clark shot a mountain-cock or cock-of-the-plains [*Centrocercus urophasianus*], a dark brown bird larger than the dunghill fowl, with a long pointed tail and a fleshy protuberance about the base of the upper chop, something like that of the turkey, though without the snout [fleshy process on the head]. In the morning,

August 21*st*,[13] he resumed his march early, and at the distance of five miles reached an Indian lodge of brush, inhabited by seven families of Shoshonees. They behaved with great civility, gave the whole party as much boiled salmon as they could eat, and added, as a present, several dried salmon and a considerable quantity of choke-cherries.

[13] "*Wednesday* 21*st*. About 7 o'clock in the morning we continued our journey down the [Lemhi] valley, and came to a few lodges of Indians where our guide lives. We remained here about two hours, during which time a number of Indians passed us, going to fish. We proceeded on the way the Indians had gone ; and one of our men went with them to the fishing-place. The valley becomes very narrow here, and a large branch of the [Salmon] river comes in a short distance

After smoking with them all he visited the fish-weir, which was about 200 yards distant. The [Lemhi] river was here divided by three small islands, which occasioned the water to pass along four channels. Of these three were narrow, and stopped by means of trees, which were stretched across and supported by willow-stakes, sufficiently near each other to prevent the passage of fish. About the center of each was (*p. 396*) placed a basket formed of willows, 18 or 20 feet in length, of a cylindrical form, terminating in a conic shape at its lower extremity; this was situated with its mouth upward, opposite an aperture in the weir. The main channel of the water was then conducted to this weir, and as the fish entered it, they became so entangled with each other that they could not move, and were taken out by untying the small end of the willow basket. The weir in the main channel was formed in a manner somewhat different; in fact, two distinct weirs were formed of poles and willow-sticks quite across the river, approaching each other obliquely with an aperture in each side near the angle. This is made by tying a number of poles together at the top, in parcels of three, which are then set up in a triangular form at the base, two of the poles being in the range desired for the weir, and the third down the stream. To these poles two ranges of other poles are next lashed horizontally with willow bark and withes, and willow-sticks are joined in with these crosswise, so as to form a kind of wicker-work from the bottom of the river to the height of three or four feet above the surface of the water. This is so thick as to prevent the fish from passing, and even in some parts, with the help of a little gravel and some stone, enables the Indians to give any direction they wish to the water. These two weirs being placed near each other, one for the purpose of catching the

below. Here we had to ascend high ground, the bottom is so narrow ; and continued on the high ground about six miles when we came again to the river, where a fine branch flows in, the valley 4 or 5 miles wide. In this branch we shot a salmon about 6 pounds weight. We travelled 20 miles this day, and encamped at a place where the mountains come close to the river." Gass, p. 124.

fish as they ascend, the other as they go down the river, are provided with two baskets, made in the form already described and placed at the apertures of the weir.

After examining these curious objects, he returned to the Indian lodges and soon passed the river to the left,[14] where an Indian brought him a tomahawk, which he said he had found in the grass near the lodge where Captain Lewis had stayed on his first visit to the village. This was a tomahawk which had been missed at the time, and supposed to be stolen ; it was, however, the only article which had been lost in our intercourse with the nation, and as even that was returned, the (*p. 397*) inference is highly honorable to the integrity of the Shoshonees.

On leaving the lodges Captain Clark crossed to the left side of the [Lemhi] river,[16] and dispatched five men to the forks of it [its confluence with Salmon river] in search of the man [Cruzatte] left behind yesterday, who had procured a horse and passed by another road, as they learned, to the forks. At the distance of 14 miles [further] they killed a very large salmon, 2½ feet long, in a creek [on the right] six miles below the forks ; and after traveling about 20 miles [in all to-day] through the valley, following the course of the river, which runs nearly northwest, halted in a small meadow on the right side [of Salmon river], under a cliff of rocks. Here they were joined by the five men who had gone in quest of Crusatte. They had been to the forks of the river, where the natives resort in great numbers for the purpose of gigging

[14] That is, passed the left hand one of the channels into which the Lemhi was divided by the islands mentioned in the last paragraph. He has now the Lemhi on his right, as before he had crossed a channel of it to examine the fish-weirs.

[15] That is, crossed the Lemhi river from its left to its right bank, so that this river is now to his left, and he proceeds down its right bank : see his map, where this crossing is marked—the one nearest to the forks of Salmon river. This crossing is about 8 miles above the confluence of the Lemhi with Salmon river ; for at 14 miles thus far to-day they killed a salmon in a creek six miles below the mouth of the Lemhi. This creek is a small branch of Salmon river from the N.E., on the right hand going down. Later, when the Expedition comes along here, it is called Salmon creek. Clark charts it, nameless, on his map of 1814, just above the spot where the dotted trail of the Expedition leaves Salmon river.

fish, of which they made our men a present of five fresh salmon. In addition to this food one deer was killed to-day.

The western [Rock river] branch of this [Salmon] river is much larger than the eastern [Lemhi river], and after we passed the junction [site of Salmon City] we found the river about 100 yards in width, rapid and shoaly, but containing only a small quantity of timber. As Captain Lewis was the first white man who [had] visited its [head-] waters, Captain Clark gave it the name of Lewis' river. The low grounds through which he had passed to-day were rich and wide, but at his camp this evening the hills begin to assume a formidable aspect. The cliff under which he lay is of a reddish-brown color; the rocks which have fallen from it are a dark-brown flintstone. Near the place are gullies of white sandstone, and quantities of a fine sand of a snowy whiteness. The mountains on each side are high and rugged, with some pine trees scattered over them.

August 22d.[16] He soon began to perceive that the Indian accounts had not exaggerated. At the distance of a mile he passed a small creek [on the right], and the points of four mountains, which were rocky, and so high that it seemed almost impossible to cross them with horses. The road lay over the sharp fragments of rocks which had fallen from the mountains, and were strewed in heaps for miles together; yet the horses, al-(*p.398*) together unshod, traveled across them as fast as the men, without detaining them a moment. They passed two bold running streams, and reached the entrance of

[16] "*Thursday 22nd.* We began our journey at 7 o'clock; and having traveled about a mile, crossed a branch of the [Salmon] river. Here the mountains came so close on the river that we could not get through the narrows, and had to cross a very high mountain about 3 miles over, and then struck the river again. . . We soon had to ascend another large mountain, and had to proceed in the same way until we had crossed 4 of them, when we came to a large creek [later Fish creek—that one which the Expedition is to go up. It is now the North fork of Salmon river] . . . we proceeded down the river; but with a great deal of difficulty; the mountains being so close, steep and rocky. The river here is about 80 yards wide and a continuous rapid, but not deep. We went about 15 miles to day, and encamped on a small island, as there was no other level place near." Gass, pp. 124, 125.

a small river,[17] where a few Indian families resided, who had not been previously acquainted with the arrival of the whites ; the guide was behind, and the woods were so thick that we came upon them unobserved, till at a very short distance. As soon as they saw us the women and children fled in great consternation ; the men offered us everything they had— the fish on the scaffolds, the dried berries, and the collars of elks' tushes worn by the children. We took only a small quantity of the food, and gave them in return some small articles which conduced very much to pacify them. The guide now coming up, explained to them who we were and the object of our visit, which seemed to relieve their fears ; still a number of the women and children did not recover from their fright, but cried during our stay, which lasted about an hour. The guide, whom we found a very intelligent, friendly old man, informed us that up this river there was a road which led over the mountains to the Missouri.

On resuming his route Captain Clark went along the steep side of a mountain about three miles and then reached the river near a small island, at the lower part of which he camped ; he here attempted to gig some fish, but could only obtain one small salmon. The river is here shoal and rapid, with many rocks scattered in various directions through its bed. On the sides of the mountains are some scattered pines, and of those on the left the tops are covered with these trees ; there are, however, but few in the low grounds through which they passed ; indeed, they had seen only a single tree fit to make a canoe, and even that was small. The country had an abundant growth of berries, and we met several women and children gathering them, who

[17] All three of these streams from the right. The "small river" is that now known as the North fork of Salmon river. When the main party comes along here they will call it Fish creek, and take the road up it over the Bitter-root mountains to Clark's river. It forks near the mountains ; its left hand fork is the one they will take. Its right fork, now known as Datang or Datongo creek, leads through the Big Hole Pass of the Rockies to a certain head (Pioneer creek) of the North fork of Wisdom or Big Hole river, and so to Missourian waters, as the old guide informs Captain Clark at the end of the paragraph.

bestowed them upon us with great liberality. Among the woods Captain Clark observed a species of woodpecker,[18] the beak [face] and tail of which are white, the wings black, and (*p. 399*) every other part of the body of a dark brown [light gray]; its size was [greater than] that of the robin, and it fed on the seeds of the pine.

August 23d.[19] Captain Clark set off very early, but as his route lay along the steep side of a mountain, over irregular and broken masses of rocks which wounded the horses' feet, he was obliged to proceed slowly. At the distance of four miles he reached the river, but the rocks here became so steep, and projected so far into the river, that there was no mode of passing except through the water. This he did for some distance, though the river was very rapid and so deep that they were forced to swim their horses. After following the edge of the water for about a mile under this steep cliff, he reached a small meadow, below which the whole current of the river beat against the right shore, on which he was, and which was formed of a solid rock perfectly inaccessible to horses. Here, too, the little track which he had been pursuing terminated. He therefore resolved to leave the horses and the greater part of the men at this place, and examine the river still further, in order to determine if there were any possibility of descending it in canoes. Having killed nothing except a single goose to-day, and the whole of their provisions having been consumed last evening,

[18] This is the remarkable bird afterward called Clark's crow, *Corvus columbianus*, by Wilson, Am. Orn. III. 1811, p. 29, pl. 20, fig. 2. It is the American nutcracker, *Nucifraga columbiana* of Audubon, Orn. Biogr. IV. 1838, p. 459, pl. 362 ; now *Picicorvus columbianus* of Prince C. L. Bonaparte, described for the first time in this paragraph, but inaccurately.

[19] " *Friday 23rd.* We proceeded down the river through dreadful narrows, where the rocks were in some places breast high, and no path or trail of any kind. . . We went on 3 [read four] miles, when Captain Clarke did not think proper to proceed further with the horses, until he should go forward, and examine the pass. So we halted on a small flatt and breakfasted on some fish the natives had given us. Captain Clarke, our guide, and three men then went on." Gass, p. 125. Here Gass remained.

it was by no means advisable to remain any length of time where they were.

He now directed the men to fish and hunt at this place till his return, and then, with his guide and three men, he proceeded, clambering over immense rocks and along the sides of lofty precipices which bordered the river, when at twelve miles' distance he reached a small meadow, the first he had seen on the river since he left his party. A little below this meadow a large creek, twelve yards wide and of some depth, discharges from the north. Here were some recent signs of an Indian camp, and the tracks of a number of horses, which must have come along a plain Indian path he now saw following the course of the creek. This stream, his guide said, led toward a large river running to the north, and was (*p. 400*) frequented by another nation [Tushepaws] for the purpose of catching fish. He remained here two hours, and having taken some small fish, made a dinner on them, with the addition of a few berries.

From the place where he had left his party to the mouth of this creek, it [Salmon river] presents one continued rapid, in which are five shoals, none of which could be passed with loaded canoes; the baggage must, therefore, be transported for a considerable distance over the steep mountains, where it would be impossible to employ horses for the relief of the men. The empty canoes must be let down the rapids by means of cords, and not even in that way without great risk to the canoes as well as the men. At one of these shoals, indeed, the rocks rise so perpendicularly from the water as to leave no hope of a passage, or even a portage, without great labor in removing rocks, and in some instances cutting away the earth. To surmount these difficulties would exhaust the strength of the party; and what was equally discouraging would waste our time and consume our provisions, of neither of which have we much to spare. The season is now far advanced, and the Indians tell us we shall shortly have snow. The salmon have so far declined that the natives themselves are hastening from the country; not an animal of any kind, larger than a pheasant or a squirrel, and of even these a few only, will then be seen in this part of the mountains; after which we shall be obliged to rely on our own stock of provisions, which will not support us more than ten days. These circumstances combine to render a passage by water impracticable in our present situation.

To descend the course of the river on horseback is the other alternative, and scarcely a more inviting one. The river is so deep that there are only a few places where it can be forded, and the rocks approach so near the water as to render it impossible to make a route along the water's edge. In crossing the mountains themselves we should have to encounter, besides their steepness, one barren sur- (*p. 401*) face of broken masses of rock, down which, in certain seasons, the torrents sweep vast quantities of stone into the river. These rocks are of a whitish-brown, toward the base of a gray color, and so hard that, on striking them with steel, they yield a fire like flint. This somber aspect is in some places scarcely relieved by a single tree, though near the river and on the creeks there is more timber, among which are some tall pines. Several of these might be made into canoes, and by lashing two of them together one of tolerable size might be formed.

After dinner Captain Clark continued his route, and at the distance of half a mile passed another creek,[20] about five yards wide. Here his guide informed him that by ascending this creek for some distance he would have a better road, and cut off a considerable bend of the river toward the south. He therefore pursued a well-beaten Indian track up this creek for about six miles; when, leaving the creek to the right, he passed over a ridge, and, after walking a mile, again met the [Salmon] river, where it flows through a meadow of about 80 acres in extent. This he passed, and then ascended

[20] *This is* the creek which Captain Clark named Berry creek, because he had nothing else to eat; six miles up which, and then over to Salmon river, finished his reconnoissance. See the bad snag about Berry creek, text of Aug. 31st.

a high and steep point of a mountain, from which the guide now pointed out where the river broke through the mountains about 20 miles distant. Near the base of the mountains a small river falls in from the south.[21]

This view was terminated by one of the loftiest mountains Captain Clark had ever seen, which was perfectly covered with snow. Toward this formidable barrier the river went directly on, and there it was, as the guide observed, that the difficulties and dangers of which he and Cameahwait had spoken commenced. After reaching the mountain, he said the river continued its course toward the north for many miles, between high perpendicular rocks, which were also scattered through its bed; it then penetrated the mountain through a narrow gap, on each side of which arose

[21] Just how far Captain Clark went down Salmon river below the confluence of the Lemhi is marked on his map, where his trail is dotted in ; but what this point corresponds to on a modern map is less easily determined. The matter can be settled by the best possible authority—his own words. He went 18 miles from the Shoshone camp to the confluence of the Lemhi with Salmon river ; his whole trip tots up 70 miles ; therefore he went 70–18=52 miles down the Salmon by the trail. Here is his itinerary of the trip, *totidem verbis*, Clark G 85, 86 :

" Course & Distance Down Columbia [=Lemhi + Salmon] river by Land, as I Decended &c

" N.W. 18 miles from the Indian Camp to the forks [of Salmon river] crossed the [Lemhi] river twice, passed several old Camps on the East side and a Camp of several lodges at a were [weir] on the West side, passed a roade on the left leading up the main West fork [*i.e.*, Salmon river above the mouth of the Lemhi] below the last Camp, several small branches falls in on each Side [of the Lemhi] a high mountain on each Side.

" N. 15° W. 14 miles to a Island [in Salmon river] passed high red Clift on the right Side passed a large Creek [on the right, later named Tower creek] at 9 miles up which a roade passes large bottom below. Several Spring runs falling from the mountain on the left. passed a creek on the right.

" N. 30° W. 2 [miles] to the top of a mountain the [Salmon] river one mile to the left.

" N. W. 10 miles with the general Course of the river, passed over the Spurs of four mountains almost inexcessable, and and two Small runs on the right to some Indian Camps at the mouth of a Small river [Fish creek of the text, North fork of Salmon river] on the right up which a road passes [which the Expedition will take to go over to Clark's Fork] passed several Island, and small bottoms between the mountains.

" West 3 miles on the right side [of Salmon river] to the assent of a mountain

perpendicularly a rock as high as the top of the mountain before them; the river then made a bend which concealed its (*p. 402*) future course from view; and as it was alike impossible to descend the river or clamber over that vast mountain, eternally covered with snow, neither he nor any of his nation had ever been lower than to a place where they could see the gap made by the river on entering the mountain. To that place he said he would conduct Captain Clark, if he desired it, by the next evening. But he was in need of no further evidence to convince him of the utter impracticability of the route before him. He had already witnessed the difficulties of part of the road; yet after all these dangers his guide, whose intelligence and fidelity he could not doubt, now assured him that the difficulties were only commencing,

passed over one Spur of the same Mountain passed 2 Islands, & a bottom in which berris were plenty.

" S. W. 5 miles to a verry bad rapid & camped [Aug. 22d], a small run on the left. Passed perpendicular Clift where we were obliged to go into the water passed several places on stones & sides of mountains, one Island & several rapids, all the way rapids at intervals.

" N.W. 3 miles high Clifts on each side no road [left horses and all but three men here, and went ahead].

" West 2 miles do do [*i. e.*, high cliffs on each side, and no road] passed bad rapids scercely possible to pass down or up [in boats].

" N. W. 6 miles to a large Creek on the Right side, passed verry bad rapids & a number of riffles, mountains high and steep very stoney no bottoms except [at] the Creek & a little above.

" South 1 mile to the mouth of of a small run [Berry creek] on the right a small Island and rapid.

" N.W. 6 miles up the Run thro' a piney countrey large and lofty hills high.

" S.W. 1 m. to the [Salmon] river at a small bottom passed over a gap in the mountn. from the top of which I could see the hollers [hollows] of the river for 20 miles to a verry high mountain on the left, at which place my guide made signs that the bad part of the river Comsd. [commenced] and [was] much worse than any I saw &c &c returned 6 bad rapids, many others.

" Miles 70." [To vicinity of Shoup, near mouth of Middle fork of Salmon R.]

This is the one and only repulse from an intended route the Expedition ever experienced. Once indeed, on the return trip, they had to fall back before the Bitter-root range; but that was simply to wait till the snow melted, when they resumed their route. It is quite certain that if Captain Clark could not make a Salmon river route, that way was impossible, with any means that the Expedition commanded.

and what he saw before him too clearly convinced him of the Indian's veracity.

He therefore determined to abandon this route, returned to the upper part of the last [Berry] creek he had passed, and reaching it an hour after dark, camped for the night.   On this creek he had seen in the morning an Indian road coming in from the north.   Disappointed in finding a route by water, Captain Clark now questioned his guide more particularly as to the direction of this road, which he seemed to understand perfectly.   He drew a map on the sand, and represented this road, as well as that passed yesterday on Berry creek, as both leading toward two forks of the same great river, where resided a nation called the Tushepaws, who, having no salmon in their river, came by these roads to the fish-weirs on Lewis' river.   He had himself been among these Tushepaws, and having once accompanied them on a fishing-party to another river, he had there seen Indians who had come across the Rocky mountains.   After a great deal of conversation, or rather signs, and a second and more particular map from his guide, Captain Clark felt persuaded that his guide knew of a road from the Shoshonee village they had left to the great river [Clark's] to the north, without coming so low down as this on a route impracticable for horses.   He was desirous of hastening his return, and therefore set out early,

(*p. 403*) *August 24th*,[22] and after descending the [Berry] creek to the [Salmon] river, stopped to breakfast on berries in

[22] " *Saturday 24th*. . . At 1 o'clock Captain Clarke and his party returned, after having been down the [Salmon] river about 12 miles. He had found it was not possible to go down, either by land or water, without much risk and trouble.   The water is so rapid and the bed of the river so rocky, that going by water appeared impracticable ; and the mountains so amazingly high, steep and rocky, that it seemed impossible to go along the river by land.   Our guide speaks of a way to sea, by going up the south fork of this river, getting on the mountains that way, and then turning to the southwest again.   Captain Clarke therefore wrote a letter to Captain Lewis, and despatched a man [Colter] on horseback to meet him ; and we all turned back up the river again, poor and uncomfortable enough, as we had nothing to eat and there is no game.   We proceeded up about 3 miles, and supperless went to rest for the night." Gass, p. 126.

the meadow above the second creek [next above Berry creek]. He then went on, but unfortunately fell from a rock and injured his leg very much ; he, however, walked as rapidly as he could, and at four in the afternoon rejoined his men. During his absence they had killed one of the mountain-cocks, a few pheasants,[23] and some small fish, on which, with haws and service-berries, they had subsisted. Captain Clark immediately sent forward a man [Colter] on horseback with a note to Captain Lewis, apprising him of the result of his inquiries,[24] and late in the afternoon set out with the rest of the party, and camped at the distance of two miles. The men were much disheartened at the bad prospect of escaping from the mountains ; and having nothing to eat but a few berries, which have made several of them sick, they all passed a disagreeable night, which was rendered more uncomfortable by a heavy dew.

August 25th. The want of provisions urged Captain Clark to return as soon as possible. He therefore set out early, and halted an hour in passing the Indian camp near the fish-weirs. These people treated him with great kindness, and though poor and dirty they willingly gave what little they possessed. They gave the whole party boiled salmon and dried berries, which were not, however, in suffi-

[23] That variety (*Bonasa umbelloides*) of the ruffed grouse (*B. umbellus*) which occurs in the northern Rocky Mountain region of the United States.

[24] Clark G 83 : " The plan I stated to Capt Lewis if he agrees with me we shall adopt is. to precure as many horses (one for each man) if possoble and to hire my present guide who I sent on to him to interegate thro' the Intptr. and proceed on by land to some navagable part of the *Columbia* river, or to the *Ocean*, depending on what provisions we can precure by the gun aded to the small stock we have on hand depending on our horses [for food] as the last resort. A second plan to divide the party, one part to attempt this defecult river with what provisions we had, and the remaindr to pass by Land on hors back Depending on our gun &c for Provisions &c. and come together occasionally on the river." (A third plan was written in the codex, but carefully erased. It was the same as the first, except that a party was to be sent back to Medicine or Sun river, and attempt to reach the Pacific that way.) Clark adds that the first plan above suggested pleased him most. This was in fact the one adopted— to proceed by land to some *navigable* Columbian waters. The situation was grave in the extreme ; and perhaps Captain Clark's good judgment in abandoning any route by way of Salmon river saved the Expedition.

cient quantities to appease their hunger. The party soon resumed their old road; but as the abstinence or strange diet had given one of the men a very severe illness, they were detained very much on his account, and it was not till late in the day they reached the cliff under which they had camped on the 21st. They immediately began to fish and hunt, in order to procure a meal. They caught several small fish, and by means of the guide obtained two salmon from a small party of women and children who, with one man, were going below to gather berries. This supplied them with about half a meal, but after dark they were regaled with a beaver which one of the hunters brought in. The other game seen in the course of the day were one (*p. 404*) deer and a herd of elk, among the pines on the side of the mountains.

August 26th. The morning was fine, and three men were dispatched ahead to hunt, while the rest were detained until nine o'clock, in order to retake some horses which had strayed away during the night. They then proceeded along the route by [past] the forks of the [Salmon] river till they reached the lower Indian camp, where they [Indians] first were when we [Captain Lewis' party had] met them.[25] The whole camp immediately flocked around them, with great appearance of cordiality; but all the spare food of the village did not amount to more than two salmon, which they gave to Captain Clark, who distributed them among his men. The hunters had not been able to kill anything, nor had Captain Clark or the greater part of the men any food during the 24 hours, till toward evening one of them shot a salmon in the river,

---

[25] A curious mistake of the text here. I make it read as Biddle intended, but that is wrong. Clark G 87 has: "Proceeded on by the way of the forks to the Indian camps at the first were," which Biddle evidently understood to mean, the place where the Indians *were* when first met by Captain Lewis, and from which place they had meanwhile moved a couple of miles up the Lemhi. But "were" is Clark's way of spelling *weir* (fish-weir); and this point (which Captain Clark had before reached on the 21st) is 15 miles or so below the upper Shoshone village on the Lemhi, near which Captain Lewis had first met the Indians. This is confirmed by Gass, who, in his itinerary of the 28th, says he went on to the upper village, and then returned to Captain Clark's camp, "a distance of 15 miles."

and a few small fish were caught, which furnished a scanty meal. The only animals they had seen were a few pigeons, some very wild hares, a great number of large black grass-hoppers [*Anabrus simplex*], and a quantity of ground-lizards.

August 27th. The men, who were engaged last night in mending their moccasins, all except one, went out hunting, but no game was to be procured. One of the men, how-ever, killed a small salmon, and the Indians made a present of another, on which the whole party made a very slight breakfast. These Indians, to whom this life is familiar, seem contented, although they depend for subsistence on the scanty productions of the fishery. But our men, who are used to hardships, but have been accustomed to have the first wants of nature regularly supplied, feel very sensibly their wretched situation; their strength is wasting away; they begin to express their apprehensions of being without food in a country perfectly destitute of any means of sup-porting life, except a few fish. In the course of the day an Indian brought into the camp five salmon, two of which Captain Clark bought and made a supper for the party.

(*p. 405*) *August 28th.*[26] There was a frost again this morn-ing. The Indians gave the party two salmon out of several which they caught in their traps, and having purchased two more, the party was enabled to subsist on them during the day. A camp of about 40 Indians from the west fork [of Salmon river] passed us to-day, on their route eastward. Our prospect of provisions is getting worse every day; the hunters, who ranged through the country in every direction where game might be reasonably expected, have seen noth-ing. The fishery is scarcely more productive, for an Indian,

[26] Gass' Journal records the return march of Captain Clark's reconnoissance under dates of 25th, 26th, and 27th, and the following is his entry for the 28th, p. 127, on which and the day following the Biddle narrative is not very clear as to the whereabouts of the parties : " *Wednesday 28th.* I went on to the upper village [of Shoshones] where I found Captain Lewis and his party buying horses. They had got 23, which, with 2 we had, made in the whole 25. I then returned to our [Captain Clark's] camp, a distance of 15 miles, and arrived there late." Captain Clark was camped there on the 26th, 27th and 28th.

who was out all day with his gig, killed only one salmon. Besides the four fish procured from the Indians, Captain Clark obtained some fish-roes in exchange for three small fish-hooks, the use of which he taught them, and which they very readily comprehended. All the men who are not engaged in hunting are occupied in making pack-saddles for the horses which Captain Lewis informed us he had bought.[27]

Tuesday, August 20th.[28] Two hunters were dispatched early in the morning, but they returned without killing anything, and the only game we procured was a beaver caught last night in a trap, which he carried off two miles before he was found. The fur of this animal is as good as any we have seen, nor does it, in fact, appear to be ever out of season on the upper branches of the Missouri. This beaver, with several dozen fine trout, gave us a plentiful subsistence for the day. The party were occupied chiefly in making pack-saddles, in the manufacture of which we supply the place of nails and boards by substituting for the first thongs of raw-hide, which answer very well, while for boards we use the handles of our oars and the plank of some boxes, the contents of which we empty into sacks made of raw-hide for the purpose. The Indians who visit us behave with the greatest decorum, and the women are busily engaged in making and mending the moccasins of the party. As we

[27] Captain Lewis had been expected by Captain Clark to join him at the lower village on the 27th. As he did not come, Captain Clark on the 28th "dispatched one man [Sergeant Gass] to the upper camp to enquire if Capt. Lewis was comeing on &c : he returned after night with a letter from Capt. Lewis informing me of his situation at the upper village," etc., Clark G 89. Gass' entry for the 28th is thus an important check on the Biddle narrative at this point ; with the extracts I give from the codex, it clears up the whole situation. On the 29th, Captain Clark went from the lower to the upper village, and there found Captain Lewis with the main party.

[28] Here the narrative of the main party, who were left at the forks of Jefferson river, is resumed from Aug. 19th (p. 520), after the special narrative of Captain Clark's reconnoissance. Captain Clark rejoined them Aug. 29th, at the upper Shoshone village, he having left two of his men with his baggage at the lower Shoshone village, and Captain Lewis having come over with the main party from the forks of the Jefferson to the upper village on the 26th.

had still some superfluous baggage which would be too heavy to carry across the mountains, it became necessary to make a (*p. 406*) cache or deposit. For this purpose we selected a spot on the bank of the [Jefferson] river, three-quarters of a mile below the camp, and three men were set to dig it, with a sentinel in the neighborhood, who was ordered, if the natives were to straggle that way, to fire a signal for the workmen to desist and separate. Toward evening the cache was completed without being perceived by the Indians, and the packages were prepared for deposit.

CHAPTER XVI.

WITH THE SHOSHONES OF LEMHI RIVER.

Freezing weather in August—Difficulty between Drewyer and a Shoshone—The cache completed—Three kinds of edible roots—Negotiations for horses—Fishing—Departure urgent through scarcity of provisions—The expected Indians arrive—The party break camp and proceed on foot with pack-horses—Wiser sick—Caprice of the Indians—Council held and the difficulty adjusted—The chief rebuked and the march resumed—A fountain-head of the Missouri passed again—Easy parturition of an Indian women en route—Edible root described—Sunflower seeds—The Indian village reached, and word received through Colter of Captain Clark's reconnoissance—Whatever the route is to be, many more horses are required—Account of the Shoshones—Their terror of the Pawkees or Minnetarees—Their wretched state—Their warriors and numerous horses—War their chief occupation—Their gayety and hardihood—Their tribal organization and domestic economy—Chastity of the women—Weapons: the bow and arrow, shield, lance, and poggamoggon—How the shields are made—Trappings of their horses—Their implements and utensils—Stature—Dress of the men—Robes, tippets, shirts, leggings, and moccasins described—Dress of the women and children—Ornaments—Fecundity—Tobacco—Intercourse with other nations, and resources—Mode of naming persons—Venereal and other diseases.

EDNESDAY, August 21st, 1805. The weather was very cold; the water which stood in the vessels exposed to the air being covered with ice a quarter of an inch thick. Ink freezes in the pen, and the low grounds are perfectly whitened with frost. After this the day proved exceedingly warm. The party were engaged in their usual occupations, and completed 20 saddles with the necessary harness. All prepared to set off as soon as the Indians should arrive. Our two hunters, who were dispatched early in the morning, did not return, so that we were obliged to encroach on our pork and corn, which we consider as the last resource when our casual supplies of game fail. After dark we carried our baggage to the cache, and deposited what we thought too cumbrous to carry with us; also, a small assortment of medicines, and all the specimens of plants, seeds, and minerals collected since leaving the falls of the Missouri.

Late to-night Drewyer, one of the hunters, returned with a fawn and a considerable quantity of Indian plunder, which he had taken by way of reprisal. While hunting that morning in the Shoshonee cove he came suddenly upon an Indian camp, at which were an old man, a young one, three women, and a boy. They showed no surprise at the sight of him; he therefore rode up to them, and after turning (*p. 408*) his horse loose to graze sat down, and began to converse with them by signs. They had just finished a repast on some roots; in about 20 minutes one of the women spoke to the rest of the party, who immediately went out, collected their horses, and began to saddle them. Having rested, Drewyer thought he would continue his hunt, and rising went to catch his horse, which was at a short distance, forgetting at the moment to take up his rifle. He had scarcely gone more than fifty paces when the Indians mounted their horses; the young man snatched up the rifle, and leaving all their baggage, they whipped up their horses and set off at full speed toward the passes of the mountains. Drewyer instantly jumped on his horse and pursued them. After running about ten miles the horses of the women nearly gave out. The women, finding Drewyer gain on them, raised dreadful cries, which induced the young man to slacken his pace; being mounted on a very fleet horse, he rode around them at a short distance. Drewyer now came up with the women, and by signs persuaded them that he did not mean to hurt them. They then stopped, and as the young man came toward them Drewyer asked him for his rifle; but the only part of the answer which he understood was Pahkee, the name by which they call their enemies, the Minnetarees of Fort du Prairie. While they were thus engaged in talking Drewyer watched his opportunity, and seeing the Indian off his guard, galloped up to him and seized his rifle. The Indian struggled for some time, but finding Drewyer getting too strong for him, had the presence of mind to open the pan and let the priming fall out. He then let go his hold, and giving his horse the whip escaped at full speed, leaving the women to the mercy of the conqueror. Drewyer then returned to where he had first seen them, where he found that their baggage had been left behind, and brought it to camp with him.

August 22d. This morning early two men were sent to complete the covering of the cache, which could not be (*p. 409*) so perfectly done during the night as to elude the search of the Indians. On examining the spoils which Drewyer had obtained, they were found to consist of several dressed and undressed skins; two bags woven with the bark of the silk-grass,[1] each containing a bushel of dried serviceberries, and about the same quantity of roots; an instrument made of bone for manufacturing flints into arrowheads, and a number of flints themselves. The flint was much of the same color and nearly as transparent as common black glass, and when cut detached itself into flakes, leaving a very sharp edge.

The roots were of three kinds, folded separately from one another in hides of buffalo made into parchment. The first is a fusiform root six inches long, about the size of a man's finger at the largest end, with radicals larger than is usual in roots of the fusiform sort. The rind is white and thin; the body is also white, mealy, and easily reducible by pounding to a substance resembling flour, like which it thickens by boiling, and is of an agreeable flavor; it is eaten frequently in its raw state, either green or dried. The second species was much mutilated, but appeared to be fibrous; it was of a cylindrical form, about the size of a small quill, hard and brittle. A part of the rind, which had not been detached in the preparation, was hard and black; but the rest of the root was perfectly white. This the Indians informed us was always boiled before eating; and on making the experiment we found that it became perfectly soft, but had a bitter taste, which was nauseous to us, though the Indians seemed to

---

[1] Silk-grass is a common name of *Yucca filamentosa*, a well-known dracæneous liliaceous plant of the Southern States, also called Adam's needle and Eve's thread; probably a related species, among those known as Spanish bayonet and dagger-plant in the West, is here meant. An above named edible root is *Lewisia rediviva*, racine amère of the French, giving name to Bitter-root mountains.

relish it ; for, on giving the roots to them, they were very heartily swallowed. The third species was a small nut [tuber] about the size of a nutmeg, of an irregularly rounded form, something like the smallest of the Jerusalem artichokes [*Helianthus tuberosus*], which on boiling we found them to resemble also in flavor ; it is certainly the best root we have seen in use among the Indians. On inquiring of the Indians from what plant these roots were (*p. 410*) procured, they informed us that none of them grew near this place.

The men were chiefly employed in dressing the skins belonging to the party who had accompanied Captain Clark. About eleven o'clock Chaboneau and his wife returned with Cameahwait, accompanied by about 50 men, with their women and children. After they had camped near us and turned loose their horses, we called a council of all the chiefs and warriors, and addressed them in a speech. Additional presents were then distributed, particularly to the two second chiefs, who had, agreeably to their promises, exerted themselves in our favor. The council was then adjourned, and all the Indians were treated with an abundant meal of boiled Indian corn and beans. The poor wretches, who had no animal food and scarcely anything but a few fish, had been almost starved, and received this new luxury with great thankfulness. Out of compliment to the chief, we gave him a few dried squashes, which we had brought from the Mandans, and he declared it was the best food he had ever tasted except sugar, a small lump of which he had received from his sister. He now declared how happy they should all be to live in a country which produced so many good things ; and we told him that it would not be long before the white men would put it in their power to live below the mountains, where they might themselves cultivate all these kinds of food, instead of wandering in the mountains. He appeared to be much pleased with this information, and the whole party being now in excellent temper after their repast, we began our purchase of horses. We soon obtained five very good ones, on very reasonable terms—that is, by giving for each horse merchandise which cost us originally about $6. We have again to admire the perfect decency and propriety of the Indians ; for though so numerous, they do not attempt to crowd round our camp or take anything which they see lying about, and whenever they borrow knives or kettles or any other article from the men, they return them with great fidelity.

(*p. 411*) Toward evening we formed a drag of bushes, and in about two hours caught 528 very good fish, most of them large trout.   Among them we observed for the first time ten or twelve trout[2] of a white or silvery color, except on the back and head, where they are of a bluish cast ; in appearance and shape they resemble exactly the speckled trout, except that they are not quite so large, though the scales are much larger; the flavor is equally good.   The greater part of the fish was distributed among the Indians.[3]

August 23d.   Our visitors seem to depend wholly on us for food ; and as the state of our provisions obliges us to be careful of our remaining stock of corn and flour, this was an additional reason for urging our departure.   But Cameah-wait requested us to wait till the arrival of another party of his nation, who were expected to-day.   Knowing that it would be in vain to oppose his wish, we consented, and two hunters were sent out with orders to go further up the south-east fork than they had hitherto been.   At the same time the chief was informed of the low state of our provisions, and advised to send out his young men to hunt.   This he recommended them to do, and most of them set out.   We

[2] This species remains to be identified.   The description indicates *Oncorhyn-chus nerka*, the common blue-backed salmon of the Columbia and its tributaries, extensively used for canning, and ranking in commercial value next to the quinnat or king salmon, *O. chavicha* or *O. quinnat.*   It attains a weight of four to eight pounds, and is usually of the color said ; but the males in the fall become tinged with red.   This salmon is also called *O. lycaodon*, and is one of the five well-established species of its genus ; they are collectively known as Pacific Salmon.   But the genus *Oncorhynchus* is not represented in any Atlantic waters.

[3] Lewis F ends at this point.   The narrative continues with a small codex, Lewis Fb, Aug. 23d–26th.   The account of the Shoshones is derived in part from Fb, in part from F and G.

then sunk our canoes by means of stones to the bottom of
the river, a situation which, better than any other, secured
them against the effects of the high waters, and the frequent fires of the plains.   The Indians promised not to
disturb them during our absence—a promise we believe the
more readily, as they are almost too lazy to take the trouble
of raising them for fire-wood.   We were desirous of purchasing some more horses, but they declined to sell any until
we reached their camp in the mountains.   Soon after starting the Indian hunters discovered a mule buck,[4] and twelve
of their horsemen pursued it for four miles.   We saw the
chase, which was very entertaining.   At length they rode it
down and killed it.   This mule buck was the largest deer of
any kind we have seen, being nearly as large as a doe elk.
Besides this they brought in another (*p. 412*) deer and three
goats [antelope] ; but instead of a general distribution of
the meat, such as we had hitherto seen among all tribes of
Indians, we observed that some families had a large share
while others received none.   On inquiring of Cameahwait
the reason of this custom, he said that meat among them
was so scarce that each hunter reserved what he killed for
the use of himself and his own family, none of the rest having any claim on what he chose to keep.   Our hunters
returned soon after with two mule-deer and three common
deer ; three of which we distributed among the families
who had received none of the game of their own hunters.
About three o'clock the expected party arrived, consisting
of 50 men, women, and children.   We now learned that
most of the Indians were on their way down the valley
toward the buffalo country, and some anxiety to accompany
them appeared to prevail among those who had promised to
assist us in crossing the mountains.   We, ourselves, were not
without some apprehension that they might leave us ; but as
they continued to say that they would return with us, nothing was said upon the subject.   We were, however, resolved
to move early in the morning, and therefore dispatched two

---

[4] That is, a male of the black-tailed or mule deer, *Cariacus macrotis.*

men to hunt in the cove and leave the game on the route we should pass to-morrow.

August 24th. As the Indians who arrived yesterday had a number of spare horses, we thought it probable they might be willing to dispose of them, and desired the chief to speak to them for that purpose. They declined giving any positive answer, but requested to see the goods which we proposed to exchange. We then produced some battle-axes which we had made at Fort Mandan, and a quantity of knives; with both of which they appeared very much pleased. We were soon able to purchase three horses [and one mule, Lewis, Fb 10] by giving for each [horse] an ax, a knife, a handkerchief, and a little paint. To this we were obliged to add a second knife, a shirt, a handkerchief and a pair of leggings [for the mule]; and such is the estimation in which those animals are held, that even at this price, which (*p. 413*) was double that [we paid] for a horse, the fellow who sold him took upon himself great merit, in having [as if he had] given away a mule to us. They now said that they had no more horses for sale; and as we had now nine of our own, two hired horses, and a mule, we began loading them as heavily as was prudent, placing the rest on the shoulders of the Indian women, and left our camp at twelve o'clock.[5]

We were all on foot, except Sacajawea, for whom her husband had purchased a horse with some articles which we gave him for that purpose; an Indian, however, had the politeness to offer Captain Lewis one of his horses to ride, which he accepted in order better to direct the march of the party. We crossed the [Jefferson] river below the forks,

[5] That the itinerary narrative may be readily resumed, it need only be remembered that Captain Lewis and the main party are still at the Two Forks of the Jefferson, to which Captain Lewis had returned Aug. 17th, after having been over the Divide, and brought some Indians with him. The canoes are left at these forks; horses are purchased, and now Captain Lewis starts with the main party from the Jefferson, to go up Prairie creek, through Shoshone cove, and over the main Divide to the upper Shoshone village on the Lemhi, there to be joined by Captain Clark and his small party, who are at this moment far down Salmon river, returning from his reconnoissance. The two parties will be together again on the 29th, excepting two men left at the lower Shoshone village.

directing our course toward the [Shoshone] cove by the route already passed, and had just reached the lower part of the cove when an Indian rode up to Captain Lewis to inform him that one of his men was very sick, and unable to come on. The party was immediately halted at a run which falls into the [Prairie] creek on the left. Captain Lewis rode back two miles, and found Wiser severely afflicted with the colic. By giving him some essence of peppermint and laudanum, he recovered sufficiently to ride the horse of Captain Lewis, who then rejoined the party on foot. When he arrived he found that the Indians, who had been impatiently expecting his return, had unloaded their horses, turned them loose, and made their camp for the night. It would have been fruitless to remonstrate, and not prudent to excite any irritation; therefore, though the sun was still high, and we had made only six miles, we thought it best to remain with them. After we camped, there fell a slight shower of rain. One of the men caught several fine trout; but Drewyer had been sent out to hunt without having killed anything. We therefore gave a little corn to those of the Indians who were actually engaged in carrying our baggage, and who had absolutely nothing to eat. We also advised Cameahwait, as we could not supply all his people with provisions, to recommend to all who (*p. 414*) were not assisting us, to go on before to their camp. This he did; but in the morning,

Sunday, August 25th, a few only followed his advice, the rest accompanying us at some distance on each side. We set out at sunrise, and after going 17 miles halted for dinner, within two miles of the narrow pass in the mountains. The Indians who were on the sides of our party had started some antelopes, but were obliged, after a pursuit of several hours, to abandon the chase. Our hunters had in the meantime brought in three deer, the greater part of which was distributed among the Indians.

While at dinner we learned by means of Sacajawea that the young men who had left us this morning carried a request from the chief that the village would break camp and meet this party to-morrow, when they would all go down the Missouri into the buffalo country. Alarmed at this new caprice of the Indians, which, if not counteracted, threatened to leave ourselves and our baggage on the mountains, or even if we reached the waters of the Columbia, to prevent our obtaining horses to go on further, Captain Lewis immediately called the three chiefs together. After smoking a pipe he asked them if they were men of their word, and if we could rely on their promises. They readily answered in the affirmative. He then asked if they had not agreed to assist us in carrying our baggage over the mountains. To this they also answered yes. " Why, then," said he, " have you requested your people to meet us to-morrow where it will be impossible for us to trade for horses, as you promised we should? If," he continued, " you had not promised to help us in transporting our goods over the mountains, we should not have attempted it, but have returned down the river; after which no white men would ever have come into your country. If you wish the whites to be your friends, to bring you arms, and to protect you from your enemies, you should never promise what you do not mean to perform. When I first met you, you doubted what I said, yet you afterward saw that (*p. 415*) I told you the truth. How, therefore, can you doubt what I now tell you? You see that I divide amongst you the meat which my hunters kill, and I promise to give all who assist us a share of whatever we have to eat. If, therefore, you intend to keep your promise, send one of the young men immediately, to order the people to remain at the village till we arrive." The two inferior chiefs then said that they had wished to keep their word and to assist us; that they had not sent for the people, but on the contrary had disapproved of that measure, which was done wholly by the first chief. Cameahwait remained silent for some time; at last he said that he knew he had done wrong, but that, seeing his people all in want of provisions, he had wished to hasten their departure for the country where their wants might be supplied. He, however, now declared that, having passed his word he would never violate it, and counter-orders were immediately sent to the village by a young man, to whom we gave a handkerchief, in order to insure dispatch and fidelity.

This difficulty being now adjusted, our march was resumed with an unusual degree of alacrity on the part of the Indians. We passed a spot where, six years ago, the Shoshonees suffered a very severe defeat from the Minnetarees; and late in the evening we reached the upper part of the cove, where the creek enters the mountains. The part of the cove on the northeast side of the creek has lately been burnt, most probably as a signal on some occasion. Here we were joined by our hunters with a single deer, which Captain Lewis gave, as a proof of his sincerity, to the women and children, and remained supperless himself. As we came along we observed several large hares, some ducks, and many cock-of-the-plains. In the low grounds of the cove were also considerable quantities of wild onions.

August 26th. The morning was excessively cold, and the ice in our vessels was nearly a quarter of an inch in thickness. We set out at sunrise and soon reached the fountain of (*p. 416*) the Missouri, where we halted for a few minutes. Then crossing the dividing ridge [6] we reached the fine spring where Captain Lewis had slept on the 12th [inst.], on his first excursion to the Shoshonee camp. The grass on the hillsides was perfectly dry and parched by the sun, but near the

---

[6] First passed by Captain Lewis, Aug. 12th, next by Captain Clark, Aug. 19th, and now by Captain Lewis again with the main party, the Expedition thus passing from Atlantic to Pacific waters, as well as from Montana into Idaho. This is the only point at which both Lewis and Clark and all the party ever crossed the Continental Divide. Captain Clark was never near the Pass by which Captain Lewis and his party returned in 1806. Captain Lewis never saw the pass by which Captain Clark and his party returned in 1806. Why, then, is not the Lemhi Pass—as it is now called—the true and only " Lewis and Clark's Pass "? It should be so designated, and the designation be officially enforced—if necessary, by an Act of Congress. The Pass that Captain Lewis made in 1806 at

spring was a fine green grass; we therefore halted for dinner, and turned our horses out to graze. To each of the Indians who were engaged in carrying our baggage was distributed a pint of corn, which they parched, then pounded, and made a sort of soup.

One of the women, who had been leading two of our pack-horses, halted at a rivulet about a mile behind, and sent on the two horses by a female friend. On inquiring of Cameah-wait the cause of her detention, he answered, with great appearance of unconcern, that she had just stopped to lie in, but would soon overtake us. In fact, we were astonished to see her in about an hour's time come on with her new-born infant, and pass us on her way to the camp, apparently in perfect health.

This wonderful facility with which the Indian women bring forth their children seems rather some benevolent gift of nature, in exempting them from pains which their savage state would render doubly grievous, than any result of habit. If, as has been imagined, a pure dry air or a cold and elevated country be obstacles to easy delivery, every difficulty incident to that operation might be expected in this part of the continent; nor can another reason, the habit of carrying heavy burdens during pregnancy, be at all applicable to the Shoshonee women, who rarely carry any burdens, since their nation possesses an abundance of horses. We have indeed been several times informed by those conversant with Indian manners, who asserted their knowledge of the fact, that Indian women pregnant by white men experience

headwaters of the Big Blackfoot and Dearborn rivers, now called "Lewis and Clark's," should be Lewis' Pass. The pass that Captain Clark made in 1806, at headwaters of Clark's and Wisdom rivers, now called Gibbon's Pass, should be Clark's Pass. It is not a sectional, still less a personal matter. It is a matter of national importance; a matter of historical significance; in such a case as this, names should not be shuffled to belie the facts and pervert history—not even if the explorers themselves intended and desired that the pass known as Lewis and Clark's should be considered to represent their mature conclusions regarding the shortest and most practicable route from the Missouri to the Columbia.

more difficulty in child-birth than when the father is an
Indian. If this account be true, it may contribute to
strengthen the belief that the easy delivery of the Indian
women is wholly constitutional.[7]

(*p. 417*) The tops of the high, irregular mountains to the
westward are still entirely covered with snow ; and the cool-
ness which the air acquires in passing them is a very agreeable relief from the heat, which has dried up the herbage on
the sides of the hills. While we stopped, the women were
busily employed in collecting the root of a plant with which
they feed their children, who, like their mothers, are nearly
half starved and in a wretched condition. It is a species
of fennel[8] which grows in the moist grounds ; the radix is
of the knobbed kind, of a long ovate form, terminating in a
single radicle, the whole being three or four inches long, and
the thickest part about the size of a man's little finger ;
when fresh it is white, firm, and crisp ; when dried and
pounded, it makes a fine white meal. Its flavor is not unlike
that of aniseed [anise-seed], though less pungent. From
one to four of these knobbed roots are attached to a single
stem, which rises to the height of three or four feet, and is
jointed, smooth, cylindric, and has several small peduncles,
one at each joint above the sheathing leaf. Its color is
deep green, as is also that of the leaf, which is sheathing,
sessile, and polipartite [*sic*—read multipartite], the divisions
being long and narrow. The flowers, which are now in
bloom, are small and numerous, with white umbelliferous
petals ; there are no root-leaves. As soon as the seeds
have matured, the roots of the present year as well as the
stem decline, and are renewed in the succeeding spring
from the little knot which unites the roots. The sunflower

---

[7] The simple fact is that Indian women are no exception to the rule of easy
delivery of all mammals which live in a state of nature, not of art.

[8] *Carum gairdneri*, an umbelliferous plant closely related to caraway, *C.
carui*, the aromatic seeds of which are so well known. It is widely distributed
in the West, and is known by its Indian name of "yamp." Another species, *C.
kellogi*, occurs in California. The fascicled tubers are an important article of
food with various tribes of Indians.

is also abundant here ; the seeds, which are now ripe, are gathered in considerable quantities, and after being pounded and rubbed between smooth stones, form a kind of meal, which is a favorite dish among the Indians.

After dinner we continued our route, and were soon met by a party of young men on horseback, who turned with us and went to the village. As soon as we were within sight of it, Cameahwait requested that we would discharge our guns ; the men were therefore drawn up in a single rank, and gave (*p. 418*) a running fire of two rounds, to the great satisfaction of the Indians. We then proceeded to the camp, where we arrived about six o'clock, and were conducted to the leathern lodge in the center of 32 others made of brush. The baggage was arranged near this tent, which Captain Lewis occupied, and surrounded by those of the men, so as to secure it from pillage. This camp was in a beautiful smooth meadow near the [Lemhi] river, about three miles above the camp where we first visited these Indians. We here found Colter, who had been sent by Captain Clark with a note apprising us that there were no hopes of a passage by water, and that the most practicable route seemed to be that mentioned by his guide, toward the north. Whatever road we meant to take, it was now necessary to provide ourselves with horses ; we therefore informed Cameahwait of our intention of going to the great river beyond the mountains, and that we wished to purchase 20 more horses. He said the Minnetarees had stolen a great number of their horses this spring, but he still hoped he could spare us that number. In order not to lose the present favorable moment, and to keep the Indians as cheerful as possible, the violins were brought out and our men danced, to the great diversion of the Indians. This mirth was the more welcome because our situation was not precisely that which would most dispose us to gayety ; for we have only a little parched corn to eat, and our means of subsistence or of success depend on the wavering temper of the natives, who may change their minds to-morrow.

The Shoshonees are a small tribe of the nation called Snake Indians,[9] a vague denomination which embraces at once the inhabitants of the southern parts of the Rocky mountains and of the plains on each side. The Shoshonees with whom we now are amount to about 100 warriors, and three times that number of women and children. Within their own recollection they formerly lived in the plains, but they have been driven into the mountains by the Pawkees, or the roving Indians of the Sascatchawain, and (*p. 419*) are now obliged to visit, occasionally and by stealth, the country of their ancestors. Their lives are indeed migratory. From the middle of May to the beginning of September they reside on the waters of the Columbia, where they consider themselves perfectly secure from the Pawkees, who have never yet found their way to that retreat. During this time they subsist chiefly on salmon, and as that fish disappears on the approach of autumn, they are obliged to seek subsistence elsewhere. They then cross the ridge to the waters of the Missouri, down which they proceed slowly and

[9] For the modern scientific classification and nomenclature of all the Shoshonean Indians, see the note, *anteà*, p. 477. In the Statistical View, prepared by Lewis in 1804-05, while he was at the Mandans, and so before he had seen any Shoshones, the account is extremely defective, being based only on Indian information. The View presents them all as *Aliatans* (from Aliatan, their language), and divides them into three main tribes: 1. "Snake Indians," from F. Gens des Serpens (and elsewhere "Serpentine" Indians) of which So-so-na', So-so-bâ, and I'-â-kâr are given as native names of three tribes. These are located "among the Rocky mountains, on the heads of the Missouri, Yellow Stone and Platte rivers." 2. "Aliatans of the West," located "among the Rocky mountains, and in the plains at the heads of the Platte and Arkansas rivers." 3. "Aliatans La Plays" (*sic*, some mangling of a French term); location, "the mountains on the borders of New Mexico, and the extensive plains at the heads of the Arkansas and Red rivers." The remarks (item "S" of the schedule) on these three nations, respectively, are as follows (English ed. of 1807, pp. 36-38):

1. "ALIATANS, *Snake Indians*. These are a very numerous and well disposed people, inhabiting a woody and mountainous country ; they are divided into three large tribes, who wander a considerable distance from each other, and are called by themselves So-so-na, So-so'-bu-bar and I-a-kar ; these are again subdivided into smaller though independent bands, the names of which I have not yet learnt ; they raise a number of horses and mules which they trade with

cautiously, till they are joined near the Three Forks by other bands, either of their own nation or of the Flatheads, with whom they associate against the common enemy. Being now strong in numbers, they venture to hunt buffalo in the plains eastward of the mountains, near which they spend the winter, till the return of the salmon invites them to the Columbia. But such is their terror of the Pawkees, that as long as they can obtain the scantiest subsistence they do not leave the interior of the mountains; and as soon as they obtain a large stock of dried meat, they again retreat, thus alternately obtaining their food at the hazard of their lives, and hiding themselves to consume it. In this loose and wandering existence they suffer the extremes of want; for two-thirds of the year they are forced to live in the mountains, passing whole weeks without meat, and with nothing to eat but a few fish and roots. Nor can anything be imagined more wretched than their condition at the present time, when the salmon is fast retiring, when roots are becoming scarce, and they have not yet acquired strength to hazard an

the Crow Indians, or are stolen by the nations on the east of them. They maintain a partial trade with the Spaniards, from whom they obtain many articles of cloathing and ironmongery, but no warlike implements.

2. "[ALIATANS] *of the West.* These people also inhabit a mountainous country, and sometimes venture on the plains east of the Rocky mountains, about the head of the Arkansas river. They have more intercourse with the Spaniards of New Mexico, than the Snake Indians [have]. They are said to be very numerous and warlike, but are badly armed. The Spaniards fear these people, and therefore take the precaution not to furnish them with any warlike implements. In their present unarmed state, they frequently commit hostilities on the Spaniards. They raise a great many horses.

3. "[ALIATANS] *La Playes* [*sic*]. These principally inhabit the rich plains from the head of the Arkansas, embracing the heads of Red river, and extending with the mountains and high lands eastwardly, as far as it is known, toward the gulph of Mexico. They possess no firearms, but are warlike and brave. They are, as well as the other Aliatans, a wandering people. Their country abounds in wild horses, besides great numbers which they raise themselves. These people, and the west Aliatans [No. 2, above] might be induced to trade with us on the upper part of the Arkansas river. I do not believe that any of the Aliatans claim a country within any particular limits."

It is a band of the first above named tribe, "So-so-ná," of Snake Indians, that Lewis and Clark now proceed to describe with such particularity.

encounter with their enemies. So insensible are they, however, to these calamities, that the Shoshonees are not only cheerful but even gay; and their character, which is more interesting than that of any Indians we have seen, has in it much of the dignity of misfortune. In their intercourse with strangers they are frank and communicative, in their dealings perfectly fair, nor have we had (*p. 420*) during our stay with them any reason to suspect that the display of all our new and valuable wealth has tempted them into a single act of dishonesty. While they have generally shared with us the little they possess, they have always abstained from begging anything from us. With their liveliness of temper, they are fond of gaudy dresses, and of all sorts of amusements, particularly games of hazard; and like most Indians are fond of boasting of their own warlike exploits, whether real or fictitious.

In their conduct toward ourselves they were kind and obliging; and though on one occasion they seemed willing to neglect us, yet we scarcely knew how to blame the treatment by which we suffered, when we recollected how few civilized chiefs would have hazarded the comforts or the subsistence of their people for the sake of a few strangers. This manliness of character may cause, or it may be formed by, the nature of their government, which is perfectly free from any restraint. Each individual is his own master, and the only control to which his conduct is subjected is the advice of a chief, supported by his influence over the opinions of the rest of the tribe. The chief himself is in fact no more than the most confidential person among the warriors, a rank neither distinguished by any external honor, nor invested by any ceremony, but gradually acquired from the good wishes of his companions, by superior merit. Such an officer has therefore strictly no power; he may recommend or advise or influence, but his commands have no effect on those who incline to disobey, and who may at any time withdraw from their voluntary allegiance. His shadowy authority, which cannot survive the confidence which supports it, often decays with the personal vigor of the chief, or is transferred to some more fortunate or favorite hero.

In their domestic economy the man is equally sovereign. He is the sole proprietor of his wives and daughters, and can barter them away or dispose of them in any manner he may think proper.   The children are seldom correct- (*p. 421*) ed ; the boys, particularly, soon become their own masters ; they are never whipped, for they say that it breaks their spirit, and that after being flogged they never recover their independence of mind, even when they grow to manhood.   A plurality of wives is very common ; but these are not generally sisters, as among the Minnetarees and Mandans, but are purchased of different fathers.   The infant daughters are often betrothed by the father to men who are grown, either for themselves or for their sons, for whom they are desirous of providing wives.   The compensation to the father is usually made in horses or mules ; and the girl remains with her parents till the age of puberty, which is thirteen or fourteen, when she is surrendered to her husband. At the same time the father often makes a present to the husband equal to what he had formerly received as the price of his daughter, though this return is optional with her parent.   Sacajawea had been contracted for in this way before she was taken prisoner, and when we brought her back her betrothed was still living.   Although he was double the age of Sacajawea and had two other wives, he claimed her ; but on finding that she had a child by her new husband, Chaboneau, he relinquished his pretensions and said he did not want her.

The chastity of the women does not appear to be held in much estimation.   The husband will, for a trifling present, lend his wife for a night to a stranger, and the loan may be protracted by increasing the value of the present.   Yet, strange as it may seem, notwithstanding this facility, any connection of this kind not authorized by the husband is considered highly offensive, and quite as disgraceful to his character as the same licentiousness in civilized societies.

The Shoshonees are not so importunate in volunteering the services of their wives as we found the Sioux to be; indeed we observed among them some women who appeared to be held in more respect than those of any nation we had seen. But the mass of the females are condemned, (*p. 422*) as among all savage nations, to the lowest and most laborious drudgery.   When the tribe is stationary they collect roots and cook; they build huts, dress skins, and make clothing; collect wood and assist in taking care of the horses on the route; load the horses and have the charge of all the baggage.   The only business of the man is to fight; he therefore takes on himself the care of his horse, the companion of his warfare; but he will descend to no other labor than to hunt and to fish.   He would consider himself degraded by being compelled to walk any distance; were he so poor as to possess only two horses, he would ride the best of them, and leave the other for his wives and children and their baggage; if he have too many wives or too much baggage for the horse, the wives have no alternative but to follow him on foot; they are not, however, often reduced to these extremities, for the stock of horses is very ample.   Notwithstanding their losses this spring they still have at least 700, among which are about forty colts and half that number of mules. There are no horses here which can be considered as wild; we have seen two only, on this side of the Muscleshell river, which were without owners; and even those, though shy, showed every mark of having been once in the possession of man.   The original stock was procured from the Spaniards, but they now raise their own.   The horses are generally very fine, of a good size, vigorous, and patient of fatigue as well as hunger.   Each warrior has one or two tied to a stake near his hut both night and day, so as to be always prepared for action.   The mules are obtained in the course of trade from the Spaniards, with whose brands several of them are marked, or stolen from them by the frontier Indians.   They are the finest animals of that kind we have ever seen, and at this distance from the Spanish colonies are very highly valued. The worst are considered as worth the price of two horses, and a good mule cannot be obtained for less than three and sometimes four horses.

(*p. 423*) We saw a bridle-bit, stirrups, and several other articles which, like the mules, came from the Spanish colonies. The Shoshonees say that they can reach those settlements in ten days' march by the route of the Yellowstone river; but we readily perceive that the Spaniards are by no means favorites. They complain that the Spaniards refuse to let them have fire-arms, under pretense that these dangerous weapons will only induce them to kill each other. In the meantime, say the Shoshonees, they are left to the mercy of the Minnetarees, who, having arms, plunder them of their horses, and put them to death without mercy. " But this should not be," said Cameahwait fiercely ; " if we had guns, instead of hiding ourselves in the mountains and living like the bears on roots and berries, we would then go down and live in the buffalo country in spite of our enemies, whom we never fear when we meet on equal terms."

As war is the chief occupation, bravery is the first virtue among the Shoshonees. None can hope to be distinguished without having given proofs of it, nor can there be any preferment or influence among the nation, without some warlike achievement. Those important events which give reputation to a warrior, and entitle him to a new name, are : killing a white bear, stealing individually the horses of the enemy, leading a party who happen to be successful either in plundering horses or destroying the enemy, and lastly, scalping a warrior. These acts seem of nearly equal dignity, but the last, that of taking an enemy's scalp, is an honor quite independent of the act of vanquishing him. To kill your adversary is of no importance unless the scalp is brought from the field of battle ; were a warrior to slay any number of his enemies in action, and others were to obtain the scalps or first touch the dead, they would have all the honors, since they have borne off the trophy.

(*p. 424*) Although thus oppressed by the Minnetarees,

the Shoshonees are still a very military people. Their cold and rugged country inures them to fatigue; their long absti- nence makes them support the dangers of mountain warfare : and worn down as we saw them, by want of sustenance, they have a look of fierce and adventurous courage. The Sho- shonee warrior always fights on horseback; he possesses a few bad guns, which are reserved exclusively for war, but his common arms are the bow and arrow, a shield, a lance, and a weapon called by the Chippeways, by whom it was formerly used, the poggamoggon [described beyond]. The bow is made of cedar or pine, covered on the outer side with sinews and glue. It is about 2½ feet long, and does not differ in shape from those used by the Sioux, Mandans, and Minnetarees. Sometimes, however, the bow is made of a single piece of the horn of an elk, covered on the back like those of wood with sinews and glue, and occasionally ornamented by a strand wrought of porcupine-quills and sinews, which is wrapped round the horn near its two ends. The bows made of the horns of the bighorn are still more prized, and are formed by glueing flat pieces of the horn together, covering the back with sinews and glue, and loading the whole with an unusual quantity of ornaments. The arrows resemble those of the other Indians, except in being more slender than any we have seen. They are contained, with the implements for striking fire, in a narrow quiver formed of different kinds of skins, though that of the otter seems to be preferred. It is just long enough to protect the arrows from the weather, and is worn on the back by means of a strap passing over the right shoulder and under the left arm. The shield is a cir- cular piece of buffalo-hide about two feet four or five inches in diameter, ornamented with feathers and a fringe of dressed leather, and adorned or deformed with paintings of strange figures. The buffalo-hide is perfectly proof against any arrow, but in the minds of the Shoshonees its power to pro- tect them is (*p. 425*) chiefly derived from the virtues which are communicated to it by the old men and jugglers. To make a shield is indeed one of their most important ceremonies; it begins by a feast to which all the warriors, old men, and jugglers are invited. After the repast a hole is dug in the ground about 18 inches in depth and of the same diameter as the intended shield ; into this hole red-hot stones are thrown and water is poured over them, till they emit a very strong hot steam. The buffalo-skin, which must be the entire hide of a male two years old, never suffered to dry since it was taken from the animal, is now laid across the hole, with the fleshy side to the ground, and stretched in every direction by as many as can take hold of it. As the skin becomes heated, the hair separates and is taken off by hand ; till at last the skin is contracted into the compass designed for the shield. It is then placed on a hide prepared into parchment, and pounded during the rest of the festival by the bare heels of those who are invited to it. This operation sometimes continues for several days, after which it is delivered to the proprietor, and declared by the old men and jugglers to be a security against arrows—provided the feast has been satisfactory, against even the bullets of their enemies. Such is the delusion that many of the Indians implicitly believe that this ceremony has given to the shield supernatural powers, and that they have no longer to fear any weapons of their enemies.

The poggamoggon is an instrument consisting of a handle 22 inches long, made of wood, covered with dressed leather, about the size of a whip-handle; at one end is a thong of two inches in length, which is tied to a round stone weighing two pounds and held in a cover of leather; at the other end is a loop of the same material, which is passed round the wrist so as to secure the hold of the instrument, with which they strike a very severe blow.

Besides these weapons, they have a kind of armor something like a coat of mail, which is formed by a great many folds (*p. 426*) of dressed antelope-skins, united by means of a mixture of glue and sand. With this they cover their own bodies and those of their horses, and find it impervious to the arrow.

The caparison of their horses is a halter and a saddle. The first is either a rope of six or seven strands of buffalo-hair plaited or twisted together, about the size of a man's finger and of great strength ; or merely a thong of raw hide, made pliant by pounding and rubbing ; the first kind is much preferred. The halter is very long, and is never taken from the neck of the horse when in constant use. One end of it is first tied round the neck in a knot and then brought down to the under jaw, round which it is formed into a simple noose, passing through the mouth ; it is then drawn up on the right side and held by the rider in his left hand, while the rest trails after him to some distance. At other times the knot is formed at a little distance from one of the ends, so as to let that end serve as a bridle, while the other trails on the ground. With these cords dangling alongside of them the horse is put to his full speed without fear of falling, and when he is turned to graze the noose is merely taken from his mouth. The saddle is formed like the pack-saddles used by the French and Spaniards, of two flat, thin boards which fit the sides of the horse, and are kept together by two cross-pieces, one before and the other behind, which rise to a considerable height, ending sometimes in a flat point extending outward, and always making the saddle deep and narrow. Under this a piece of buffalo-skin, with the hair on, is placed so as to prevent the rubbing of the boards, and when they mount they throw a piece of skin or robe over the saddle, which has no permanent cover. When stirrups are used, they consist of wood covered with leather ; but stirrups and saddles are conveniences reserved for old men and women. The young warriors rarely use anything except a small leather pad stuffed with hair, and secured by a girth made of a leathern thong. In this way they ride with great expertness, and they have a particular dex-(*p. 427*) terity in catching the horse when he is running at large. If he will not immediately submit when they wish to take him, they make a noose in the rope, and although the horse may be at a distance, or even running, rarely fail to fix it on his neck; and such is the docility of the animal that, however unruly he may seem, he surrenders as soon as he feels the rope on him. This cord is so useful in this way that it is never dispensed with, even when they use the Spanish bridle, which they prefer and always procure when they have it in their power. The horse becomes almost an object of attachment; a favorite is frequently painted and has his ears cut into various shapes; the mane and tail, which are never drawn or trimmed, are decorated with feathers of birds; and sometimes a warrior suspends at the breast of his horse the finest ornaments he possesses.

Thus armed and mounted the Shoshonee is a formidable enemy, even with the feeble weapons which he is obliged to use. When they attack at full speed they bend forward and cover their bodies with the shield, while with the right hand they shoot under the horse's neck.

The only articles of metal which the Shoshonees possess are a few bad knives, some brass kettles, some bracelets or arm-bands of iron and brass, a few buttons worn as ornaments in their hair, one or two spear-heads about a foot in length, and some heads for arrows made of iron and brass. All these they obtained in trading with the Crow or Rocky Mountain Indians, who live on the Yellowstone. The few bridle-bits and stirrups they procured from the Spanish colonies.

The instrument which supplies the place of a knife among them is a piece of flint of no regular form, the sharp part of it not more than one or two inches long; the edge of this is renewed, and the flint itself is formed into heads for arrows, by means of the point of a deer or elk horn, an instrument which they use with great art and ingenuity. They have no axes or hatchets, all the wood being cut with (*p. 428*) flint or elk-horn, the latter of which is always used as a wedge in splitting wood. Their utensils consist, besides the brass kettles, of pots in the form of a jar, made either of earth or of a stone found in the hills between Madison and Jefferson rivers, which, though soft and white in its natural state, becomes very hard and black after exposure to the fire.   The horns of the buffalo and bighorn supply them with spoons.

The fire is always kindled by means of a blunt arrow and a piece of well-seasoned wood of a soft, spongy kind, such as the willow or cottonwood.[10]

The Shoshonees are of diminutive stature, with thick ankles, flat feet, and crooked legs, and are, generally speaking, worse formed than any nation of Indians we have seen. Their complexion resembles that of the Sioux, and is darker than that of the Minnetarees, Mandans, or Shawnees.   The hair in both sexes is suffered to fall loosely over the face and down the shoulders; some men, however, divide it by means of thongs of dressed leather or otter-skin into two equal cues, which hang over the ears and are drawn down in front of the body; but at the present moment, when the nation is afflicted by the loss of so many relations killed in war, most of them have their hair cut quite short in the neck, and Cameahwait has the hair cut short all over his head, this being the customary mourning for deceased kindred.

The dress of the men consists of a robe, a tippet, a shirt, long leggings, and moccasins.   The robes are formed most commonly of the skins of antelope, bighorn, or deer, though, when it can be procured, buffalo-hide is preferred.   Sometimes they are made of beaver, moonax,[11] or small wolves, and frequently, during the summer, of elk-skin.   These are dressed with the hair on, and reach about as low as the middle of the leg.   They are worn loosely over the shoulders, the sides being at pleasure either left open or drawn together by the hand, and in cold weather kept close by a girdle round the waist.   This robe answers the pur- (*p. 429*)

[10] The arrow being held upright upon a horizontal piece of the other wood, and twirled rapidly with reciprocal motion, in the palms of the hands, till the continued friction generates heat enough to make a spark.

[11] *Sic*—read monax, and understand not the common marmot or woodchuck, *Arctomys monax*, but the yellow-bellied marmot of the Rocky mountains, *Arctomys flaviventer*.

pose of a cloak during the day, and at night is their only covering.

The tippet is the most elegant article of Indian dress we have ever seen. The neck or collar of it is a strip about four or five inches wide, cut from the back of the otter-skin, the nose and eyes forming one extremity, the tail another. This being dressed with the fur on, they attach to one edge of it 100 to 250 little rolls of ermine-skin, beginning at the ear, and proceeding toward the tail. These ermine-skins are the same kind of narrow strips from the back of that animal, which are sewed round a small cord of twisted silk-grass, thick enough to make the skin taper toward the tail which hangs from the end, and are generally about the size of a large quill. These are tied at the head into little bundles of two, three, or more, according to the caprice of the wearer, and then suspended from the collar; and a broad fringe of ermine-skin is fixed so as to cover the parts where they unite, which might have a coarse appearance. Little tassels of fringe of the same materials are also fastened to the extremities of the tail, so as to show its black color to greater advantage. The center of the collar is further orna-mented with the shells of the pearl-oyster.[12] Thus adorned, the collar is worn close around the neck, and the little rolls fall down over the shoulders nearly to the waist, so as to form a sort of short cloak, which has a very handsome appearance. These tippets are very highly esteemed, and are given or disposed of on important occasions only. The ermine is the fur known to the northwest traders by the name of the white weasel, but is the genuine ermine;[13] and

[12] Doubtless bits of abalone-shell (species of *Haliotis*), highly lustrous, common on the Pacific coast of the United States, and an article of commerce which these Indians could procure indirectly from the Spaniards.

[13] The true ermine of Europe, Asia, and North America is the stoat, *Putorius erminea*, which in winter is pure white, or white with a slight yellow tint, except the black tip of the tail. The species actually in view here is doubtless *P. longicauda*, technically distinct, but so much like *P. erminea* as to be prac-tically the same animal for ornamental and commercial purposes. See note [14], p. 191.

by encouraging the Indians to take them, might no doubt be rendered a valuable branch of trade. These animals must be very abundant, for the tippets are in great numbers, and the construction of each requires at least 100 skins.

The shirt is a covering of dressed skin without the hair, made of the hide of the antelope, deer, bighorn, or (*p. 430*) elk, though the last is more rarely used than any other for this purpose. It fits the body loosely, and reaches halfway down the thigh. The aperture at the top is wide enough to admit the head, and has no collar, but is either left square, or most frequently terminates in the tail of the animal, which is left entire, so as to fold outward, though sometimes the edges are cut into a fringe, and ornamented with quills of the porcupine. The seams of the shirt are on the sides, richly fringed and adorned with porcupine-quills, to within five or six inches of the sleeve, where the seam is left open, as is also the under side of the sleeve from the shoulder to the elbow, whence it fits closely round the arm as low as the wrist, and has no fringe like the side-seam and the under part of the sleeve above the elbow. It is kept up by wide shoulder-straps, on which the manufacturer displays his taste by the variety of figures wrought with porcupine-quills of different colors, and sometimes with beads when they can be obtained. The lower end of the shirt retains the natural shape of the fore legs and neck of the skin, with the addition of a slight fringe; the hair too is left on the tail and near each hoof, part of which last is retained and split into a fringe.

The leggings are generally made of antelope-skins, dressed without the hair, and with the legs, tail, and neck hanging to them. Each legging is formed of a skin nearly entire, and reaches from the ankle to the upper part of the thigh; the legs of the skin being tucked before and behind under a girdle round the waist. It fits closely to the leg, the tail being worn upward; the neck, highly ornamented with fringe and porcupine-quills, drags on the ground behind the heels. As the legs of the animal are tied round the girdle, the wide part of the skin is drawn so high as to conceal the parts usually kept from view; in which respect their dress is much more decent than that of any nation of Indians on the Missouri. The seams of the leggings down the sides are also fringed and ornamented, and occasionally (*p. 431*) decorated with tufts of hair taken from enemies whom they have slain. In making all these dresses, their only thread is the sinew taken from the back and loins of deer, elk, buffalo, or other animal.

The moccasin is of the deer-, elk-, or buffalo-skin, dressed without the hair; though in winter they use the buffalo-skin with the hairy side inward, as do most of the Indians who inhabit the buffalo country. Like the Mandan moccasin, it is made with a single seam on the outer edge, and sewed up behind, a hole being left at the instep to admit the foot. It is variously ornamented with figures wrought with porcupine-quills, and sometimes the young men most fond of dress cover it with the skin of a polecat, and trail at their heels the tail of the animal.

The dress of the women consists of the same articles as that of their husbands. The robe, though smaller, is worn in the same way; the moccasins are precisely similar. The shirt or chemise, which reaches halfway down the leg, is in the same form, except that there is no shoulder-strap, the seam coming quite up to the shoulder; though for women who give suck both sides are open almost down to the waist. It is also ornamented in the same way with the addition of little patches of red cloth, edged round with beads at the skirts. The chief ornament is over the breast, where there are curious figures made with the usual luxury of porcupine-quills. Like the men they have a girdle round the waist, and when either sex wishes to disengage the arm, it is drawn up through the hole near the shoulder, and the lower part of the sleeve is thrown behind the body.

Children alone wear beads around their necks; grown persons of both sexes prefer them suspended in little bunches from the ear, sometimes intermixed with triangular pieces of the shell of the pearl-oyster. Sometimes the men tie them in the same way to the hair of the forepart of the head, and increase the beauty of it by adding the wings and tails of birds, particularly the feathers of the great eagle (*p. 432*) or calumet-bird, of which they are extremely fond. The collars are formed either of sea-shells procured from their relations to the southwest, or of the sweet-scented grass which grows in the neighborhood, and which they twist or plait together, to the thickness of a man's finger, and then cover with porcupine-quills of various colors. The first of these is worn indiscriminately by both sexes, the second is principally confined to the men, while a string of elks' tusks is a collar almost peculiar to the women and children. Another collar worn by the men is a string of round bones like the joints of a fish's back; but the collar most preferred, because most honorable, is one of the claws of the brown bear. To kill one of these animals is as distinguished an achievement as to have put to death an enemy, and in fact, with their weapons, is a more dangerous trial of courage. These claws are suspended on a thong of dressed leather, and being ornamented with beads, are worn round the neck by the warriors with great pride. The men also frequently wear the skin of a fox, or a strip of otter-skin, round the head in the form of a bandeau.

In short, the dress of the Shoshonees is as convenient and decent as that of any Indians we have seen.

They have many more children than might have been expected, considering their precarious means of support and their wandering life. This inconvenience is, however, balanced by the wonderful felicity with which their females undergo the operation of childbirth. In the most advanced state of pregnancy they continue their usual occupations, which are scarcely interrupted longer than the mere time of bringing the child into the world.

The old men are few in number, and do not appear to be treated with much tenderness or respect.

The tobacco used by the Shoshonees is not cultivated

among them, but obtained from the Indians of the Rocky mountains, and from some of the bands of their own nation who live south of them.   It is the same plant which is in use among the Minnetarees, Mandans, and Ricaras.

(*p. 433*) Their chief intercourse with other nations seems to consist in their association with other Snake Indians, and with the Flatheads when they go eastward to hunt buffalo, or during the occasional visits made by the Flatheads to the waters of the Columbia for the purpose of fishing.   Their intercourse with the Spaniards is much more rare; it furnishes them with a few articles, such as mules, some bridles and other ornaments for horses, which, as well as some of their kitchen utensils, are also furnished by the bands of Snake Indians from the Yellowstone.   The pearl ornaments which they esteem so highly come from other bands, whom they represent as their friends and relations, living to the southwest, beyond the barren plains on the other side of the mountains.   These relations, they say, inhabit a good country, abounding with elk, deer, bear, and antelope, where horses and mules are much more abundant than they are here—or, to use their own expression, " as numerous as the grass of the plains."

The names of these Indians vary in the course of their life. Originally given in childhood, from the mere necessity of distinguishing objects, or from some accidental resemblance to external objects, the young warrior is impatient to change it by some achievement of his own.   Any important event—the stealing of horses, the scalping of an enemy, or the killing of a brown bear—entitles him at once to a new name, which he then selects for himself, and it is confirmed by the nation.   Sometimes the two names subsist together; thus, the chief Cameahwait, which means " One Who Never Walks," has the war-name of Tooettecone, or " Black Gun," which he acquired when he first signalized himself. As each new action gives a warrior a right to change his name, many of them have several in the course of their lives. To give to a friend one's own name is an act of high courtesy, and a pledge, like that of pulling off the moccasin, of sincerity and hospitality. The chief in this way gave his name to Cap- (*p. 434*) tain Clark when he first arrived, and he was afterward known among the Shoshonees by the name of Cameahwait.[14]

The diseases incident to this state of life may be supposed to be few, and chiefly the results of accidents. We were particularly anxious to ascertain whether they had any knowledge of the venereal disorder. After inquiring by means of the interpreter and his wife, we learnt that they sometimes suffered from it, and that they most usually die with it ; nor could we discover what was their remedy. It is possible that this disease may have reached them in their circuitous communications with the whites through the intermediate Indians ; but the situation of the Shoshonees is so insulated that it is not probable that it could have reached them in this way, and the existence of such a disorder in the Rocky mountains seems rather a proof of its being aboriginal.

[14] Text variant from codex here : see note [1] p. 509.

CHAPTER XVII.

IN THE BITTER ROOT MOUNTAINS AND DOWN THE KOOSKOOSKEE.

Discussion of a route—More horses purchased—The best portage over the Great Divide from the forks of the Jefferson to the east fork of Lewis' river—Captain Clark rejoins the main party, Aug. 29th—They take leave of the Shoshones and proceed—Salmon creek— Tower creek—They go up Fish creek—West branch of Fish creek—Delays and accidents— Last thermometer broken—Heavy snow—Large camp of Ootlashoot Indians—Council held with them—Their appearance and language—Clark's river reached and named—Down Clark's river—Several creeks passed—A species of prickly-pear—Scattering creek—A large road in the valley of Clark's river—Direct route to headwaters of the Missouri, which might be reached, hence four days' journey, at a point about 30 miles above the Gates of the Rocky mountains—Traveler's-rest creek—Hunters sent out—Below Traveler's-rest creek is a river from the east by which Indians go to the Missouri—Tushepaw Indians— Traveler's-rest creek forks—West fork taken—A mountain crossed—Horses strayed—Game scarce—Hot springs—Sources of this creek left and Glade creek followed along its right side to its forks—Abandoned Tushepaw camp and fish-weirs—Difficult mountains crossed— Supposed Kooskooskee river—The party reduced to killing a horse for food—A creek therefore named Colt-killed—Rugged mountains on every hand—Snow all day—Out of pro-visions—Another horse killed—Captain Clark forges ahead with six hunters to Hungry creek—The main party follows—Captain Clark goes up Hungry creek and over mountains beyond it—The main party follows—Captain Clark reaches a large creek, which he descends to an Indian village—Sumptuously treated by the chief—The main party follows—A horse missing—Vegetable productions—Captain Clark sick from having enough to eat—Chopun-nish or Pierced-nose Indians—The chief's information as to the route—Men sent back to Captain Lewis' party with provisions—Captain Clark proceeds to the camp of Chief Twisted-hair—The main party reaches the village—Twisted-hair's elk-skin chart of the Kooskooskee and its tributaries—Council with the Indians—Presents given—Provisions purchased— Captain Lewis and others sick from having enough to eat—Captain Clark seeks timber for canoes—The party proceeds to build canoes—Visited by many Indians from below—Their 38 horses branded and intrusted to Indians—The canoes launched, and loaded—Down the Kooskooskee—Shoals and rapids—A canoe founders—Desertion of the old Shoshone guide and his son—A crazy squaw—Rugged rapids named—The party reduced to eating dogs, which they relish—Confluence of the Kooskooskee with a larger river from the south—This is the main stream of Lewis' river—Description of the two rivers—Account of the Chopunnish Indians—Three kinds of prickly-pear—The Expedition has not reached the Columbia river on Oct. 10th, 1805.

TUESDAY, August 27th, 1805. We were now occupied in determining our route and procuring horses from the Indians. The old guide who had been sent on by Captain Clark confirmed, by means of our interpreter, what he had already asserted of a road up Berry creek which would lead to Indian establishments on another branch of the Columbia; his reports, however, were contradicted by all the Shoshonees. This representation we ascribed to a wish on their part to keep us with them during the winter, as well for the protection we might afford against their enemies as for the purpose of consuming our merchandise among them; and as the old man promised to conduct us himself, that route seemed to be the most eligible. We were able to procure some horses, though not enough for all our purposes. This traffic, and our inquiries and councils with the Indians, consumed the remainder of the day.

August 28th.[1] The purchase of horses was resumed, and our stock raised to 22. Having now crossed more than once [Captain Lewis thrice, Captain Clark once] the country which separates the headwaters of the Missouri from those of the Columbia, we can designate the easiest and most expeditious route for a portage. It is as follows:[2]

[1] This day Sergeant Gass, who had been on Captain Clark's reconnoissance, returned to Captain Lewis' camp at the upper Shoshone village, and then went back to his own at the lower village. See note at previous entry of Aug. 28th.

[2] This most important itinerary stands as follows in Clark G 90:

"Course Distance &c Over the Portage from the Waters of the Missouri to the Waters of the Columbia River.—

"N. 60° W. 5 miles to a Point of a hill on the right Passed Several points of high land bottom wide only 3 small trees

"S. 80° W. 10 miles to a place the high land approach within 200 yards, Creek 10 yds. wide

"S.W. 5 miles to a narrow part of the bottom passed a Creek on each Side, a place the Indians were massicreed, a road coms in on the right

"S. 70° W. 2 miles to a Creek on the right

"S. 80° W. 3 miles to a rockey point opsd. [opposite] a Pine thicket on the left, passed a run from the right

"West 3 miles to the head Spring of the Missouri near the top of a dividing mountain at a gap

"S. 80° W. 6 miles to a run from the right, passed Several Small Streams & Spring runs running to my left, and down a Drean [drain]

"N. 80° W. 4 miles to the East fork [Lemhi river] of the Lewis's River 40 yds. wide a an Snake Indian Camp of 25 Lodges passed over hilley land all the way from the dividing ridge.

"Miles 38."

For the days when Captain Clark was making this Pass the entries are as follows, Clark G 68–70:

Aug. 18th. "We proceeded on thro' a wide leavel Vallee without wood except Willows & Srubs for 15 miles and Encamped at a place the high lands approach

(*p. 436*) From the forks of the [Jefferson] river N. 60° W.
five miles, to the point of a hill on the right; then S. 80° W.
ten miles, to a spot where the creek is ten miles [yards] wide,
and the highlands approach within 200 yards; S.W. five
miles, to a narrow part of the bottom; then turning S. 70°
W. two miles, to a creek on the right; thence S. 80° W.
three miles, to a rocky point opposite a thicket of pines on
the left; from that place W. three miles, to the gap where is
the fountain of the Missouri; on leaving this fountain S. 80°
W. six miles, across the dividing ridge [and down], to a run
from the right, passing several small streams; [thence] N.

within 200 yards in 2 points the River [Prairie creek] here only 10 yards wide
Several Small Streams branching out on each side below. . .   The Course from
the forks is West 9 miles N. 60° W. 6 miles.   [These 15 miles are elsewhere
made N. 60° W. 5 miles+S. 80° W. 10 miles]. . ."

Aug. 19th. " Proceeded on through a wide leavel vallee . . . this vallee continues 5 miles & and then becoms narrow, the beaver has Damed up the River
in many places we proceeded on up the main branch with a gradeal assent to the
head and passed over a low mountain and Decended a Steep Decent to a butifull
Stream, passed over a Second hill of a verry Steep assent & thro' a hilley cointrey
for 8 miles an Encamped on a Small Stream. . . ."

Aug. 20th. " Procceded on thro' a hilley countrey to the camp of the Indians
on a branch of the Columbia River, . . ."

Lewis' river is named in these terms : " I shall in justice to Capt. Lewis who
was the first white man ever on this fork of the Columbia call this Louis's river,"
Clark G 75.   The name stands elsewhere Lewis's, once " Louises."

I was surprised to find that no map charts Shoshone cove, Prairie creek, and
the so-called Lemhi Pass, correctly, and was therefore obliged to construct a map
for myself, from Clark's courses and distances.   I find the closest approximation
to the facts in the case on the Milit. map Dept. Dakota, 1891, and G. L. O. map,
1892.   Comparing my chart, projected on a scale of two miles to the inch, and
filled in with every detail given by Clark, I can identify Swartz, Painter, Coyote,
Bloody Dick, and Trail creeks (besides the large southern branch on which is
Horse Prairie town) of the maps just said ; and Trail creek leads up to the "fountain-head of the Missouri," not more than five miles south of 45° N.   Assuming the " forks of the Missouri," *i. e.*, the mouth of Prairie creek, to be on or very
close to 45° N.—and all my maps agree on this point—I provisionally determine the latitude of the fountain to be 44° 55′ 33″ (without correction for the magnetic variation).   Prairie creek is a nearly west-east stream on the whole, from
source to mouth, though very crooked in meandering Shoshone cove.   But the
maps will have it that this creek heads much further south.   Some make the Pass S.
W., and then run a stream N.W. up from the Lemhi to the Pass to connect with the
source of Prairie creek.   This is unquestionably wrong.   Observe Clark's last three

80° W. four miles, over hilly ground, to the east [Lemhi] fork of Lewis' river, which is here 40 yards wide.

August 29th.[3] Captain Clark joined us this morning, and we continued our bargains for horses. The late misfortunes of the Shoshonees make the price higher than common, so that one horse [which Captain Clark purchased] cost a pistol, 100 balls, some powder, and a knife; another was exchanged for a musket; in this way we obtained 29. The horses themselves are young and vigorous; but they are very poor, and most of them have sore backs in consequence of the roughness of the Shoshonee saddle. We are,

courses toward the Pass (S. 70° W. 2 miles ; S. 80° W. 3 miles ; W. 3 miles) ; see how little southing he makes in these eight miles, and note that he comes due *west* to the Pass. From the Pass toward the Lemhi he goes *west* six miles with only 10° southing ; then *west* again four miles with 10° *northing*—these ten miles being practically due west. For 18 miles, then, from Shoshone cove, over the divide, and down to the Lemhi, Clark went west (by compass), with scarcely any southing. Then he did not *follow down* any creek from the Pass to the Lemhi. He *crossed* "several runs," all going to his left ; then he *crossed* a larger one, also going to the left. I believe that that stream which the engravers run up from the Lemhi river N.E. to the Pass is a map-myth, which ought to be called Ghost creek. Nobody knows what its name is. On applying for a name to Mr. Henry Gannett, Chief Topographer of the U. S. Geological Survey, he replies : " I find no name for the small stream of the Lemhi river which flows out of the so-called Lemhi Pass, . . . I do not believe that a name could be found on any map " (letter of Feb. 21st, 1893). When my Ghost creek, which Clark crossed but never went down, in going from the Pass to the Lemhi, is properly located, it will be found to head north of 45°, and flow southward along the main divide, before it curves westward to join the Lemhi river, near the present site of Fort Lemhi, but well within the northern boundary of the Lemhi Indian Reservation.

³ " I left our baggage in possession of 2 men and proceeded on up [from the lower Shoshone village] to join Capt. Lewis at the upper village," Clark G 91.

Gass, p. 128, enters to-day : "*Thursday* 29*th*. Captain Clarke and all the men except myself and another, who remained to keep camp and prepare pack-saddles, went up to Captain Lewis' camp. While I lay here to-day, one of the natives showed me their method of producing fire, which is somewhat curious. They have two sticks ready for the operation, one about 9 and the other 18 inches long. The short stick they lay down flat and rub [twirl] the end of the other upon it in a perpendicular direction for a few minutes ; and the friction raises a kind of dust, which in a short time takes fire." I first witnessed this operation among the Yavasupai Indians in Cataract cañon, a side cañon of the Grand Cañon of the Colorado, in Arizona, in 1879. The longer stick is of very hard wood, like the shaft of an arrow in caliber ; the other is broad and

therefore, afraid of loading them too heavily, and are anxious to obtain one at least for each man, to carry the baggage or the man himself, and in the last resource to serve as food; but with all our exertions we could not provide all our men with horses. We have, however, been fortunate in obtaining for the last three days a sufficient supply of flesh, our hunters having killed two or three deer every day.

August 30th. The weather was fine ; having now made all our purchases, we loaded our horses and prepared to start. The greater part of the band, who had delayed their journey on our account, were also ready to depart. We took leave of the Shoshonees, who set out on their visit to the Missouri at the same time that we, accompanied by the old guide, his four sons, and another Indian, began (*p. 437*) the descent of the [Lemhi] river, along the same road which Captain Clark had previously pursued. After riding twelve miles we camped[4] on the south bank of this river, and as the hunters had brought in three deer early in the morning, we did not feel the want of provisions.

August 31st.[5] At sunrise we resumed our journey, and

flat ; both are of course quite dry. In time the flat piece, if often used, gets a number of little burnt holes, each one showing where fire had been made. The friction is increased by a little dry sand. The upright stick is twirled between the palms of the hand, rapidly, back and forth. As soon as a spark appears it is blown by the breath, till strong enough to set fire to other bits of wood.

[4] This camp must be fixed, or we shall be lost to-morrow. It is on the south bank of the Lemhi river, twelve miles by text and codex from the upper Shoshone village whence the Expedition started this morning. It is therefore above the lower Shoshone village (where Gass and another are to-day, to be picked up as the Expedition comes along to-morrow) ; it is at or very near Captain Clark's camp of Aug. 20th ; and it is about eight miles above the forks of Salmon river.

[5] To-day's itinerary is simply unintelligible. To follow the text literally would be a journey of some 70 miles, from Salmon creek to " Berry " creek, and back to Tower creek. Mr. Biddle did a very rare if not unique thing for him—he " pied " two creeks. " Berry " creek is over 30 miles from any point of to-day's march, and should not appear in the text at all. It slipped in here by sheer inadvertence ; there is not a word about it in the codex—though there is a passage in Clark G 93 (see below) where I can see just how Homer nodded for a

halted for three hours on Salmon creek, to let the horses graze. We then proceeded to the stream called Berry [read Tower] creek, 18 miles from the camp of last night. As we passed along, the valleys and prairies were on fire in several places, in order to collect the bands of the Shoshonees and the Flatheads, for their journey to the Missouri. The weather was warm and sultry; but the only inconvenience which we apprehend is a dearth of food, of which we had to-day an abundance, having procured a deer, a goose, one duck, and a prairie-fowl. On reaching Tower creek we left the former track of Captain Clark, and began to explore the new route, which is our last hope of getting out of the

moment, and wrote "Berry" for Tower. By referring back to our text for Clark's reconnoissance of Aug. 23d (p. 533), we find him on Berry creek at the very terminus of his 70-mile trip. He goes up it six miles, then passes to the left one mile, to a point where he views the further course of Salmon river for 20 miles ; then he comes back to Berry creek, camps there, and on the 24th begins his return. He calls it Berry creek, because he had nothing to eat but some berries. Biddle has Berry creek all right there ; it is the only creek Clark named for that reconnoissance, and he did not give it any name till he revised his manuscript at St. Louis, after 1806 ! This I know, because it is a red-ink interlineation in the codex, in the single place where "Berry" is written (G 81). There the codex speaks of a road up it, etc., being that which Captain Clark took Aug. 23d. Now, on Aug. 31st, the Expedition takes a road up *Tower* creek ; and in a sad moment Biddle slips in "Berry" creek, to the confusion of all previous commentators. Clark G 93 confirms this correction, and makes the route of Aug. 31st perfectly clear : " Set out before Sun rise, as we passed the lodges [lower Shoshone village on the Lemhi] at which place I had encamped for thre nights [Aug. 26th, 27th, 28th] and left 2 men [Gass and another], those 2 men joined us, and we proceeded on in the same rout I decended the 21st Instant. halted 3 hours on Sammon creek to Let our horses graze. . . we proceeded on the road on which I had decended as far as the 1st run [*i. e.*, Tower creek. Here is where Biddle tripped, and sent the whole Expedition to-day as far as Clark had descended Salmon river on his whole reconnoissance, *i. e.*, to Berry creek!] below [Salmon creek, on the right], & left the road [along Salmon river] and proceeded up the run [Tower creek] in a tolerable road 4 miles & Encamped."

The "Salmon creek" of the text must of course not be confounded with Salmon *river*. It is a considerable affluent of the latter, on the right, some six miles below the forks. It is so called because here Captain Clark got his 2½ foot salmon, Aug. 21st (p. 528). Tower creek is the next affluent of Salmon river, on the right. It is named from a "remarkable rock resembling Perimeds [pyramids] on the Left Side," two or three miles from its mouth, Clark G 96. By text and

mountains. For four miles the road, which is tolerably plain, led us along Berry [read Tower] creek to some old Indian lodges, where we camped for the night.

Sunday, September 1st, 1805. We followed the same road, which here left the [Tower] creek and turned to the north-west across the hills. During all day we were riding over these hills, from which are many drains and small streams running into the [Salmon] river to the left, and at the distance of 18 miles came to a large creek, called Fish[6] creek, emptying into the Columbia [*i. e.*, Salmon river], which is about six miles from us. It had rained in the course of the day, and commenced raining again toward evening. We therefore determined not to leave the low grounds to-night, and after going up Fish creek four miles, formed our camp. The country over which we passed is well watered, but poor

codex to-day's march is 18 miles to the mouth of Tower creek. Nearly half of this way is along the Lemhi ; so Tower creek discharges into Salmon river nine or ten miles below the forks. It should thus be identifiable, in connection with the pyramidal rock formation which the codex gives ; but its present name I have not learned. Salmon creek may be the one now called Carmen. On either Salmon or Tower creek is now a place called Boyle's ; which I should not be surprised to discover as the spot where the Expedition camps this Aug. 31st, 1805. To complete the record of this unlucky day, I transcribe Gass, p. 128 :

" *Saturday* 31*st*. They all [the main party] came down to our camp [where Gass had stayed with one man], and we proceeded on [down the Lemhi river] with 27 horses and one mule. Our old guide, after consulting with the Indians, thought it was better to go along the north side of the Columbia [*i. e.*, the Lemhi and Salmon], than on the south side. We therefore proceeded down, the same way Captain Clarke had been before, 30 [read 18] miles, and then turned up a [Tower] creek that comes in from the north, and camped on it about 3 miles and a half from the mouth."

[6] From the Indian fishing-camp Captain Clark had observed at its mouth, Aug. 22d and 25th, when he passed each way (see p. 530). This is the largest tributary of Salmon river from the north for many miles, now known as the North fork of that river. It falls in nearly opposite a corresponding stream from the south, called Napias creek. The cross-country route of to-day cannot be disposed of in one short paragraph, if we are to trail the Expedition through these mountains. Starting from a point four miles up Tower creek, Clark G 96 may be edited as follows : N. 80° W. 1½ m. to top of a high hill. N. 65° W. 1½ m. to top of a hill, passing heads of a drain to our left. N. 55° W. 3½ m. to top of a high hill, past two forks of a creek, 1st large and bold, 2d small. S. 80° W. 1½ m. down a ravine to a run. N. 80° W. 3½ m. to top of a high hill, passing a

and rugged or stony, except the bottoms of Fish creek, and even these are narrow. Two men were sent to purchase fish of the Indians at the mouth of the creek, and with the dried fish (*p. 438*) which they obtained, and a deer and a few salmon killed by the party, we were still well supplied. Two bears also were wounded, but we could procure neither of them.

September 2d. This morning all the Indians left us, except the old guide, who now conducted us up Fish creek. At 1½ miles we passed a branch of the river coming in through a low ground covered with pines on the left ; 2½ miles further is a second branch from the right ; after continuing our route along the hills covered with pines, and a low ground of the same growth, we arrived, at the distance of 3½ miles, at the forks of the creek.[7] The road which we

branch at ¼ of a mile, and a hill at 1 mile. N. 35° W. 2½ m. to top of a high hill. N. 25° W. 1½ m. to ditto, passing a branch to the left at ½ a mile. N. 80° W. 2½ m. descending a steep winding hill to Fish creek. N. 12° W. 2 m. up this creek to a bluff point. Total 20 miles. On plotting these courses and distances on a sufficiently large scale (mile to inch), I find the zigzag line to tally wonderfully well with the best map before me. The route is about W. N. W., and corresponds in general, though not in detail, to the present road from Boyle's (see last note) to Gibbonsville (on or near main forks of Fish creek) ; but strikes Fish creek lower down—only eight miles above its mouth, and 7½ below its main forks. The Expedition crosses four streams making to the left, which will be found charted, perhaps not by name, on a sufficiently good map. These correspond to the four " spurs of mountains " which Captain Clark crossed over on Aug. 21st, and two of them are the " two bold running streams " of the text of that date.

The way hence to a head of Traveler's-rest creek, on the summit of the Bitter-root mountains (Sept. 13th), is as plain as a turnpike flanked with telegraph-poles.

[7] Locality of Gibbonsville. The " east " fork of Fish creek is now called Datang or Datongo creek. It comes from the N. E., and the road which the text mentions as going up its east side " to the Missouri " leads to Big Hole Pass, over the main divide, to the head of Pioneer creek, a side-source of Big Hole or Wisdom river, and so to the Missouri watershed. About the mouth of Pioneer creek was the noted battle of the Big Hole, as it is called in military circles, Aug. 9th and 10th, 1877. Captain Clark will pass over this battle-ground, or close by it, on his return trip in 1806. The lower branch of Fish creek, which the text mentions as coming from the right hand, is now called Sheep creek. It runs about west from the main divide, to join Fish creek. The " west " fork of Fish creek, up which the Expedition now proceeds to cut their way, takes them toward the crest

were following now turned up the east side of these forks, and, as our guide informed us, led to the Missouri. We were therefore left without any track; but as no time was to be lost we began to cut our road up the west branch of the creek. This we effected with much difficulty; the thickets of trees and brush through which we were obliged to cut our way required great labor; the road itself was over the steep and rocky sides of the hills, where the horses could not move without danger of slipping down, while their feet were bruised by the rocks and stumps of trees. Accustomed as these animals were to this kind of life, they suffered severely; several of them fell to some distance down the sides of the hills, some turned over with the baggage, one was crippled, and two gave out, exhausted with fatigue. After crossing the creek several times we at last made five [read 7½] miles, with great fatigue and labor, and camped on the left side of the creek in a small stony low ground. It was not, however, till after dark that the whole party was collected; and then, as it rained and we had killed nothing, we passed an uncomfortable night. The party had been too busily occupied with the horses to make any hunting excursion; and though, as we came along Fish creek, we saw many beaver-dams, we saw none of the animals themselves.

(*p. 439*) *September* 3*d*. The horses were very stiff and weary. We sent back two men for the load of the horse which had been crippled yesterday, and which we had been forced to leave two miles behind. On their return we set out at eight o'clock and proceeded up the creek, making a passage through the brush and timber along its borders. The country is generally supplied with pine, and in the low grounds is a great abundance of fir-trees and underbrush. The [Bitter-root] mountains are high and rugged; those to

of the Bitter-root mountains. By Clark G 97 they go N. 60° W. 2½ m., N. 35° W. 3 m., N. 50° W. 2 m., and thus make 7½ miles (not "five" as per text); at 6½ miles up this fork they pass a run on the right hand (now called Pierce creek); they camp on the left hand side or right bank of this fork of Fish creek; total miles to-day, 15.

the east of us are covered with snow. With all our precautions the horses were very much injured in passing over the ridges and steep points of the hills; to add to the difficulty, at the distance of 11 miles the high mountains closed [in on] the creek, so that we were obliged to leave the creek to the right and cross the mountain [7,000 feet or more] abruptly. The ascent was here so steep that several of the horses slipped and hurt themselves; but at last we succeeded in crossing the mountain, and camped on a small branch of [the north fork of] Fish creek. We had now made 14 miles,[8] in a direction nearly north from the [Salmon] river; but this distance, though short, was very fatiguing, and rendered still more disagreeable by the rain, which began at three o'clock. At dusk it commenced snowing, and continued till the ground was covered to the depth of two inches, when it changed into sleet. We here met with a serious misfortune, the last of our thermometers being broken by accident. After making a scanty supper on a little corn and a few pheasants [ruffed grouse, *Bonasa umbelloides*], killed in the course of the day, we laid down to sleep. The next morning,

September 4th, we found everything frozen, and the ground covered with snow. We were obliged to wait some time in order to thaw the covers of the baggage, after which we began our journey at eight o'clock. We crossed a high mountain [of the Bitter-root range] which forms the dividing ridge [9] between the waters of the [Fish] creek we had

[8] From camp; so Clark G 97, but only eight miles by G 98. The discrepancy is rather apparent than real; the longer distance is the way they knocked about the rocks; the shorter, their actual advance. Courses and distances to-day, digested concisely from G 97, are: N. 25° W. 2½ m., to a small branch, left; hilly; thick woods. N. 15° W. 2 m., to a branch, right. N. 22° W. 2½ m., to a branch, left, passing one, left, and several springs, right; hilly; stony; windfalls. N. 18° E. 2 m., winding about to a high point; passed a run on the right. N. 32° W. 2 m., on side of a steep ridge to top of a high hill, no road; passed two runs, left. N. 40° W. 3 m., leaving the creek to the right and passing over a high pine mtn. to head of a drain running to the left. Total of 14 miles. This is all up-hill work; and camp is near the summit of the dividing ridge, to be surmounted within the first six miles to-morrow.

[9] Consequently passing from Idaho back into Montana at this point, but not

been ascending and those [of Clark's river] running to the north and west. We had not gone more than six miles over the snow when we reached the head of a stream [Camp creek, a branch of Ross' fork of Clark's river, as named beyond] (*p. 440*) from the right, which directed its course more to the westward. We descended the steep sides of the hills along its border, and at the distance of three miles found a small branch coming in from the east. We saw several of the argalia [bighorns], but they were too shy to be killed, and we therefore made a dinner from a deer shot by one of the hunters. Then we pursued the course of the stream for three miles, till it emptied into a river [Ross' fork] from the east. In the wide valley [Ross' Hole] at their junction, we discovered a large camp of Indians. When we reached them and alighted from our horses we were received with great cordiality. A council was immediately assembled, white robes were thrown over our shoulders, and the pipe of

recrossing from the Pacific to the Atlantic watershed. They had passed this Continental Divide from Shoshone cove (Montana into Idaho), gone down the Lemhi, thence down Salmon river to Fish creek, up this creek to its forks, up the left-hand fork, and so over the inter-state boundary mountains and into Montana again. This is a very notable point in the journey among the Bitter-root mountains, and must be fixed in mind. It is easily illustrated. Let the letter **Y** stand for mountain ridges. As the reader faces it, the right hand branch and the stem are together the main Rockies or Continental Divide. The left hand branch alone is the Bitter-root mountains, separating the watershed of Lewis' river from that of Clark's river. The left hand branch and the stem are together the boundary between Montana and Idaho. The Expedition approaches the foot of the stem, from east to west—from reader's right to left ; crosses there, consequently from Atlantic to Pacific waters, and also from Montana to Idaho ; goes roundabout up west or left side of main stem, in Idaho and in Lewis' river basin ; strikes left branch close to the crotch ; crosses this, thus passing from Idaho into Montana again, and also from Lewis' to Clark's river basin, but not from Pacific to Atlantic waters. Right in the crotch is a valley or " hole," where the Rockies adjoin the Bitter-root range. This is now called Ross' Hole. Its main stream is Ross' fork of Clark's river, from the east ; the Expedition reaches this by following down a creek, now Camp creek, as soon as they pass the Divide. This is the spot we must remember, as it is our starting-point to go north down Clark's river to Traveler's-rest creek ; moreover, Captain Clark and his party will be here again next year.

Courses and distances for Sept. 4th, briefly by Clark G 97, are : N. 10° W.

peace was introduced. After this ceremony, as it was too late to go any further, we camped, and continued smoking and conversing with the chiefs to a late hour.

September 5th. We assembled the chiefs and warriors, and informed them who we were, and the purpose for which we visited their country. All this was, however, conveyed to them through so many different languages that it was not comprehended without difficulty. We therefore proceeded to the more intelligible language of presents, and made four chiefs by giving a medal and a small quantity of tobacco to each. We received in turn from the principal chief a present consisting of the skins of a braro blaireau, an otter, and two antelopes, and were treated by the women to some dried roots and berries. We then began to traffic for horses, and succeeded in exchanging seven, purchasing 11, for which we gave a few articles of merchandise.

This camp consists of 33 lodges, in which were about 400 souls, among whom 80 were men. They are called Ootlashoots,[10] and represent themselves as one band of a nation

6 m. on a direct course over a high snowy mountain and down a drain of Flathead (*i. e.*, Clark's) river to a fork on the right, along the side of a *Dividing ridge* to the right. N. 18° W. 3 m. down the run to a run on the left. N. 35° W. 3 m. down this run to "the river which comes from the east," *i. e.*, Ross' fork of Clark's, in a wide valley, *i. e.*, Ross' Hole, where is the Ootlashoot village. Total 12 miles.

My impression is that the friendly old Shoshone guide, whose name history has not recorded, but to whom the United States should feel as much indebted as Lewis and Clark were, *intended* to fetch the Expedition over the Bitter-root range further west, and strike some branch of the western (Nez-percé) fork of Clark's river, instead of the eastern (Ross') ; but that he lost his way Sept. 3d, and then bluffed the thing through the other way. This seems to be what Gass means by saying, p. 131, that the creek they camped on Sept. 3d, "was not the creek our guide wished to have come upon." Perhaps, however, it was only a question of a better or worse way over to Ross' fork.

By "Clark's river," in this note, I am of course to be understood to mean that stream which results from the confluence of Ross' fork and Nez-percé creek. It is now known by the alternative names of Bitter-root and St. Mary's river, running north in the Bitter-root valley, and washing the foot of the mountain range of this name. On this point, see the note beyond, p. 586.

[10] "Oat-la-shoot 430 Souls" Clark's map, 1814, conspicuously ; Eoote-lashschute, Clark G 100 ; "Captain Clarke . . . calls them the Oleachshoot band of

called Tushepaws," a numerous people of 450 lodges, residing on the heads of the Missouri and Columbia rivers, and some of them lower down the latter river. In person these (*p. 441*) Indians are stout, and their complexion is lighter than that common among Indians. The hair of the men is worn in cues of otter-skin, falling in front over the shoulders. A shirt of dressed skin covers the body to the knee, and on this is worn occasionally a robe. To these are added leggings and moccasins. The women suffer their hair to fall in disorder over the face and shoulders, and their chief article of covering is a long shirt of skin, reaching down to the ankles and tied around the waist. In other respects, as also in the few ornaments which they possess, their appearance is similar to that of the Shoshonees. There is, however, a difference between the language of these people, which is still further increased by the very extraordinary pronunciation of the Ootlashoots. Their words have all a remarkably guttural sound; there is nothing which seems to represent the tone

the Tucknapax," Gass, p. 132 ; codices variant to the usual extent. Clark G 100 describes their speech as "a gugling kind of languaje Spoken much thro the throught "—which is richer than what Mr. Biddle makes of it, below.

11 " Tussapa " in Gass ; Tut-see'-wâs in Lewis' Statistical View, p. 35 of the English ed. 1807. These are of different linguistic stock from any Indians the Expedition has hitherto encountered, belonging to the extensive and much split-up Salishan family, or " Flatheads " in a broad, loose sense. They are here met at about the extreme southwest point of their geographical distribution. The " Flatheads " of the Statistical View are located " on the west side of a large river, lying west of the Rocky mountains, and running north, supposed to be the south fork of the Columbia river." This river, " running north," is the very one the Expedition is now on ; but it is a headwater of the *north branch* of the Columbia, *i. e.*, the westernmost of three principal affluents which unite to form the Missoula, this westernmost affluent being that upon which the name of " Clark's river " was originally based. When Gallatin, in 1836, named the Salish Indians, or Flatheads only, he had this very tribe in view, as appears from his locating it doubtfully on " either the most southern branch of Clarke's river or the most northern branch of Lewis' river "—the former being the correct supposition. The remarks upon the Flatheads presented in the Statistical View are vague, and merely rest upon information derived from the Minnetarees, who had taken some Flathead prisoners and brought them to their own village on the Missouri. For an account of the whole Salishan stock, in its modern classification and nomenclature, see the note beyond.

of their speaking more exactly than the clucking of a fowl, or the noise of a parrot. This peculiarity renders their voices scarcely audible, except at a short distance; and, when many of them are talking, forms a strange confusion of sounds. The common conversation we overheard consisted of low guttural sounds occasionally broken by a loud word or two, after which it would relapse and scarcely be distinguished. They seemed kind and friendly, and willingly shared with us berries and roots, which formed their only stock of provisions. Their only wealth is their horses, which are very fine, and so numerous that this party had with them at least 500.

September 6th. We continued [remained] this morning with the Ootlashoots, from whom we purchased two more horses, and procured a vocabulary of their language. The Ootlashoots set off about two o'clock [p. m.] to join the different bands who were collecting at the Three Forks of the Missouri. We ourselves proceeded at the same time, taking a direction N. 30° W. We crossed, within the distance of 1½ miles, a small river from the right, and a creek coming in from the north.[12] This river is the main stream which, when it reaches the end (*p. 442*) of the valley, where the mountains close in upon it, is [has already been] joined by the river [*i. e.*, Camp creek] on which we camped last evening, as well as by the [other] creek just mentioned. To the river thus formed[13] we gave the name of Captain Clark, he being the first white man who had ever visited its waters. At

[12] A misleading sentence. Being already on Ross' fork, at the mouth of Camp creek, what is this *other* river they crossed? There is no other; this " small river" is Ross' fork itself. Clark G 104, Sept. 6th, first course and distance, has : " N. 30° W. 5 miles crossing the river and a creek at 1½ miles." Nothing could be plainer. They started from the south or left bank of Ross' fork ; crossed *it* to the north or right bank, down which they go ; at 1½ miles they cross a creek. This is from the N.E., on their right ; Clark charts it, nameless (see the trace at the letter " 4 " of the " 430 souls " there inscribed). Below this creek, Ross' fork runs into a cañon ; to avoid which, the road goes over a small mountain, which helps to shut in Ross' Hole on the west.

[13] The confluence here indicated is a little south of lat. 46° N., and a little west of long. 114° W. The streams making it will be found on any good

the end of five miles on this course we had crossed the valley, and reached the top of a mountain covered with pine; this we descended along the steep sides and ravines for 1½ miles, when we came to a spot on the river where the Ootlashoots had camped a few days before. We then followed the course of the river, which is from 25 to 30 yards wide, shallow and stony, with the low grounds on its borders narrow. Within the distance of 3½ miles we crossed it several times, and, passing a run on each side, camped on its right bank, after making [finishing] ten miles during the afternoon [ten miles in all to-day, Clark G 104]. The horses were turned out to graze; but those we had lately bought were secured and watched, lest they should escape, or be stolen by their former owners. Our stock of flour was now exhausted; we had but little corn, and as our hunters had killed nothing

map (best on G. L. O. of 1892). The one river thus formed on Clark's map is marked "Main Fork," i. e., of "Clark's river." This is the actual point where Clark's river is named—the Expedition knowing nothing further of it at this time. It is by courtesy that Captain Clark is said to be the first white man who had ever visited its waters. That intrepid explorer had gone ahead of the main party down the Lemhi, and down Salmon river a piece, and had returned, finding that way impracticable; but he had never seen a drop of water of Clark's river till he, with the whole party, crossed the divide of the Bitter-root range on Sept. 4th. Captain Lewis bestowed the name, with the most eminent appropriateness, and with all the consideration so justly due to Captain Clark. The later history of the name I will give in the sequel; it has fared but little better than the name of "Lewis' river," at the hands of those who should have kept their hands off the whole thing. Clark's river of our present text became known as the Bitter-root river, and was also called Mary's, or St. Mary's; but who she was, or what she had to do with Clark's river, nobody knows except Father De Smet, perhaps. The stream joins Hellgate river near Missoula; their united waters thence acquire the latter name, and run into Pend d'Oreille lake; on emerging from which, the great river retakes the name of Clark's, which it should never have lost, and empties into the Columbia at 49° N. Some geographers attach the name of Clark's to the river from its confluence with the Hellgate to the Columbia; which I think is the least that can be done with any regard for the amenities in the case. (Note[13], p. 991.)

Whatever its name, this branch of Clark's river, on which we now are, runs north, with an average course almost meridional, along the eastern base of the Bitter-root mountains, in Missoula Co., Mont., and receives Hellgate river a very short distance due west of Missoula. Clark makes its course 88 miles from the formation of the river, in the above paragraph, to its mouth (76 miles to Traveler's-rest creek). In this course it receives very many—40 or more—short

except two pheasants [ruffed grouse], our supper consisted chiefly of berries.

September 7th. The greater part of the day the weather was dark and rainy. We continued through the narrow low grounds along the river, till at the distance of six miles we came to a large creek [Nez-percé fork [14]] from the left, after which the bottoms widen. Four miles lower is another [Tin Cup] creek on the same side, and the valley now extends from one to three miles, the mountains on the left being high [7,000 feet or more] and bald, with snow on the summits, while the country to the right is open and hilly. Four miles beyond this is a [Rock] creek, running from the snow-topped mountains, and several runs on both sides of the river. Two miles from this last is another [Lost Horse] creek on the left. The afternoon was now far advanced; but not being able to find a fit place to camp we continued six miles

streams, east and west, not all of which have names. The most notable of these is the Nez-percé river, from the S.W., formed of two main branches, one of which arises in the mountains which the Expedition has just crossed. The other and more westerly branch comes from the Nez-percé Pass of the Bitter-root range, and thus leads to the *Southern* Nez-percé trail westward—the same that was taken by Mr. A. W. Tinkham, C. E., of Governor I. I. Stevens' party, on the trip for Fort Benton to Wallawalla, Oct. 31 to Dec. 30, 1853. This difficult route is described in P. R. R. Rep. XII. pt. i, 1860, pp. 164–166, and marked on the map accompanying Stevens' Report. Clark's 1814 map charts this river as the " West fork " of his " Main fork " of Clark's river ; but as he never saw it except at its mouth, it could only be traced by conjecture, and is in fact laid down far out of the way. This is the " large creek from the left " of to-morrow's text.

The Expedition will go due north down this " Main Fork of Clark's river," nearly to its mouth, but little south of Missoula City, and then turn abruptly west up a creek (Traveler's-rest), and so on over several ranges of the Bitter-root mountains to the main forks of the Kooskooskee or Clearwater river, which empties into the Snake, and that into the Columbia.

[14] See last note, where this notable stream is characterized. Its mouth is nearly up to 46° N., and little west of 114° W. The Expedition has thus made about one degree of northing since they left the Shoshone camp on the Lemhi, and been coming on an average course almost due north since they left Salmon river at the mouth of Fish creek, its North fork. Hereabouts was the site of Doolittle's ; above this, on Ross' fork, is a place named Sula. Nearly opposite Nez-percé fork is a small creek, called Rye, or Rye Grass, from the right or east, which the text does not notice ; higher up is Marsh creek, on the same side.

further, till after dark, when we halted for the night.[15]   The river here is still shallow and stony, but is increased to the width (*p. 443*) of 50 yards.   The valley through which we passed is of a poor soil, and its fertility is injured by the quantity of stone scattered over it.   We met two horses, which had strayed from the Indians and were now quite wild. No fish were to be seen in the river, but we obtained a very agreeable supply of two deer, two cranes, and two pheasants.

Sunday, September 8th.   We set out early.   The snow-topped hills on the left approached the river near our camp ; but we soon reached a valley four or five miles wide, through which we followed the course of the river in a direction due north.   We passed three creeks on the right, and several runs emptying into the opposite side of the river.[16]   At the distance of 11 miles the river turned more toward the west.   We pursued it for twelve miles, and camped near a large creek coming in from the right, which, from its being

[15] About the present site of Grantsdale, having made 22 miles to-day.   Checking the text by the codex, and adjusting the wide discrepancies among the several maps before me, I have no hesitation in making the identifications I have bracketed in the text.   Rock creek is easily recognized by a lake (Rock or Como) into and out of which it runs.   The most considerable stream before this is Tin Cup creek, left, with Derby at or near its mouth ; and the next below Rock are Lick and Lost Horse, both on the left.   At mouth of Rock creek is a place called Como.   The principal stream on the right passed to-day is one called Child's, or Weeping Child, or Sleeping Child, to which different mappists play wet-nurse at various points for some ten miles along the river—no wonder the infant wept at such cartography.   Finally, Kamas, Camas, or Quamash creek comes in on the left, near Grantsdale.   These identifications are exclusive of several nameless creeks or runs on each side passed to-day.   Grantsdale is the present or a very recent terminus of the Missoula and Bitter-root branch of the N. P. R. R.

[16] This curt clause does too much duty, and must be expanded.   Clark G 105 has for first course of Sept. 8th : " North 11 miles to a small run on the right side, passed a large creek at 1 mile, one at 4 miles and a small one at 8 miles, thro' a open vally of 4 or 5 miles wide call'd Horse Vally."   Which being interpreted means : Large creek from the right, first below Grantsdale, now called Skalkaho, Skakaho, or Shakaho ; near it is railroad station of Hamilton. Next below, right, is Gird's creek.   The third one of the creeks on the right which the codex specifies, is now called Willow creek ; on it is Corvallis.   The " small run on the right," at the end of this course, is now Birch creek, or some stream close by it.   Here or hereabouts is the place where on Oct. 8th, 1853,

divided into four different channels, we called Scattering creek.[17] The valley continues to be a poor stony land, with scarcely any timber, except some pine-trees along the waters and partially scattered on the hills to the right, which, as well as those on the left, have snow on them. The plant which forces itself most on our attention is a species of prickly-pear very common on this part of the river. It grows in clusters, in an oval form about the size of a pigeon's egg, and its thorns are so strong and bearded that, when it penetrates our feet, it brings away the pear itself. We saw two mares and a colt, which, like the horses seen yesterday, seemed to have lost themselves and become wild. Our game to-day consisted of two deer, an elk, and a prairie-fowl.

September 9th. We resumed our journey through the valley, and [not yet] leaving the road on our right [we first] crossed Scattering creek; [we then proceeded, and next]

Lieutenant John Mullan, U. S. A., established the post he named Cantonment Stevens, in honor of Governor Isaac I. Stevens, who conducted the explorations and surveys for a railroad route along the 47th and 49th parallels in 1853–55 (see P. R. R. Rep. XII. pt. i, 1860, p. 181, col'd pl. lix., and map.) Stevensville is now lower down the river, near old Fort Owen: see next note. Among the "several runs" of the text, from the left, are: Upper Big creek; Mill creek; Burr creek; Sweathouse creek, by which is railroad station Victor, 15 miles below Grantsdale (Victor was English name of a noted Flathead chief); Lower Big creek; and Kootenay creek, which falls in opposite Willoughby creek.

[17] Second lap to-day is, Clark G 105: "N. 12° W. 12 [miles] through the said [Horse] Vallie to a large creek from the right divided into 4 different channels, Scattered creek," elsewhere Scattery; also Scattering, as per text. The channels have changed since 1805, and no detailed identifications are possible. One of them corresponds to what is now called Burnt Fork creek. Here is present town of Stevensville, on the railroad; and Big Timber creek falls in on the other side of the river. Stevensville was located just above an establishment called Fort Owen, from two brothers of that name, ranchers, and the first settlers in the valley. Fort Owen was built on the site of a Flathead village. For a view of it, and another of the river near it, see P. R. R. Rep. XII. pt. i. pll. xxx. and lxvi. In this Report Governor Stevens pays his respects to Lewis and Clark, p. 122: "I would earnestly urge all persons desirous to know the minute details of the topography of this valley to study carefully the narrative of Lewis and Clark; for to us it was a matter of the greatest gratification, with their narrative in hand, to pass through this valley and realize the fidelity and graphic character of their descriptions."

halted, at the distance of [ten or] twelve miles, on a small
run from the east, where we breakfasted on the remains of
yesterday's hunt.   We here took a meridian altitude, which
gave the latitude of 46° 41' 38" 9'''.   We then continued,
and at the distance of four [or five] miles passed over to the
left bank of the river, where we found a large road through
the valley.   At (*p. 444*) this place[18] [this river is] is a handsome stream of very clear water, 100 yards wide, with low
banks, and a bed formed entirely of gravel.   It has every
appearance of being navigable ; but as it contains no salmon,
we presume there must be some fall below which obstructs
their passage.   Our guide could not inform us where this
river discharged its waters [into Pend d'Oreille lake] ; he
said that as far as he knew its course it ran along the [Bitter-
root and Cœur d'Alene] mountains to the north [-west], and
that not far from our present position it was joined by
another stream [Hellgate river] nearly as large as itself,
which rises in the [Rocky] mountains to the east near the
Missouri, and flows through an extensive [Deer Lodge] valley or open prairie.   Through this prairie is the great Indian

[18] I do not read the codex for Sept. 9th quite as Mr. Biddle seems to have
understood it.   Clark G 103 has : " Proceeded on thro' a plain as yesterday
down the Valley crossed a large creek called Scattering on which Cotton trees
grew at 1½ miles, a small one at 10 miles, both from the right, [crossed] the
main river at 15 miles & [at 6 miles further] Encamped on a large Creek from
the left which we Call Travelers rest Creek."   Nothing could be plainer.   They
continued along the right bank of the river for 15 miles, crossed it, and went
along the left bank six miles to Traveler's-rest creek.   They did not leave any
road to the right till they crossed the river.   At 1½ miles they first crossed the
last channel of Scattering creek; at ten miles (the " twelve miles " of the text) they
halted at a run from the east, where they breakfasted and took the observation ;
at five miles beyond this they crossed the river ; whence it was six miles along its
left bank to Traveler's-rest ; total 21 miles to-day.   Clark G 103 and 105 are
discrepant in some details, but in nothing more than a mile or two for certain
points in the day's march ; which slight discrepancies may be safely disregarded.
The creek from the right, at which they breakfasted, is that nearly opposite
whose mouth is now Florence, given as eight miles by rail below Stevensville.
Near the place they crossed the river is now town of Carlton, on creek of
same name, from the left or west ; and Carlton is given as six miles by rail
from Lou Lou, which is at the mouth of Traveler's-rest.   Several other creeks
are passed to-day.

road to the waters of the Missouri; so direct is the route that, in four days' journey from this place, we might reach the Missouri, about 30 miles above what we called the Gates of the Rocky Mountains, or the spot where the valley of that river widens into an extensive plain on entering the chain of mountains.

At ten miles from our camp is a small creek falling in from the east,[19] five [or six] miles below which we halted at a large stream which empties itself on the west side of the river. This is a fine bold creek of clear water, about 20 yards wide, which we called Traveler's-rest[20] creek; for, as our guide told us that we should here leave the river, we determined to remain for the purpose of making celestial observations and collecting some food, as the country through which we are to pass has no game for a great distance.

The valley of the river through which we have been passing is generally a prairie from five to six miles in width, and with a cold, gravelly, white soil. The timber which it possesses is almost exclusively pine, chiefly of the long-leaved kind, with some spruce, and a species of fir resembling the Scotch fir. Near the water-courses are also seen a few narrow-leaved cottonwood trees; the only underbrush is the redwood, honeysuckle, and rosebushes. Our game was four deer, three geese, four ducks, and three prairie-fowls; one of the hunters, also, brought in a red-headed [pileated] (*p. 445*) wood-pecker [*Ceophlæus pileatus*], of the large kind common in the United States, but the first of the kind we have seen since leaving the Illinois.

[19] This statement I do not understand, and cannot explain, unless it duplicates what is said of the "run from the east" in the preceding paragraph. Some 14 or 16 miles of to-day's march are already passed, and the Expedition is on the left side of the river, only five or six miles from Traveler's-rest.

[20] The Expedition will go up this creek, nearly due west, and in this way get over the first Bitter-root range, which separates them from headwaters of the Kooskooskee or Clearwater river. It is a very notable stream in the annals of the Expedition, la crique du Repos du Voyageur of Gass' French editor, Lalle-mant, but now called Lo Lo, Lou Lou, or Lu Lu fork of the Bitter-root or St. Mary's river; town of same name at its mouth, 15 miles by rail from Missoula City, and somewhat less from the confluence of Hellgate river.

September 10*th.* The morning being fair all the hunters were sent out, and the rest of the party employed in repairing their clothes. Two of them were sent to the junction of that river from the east along which the Indians go to the Missouri. It is about seven miles below Traveler's-rest creek; the country [low land] at the forks is seven or eight miles wide, level and open, but with little timber. Its course is to the north, and we incline to believe that this is the river which the Minnetarees described to us as running from south to north along the west side of the Rocky mountains, not far from the sources of Medicine [Sun] river. There is, moreover, reason to suppose that, after going as far northward as the headwaters of that river, it turns to the westward and joins the Tacootchetessee.[21]

Toward evening one of the hunters returned with three Indians, whom he had met in his excursion up Traveler's-rest creek. As soon as they saw him they prepared to attack him with arrows ; but he quieted them by laying down his gun and advancing toward them, and soon persuaded them to come to camp. Our Shoshonee guide could not speak the language of these people, but by the universal language of signs and gesticulations, which is perfectly intelligible among the Indians, he found that these were

[21] Here meaning the Columbia itself, to make the context true, though the " Tacootchetessee" is really Fraser's river. The text is quite correct, in the sense that the Missoula, formed by the confluence of Hellgate river and St. Mary's fork, flows in a general N.W. course, between the Rocky mountains and the Bitterroot and Cœur d'Alene ranges, into Pend d'Oreille lake, emerging from which it continues (as Clark's fork of the Columbia of modern geography) into the Columbia itself at 49° N.

Fraser's is the next great river which reaches the Pacific north of the Columbia. It seems to have been missed, or only suspected, by the early navigators. In June, 1793, it was navigated in its upper reaches by Sir Alexander Mackenzie, who called it by its Indian name Taoutche-tesse, said to mean " great river." It was supposed to be a branch of the Columbia. After 1806, Mr. D. W. Harmon, of the Northwest Company, explored some of its upper parts ; see his Journal. In 1810, Mr. Fraser, another agent of the same company, traced it toward its sources, and showed that it did not join the Columbia ; it has since been generally known by his name. Sir George Simpson, Governor of the Hudson's Bay Company's Territory, explored the whole river in 1828.

three Tushepaw [see note, *anteà*, p. 584] Flatheads, in pursuit of two men, supposed to be Shoshonees, who had stolen 23 of their horses. We gave them some boiled venison and a few presents, such as a fishhook, a steel to strike fire, and a little powder; but they seemed better pleased with a piece of ribbon which we tied in the hair of each of them. They were in such haste, lest their horses should be carried off, that two of them set out after sunset in quest of the robbers; the third, however, was persuaded to remain with us and conduct us to his relations. These he said were numerous, and resided on the Columbia in the plain below (*p. 446*) the mountains. From that place, he added, the river was navigable to the ocean; that some of his relations had been there last fall and seen an old white man, who resided there by himself, and who gave them some handkerchiefs like those we have. The distance from this place is five "sleeps," or days' journey. When our hunters had all joined us, we found that our provisions consisted of four deer, a beaver, and three grouse.

The observation of to-day gave 46° 48' 28" as the latitude of [the mouth of] Traveler's-rest creek.

September 11th. Two of our horses having strayed away, we were detained all the morning before they were caught. In the meantime our Tushepaw Indian became impatient of the delay, and set out to return home alone. As usual, we had dispatched four of our best hunters ahead. As we hoped with their aid and our present stock of provisions to subsist on the route, we proceeded at three o'clock up the right [hand] side of the [Traveler's-rest [22]] creek, and camped

[22] In 1854, Lieutenant John Mullan, U.S.A., crossed the Bitter-root mountains by this trail. On the summit he found a hot spring, with a temperature of 132° F., around which was fine prairie camping-ground. " This route is nearly one and the same as that followed by Lewis and Clark in 1805, the Lou-Lou fork being their Travellers' Rest creek, and the hot springs referred to are those spoken of by these indefatigable explorers," Stevens, P. R. R. Rep. XII. pt. i., 1860, p. 180, where particulars are given of Lieutenant Mullan's route of Sept.– Oct., 1854. This route is very clearly shown on Governor Stevens' large folding map, bound in the volume cited, and the narrative of this trip is illustrated with two colored plates—pl. lvii. showing the entrance to the Bitter-root mountains

under some old Indian huts at the distance of seven miles. The road was plain and good ; the valley, however, narrower than that which we left, and bordered by high and rugged hills to the right, while the mountains on the left were covered with snow. The day was fair and warm, the wind from the northwest.

September 12*th.* There was a white frost this morning. We proceeded [up Traveler's-rest creek] at seven o'clock, and soon passed a stream falling in on the right, near which was an old Indian camp, with a bath or sweating-house covered with earth. At two miles' distance we ascended a high [hill], and thence continued through a hilly and thickly timbered country for nine miles, when we came to the forks of the creek, where the road branches up each fork. We followed the western route, and finding that the creek made a considerable bend at the distance of four miles, crossed a high mountain in order to avoid the circuit. The road had been very bad during the first part of the day, but the passage of the mountain, which was (*p. 447*) eight miles across, was very painful to the horses, as we were obliged to go over steep, stony sides of hills and along the hollows and ravines, rendered more disagreeable by fallen timber, chiefly pine, spruce-pine, and fir. We at length reached the creek [Traveler's-rest again], having made 23 miles of a route so difficult

by the Lo Lo Fork or Traveler's-rest creek, and pl. lxviii. giving a view of the hot springs near a source of this stream in the Bitter-root mountains, looking west. The " Northern Nez-percé trail," as this route came to be called, which was followed approximately by Lewis and Clark, is described thus by Stevens, (P.R.R. Rep. XII. pt. i., p. 248, 1860) : " The northern Nez Percé trail is in character much the same [as the southern one of this name], but its course is more direct. It passes up the valley of the Lou-Lou branch of the Bitter Root, (Traveller's Rest creek of Lewis and Clark,) and, crossing to a northern branch of the Kooskooskia, winds along the heads of branches flowing into this and the Pelouse (?) in a southerly direction, till it comes out on the Great Plain at the same place as the southern trail. The distance travelled across mountains by this route is about 120 miles. The mountain dividing the waters which flow east and west is lower than some of those crossed in going up Lou-Lou creek, but covered with pine and fallen timber. This may be found a tolerable wagon route from valley to valley [Bitter-root to Kooskooskee], if the timber which now obstructs them shall be found the only obstacle."

that some of the party did not join us before ten o'clock. We found the account of the scantiness of game to be but too true, as we were not able to procure anything during the whole of yesterday, and to-day killed only a single pheasant. Along the road we observed many of the pine-trees peeled off, which is done by the Indians to procure the inner bark for food in the spring.

September 13*th.* Two of the horses strayed away during the night, and one of them being Captain Lewis', he remained with four men to search for them while we proceeded up the creek [Traveler's-rest]. At the distance of two miles we came to several springs issuing from large rocks of a coarse, hard grit, and nearly boiling hot. These seem to be much frequented, as there are several paths made by elk, deer, and other animals, near one of the springs a hole or Indian bath, and roads leading in different directions. These embarrassed our guide, who, mistaking the road, took us three miles out of the proper course over an exceedingly bad route. We then fell into the right road, and proceeded on very well, till, having made five miles, we stopped to refresh the horses. Captain Lewis here joined us ; but not having been able to find his horse, two men were sent back to continue the search. We then proceeded along the same kind of country which we passed yesterday, and after crossing a mountain [23] and leaving the sources of Traveler's-rest creek on the left, reached, after five miles'

[23] Thus crossing the main divide of the Bitter-root mountains from the Missoula watershed on the east to the basin of the Kooskooskee or Clearwater on the west, and so passing over from Montana into Idaho (Shoshone county). This " new creek " which the Expedition strikes, and calls Glade creek, is one of the headwaters of the Kooskooskee or Clearwater river. The party at this point is nearly due west of Pierce City. The mountain they have passed is at least 7,000 feet high. The pass just now made is known as the Lo Lo Pass, from the creek which the Expedition has ascended. Hence the route is to be from east to west, right across Idaho, to the main forks of the Kooskooskee ; and thence, by canoes built there, down to Lewiston at the junction of the Kooskooskee with the Snake, thus finishing with Idaho and reaching Washington. The land journey is 150 miles (roundly). As already intimated, the track of the Expedition is approximately the old Northern Nez-percé trail, also called the Lo Lo trail. It is

riding, a small creek which came in from the left hand, passing through open glades, some of which were half a mile wide. The road, which had been as usual rugged and stony, became firm, plain, and level after quitting the head of Traveler's-rest. We followed [down] the course of this new [Glade] creek (*p. 448*) for two miles, and camped[24] at a spot where the mountains close in on each side. Other mountains, covered with snow, are in view to the southeast and southwest. We were somewhat more fortunate to-day in killing a deer, and several pheasants, which were of the common species, except that the tail was black.

September 14*th*. The day was very cloudy with rain and hail in the valleys, while on the top of the mountains some snow fell. We proceeded early, continuing along the right side of Glade creek, crossed a high [about 7,000 feet] mountain, and at the distance of six miles reached the place where it [Glade creek] is joined by another branch of equal size from the right [thus composing the Kooskooskee river]. Near these forks the Tushepaws have had a camp, which is but

approximately the Mullan trail of September, 1854, as charted on Stevens' map. It likewise approaches to some extent the southern border of Shoshone county. But with half-a-dozen of the best modern maps of Idaho before me, there is not one on which I can dot the trail of the Expedition in detail. The country has not yet been sectionized, and our topographical knowledge is still too vague to be of any exact use. I propose to follow Lewis and Clark's footsteps across these mountains. They were never spirited from one point to any other; they stepped off every foot of the way. Clark's detailed courses and distances have never before been published. I give them complete. If the ascribed distances do not suit modern measurements, that is no affair of mine. If the creeks run the wrong way on paper, they run the right way on the ground that Lewis and Clark went over, and the maps can be re-constructed, upon determination of the correction of Clark's compass-courses required for the magnetic variation.

[24] Sept. 13th, Clark G 130: "S.W. 2 miles up the said [Traveler's-rest] creek bad road rockey steep hill sides falling timber to *hot* springs on the right of the creek boiling out of a corse gritty stones, &c. S. 30° W. 3 miles passing a bad falling timber to the Creek on our left passed 3 small Streams from our right. S. 30° W. 7 miles over a mountain and on a dividing [plateau now known as Summit Prairie] of flat gladey land to a [Glade] Creek in a glade of ½ a mile in width, & keeping down this Creek two miles." So from the fixed point of the hot springs, the course is straight for ten miles S. 30° W. to a point on Glade creek, which creek comes from the left or east, and is flowing westwardly.

recently abandoned ; for the grass is entirely destroyed by horses, and two fish-weirs across the creek are still remaining ; no fish were, however, to be seen. We here passed over to the left side of the [Glade] creek, and began the ascent of a very high and steep mountain, nine miles across. On reaching the other side we found a large branch [Colt-killed, of the Kooskooskee] from the left, which seems to rise in the snowy mountains to the south and southeast. We [crossed the main stream, Clark G 111, and] continued along the creek [*i. e.*, down right bank of the Kooskooskee] two miles further; when, night coming on, we camped[25] opposite a small island, at the mouth of a branch [which fell in] on the right side of the [Kooskooskee] river. The mountains which we crossed to-day were much more difficult than those of yesterday ; the last was particularly fatiguing, being steep and stony, broken by fallen timber, and thickly overgrown by pine, spruce, fir, hackmatack, and tamarac. Although we had made only 17 miles, we were all very weary. The whole stock of animal food being now exhausted, we therefore killed a colt, on which we made a hearty supper. From this incident we called the last creek we had passed, [coming] from the south, Colt-killed creek. The river itself is 80 yards wide, with a swift current and a stony channel. Its Indian name is Kooskooskee.[26]

[25] Sept. 14th, Clark G 131 : " S. 80° W. 6 miles over a high mountanious country thickly covered with pine spruce &c to the forks of the Creek, one of equal size falling in from the right passing much falling timber. S. 60° W. over a high mountain steep and almost inexcessable leaving the creek to our right hand to the forks, a [Colt-killed] creek of equal size falling in from the *left* 2 fish dams or Weares across the North [Kooskooskee] fork to catch Salmon. S. 70° W. 2 miles down the river Kooskooske to a small branch on the right side killed and eate Coalt." Thus 17 miles, much of it " in the air " over two mountains, to a point on the supposed Kooskooskee river, two miles below a considerable branch from the *south;* camp on *right* bank of the river, at mouth of an unnamed creek from the *north.* (Codex has a crossing not given by Biddle.)

[26] This name variable as usual in spelllng ; *c* or *k* in one, two, or three places ; single or double *o* and *s ;* ending *ee, e, i, ie, ia;* the syllables sometimes hyphenated, or separated. It will frequently recur as the narrative proceeds, and its application will vary as the Expedition learns more of the geography of the unknown region now being explored. " Kooskooskee " is the Indian name of the river

(*p. 449*) *Sunday, September* 15*th*. At an early hour we proceeded along the right side of the Kooskooskee, over steep, rocky points of land, till at the distance of four miles we reached an old Indian fishing-place. The road here turned to the right of the water, and began to ascend a mountain. But the fire and wind had prostrated or dried almost all the timber on the south side, and the ascents were so steep that we were forced to wind in every direction round the high knobs, which constantly impeded our progress. Several of the horses lost their foot-hold and slipped; one of them, which was loaded with a desk and small trunk, rolled over and over for 40 yards, till his fall was stopped by a tree. The desk was broken, but the poor animal escaped without much injury. After clambering in this way for four miles, we came to a high, snowy part of the mountain, where was a spring of water, at which we halted two hours to refresh our horses.

On leaving this spring this road continued as bad as it was below, and the timber more abundant. At four miles we reached the top of the mountain ; foreseeing no chance of meeting with water, we camped[27] on the northern side of this mountain, near an old bank of snow three feet deep. Some of this we melted, and supped on the remains of the colt killed yesterday. Our only game to-day was two pheasants; the horses, on which we calculated as a last resource, began

now called the Clearwater, rising in the Bitter-root mountains, draining the country west of these mountains and north of the Salmon river watershed, and falling into the Snake at county town of Lewiston, Nez-Percé Co., a little west of Fort Lapwai. Under date of Oct. 7th it is said that the Kooskooskee is only so called downward from " its forks," *i. e.*, where the main North fork of the Clearwater falls in. But this is immaterial, for " Clearwater " is now the name of the main stream to its proper head in the Bitter-root mountains.

[27] Sept. 15th, Clark G 131 : " West 4 miles down the River, passing over four high steep hills to a run at an old Indn. encampment. N.W. 8 miles ascending a ruged mountain winding in every direction passing over high stoney knobs, passed a spring on our right at 4 miles to a high part of the mountain on which was snow." Note this *northwest* course, away from the river ; camp also on *north side* of a mtn. Most of the way was zigzag as well as in the air, and actual advance may not have been over six or eight miles for the twelve traveled.

to fail us, for two of them were so poor and worn out with
fatigue that we were obliged to leave them behind. All
around us are high rugged mountains, among which is a
lofty range from southeast to northwest, whose tops are
without timber, and in some places covered with snow.
The night was cloudy and very cold. Three hours before
daybreak,

September 16*th*, it began to snow and continued all day,
so that by evening it was six or eight inches deep. This
covered the track so completely that we were obliged
constantly to halt and examine, lest we should lose the
route. (*p. 450*) In many places we had nothing to guide us
except the branches of the trees, which, being low, had been
rubbed by the burdens of the Indian horses. The road was,
like that of yesterday, along steep hillsides, obstructed with
fallen timber and a growth of eight different species of pine,
so thickly strewed that the snow fell from them as we passed ;
this kept us continually wet to the skin, and so cold that
we were anxious lest our feet should be frozen, as we had
only thin moccasins to defend them.

At noon we halted to let the horses feed on some long
grass on the south side of the mountain, and endeavored
by making-fires to keep ourselves warm. As soon as the
horses were refreshed, Captain Clark went ahead with one
man, at the distance of six miles reached a stream [28] from
[the left to] the right, and prepared fires by the time of our
arrival at dusk. We here camped in a piece of low ground,
thickly timbered, but scarcely large enough to permit us

[28] Worst possible snag in this stream, "from the right." Read *from the left
to the right :* "A small branch passing to the right," Clark G 114, Sept. 16th ;
and again, Clark G 132, Sept. 16 : "S. 75° W. 13 miles on the mountain passing
emencely high and ruged knobs of the mounts. in snow from 4 to 6 inches deep,
much falling timber, snow continued to fall passed thro a country thickly
timbered with 8 destunct kinds of pine to *a small branch passing to our right.*"
Perhaps no passage in this itinerary has done more to "throw off " the L. and C.
trail than this unlucky slip. The Expedition at this point is away from the
main Kooskooskee altogether, a mountain intervening, and has struck on a creek
flowing *northward*. It is therefore a separate watershed from that of the *main*
Kooskooskee basin. See itinerary of June 27th, p. 1056.

to lie level. We had now made 13 miles. We were all very wet, cold, and hungry. Though before setting out this morning we had seen four deer, yet we could not procure any of them, and were obliged to kill a second colt for our supper.

September 17*th.* Our horses became so much scattered during the night that we were detained till one o'clock before they were all collected. We then continued our route over high, rough knobs,[29] and several drains and springs, along a ridge of country separating the waters of two small rivers. The road was still difficult; several of the horses fell and injured themselves very much, so that we were unable to advance more than ten miles to a small stream [running southward, to our left], on which we camped.

We had killed a few pheasants; but these being insufficient for our subsistence, we killed another of the colts. This want of provisions, the extreme fatigue to which we were subjected, and the dreary prospects before us, began to dispirit the men. It was therefore agreed that Cap- (*p. 451*) tain Clark should go on ahead with six hunters, and endeavor to kill something for the support of the party. He therefore set out,[30]

September 18*th,* early in the morning, in hopes of finding a level country from which he might send back some game. His route lay S. 85° W., along the same high dividing ridge, and the road was still very bad; but he moved on rapidly, and at the distance of 20 miles was rejoiced on discovering

[29] Sept. 17th, Clark G 132 : " S. 50° W. 10 miles over high knobs of the mountn. emencely dificuelt, passed 3 Dreans [drains] to our right [and came to] one which passes to our left on the top of a high mountain, passing on [going along] a dividing ridge." This is nearly a southwest course, and with more actual advance for the miles traveled than yesterday and the day before that, as it is along a dividing ridge; it takes them past several runs to the north, and brings them to camp at a run to the south. They have therefore crossed a divide, and are again on a southern watershed—not that of the main Kooskooskee, but of its tributary, the Lo Lo fork, otherwise known as the Nahwah river.

[30] Two parallel narratives continue hence to Sept. 23d. The situation was grave. " A coalt being the most useless part of our stock, he fell a Prey to our appetites," Clark G 116.

far off an extensive plain toward the west and southwest, bounded by a high mountain. He halted an hour to let the horses eat a little grass on the hill-sides, and then went on 12½ miles till he reached a bold creek running to the left, on which he camped. To this stream he gave the very appropriate name of Hungry[31] creek; for having procured no game, the party had nothing to eat.

In the meantime we were detained till after eight o'clock by the loss of one of our horses, which had strayed away and could not be found. We then proceeded, but having soon finished the remainder of the colt killed yesterday, felt the want of provisions ; which was more sensible from our meeting with no water till, toward nightfall, we found some in a ravine among the hills. By pushing our horses to their utmost strength, we made 18 miles. We then melted some snow, and supped on a little portable soup, a few canisters of which, with about 20 [pounds'] weight of bear's oil, are our only remaining means of subsistence. Our guns are scarcely of any service, for there is no living creature in these mountains, except a few small pheasants, a small species of gray squirrel, and a blue bird of the vulture kind[32] about the size of a turtle-dove or jay ; even these are difficult to shoot.

September 19*th*. Captain Clark proceeded up the [Hungry] creek, along which the road was more steep and stony than any he had yet passed. At six miles' distance he reached a small (*p. 452*) plain, where he fortunately found a horse, on which he breakfasted, and hung the rest on a tree for the

[31] " A bold running Creek passing to the left which I call Hungery Creek as at that place we had nothing to eate," Clark G 117. " S. 85° W. 32 miles to Hungary Creek passing to our left, passed a branch & several springs which passes to our right, keeping a Dividing ridge," etc., Clark G 132. This long course, nearly west, is on the divide between the waters of Lo Lo fork or Nahwah river on the south, and other tributaries of the Kooskooskee system to the north ; as Hungry creek runs to the left, southward, it is supposably a branch of the former river ; on which supposition it may be identifiable with the Musselshell creek of present maps, or a branch of this.

[32] Meaning probably *Gymnokitta cyanocephala;* see note [6], p. 454. The squirrel is *Sciurus fremonti*, a western variety of the common squirrel, *S. hudsonius*.

party in the rear. Two miles beyond this he left the creek, [to his right] and crossed three high mountains, rendered almost impassable from the steepness of the ascent and the quantity of fallen timber. After clambering over these ridges and mountains, and passing the heads of some branches of Hungry creek, he came to a large [Collins'] creek running westward [passing to our left, Clark G 117]. This he followed for four miles, and then turned to the right down the mountain, till he came to a small creek [running] to the left. Here he halted, having made 22 miles on his course, S. 80° W., though the winding route over the mountains almost doubled the distance.[33] On descending the last mountain, the heat became much more sensible, after the extreme cold he had experienced for several days past. Besides the breakfast in the morning, two pheasants were their only food during the day ; the only [other] kinds of birds they saw were the bluejay [*Cyanocitta stelleri*], a small white-headed hawk [?], a larger hawk, crows, and ravens.

[33] Clark G 132, Sept 19th : " S. 80° W. 22 miles on our course thro' emencely bad falling timber the greater part of the way. Keeping up the [Hungry] creek for 8 miles, at 6 passed thro a small Plain where we killed a horse, the road up the Creek stoney hill sides much worse than any we have passed left the Creek to our right and passd. over a mountain and the heads of some branches of hungary Creek. over ridges and thro' much falling timber & two other high mountains of like description to a large [Collins'] creek running west. kept down [this creek] 4 miles and left it to our left and passed over a mountain as bad as usual to a Branch which runs to our left." This steady westward course which Captain Clark is holding does not agree at all with the meanders of this part of the 1854 Mullan trail as dotted on the Stevens map, which fetches out much further south, by Kamai or Komeyer creek (Commearp creek of our text of May and June, 1806, now known as Lawyer's Cañon creek), and thus south of Lo Lo fork. Observe how nearly Captain Clark holds to west—his southings are mostly 20° or less ; and I believe the simple, slightly curved line which you see on his 1814 map, as representing the L. and C. trail on a very small scale, is the most nearly accurate delineation we have of this " Lo Lo " route. It is true that he runs Hungry creek due south into the Kooskooskee itself, and therefore cuts Collins' creek down to a short westward run ; but that does not obscure his route. This Collins' creek is what is now called the Nahwah river, or Lo Lo fork of the Kooskooskee ; and Hungry creek is one of its northern tributaries. Clark is all right, as usual ; next lap will fetch him out of the mountains, and we can turn to our modern maps again.

We followed soon after sunrise. At six miles the ridge terminated, and we had before us the cheering prospect of the large plain to the southwest. On leaving the ridge we again ascended and went down several mountains; six miles further we came to Hungry creek, where it was 15 yards wide, and received the waters of a branch from the north. We went up it on a course nearly due west, and at three miles crossed a second branch flowing from the same quarter. The country is thickly covered with pine timber, of which we have enumerated eight distinct species. Three miles beyond this last branch of Hungry creek we camped, after a fatiguing route of 18 miles.

The road along the creek is a narrow rocky path near the borders of very high precipices, from which a fall seems almost inevitable destruction. One of our horses slipped and rolled over with his load down the hill-side, which was nearly perpendicular and strewed with large irregular rocks, (*p. 453*) nearly 100 yards, and did not stop till he fell into the creek. We all expected he was killed; but to our astonishment, on taking off his load he rose, seemed but little injured, and in 20 minutes proceeded with his load. Having no other provision we took some portable soup, our only refreshment during the day. This abstinence, joined with fatigue, has a visible effect on our health. The men are growing weak and losing their flesh very fast; several are afflicted with dysentery, and eruptions of the skin are very common.

September 20th.[34] Captain Clark went on through a country as rugged as usual, till, on passing a low mountain, he came at the distance of four miles to the forks of a large creek.

[34] Clark G 133, Sept. 20th: "S. 60° W. 12 miles to the Low Country at the foot of the Mountain, passed over into the forks of a large Creek at 4 miles. Kept down this Creek 2 miles and left it to our left hand, passing on a dividing ridge, passed some dreans [drains] to our left. West 6 miles to an Pierced nose Indian Village in a Small Plain passd. thro a open pine Countery crossed 2 runs passing to our left. N. 70° W. 2 miles to a 2d. Village passing through the open plains covered with horses &c & Indian womin diging roots." Total 20 miles, little south of west on the whole. I understand that Captain Clark

Down this he kept on a course S. 60° W. for two miles; then, turning to the right, continued over a dividing ridge where were the heads of several small streams, and at twelve miles' [total] distance descended the last of the Rocky mountains [Bitter-root ranges] and reached the level country. A beautiful open plain, partially supplied with pine, now presented itself. He continued for five miles, when he discovered three Indian boys who, on observing the party, ran off and hid themselves in the grass. Captain Clark immediately alighted, and giving his horse and gun to one of the men, went after the boys. He soon relieved their apprehensions, and sent them forward to a village about a mile off, with presents of small pieces of ribbon.

Soon after the boys reached home, a man came out to meet the party, with great caution; but he conducted them to a large tent in the village, and all the inhabitants gathered round to view with a mixture of fear and pleasure these wonderful strangers. The conductor now informed Captain Clark, by signs, that the spacious tent was the residence of the great chief, who had set out three days ago with all the warriors to attack some of their enemies toward the southwest; that he would not return before 15 or 18 days, and that in the meantime there were only a few men left to guard the wo- (*p. 454*) men and children. They now set before them a small piece of buffalo-meat, some dried salmon, berries, and several kinds of roots. Among these last is one which is round, much like an onion in appearance, and sweet to the taste. It is called quamash, and is eaten either in its natural state, or boiled into a kind of soup, or made into a cake, which is then called pasheco.[35] After the long absti-

---

comes out on the Weippe prairie, north of the Nahwah river or Lo Lo Fork, in the vicinity of the present town of Weippe, and keeps on to a point some 12 or 15 miles above the mouth of the creek now called Flores or Jim Ford's, which he will call Village creek, and which runs into the Kooskooskee from the east. He is still in Shoshone Co., and is approaching the eastern border of the present Nez-percé Indian Reservation. This low country is plainly lettered " Quamash Flats " on his map of 1814.

[35] " Quawmash or passhico," Clark G 119, and in great profusion of spellings.

nence this was a sumptuous treat. They returned the kindness of the people by a few small presents, and then went on in company with one of the chiefs to a second village in the same plain, at the distance of two miles. Here the party were treated with great kindness, and passed the night. The hunters were sent out, but, though they saw some tracks of deer, were not able to procure anything.

We were detained till ten o'clock before we could collect our scattered horses; we then proceeded for two miles, when to our great joy we found the horse which Captain Clark had killed; also a note apprising us of his intention of going to the plains toward the southwest, and collecting provisions by the time we reached him. At one o'clock we halted on a small stream, and made a hearty meal of horse-flesh. On examination it now appeared that one of the horses was missing, and the man in whose charge he had been was directed to return and search for him. He came back in about two hours without having been able to find the horse; but as the load was too valuable to be lost, two of the best woodsmen were directed to continue the search, while we proceeded. Our general course was S. 25° W.,[36] through a thick forest of large pine, which has fallen in many places and very much obstructs the road. After making about 15 miles we camped on a ridge, where we could find but little grass and no water. We succeeded, however, in procuring some from a distance, and supped on the remainder of the horse.

in the codices, *passim ;* as, for the former word, quamas, kamash, kamas, camash, camas, commis, commas, etc.; for the latter, pashequaw, pashequa, etc.; The usual spellings are now camas or kamas, and camass ; from the latter form is the New Latin generic name *Camassia.* This is applied to a genus of bulbous liliaceous plants of North America, nearly related to *Scilla* (squill), with long linear leaves and a scape with blue flowers in a raceme. The name is Indian. There are two Western species, *C. esculenta* and *C. leichlini,* growing in moist meadows from California to British Columbia and Montana. Our text will have much to say of these important food-plants.

[36] *Sic*—but read S. 85° W. See Clark's course of Sept. 18th, p. 601. The Expedition is on his trail.

On descending the heights of the mountains the soil becomes gradually more fertile, and the land through which (*p. 455*) we passed this evening is of an excellent quality. It has a dark gray soil, though it is very broken, with large masses of gray freestone above the ground in many places. Among the vegetable productions we distinguished the alder [*Alnus incana ?*], honeysuckle, and huckleberry [like those which are] common in the United States, and a species of honeysuckle known only westward of the Rocky mountains, which rises to the height of about four feet and bears a white berry. There is also a plant resembling the choke-cherry, which grows in thick clumps eight or ten feet high, and bears a black berry with a single stone and of a sweetish taste. The arbor vitæ [*Thuja occidentalis ?*], is very common and grows to a great size, being from two to six feet in diameter.

Saturday, September 21st. The free use of food, to which he had not been accustomed, made Captain Clark very sick,[37] both yesterday evening and during the whole of to-day. He therefore sent out all the hunters and remained himself at the village, as well on account of his sickness as for the purpose of avoiding suspicion and collecting information from the Indians as to the route.

The two villages consist of about thirty double tents, and the inhabitants call themselves Chopunnish or Pierced-nose.[38] The chief drew a chart of the river, and explained

[37] " I am very sick to day and puke which relieves me," Clark G 121.

[38] Nez-Percé Indians of the French, the leading tribe of the Shahaptian family of modern classification and nomenclature.

Gallatin's map of 1836 presents the name Sahaptin, referring only to the Nez-Percé tribe, of whose linguistic affinities he knew nothing, however. The name Shahaptan was based by Scouler in 1841 (Journ. Roy. Geogr. Soc. XI., p. 225) upon vocabularies collected by Tolmie, and included three tribes, viz.: Shahaptan or Nez-Percé, Kliketat, and Okanagan—the latter, however, proving to be of a different (Salishan or Flathead) linguistic stock. The word itself is Salishan, but its meaning is unknown. In 1847 Pritchard (Phys. Hist. Mankind, V., p. 428) followed Scouler in using this name, which he applied to two groups of Indians : Nez Percés proper, of the mountains, and Polanches, of the plains ; his use of the term covers the Kliketat and Okanagan, thus including

that a greater chief than himself, who governed this village and was called Twisted-hair, was now fishing at the distance of half a day's ride down the river. His chart made the Kooskooskee fork a little below his camp, a second fork was below, still further on a large branch flowed in on each side, below which the river passed the mountains. Here was a great fall of water, near which lived white people, from whom were procured the white beads and brass ornaments worn by the women.

A chief of another band made a visit this morning, and smoked with Captain Clark. The hunters returned without having been able to kill anything; Captain Clark purchased as much dried salmon, roots, and berries as he could, (*p. 456*) with the few articles he chanced to have in his pockets; and having sent them by one of the men and a hired Indian back to Captain Lewis, he went on toward the

a Salishan tribe. The Sahaptin of Hale (U. S. Expl. Exped. VI. 1846, pp. 19C, 212, 552) includes the Nez Percés, Walla-Wallas, Pelooses, Yakemas, and Klikatats. Gallatin follows Hale, in Trans. Amer. Ethn. Soc. II. 1848. Gallatin in Schoolcraft, III. 1853, p. 402, covers Nez-percés and Wallawallas. The Sahaptin of Latham's works is nearly synonymous with the Shahaptian family as now understood, but includes certain members of another stock (Waiilatpu); and the same is to be said of Keane's Sahaptin. The Shahaptani of Tolmie and Dawson, Comp. Vocabs. 1884, p. 78, notes the Whulwhaipum tribe. Under the name Sahaptin, Gatschet, Mag. Amer. Hist. 1877, p. 168, defined the family as now accepted, and gave a list of the tribes.

The habitat of these tribes was along the waters of the Columbia and its tributaries from the Cascade range on the west to the Bitter-root mountains on the east, and from about 46° N. on the north to 44° N. on the south. Their neighbors on the N.W., N., and N.E. were Salishan tribes ; on the S., Shoshonean ; on the W., Chinookan and Waiilatpuan ; Chinook territory extended into Shahaptian along the Columbia itself to the Dalles, and some Waiilatpuan stock was isolated in Shahaptian territory further up this river.

Latest returns of Shahaptian Indians are as follows :

1. *Chopunnish*, 1,515, on Nez Percé Reservation, Idaho.
2. *Klikitat*, perhaps half of 330 Indians on Yakama Reservation, Washington.
3. *Paloos*, census uncertain, on Yakama Reservation.
4. *Tenaino*, 69, Warm Springs Reservation, Oregon.
5. *Tyigh*, 430, with the Tenainos.
6. *Umatilla*, 179, on Umatilla Reservation, Oregon.
7. *Walla-walla*, 405, on Walla-walla Reservation, Oregon.

camp of Twisted-hair. It was four o'clock before he set out, and the night soon came on; but having met an Indian coming from the river, they engaged him, by a present of a neckcloth, to guide them to Twisted-hair's camp. For twelve miles they proceeded through the plain before they reached the river-hills, which are very high and steep. The whole valley from these hills to the Rocky mountains is a beautiful level country, with a rich soil covered with grass. There is, however, but little timber, and the ground is badly watered. The plain is so much lower than the surrounding hills, or so much sheltered by them, that the weather is quite warm, while the cold of the mountains is extreme. From the top of the river-hills they proceeded down for three miles till they reached the water-side [Kooskooskee river, at mouth of Village creek from the east],³⁹ near midnight. Here they found a small camp of five squaws and three children, the chief himself being camped, with two others, on a small island in the river; the guide called to him, and he soon came over. Captain Clark gave him a medal, and they smoked together till one o'clock.

We could not set out till eleven o'clock; because, being obliged in the evening to loosen our horses to enable them to find subsistence, it is always difficult to collect them in the morning. At that hour we continued along the ridge on which we had slept, and at 1½ miles reached a large creek running to our left, just above its junction with one of its branches. We proceeded down the low grounds of this creek, which are level, wide, and heavily timbered; but turned to the right at the distance of 2½ miles, and began to pass the broken and hilly country; the thick timber had fallen in so many places that we could scarcely make our

³⁹ Clark G 133, Sept 21st: "N. 80° W. 12 miles thro an open leavel rich pine countery to the top of the river hills passed no water. S. 70° W. 3 miles down a steep hill to the [Kooskooskee] river at the mouth of a small [Village, now Flores or Jim Ford's] creek on which the Indian village is situated—" the camp of the Twisted hare," *sic*, Clark G 121. This creek is nameless in Clark G, and hence no name appears in Biddle; it is called Village creek in another codex.

way. After going five miles we passed the creek on which
Captain Clark had camped during the night of the 19th, and
continued five miles further over the (*p. 457*) same kind of
road, till we came to the forks of a large creek. We crossed
the northern branch of this stream, and proceeded down it
on the west side for a mile. Here we found a small plain
where there was tolerable grass for the horses, and therefore remained during the night, having made 15 miles, on a
course S. 30° W.[40]

The arbor vitæ [*Thuja occidentalis*] increases in size and
quantity as we advance, some of the trees we passed to-day
being capable of forming periogues at least 45 feet in length.
We were so fortunate also as to kill a few pheasants and
a prairie-wolf, which, with the remainder of the horse, supplied us with one meal, the last of our provisions ; our food
for the morrow being wholly dependent on the chance of
our guns.

Sunday, September 22d. Captain Clark passed over to the
island with Twisted-hair, who seemed to be cheerful and sin-
cere in his conduct. The river at this place is about 160
yards wide, but interrupted by shoals ; the low grounds on
its borders are narrow. The hunters brought in three deer ;
after which Captain Clark left his party, and, accompanied
by Twisted-hair and his son, rode back to the village, where
he arrived about sunset. They then walked up together to
the second village, where we had just arrived.

We had intended to set out early ; but one of the men
having neglected to hobble his horse, he strayed away, and
we were obliged to wait till nearly twelve o'clock. We then
proceeded on a western course for 2½ miles, when we met
the hunters sent by Captain Clark from the village 7½ miles
distant, with provisions. This supply was most seasona-
ble, as we had tasted nothing since last night ; and the fish,

---

[40] *Sic*—but read S. 80° W. See Clark's course of Sept. 19th, p. 602. The
Expedition is on his trail.

roots, and berries, in addition to a crow which we had killed on the route, completely satisfied our hunger.   After this refreshment we proceeded in much better spirits, and at a few miles were overtaken by the two men who had been sent back after a horse on the 20th.   They were perfectly exhausted with the fa- (*p. 458*) tigue of walking and the want of food ; but, as we had two spare horses, they were mounted and brought on to the village.

They had set out about three o'clock in the afternoon of the 20*th* with one horse between them; after crossing the mountain they came to the place where we had eaten the horse.   Here they camped, and having no food made a fire and roasted the head of the horse, which even our appetites had spared, and supped on the ears, skin, and lips of the animal.   The next morning, 21*st*, they found the track of the horse ; pursuing it, they recovered the saddle-bags, and at length, about eleven o'clock, the horse himself.   Being now both mounted, they set out to return, and slept at a small stream ; during the day they had nothing at all except two pheasants, which were so torn to pieces by the shot that the head and legs were the only parts fit for food.   In this situation they found the next morning, 22*d*, that during the night their horses had run away or been stolen by the Indians.   They searched for them until nine o'clock, when seeing that they could not recover them, and fearful of starving if they remained where they were, they set out on foot to join us, carrying the saddle-bags alternately.   They walked as fast as they could during the day, till they reached us in a deplorable state of weakness and inanition.

As we approached the village most of the women, though apprised of our being expected, fled with their children into the neighboring woods.   The men, however, received us without any apprehension, and gave us a plentiful supply of provisions.   The plains were now crowded with Indians, who came to see the persons of the whites, and the strange things they brought with them ; but, as our guide was a perfect stranger to their language, we could converse by signs only. Our inquiries were chiefly directed to the situation of the country, the courses of the rivers, and the Indian villages, of all which we received information from several of the Indians ; and as their accounts varied but little from each other, we were induced to place confidence (*p. 459*) in them. Among others, Twisted-hair drew a chart of the river on a white elk-skin. According to this, the Koos-kooskee forks [confluence of its North fork] a few miles from this place ; two days toward the south is another and larger fork [confluence of Snake river], on which the Shoshonee or Snake Indians fish ; five days' journey further is a large river from the northwest [*i. e.*, the Columbia itself] into which Clark's river empties ; from the mouth of that river [*i. e.*, confluence of the Snake with the Columbia] to the falls is five days' journey further ; on all the forks as well as on the main river great numbers of Indians reside, and at the falls are establishments of whites [not so then]. This was the story of Twisted-hair.

Monday, September 23d. The chiefs and warriors were all assembled this morning, and we explained to them where we came from, the objects of our visiting them, and our pacific intentions toward all the Indians. This being conveyed by signs, might not have been perfectly comprehended, but appeared to give perfect satisfaction. We now gave a medal to two of the chiefs, a shirt in addition to the medal already received by Twisted-hair, and delivered a flag and a hand-kerchief for the grand chief on his return. To these were added a knife, a handkerchief, and a small piece of tobacco for each chief. The inhabitants did not give us any pro-visions gratuitously. We therefore purchased a quantity of fish, berries (chiefly red haws), and roots ; and in the after-noon went on to the second village. Twisted-hair intro-duced us into his own tent, which consisted, however, of noth-ing more than pine-bushes and bark, and gave us some dried salmon boiled. We continued our purchases, and obtained as much provision as our horses could carry in their present weak condition as far as the river. The men exchanged a few old canisters for dressed elk-skins, of which they made shirts. Great crowds of the natives were round us all night, but we have not yet missed anything except a knife and a few other articles stolen yesterday from a shot-pouch. At dark we had a hard wind from the southwest accompanied with rain which lasted half an hour ; but in the morning,

(*p. 460*) *September 24th*, the weather was fair. We sent back Colter in search of the horses lost in the mountains, and having collected the rest set out at ten o'clock along the same route already passed by Captain Clark toward the river. All around the village the women are busily employed in gathering and dressing the pasheco-root, of which large quantities are heaped in piles over the plain. We now felt severely the consequence of eating heartily after our late privations. Captain Lewis and two of the men were taken very ill last evening ; to-day he could hardly sit on his horse, while others were obliged to be put on horseback, and some, from extreme weakness and pain, were forced to lie down alongside of the road for some time. At sunset we reached the island where the hunters had been left on the 22d. They had been unsuccessful, having killed only two deer since that time, and two of them were very sick. A little below this island is a larger one on which we camped,[41] and administered Rush's pills to the sick.

September 25th. The weather was very hot and oppressive to the party, most of whom are now complaining of sickness. Our situation, indeed, rendered it necessary to husband our remaining strength, and it was determined to proceed down the river in canoes. Captain Clark therefore set out with Twisted-hair and two young men, in quest of timber for canoes. As he went down the river he crossed at the distance of a mile a creek from the right, which from the rocks that obstructed its passage, he called Rockdam[42]

[41] In the Kooskooskee river, a mile or so above Rockdam or Oro Fino creek. See next note.

[42] Now called Oro Fino, in Spanish. This is the creek on one of whose upper reaches is Pierce City, county seat of Shoshone Co., Idaho.

river. The hills along the river are high and steep ; the low grounds are narrow, and the navigation of the river is embarrassed by two rapids. At the distance of three miles further he reached two nearly equal forks[43] of the river, one of which flowed in from the north. Here he rested for an hour, and cooked a few salmon, which one of the Indians caught with a gig. Here he was joined by two canoes of Indians from below ; they were long, steady, (*p. 461*) and loaded with the furniture and provisions of two families. He now crossed the south fork [main stream of the Clearwater or Kooskooskee], and returned to the camp on the south side, through a narrow pine-bottom the greater part of the way, in which was found much fine timber for canoes. One of the Indian boats, with two men, set out at the same time ; and such was their dexterity in managing the pole that they reached camp within fifteen minutes after him, though they had to drag the canoe over three rapids. He found Captain Lewis and

[43] Confluence of the North fork of the Kooskooskee or Clearwater with this river itself. Clark G 134, starting from Village (Flores) creek : " West 3 miles down the river to the mouth of a large Creek I call rock Dam on the right side, passing a bad road on a steep hill side and place the Indians catch fish at 2 Islands river about 150 yds. wide and is the one we killed the 1st Coalt on. N. 70° W. 2 miles down the Kosskosske River to a rapid at a graveley Island Hills high & Steep Small bottoms covered with pine passed 2 rapids. S. 75° W. 3 miles to the forks of the river the N.W. fork as large as the [other, I call it the] Chopunnish River. Crossed to the South Side and formed a camp to build Canoes &c. in a Small Pine bottom opposit a riffle in the South fok &c." That was a wonderful inference the great geographer drew—that here again was the same river on which the first colt was killed—considering that he never saw it from Colt-killed creek to Village creek, and meanwhile crossed mountain after mountain, with creeks running both to the right and to the left. The total distance, from mouth of Traveler's-rest creek to the present camp, by one codex is 190 miles, by another 184 ; the crow-flight distance is very much less, because the trail is so crooked, both in the vertical and horizontal planes. Having been neither frozen nor starved quite to death—having survived camass roots, tartar emetic, and Rush's pills—the explorers have reached navigable Columbian waters, by riding and eating their horses. They call this place Canoe Camp, because they build boats here. We have them once more between river-banks ; by the grace of God, good luck, and especially good steering, the Expedition will shoot every rapid without drowning anybody, down the Kooskooskee, down the Snake, and down the Columbia, to the Pacific Ocean.

several of the men still very sick; and distributed, to such as were in need of it, salts and tartar emetic."[44]

September 26th.[45] Having resolved to go down to some spot calculated for building canoes, we set out early this morning, proceeded five miles, and camped on low ground on the south, opposite the forks of the river. But so weak were the men that several were taken sick in coming down, the weather being oppressively hot. Two chiefs and their families followed us, and camped with a great number of horses near us; soon after our arrival we were joined by two Indians, who came down the north fork on a raft. We purchased some fresh salmon, and having distributed axes and portioned off the labor of the party, we began,

Friday, 27th, at an early hour, the preparations for making five canoes. But few of the men, however, were able to work, and of these several were soon taken ill, as the day proved very hot. The hunters returned without any game, and seriously indisposed; so that nearly the whole party was now ill. We procured some fresh salmon; and Colter, who now returned with one of the horses, brought half a deer, which was very nourishing to the invalids. Several Indians from a camp below came up to see us.

September 28th. The men continue ill, though some of those first attacked are recovering. Their general complaint is a heaviness at the stomach, and a lax which is rendered more painful by the heat of the weather and the (*p. 462*) diet

44 " I administered Salts, Pils, Galip [jalap], Tarter emitic &c.," Clark G 127. What the "and so forth " was the codex does not say; yet we know that but one man died during the Expedition.

45 Gass, p. 143, gives an interesting natural history note at this date. " There appears to be a kind of sheep in this country, besides the Ibex or mountain sheep [*Ovis montana*], and which have wool on. I saw some of the skins, which the natives had, with wool four inches long, and as fine, white and soft as any I had ever seen." This, of course, is the Rocky Mountain goat, *Haplocerus montanus.* Putting ourselves back to 1805, we cannot wonder at the confusion that arose between these two animals, neither of which had at that time been recognized by science. It was a sufficiently perplexing case—goats with wool mistaken for sheep, and sheep without wool mistaken for ibexes. See the note, p. 327, and the chapter devoted to natural history, beyond.

of fish and roots to which they are confined, as no game is to be procured. A number of Indians collect about us in the course of the day, to gaze at the strange appearance of everything belonging to us.

September 29th. The morning was cool, the wind from the southwest ; but in the afternoon the heat returned. The men continue ill; but all those who are able to work are occupied at the canoes. The spirits of the party were much recruited by three deer brought in by the hunters.

September 30th. The sick began to recruit their strength, the morning being fair and pleasant. The Indians pass in great numbers up and down the river, and we observe large quantities of small ducks going down this morning.

Tuesday, October 1st, 1805. The morning was cool, the wind easterly ; but the latter part of the day was warm. We were visited by several Indians from the tribes below, and others from the main south fork. To two of the most distinguished men we made presents of a ring and broach, and to each of five others a piece of ribbon, a little tobacco, and the fifth part of a neckcloth. We now dried our clothes and other articles, and selected some articles, such as the Indians admire, in order to purchase some provisions; as we have nothing left except a little dried fish, which operates as a complete purgative.

October 2d. The day was very warm. Two men were sent to the village with a quantity of these articles to purchase food. We are now reduced to roots, which produce violent pains in the stomach. Our work continued as usual, and many of the party are convalescent. The hunters returned in the afternoon with nothing but a small prairie-wolf ; so that, our provisions being exhausted, we killed one of the horses to eat and provide soup for the sick.

October 3d. The fine cool morning and easterly wind had an agreeable effect upon the party, most of whom (*p. 463*) are now able to work.⁴⁶ The Indians from below

⁴⁶ " All the men are now able to work ; but the greater number are very weak. To save them from hard labour, we have adopted the Indian method of

left us, and we were visited by others from different quarters.

October 4th. Again we had a cool east wind from the mountains. The men were now much better, and Captain Lewis himself was so far recovered as to walk about a little. Three Indians arrived to-day from the great [Snake] river to the south. The two men also returned from the village with roots and fish; and as the flesh of the horse killed yesterday was exhausted, we were confined to that diet, atthough it was unwholesome as well as unpleasant. The afternoon was warm.

October 5th. The wind easterly and the weather cool. The canoes being nearly finished, it became necessary to dispose of our horses. They were therefore collected, to the number of 38, and being branded and marked were delivered to three Indians, the two brothers and the son of a chief, who promises to accompany us down the river. To each of these men we gave a knife and some small articles, and they agreed to take good care of the horses till our return. The hunters with all their diligence are unable to kill anything, the hills being high and rugged, and the woods too dry to hunt deer, which is the only game in the country. We therefore continue to eat dried fish and roots, which are purchased from the squaws by means of small presents, chiefly white beads, of which they are extravagantly fond. Some of these roots seem to possess very active properties; for, after supping on them this evening, we were swelled to such a degree as to be scarcely able to breathe for several hours. Toward night we launched two canoes, which proved to be very good.

October 6th. This morning is again cool and the wind easterly. The general course of the wind seems to resemble

burning out the canoes," Gass, p. 144. Both the captains had suffered severely, and scarcely a man escaped diarrhœa or dysentery. They had come from snowy mountains, gaunt as famished wolves, into a sultry valley, and suddenly changed their fare from scant rations of horse-flesh to a full diet of fish and roots. Taken in sufficient quantity, camass is both emetic and purgative to those who are not accustomed to eat it.

that which we observed on the east side of the mountain. While on the headwaters of the Missouri we had every morning a cool wind from the west. At this place a cool breeze springs up during the latter part of the night, or near (*p. 464*) daybreak, and continues till seven or eight o'clock, when it subsides, and the latter part of the day is warm. Captain Lewis is not so well as he was, and Captain Clark was also taken ill. We buried all our saddles in a cache near the river, about half a mile below, and deposited at the same time a canister of powder and a bag of balls. The time which could be spared from our labors on the canoes was devoted to some astronomical observations.[47] The latitude of our camp, as deduced from the mean of two observations, is 46° 34' 56" 3''' north.

October 7th. This morning all the canoes were put in the water and loaded, the oars fixed, and every preparation made for setting out.[48] But when we were all ready, the two chiefs who had promised to accompany us were not to be found, and at the same time we missed a pipe-tomahawk. We therefore proceeded without them.[49] Below the forks this river is called the Kooskooskee; it is a clear rapid stream, with a number of shoals and difficult places. For some

[47] Given in full, Clark G 129 and 136; others, G 138, 139. The latitude deduced is very close—one of the best determinations made.

[48] Canoe Camp, at junction of the North fork with the main stream, whence the Expedition starts to-day, is at the point where the Kooskooskee is conventionally divided into "Upper" and "Lower." The latter course is about 40 miles; first 17 m. a little N. of W., then nine m. about S.W., then nearly due W. to Lewiston, at the confluence of the Kooskooskee with the Snake. The principal tributary in this course is Colter's or Potlatch creek, from the north; the best known is Lapwai, Lapway, or Lapwah creek, from the south; there are five or six others. Besides various cobblestone bars and minor "riffles," as they are called by the river-men, several rapids obstruct the navigation of the river, as the Expedition learns to its cost. Some of these are noted by name, beyond.

[49] "The morning of the 7th was pleasant, and we put the last of our canoes into the water; loaded them, and found that they carried all our baggage with convenience. We had four large canoes; and one small one, to look ahead. About 3 o'clock in the afternoon we began our voyage down the river, and found the rapids in some places very dangerous. One of our canoes sprung a leak. We therefore halted and mended her, after going 20 miles." Gass, p. 145.

miles the hills are steep and the low grounds narrow; then succeeds an open country with a few trees scattered along the river. At the distance of nine miles is a small creek[50] on the left. We passed in the course of the day ten rapids, in descending which one of the canoes struck a rock, and sprung a leak; we however continued for 19 miles, and camped on the left side of the river, opposite the mouth of a small run. Here the canoe was unloaded and repaired, and two lead canisters of powder were deposited. Several camps of Indians were on the sides of the river, but we had little intercourse with any of them.

October 8th. We set out at nine o'clock. At 8½ miles we passed an island; 4½ miles lower, a second island, opposite a small creek on the left side of the river. Five miles lower is another island, on the left; 1½ miles below which is a fourth. At a short distance from this is a large creek[51] from the right, to which we gave the name of Colter's creek, from [John] Colter, one of the men. (*p. 465*) We had left this creek about 1½ miles, and were passing the last of 15 rapids which we had been fortunate enough to escape, when one of the canoes struck; a hole being made in her side, she immediately filled and sunk.[52] The men, several of whom could not swim, clung to the boat till one of our canoes could be unloaded, and with the assistance of an Indian

[50] In fact there are two creeks, from the south or left, falling in close together. The upper one of these is now called Big Cañon creek; the lower, Jack's creek. At to-night's camp, the "small run," from the north, is Bed-rock creek. Among rapids passed to-day are: Steamboat riffle, 500 feet long; Saddle-bag rapid, 400 feet; Big Eddy, 400 feet; and Tenpowwee, 1,000 feet or more.

[51] This is the principal tributary of the Lower Kooskooskee; a much branched stream, arising by many affluents in the Thatuna Hills to the north, in Latah Co., and discharging in Nez-percé Co. It is marked "Pottock Cr." on the G. L. O. map of 1879; elsewhere Puttock and Pollock, but the name oftener goes as Potlatch, or in some similar form. These are all doubtless renderings of an Indian word. The above "small creek," left, is now called Cottonwood.

[52] "In passing through a rapid, I had my canoe stove, and she sunk. Fortunately the water was not more than waist deep, so our lives and baggage were saved, though the latter was wet." Gass, p 145.

boat they were all brought to shore. All the goods were so wet that we were obliged to halt for the night and spread them out to dry. While all this was exhibited it was necessary to place two sentinels over the merchandise; for we found that the Indians, though kind and disposed to give us every aid during our distress, could not resist the temptation of pilfering some of the small articles. We passed, during our route of 20 miles to-day, several camps of Indians on the islands and near the rapids, which places are chosen as most convenient for taking salmon. At one of these camps we found our two chiefs who, after promising to descend the river with us, had left us; they however willingly came on board after we had gone through the ceremony of smoking.

October 9th. The morning was as usual cool; but as the weather both yesterday and to-day was cloudy, our merchandise dried but slowly. The boat, though much injured, was repaired by ten o'clock so as to be perfectly fit for service; but we were obliged to remain during the day till the articles were sufficiently dry to be reloaded. The interval we employed in purchasing fish for the voyage, and conversing with the Indians. In the afternoon we were surprised at hearing that our old Shoshonee guide and his son had left us and had been seen running up the river several miles above. As he had never given any notice of his intention, nor had even received his pay for guiding us, we could not imagine the cause of his desertion; nor did he ever return to explain his conduct. We requested the chief to send a horseman after him to request that he would return and receive what we owed him. From this, however, he dissuaded us, and said (*p. 466*) very frankly that his nation, the Chopunnish, would take from the old man any presents that he might have on passing their camp. The Indians came about our camp at night, and were very gay and good-humored with the men. Among other exhibitions was that of a squaw who appeared to be crazy. She sang in a wild, incoherent manner, and offered to the spectators all the little articles she possessed, scarifying herself in a horrid manner if anyone refused her present. She seemed to be an object of pity among the Indians, who suffered her to do as she pleased without interruption.[53]

October 10*th*. A fine morning. We loaded the canoes and set off at seven o'clock. At the distance of 2½ miles we had passed three islands, the last of which is opposite a small stream on the right.[54] Within the following 3½ miles is another island and a creek on the left,[55] with wide low grounds, containing willow and cottonwood trees, on which were three tents of Indians. Two miles lower is the head of a large island; 6½ miles further we halted at a camp of eight lodges on the left, in order to view a rapid before us. We had already passed eight, some of them difficult; but this was worse than any of them, being a very hazardous ripple strewed with rocks. We here purchased roots and dined with the Indians. Among them was a man from the falls [of the Columbia], who says that he saw white people

[53] "*Wednesday* 9*th*. We stayed here during the whole of this day, which was very pleasant, and repaired our canoe. In the evening we got her completed and all the baggage dry. Here our old Snake guide deserted and took his son with him. I suspect he was afraid of being cast away passing the rapids. At dark one of the squaws, who keep about us, took a crazy fit, and cut her arms from the wrists to the shoulders, with a flint; and the natives had great trouble and difficulty in getting her pacified. We have some Frenchmen, who prefer dog-flesh to fish; and they here got two or three dogs from the Indians." Gass, p. 146.

[54] Not identified. I find no stream from the north between Colter's or Potlatch and Lapwai. Below the latter is one on the right, called Holwai on some maps, Hatwai on others. Some of the named rapids, in the last 20 miles above Lewiston, are: Kent's chute; Island rapid; Reuben's rapid; and Upper and Lower Lewiston shoals. Reuben's is the Rugged rapid of the text.

[55] Near the mouth of which creek is the site of Fort Lapwai, Nez-percé Co., Idaho. This was discontinued as a military post a few years ago, about 1886; the Indian Agency is near that place, and the buildings are used for schools and other purposes. This locality was first settled upon in 1836, or about that year, when the first house was built by the missionary, Dr. Spaulding. This was originally a two-story house, but now only the ground floor remains. Dr. Spaulding set up a printing-office, and ran off the New Testament in the Nez-percé language. His press is now a relic in the State Library at Salem, Ore. The establishment is marked " Old Mission," on Stevens' map. Abandoned 1847.

at that place, and is very desirous of going down with us; an offer which, however, we declined. Just above this camp we had passed a tent, near which was an Indian bathing himself in a small pond or hole of water, warmed by throwing in hot stones.

After finishing our meal we descended the rapid with no injury, except to one of our boats, which ran against a rock, but in the course of an hour was brought off with only a small split in her side.[56] This ripple, from its appearance and difficulty, we named Rugged rapid. We went on over five other rapids of a less dangerous kind; at the distance of five (*p. 467*) miles we reached a large fork [*i. e.*, Snake river itself] of the [Kooskooskee] river from the south; and after coming [having now come] 20 miles halted below the junction [confluence of the Kooskooskee with the Snake] on the right side of the river [near present site of Lewiston,[57] Idaho, adjoining Washington].

[56] " *Thursday* 10*th*. We had a fine morning; embarked early, and passed over some very bad rapids. In passing over one [Rugged rapid] a canoe sprung a leak, but did not sink; though the greater part of the loading was wet; and we had to stop and dry it. We stopped a short distance above the junction of this with another large river [the Snake]. The natives call this eastern branch Koos-koos-ke, and the western [southern] Ki-mo-ee-nem. Yesterday evening I had a fit of the ague and have been very unwell to-day: so much so that I am unable to steer my canoe." Gass, p. 146. All the party had been sick, with their miserable diet and other hardships; and things must have been bad indeed to disable the sturdy sergeant. His drenching on the 8th, when his canoe sunk, probably did it for him, considering he was already affected with the prevailing bowel complaint. In fact, water never seemed to agree with Patrick. He lived chiefly on whisky for fifty years or more after he got home from the Expedition, and when he finally gave up his almost centennial ghost it was after a ducking in the river the Campbellites gave him on his initiation into the mysteries of their religion.

[57] Lewiston is commonly supposed to have been named for Captain Lewis. I have no reason to doubt this, but have not looked up the record. Next after Lewis and Clark, the first white men in this country were the overland Astorians under Hunt and Stuart, in 1812. They came by way of the Snake river, having lost several men by drowning and other casualties. If one wishes to know how *not* to take a party across the continent, let him turn from the present narrative of how to do it, and read Irving's Astoria. Lewiston was first settled in May, 1861, according to affidavit of Levi Ankeney, in the U. S. Land

Our arrival soon attracted the attention of the Indians, who flocked in all directions to see us. In the evening the Indian from the falls, whom we had seen at Rugged rapid, joined us with his son in a small canoe, and insisted on accompanying us to the falls. Being again reduced to fish and roots, we made an experiment to vary our food by purchasing a few dogs, and after having been accustomed to horse-flesh, felt no disrelish for this new dish. The Chopunnish have great numbers of dogs, which they employ for domestic purposes, but never eat; and our using the flesh of that animal soon brought us into ridicule as dog-eaters.

The country at the junction of the two rivers [Kooskooskee or Clearwater with Kimooenim or Snake] is an open plain on all sides, broken toward the left by a distant ridge of high land, thinly covered with timber. This is the only body of timber which the country possesses; for at the forks [of the Kooskooskee] there is not a tree to be seen, and during almost the whole descent of 60 miles down the Kooskooskee from its forks there are very few. This southern branch [*i. e.*, Snake river] is in fact the main stream of Lewis' river, on which we camped when among the Shoshonees.[58] The Indians inform us that it is navigable for 60

Office, made by him for entry of the town site. It was incorporated by the Legislature of Washington Territory in 1863, by the name of the City of Lewiston. Mr. James E. Babb of that place, who gives me some of these points, replies to a question, that the Lewistonians habitually call their river Clearwater, and not by its Indian name. When the city was chartered an attempt was made to name it by the Indian word Sheminakum, meaning "forks of the rivers," by which the Indians knew the place. The town is immediately east of the meridian of 117° W., which separates Idaho from Washington; into which latter state the Expedition now passes.

[58] To appreciate this statement, we must remember: 1st. "Lewis' river" started from that one of its sources which is nearest that source of the Jefferson or Missouri which the Expedition ascended to its supposed fountain-head, when the travelers were ignorant of everything before them. 2d. "Lewis' river" was therefore the Lemhi river, which flows into Salmon river, which flows into Snake river, which flows into the Columbia. 3d. Captain Clark had been bluffed back in descending the Lemhi and some little way down Salmon river; that route being abandoned, the party knew nothing further of "Lewis' river." 4th. Then they went north up Fish creek and down "Clark's river" to Traveler's-

miles [further up]; that not far from its mouth [where we now are] it receives a branch [Grande Ronde river] from the south; and a second and larger branch [Salmon river], two days' march up and nearly parallel to the first Chopunnish villages we met near the mountains. This branch is called Pawnashte, and is the residence of a chief, who, according to their expression, has more horses than he can count. The [Snake] river has many rapids, near which are situated many fishing-camps; there being ten establishments of this [kind] before reaching the first southern branch—one on that stream, five between that and the Pawnashte, one on that river, and two above it; besides many other Indians who reside high up on the more distant waters of this river. (*p. 468*) All these Indians belong to the Chopunnish nation, and live in tents of an oblong form, covered with flat roofs.

rest creek; up this creek, and across country west, over to the main forks of the Kooskooskee or Clearwater river, which latter they descended to its confluence with Snake river. 5th. Here they naturally think they have struck the main stream of " Lewis' river," on which they had camped when among the Shoshones; so " Lewis' river," as at the present moment regarded by them, is the course of the Lemhi into the Salmon, of the Salmon into the Snake, and of the Snake down to the point where they now are, where the Kooskooskee or Clearwater flows into it. 6th. As will be seen by the following paragraph, they here find the Kooskooskee only 150 yards wide, as against 250 of " Lewis' river"; so they now run " Lewis' river " as the " main stream " down to the Columbia itself, as we shall see further on (Oct. 17th), where they make " Lewis' river " 575 yards wide, and the Columbia 960. 7th. Hence, " Lewis' river " as heretofore faultily indicated, was no real single river, but a composite of several. " Lewis' river," consequently, does not appear on all modern maps, the name having lapsed, unfortunately.

But I think it could properly be restored, and this should be done. We are not bound to be held by the first mistaken naming in the text, if the same text subsequently adjusts the name to its proper significance, charts this adjustment correctly, and publishes the new determination in the same book with the original naming. Clark's map is perfectly clear on all the main points. He starts Lewis' river from its confluence with the Columbia. The Kooskooskee is its first large branch. Then it forks; at these forks the present Snake river becomes the " South Fork of Lewis's R." much more extensive than the " North Fork of Lewis's R.," which is now Salmon river. This is sound and simple nomenclature; it is also correct geography. The great stream that rises in and about Lake Henry, and empties into the Columbia, is Lewis' river, by the clear intent of William Clark, who discovered, described, charted, and named it.

At its mouth Lewis' river is about 250 yards wide, and its water is of a greenish-blue color. The Kooskooskee, whose waters are clear as crystal, is 150 yards in width; after the union the river enlarges to the space of 300 yards. At the point of the union is an Indian cabin, and in Lewis' river a small island.

The Chopunnish or Pierced-nose nation, who reside on the Kooskooskee and Lewis' [Kimooenim] rivers, are in person stout, portly, well-looking men; the women are small, with good features and generally handsome, though the complexion of both sexes is darker than that of the Tushe-paws. In dress they resemble that nation, being fond of displaying their ornaments. The buffalo or elk-skin robe decorated with beads; sea-shells, chiefly mother-of-pearl, attached to an otter-skin collar and hung in the hair, which falls in front in two cues; feathers, paints of different kinds, principally white, green, and light blue, all of which they find in their own country; these are the chief orna-ments they use. In the winter they wear a short shirt of dressed skins, long painted leggings and moccasins, and a plait of twisted grass round the neck. The dress of the women is more simple, consisting of a long shirt of argalia [argali] or ibex [bighorn] skin, reaching down to the ankles, without a girdle; to this are tied little pieces of brass, shells, and other small articles; but the head is not at all orna-mented. The dress of the female is indeed more modest, and more studiously so, than any we have observed; though the other sex is careless of the indelicacy of exposure.

The Chopunnish have very few amusements, for their life is painful and laborious; all their exertions are necessary to carn even their precarious subsistence. During (*p. 469*) the summer and autumn they are busily occupied in fishing for salmon and collecting their winter store of roots. In winter they hunt the deer on snow-shoes over the plains, and toward spring cross the mountains to the Missouri for the purpose of trafficking for buffalo-robe. The inconveniences of their comfortless life are increased by frequent encounters with their enemies from the west, who drive them over the mountains with the loss of their horses, and sometimes the lives of many of the nation. Though originally the same people, their dialect varies very perceptibly from that of the Tushepaws [Salishan stock]. Their treatment of us differed much from the kind and disinterested services of the Shoshonees. They are indeed selfish and avaricious ; they part very reluctantly with every article of food or clothing ; and while they expect a recompense for every service, however small, do not concern themselves about reciprocating any presents we may give them. They are generally healthy, the only disorders which we have had occasion to remark being of a scrofulous kind ; for these, as well as for the amusement of those who are in good health, hot and cold bathing is very commonly used.

The soil of these prairies is of a light yellow clay, intermixed with small smooth grass ; it is barren, producing little more than a bearded grass about three inches high, and a prickly-pear, of which we found three species. The first is of the broad-leaved kind, common to the Missouri. The second has a leaf of a globular form, and is also frequent on the upper part of the Missouri, particularly after it enters the Rocky mountains. The third is peculiar to this country, and is much more inconvenient than the other two. It consists of small, thick leaves of circular form, which grow from the margin of each other as in the broad-leaved pear of the Missouri ; but these leaves are armed with a greater number of thorns, which are stronger and (*470*) appear to be barbed ; and as the leaf itself is very slightly attached to the stem, as soon as one thorn touches the moccasin it adheres and brings with it the leaf, which is accompanied by a reinforcement of thorns.[59]

[59] Codex G ends here. The narrative continues directly with Codex H, also a Clark.

CHAPTER XVIII.

DOWN THE SNAKE AND COLUMBIA RIVERS.

The Expedition continues down the Snake from the junction of the Kooskooskee river—Indian camp and traffic—Indian sweat-bath—Many rapids passed—Indian burial-places—A dangerous rapid two miles long—Kimooenim creek—Drewyer's river—Indian fishing-establishments—Accident at a dangerous rapid three miles long—Indian timber appropriated—Difficult rapids—A fall of the river where a portage of nearly a mile is made—The Expedition reaches the Columbia river, Oct. 16th, 1805—A procession of nearly 200 Indians advances to meet the party with music—Smoking and other ceremonies—Snake river now regarded as the main stream of Lewis' river, 575 yards wide at its mouth, the Columbia being 960 yards at the confluence—The Indians call themselves Sokulks—Account of these Indians—Captain Clark with two men ascends the Columbia a few miles—His reception by the Indians—Vast multitude of salmon—Tapteal river, a western tributary of the Columbia—The party holds council with the Indians, obtains a sketch of the Columbia, and lays in stores—The party proceeds down the Columbia—Indians continually passed drying fish—Visit of and conference with Indians—Bad rapids passed—Captain Clark ascends a cliff and sights a mountain supposed to be Mt. St. Helena—He visits some Indians, whose fears that he had fallen from the clouds are allayed—He practices some natural magic—The party proceeds—Visited by many Pishquitpaw Indians—Pelican rapids—Extensive Indian burial-place described—Islands, rapids, and tributaries—Highlands on the right.

FRIDAY, October 11th, 1805.[1] This morning the wind was from the east and the weather cloudy. We set out early, and at the distance of a mile and a half reached a point of rocks in a bend of the river toward the left, near which was an old Indian house, and a meadow on the opposite bank. Here the hills came down toward the water, and formed by the rocks which have fallen from their sides a rapid, over which we dragged the canoes. We passed, a mile and a half further, two Indian lodges in a bend toward the right, and at six miles [or more] from our camp of last evening reached the mouth of a brook on the left.[2] Just above

[1] Vol. II. of the History opens with a Clark, Codex H, beginning at this date, and ending Nov. 19th, 1805. The present chapter xviii. is chapter i. of the original edition, and so on. The reader will also note that a new pagination (in the textual parentheses) begins here with p. 1 of the original Vol. II.

[2] In Asotin Co., Wash., at the elbow made by the river in turning from west northward ; charted by Clark, nameless ; Alpahwah creek of Stevens' map, now variously Alpowah, Alpoway, Alpowai, Alpowa, etc. It is a notable stream in connection with the overland route of Expedition in 1806, from Wallawalla to

this stream we stopped for breakfast at a large camp of Indians on the same side. We soon began to trade with them for a stock of provisions, and were so fortunate as to purchase (*p. 2*) seven dogs and all the fish they would spare.

While this traffic was going on we observed a vapor bath or sweating-house, in a different form from that used on the frontier of the United States or in the Rocky mountains. It was a hollow square six or eight feet deep, formed in the river bank by damming up with mud the other three sides and covering the whole completely, except an aperture about two feet wide at the top. The bathers descend by this hole, taking with them a number of heated stones and jugs of water; after being seated round the room they throw the water on the stones till the steam becomes of a temperature sufficiently high for their purposes. The baths of the Indians in the Rocky mountains are of different sizes, the most common being made of mud and sticks like an oven, but the mode of raising the steam is exactly the same. Among both these nations it is very uncommon for a man to bathe alone ; he is generally accompanied by one or sometimes several of his acquaintances ; indeed, it is so essentially a social amusement, that to decline going in to bathe when invited by a friend is one of the highest indignities which can be offered to him. The Indians on the frontier generally use a bath which will accommodate only one person, formed of a wicker-work of willows about four feet high, arched at the top, and covered with skins. In this the patient sits, till by means of the heated stones and water he has perspired sufficiently. Almost universally these baths are in the neighborhood of running water, into which the Indians plunge immediately on coming out of the vapor bath, and sometimes return again and subject themselves to a second perspiration. This

this point. Here the railroad from Lewiston leaves the Snake to pass on to the Tukanon river. In the bend of the Snake opposite, is or was a place called Red Wolf ; near which falls in, from the right, Steptoe creek, unnoticed in our text.

" Here we got more fish and dogs. Most of our people having been accustomed to meat, do not relish the fish, but prefer dog meat ; which, when well cooked, tastes very well." Gass, p. 147, Oct. 11th.

practice is, however, less frequent among our neighboring nations than those to the westward.   This bath is employed either for pleasure or for health, and is used indiscriminately for rheumatism, venereal—in short, for all kinds of diseases.

On leaving this camp we passed two more rapids and some swift water, and at the distance of 4½ (*p. 3*) miles reached one which was much more difficult to pass.   Three miles beyond this rapid are three huts of Indians on the right, where we stopped and obtained in exchange for a few trifles some pashequa-roots,[3] five dogs, and a small quantity of dried fish.   We made our dinner on part of each of these articles, and then proceeded without any obstruction, till after making 12½ miles we came to a stony island on the right side of the river, opposite which is a rapid; and a second is at its lower point.   About 3½ miles beyond the island is a small brook[4] which empties into a bend on the right, where we camped at two Indian huts, which are now inhabited.   Here we met two Indians belonging to a nation who reside at the mouth of this river.   We made 31 miles to-day, though the weather was warm, and we found the current obstructed by nine different rapids, more or less difficult to pass.

All these rapids are fishing-places of great resort in the season ; as we passed we observed near them slabs and pieces of split timber raised from the ground, and some entire houses which are vacant at present, but will be occupied as soon as the Indians return from the plains on both sides of the river, where our chief informs us they are now hunting antelope.   Near each of these houses is a small collection of graves, the burial-places of those who frequent these establishments.   The dead are wrapped in robes of skins and deposited in graves, which are covered over with earth and marked or secured by little pickets or pieces of wood stuck

[3] Heretofore spelled *pasheco*. Clark H 5 has "pash-he-quar." See note [35], p. 604.
[4] Almota, Alemata, Alenota, etc., creek, a small forked stream in Whitman Co. Clark charts it, nameless ; town and rapids of same name. A lesser creek on same side passed unnoticed some miles above ; this is Wawawa creek.

promiscuously over and around it. The country on both
sides, after mounting a steep ascent of about 200 feet, becomes an open, level, and fertile plain ; which is, however, as
well as the borders of the river itself, perfectly destitute of
any kind of timber, the chief growth which we observed
consisting of a few low blackberries.   We killed some geese
and ducks.   The wind in the after part of the day changed
to the southwest and became high ; but in the morning,

(*p. 4*) *October* 12*th*, it shifted to the east, and we had a fair
cool morning.   After purchasing all the provisions the Indians would spare, which amounted to only three dogs and
a few fish, we proceeded.   We soon reached a small island,
and in the course of three miles passed three other islands
nearly opposite each other, and a bad rapid on the left in the
neighborhood of them.   Within the following seven miles we
passed a small rapid and an island on the left, another stony
island and a rapid on the right, just below which a brook [5]
comes in on the same side, and came to a bend toward the
right opposite a small island.   From this place we saw some
Indians on the hills ; but they were too far off for us to have
any intercourse, and showed no disposition to approach us.
After going two miles to a bend toward the left, we found
that the plains, which till now had formed rugged cliffs over
the river, leaving small and narrow bottoms, became much
lower on both sides.   The river itself widens to 400 yards and
continues for the same width, the country rising by a gentle
ascent toward the high plains.   At 2½ miles is a small creek [6]
on the left, opposite an island.   For the three following
miles the country is low and open on both sides, after which
it gradually rises till we reached a bend of the river toward
the right, 3½ miles further, in the course of which we passed
[Brown's Ferry] a rapid and an island.   The wind now
changed to the southwest and became violent.   We passed
an island at the distance of four miles ; another one mile

---

[5] Penawa, Penawawa, or Penowawa creek, Whitman Co.; charted by Clark,
nameless ; place of same name at or near its mouth ; Cran's ferry.

[6] Dead Man's creek, running westerly in Garfield Co.; town of Reform.

beyond it, where the water was swift and shallow; and two miles further, a rapid at the upper point of a small stony island. We went along this island by the mouth of a brook[7] on the right, and camped on the same side opposite a small island, close under the left shore.

Our day's journey had been 30 miles, and we might have gone still further; but as the evening was coming on we halted at the [upper] end of a rapid, which the Indians represented as dangerous to pass, for the purpose of examining it be- (*p. 5*) fore we set out in the morning. The country has much the same appearance as tha twe passed yesterday, consisting of open plains, which, when they approach the water, are faced with a dark-colored rugged stone. The river is, as usual, much obstructed by islands and rapids, some of which are difficult to pass. Neither the plains nor the borders of the rivers possess any timber, except a few hackberry [*Celtis reticulata*] bushes and willows; and as there is not much driftwood, fuel is very scarce.

October 13*th*. The morning was windy and dark; the rain, which began before daylight, continued till near twelve o'clock. Having viewed very accurately the whole of this rapid, we set out, the Indians going on before us to pilot the canoes. We found it, as had been reported, very dangerous, about two miles in length and strewed with rocks in every direction, so as to require great dexterity to avoid running against them. We however passed through the channel, which is toward the left and about the center of the rapid, without meeting with any accident. Two miles below it we had another bad rapid, a mile beyond which is a large creek in a bend to the left. This is called [by us] Kimooenim[8] creek.

[7] A small stream, now known as Texas Rapids or Alkali Flats creek, meandered by the Oregon Railway and Navigation Company's track; opposite its mouth is town of Riparia. It is notable in connection with the dangerous rapids which begin here. These are described in the text following. They are now known as the Texas rapids. On shooting them, we are presently brought to the two largest branches of the Snake below the Kooskooskee, from the left and right, respectively.

[8] "Ki-moo'-e-nimm," Clark H 7; the Tukenon, Tukanon, Tokanon, Tu-

On leaving it the river soon became crowded with rough black rocks, till at the distance of a mile it forms a rapid which continues for four miles, during the latter part of which, for a mile and a half, the whole river is compressed into a narrow channel, not more than 25 yards wide. The water happened to be low as we passed, but during high water the navigation must be very difficult. Immediately at the end of this rapid is a large stream in a bend to the right, which we called Drewyer's[9] river, after George Drewyer, one of the party. A little below the mouth of this river is a large fishing-establishment, where are the scaffolds and timbers of several houses piled up against each other; and the meadow adjoining contains a number of holes, which seem to have been used as (*p. 6*) places of deposits for fish for a great length of time. There were no entire houses standing, and we saw only two Indians who had visited the narrows; but we were overtaken by two others, who accompanied us on horseback down the river, informing us that they meant to proceed by land down to the great river. At 9½ miles below Drewyer's river we passed another rapid, and 3½ miles further reached some high cliffs in a bend to the left. Here, after passing the timbers of a house which were preserved on forks, we camped on the right side near a collection of graves, such as we had seen above. The country was still an open plain without timber, and our day's journey had no variety, except the fishing-

canon, Tucannon, Tuscanon, etc., river, emptying in Columbia Co., near the boundary of Wallawalla Co.; old Fort Taylor and Grange City at its mouth. This is the most considerable tributary that comes into the Snake from the left or south, below the Kooskooskee. Clark charts it, by name. Its main fork is the Patahaha or Pataha, on which is Pomeroy, the county seat of Garfield Co. The railroad from Lewiston meanders it.

[9] So Clark H 7 ; Pavillon or Pavilion river, as S. Parker's map, 1838 ; "Pavion" river in Irving's Astoria ; Flag river, Wilkes' map, 1841 ; now Peluse or Palouse river, whose name has been spelled in various other ways. It runs chiefly in Whitman Co., then separates this from Adams and Franklin, and falls into the Snake from the north, nearly opposite the boundary between Columbia and Wallawalla counties. This is the largest tributary of the Snake below the Kooskooskee, and the only one of any considerable size on that side.

houses which are scattered near the situations convenient for fishing, but are now empty. Our two Indian companions spent the night with us.

October 14th. The wind was high from the southwest during the evening; this morning it changed to the west and the weather became very cold until about twelve o'clock, when it shifted to the southwest and continued in that quarter during the rest of the day. We set out early, and after passing some swift water reached at 2½ miles a rock [Monumental] of very singular appearance. It was situated on a point to the left, at some distance from the ascending country, was very high and large, and resembled in shape the hull of a ship. At five miles we passed a rapid; at eight another rapid and a small island on the right; and at 10½ a small island on the right. We halted a mile and a half below, for the purpose of examining a much larger and more dangerous rapid than those we had yet passed. It was three miles in length and very difficult to navigate. We had scarcely set out, when three of the canoes stuck fast in endeavoring to avoid the rocks in the channel; soon after, in passing two small rocky islands, one of the canoes struck a rock, but was prevented from upsetting; and fortunately we all arrived safe at the lower end of the rapid. Here we dined; we then proceeded and soon reach- (*p. 7*) ed another [Pine-tree] rapid on both sides of the river, which was divided by an island.

As we were descending it, one of the boats was driven crosswise against a rock in the middle of the current. The crew attempted to get her off, but the waves dashed over her, and she soon filled; they got out on the rock, and held her above water with great exertion, till another canoe was unloaded and sent to her relief; but they could not prevent a great deal of her baggage from floating down the stream. As soon as she was lightened she was hurried down the channel, leaving the crew on the rock. They were brought off by the rest of the party; the canoe itself, and nearly all that had been washed overboard, was recovered. The chief loss was the bedding of two of the men, a tomahawk, and some small articles. But all the rest were wet; and though by drying we were able to save the powder, all the loose packages of which were in this boat, yet we lost all the roots and other provisions, which were spoilt by the water.[10] In order to diminish the loss as far as was in our power, we halted for the night on an island, and exposed everything to dry.

On landing we found some split timber for houses, which the Indians had very securely covered with stone, and also a place where they had deposited their fish. We had hitherto abstained scrupulously from taking anything belonging to the Indians, but on this occasion we were compelled to depart from this rule; and, as there was no other timber to be found in any direction for firewood, and no owner appeared from whom it could be purchased, we used a part of these split planks, bearing in mind our obligation to repay the proprietor whenever we should discover him. The only game we observed was geese and ducks; of the latter we killed some, including a few blue-winged teal [*Querquedula discors*]. Our journey was 15 miles in length.

October 15*th.* The morning was fair. Being obliged to remain for the purpose of drying the baggage, we sent out the hunters to the plains; they returned at ten o'clock, (*p. 8*) without having seen even the tracks of any large game, but brought in three geese and two ducks. The plains are waving, and as we walked in them we could plainly discover a range of mountains bearing southeast and northwest, becoming higher as they advanced toward the north, the nearest point bearing south about 60 miles from us. Our stores being sufficiently dry to be reloaded, and as we shall be obliged to stop for the purpose of making some celestial observations at the mouth of the river, which cannot be at a great distance, we concluded to embark and

---

[10] " *Monday* 14*th.* About 1 o'clock a canoe hit a rock, and part of her sunk, and a number of the things floated out. With the assistance of the other canoes all the men got safe to shore ; but the baggage was wet, and some articles were lost." Gass, p. 148. (Pine-tree rapids, 30 m. below Palouse river.)

complete the drying at that place ; we therefore set out at two o'clock.

For the first four miles we passed three islands, at the lower points of which were the same number of rapids, besides a fourth at a distance from them.   During the next ten miles we passed eight islands and three more rapids, and reached a point of rocks on the left side.   The islands were of various sizes, but were all composed of round stone and sand ; the rapids were in many places difficult and dangerous to pass.   About this place the country becomes lower than usual, the ground over the river not being higher than 90 or 100 feet, and extending back into a waving plain." Soon after leaving this point of rocks we entered a narrow channel formed by the projecting cliffs of the bank, which rise nearly perpendicularly from the water.   The river is not, however, rapid, but gentle and smooth during its confinement, which lasts for three miles, when it falls, or rather widens, into a kind of basin nearly round, without any perceptible current.   After passing through this basin we were joined by the three Indians who had piloted us through the rapids since we left the forks, and who, in company with our two chiefs, had gone before us.   They had now halted here to warn us of a dangerous [Fish-hook] rapid, which begins at the lower point of the basin.   As the day was too far spent to descend it, we determined to examine before we attempted it.

We therefore landed near an island at the head of the rapid, and studied particularly all its narrow and difficult (*p. 9*) parts.   The spot where we landed was an old fishing-establishment, of which there yet remained the timbers of a house carefully raised on scaffolds to protect them against the spring tide.   Not being able to procure any other fuel, and the night being cold, we were again obliged to use the property of the Indians, who still remain in the plains hunt-

[11] The general elevation of the flat country on both sides of the river along here is only 1,000 feet or a little more above sea-level, and the immediate valley of the river is less than this, by the amount noted in the text.   To-day, Jim Ford's and other islands passed ; then the cañon, and camp on Rattlesnake flats, above Fish-hook rapids.

ing antelope. Our progress was only 20 miles, in consequence of the difficulty of passing the rapids. Our game
consisted of two teal.

October 16th. Having examined these rapids, which we
found more difficult than the report of the Indians had induced us to believe, we set out early; and putting our
Indian guide in front, our smallest canoe next, and the rest
in succession, began the descent. The passage proved to be
very disagreeable, as there is a continuation of shoals extending from bank to bank for the distance of three miles, during which the channel is narrow, crooked, and obstructed by
large rocks in every direction, so as to require great dexterity
to avoid being dashed on them. We got through the rapids
with no injury to any of the boats except the hindmost,
which ran on a rock; but by the assistance of the other
boats and of the Indians, who were very alert, she escaped,
though the baggage she contained was wet. Within three
miles after leaving this rapid we passed three small islands,
on one of which were the parts of a house put on scaffolds,
as usual. We soon after came to a rapid at the lower
extremity of three small islands, and a second at the distance
of 1½ miles below them; reaching, six miles below the great
rapid, a point of rocks at a rapid opposite the upper point of
a small island on the left. Three miles further is another
rapid; and two miles beyond this a very bad [Five-mile]
rapid, or rather a fall of the river. This, on examination,
proved so difficult to pass, that we thought it imprudent to
attempt, and therefore unloaded the canoes and made a portage of three-quarters of a mile. This rapid, which is of
about the same extent, is much broken by rocks and shoals,
(*p. 10*) and has a small island in it on the right side.

After crossing by land we halted for dinner, and whilst we
were eating were visited by five Indians, who came up the
river on foot in great haste. We received them kindly,
smoked with them, and gave them a piece of tobacco to
smoke with their tribe. On receiving the present they set
out to return, and continued running as fast as they could

while they remained in sight. Their curiosity had been excited by the accounts of our two chiefs, who had gone on in order to apprise the tribes of our approach and of our friendly disposition toward them. After dinner we reloaded the canoes and proceeded. We soon passed a rapid opposite the upper point of a sandy island on the left, which has a smaller island near it. At three miles is a gravelly bar in the river; four miles beyond this the Kimooenim[12] empties into the Columbia, and at its mouth has an island just below a small rapid.

We halted above the point of junction, on the Kimooenim, to confer with the Indians, who had collected in great numbers to receive us. On landing we were met by our two chiefs, to whose good offices we were indebted for this reception, and also the two Indians who had passed us a few days since on horseback; one of whom appeared to be a man of influence, and harangued the Indians on our arrival. After smoking with the Indians, we formed a camp at the point where the two rivers unite, near to which we found some driftwood, and were supplied by our two old chiefs with the stalks of willows and some small bushes for fuel.

We had scarcely fixed the camp and got the fires prepared, when a chief came from the Indian camp about a quarter of a mile up the Columbia, at the head of nearly 200

[12] That is, of course, the Snake itself; see note [58] p. 621. The double employ of the name Kimooenim, for the Snake river and for one of its small tributaries (see note, Oct. 13th), is confusing. Perhaps the distinction in the explorers' minds was Kimooenim *river* and Kimooenim *creek*, the latter being the phrase used by them Oct. 13th. More probably, however, it was an editorial oversight to allow Kimooenim to appear in print anywhere as a name of the Snake or Lewis' river. Clark H 15, 23, 24 erases Kimooenim with care and over-writes "**Lewis's**" in very bold letters. The name Kimooenim being thus set aside from Snake river, the matter of Lewis' river was clinched, as it were, by calling another stream Kimooenim. We should expect some sign of feeling at this moment, when the long-sought Columbia is first actually reached; but Clark H 12 is unmoved: "After getting safely over the rapid and haveing taken Dinner set out and proceeded on seven miles to the junction of this river and the Columbia which joins from the N.W. passed a rapid two Islands and a graveley bare [gravelly bar] and imediately [camped] in the mouth [of a] rapid above an Island." Gass views the Columbia with equal simplicity of statement.

men. They formed a regular procession, keeping time to the noise, rather the music of their drums, which they accompanied with their voices. As they advanced they formed a semicircle around us, and continued singing for some time. We then smoked with them all and communicated, as well as we could by signs, our friendly intentions toward all (*p. 11*) nations, and our joy at finding ourselves surrounded by our children. We then proceeded to distribute presents to them, giving the principal chief a large medal, a shirt, and handkerchief ; to the second chief a medal of smaller size ; and to a third chief, who came down from some of the upper villages, a small medal and a handkerchief. This ceremony being concluded, they left us ; but in the course of the afternoon several of them returned, and remained with us till a late hour. After they had dispersed we proceeded to purchase provisions, and were enabled to collect seven dogs, to which some of the Indians added small presents of fish, and one of them gave us 20 pounds of fat dried horse-flesh.

October 17*th*. The day being fair we were occupied in making the necessary observations for determining our longitude, and obtained a meridian altitude, from which it appeared that we were in latitude 46° 15′ 13″ 9‴.[13] We also measured the two rivers by angles, and found that at the junction the Columbia is 960 yards wide, and Lewis' [Snake : see note, Oct. 10th] river 575 ; but soon after they unite the former widens to the space of from one to three miles, including the islands.[14] From the point of junction the country is

[13] A close observation, but little too far south. The longitude 119° W., or a trifle more. In the angle of junction of the Snake with the Columbia is Ainsworth, and near this Pasco, Wash., where the North Pacific meets the Oregon railway—the latter crossing Snake river to make the junction, the former crossing the Columbia to run on west and northwest in Washington. Three counties come together here—Franklin, Wallawalla, and Yakima. The north (right) bank of the Snake, and the north (left) bank of the Columbia, are in Franklin Co. Some ten miles direct above the confluence of the rivers the Yakima comes into the Columbia from the west, and for a considerable distance the N. P. R. R. follows the course of the Yakima.

[14] With his usual sagacity, Gass (p. 151) makes a remark about the important

a continued plain, low near the water, from which it rises gradually, and the only elevation to be seen is a range of high country running from northeast to southwest, where it joins a range of mountains from the southwest, and is on the opposite side about two miles from the Columbia. There is on this plain no tree, and scarcely any shrubs, except a few willow-bushes; even of smaller plants there is not much more than the prickly-pear, which is in great abundance, and is even more thorny and troublesome than any we have yet seen. During this time the principal chief came down with several of his warriors, and smoked with us. We were also visited by several men and women, who offered dogs and fish for sale; but as the fish was out of season, and at present (*p. 12*) abundant in the river, we contented ourselves with purchasing all the dogs we could obtain.

The nation among which we now are call themselves Sokulks; with them are united a few of another nation, who reside on a western branch which empties into the Columbia a few miles above the mouth of the latter river, and whose name is Chimnapum [Chimnahpum, or Cuimnapum]. The languages of these two nations,[15] of each of which we obtained a vocabulary, differ but little from each other, or from that of the Chopunnish who inhabit the Kooskooskee and Lewis' river. In their dress and general appearance they also much resemble those nations; the men wearing a robe of deer- or antelope-skin, under which a few of them have a short

matter of " Lewis' river " already explained, as finally determined by our authors. After remarking that " the small river, which we called Flathead and afterwards Clarke's river, is a branch of the Great Columbia, and running a northwest course, falls into it a considerable distance above this place; we therefore never passed the mouth of that river," he continues: " The Columbia is here 860 yards wide, and the Ki-moo-ee-nem (*called Lewis's river from its junction with the Koos-koos-ke*) 475 yards," *i. e.*, the name now extends to the mouth of the Snake. He makes each measurement 100 yards less than Lewis and Clark do.

[15] Agreeably with this indication of their linguistic affinities, these two nations are referable to the Shahaptian family. On Clark's map the Sokulks, 3,000 souls, are located on the Columbia itself, considerably north of the entrance of the Snake. On this map the " Chimnahpuns," 2,000 souls, are marked on the " Tapctctc " river, *i. e.*, on the Yakima.

leathern shirt. The most striking difference between them is among the females, the Sokulk women being more inclined to corpulency than any we have yet seen; their stature is low, their faces are broad, and their heads flattened in such a manner that the forehead is in a straight line from the nose to the crown of the head; their eyes are of a dirty sable, their hair is coarse and black, and braided as above without ornament of any kind. Instead of wearing, as do the Chopunnish, long leathern shirts highly decorated with beads and shells, the Sokulk females have no other covering but a truss or piece of leather tied round the hips and then drawn tight between the legs. The ornaments usually worn by both sexes are large blue or white beads, either pendant from their ears, or around the neck, wrists, and arms; they have, likewise, bracelets of brass, copper, and horn, and some trinkets of shells, fish-bones, and curious feathers. The houses of the Sokulks are made of large mats of rushes, and are generally of square or oblong form, varying in length from 15 to 60 feet, and supported in the inside by poles or forks about six feet high; the top is covered with mats, leaving a space of 12 or 15 inches the whole length of the house, for the purpose of admitting the light and suffering the smoke to pass through; the roof is nearly flat, which seems to indicate (*p. 13*) that rains are not common in this open country; the house is not divided into apartments, the fire being in the middle of the large room, immediately under the hole in the roof; the rooms are ornamented with their nets, gigs, and other fishing-tackle, as well as the bow for each inhabitant, and a large quiver of arrows, which are headed with flints.

The Sokulks seem to be of mild and peaceable disposition, and live in a state of comparative happiness. The men, like those on the Kimooenim [Lewis' river], are said to content themselves with a single wife, with whom we observe the husband shares the labors of procuring subsistence much more than is usual among savages. What may be considered as an unequivocal proof of their good disposition is the great respect which is shown to old age. Among other marks of it, we observed in one of the houses an old woman perfectly blind, who we were informed had lived more than a hundred winters. In this state of decrepitude, she occupied the best position in the house, seemed to be treated with great kindness, and whatever she said was listened to with much attention. They are by no means intrusive, and as their fisheries supply them with a competent, if not an abundant subsistence, although they receive thankfully whatever we choose to give, they do not importune us by begging. Fish is their chief food, except roots and casual supplies of antelope, which latter, to those who have only bows and arrows, must be very scanty. This diet may be the direct or the remote cause of the chief disorder which prevails among them, as well as among the Flatheads on the Kooskooskee and Lewis' rivers. With all these Indians a bad soreness of the eyes is a very common disorder, which is suffered to ripen by neglect, till many are deprived of one of their eyes, and some have totally lost the use of both. This dreadful calamity may reasonably, we think, be imputed to the constant reflection of the sun on the waters, where they are constantly (*p. 14*) fishing in the spring, summer, and fall, and during the rest of the year on the snows of a country which affords no object to relieve the sight.

Among the Sokulks, indeed among all the tribes whose chief subsistence is fish, we have observed that bad teeth are very general; some have the teeth, particularly those of the upper jaw, worn down to the gums, and many of both sexes, even of middle age, have lost them almost entirely. This decay of the teeth is a circumstance very unusual among Indians, either of the mountains or the plains, and seems peculiar to the inhabitants of the Columbia. We cannot avoid regarding as one principal cause of it the manner in which they eat their food. The roots are swallowed as they are dug from the ground, frequently covered with a gritty sand; so little idea have they that this is offensive, that all the roots they offer us for sale are in the same condition.

A second principal cause may be their great use of dried salmon, the bad effects of which are most probably increased by their mode of using it, which is simply to warm and then swallow the rind, scales, and flesh without any preparation. The Sokulks possess but few horses, the greater part of their labors being performed in canoes. Their amusements are similar to those of the Missouri Indians.

In the course of the day Captain Clark, in a small canoe with two men, ascended the Columbia. At the distance of five miles he passed an island in the middle of the river, at the head of which is a small and not dangerous rapid. On the left bank of the river opposite this river is a fishing-place, consisting of three mat-houses. Here were great quantities of salmon drying on scaffolds; and indeed from the mouth of the river upward he saw immense numbers of dead salmon strewed along the shore or floating on the surface of the water, which is so clear that the salmon may be seen swimming in the water at the depth of 15 or 20 feet. The Indians, who had collected on the banks (*p. 15*) to view him, now joined him in 18 canoes, and accompanied him up the river. A mile above the rapids he came to the lower point of an island where the course of the river, which had been from its mouth [confluence with Lewis' river] N. 83° W., became due west. He proceeded in that direction, till, observing three houses of mats at a short distance, he landed to visit them.

On entering one of the houses he found it crowded with men, women, and children, who immediately provided a mat for him to sit on, and one of the party undertook to prepare something to eat. He began by bringing in a piece of pine-wood that had drifted down the river, which he split into small pieces with a wedge made of elk-horn, by means of a mallet of stone curiously carved. The pieces were then laid on the fire, and several round stones placed upon them. One of the squaws now brought a bucket of water, in which was a large salmon about half dried; and as the stones became heated, they were put into the bucket till the salmon was sufficiently boiled for use. It was then taken out, put on a platter of rushes neatly made, and laid before Captain Clark; another was boiled for each of his men. During these preparations he smoked with those about him who would accept of tobacco; but very few were desirous of smoking, a custom which is not general among them, and chiefly used as a matter of form in great ceremonies.

After eating the fish, which was of an excellent flavor, Captain Clark set out and, at the distance of four miles from the last island, came to the lower point of another near the left shore, where he halted at two large mat-houses. Here, as at the three houses below, the inhabitants were occupied in splitting and drying salmon. The multitudes of this fish are almost inconceivable. The water is so clear that they can readily be seen at the depth of 15 or 20 feet; but at this season they float in such quantities down the stream, and are drifted ashore, that the Indians have only to collect, split, and dry them on the scaffolds. Where they procure the (*p. 16*) timber of which these scaffolds are composed he could not learn; but as there is nothing but willow-bushes to be seen for a great distance from this place, it rendered very probable what the Indians assured him by signs, that they often used dried fish as fuel for the common occasions of cooking.

From this island they showed him the entrance of the western branch of the Columbia, called the Tapteal,[16] which, as far as could be seen, bears nearly west and empties about eight miles above into the Columbia, the general course of which is northwest. Toward the southwest a range of high-land runs parallel to the river, at the distance of two miles

---

[16] Elsewhere printed Tapteel and Tapteet; on Clark's map Tapetete; in Clark H 32 Tâpe-têtt, and 33 Ta-pe-tett, with a colored sketch map locating various tribes on this river, the Columbia, Lewis', and the Kooskooskee. This is the Yakima or Yakama river, heading by numerous affluents in the Cascade range of Washington, and flowing in a general southeast course to its confluence with the Columbia in Yakima Co. The N. P. R. R. follows up this river, approximately, toward points on Puget's Sound. Two islands in the Columbia, possibly corresponding to the two of the text, are now called Glover and Beckwith.

on the left; while on the right the country is low and covered with prickly-pear, and a weed or plant two or three feet high, resembling whin. Eastward is a range of [the Blue] mountains, 50 or 60 miles distant, which bears north and south; but neither in the low grounds nor in the highlands is any timber to be seen.

The evening coming on, he determined not to proceed further than the island, and therefore returned to camp, accompanied by three canoes, which contained 20 Indians. In the course of his excursion he shot several grouse and ducks, and received some presents of fish, for which he gave in return small pieces of ribbon. He also killed a prairie-cock, an animal of the pheasant kind, but about the size of a small turkey. It measured from the beak to the end of the toe 30¾ inches, from the extremity of the wings 42 inches, and the feathers of the tail were 13 inches long. This bird we have seen nowhere except on this river. Its chief food is grasshoppers, and the seed of the wild plant which is peculiar to this river and the upper parts of the Missouri.[17]

The men availed themselves of this day's rest to mend their clothes, dress skins, and put their arms in complete order—an object always of primary concern, but particularly at a moment when we are surrounded by so many strangers.

(*p. 17*) *October 18th.* We were visited this morning by several canoes of Indians, who joined those already with us, and soon opened a numerous council. We informed them, as we had done all the other Indian nations, of our friendship for them, and of our desire to promote peace among all our red children in this country. This was conveyed by signs through the means of our two chiefs, and seemed to be perfectly understood. We then made a second chief, and gave to all the chiefs a string of wampum, in remembrance of what we had said. During the conference four men came in a canoe from a large camp on an island about eight miles

[17] This bird is the sage-grouse, *Centrocercus urophasianus*, already repeatedly noticed. In saying they have not seen it anywhere except on this river, the explorers may be understood as excluding the rest of the country in this vicinity.

below, but after staying a few minutes returned without saying a word to us. We now procured from the principal chief and one of the Cuimnapum [Chimnapum] nation a sketch of the Columbia, and the tribes of his nation living along its banks and those of the Tapteet [or Tapteal]. They drew it with a piece of coal on a robe ; and afterward transferred to paper [being now on Clark H 33], it exhibited a valuable specimen of Indian delineation.

Having completed the purposes of our stay, we now began to lay in our stores. Fish being out of season, we purchased forty dogs, for which we gave small articles, such as bells, thimbles, knitting-needles, brass wire, and a few beads, an exchange with which they all seemed perfectly satisfied. These dogs, with six prairie-cocks killed this morning, formed a plentiful supply for the present. We here left our guide and the two young men who had accompanied him, two of the three being unwilling to go any further, and the third being of no use, as he was not acquainted with the river below. We therefore took no Indians but our two chiefs, and resumed our journey in the presence of many of the Sokulks, who came to witness our departure. The morning was cool and fair, and the wind from the southeast.

Soon after proceeding, we passed the island in the mouth of Lewis' [Snake] river, and at eight miles reached a larger island, which extends three (*p. 18*) miles in length. On going down by this island there is another on the right, which commences about the middle of it and continues for 3½ miles. While they continue parallel to each other, they occasion a rapid near the lower extremity of the first island, opposite which on the second island are nine lodges built of mats, intended for the accommodation of the fishermen, of whom we saw great numbers, and vast quantities of dried fish on their scaffolds.

On reaching the lower point of the island, we landed to examine a bad [Homly] rapid, and then undertook the passage, which is very difficult, as the channel lies between two small islands, with two others still smaller near the left side of the river. Here were two Indian houses, the inhabitants of which were as usual drying fish. We passed the rapid without injury, and 14½ miles from the mouth of Lewis' river came to an island near the right shore, on which were two other houses of Indians, pursuing the customary occupation. At 1½ miles beyond this place is the mouth of a small brook[18], under a high hill on the left. It seems to run during its whole course through the high country, which begins at this place and rises to the height of 200 feet, forming cliffs of rugged black rocks which project a considerable distance into the river. Here we observed a mountain to the S.W., the form of which is conical, and its top covered with snow. We followed the river as it entered these high lands, and at the distance of two miles reached three islands, one on each side of the river, and a third in the middle, on which were two houses, where the Indians were drying fish opposite a small rapid. Near these a fourth island begins, close to the right shore, where were nine lodges of Indians, all employed with their fish. As we passed they called to us to land; but as night was coming on, and there was no appearance of wood in the neighborhood, we went on about a (*p. 19*) mile further, till, observing a log that had drifted down the river, we landed near it on the left side, and formed our camp[19] under a high hill, having made 20 miles to-day.

Directly opposite us were five houses of Indians, who were drying fish on the same island where we had passed the nine lodges, and on the other side of the river we saw a number

[18] "At the comencement of this high Countrey on Lard Side a small riverlet falls in which appears to [have] passed under the high country in its whole cose [course]. Saw a mountain bearing S.W. conocal form covered with Snow," Clark H 35. This river is the Wallawalla, to be more particularly noted on our return trip, April 29th, 1806 ; Wallula at its mouth. The mountain is Mt. Hood.

[19] Judging by the mileage, this camp is on or barely over the border of Washington—if past 46° N., it is in Oregon. This parallel of latitude bounds the two States westward to the meridian of 119° W., whence to the Pacific they are separated by the Columbia river. To-day's voyage has been nearly south ; the Columbia crosses the intersection of 49° N. with 119° W.; and from this point the Expedition will have Washington on the right or north, and Oregon on the left or south.

of horses feeding. Soon after landing we were informed by our chief that the large camp of nine houses belonged to the first chief of all the tribes in this quarter, and that he had called to request us to land and pass the night with him, as he had plenty of wood for us. This intelligence would have been very acceptable if it had been explained sooner, for we were obliged to use dried willows for fuel to cook with, not being able to burn the drift-log which had tempted us to land. We now sent the two chiefs along the left side of the river to invite the great chief down to spend the night with us. He came at a late hour, accompanied by 20 men, bringing a basket of mashed berries, which he left as a present for us, and formed a camp at a short distance from us. The next morning,

Saturday, October 19th, the great chief, with two of his inferior chiefs and a third belonging to a band on the river below, made us a visit at a very early hour. The first of these was called Yelleppit [or Yellept': see April 26th, beyond]—a handsome, well-proportioned man, about 5 feet 8 inches high, and 35 years of age, with a bold and dignified countenance; the rest were not distinguished in their appearance. We smoked with them, and after making a speech, gave a medal, a handkerchief, and a string of wampum to Yelleppit, but a string of wampum only to the inferior chiefs. He requested us to remain till the middle of the day, in order that all his nation might come and see us; but we excused ourselves by telling him that on our return we would spend two or three days with him. This conference detained us till nine o'clock, by which time great numbers of the Indians had come down to visit us. On (p. 20) leaving them we went on for eight miles, when we came to an island near the left shore, which continued six miles in length. At its lower extremity is a small island on which are five houses, at present vacant, though the scaffolds of fish are as usual abundant. A short distance below are two more islands, one of them near the middle of the river. On this there were seven houses, but as soon as the Indians, who were drying fish, saw us, they fled to their houses, and not one of them appeared till we had passed; when they came out in greater numbers than is usual for houses of that size, which induced us to think that the inhabitants of the five lodges had been alarmed at our approach and taken refuge with them. We were very desirous of landing in order to relieve their apprehensions, but as there was a bad rapid along the island all our care was necessary to prevent injury to the canoes. At the foot of this rapid is a rock on the left shore, which is 14 miles from our camp of last night and resembles a hat in shape.

Four miles beyond this island we came to a rapid, from the appearance of which it was judged prudent to examine it. After landing for that purpose on the left side we began to enter the channel, which is close under the opposite shore. It is a very dangerous rapid, strewed with high rocks and rocky islands, and in many places obstructed by shoals, over which the canoes had to be hauled, so that we were more than two hours in passing through the rapids, which extend for the same number of miles. The rapid has several small islands, and banks of muscleshells [20] are spread along the river in several places.

In order to lighten the boats Captain Clark, with the two chiefs, the interpreter and his wife, had walked across the low grounds on the left to the foot of the rapids. On the way Captain Clark ascended a cliff about 200 feet above the water, from which he saw that the country on both sides of the river, immediately from its cliffs, was low and spread into a level plain, extending (*p. 21*) for a great distance on all sides. To the west, at the distance of about 150 miles, is a very high mountain covered with snow, which from its direction and appearance he supposed to be Mount St. Helens,[21] laid down by Vancouver as visible from the mouth

[20] Whence called Muscleshell rapid, in the Summary Statement; now known as Yumatilla rapids. These mussels are species of fresh-water *Unionidæ*.

[21] No doubt correctly identified. Mt. St. Helen, Helen's, Helens, or Helena, is one of the three highest peaks of the Cascade range north of the Columbia, in

of the Columbia. There is also another mountain [Mt. Hood] of a conical form, whose top is covered with snow, in a southwest direction.

As Captain Clark arrived at the lower end of the rapid before any, except one of the small canoes, he sat down on a rock to wait for them; and seeing a crane fly across the river, shot it, and it fell near him. Several Indians had been before this passing on the opposite side toward the rapids, and ~ome few who had been nearly in front of him, being alarmed either at his appearance or the report of the gun, fled to their houses. Captain Clark was afraid that these people had not yet heard that white men were coming; therefore, in order to allay their uneasiness before the whole party should arrive, he got into the small canoe with three men [Drewyer and J. and R. Fields], rowed over toward the houses, and while crossing shot a duck, which fell into the water. As he approached, no person was to be seen except three men in the plains, and they too fled as he came near the shore. He landed before five houses close to each other, but no one appeared, and the doors, which were of mat, were closed. He went toward one of them with a pipe in his hand, and pushing aside the mat, entered the lodge, where he found 32 persons, chiefly men and women, with a few children, all in the greatest consternation; some hanging down their heads, others crying and wringing their hands. He went up to them all and shook hands with them in the most friendly manner; but their apprehensions, which had for a moment subsided, revived on his taking out a burning-glass, as there was no roof to the house, and lighting his pipe. He then offered it to some of the men, distributed among the women and children some small trinkets which he carried about him, and gradually restored some

Cowlitz Co., Wash.; altitude given as 9,750 feet. East of this peak is Mt. Adams, in Yakima county, and north of them both is Mt. Ranier, Rainier, or Regnier. These peaks are about halfway from where the Expedition now is to the sea-coast. Nearly due south of them, across the Columbia and therefore in Oregon, the Cascade range presents the bold peaks, Mts. Hood and Jefferson.

tranquil- (*p. 22*) lity among them. He then left this house, and directing each of the men to go into a house, went himself to a second. Here he found the inhabitants more terrified than those he had first seen; but he succeeded in pacifying them, and then visited the other houses, where the men had been equally successful.[22]

After leaving the houses he went out to sit on a rock, and beckoned to some of the men to come and smoke with him; but none of them ventured to join him till the canoes arrived with the two chiefs, who immediately explained our pacific intentions toward them. Soon afterward the interpreter's wife landed, and her presence dissipated all doubts of our being well-disposed, since in this country no woman ever accompanies a war-party. They therefore all came out and seemed perfectly reconciled; nor could we indeed blame them for their terrors, which were perfectly natural. They told the two chiefs that they knew we were not men, for they had seen us fall from the clouds. In fact, unperceived by them, Captain Clark had shot the white crane, which they had seen fall just before he appeared to their eyes; the duck which he had killed also fell close by him, and as there were a few clouds flying over at the moment, they connected the fall of the birds with his sudden appearance, and believed that he had himself dropped from the clouds; the noise of the rifle, which they had never heard before, being considered merely as the sound to announce so extraordinary an event. This belief was strengthened when, on entering the room, he brought down fire from heaven by means of his burning-glass. We soon convinced them satisfactorily that we were only mortals, and after one of our chiefs had explained our history and objects, we all smoked together in great harmony. These people do not speak precisely the same language as the Indians above, but understand them in conversation. In a short time we were joined by many

[22] "I then entered the third 4th & fifth Lodge which I found somewhat passified, the three men Drewer Jo. & R. Fields, haveing useed everey means in their power," etc., Clark H 40.

of the inhabitants from below, several of them on horse-back; all were pleased to see us, and to exchange their fish and berries for a few trinkets.

(*p. 23*) We remained here to dine, and then proceeded. At half a mile the hilly country on the right side of the river ceased; at 11 miles we found a small rapid, and a mile further came to a small island on the left, where there were some willows. Since we left the five lodges we [have] passed 20 more, dispersed along the river at different parts of the valley on the right; but as they were now apprised of our coming, they showed no signs of alarm. On leaving the island, we passed three miles further along a country which is low on both sides of the river, and camped [23] under some willow-trees, on the left, having made 36 miles to-day.

Immediately opposite us is an island close to the left shore, and another in the middle of the river, on which are 24 houses of Indians, all engaged in drying fish. We had scarcely landed before about a hundred of them came over in their boats to visit us, bringing with them a present of some wood, which was very acceptable. We received them in as kind a manner as we could, smoked with all of them, and gave the principal chief a string of wampum; but the highest satisfaction they enjoyed was the music of two of our violins [Cruzatte's and Gibson's], with which they seemed much delighted. They remained all night at our fires. This tribe is a branch of the nation called Pishquitpaws,[24] and can raise about 350 men. In dress they resemble the Indians near the forks of the Columbia, except that their robes are smaller, and do not reach lower than the waist; indeed, three-fourths of them have scarcely any robes at all.

[23] In Oregon, in Umatilla Co., or somewhat over the border of the lately established Morrow Co. Camp is six or seven miles below the mouth of Umatilla river (which has been passed unnoticed), as we see by comparing Apr. 26th, beyond. See p. 969, and note [23], p. 970.

[24] Or Pishquitpahs, Clark's map, " 2,600 souls"; Pischquitpa's, Clark H 42. This is the same as Pishquow, one of the many (more than 60) tribes of the greatly subdivided Salishan family. See note [29], p. 973.

The dress of the females is equally scanty; for they wear only a small piece of a robe which covers their shoulders and neck, and reaches down the back to the waist, where it is attached by a piece of leather tied tight around the body; their breasts, which are thus exposed to view, are large, ill-shaped, and suffered to hang down very low; their cheek-bones are high, their heads flattened, and their persons in general adorned with scarcely any ornaments. Both sexes are employed in curing fish, of which they have great quantities on their scaffolds.

(*p. 24*) *Sunday, October* 20*th*. The morning was cool, the wind from the southwest. Our appearance had excited the curiosity of the neighborhood so much that before we set out about 200 Indians had collected to see us; and as we were desirous of conciliating their friendship, we remained to smoke and confer with them till breakfast. We then took our repast, which consisted wholly of dog-flesh, and proceeded. We passed three vacant houses near our camp, and at six miles reached the head of a rapid, on descending which we soon came to another, very difficult and dangerous. It is formed by a chain of large black rocks, stretching from the right side of the river, and, with several small islands on the left, nearly chokes the channel of the river. To this place we gave the name of the Pelican rapid, from seeing a number of [white] pelicans and black cormorants about it.[25] Just below it is a small island near the right shore, where are four houses of Indians, all busy in drying fish. At 16 miles from our camp we reached a bend to the left, opposite a large island, and at one o'clock halted for dinner on the lower point of an island on the right side of the channel. Close to this was a larger island on the same side, and on the left bank of the river a small one, a little below.

We landed near some Indian huts, and counted on this cluster of three islands 17 of their houses filled with inhabit-

[25] These pelicans, like all those heretofore mentioned, are of the species *Pelecanus erythrorhynchus.* The cormorants cannot be specified, but were probably *Phalacrocorax dilophus.*

ants, resembling in every respect those higher up the river;
they were busy in preparing fish. We purchased of them
some dried fish, which were not good, and a few berries, on
which we dined; and then walked to the head of the island
for the purpose of examining a vault, which we had marked
in coming along.

This place, in which the dead are deposited, is a building
about 60 feet long and 12 feet wide, formed by placing in
the ground poles or forks six feet high, across which a long
pole is extended the whole length of the structure; against
this ridge-pole are placed broad boards and pieces of canoes,
in a slanting direction, so as to form a shed. It stands east
and west, and neither of the (*p. 25*) extremities is closed.
On entering the western end we observed a number of bodies
wrapped carefully in leather robes, and arranged in rows on
boards, which were then covered with a mat. This was the
part destined for those who had recently died; a little further on, bones half decayed were scattered about, and in the
center of the building was a large pile of them heaped promiscuously on each other. At the eastern extremity was a
mat, on which 21 skulls were placed in a circular form; the
mode of interment being first to wrap the body in robes, then
as it decays to throw the bones into the heap, and place the
skulls together. From the different boards and pieces of
canoes which form the vault were suspended, on the inside,
fishing-nets, baskets, wooden bowls, robes, skins, trenchers,
and trinkets of various kinds, obviously intended as offerings
of affection to deceased relatives. On the outside of the
vault were the skeletons of several horses, and great quantities of their bones were in the neighborhood, which induced
us to believe that these animals were most probably sacrificed at the funeral rites of their masters.

Having dined we proceeded past a small island, where
were four huts of Indians, and at the lower extremity a bad
rapid. Half a mile beyond this, at the distance of 24 [miles]
from our camp, we came to the commencement of the high
lands on the right, which are the first we have seen on that

side since near the Muscleshell rapids, leaving a valley 40 miles in extent. Eight miles lower we passed a large island in the middle of the river, below which are 11 small islands, five on the right, the same number on the left, and one in the middle of the stream. A brook falls in on the right side, and a small rivulet empties itself behind one of the islands. The country on the right consists of high and rugged hills ; the left is a low plain with no timber on either side, except a few small willow-bushes along the banks ; though a few miles after leaving these islands the country on the left rises to the same height with that opposite (*p. 26*) it, and becomes an undulating plain. Two miles after passing a small rapid we reached a point of high land in a bend toward the right, and camped [26] for the evening, after a journey of 42 miles. The river has been about a quarter of a mile in width, with a current much more uniform than it was during the last two days. We killed two speckled [27] gulls, and several ducks of a delicious flavor.

[26] In Klikitat Co., Wash., a matter of some 30 river-miles, by L. and C.'s esti-mates, above the mouth of Lepage's or John Day's river ; but the narrative hardly enables us to speak with confidence on this point. Castle Rock., Ore., seems to have been passed after dinner. Below this come : Alder creek, right ; Willow creek, *left ;* Pine creek (Olive creek of Symons), right ; Wood creek (Pine creek of Symons), right. Willow creek is the largest stream on the Oregon side between the Yumatilla and John Day ; it falls in at Willows, on the boundary between Morrow and Gilliam counties. This is probably one of the two streams mentioned in the text, and Pine creek the other. If so, camp may be located below the latter stream, and above Wood creek, at a point some ten miles above Owyhee rapids. The assigned mileages—42 to-day and 33 to-morrow—favor this adjustment of the actual distances between known points.

[27] Therefore immature birds, but of what species it is useless to conjecture.

CHAPTER XIX.

DOWN THE COLUMBIA TO TIDE-WATER.

MONDAY, October 21st, 1805. The morning was cool, and the wind from the southwest. At 5½ miles we passed a small island; 1½ miles further, another in the middle of the river, which has some rapid water near its head; and opposite its lower extremity, eight cabins of Indians on the right side. We landed near them to breakfast; but such is the scarcity of wood, that last evening we had not been able to collect anything except dry willows, not more than barely sufficient to cook our supper, and this morning we could not find enough even to prepare breakfast. The Indians received us with great kindness, and examined everything they saw with much attention. In their appearance and employments, as well as in their language,

they do not differ from those higher up the river. The dress
is nearly the same; that of the men consisting of nothing
but a short robe of deer- or goat-skin; while the women wear
only a piece of dressed skin, falling from the neck so as to
cover the front of the body as low as the waist, and a bandage tied round the body and passing between the legs, over
which a short robe of deer- or antelope-skin is occasionally
thrown. Here we saw two blankets of scarlet and one of
(*p. 28*) blue cloth, and also a sailor's round jacket; but we
obtained only a few pounded roots, and some fish, for which
we of course paid them. Among other things we observed
some acorns, the fruit of the white-oak [*Quercus garryana*].
These they use as food either raw or roasted, and on inquiry
informed us that they were procured from the Indians who
live near the Great Falls. This place they designate by a
name very commonly applied to it by the Indians and highly
expressive, the word " Timm,"[1] which they pronounce so as
to make it perfectly represent the sound of a distant cataract.

After breakfast we resumed our journey, and in the course
of three miles passed a rapid [Owyhee] where large rocks
were strewed across the river, and at the head of which on
the right shore were two huts of Indians. We stopped here
for the purpose of examining it, as we always do when any
danger is to be apprehended, and send round by land all
those who cannot swim. Five [?] miles further is another
[Rock Creek] rapid, formed by large rocks projecting from
each side, above which were five huts of Indians on the right
side, occupied, like those we had already seen, in drying
fish. One mile below this is the lower point of an island
close to the right side, opposite which on that shore are two
Indian huts.

On the left side of the river at this place are immense
piles of rocks, which seem to have slipped from the cliffs

[1] According to Parker's Journal, the word is " Tum," reduplicated " Tum-tum,"
and the same expression is used by the Indians to indicate the beating of the
heart. The latter sounds differently to us, and is commonly indicated as to its
phonetic quality by different consonants, as " lub-tub," or " lup-tup."

under which they lie; they continue till, spreading still further into the river, at the distance of a mile from the island
they occasion a very dangerous rapid [Squally Hook]; a
little below which on the right side are five huts. For many
miles the river is now narrow and obstructed with very large
rocks thrown into its channel; the hills continue high and
covered, as is very rarely the case, with a few low pine-trees
on their tops. Between three and four miles below the last
rapid occurs a second [Indian], which is also difficult, and
three miles below it is a small river, which seems to rise in
the open plains to the southeast, and falls in on the left. It
is 40 yards wide at its mouth, but discharges only a small
quantity of water (*p. 29*) at present. We gave it the name of
Lepage's river, from [Baptiste] Lepage, one of our company.
Near this little river [now known as the John Day²] and
immediately below it, we had to encounter a new rapid.
The river is crowded in every direction with large rocks and
small rocky islands; the passage is crooked and difficult, and
for two miles we were obliged to wind with great care along
the narrow channels and between the huge rocks. At the
end of this rapid are four huts of Indians on the right, and
two miles below five more huts on the same side. Here
we landed and passed the night, after making 33 miles.

The inhabitants of these huts explained to us that they were
the relations of those who live at the Great Falls. They appear to be of the same nation with those we have seen above,

² John Day, for whom this river and these rapids were named, was a Virginian
or Kentuckian backwoodsman, who joined Hunt's Astoria overland expedition at his camp on the Missouri, at the mouth of the Nadawa, in the winter of
1811-12. He had then been for some years on the Missouri, in the employ of
Mr. Crooks and other traders; was 40 years old, 6 feet 2 inches tall, straight
and sinewy, and a crack shot still, though he had lived fast and injured himself
by his excesses. Like all the rest of these overland Astorians, he suffered terrible hardships and privations in the Snake river country, though he reached
Astoria alive. On a return trip up the Columbia he went insane, and twice
attempted suicide, in July, 1812. They sent him back to Astoria with the assistance of some Indians, but his mind was gone and his constitution shattered. He
died within a year. See the story of him in Irving's Astoria, especially at pp.
138 and 360. (There is another John Day river, near Point William.)

whom, indeed, they resemble in everything except that their language, though the same, has some words different.   They all have pierced noses, and the men, when in full dress, wear a long tapering piece of shell or bead through the nose. These people did not, however, receive us with the same cordiality to which we have been accustomed.   They were poor, but we were able to purchase from them some wood to make a fire for supper, though they have but little, which they say they bring from the Great Falls.   The hills in this neighborhood are high and rugged; a few scattered trees, either small pine or scrubby white-oak, are occasionally seen on them.   From the last rapids we also observed the conical mountain [Mt. Hood] toward the southwest, which the Indians say is not far to the [our] left of the Great Falls.   From its vicinity to that place we called it the Timm or Falls mountain.   The country through which we passed is furnished with several fine springs, which rise either high up the sides of the hills, or else in the river meadows, and discharge into the Columbia.

We could not help remarking that almost universally the fishing establishments of the Indians, both on the Columbia and the waters of Lewis' [Snake] river, are on the right bank. On inquiry we were led to believe that the (*p. 30*) reason may be found in their fear of the Snake Indians; between whom and themselves, considering the warlike temper of that people, and the peaceful habits of the river tribes, it is very natural that the latter should be anxious to interpose so good a barrier.   These Indians are described as residing on a great river to the south, and always at war with the people of this neighborhood.   One of our chiefs pointed out to-day a spot on the left where, not many years ago, a great battle was fought, in which numbers of both nations were killed.

We were agreeably surprised this evening by a present of some very good beer, made [by John Collins] out of the remains of bread composed of the pasheco-quamash, part of the stores we had laid in at the head of the Kooskooskee, which by frequent exposure had become sour and molded.

October 22d. The morning was fair and calm. We left our camp at nine o'clock, and after going on for six miles came to the head of an island and a very bad [Hellgate] rapid, where the rocks are scattered nearly across the river. Just above this and on the right are six huts of Indians. At the distance of two miles below are five more huts; the inhabitants of which are engaged in drying fish, and some of them are in their canoes killing fish with gigs. Opposite this establishment is a small island in a bend toward the right, on which there were such quantities of fish that we counted 20 stacks of dried and pounded salmon. This small island is at the upper point of one much larger, the sides of which are high uneven rocks, jutting over the water; here there is a bad rapid. The island continues for four miles, and at the middle of it is a large river, which appears to come from the southeast, and empties on the left. We landed just above its mouth in order to examine it, and soon found the route intercepted by a deep, narrow channel, running into the Columbia above the large entrance, so as to form a dry and rich island about 400 yards wide and 800 long. Here, as along the grounds of the (*p. 31*) river, the natives had been digging large quantities of roots, as the soil was turned up in many places. We reached this river about a quarter of a mile above its mouth, at a place where a large body of water is compressed within a channel about 200 yards wide, where it foams over rocks, many of which are above the surface of the water. These narrows are the end of a rapid which extends two miles back, where the river is closely confined between two high hills, below which it is divided by numbers of large rocks and small islands, covered with a low growth of timber. This river, which is called by the Indians Towahnahiooks,[3] is 200 yards wide at its mouth, has a very rapid

[3] Thrice Towarnehiooks, Clark H 52, etc.; Towannehooks, H 69; To-war-na-he-ooks, Clark's map. This is the Des Chutes river of modern geography, one of the largest southern tributaries of the Columbia. It rises in southern Oregon,

current, and contributes about one-fourth as much water as the Columbia possesses before the junction. Immediately at the entrance are three sand-islands, and near it the head of an island which runs parallel to the large rocky island.

We now returned to our boats, and passing the mouth of the Towahnahiooks went between the islands. At the distance of two miles we reached the lower end of this rocky island, where were eight huts of Indians. Here we saw some large logs of wood, which had been most probably rafted down the Towahnahiooks; and a mile below, on the right bank, were 16 lodges of Indians, with whom we stopped to smoke. Then, at the distance of about a mile, we passed six more huts on the same side, nearly opposite the lower extremity of the island, which has its upper end in the mouth of the Towahnahiooks. Two miles below we came to 17 huts [of Eneeshurs] on the right side of the river, situated at the commencement of the pitch which includes the Great Falls.⁴ Here we halted, and immediately on landing walked down, accompanied by an old Indian from the huts, in order to examine the falls and ascertain on which side we could make a portage most easily.

about Diamond peak and other mountains of the Cascade range, and flows about north through Wasco county, with numerous tributaries all along its course, but especially on the west side, draining the eastern watershed of the range named.

Gass, p. 153, has: " *Tuesday 22d.* . . At 10 o'clock we came to a large island, where the river has cut its way through the point of a high hill. Opposite to this island a large river comes in on the south side, called by the natives the Sho-sho-ne or Snake-Indian river, and which has large rapids, close to its mouth. This, or the Ki-moo-ee-nem, is the same river, whose head waters we saw at the Snake nation." This was a natural enough surmise, especially if the Indians gave the name of Shoshone or Snake to the Des Chutes river.

⁴ For the Great Falls, now about to be described, see plate. "The first pitch of this falls is 20 feet perpendicular, then passing thro' a narrow chancl for 1 mile to a rapid of about 8 feet fall below which the water has no perceptable fall but verry rapid, See Sketch No. 1," Clark H 57. This sketch, colored, from which the plate was engraved, occupies Clark H 1, overrunning a little on the flyleaf. The scale is 200 yards to the inch; the Biddle plate is slightly reduced. The starboard portage, 1,200 yards, by which baggage was taken down, is marked "Portage"; the larboard one, 457 yards, over which canoes were hauled, is dotted, but not lettered. At head of the falls is Celilo, Ore.

We soon discovered that the nearest route was on the right side, and therefore dropped down to the head of the rapid, unloaded the canoes, and took all the baggage over by land to (*p. 32*) the foot of the rapid.   The distance is 1,200 yards.   On setting out we crossed a solid rock, about one-third of the whole distance ; then reached a space 200 yards wide, which forms a hollow, where the loose sand from the low grounds has been driven by the winds, is steep and loose, and therefore disagreeable to pass; the rest of the route is over firm and solid ground.   The labor of crossing would have been very inconvenient if the Indians had not assisted us in carrying some of the heavy articles on their horses; but for this service they repaid themselves so adroitly that, on reaching the foot of the rapids, we formed a camp in a position which might secure us from the pilfering of the natives, which we apprehend much more than we do their hostilities.   [We made 19 miles to-day, Clark H 56.]

Near our camp are five large huts of Indians engaged in drying fish and preparing it for the market.   The manner of doing this is by first opening the fish and exposing it to the sun on scaffolds.   When it is sufficiently dried it is pounded between two stones till it is pulverized, and is then placed in a basket about two feet long and one in diameter, neatly made of grass and rushes, and lined with the skin of a salmon stretched and dried for the purpose.   Here the fish are pressed down as hard as possible, and the top is covered with fish-skins, which are secured by cords through the holes of the basket.   These baskets are then placed in some dry situation, the corded part upward, seven being usually placed as close as they can be put together, and five on the top of these.   The whole is then wrapped up in mats, and made fast by cords, over which mats are again thrown.   Twelve of these baskets, each of which contains from 90 to 100 pounds, form a stack, which is left exposed till it is sent to market.   The fish thus preserved keep sound and sweet for several years, and great quantities, they inform us, are sent to the Indians who live below the falls, whence it finds its way to the whites who visit the mouth of the Columbia. We ob- (*p. 33*) serve, both near the lodges and on the rocks in the river, great numbers of stacks of these pounded fish.

Besides fish, these people supplied us with filberts [*Corylus rostrata*] and berries, and we purchased a dog for supper; but it was with much difficulty that we were able to buy wood enough to cook it. In the course of the day we were visited by many Indians, from whom we learned that the principal chiefs of the bands residing in this neighborhood are now hunting in the mountains toward the southwest. On that side of the river none of the Indians have any permanent habitations; and on inquiry we were confirmed in our belief that it was for fear of attacks from the Snake Indians, with whom they are at war. This nation they represent as very numerous and residing in a great number of villages on the Towahnahiooks, where they live principally on salmon. That river, they add, is not obstructed by rapids above its mouth, but there becomes large and reaches to a considerable distance; the first villages of the Snake Indians on that river being twelve days' journey on a course about southeast from this place.

October 23*d*. Having ascertained from the Indians, and by actual examination, the best mode of bringing down the canoes, it was found necessary, as the river was divided into several narrow channels by rocks and islands, to follow the route adopted by the Indians themselves. This operation Captain Clark began this morning, and, after crossing to the other side of the river, hauled the canoes over a point of land, to avoid the perpendicular fall of 20 feet. At the distance of 457 yards we reached the water, and embarked at a place where a long rocky island compresses the channel of the river within the space of 150 yards, so as to form nearly a semicircle. On leaving this rocky island the channel is somewhat wider; but a second and much larger island of hard black rock still divides it from the main stream, while on the left shore it is closely bordered (*p. 34*) by perpendicular rocks. Having descended in this way for a mile, we reached a pitch of the river, which being divided by two large rocks, descends with great rapidity down a fall eight feet in height.   As the boats could not be navigated down this steep descent, we were obliged to land, and let them down as slowly as possible by strong ropes of elk-skin, which we had prepared for the purpose.   They all passed in safety except one, which, being loosed by the breaking of the ropes, was driven down, but was recovered by the Indians below. With this rapid ends the first pitch of the Great Falls, which is not great in point of height, and remarkable only for the singular manner in which the rocks have divided its channel.[5]

From the marks everywhere perceivable at the falls, it is obvious that in high floods, which must be in the spring, the water below the falls rises nearly to a level with that above them.   Of this rise, which is occasioned by some obstructions which we do not as yet know, the salmon must avail themselves to pass up the river in such multitudes that this fish is almost the only one caught in great abundance above the falls ; but below that place we observe the salmon-trout, and the heads of a species of trout smaller than the salmon-trout, which is in great quantities, and which they are now burying, to be used as their winter food.   A hole of any size being dug, the sides and bottom are lined with straw, over which skins are laid ; on these the fish, after being well dried,

---

[5] " *Wednesday* 23*rd.*   At 9 o'clock in the forenoon all hands, but three left to keep camp, went up and took the canoes over to the south side ; as the natives said that was the best side of the river to take them down.   Here we had to drag them 450 yards round the first pitch which is 20 feet perpendicular.   We then put them into the water and let them down the rest of the way by cords. The whole height of the falls is 37 feet 8 inches, in a distance of 1200 yards . . . The high water mark below the falls is 48 feet, and above them only 10 feet 4 inches : so that in high water there is nothing but a rapid, and the salmon can pass up without difficulty.   The reason of this rise in the water below the falls is, that for three miles down the river is so confined by rocks (being not more than 70 yards wide) that it cannot discharge the water as fast as it comes over the falls, until what is deficient in breadth is made up in depth.   About the great pitch the appearance of the place is terrifying, with vast rocks, and the river below the pitch foaming through different channels."   Gass, p. 155.

are laid, covered with other skins, and the hole is closed with a layer of earth 12 or 15 inches deep.

About three o'clock we reached the lower camp, but our joy at having accomplished this object was somewhat diminished by the persecution of a new acquaintance. On reaching the upper point of the portage, we found that the Indians had camped there not long since, and had left behind them multitudes of fleas. These sagacious animals were so pleased to exchange the straw and fish-skins, in which they had been living, for some better residence, that we were soon (*p. 35*) covered with them, and during the portage the men were obliged to strip to the skin in order to brush them from their bodies.[6] They were not, however, so easily dislodged from our clothes, and accompanied us in great numbers to our camp.

We saw no game except a sea-otter [*Enhydris marina*], which was shot in the narrow channel as we came down, but we could not get it. Having therefore scarcely any provisions, we purchased eight small fat dogs, a food to which we are now compelled to have recourse, for the Indians are very unwilling to sell us any of their good fish, which they reserve for the market below. Fortunately, however, the habit of using this animal has completely overcome the repugnance which we felt at first, and dog, if not a favorite dish, is always an acceptable one. The meridian altitude of to-day gives 45° 42' 57" 3''' N. as the latitude of our camp.

On the beach near the Indian huts we observed two canoes of a different shape and size from any which we had hitherto seen. One of these we got in exchange for our smallest canoe, giving a hatchet and a few trinkets to the owner, who

[6] " I with the greater part of the men crossed in the canoes to opposite [left] side above the falls and hauled them across the portage of 457 yards. . . I accomplished this necessary business and landed safe with all the canoes at our camp below the falls by 3 o'clock P. M., nearly covered with flees which were so thick among the straw and fish skins at the upper part of the portage at which place the nativs had been camped not long since ; that every man of the party was obliged to strip naked dureing the time of takeing over the canoes, that they might have an oppertunity of brushing the flees of their legs and bodies," Clark H 56.

said he had purchased it from a white man below the falls, by giving him a horse. These canoes are very beautifully made; they are wide in the middle and tapering toward each end, with curious figures carved on the bow. They are thin, but being strengthened by cross-bars about an inch in diameter, which are tied with strong pieces of bark through holes in the sides, are able to bear very heavy burdens, and seem calculated to live in the roughest water.

A great number of Indians both from above and below the falls visited us to-day, and toward evening we were informed by one of the chiefs who had accompanied us that he had overheard that the Indians below intended to attack us as we went down the river. Being at all times ready for any attempt of that sort, we were not under greater apprehensions than usual at this intelligence. We therefore only (*p. 36*) re-examined our arms, and increased the ammunition to 100 rounds. Our chiefs, who had not the same motives of confidence, were by no means so much at their ease, and when at night they saw the Indians leave us earlier than usual, their suspicions of an intended attack were confirmed, and they were very much alarmed.

October 24th. The Indians approached us with apparent caution, and behaved with more than usual reserve. Our two chiefs, by whom these circumstances were not unobserved, now told us that they wished to return home; that they could be no longer of any service to us; that they could not understand the language of the people below the falls; that those people formed a different nation from their own; that the two people had been at war with each other; and that as the Indians had expressed are solution to attack us, they would certainly kill them. We endeavored to quiet their fears, and requested them to stay two nights longer, in which time we would see the Indians below, and make a peace between the two nations. They replied that they were anxious to return and see their horses. We however insisted on their remaining with us, not only in hopes of bringing about an accommodation between them and their enemies,

but because they might be able to detect any hostile designs
against us, and also assist us in passing the next falls, which
are not far off, and represented as very difficult. They at
length agreed to stay with us two nights longer.

About nine o'clock we proceeded, and on leaving our camp
near the lower fall, found the river about 400 yards wide,
with a current more rapid than usual, though with no perceptible descent. At the distance of 2½ miles the river
widened into a large bend or basin on the right, at the
beginning of which were three huts of Indians. At the
extremity of this basin stands a high black rock, which,
rising perpendicularly from the right shore, seems to run
wholly across the river; so totally indeed does it appear to
stop the passage that we could not see where the water
escaped, except that the current ap- (*p. 37*) peared to be
drawn with more than usual velocity to the left of the rock,
where was a great roaring. We landed at the huts of the
Indians, who went with us to the top of this rock, from
which we saw all the difficulties of the channel. We were no
longer at a loss to account for the rising of the river at the
falls, for this tremendous rock stretches across the river to
meet the high hills of the left shore, leaving a channel only
45 yards wide, through which the whole body of the Columbia
must press its way [*i. e.*, Short Narrows⁷]. The water, thus
forced into so narrow a channel, is thrown into whirls, and
swells and boils in every part with the wildest agitation. But
the alternative of carrying the boats over this high rock was
almost impossible in our present situation ; and as the chief
danger seemed to be, not from any rocks in the channel, but
from the great waves and whirlpools, we resolved to try the

---

⁷ We must see Captain Clark in the act of shooting the Short Narrows : " As the
portage of our canoes over this high rock would be impossible with our Strength,
and the only danger in passing thro those narrows was the whorls and swills
arriseing from the compression of the water, and which I thought (as also our
principal waterman Peter Crusat) by good stearing we could pass down safe,
accordingly I deturmined to pass through this place not with standing the horred
appearance of this agitated gut swelling, boiling & whorling in every direction
which from the top of the rock did not appear as bad as when I was in it [italics
mine] ; however we passed safe to the astonishment of the Inds," H 61.

passage in our boats, in hopes of being able by dexterous steering to escape. This we attempted, and with great care were able to get through, to the astonishment of all the Indians of the huts we had just passed, who now collected to see us from the top of the rock. The channel continues thus confined for a space of about half a mile, when the rock ceased. We passed a single Indian hut at its foot, where the river again enlarges to the width of 200 yards, and at the distance of a mile and a half stopped to view a very bad rapid ; this is formed by two rocky islands which divide the channel, the lower and larger of which is in the middle of the river. The appearance of this place was so unpromising that we unloaded all the most valuable articles, such as guns, ammunition, our papers, etc., and sent them by land, with all the men that could not swim, to the extremity of these rapids. We then descended with the canoes, two at a time ; though the canoes took in some water, we all went through safely ; after which we made two miles, stopped in a deep bend of the river toward the right, and camped a little above a large [Echeloot] village of 21 (*p. 38*) houses. Here we landed ; and as it was late before all the canoes joined us, we were obliged to remain this evening, the difficulties of the navigation having permitted us to make only six miles.

This village is situated at the extremity of a deep bend toward the right, immediately above a ledge of high rocks, 20 feet above the marks of the highest flood, but broken in several places, so as to form channels which are at present dry, extending nearly across the river ; this forms the second fall, or the place most probably which the Indians indicate by the word " Timm " [see note, p. 664]. While the canoes were coming on, Captain Clark walked with two men down to examine the channels. On the rocks the Indians are accustomed to dry fish ; and as the season for that purpose is now over, the poles which they use are tied up very securely in bundles, and placed on the scaffolds. The stock of fish dried and pounded was so abundant that he counted 107 of them, making more than 10,000 pounds of that provision.

After examining the [Long] narrows as well as the lateness of the hour would permit, he returned to the village through a rocky, open country, infested with polecats [skunks].

This village, the residence of a tribe called the Echeloots, consists of 21 houses, scattered promiscuously over an elevated situation, near a mound about 30 feet above the common level, which has some remains of houses on it, and bears every appearance of being artificial. The houses, which are the first wooden buildings we have seen since leaving the Illinois country, are nearly equal in size, and exhibit a very singular appearance. A large hole, 20 feet wide and 30 in length, is dug to the depth of 6 feet. The sides are then lined with split pieces of timber, rising just above the surface of the ground, which are smoothed to the same width by burning, or shaved with small iron axes. These timbers are secured in their erect position by a pole stretched along the side of the building near the eaves, and supported on a strong post fixed at each (*p. 39*) corner. The timbers at the gable ends rise gradually higher, the middle pieces being the broadest. At the top of these is a sort of semicircle, made to receive a ridge-pole the whole length of the house, propped by an additional post in the middle and forming the top of the roof. From this ridge-pole to the eaves of the house are placed a number of small poles or rafters, secured at each end by fibers of the cedar. On these poles, which are connected by small transverse bars of wood, is laid a covering of the white cedar, or arbor vitæ, kept on by the strands of the cedar fibers; but a small distance along the whole length of the ridge-pole is left uncovered for the purpose of lighting and permitting the smoke to pass through. The roof thus formed has a descent about equal to that common among us, and near the eaves is perforated with a number of small holes, made most probably to discharge arrows in case of an attack. The only entrance is by a small door at the gable end, cut out of the middle piece of timber, 29½ inches high, and 14 inches broad, reaching only 18 inches above the earth. Before this hole is hung a mat; on pushing it aside and crawling through, the descent is by a small wooden ladder, made in the form of those used among us. One-half of the inside is used as a place of deposit for dried fish, of which large quantities are stored away, and with a few baskets of berries form the only family provisions; the other half, adjoining the door, remains for the accommodation of the family. On each side are arranged near the walls small beds of mats placed on little scaffolds or bedsteads, raised from 18 inches to 3 feet from the ground; and in the middle of the vacant space is the fire, or sometimes two or three fires, when, as is usually the case, the house contains three families.

The inhabitants received us with great kindness, invited us to their houses, and in the evening, after our camp had been formed, came in great numbers to see us. Accompanying them was a principal chief and several of the warriors (*p. 40*) of the nation below the great narrows. We made use of this opportunity to attempt a reconciliation between them and our two chiefs, and to put an end to the war which had disturbed the two nations. By representing to the chiefs the evils which this war inflicted on them, and the wants and privations to which it subjects them, they soon became disposed to conciliate each other; and we had some reason to be satisfied with the sincerity of the mutual professions that the war should no longer continue, and that in future they would live in peace with each other. On concluding this negotiation we proceeded to invest the chief with the insignia of command, a medal, and some small articles of clothing; after which the violin [Cruzatte's] was produced and our men danced, to the great delight of the Indians, who remained with us till a late hour.

October 25th. We walked down with several of the Indians to view that part of the [Long] narrows which they represented as most dangerous. We found it very difficult; but, as with our large canoes the portage was impracticable, we concluded to carry our most valuable articles by land, and then hazard the passage. We therefore returned to the village, and after sending some of the party with our best stores to make a portage, and fixing others on the rock to assist with ropes the canoes that might meet with any difficulty, we began the descent, in the presence of great numbers of Indians who had collected to witness this exploit. The channel for three miles is worn through a hard rough black rock from 50 to 100 yards wide, in which the water swells and boils in a tremendous manner. The first three canoes escaped very well; the fourth, however, had nearly filled with water; the fifth passed through with only a small quantity of water over her. At half a mile we had got through the worst part; and having reloaded our canoes went on very well for 2½ miles, except that one of the boats was nearly lost by running against a rock. At the end of this channel of three (*p. 41*) miles, in which the Indians inform us they catch as many salmon as they wish, we reached a deep basin or bend of the river toward the right, near the entrance of which are two rocks. We crossed this basin, which has a quiet and gentle current, and at the distance of a mile from its commencement, a little below where the river resumes its channel, reached a rock which divides it [above Holman's creek].

At this place we met our old chiefs, who, when we began the portage, had walked down to a village below to smoke a pipe of friendship on the renewal of peace. Just after our meeting we saw a chief of the village above, with a party who had been out hunting, and were then crossing the river with their horses on their way home. We landed to smoke with this chief, whom we found a bold-looking man of pleasing appearance, about 50 years of age, dressed in a war-jacket, a cap, leggings, and moccasins. We presented him with a medal and other small articles, and he gave us some meat, of which he had been able to procure but little; for on his route he had met with a war-party of Indians from the Towahnahiooks, with whom there was a battle. We here smoked a parting pipe with our two faithful friends, the chiefs who had accompanied us from the heads of the river, and who now had each bought a horse, intending to go home by land.

On leaving this rock the river is gentle, but strewed with a great number of rocks for a few miles, when it becomes a beautiful still stream about half a mile wide. At five miles from the large bend we came to the mouth of a [Mill] creek 20 yards wide, heading in the range of mountains which runs S.S.W. and S.W. for a long distance, and discharging a considerable quantity of water; it is called by the Indians Quenett.[8] We halted below it under a high point of rocks on the left; and as it was necessary to make some celestial observations, we formed a [Fort Rock] camp on top of the rocks. This situation is perfectly well calculated for defense in case the Indians should incline to attack us, for the rocks form a sort of natural fortification, with the aid of (*p. 42*) the river and creek; it is also convenient to hunt along the foot of the mountains to the west and southwest, where there are several species of timber which form fine coverts for game. From this rock the pinnacle of the round mountain covered with snow, which we had seen a short distance below the forks of the Columbia, and which we had called the Falls or Timm mountain, is S. 43° W., about 37 miles distant.[9] The face of the country on both sides of the river, above and below the falls, is steep, rugged, and rocky, with a very small proportion of herbage, and no timber except a few bushes; the hills to the west, however, have some scattered pine, white-oak, and other kinds of trees. All the timber used by the people at the upper falls is rafted down the Towahnahiooks; and those who live at the head of the [Long] narrows we have just passed bring their wood in the same way from this creek to the lower part of these narrows, from which it is carried three miles by land to their habitations.

[8] So Clark H 75. The name is Salish, and the same as that of a Salishan tribe variously spelled Queniult, Queniut, Quinaielt, Quiniilt, Quinult, Quinaitle, Kwiniault, etc. Now Mill creek; town of The Dalles here, opposite Rockdale. This camp is named Fort Rock on their return in 1806.

[9] " The pinical of the round toped mountain which we saw a short distance below the forks of this river [confluence of the Snake], is S. 43° W. of us and abt. 37 miles ; it is at this time toped with snow we call this the falls mountain or timms mountain," Clark H 69, interlined " This the Mount Hood of Vancouver."

Both above and below, as well as in the narrows, we saw a great number of sea-otters [*Enhydris marina*, a species of *Mustelidæ*] or seals [species of *Phocidæ*]. This evening one deer was killed, and great signs of that animal were seen near the camp. In the creek we shot a goose, and saw much appearance of beaver. One of the party also saw a fish, which he took to be a drum-fish. Among the willows we found several snares set by the natives for the purpose of catching wolves.

October 26th. The morning was fine. We sent six men to hunt, and to collect rosin to pitch the canoes, which, by being frequently hauled over rocks, have become very leaky. The canoes were also brought out to dry, and on examination it was found that many of the articles had become spoiled by being repeatedly wet. We were occupied with the observations [10] necessary to determine our longitude, and with conferences among the Indians, many of whom came on horseback to the opposite shore in the forepart of the day, and showed some anxiety to cross over to us. We did not, (*p. 43*) however, think it proper to send for them; but toward evening two chiefs, with 15 men, came over in a small canoe. They proved to be the two principal chiefs of the tribes at and above the falls, who had been absent on a hunting excursion as we passed their residence. Each of them on their arrival made us a present of deer's flesh, and small white cakes made of roots. Being anxious to ingratiate ourselves in their favor, so as to insure a friendly reception on our return, we treated them with all the kindness we could show; we acknowledged the chiefs, gave a medal of the small size, a red silk handkerchief, an armband, a knife, and a piece of paint to each chief, small presents to several of the party, and half a deer. These attentions were not lost on the Indians, who appeared very well pleased with them. At night a fire was made in the middle of our camp, and as the Indians sat round it our men danced to the music of the violin [Cruzatte's], which so delighted them that several resolved to remain with us all night; the rest crossed

[10] In full, Clark H 71. The Dalles (town) is abt. 9 m. W. of long. 121°.

the river. All the tribes in this neighborhood are at war
with the Snake Indians, whom they all describe as living on
the Towahnahiooks [Des Chutes river], and whose nearest
town is said to be four days' march from this place, in a
direction nearly southwest.   There has lately been a battle
between these tribes, but we could not ascertain the loss on
either side.

The water rose to-day eight inches—a rise which we could
only ascribe to the circumstance of the wind's having been
up the river for the last 24 hours, since the influence of the
tide cannot be sensible here on account of the falls [Cascades]
below.   The hunters returned in the evening; they had seen
the tracks of elk and bear in the mountains, and killed five
deer, four very large gray squirrels [*Sciurus fossor*], and a
grouse; they inform us that the country off the river is
broken, stony, and thinly timbered with pine and white-oak.
Besides these delicacies one of the men killed with a gig a
salmon-trout which, being fried in some bear's oil which had
been given to us by the chief whom we met this morning below the narrows, (*p. 44*) furnished a dish of very delightful
flavor.   A number of white cranes [*Grus americana*] were also
seen flying in different directions, but at such a height that
we could not procure any of them.   The fleas, with which we
had contracted an intimacy at the falls, are so unwilling to
leave us that the men are obliged to throw off all their
clothes in order to relieve themselves from their persecution.

Sunday, October 27th.   The wind was high from the westward during last night and this morning, but the weather
being fair we continued our celestial observations.   The two
chiefs who remained with us were joined by seven Indians,
who came in a canoe from below.   To these men we were
very particular in our attentions; we smoked and eat with
them; but some of them, who were tempted by the sight
of our goods exposed to dry, wished to take liberties with
them; to which we were under the necessity of putting an
immediate check; which restraint displeased them so much
that they returned down the river in very ill humor.   The

two chiefs, however, remained with us till the evening, when they crossed the river to their party.

Before they went we procured from them a vocabulary of the Echeloot, their native language, and on comparison were surprised at its difference from that of the Eneeshur tongue.[11] In fact, though the Echeloots, who live at the Great Narrows, are not more than six miles from the Eneeshurs or residents at and above the Great Falls, the two people are separated by a broad distinction of language.   The Eneeshurs are understood by all the tribes residing on the Columbia above the Falls; but at that place they meet with the unintelligible language of the Echeloots, which then descends the river to a considerable distance.   Yet the variation may possibly be rather a deep shade of dialect than a radical difference, since among both [tribes] many words are the same, and the identity cannot be accounted for by supposing that their neighborhood has interwoven them into their daily conversations, because the same words are equally familiar among all the Flathead bands which we have passed.   (*p. 45*) To all these tribes the strange clucking or guttural noise which first struck us is common.   They also flatten the heads of their children in nearly the same manner; but we now begin

[11] This statement well illustrates the great attention paid by Lewis and Clark to ethnology, and the discernment they showed in discriminating similar appearing Indians who were nevertheless of distinct linguistic stocks, at a time when modern scientific classification had no existence.   They were pioneers in ethnography as in geography.   The Eneeshurs, elsewhere Eneshures and Eneshurs, were a tribe of the Shahaptian family, for most of our knowledge of whom we are indebted to these pages of Lewis and Clark, as these Indians are extinct, or at least unknown by the name here given them.   On the other hand, the Echeloots are a tribe of the Chinookan family, of which great division we shall see many other tribes as the Expedition descends the river to its mouth.   Their name is elsewhere spelled Eskcloot and Eloot, Hellwit, Tilheillewit, etc.   Clark H 75 has "Echelute."   The form Echeloot, here given by our authors, is the accepted one in present classification.   In Powell's enumeration of Upper Chinookans, the Echeloots are named as one of nine principal tribes.   On Clark's map they are marked next below the Eneeshurs and next above the Chilluckittequaws; census 1,000 souls.   The wretched Chaboneau had a hard time of it with the Columbia River Indians.   "Some words with Shabono, our interpreter, about his duty," Clark H 74—and we may be sure those same words were significant.

SIGNS OF CIVILIZATION—CHILLUCKITTEQUAWS. 673

to observe that the heads of males, as well as of the other sex, are subjected to this operation, whereas among the mountains custom has confined it almost to the females. The hunters brought home four deer, one grouse, and a squirrel.

October 28th. The morning was again cool and windy. Having dried our goods, we were about setting out, when three canoes came from above to visit us, and at the same time two others from below arrived for the same purpose. Among these last was an Indian who wore his hair in a cue and had on a round hat and a sailor's jacket, which he said he had obtained from the people below the great rapids, who bought them from the whites. This interview detained us till nine o'clock, when we proceeded down the river, which is now bordered with cliffs of loose dark colored rocks about 90 feet high, with a thin covering of pines and other small trees. At the distance of four miles we reached a small village of eight houses under some high rocks on the right [at or near Crate's Point], with a small [Cheneweth] creek on the opposite side of the river.

We landed and found the houses similar to those we had seen at the great narrows ; on entering one of them we saw a British musket, a cutlass, and several brass tea-kettles, of which they seemed to be very fond. There were figures of men, birds, and different animals, which were cut and painted on the boards which form the sides of the room ; though the workmanship of these uncouth figures was very rough, they were as highly estemed by the Indians as the finest frescoes of more civilized people. This tribe is called the Chilluckittequaw ;[12] their language, though somewhat different from that of the Echeloots, has many of the same words, and is sufficiently intelligible to the neighboring Indians. We procured from them a vocabulary, and then, after buying five

[12] So Clark H 76. A tribe of the Chinookan family, for most of our information concerning whom we are indebted to these pages. The name is preserved in this form ; but no Indians are now known by this name. They are marked on Clark's map on the Columbia, between the Echeloots and the Smackshops ; population 2,400 souls. Name stands Chee-luck-it-te-quar on Clark H 2.

small dogs, some dried berries, (*p. 46*) and a white bread or cake made of roots, we left them. The wind, however, rose so high that we were obliged, after going one mile, to land on the left side, opposite a rocky island, and pass the day there. We formed our camp in a niche above a point of high rocks, as this was the only safe harbor we could find, and submitted to the inconvenience of lying on the sand exposed to the wind and rain during all the evening. The high wind, which obliged us to consult the safety of our boats by not venturing further, did not at all prevent the Indians from navigating the river.

We had not been long on shore before a canoe with a man, his wife, and two children came from below through the high waves with a few roots to sell ; and soon after we were visited by many Indians from the village above, with whom we smoked and conversed. The canoes used by these people are like those already described, built of white cedar or pine, very light, wide in the middle and tapering toward the ends, the bow being raised and ornamented with carvings of the heads of animals. As the canoe is the vehicle of transportation, the Indians have acquired great dexterity in its management, and guide it safely over the highest waves. They have among their utensils bowls and baskets very neatly made of small bark and grass, in which they boil their provisions. The only game seen to-day were two deer, of which only one was killed ; the other was wounded, but escaped.

October 29th. The morning was still cloudy and the wind from the west, but as it had abated its violence we set out at daylight. At the distance of four miles we passed a creek on the right [?], one mile below which is a village of seven houses on the same side. This is the residence of the principal chief of the Chilluckittequaw nation, whom we now found to be the same between whom and our two chiefs we had made a peace at the Echeloot village. He received us very kindly and set before us pounded fish, filberts, [and other] nuts, berries of the sacacommis [*Arctostaphylos uva-*

ursi], and white bread made of roots.   We gave in return a
bracelet of ribbon to each of the (*p. 47*) women of the house,
with which they were very much pleased.   The chief had several articles, such as scarlet and blue cloth, a sword, a jacket
and a hat, which must have been procured from the whites;
and on one side of the room were two wide split boards placed
together [edge to edge], so as to make space [be wide enough]
for a rude figure of a man cut and painted on them.   On pointing to this and asking him what it meant, he said something,
of which all we understood was " good," and then stepped to
the image and brought out his bow and quiver, which, with
some other warlike instruments, were kept behind it.

The chief then directed his wife to hand him his medicine-
bag, from which he brought out 14 fore-fingers, which he
told us had once belonged to the same number of his enemies
whom he had killed in fighting with the nations to the southeast, to which place he pointed; alluding, no doubt, to the
Snake Indians, the common enemy of the nations on the
Columbia.   This bag is about two feet in length, containing
roots, pounded dirt, etc., which the Indians only know how
to appreciate.   It is suspended in the middle of the lodge,
and it is supposed to be a species of sacrilege to be touched
by any but the owner.   It is an object of religious fear, and
from its sanctity is the safest place to deposit their medals
and their more valuable articles.   The Indians have likewise
small bags which they preserve in their great medicine-bag,
whence they are taken and worn around their waists and
necks, as amulets against real or imaginary evils.   This was
the first time we had ever known Indians to carry from the
field any trophy except the scalp.   The fingers were shown
with great exultation, and after a harangue, which we were
left to presume was in praise of his exploits, they were carefully replaced among the valuable contents of the red medicine-bag.[13]   This village being part of the same nation

[13] " The chief pointed [out] those fingers with several other articles which **was**
in his bag red and securely put them back, haveing first made a short harrang
which I suppose was bragging," Clark H 79.   How many of his enemies the

with the village we passed above, the language of the two is the same; their houses are of similar form and materials, and calculated to contain about 30 souls.[14] The inhabitants were unusually hospitable and good- (*p. 48*) humored, so that we gave to the place the name of Friendly village.

We breakfasted here, and after purchasing twelve dogs, four sacks of fish, and a few dried berries, proceeded on our journey. The hills we passed are high, with steep rocky sides, some pine and white-oak, and an undergrowth of shrubs scattered over them. Four miles below this village is a small river [Klikitat] on the right side; immediately below is a village of Chilluckittequaws, consisting of 11 houses. Here we landed and smoked a pipe with the inhabitants, who were very cheerful and friendly. They as well as the people of the last village inform us that this river comes a considerable distance from the N.N.E.; that it has a great number of falls, which prevent the salmon from passing up, and that there are ten nations residing on it, who subsist on berries, or such game as they can procure with their bows and arrows. At its mouth the river is 60 yards wide, and has a deep and very rapid channel. From the number of falls of which the Indians spoke we gave it the name of Cataract[15] river. We purchased four dogs, and then proceeded.

The country as we advance is more rocky and broken, and the pine and low white-oak on the hills increase in great quantity. Three miles below Cataract river we passed three

chief really had killed must ever remain a mystery; for fourteen fingers might mean from two to fourteen persons, and Clark H has not a word about their being all fore-fingers, though "different fingers, not little or middle fingers," is there interlined.

[14] In Indian censuses "souls" always means "people all told," or "total population"; the antithesis being "men," *i. e.*, those able to bear arms, usually estimated at one-fifth to one-fourth of the "souls."

[15] "Catterack" river, Clark H 90. Now known as Klikitat, Klickitat, Kliketat, etc., river, and giving name to Klikitat Co., Wash., of which the Columbia forms the southern boundary from the mouth of Wallawalla river to a little below the Klikitat. Klikitat Co. is bounded on the north by Yakima Co., on the east adjoins Wallawalla Co., and on the west Skamania Co. Across the Columbia, in Oregon, are Umatilla, Morrow, Gilliam, Sherman, and Wasco counties.

large rocks in the river; that in the middle is large and longer than the rest, and from the circumstance of its having several square vaults on it, obtained the name of Sepulcher island [Klikitat name Memaloose Alahee—"Land of the Dead."] A short distance below are two huts of Indians on the right. The river now widens, and in three miles we came to two more houses on the right, one mile beyond which is a rocky island in a bend of the river toward the left. Within the next six miles we passed 14 huts of Indians scattered on the right bank, and then reached the entrance of a river on the left, which we called Labieshe's [Labiche's[16]] river, after Labieshe, one of our party. Just above this river is a low ground more thickly timbered than usual, and in front are four huts of Indians on the bank, which are the first we have seen on that side of the Columbia. The ex-(*p. 49*) ception may be occasioned by this spot being more than usually protected from the approach of enemies by the creek and the thick wood behind.

We again embarked, and at the distance of a mile passed the mouth of a rapid creek on the right, 18 yards wide. In this creek the Indians whom we left take their fish, and from the number of canoes which were in it we called it Canoe[17] creek. Opposite this creek is a large sand-bar, which continues for four miles along the left side of the river. Just below this a beautiful cascade falls in on the left, over a precipice of rock 100 feet in height. One mile further are four Indian huts in the low ground on the left, and two miles beyond this is a point of land on the right, where the mountains become high on both sides, and possess more timber and greater varieties of it than hitherto, while those on the left are covered with snow. One mile from this point

[16] " From the mouth of the little river which we shall call Labeashe River, the falls mountain [Mt. Hood] is south," Clark H 81. Now Hood or Hood's river, after the name of the mountain. Between this and the Klikitat are Mosier's (left), Major's (right), and several lesser creeks, passed unnoticed.

[17] Now White Salmon river, a considerable stream heading in Skamania and the S.W. corner of Yakima counties, about Mt. Adams, and falling into the Columbia on the western border of Klikitat Co. Also called Nikepun river.

we halted for the night at three Indian huts on the right [Skamania Co., Wash.], having made 32 miles.

On our first arrival they seemed surprised, but not alarmed, and we soon became intimate by means of smoking and our favorite entertainment for the Indians, the violin. They gave us fruit, roots, and root-bread, and we purchased from them three dogs. The houses of these people are similar to those of the Indians above, and their language is the same; their dress also, consisting of robes or skins of wolves, deer, elk, and wildcat [loucirvia, Clark H 82], is made nearly after the same model; their hair is worn in plaits down each shoulder, and round their neck is put a strip of some skin with the tail of the animal hanging down over the breast; like the Indians above, they are fond of otter-skins, and give a great price for them. We here saw the skin of a mountain sheep,[18] which they say lives among the rocks in the mountains; the skin was covered with white hair; the wool was long, thick, and coarse, with long coarse hair on the top of the neck and on the back, resembling somewhat the bristles of a goat. Im- (*p. 50*) mediately behind the village is a pond, in which were great numbers of small swan.

October 30*th.* A moderate rain fell during all last night, but the morning was cool; and, after taking a scanty breakfast of deer, we proceeded. The river is now about three-quarters of a mile wide, with a current so gentle that it does not exceed one mile and a half an hour; but its course is obstructed by the projection of large rocks, which seem to have fallen promiscuously from the mountains into the bed of the river. On the left side four different streams[19] of water empty in cascades from the hills. What is, however, most singular is that there are stumps of pine-trees scattered for

[18] This is not the mountain sheep, argali, or bighorn (*Ovis montana*), already repeatedly mentioned in this work; but the mountain goat (*Haplocerus montanus*), a totally different animal, here first noticed by our authors, whose unfortunate slip in naming it led to a long series of subsequent misapprehensions. See the natural history chapter beyond. "Loucirvia" is *Lynx rufus fasciatus*.

[19] For these four cascades, and a fifth on p. 677, see p. 937. For Little White Salmon river, here unnoticed, compare Little Lake river, p. 1262.

some distance in the river, which has the appearance of being dammed below and forced to encroach on the shore. These obstructions continued to the distance of twelve miles, when we came to the mouth of a river on the right, where wc landed.

We found it 60 yards wide, and its banks possess two kinds of timber which we had not hitherto seen. One is a very large species of ash; the other resembles in its bark the beech, but the tree itself is smaller, as also are the leaves. We called this stream Crusatte's [or Cruzatte's] river, after Crusatte, one of our men.[20] Opposite its mouth the Columbia widens to the distance of a mile, with a large sand-bar, and large stones and rocks scattered through the channel. We here saw several of the large buzzards,[21] which are of the size of the largest eagle, with the under part of their wings white: we also shot a deer and three ducks, on part of which we dined, and then continued down the Columbia.

Above Crusatte's river the low grounds are about three-quarters of a mile wide, rising gradually to the hills, with a rich soil covered with grass, fern, and other small under-growth; but below, the country rises with a steep ascent, and soon the mountains approach the river with steep rugged sides, covered with a very thick growth of pine, cedar, cottonwood, and oak. The river is still strewed with large rocks. At 2½ miles below (*p. 51*) Crusatte's river is a large creek[22]

[20] "We call this little river ["Ash" erascd and interlined] New Timber river from a species of ["that wood" erased and interlined] ash which grows on its bank of a verry large [size] and different from any we had before seen, and a timber resembling the beech in bark but different in its leaf which is smaller, and the tree smaller," Clark H 84. It was dedicated to Cruzatte by an after-thought, as no such name appears anywhere along here. It is now known as Wind river, in Skamania Co. falling in just above town of Sprague. The "new timber" is the broad-leaved maple, *Acer macrophyllum*. See the chapter on botany, No. 23.

[21] Californian condor, *Pseudogryphus californianus*, as large as the Andean.

[22] Several creeks fall in on the right, in Skamania Co., between Cruzatte's or Wind river and the head of the "great shoot." Two of them are named Smith's and Rock. The Expedition now reaches the famous Cascades of the Columbia. We have swept down the great river very rapidly, and its dangerous places have

on the right, with a small island in the mouth. Just below this creek we passed along the right side of three small islands on the right bank of the river, with a larger island on the opposite side, and landed on an island very near the right shore at the head of the Great Shoot,[23] opposite two smaller islands at the fall or shoot itself. Just above the island on which we camped is a small village of eight large houses in a bend on the right, where the country, from having been very mountainous, becomes low for a short distance. We made 15 miles to-day, during all which time we were kept constantly wet with the rain ; but as we were able to get on this island some of the ash, which we saw for the first time to-day, and which makes a tolerable fire, we were as comfortable as the moistness of the evening would permit.

As soon as we landed, Captain Lewis went with five men [up] to the village, which is situated near the river, with ponds[24] in the low grounds behind. The greater part of the inhabitants were absent collecting roots down the river; the few, however, who were at home treated him very kindly, and gave him berries, nuts, and fish; in the house were a gun and several articles which must have been procured from the whites; but not being able to procure any information, he returned to the island. Captain Clark had in the meantime gone down to examine the shoot and discover the best route for a portage. He followed an Indian path which, at the

required such watching to avoid capsizing or foundering, that less attention has been paid to the smaller streams making in on either hand. These we shall observe more scrutinously as we stem the current next spring.

[23] "Shute," Clark H 85; commonly in French form, chute. The great chute is a part of the Cascades of the Columbia, and is shown on the plate. This, as engraved for the original edition and now reproduced in facsimile, is slightly reduced from the original pen-and-ink sketch map, which occupies Clark H 4, on a scale of 426 poles to the inch.

[24] See the plate, where the "village of 8 houses," and one of the ponds, are clearly shown. This pond is marked Trout lake on some maps. Some of the creeks connected with it, or close by, are shown on the plate ; one lower down is called Hamilton creek. Across the river, in Oregon, along the railroad, are places called Cascade Locks and Bonneville. The town of Cascades is a little lower down, in Washington. The island on which is camp is that largest one, on the right, to which the right hand one of the three arrows flying abreast points.

distance of a mile, led to a village on an elevated situation, the houses of which had been large and built in a different form from any we had yet seen, but which had been lately abandoned, the greater part of the boards having been put into a pond near the village; this was most probably for the purpose of drowning the fleas, which were in immense quantities near the houses. After going about three miles the night obliged him to return to camp. He resumed his search in the morning,

(*p. 52*) *October* 31*st*, through the rain. At the extremity of the basin, in which is situated the island where we camped, several rocks and rocky islands are interspersed through the bed of the river. The rocks on each side have fallen down from the mountains; that on the left being high, and on the right the hill itself, which is lower, slipping into the river; so that the current is here compressed within a space of 150 yards. Within this narrow limit it runs for 400 yards with great rapidity, swelling over the rocks with a fall of about 20 feet; it then widens to 200 paces, and the current for a short distance becomes gentle; but at the distance of a mile and a half, opposite the old village mentioned yesterday, it is obstructed by a very bad rapid, where the waves are unusually high; the river being confined between large rocks, many of which are at the surface of the water. Captain Clark proceeded along the same path he had taken before, which led him through a thick wood and along a hillside, till 2½ miles below the shoots [chutes] he struck the river at the place whence the Indians make their portage to the head of the shoot. He here sent Crusatte, the principal waterman, up the stream, to examine if it were practicable to bring the canoes down the water. In the meantime he, with Joseph Fields, continued his route down the river, along which the rapids seemed to stretch as far as he could see. At half a mile below the end of the portage he came to a house, the only remnant of a town which, from its appearance, must have been of great antiquity. The house was uninhabited; being old and decayed, he felt no disposition to encounter the fleas which abound in every situation of that kind, and therefore did not enter.

About half a mile below this house, in a very thick part of the woods, is an ancient burial place. It consists of eight vaults made of pine or cedar boards closely connected, about eight feet square and six in height; the top covered with wide boards sloping a little, so as (*p. 53*) to convey off the rain. The direction of all of these vaults is east and west, the door being on the eastern side, partially stopped with wide boards decorated with rude pictures of men and other animals. On entering he found in some of them four dead bodies, carefully wrapped in skins, tied with cords of grass and bark, lying on a mat, in a direction east and west. The other vaults contained only bones, which were in some of them piled to the height of four feet. On the tops of the vaults, and on poles attached to them, hung brass kettles and frying-pans with holes in their bottoms, baskets, bowls, sea-shells, skins, pieces of cloth, hair, bags of trinkets and small bones—the offerings of friendship or affection, which have been saved by a pious veneration from the ferocity of war, or the more dangerous temptations of individual gain. The whole of the walls as well as the door were decorated with strange figures cut and painted on them; and besides were several wooden images of men, some so old and decayed as to have almost lost their shape, which were all placed against the sides of the vaults. These images, as well as those in the houses we have lately seen, do not appear to be at all the objects of adoration; in this place they were most probably intended as resemblances of those whose decease they indicate; when we observe them in houses, they occupy the most conspicuous part, but are treated more like ornaments than objects of worship. Near the vaults which are standing are the remains of others on the ground completely rotted and covered with moss; and as they are formed of the most durable pine and cedar timber, there is every appearance that for a very long series of years this retired spot has been the depository for the Indians near this place.

After examining this place Captain Clark went on, and found the river as before strewed with large rocks, against which the water ran with great rapidity. Just below the vaults the mountain, which is but low on the right side, leaves the river, and is succeeded by an open stony level, which extends down the (*p. 54*) river, while on the left the mountain is still high and rugged. At two miles' distance he came to a village of four houses, which were now vacant and the doors barred up. On looking in he saw the usual quantity of utensils still remaining, from which he concluded that the inhabitants were at no great distance collecting roots or hunting, in order to lay in their supply of food for the winter. He left them and went on three miles to a difficult rocky rapid, which was the last in view. Here, on the right, are the remains of a large and ancient village, which could be plainly traced by the holes for the houses and the deposits for fish. After he had examined these rapids and the neighboring country he returned to camp by the same route. The only game he obtained was a sand-hill crane.

In the meantime we had been occupied in preparations for making the portage, and in conference with the Indians, who came down from the village to visit us. Toward evening two canoes arrived from the village at the mouth of Cataract [Klikitat] river, loaded with fish and bear's grease for the market below. As soon as they landed they unloaded the canoes, turned them upside down on the beach, and camped under a shelving rock near our camp.

We had an opportunity of seeing to-day the hardihood of the Indians of the neighboring village. One of the men shot a goose, which fell into the river and was floating rapidly toward the great shoot, when an Indian observing it plunged in after it. The whole mass of the waters of the Columbia, just preparing to descend its narrow channel, carried the animal down with great rapidity. The Indian followed it fearlessly to within 150 feet of the rocks, where he would inevitably have been dashed to pieces; but seizing his prey he turned round and swam ashore with great composure. We very willingly relinquished our right to the bird in favor of the Indian who had thus saved it at the imminent hazard of his life; he immediately set to work and picked off about half the feathers, and then, without opening it, ran a stick through it and carried it off to roast.

(*p. 55*) *Friday, November* 1*st*, 1805. The morning was cool and the wind high from the northeast. The Indians who arrived last night took their empty canoes on their shoulders and carried them below the great shoot, where they put them in the water and brought them down the rapid, till at the distance of 2½ miles they stopped to take in their loading, which they had been afraid to trust in the last rapid, and had therefore carried by land from the head of the shoot. After their example we carried our small canoe and all the baggage across the slippery rocks to the foot of the shoot. The four large canoes were next brought down by slipping them along poles, placed from one rock to another, and in some places by using, partially, streams which escaped alongside of the river. We were not, however, able to bring them across without three of them receiving injuries which obliged us to stop at the end of the shoot to repair them. At this shoot we saw great numbers of sea-otters; but they are so shy that it is difficult to reach them with the musket; one of them that was wounded sunk and was lost. Having by this portage avoided the rapid and shoot of 400 yards in length, we re-embarked, passed at a mile and a half the bad rapid opposite the old village on the right, and making our way through the rocks saw the house just below the end of the portage, and the eight vaults near it; and at the distance of four miles from the head of the shoot reached a high rock, which forms the upper part of an island [Brant] near the left shore. Between this island and the right shore we proceeded, leaving at the distance of a mile and a half the village of four houses on our right, and a mile and a half lower came to the head of a rapid near the village on the right. Here we halted for the night, having made only seven miles from the head of the shoot. During the whole of the passage the river is very much obstructed by rocks. The island,[25] which is about three miles long, reaches to the rapid which (*p. 56*) its lower extremity contributes to form. The meridian altitude of to-day gave us the latitude of 45° 44′ 3″ N.

As we passed the village of four houses, we found that the inhabitants had returned, and stopped to visit them. The houses are similar to those already described, but larger, from 35 to 50 feet long and 30 feet wide, being sunk in the ground about six feet, and raised the same height above. Their beds are raised about 4½ feet above the floor ; the ascent is by a new painted ladder, with which every family is provided, and under them are stored their dried fish, while the space between the part of the bed on which they lie and the wall of the house is occupied by the nuts, roots, berries, and other provisions, which are spread on mats. The fireplace is about eight feet long and six feet wide, sunk a foot below the floor, secured by a frame, with mats placed around for the family to sit on. In all of the houses are images of men of different shapes, placed as ornaments in the parts of the house where they are most seen. They gave us nuts, berries, and some dried fish to eat, and we purchased, among other articles, a hat made after their own taste, such as they wear, without a brim. They ask high prices for all that they sell, observing that the whites below pay dearly for all which they carry there.

We cannot learn precisely the nature of the trade carried on by the Indians with the inhabitants below. But as their knowledge of the whites seems to be very imperfect, and as the only articles which they carry to market, such as pounded fish, bear-grass, and roots, cannot be an object of much foreign traffic, their intercourse appears to be an intermediate

[25] "Brant island" of our plate; camp on right bank of the river, at point marked "Village," opposite head of "Strawberry island" of the plate, with the "Broad Run" back of camp. The Expedition is close by town of Cascades, county seat of Skamania Co., Wash. The assigned latitude is but a trifle out—a little too far north—45° 34′ would be nearer right.

trade with the natives near the mouth of the Columbia. From them these people obtain, in exchange for their fish, roots, and bear-grass, blue and white beads, copper tea-kettles, brass armbands, some scarlet and blue robes, and a few articles of old European clothing. But their great object is to obtain beads, an article which holds the first place in their ideas of (*p. 57*) relative value, and to procure which they will sacrifice their last article of clothing or last mouthful of food. Independently of their fondness for them as an ornament, these beads are the medium of trade, by which they obtain from the Indians still higher up the river, robes, skins, chappelel [*sic*] bread, bear-grass, etc. Those Indians in turn employ them to procure from the Indians in the Rocky mountains, bear-grass, pachico-roots [*sic*], robes, etc.

These Indians are rather below the common size, with high cheek-bones; their noses are pierced, and in full dress ornamented with a tapering piece of white shell or wampum about two inches long. Their eyes are exceedingly sore and weak; many of them have only a single eye, and some are perfectly blind. Their teeth prematurely decay, and in frequent instances are altogether worn away. Their general health, however, seems to be good, the only disorder we have remarked being tumors in different parts of the body. The women are small and homely in their appearance, their legs and thighs much swelled, and their knees remarkably large—deformities which are no doubt owing to the manner in which they sit on their hams. They go nearly naked, having only a piece of leather tied round the breast, falling thence nearly as low as the waist; a small robe about three feet square, and a piece of leather, which ill supplies the place of a cover, tied between their legs. Their hair is suffered to hang loose in every direction, and in their persons, as well as in their cookery, they are filthy to a most disgusting degree. We here observe that the women universally have their heads flattened, and in many of the villages we have lately seen the female children undergoing this operation.

CHAPTER XX.

COLUMBIAN TIDE-WATER TO THE PACIFIC OCEAN.

Last rapids and portage—Appearance of tide-water—Strawberry island—Beacon rock—Quicksand river—Seal creek—Mt. Hood in the distance—Diamond island—Multnomah river—Wappatoo roots—Indians in sailors' dress—Their canoes—Canoe-image island—Mt. St. Helena in full view—Visits from Indians—The Columbia valley described and named—Coweliske river—Deserted villages—Wahkiacum Indians described—Roar of breakers heard, and the ocean viewed, Nov. 7th, 1805—The party coasts an inlet called Shallow bay—Seasickness—Camp on a point of Shallow bay—A wet night and bad camp—Another poor camp—Canoes at the mercy of the waves—Visit from Cathlamah Indians—A gale of wind—Captain Clark explores—Dried fish the only food—Difficulty with some Indians—Captain Lewis explores—The party leaves Point Distress, the miserable spot of their week's detention—Serious trouble with Indians—Good camp made on the beach (at Chinook Point) near a deserted village, in full view of the ocean—Captain Lewis returns, having coasted Haley's bay to Cape Disappointment—Chinnook Indians—Captain Clark explores with eleven men—Chinnook river—Across the bay is Point Round or Point Adams—Columbian black-tailed deer—Point Lewis named.

SATURDAY, November 2d, 1805. We now examined the rapid below more particularly, and the danger appearing to be too great for the loaded canoes, all those who could not swim were sent with the baggage by land. The canoes then passed safely, and were reloaded. At the foot of the rapid we took a meridian altitude of 59° 45' 45". Just as we were setting out seven squaws arrived across the portage, loaded with dried fish and bear-grass, neatly packed in bundles, and soon after four Indians came down the rapid in a large canoe. After breakfast we left our camp at one o'clock, passed the upper point of an island which is separated from the right shore by a narrow channel through which in high tides the water passes. But at present it contains no running water, and a creek [Hamilton] which falls into it from the mountains on the right is in the same dry condition, though it has the marks of discharging immense torrents at some seasons. The island thus made is three miles in length and about one in width; its situation is high and open; the land is rich, and at this time covered with grass and a great number of strawberry-vines [*Fragaria vesca ?*], from which we gave it the name of Strawberry island [see the plate]. In several places we observed that the Indians had (*p. 59*) been digging for roots; indeed the whole island bears every appearance of having been at some period in a state of cultivation. On the left side of the river the low ground is narrow and open.

The rapid we have just passed is the last of all the descents of the Columbia. At this place the first tide-water commences, and the river in consequence widens immediately below the rapid. As we descended we reached, at the distance of one mile from the rapid, a creek under a bluff on the left; at three miles is the lower point of Strawberry island. To this immediately succeed three small islands covered with wood. In the meadow to the right, at some distance from the hills, stands a perpendicular rock about 800 feet high and 400 yards around the base. This we called Beacon[1] rock. Just below is an Indian village of nine houses, situated between two small creeks. At this village the river widens to nearly a mile in extent; the low grounds become wider, and they as well as the mountains on each side are covered with pine, spruce-pine, cottonwood, a species of ash, and some alder. After being so long accustomed to the dreary nakedness of the country above, the change is as grateful to the eye as it is useful in supplying us with fuel. Four miles from the village is a point of land on the right, where the hills become lower, but are still thickly timbered. The river is now about two miles wide, the current smooth and gentle, and the effect of the tide has been sensible since leaving the

---

[1] " Beaten " rock, Clark H 91, Oct. 31st, when Brant and Strawberry islands are also first named. Perhaps the most famous landmark on the Columbia, as it stands at the head of tide-water, besides being so conspicuous an object in itself. It is visible some 20 miles below. The creek to the left, opposite Strawberry island, is now called Plum creek. There are several other small streams along here on the Oregon side, in Multnomah Co., which extends from above the Cascades to below Portland. On the Washington side, Clark or Clarke Co. succeeds Skamania ; the bold headland called Cape Horn marks their bounds.

rapid. Six miles lower is a rock rising from the middle of the river to the height of 100 feet, and about 80 yards [2] at its base. We continued six miles further, and halted for the night under a high projecting rock on the left side of the river, opposite the point of a large meadow.

The mountains, which, from the great shoot to this place, are high, rugged, and thickly covered with timber, chiefly of the pine species, here leave the river on each side; the river becomes 2½ miles in width; the low grounds are extensive (*p. 60*) and well supplied with wood. The Indians whom we left at the portage passed us on their way down the river, and seven others, who were descending in a canoe for the purpose of trading below, camped with us. We had made from the foot of the great shoot 29 miles to-day. [3] The ebb tide rose at our camp about nine inches; the flood must rise much higher. We saw great numbers of water-fowl, such as swan, geese, ducks of various kinds, gulls, plovers, and the white and gray brant, of which last we killed 18.

November 3*d.* We were detained until ten o'clock by a fog so thick that a man could not be discerned at the distance of 50 steps. As soon as it cleared off we set out in company with our new Indian acquaintances, who came from a village near the Great Falls. The low grounds along the river are covered so thickly with rushes, vines, and other small growth that they are almost impassable. At the distance of three miles we reached the mouth of a river on the left, which seemed to lose its waters in a sand-bar opposite, the stream itself being only a few inches in depth. But, on attempting to wade across, we discovered that the bed was a very bad quicksand, too deep to be passed on foot. We went up a mile and a half to examine this river, and found

---

[2] In circumference. "Passed a rock near the middle of the river about 100 feet high and 80 feet Diameter," Clark H 99. This would be about 80 yards around.

[3] That is, to-night's camp is 29 miles from the foot of the "great shoot"; about one-fourth of which distance, however, was made yesterday. Some notable points passed are Multnomah falls, Sunday island, Table rock, and Cape Horn. Camp is about halfway between Cascades and Vancouver.

it to be at this distance a very considerable stream, 120 yards wide at its narrowest part, with several small islands. Its character resembles very much that of the river Platte. It drives its quicksand over the low grounds with great impetuosity, and such is the quantity of coarse sand which it discharges that the accumulation has formed a large sand-bar or island, three miles long and a mile and a half wide, which divides the waters of the quicksand river into two channels. This sand-island compresses the Columbia within a space of half a mile, and throws its whole current against the right shore. Opposite this river, which we call Quicksand⁴ river, is a large creek, to which we give the name of Seal⁵ river. The first appears to pass through the low country, at the foot of the high (*p. 61*) range of mountains toward the southeast, while the second, as well as all the large creeks on the right side of the Columbia, rises in the same ridge of mountains N.N.E. from this place. The mountain, which we have [rightly] supposed to be the Mount Hood of Vancouver, bears S. 85° E. about 47 miles from the mouth of the Quicksand river.

After dinner we proceeded, and at the distance of three miles reached the lower mouth of Quicksand river. On the opposite side a large creek falls in near the head of an island, which extends for 3½ miles down the river; it is a mile and a half in width, rocky at the upper end, and has some timber round its borders; but in the middle is open and has several ponds. Half a mile lower is another island in the middle of the river, to which, from its appearance, we gave the name of Diamond island.⁶ Here we met 15 Indians

⁴ Quicksand river is now trivially called Sandy river. It drains western slopes of Mt. Hood by many affluents, in Clackamas Co., Ore., and flows with a general N.W. course, to discharge into the Columbia through Multnomah Co.

⁵ Now Washougal river, rising in Skamania Co., about Saddle Peak, and discharging in the S.E. corner of Clark or Clarke Co., Wash.

⁶ Both these islands appear on any good map, the lower one (Diamond, now called Government) much the larger of the two, with its lower end nearly north of East Portland, Multnomah Co., Ore., and not much above Vancouver, Wash. Captain Broughton of the ship " Chatham," one of Captain Vancouver's lieu-

ascending the river in two canoes ; but the only information we could procure from them was that they had seen three vessels, which we presume to be European, at the mouth of the Columbia. We went along its right side for three miles, and camped opposite it [at or near Fisher's Landing], after making to-day 13 miles.

A canoe soon after arrived from the village at the foot of the last rapid, with an Indian and his family, consisting of a wife, three children, and a woman who had been taken prisoner from the Snake Indians, living on a river from the south, which we afterward found to be the Multnomah.[7] Sacajawea was immediately introduced to her, in hopes that, being a Snake Indian, they might understand each other; but their language was not sufficiently intelligible to permit them to converse together. The Indian had a gun with a brass barrel and cock, which he appeared to value highly.

Below Quicksand river the country is low, rich, and thickly wooded on each side of the river. The islands have less timber, but are furnished with a number of ponds near which are vast quantities of fowls, such as swan, geese, brants, cranes, storks, white gulls, cormorants, and plovers. The river is wide and contains a great number of sea-otters [*Enhy-*

tenants, ascended the river as far as the point where Fort Vancouver was built, taking possession of the Columbia river and country in the name of his Britannic Majesty, Oct. 31st, 1792.

[7] The Expedition missed this great river in going down the Columbia, its mouth being hidden by islands. Clark H 102 interlines " Mulknoma " in red ink. It is one of the three largest southern tributaries of the Columbia after the Snake— these being the John Day, Des Chutes, and Multnomah. An alternative name is Willamette, and these two have been much confused in their respective applications to great or less extents of this large stream. Multnomah was properly the name of the river only for a short section from its mouth, along which extent lived the Multnomah Indians, among the tribes grouped by Lewis and Clark as " Wappatoo " Indians, from the name of the root affording much of their subsistence. Thus Parker says in his Journal, p. 161, " the name Multnomah is given to a small section of this river, from the name of a tribe of Indians who once resided about 6 miles on both sides from its confluence with the Columbia to the branch which flows down the southern side of Wâppatoo Island ; above this section it is called the Willamette." The Rev. Parker, who knew nothing about it himself, got his information from Donald Mackenzie, who was of the family

dris marina]. (*p. 62*) In the evening the hunters brought in game for a sumptuous supper, which we shared with the Indians, both parties of whom spent the night with us.

November 4th.[8] The weather was cloudy and cool, and the wind from the west. During the night the tide rose 18 inches near our camp. We set out about eight o'clock, and at the distance of three miles came to the lower end of Diamond island. It is six miles long, nearly three in width, and, like the other islands, thinly covered with timber; it has a number of ponds or small lakes scattered over its surface. Besides the animals already mentioned, we shot a deer on it this morning. Near the end of Diamond island are two others, separated by a narrow channel filled at high tide only, which continue on the right for the distance of three miles; and, like the adjacent low grounds, are thickly covered with pine. Just below the last we landed on the left bank of the river, at a village of 25 houses. All of these were thatched with straw and built of bark, except one which was about 50 feet long, built of boards in the form of those higher up the river; from which it differed, however, in being completely above ground and covered with broad split boards. This village contains about 200 men of the Skilloot[9] nation, who seem well provided with canoes, of which

of the famous Sir Alexander, and himself a Chief Factor of the Hudson's Bay Company. He was a great traveler, and one of the overland Astorians, in 1811–12. He explored the Multnomah for several hundred miles. Another great traveler and trader, Henry, considered Wallamut to be properly the name of only the falls of the river. The latter word occurs in a profusion of spellings, among which we find, of course, Williamette; but this is an Indian word, and not our name William with a diminutive suffix in French feminine form. Multnomah is also the name of the county in Oregon, along the Columbia, intervening between Wasco Co. on the east, and Washington and Columbia counties on the west and north, with Portland as its principal city. This name is now usually extended to the whole river, to the principal branch of which the name Willamette is correspondingly restricted. It is also spelled Multnoma and in various other ways. The Indians of this name are a Chinookan tribe; the word is a corruption of Nematlnomaq, signifying " down river."

[8] For various important matters of this date, compare March 30th, beyond.

[9] A Chinookan tribe, no longer known as such by this name, for most our information respecting whom we are indebted to these pages.

there were at least 52, some of them very large, drawn up in front of the village.

On landing we found the Indian from above who had left us this morning, and who now invited us into a lodge of which he appeared to own a part. Here he treated us with a root, round in shape, and about the size of a small Irish potato, which they call wappatoo.[10] This is the common arrowhead or sagittifolia [of North America, *Sagittaria variabilis*, another species of which genus (*S. sinensis*) is] so much cultivated by the Chinese; when roasted in the embers till it becomes soft it has an agreeable taste, and is a very good substitute for bread.

After purchasing some more of this root, we resumed our journey, and at seven (*p. 63*) miles' distance came to the head of a large island near the left. On the right shore is a fine open prairie for about a mile, back of which the country rises and is supplied with timber, such as white-oak [*Quercus garryana*], pine of different kinds, wild crab [*Pirus rivularis*], and several species of undergrowth, while along the borders of the river there are only a few cottonwood and ash [*Fraxinus oregana*] trees. In this prairie were also signs of deer and elk.

When we landed for dinner, a number of Indians from the last village came down for the purpose, as we supposed, of paying us a friendly visit, as they had put on their favorite dresses. In addition to their usual covering they had scarlet and blue blankets, sailors' jackets and trousers, shirts and hats. They had all of them either war-axes, spears, and bows and arrows, or muskets and pistols, with tin powder-flasks. We smoked with them and endeavored to show them every attention, but we soon found them very assuming and disagreeable companions. While we were eating, they stole the pipe with which they were smoking, and the

[10] " We got some dogs and roots from the natives. The roots are of a superior quality to any I had before seen : they are called *whapto;* resemble a potatoe when cooked, and are about as big as a hen egg," Gass, p. 160, Nov. 4th ; elsewhere *wapto*. In the codices usually as in the text, but with some fluctuation. The plant, *Sagittaria variabilis*, is one of the best-known members of the monocotyledonous order *Alismaceæ*.

greatcoat of one of the men.   We immediately searched them all, and discovered the coat stuffed under the root of a tree near where they were sitting; but the pipe we could not recover.   Finding us determined not to suffer any imposition, and discontented with them, they showed their displeasure in the only way which they dared, by returning in an ill-humor to their village.

We then proceeded and soon met two canoes, with twelve men of the same Skilloot nation, who were on their way from below.   The larger of the canoes was ornamented with the figure of a bear in the bow and a man in the stern, both nearly as large as life, both made of painted wood and very neatly fixed to the boat.   In the same canoe were two Indians, finely dressed and with round hats.   This circumstance induced us to give the name of Image-canoe[11] to the large island, the lower end of which we now passed at the distance of nine miles from its head.   We had seen two smaller islands to the right, and three more near its lower (*p. 64*) extremity.   The Indians in the canoe here made signs that there was a village behind those islands, and indeed we presumed there was a channel on that [left] side of the river, for one of the canoes passed in that direction between the small islands; but we were anxious to press forward, and therefore did not stop to examine more minutely.   The river was now about a mile and a half in width, with a gentle current; the bottoms were extensive and low, but not subject to be overflowed.   Three miles below Image-canoe island we came to four large houses on the left side, at which place we had a full view of the mountain which we first saw on the 19th of October, from the Muscleshell rapid, and which we now find to be the Mount St. Helen[12] of Vancouver. It bears N. 25° E., about 90 miles distant; it rises in the

[11] Image-canoe is really three islands, the separateness of which was not noted.   In passing it the Expedition goes by a historic spot on the north bank of the river, where is the present site of Vancouver, county seat of Clark Co.

[12] " Mt. Helien, which is perhaps the highest penical in America," Clark H 106 ; variously called Helen, Helen's, and Helena, besides several misspellings. Gass, p. 160, identifies it as " Mount Rainy," which his French translator, Lalle-

form of a sugar-loaf to a very great height, and is covered with snow. A mile lower we passed a single house on the left and another on the right. The Indians had now learnt so much of us that their curiosity was without any mixture of fear, and their visits became very frequent and troublesome. We therefore continued on till after night, in hopes of getting rid of them; but after passing a village on each side, which on account of the lateness of the hour we saw indistinctly, we found there was no escaping from their importunities. We therefore landed at the distance of seven miles below Image-canoe island, and camped [13] near a single house on the right, having made during the day 29 miles.

The Skilloots whom we passed to-day speak a language somewhat different from that of the Echeloots or Chilluckittequaws near the long narrows. Their dress is similar, except that the Skilloots possess more articles procured from the white traders; and there is a further difference between them, inasmuch as the Skilloots, both males and females, have the head flattened. Their principal food is fish and wappatoo-roots, with some elk and deer, in killing which with their arrows they seem very expert; for (*p. 65*) during the short time we remained at the village three deer were brought in. We also observed there a tame brairo.

As soon as we landed we were visited by two canoes loaded with Indians, from whom we purchased a few roots. The grounds along the river continue low and rich, and among the shrubs which cover them is a large quantity of vines [*Rubus spectabilis*], resembling the raspberry. On the right the low grounds are terminated at the distance of five miles by a range of high hills covered with tall timber, and running southeast and northwest. The game as usual very abundant; among other birds we observe some white geese with a part of their wings black [*Chen hyperboreus*].

mant, renders Mont Pluvieux, with a sage note.: " Il serait possible qu'il y eût ici une faute d'impression, et que *Mont Rainy* fût le Mont Rainier," etc.

[13] At Knapp's Landing, Clark Co., Wash., just above Halfway point and Post Office Lake, and 5½ m. below mouth of the Multnomah.

November 5*th.* Our choice of a camp had been very unfortunate; for on a sand-island opposite us were immense numbers of geese, swan, ducks, and other wild fowl, which during the whole night serenaded us with a confusion of noises which completely prevented our sleeping. During the latter part of the night it rained, and we therefore willingly left camp at an early hour. We passed at three miles a small prairie, where the river is only three-quarters of a mile in width, and soon after two houses on the left, half a mile distant from each other; from one of which three men came in a canoe merely to look at us, and having done so returned home. At eight miles we came to the lower point of an island [Bachelor's; Lewis' and Lake rivers empty here], separated from the right side by a narrow channel, on which, a short distance above the end of the island, is situated a large village. It is built more compactly than the generality of the Indian villages, and the front has 14 houses, which are ranged for a quarter of a mile along the channel. As soon as we were discovered seven canoes came out to see us, and after some traffic, during which they seemed well disposed and orderly, accompanied us a short distance below. The river here again widens to the space of a mile and a half. As we descended we soon observed, behind a sharp [Warrior] point of rocks, a channel [Willamette slough] a quarter of a mile wide, which we suppose must be (*p. 66*) the one taken by the canoes yesterday on leaving Image-canoe island. A mile below this channel are some low cliffs of rocks [left, between St. Helen's and Columbia City, Ore.], near which is a large island on the right side [shoals and jetty there now], and two small islands a little further on [Burke's and Martin's, below Maxwell's point]. Here we met two canoes ascending the river. At this place the shore on the right becomes bold and rocky, and the bank is bordered by a range of high hills covered with a thick growth of pine; on the other side is an extensive low [Deer] island, separated from the left side by a narrow channel [Deer Island slough].

Here we stopped to dine, and found the island open, with

an abundant growth of grass, and a number of ponds well supplied with fowls ; at the lower extremity are the remains of an old village. We procured a swan, several ducks, and a brant, and saw some deer on the island. Besides this island, the lower extremity of which is [less than] 17 miles from the channel just mentioned, we passed two or three smaller ones in the same distance [as already said]. Here the hills on the right retire from the river, leaving a high plain, between which, on the left bank, a range of high hills, running south-east and covered with pine, forms a bold and rocky shore. At the distance of six miles, however, these hills again return and close the river on both sides.

We proceeded on [past Kalama], and at four miles reached a creek [14] on the right, about 20 yards in width, immediately below which is an old village. Three miles further, at the distance of 32 miles from our camp of last night, we halted under a point of highland, with thick pine trees, on the left bank of the river [opposite Carroll's bluff]. Before landing we met two canoes, the largest of which had at the bow the image of a bear, and that of a man on the stern. There were 26 Indians on board, but they all proceeded upward, and we were left, for the first time since we reached the waters of the Columbia, without any of the natives during the night. Besides the game already mentioned, we killed a grouse much larger than the common size, and observed along the shore a number of striped snakes [*Eutænia pickeringi*].

The river is here deep, and about a mile and a half in width. (*p. 67*) Here too the ridge of low mountains [Coast range] running northwest and southeast crosses the river, and forms the western boundary of the plain through which we have just passed. This great plain or valley begins above the mouth of Quicksand river, and is about 60 miles wide in a straight line, while on the right and left it extends to a

[14] Kalama river, Cowlitz Co., Wash.; county town of same name 2 m. above its mouth, about 46° N.; Sandy island opposite the town ; Coffin Rock opposite the river. In reaching this point, only some six or eight miles above the Cow-litz river, the Expedition has missed a much larger river on the right, now called Lewis' river. It is that charted by Clark as Chah-wah-na-hi-ooks.

great distance. It is a fertile and delightful country, shaded by thick groves of tall timber, watered by small ponds, and running on both sides of the river. The soil is rich and capable of any species of culture; but in the present condition of the Indians, its chief production is the wappatoo-root, which grows spontaneously and exclusively in this region. Sheltered as it is on both sides, the temperature is much milder than that of the surrounding country; for even at this season of the year we observe very little appearance of frost. During its whole extent it is inhabited by numerous tribes of Indians, who either reside in it permanently, or visit its waters in quest of fish and wappatoo-roots. We gave it the name of the [Wappatoo or] Columbia valley.

November 6th. The morning was cool, wet, and rainy. We proceeded at an early hour between the high hills on both sides of the river, till at the distance of four miles we came to two tents of Indians in a small plain on the left [Rainier], where the hills on the right recede a few miles from the river, and a long narrow island stretches along the right shore. Behind this island is the mouth of a large river, 150 yards wide, called by the Indians Coweliske.[15] We halted for dinner on the island, but the redwood [*Cornus pubescens?*] and green-briar [*Rubus ursinus*] are so interwoven with pine, alder [*Alnusrubra* or *A. rhombifolia*], ash, a species of beech, and other trees, that the woods form a thicket, which our hunters could not penetrate. Below the mouth of the Coweliske a very remarkable knob rises from the water's edge to the height of 80 feet, being 200 paces round the base; as it is in a low part of the island, at some distance from the high grounds, its appearance is very singular [Mt. Coffin].

On setting out after dinner (*p. 68*) we overtook two canoes going down to trade; one of the Indians, who spoke a few words of English, mentioned that the principal person

[15] Or Coweliskee, as Clark H 111 and map; Coweleskee in Irving's Astoria; the Cowlitz river, so called from a once populous and powerful Salishan tribe, whose remnants are now on Puyallup Reservation, Wash. Freeport and Monticello at its mouth. Cowlitz is also the present name of the county next east of Wahkiacum, south of Lewis, north of Clark, and west of Skamania.

who traded with them was a Mr. Haley; and he showed a bow of iron and several other things, which he said Mr. Haley had given him.   Nine miles below that river is a creek on the same [side]; and between them are three smaller islands, one on the left shore, the other [Walker's] about the middle of the river, and a third [Fisher's] near the lower end of the long narrow island,[16] opposite a high cliff of black rocks on the left, 16 miles from our camp.   Here we were overtaken by the Indians from the two tents we passed in the morning, from whom we now purchased wappatoo-roots, salmon, trout, and two beaver-skins, for which last we gave five small fish-hooks.   At these cliffs [Green's point] the mountains, which had continued high and rugged on the left, retired from the river, and as the hills on the other side had left the water at the Coweliske, a beautiful extensive plain now presented itself before us.   For a few miles we passed alongside an island [Grim's] a mile in width and three miles long, below which is a smaller island [Gull].   Here the high rugged hills, thickly covered with timber, border the right bank of the river and terminate the low grounds.   These were supplied with common rushes, grass, and nettles in the moister parts with the bulrushes and flags, and along the water's edge with willows.   Here also were two ancient villages, now abandoned by their inhabitants, of whom no vestige remains, except two small dogs, almost starved, and a prodigious quantity of fleas.   After crossing the plain and [thus] making five miles, we proceeded through the hills for eight miles [passing Wallace's island].   The river is about a

[16] Text makes this "long narrow island" 16—4=12 miles, in the length of which were the smaller islands.   It is now incompletely isolated by a (Big) slough, into which Coal creek falls.   By U. S. Coast Surv. charts (scale 1 to 40,000) the following is the situation: 1. Cottonwood isl., 2 m. long, just above mo. Cowlitz river (not in the text).   2. A long lowland, left, incompletely isolated by Rinearson's slough; Cedar Ldg. at its head; Mt. Coffin opposite; corresponding to first of "three smaller" islands.   3. Walker's, in mid-river, opp. Mt. Solo. 4. Fisher's, right, nearly opp. Green's point.   5. Grim's, left, 2 m. long, by which fall in Big slough, and Nequally and Negisticook creeks, right.   6. Gull island, right, very small, near end of Grim's.   7. Wallace's, left, 3 m. long.   See p. 909.

mile in width, and the hills are so steep that we could not for several miles find a place sufficiently flat to suffer us to sleep in a level position; at length, by removing some large stones, we cleared a place fit for our purpose above the reach of the tide, and after a journey of 29 miles slept among the smaller stones under a mountain to the right [one mile below Cape Horn]. The weather was rainy during the whole day; (*p. 69*) we therefore made large fires to dry our bedding and to kill the fleas, which have accumulated upon us at every old village we have passed.

November 7th. The morning was rainy, and the fog so thick that we could not see across the river. We observed, however, opposite our camp, the upper point of an island [Puget's [17]], between which and the steep hills on the right we proceeded for five miles [site of Cathlamet]. Three miles lower is the beginning of an island separated from the right shore by a narrow channel; down this we proceeded under the direction of some Indians, whom we had just met going up the river, and who returned in order to show us their village. It consists of four houses only, situated on this channel behind several marshy islands formed by two small creeks. On our arrival they gave us some fish, and we afterward purchased some wappatoo-roots, fish, three dogs, and two otter-skins, for which we gave fish-hooks chiefly, that being an article of which they are very fond.

These people seem to be of a different nation from those we have just passed; they are low in stature, ill shaped, and all have their heads flattened. They call themselves Wahkiacum,[18] and their language differs from that of the tribes above, with whom they trade for wappatoo-roots. The houses are built in a different style, being raised entirely

[17] This island, five miles long, is now known as Puget or Puget's. Nearly opposite its lower end is Cathlamet, county town of Wahkiacum. Three islands lower down, close under the right shore, are Hunting, Cathlamet, and Skumaquea, Skamokawa, or Skomaukie; near the latter a creek of the same name falls in, which is one of the two mentioned in the text. Opposite are the large Tenasillihee and several smaller islands.

[18] First Warciâcum, altered to Warkiâcum, Clark 114; Wahkiakume, Clark's

above ground, with the eaves about five feet high and the door at the corner.   Near the end, opposite this door, is a single fireplace, round which are the beds, raised four feet from the floor of earth ; over the fire are hung the fresh fish, which, when dried, are stowed away with the wappatoo-roots under the beds.   The dress of the men is like that of the people above, but the women are clad in a peculiar manner, the robe not reaching lower than the hip, and the body being covered in cold weather by a sort of corset of fur, curiously plaited and reaching from the arms to the hip; added to this is a sort of petticoat, or rather tissue of white cedar bark, bruised or broken into small strands, and woven (*p. 70*) into a girdle by several cords of the same material. Being tied round the middle, these strands hang down as low as the knee in front, and to the mid-leg behind ; they are of sufficient thickness to answer the purpose of conceal-ment whilst the female stands in an erect position, but in any other attitude form but a very ineffectual defense. Sometimes the tissue is strings of silk-grass, twisted and knotted at the end.

After remaining with them about an hour, we proceeded down the channel with an Indian dressed in a sailor's jacket for our pilot, and on reaching the main channel were visited by some Indians who have a temporary residence on a marshy [Tenasillihee] island in the middle of the river, where is a great abundance of water-fowl.   Here the mountainous country again approaches the river on the left, and a higher [Saddle] mountain is distinguished toward the southwest. At a distance of 20 miles from our camp we halted at a vil-lage of Wahkiacums, consisting of seven ill-looking houses, built in the same form with those above, and situated at the

map.   This word preserves an orthography made for it by Lewis and Clark, and is now the name of a county in Washington, on the Columbia, west of Cowlitz and east of Pacific.   The Wahkiacum is one of about nine tribes of the Upper Chinooks (the Lower Chinooks being only the genuine Chinooks and the Clat-sops).   These ten or twelve principal tribes constitute the Chinookan stock, or family, inhabiting the Columbia from its mouth to the Dalles.   The Wahkiacum tribe was named from its chief ; it has been lost sight of as a tribe since 1850.

foot of the high hills on the right, behind two small marshy islands. We merely stopped to purchase some food and two beaver-skins, and then proceeded. Opposite to these islands the hills on the left retire, and the river widens into a kind of bay crowded with low islands, subject to be over-flowed occasionally by the tide.

We had not gone far from this village when the fog cleared off, and we enjoyed the delightful prospect of the ocean—that ocean,[19] the object of all our labors, the reward of all our anxieties. This cheering view exhilarated the spirits of all the party, who were still more delighted on hearing the distant roar of the breakers. We went on with great cheerfulness under the high mountainous country which continued along the right bank [passing Three Tree and Jim Crow points]; the shore was, however, so bold and rocky that we could not, until after going 14 miles from the last village, find any spot fit for a camp [opposite Pillar Rock]. At that distance, having made during the day 34 miles, we spread our mats on the ground, and passed the night in the rain. Here we were joined by our (*p. 71*) small canoe, which had been separated from us during the fog this morning. Two Indians from the last village also accompanied us to the camp; but, having detected them in stealing a knife, they were sent off.

November 8th. It rained this morning, and having changed the clothing which had been wet during yesterday's rain, we did not set out till nine o'clock. Immediately opposite our camp is a [Pillar] rock at the distance of [half] a mile in the river, about 20 feet in diameter and 50 in height; toward the southwest are some high mountains, one of which

[19] Clark H 117 has: " Encamped under a high hill on the Stard. side opposit to a rock situated half a mile from the shore, about 50 feet high and 20 feet Deamieter." This is Pillar rock, one mile below Jim Crow point, where camp was pitched on the memorable day that the Pacific was sighted. " Great joy in camp," writes the great captain, who so seldom betrays a feeling, or indulges a sentiment ; " we are in *view* of the *Ocian*, this great Pacific Octian which we have been so long anxious to see, and the roreing or noise made by the waves brakeing on the rockey shores (as I suppose) may be heard distictly." And H 147, same date : " Ocian in view ! O ! the joy."

is covered with snow at the top. We proceeded past several low islands in the bay or bend to the left of the river, which is here five or six miles wide. We were here overtaken by three Indians in a canoe, who had salmon to sell. On the right side we passed an old village, and then, at the distance of three miles, entered an inlet [rounding Yellow bluffs], or niche, about six miles across, making a deep bend of nearly five miles into the hills on the right shore, where it receives the waters of several creeks. We coasted along this inlet, which, from its little depth, we called Shallow [20] bay; and at the bottom of it halted to dine near the remains of an old village, from which, however, we kept at a cautious distance, as it was occupied by great numbers of fleas. At this place we observed a number of fowl, among which we killed a goose, and two ducks exactly resembling in appearance and flavor the canvasback duck of the Susquehannah. After dinner the three Indians left us. We then took advantage of the returning tide to go on about three miles to a point on the right, eight miles [direct] distant from our camp; but here the waves ran so high, and dashed about our canoes so much that several of the men became seasick. It was therefore judged imprudent to go on in the present state of the weather, and we landed at the point [Gray's; Cape Swell of Gass]. The situation was extremely uncomfortable; the high hills jutted in so closely that there was not room for us to lie level, or to secure our baggage free from the tide, and the water of the river was too salt to be used; but (p. 72) the waves increased every moment so much that we could not move from the spot with safety. We therefore fixed ourselves on the beach left by the ebb tide, and having raised the baggage on poles, passed a disagreeable night, the rain

[20] Well within the mouth of the Columbia, on the north side, in the S.W. corner of Wahkiacum Co., adjoining Pacific Co., Wash.—not to be confounded with Shoalwater bay, on the Pacific coast, north of Cape Disappointment. "Call it the Shallow nitch," Clark H 118, with "Bay" red-inked over "nitch." This is now Gray's bay; Gray's point forms the seaward one of its bounds, and Yellow bluffs the landward; Gray's and Alamicut rivers are the two principal streams falling into it.

during the day having wet us completely, as indeed we have been for some days.

November 9th. Fortunately for us, the tide did not rise as high as our camp during the night; but being accompanied by high winds from the south, the canoes, which we could not place beyond its reach, were filled with water, and were saved with much difficulty. Our position was very uncomfortable, but as it was impossible to move from it, we waited for a change of weather. It rained, however, during the whole day, and at two o'clock in the afternoon the flood tide set in, accompanied by a high wind from the south, which, about four o'clock, shifted to the southwest and blew almost a gale directly from the sea. The immense waves now broke over the place where we were camped; the large trees, some of them five or six feet thick, which had lodged at the point, were drifted over our camp, and the utmost vigilance of every man could scarcely save our canoes from being crushed to pieces. We remained in the water, and drenched with rain, during the rest of the day, our only food being some dried fish and some rain-water which we caught. Yet, though wet and cold, and some of them sick from using salt water, the men were cheerful, and full of anxiety to see more of the ocean. The rain continued all night.

Sunday, November 10th. This morning the wind lulled, and the waves not being so high, we loaded our canoes and proceeded. The mountains on the right are high, covered with timber, chiefly pine, and descend in a bold and rocky shore to the water. We went through a deep niche and several inlets on the right [past Cementville and Cliff Point], while on the opposite side is a large bay, above which the hills are close on the river. At the distance of ten miles the wind rose from the north- (*p. 73*) west, and the waves became so high that we were forced to return for two miles to a place where we could with safety unload. Here we landed at the mouth of a small run, and, having placed our baggage on a pile of drifted logs, waited until low water. The river then appeared more calm; we therefore started.

but after going a mile found the waves too high for our canoes, and were obliged to put to shore. We unloaded the canoes; and having placed the baggage on a rock above the reach of the tide, camped[21] on some drift-logs, which formed the only place where we could lie, the hills rising steep over our heads to the height of 500 feet. All our baggage, as well as ourselves, were thoroughly wet with the rain, which did not cease during the day; it continued violently during the night, in the course of which the tide reached the logs on which we lay, and set them afloat.

November 11*th*. The wind was still high from the southwest, and drove the waves against the shore with great fury; the rain too fell in torrents, and not only drenched us to the skin, but loosened the stones on the hillsides, which then came rolling down upon us. In this comfortless situation we remained all day, wet, cold, with nothing but dried fish to satisfy our hunger; the canoes in one place at the mercy of the waves, the baggage in another, and all the men scattered on floating logs, or sheltering themselves in the crevices of the rocks and hillsides. A hunter [J. Fields] was dispatched in hopes of finding some fresh meat; but the hills were so steep, and so covered with undergrowth and fallen timber, that he could not penetrate them, and he was forced to return. About twelve o'clock we were visited by five Indians in a canoe; they came from [Warren's Landing] above this place, on the opposite side of the river; their language much resembles that of the Wahkiacums, and they call themselves Cathlamahs.[22] In person they are small,

---

[21] The Expedition undertook to round Point Ellice, and were beaten back, as their miserable dug-outs were unmanageable in such a sea. Clark H 148 calls this Point Distress, which name appears also on his MS. map, I 152, but not on the engraved plate. This is Blustry Point of Gass, p. 167.

[22] Clark H 123, first Calt-har-mar, scored and overwritten Cath-lah-ma; now spelled Cathlamet, but more properly would be Katla'mat. They were one of the several tribes of Upper Chinookans who fished the Columbia as low down as Astoria. The name was also applied to the village of these Indians, and Cathlamet is now the principal town of Wahkiacum or Wahkiakum Co., Wash. The Katla'mats are credited with 300 souls on Clark's map; these were reduced to a population of 58 in 1849. There is now no such tribe officially recognized.

ill made, and badly clothed; though one of them had on a sailor's round jacket and pantaloons, which, as he explained by signs, he had received from the (*p. 74*) whites below the point. We purchased from them 13 red char, a fish which we found very excellent. After some time they went aboard the boat and crossed the river, which is here five miles wide, through a very heavy sea.

November 12*th.* About three o'clock a tremendous gale of wind arose, accompanied with lightning, thunder, and hail; at six it became light for a short time, but a violent rain soon began and lasted during the day. During this storm one of our boats, secured by being sunk with great quantities of stone, got loose; but, drifting against a rock, was recovered without having received much injury. Our situation became now much more dangerous, for the waves were driven with fury against the rocks and trees, which till now had afforded us refuge. We therefore took advantage of a low tide, and moved about half a mile round a point to a small brook, which we had not observed till now on account of the thick bushes and driftwood which concealed its mouth. Here we were more safe; but still cold and wet, our clothes and bedding rotten as well as wet, our baggage at a distance, and the canoes—our only means of escape from this place—at the mercy of the waves. We were, however, fortunate enough to enjoy good health, and even had the luxury of getting some fresh salmon and three salmon-trout in the brook. Three of the men [Gibson, Bratton, Willard] attempted to go round a point in our small Indian canoe, but the high waves rendered her quite unmanageable—these boats requiring the seamanship of the natives themselves to make them live in so rough a sea.

November 13*th.* During the night we had short intervals of fair weather, but it began to rain in the morning and continued through the day. In order to obtain a view of the country below, Captain Clark followed up the course of the brook, and with much fatigue, after walking three miles, ascended the first spur of the mountains. The whole lower

country was covered with almost impenetrable thick- (*p. 75*)
ets of small pine, with which is mixed a species of plant
[*Cratægus rivularis*] resembling arrow-wood, 12 or 15 feet
high, with a thorny stem, almost interwoven with each other,
and scattered among the fern and fallen timber.   There is
also a red berry [*Smilacina sessilifolia*], somewhat like the
Solomon's seal, which is called by the natives solme, and
used as an article of diet.   This thick growth rendered traveling almost impossible, and it was made more fatiguing by
the steepness of the mountain, which was so great as to
oblige him to draw himself up by means of the bushes.
The timber on the hills is chiefly of a large tall species of
pine, many of them 8 or 10 feet in diameter at the stump,
and rising sometimes more than 100 feet in height.   The
hail which fell two nights since is still to be seen on the
mountains.   There was no game, and no trace of any, except some old signs of elk.   The cloudy weather prevented
his seeing to any distance; he therefore returned to camp,
and sent three men [Colter, Willard, Shannon] in the Indian
canoe to try if they could double the point [Ellice or Dis-
tress] and find some safer harbor for our canoes.   At every
flood tide the seas break in great swells against the rocks,
and drift the trees among our establishment, so as to render
it very insecure.   We were confined as usual to dried fish,
which is our last resource.

November 14th.   It rained without intermission during last
night; to-day the wind too was very high, and one of our
canoes was much injured by being dashed against rocks.
Five Indians from below came to us in a canoe, and three of
them, having landed, informed us that they had seen the men
sent down yesterday.   At this moment one of them [Colter]
arrived, and informed us that these Indians had stolen his
gig and basket.   We therefore ordered the two women who
remained in the canoe to restore them; but this they refused,
till we threatened to shoot, when they gave back the articles, and we then ordered them to leave us.   They were of
the Wahkiacum nation.   The man [Colter] now informed us

that they had gone round the point as far as the high sea would suffer (*p. 76*) them in the canoe, and then landed; that in the night he had separated from his companions, who had gone further down, and that at no great distance from where we are is a beautiful sand-beach and a good harbor. Captain Lewis concluded to examine more minutely the lower part of the bay [Haley's]; taking one of the large canoes he was landed at the point [Ellice], whence he proceeded by land with four men [Drewyer, J. and R. Fields, and Frazier], and the canoe returned nearly filled with water.

November 15*th*. It continued raining all night, but in the morning the weather became calm and fair. We therefore began to prepare for setting out; but before we were ready a high wind sprang up from the southeast, and obliged us to remain. The sun shone until one o'clock, and we were thus enabled to dry our bedding and examine our baggage. The rain, which has continued for the last ten days without an interval of more than two hours, has completely wet all our merchandise, spoiled some of our fish, destroyed the robes, and rotted nearly half of our few remaining articles of clothing, particularly the leather dresses. About three o'clock the wind fell; we instantly loaded the canoes, and left the miserable spot to which we have been confined the last six days. On turning the point we came to the sand-beach, through which runs a small stream from the hills; at the mouth of this is an ancient [Chinook] village of 36 houses, which has at present no inhabitants except fleas.

Here we met Shannon, who had been sent back to meet us by Captain Lewis. The day Shannon left us in the canoe, he and Willard proceeded till they met a party of 20 Indians, who, having never heard of us, did not know where they [our men] came from; they, however, behaved with so much civility, and seemed so anxious that the men should go with them toward the sea, that their suspicions were excited, and they declined going on. The Indians, however, would not leave them; the men being confirmed in their suspicions, and fearful that if they went into the woods to sleep they would be cut to pieces in the night, (*p. 77*) thought it best to pass the night in the midst of the Indians. They therefore made a fire, and after talking with them to a late hour, laid down with their rifles under their heads. As they awoke that morning they found that the Indians had stolen and concealed their guns. Having demanded then in vain, Shannon seized a club, and was about assaulting one of the Indians, whom he suspected as a thief, when another Indian began to load a fowling-piece with the intention of shooting him. He therefore stopped, and explained by signs that if they did not give up the guns a large party would come down the river before the sun rose to such a height, and put every one of them to death. Fortunately, Captain Lewis and his party appeared at this time. The terrified Indians immediately brought the guns, and five of them came on with Shannon. To these men we declared that if ever anyone of their nation stole anything from us, he should be instantly shot.[23] They reside to the north of this place, and speak a language different from that of the people higher up the river.

It was now apparent that the sea was at all times too rough for us to proceed further down the bay by water. We therefore landed, and having chosen the best spot we could select, made our camp[24] of boards from the old [Chinook] village. We were now situated comfortably, and being visited by four Wahkiacums with wappatoo-roots, were enabled to make an agreeable addition to our food.

November 16*th.*[25] The morning was clear and beautiful.

[23] " I told those Indians who accompanied Shannon that they should not come near us, and if any one of their nation stold anything from us, I would have him Shot, which they understoot verry well," Clark H 129.

[24] This camp was at the S.E. or landward end of Haley's (Baker's) bay, just inside Chinook Point (Point Open-slope of Gass), a mile above a point of rocks 40 feet high, and the same below where Chinook town now stands, on the site of the old Chinook village already mentioned.

[25] At this date, Clark H 131, the narrative is interrupted in the codex, and H 132–148 is tabular: " Course Distance & Remarks Decending the Columbia from the Lewis's [Snake] River," etc., Oct. 18th–Nov. 16th. The " remark " for the course of Nov. 7th is hardly statistical—" Ocian in View ! O ! the joy."

We therefore put out all our baggage to dry, and sent several of the party to hunt. Our camp is in full view of the ocean, on the bay laid down by Vancouver, which we distintinguish by the name of Haley's[26] bay, from a trader who visits the Indians here, and is a great favorite among them. The meridian altitude of this day gave 46° 19' 11" 7''' as the latitude of our camp. The wind was strong from the southwest, and the waves were very high ; yet the Indians were passing up and down the bay in canoes, and several of them camped near us. We smoked with them, but after our recent (*p. 78*) experience of their thievish disposition treated them with caution. Though so much exposed to the bad weather, none of the party have suffered, except one, who has a violent cold, in consequence of sleeping for several nights in wet leather. The hunters brought in two deer, a crane, some geese and ducks, and several brant, three of which [snow-geese] were white, except a black part of the wing, and much larger than the gray brant, which is itself a size beyond the duck.

Sunday, November 17*th*. A fair, cool morning and an easterly wind. The tide rises at this place 8½ feet, and rolls over the beach in great waves.

About one o'clock Captain Lewis returned, after having coasted down Haley's bay to Cape Disappointment [see beyond], and some distance to the north along the seacoast. He was followed by several Chinnooks,[27] among whom were

The tables make the ocean 165 miles from Quicksand river, 190 from the first rapid on the Columbia, and 4142 from the mouth of the Missouri. Then the narrative resumes, including Nov. 17th and 18th, breaking off on p. 152, in the midst of Nov. 19th, with the remark, '' See another book for particulars.'' This other book is Codex I, directly continuous with H.

[26] North side of the mouth of the Columbia, just inside Cape Disappointment, in Pacific Co., Wash. The latitude as determined is nearly right (46° 14½'.) Now Baker's bay, though still sometimes called Rogue's harbor, after Gass, who so named it from the way the Chinooks had treated Shannon and Willard.

[27] Preferably and usually spelled *Chinook*, as Gass has it, and after him Gallatin in Trans. and Coll. Amer. Antiq. Soc. II. 1836, pp. 134, 306, and Hale, U. S. Explor. Exped. VI. 1846, p. 198. The orthography has fluctuated also to *Cheenook* and *Chinuk*, as Latham, Journ. Ethnol. Soc. London,

the principal chief and his family. They made us a present of a boiled root, very much like the common licorice in taste and size, called culwhamo [*Glycyrrhiza lepidota*] ; in return we gave double the value of their present, and now learned the danger of accepting anything from them, since no return, even if ten times the value of their gift, can satisfy them. We were chiefly occupied in hunting, and were able to procure three deer, four brant, and two ducks, and also saw some signs of elk. Captain Clark now prepared for an excursion down the bay,[28] and accordingly started [by land],

November 18*th*, accompanied by 11 men. He proceeded along the beach one mile to a point of rocks about 40 feet high, where the hills retire, leaving a wide beach [White's Point] and a number of ponds covered with water-fowl, beween which and the mountain is a narrow bottom of alder and small balsam trees. Seven miles from the rocks is the entrance of a creek, or rather a drain, from the ponds and hills, where is a cabin of Chinnooks. The cabin contained some children, and four women, one of whom was in a most miserable state, covered with ulcers, proceeding, as we (*p. 79*)

I. 1848, p. 236, and Nat. Hist. Man. 1850, p. 317 ; to *Tshinooh* of Gallatin in Schoolcraft's Indian Tribes, and to *Tshinuk* and *Tschinuk* of Buschmann and Berghaus. The word now gives name to the Chinookan stock or family of Indians, of Powell's classification. In this sense Chinookans include a number of tribes which lived from the mouth of the Columbia to the Dalles, about 200 miles, chiefly on the north side, and whose villages also extended coastwise for some 20 miles south of Point Adams, and northward nearly the whole extent of Shoalwater bay. These were the principal tribe of their stock. In the Estimate of the Western Indians Lewis and Clark understate their then population ; Clark's map marks only 400 souls. The Chinookans are divided into the Chinooks most properly so called, and Clatsops, these two forming the Lower Chinookan tribes ; and into Upper Chinookan (or Watlala) tribes, named as Cathlamet, Cathlapotle, Chilluckquittequaw, Clackama, Cooniac, Echeloot, Multnoma, Wahkiacum, and Wasco. The remnants of all these tribes are now only about 500 to 600 in number, on several Indian reservations. There were recently 288 Wascos on the Warm Springs Reservation, Oregon, and 150 of them on the Yakama Reservation in Washington. A few families of one of the lower tribes live or lately lived near Freeport, Wash. The Chinooks proper are nearly if not quite extinct.

[28] Down Haley's Bay to Cape Disappointment, round the cape, up the coast several miles and back, across neck of the peninsula, and by the bay to camp.

imagine, from venereal disease, with which several of the Chinnooks we have seen appear to be afflicted. We were taken across in a canoe by two squaws, to each of whom we gave a fish-hook, and then, coasting along the bay, passed at two miles the low bluff of a small hill, below which are the ruins of some old huts, and close to it the remains of a whale. The country is low, open, and marshy [slashey, Clark], interspersed with some high pine and a thick undergrowth. Five miles from the creek we came to a stream 40 yards wide at low water, which we called Chinnook river.[29] The hills up this river and toward the bay are not high, but very thickly covered with large pine of several species; in many places pine trees, three or four feet in thickness, are seen growing on the bodies of large trees, which, though fallen and covered with moss, were in part sound. Here we dined on some brant and plover, killed as we came along,[30] and after crossing in a boat lying in the sand near some old houses, proceeded along a bluff of yellow clay and soft stone to a little bay or harbor, into which a drain from some ponds empties. At this harbor the land is low, but as we went on it rose to hills of 80 or 90 feet above the water. At the distance of one mile is a second bay, and a mile beyond it a small, rocky island in a deep bend, which seems to afford a very good harbor, where the natives inform us European vessels anchor for the purpose of trading.[31] We went on around another bay, in

[29] Rogue's-harbour creek, Gass, p. 167 ; la crique des Voleurs of his French editor, p. 263; now Wanachute creek, as G. L. O. map, 1891, or Wallacut river, as U. S. Coast Surv. chart, 1892. It is the *other* one of the two main streams falling into Haley's bay, unnamed by L. and C., that is now known as Chinook creek or river.

[30] And here R. Fields killed a Californian condor, *Pseudogryphus californianus*, which Clark H 150 carefully describes. It measured 9½ feet from tip to tip, 3 feet 10¼ inches from the point of the bill to the end of the tail, the tail 14½ inches, the head and beak 6½ inches. This is one of the earliest measurements ever made in detail of this famous vulture, which is quite as large as the more celebrated Andean condor, *Sarcorhamphus gryphus*.

[31] " Here I found Capt. Lewis's name on a tree. I also engraved my name, & by land [*i. e.*, the words " by land "] the day of the month and the year, as also [did] several of the men," Clark H 151. The eleven men on this reconnoissance, besides their leader, were Ordway, Pryor, J. and R. Fields, Shannon, Bratton, Colter, Wiser, Labiche, " Shabono," and York, Clark H 150.

which is a second small island of rocks, and crossed a small stream, which rises in a pond near the seacoast, and after running through a low isthmus [Fort Canby here] empties into the bay. This narrow, low ground, about 200 or 300 yards wide, separates from the main hills a kind of peninsula, the extremity of which is two miles from the anchoring place.

This spot, which was called Cape Disappointment,[32] is an elevated, circular knob, rising with a steep ascent 150 or 160 feet above the water, formed like the whole shore of the

[32] From the text it might be gathered that this name was given by Lewis and Clark; but what they mean is, that they identified the place as Cape Disappointment. The history of the discovery of the mouth of the Columbia, and the naming of this cape, may be here epitomized. I prepare it from M'Vickar's Introduction to his digest of Lewis and Clark, 1842. In 1774, for the first time since the voyage of Viscaino in 1602, the examination of the coast was directed by Spanish authorities of Mexico, and Juan Perez was instructed to proceed north to 60° N. Perez went to 54° N., and on his return entered at 49½° a bay he called San Lorenzo, probably Nootka Sound of Captain Cook. Next year, 1775, the Spanish Viceroy sent two vessels, under Heceta and Bodega, who went together only as far as the Straits of San Juan de Fuca. Bodega pushed further north, but Heceta was ordered to return to Monterey. On this return voyage he discovered a promontory which he called San Roque, and immediately south of it an opening in the land, as of a harbor or the mouth of a river. This should be the Columbia; and San Roque, Cape Disappointment, as afterward so named. Meantime Captain Cook, on his second voyage, made land 100 miles north of Cape Mendocino, March 7th, 1778; held northward and passed the mouth of the Columbia on a stormy night, thus missing it; and March 29th reached the inlet he first called King George's Sound, and later Nootka. In 1785 Lapeyrouse was sent out to prepare the way for the French fur-trade by examining the coast. He made land near Mt. St. Elias, and coasted down to Monterey. In 1787 began the first voyages from the United States. The ship "Columbia," John Kendrick, 200 tons, and the sloop "Washington," Robert Gray, 90 tons, sailed from Boston Sept. 30th, 1787, and doubled Cape Horn together. The "Washington" reached Nootka Sept. 17th, 1788, was soon joined by the "Columbia," and both wintered there. They returned by way of the Cape of Good Hope, reaching Boston Aug. 9th, 1790. Between 1785 and 1790 important surveys of the coast were made by both British and American vessels engaged in the fur-trade. The most interesting was the voyage of Captain John Meares, from Macao, in the "Felice," under the Portuguese flag, to discover the opening which had been noted by Heceta in 1775. This had been charted as "Entrada de Heceta," or "Entrada de Asuncion," sometimes as "Rio de San Roque." Meares finished his examination by calling the opening "*Deception Bay*," and the promontory "*Cape Disappointment*." He makes the lati-

(*p. 80*) bay, as well as of the seacoast, and covered with thick timber on the inner side, but open and grassy in the exposure next the sea. From this cape a high point of land [33] bears S. 20° W., about 25 miles distant. In the range between these two eminences is the opposite point of the bay, a very low ground, which has been variously called Cape Rond by Lapeyrouse, and Point Adams by Vancouver [see preceding note]. The water for a great distance off the mouth of the river appears very shallow, and within the mouth nearest to Point Adams is a large sand-bar, almost covered at high tide.

tude 49° 10' N. and concludes : "We can now with safety assert that no such river as that of Saint Roc exists, as laid down in Spanish charts."

The actual discovery and naming of the Columbia were American, of date 1791. Among the seven American vessels which that year reached the North Pacific was the ship "Columbia," Captain Gray, which sailed from Boston Sept. 27th, 1790, and touched the coast a little north of Cape Mendocino. Coasting on toward Nootka, Captain Gray observed an opening at 49° 16 , discharging a current so strong that he could not stem it, though he tried for nine days. He was satisfied that he had discovered the mouth of a great river. He then sailed on to Nootka, made his winter station in September, 1791, and built Fort Defiance. Here he also built and launched the schooner "Enterprise."

Meanwhile, in 1791, Captain Vancouver and Lieutenant Broughton were dispatched from England in the British vessels "Discovery" and "Chatham," to receive the surrender from the Spanish of a port on Nootka Sound. On the 27th of April, 1792, Vancouver passed with a careless glance the cape and bay Meares had called "Disappointment" and "Deception," entering in his log-book, "not considering this opening worthy of more attention, I continued our course to the northwest," etc. Two days afterward he met the American ship "Columbia," and Captain Gray informed him that he (Gray) had been "off the mouth of a river, in latitude 46° 10', where the outset or reflux was so strong as to prevent his entering for nine days." Vancouver kept on north, in his incredulity, while Gray again sought the mouth of the river. He reached it May 11th, 1792, crossed the bar, and found himself in water so fresh that he filled the ship's casks within ten miles of the ocean. Gray named the river *Columbia*, after his own vessel ; Cape Disappointment he named Cape *Hancock ;* the opposite cape he named Cape *Adams*. These names which the Yankee patriot bestowed have since held on some maps, and not on others. "The name of the good ship 'Columbia,'" adds M'Vickar, "will flow with the waters of the bold river as long as grass grows or water runs in the valleys of the Rocky Mountains."

[33] "Which we shall call Clark's point of view," Clark H 152, here first mentioned, as the codices run : but see Jan. 8th, 1806. Captain Clark of course did not give his own name to the point. Gass' French editor makes it l'Observatoire de Clarke, p. 281. This bold promontony is False Tillamook Head.

We could not ascertain the direction of the deepest channel, for the waves break with tremendous force the whole distance across the bay; but the Indians point nearer to the opposite side as the best passage. After remaining some time on this elevation, we descended across the low isthmus, and reached the ocean at the foot of a high hill [McKenzie head], about a mile in circumference, projecting into the sea. We crossed this hill, which is open and has a growth of high coarse grass, and camped on the north side of it, having made 19 miles. Besides the pounded fish and brant, we had for supper a flounder, which we picked up on the beach.

November 19*th*.[34] In the night it began to rain and continued till eleven o'clock. Two hunters were sent on to kill something for breakfast, and the rest of the party, after drying their blankets, soon followed. At three miles we overtook the hunters and breakfasted on a small deer which they had been fortunate enough to kill. This, like all those we have seen on this coast, are much darker than our common deer. Their bodies, too, are deeper, their legs shorter, and their eyes larger. The branches of the horns are similar, but the upper part of the tail is black, from the root to the end; and they do not leap, but jump like sheep frightened.[35]

We then continued over rugged hills and steep hollows near the sea, on a course about N. 20° W., in a direct line from the cape till at the distance of five miles (*p. 81*) we reached a point of high land; below which a sandy beach extends, in a direction N. 10° W., to another high point[36]

[34] Codex H ends in the midst of this date. Nov. 19th is picked up afresh at p. 34 of Clark I—the matter of this codex which precedes p. 34 being statistical, meteorological, etc. Codex I runs to Jan. 29th, 1806, without break in the Journal from Codex H.

[35] This is the original description of the Columbian black-tailed deer, *Cariacus columbianus*, which is quite distinct from the Missourian black-tailed or mule-deer, *C. macrotis*, and from the common white-tailed or Virginian deer, *C. virginianus*. In the text "leap" is a mistake for *lope*, Clark I 35.

[36] "This point I have taken the liberty of calling after my particular friend Lewis," Clark I 34. This elevation is near the entrance of Shoalwater bay. (Adjust all Clark's compass-bearings about the mouth of the Columbia for a magnetic variation of 21° 30' E.)

about twenty miles distant.   This eminence we distinguished
by the name of Point Lewis.   It is there that the highlands,
which at the commencement of the sandy beach recede
toward Chinnook river, again approach the ocean.   The intermediate country is low, with many small ponds, crowded
with birds and watered by the Chinnook, on the borders of
which resides the nation of the same name.   We went four
miles along the sandy beach to a small pine-tree, on which
Captain Clark marked his name, with the year and day, and
then returned to the foot of the hills, passing on the shore
a sturgeon [*Acipenser transmontanus*] ten feet long, and
several joints of the backbone of a whale, both of which
seem to have been thrown ashore and foundered.   After
dining on the remains of the small deer, we crossed in a
southeastern direction to the [Haley's] bay, where we
arrived at the distance of two miles [at Ilwaco]; then we
continued along the bay, crossed Chinnook [Wallacut]
river, and camped on its upper side in a sandy bottom.

November 20th.   It rained in the course of the night.   A
hunter [Labiche], dispatched early to kill some food, returned
with eight ducks, on which we breakfasted, and then followed the course of the bay to the [present Chinook] creek
or outlet of the ponds.   It was now high tide, the stream
300 yards wide, and no person in the cabin to take us across.
We therefore made a small raft, on which one of the men
[R. Fields] passed and brought a canoe to carry us over.
As we went along the beach we were overtaken by several
Indians, who gave us dried sturgeon and wappatoo-roots,
and soon met several parties of Chinnooks returning from
the camp.   When we arrived there we found many Chinnooks; two of them being chiefs, we went through the
ceremony of giving to each a medal, and to the most
distinguished a flag.   Their names were Comcommoly[37]
and Chillahlawil.   One of the Indians had a robe made of

[37] " This one-eyed potentate, Comcomly," as Washington Irving calls him, still
lived and reigned over the amphibious Chinnooks of fishy odor and renown, in
1812, when McDougal of the Astorians indulged the romance of marrying the
chieftain's daughter.   How the sagacious savage played the father-in-law, and

two sea-otter skins, the fur of which was the most beautiful we had ever seen.   The owner at first resisted (*p. 82*) every temptation to part with it, but at length could not resist the offer of a belt of blue beads which Chaboneau's wife wore around her waist.[38]   During our absence the camp had been visited by many Indians, and the men who had been employed in hunting killed several deer and a variety of wild fowls.

November 21st.   The morning was cloudy, and from noon till night it rained.   The wind was high from the southeast, and the sea so rough that the water reached our camp. Most of the Chinnooks returned home ; but we were visited in the course of the day by people of different bands in the neighborhood, among whom are the Chiltz,[39] a nation residing on the seacoast near Point Lewis, and the Clatsops,[40] who live immediately opposite [us], on the south side of the Columbia.   A chief from the grand rapid also came to see us, and we gave him a medal.   To each of our visitors we made a present of a small piece of ribbon, and purchased some cranberries and some articles of their manufacture, such as mats and household furniture, for all which we paid high prices.   After we had been relieved from these Indians, we were surprised at a visit of a different kind.   An old woman, the wife of a Chinnook chief, came with six young women, her daughters and nieces, and having deliberately camped near us, proceeded to cultivate an intimacy between our men and her fair wards.

how the unctuous nuptials slid on into the piscivorous honeymoon, forms an irresistibly humorous chapter in Astoria, pp. 461-464.

[38] " We procured it for a belt of blue beeds of our interpreter Shabono wore around her waste," Clark I 37.

[39] These Chiltz, elsewhere Chilts, are the Chehalis, a collective name, as applied by various authors covering half a dozen different Salishan tribes on the Chehalis river, Gray's harbor, and Shoalwater bay.   Clark charts "Chiltz 800 souls."   Chehalis is now name of the county seat of Lewis Co., Wash.

[40] One of the two tribes of Lower Chinookans (the regular Chinooks being the other), with whom the Expedition is about to winter.   This tribe gave name to Fort Clatsop, and also to Clatsop Co., Ore., on the coast immediately south of the Columbia.

CHAPTER XXI.

THE ESTABLISHMENT OF FORT CLATSOP.

Bad weather and high seas—Clatsops—Having examined the coast, the party must select a site for their winter-quarters—Various considerations—They decide to cross the mouth of the Columbia to the south side—They proceed to Shallow bay—They pass Seal islands and reach the south shore near a point they name Point Samuel—They enter a channel separating a large island from the mainland—Here are Cathlamahs—The party passes on to Kekemahke creek, and to a knob they name Point William—Exposed camp on the seaward side of Point William—Captain Lewis explores further, and hunters go out— Animals and plants observed—Bad food causes much sickness—First elk killed west of the Rockies—Seamanship of the Clatsops—Captain Lewis returns—He has found a place for a winter camp—The party detained by rain, wind, and wave—They round a point into a bay, called Meriwether's, which receives several streams, one of them Netul river— They ascend the Netul three miles and camp in a grove of pines—This spot selected for winter-quarters—Captain Clark proceeds to explore the coast—Is invited to a village of Clatsops—Indian gambling—Captain Clark shows himself a crack shot, and returns to camp—The party engaged in felling trees and building cabins—Continuous rain—Visit from Clatsops—Wappatoo and shanataque—Progress of the buildings—Hardships of the hunters—Rain, rain, rain, snow, hail, more rain—Clatsops come to trade—Their females offended, and why—Chistmas celebrated—Calamitous fleas—Culhomo roots—Men sent to the seacoast to make salt—The fort picketed—Trade with Wahkiacums—Fort Clatsop completed, Dec. 30th—Military regulations—New Year's day saluted—Dog-flesh and whale-blubber—The salt-makers—A party to go 35 miles to see a stranded whale—First pleasant evening for two months.

FRIDAY, November 22d, 1805. It rained during the whole night; about daylight a tremendous gale of wind arose from the S.S.E., and continued during the whole day with great violence. The sea runs so high that the water comes into our camp, which the rain prevents us from leaving.[1] We purchased from the old squaw, for arm-bands and rings, a few wappatoo-roots, on which we subsisted. They are nearly equal in flavor to the Irish potato, and afford a very good substitute for bread. The bad weather has driven several Indians to our camp, but they are still under the terrors of the threat which we made on first seeing them, and now behave with the greatest decency.

---

[1] "O! how horriable is the day waves brakeing with great violence against the shore throwing the water into our camp, &c.," Clark I 40.

November 23d. The rain continued through the night, but the morning was calm and cloudy. The hunters were sent out and killed three deer, four brant, and three ducks. Toward evening seven Clatsops came over in a canoe, with two skins of the sea-otter. To this article they attach an extravagant value, and their demands for it were so high that we were [too] fearful of reducing our small stock of merchandise, (*p. 84*) on which we must depend for subsistence as we return, to venture on purchasing. To ascertain, however, their ideas as to the value of different objects, we offered for one of the skins a watch, a handkerchief, an American dollar, and a bunch of red beads; but neither the curious mechanism of the watch, nor even the red beads, could tempt the Indian; he refused the offer, but asked for tia-comoshack or chief beads—the most common sort of coarse blue-colored beads—the article beyond all price in their estimation. Of these blue beads we have but few, and therefore reserve them for more necessitous circumstances.

November 24th. The morning being fair, we dried our wet articles and sent out the hunters, but they returned with only a single brant. In the evening a chief and several men of the Chinnooks came to see us; we smoked with them, and bought a sea-otter skin for some blue beads. Having now examined the coast, it became necessary to decide on the spot for our wintering-quarters. The people of the country subsist chiefly on dried fish and roots; but of these there does not seem to be a sufficient quantity for our support, even were we able to purchase, and the extravagant prices as well as our small store of merchandise forbid us to depend on that resource. We must therefore rely for subsistence on our arms, and be guided in the choice of our residence by the abundance of game which any particular spot may offer. The Indians say that deer are most numerous at some distance above on the river, but that the country on the opposite side of the bay is better supplied with elk, an animal much larger and more easily killed than deer, with a skin better fitted for clothing, and the meat of which is more nutritive during the winter, when they are both poor. The climate is obviously much milder here than above the first range of mountains, for the Indians are thinly clad, and say they have little snow; indeed since our arrival the weather has been very warm, sometimes disagreeably so ; and dressed as we are altogether in leather, the (*p. 85*) cold would be very unpleasant if not injurious. The neighborhood of the sea is moreover recommended by the facility of supplying ourselves with salt, and the hope of meeting some of the trading-vessels, which are expected in about three months, and from which we may procure a fresh supply of trinkets for our route homeward. These considerations [2] induce us to determine on visiting the opposite side of the bay ; and if there be an appearance of much game, to establish ourselves there during the winter. Next day,

November 25*th,* however, the wind was too high to suffer us to cross the river; but as it blew generally from the E.S.E., the coast on the north was in some degree sheltered by the highlands. We therefore set out, and keeping near the shore, halted for dinner in Shallow bay ; and after dark reached a spot, near a [Pillar] rock at some distance in the river, close to our former camp of the 7th inst. On leaving our camp, seven Clatsops accompanied us in a canoe; but after

[2] Were reached by consultation with the whole party, a rare thing in military life. Gass, p. 169, records the circumstance thus : " At night the party were consulted by the Commanding Officers, as to the place most proper for winter quarters ; and most of them were of opinion, that it would be best, in the first place, to go over to the south side of the river, and ascertain whether good hunting ground could be found there. Should that be the case, it would be a more eligible place than higher up the river, on account of getting salt, as that is a very scarce article with us." The decision seems to have been judicious. In the dismal semi-aquatic life to which the party is about to be condemned, living in almost continuous rain for four months, in miserable sheds, like muskrats in their holes, they will have nothing to do but shoot elk for a living, make salt to season their meat, and dicker with the natives.

When Astoria was established, next door to Fort Clatsop, a ship was sent to meet the overland party at the mouth of the Columbia, and it was not Mr. Astor's fault that the " Tonquin" was blown up. One naturally wonders why President Jefferson did not take the same care of his Expedition. The advantage of such an arrangement is so self-evident, that there must have been some strong

going a few miles crossed the bay through immensely high waves, leaving us in admiration at the dexterity with which they threw aside each wave as it threatened to come over their canoe. The evening was cloudy, and in the morning, *November 26th*, it rained. We set out with the wind from the E.N.E., and a short distance above the rock near our camp began to cross the river. We passed between some low, marshy islands, which we called Seal islands, and reached the south side of the Columbia at a bottom three miles below a point, to which we gave the name of Point Samuel.[3] After going along the shore for five miles, we entered a channel 200 yards in width, which separates from the mainland a large, but low island. On this channel, at the foot of some highlands, is a village, where we landed [Warren's Landing]. It consists of nine large wooden houses, inhabited by a tribe called Cathlamahs, who seem to differ neither in dress, language, nor manners from the Chinnooks and Wahkiacums ; like whom they live chiefly (*p. 86*) on fish and wappatoo-roots. We found, however, as we hoped, some elk meat. After dining on some fresh fish and roots, which we purchased from them at an immoderate price, we coasted along a deep bend of the river toward the south, and at night camped under a high hill. All the way from the village the land is

reason why it was not made. It could not have been overlooked ; it must have been discussed, and rejected. In correspondence on this subject with an eminent English scholar and scientist—whose name, however, I have no authority for using here—it has been suggested that the reason must have been political. A ship for this purpose would have needed special equipment; her destination would have excited the curiosity, and perhaps aroused the suspicions, of foreign governments. England might not have cared, as she had her hands full of other business at that time ; but there was Spain, always extremely jealous of her colonial possessions, and still powerful on the seas in 1804—for she did not get her quietus from Nelson at Trafalgar till Oct. 21st, 1805, when L. and C. were nearing the Great Falls of the Columbia. It was not the policy of the United States to be on any but a friendly footing with Spain in 1804, and Spain would have resented anything that looked like interference with her affairs on the Pacific coast.

[3] After Samuel Lewis, a relative of Captain Lewis ? This name appears as that of the copyist of Clark's map of 1814—" Copied by Samuel Lewis from the Original Drawing of Wm. Clark." Now Cathlamet Point. One of the several islands is still called Seal. Dinner served at Warren's Landing.

high, and has a thick growth of pine, balsam, and other timber; but as it was still raining very hard, it was with difficulty we procured wood enough to make fires. Soon after we landed, three Indians from the Cathlamah village came down with wappatoo-roots, some of which we purchased with fish-hooks. At daylight the next morning,

November 27th, eleven more came down with provisions, skins, and mats for sale; but the prices were too high for our reduced finances, and we bought nothing. As we were preparing to set out we missed an ax, which we found under the robe of one of the Indians; they were all prohibited in consequence from following us. We went on in the rain, which had continued through the night, and passing between a number of islands came to a small river, called by the Indians Kekemahke.[4] We afterward came to a very remarkable knob of land, projecting about a mile and a half toward Shallow bay, and about four miles round, while the neck of land which connects it to the main shore is not more than 50 yards wide. We went round this projection, which we named Point William;[5] but the waves then became so high that we could not venture any further. We therefore landed on a beautiful shore of pebbles of various colors, and camped near an old Indian hut on the isthmus. In drawing our canoes in shore, we had the misfortune to make a split two feet long in one of them. This isthmus opposes a formidable barrier to the sea; for we now found that the water below is salt, while that above is fresh and well-tasted. It rained hard during the whole day; it continued all night, and in the morning,

(*p. 87*) *November 28th,* began more violently, attended with a high wind from the southwest. It was now impossible to proceed on so rough a sea. We therefore sent several

---

[4] Kekemarke, Clark I 46; Kekemarque, I 50; now the John Day, a small stream emptying into Cathlamet bay, in which the Expedition continues until they round Point William, or Tongue point; at its mouth is the point also called John Day's. See note[2] p. 655.

[5] After the Christian name of Captain Clark, Clark I 46. Now Tongue point.

men to hunt, and the rest of us remained during the day in a situation the most cheerless and uncomfortable. On this little neck of land we are exposed, with a miserable covering which does not deserve the name of a shelter, to the violence of the winds ; all our bedding and stores, as well as our bodies, are completely wet ; our clothes are rotting with constant exposure, and we have no food except the dried fish brought from the falls,[6] to which we are again reduced. The hunters all returned hungry and drenched with rain, having seen neither deer nor elk, and the swan and brant were too shy to be approached. At noon the wind shifted to the northwest, and blew with such tremendous fury that many trees were blown down near us. This gale lasted with short intervals during the whole night ; but toward morning,

November 29th, the wind lulled, though the rain continued, and the waves were still high. Captain Lewis took the Indian canoe, which is better calculated for rough weather, and with five men went down to a small [Meriwether's, now Young's] bay below us, where we expected to find elk. Three other men set out at the same time to hunt in different directions, and the rest remained round the smoke of our fires drying leather, in order to make some new clothes. The night brought only a continuation of rain and hail, with short intervals of fair weather.

November 30th. It cleared up about nine o'clock, and the sun shone for several hours. Other hunters were now sent out, and we passed the remainder of the day in drying our merchandise, so long exposed. Several of the men complain of disorders in their bowels, which can be ascribed only to their diet of pounded fish[7] mixed with salt water; they are therefore directed to use for that purpose the fresh

---

[6] Great Falls of the Columbia. " O ! how disagreeable is our situation during this dreadfull weather," Clark I 47. The weather did not improve much for three months, but the party got housed after a fashion before January.

[7] " The squar gave me a piece of bread made of flour which she had reserved for her child and carefully kept untill this time, which has unfortunately got wet and a little sour—this bread I eate with great satisfaction, it being the only mouthfull I had tasted for several months past," Clark I 49.

water above the point.   The hunters had (*p. 88*) seen three elk, but could not obtain any of them ; they however brought in three hawks, and a few black ducks [coots (*Fulica americana*)] of a species common in the United States, living in large flocks and feeding on grass ; they are distinguished by a sharp white beak, toes separate, and no craw.   Besides these wild-fowl, there are in this neighborhood a large kind of buzzard [vulture] with [partly] white wings [*Pseudogryphus californianus*], the gray and the bald eagle [young and adult *Haliaëtus leucocephalus*], the large red-tailed hawk [*Buteo borealis calurus*], the blue magpie [Steller's jay (*Cyanocitta stelleri*)], and great numbers of ravens and crows [*Corvus caurinus*].   We observe, however, few small birds, the one which has most attracted our attention being a small brown bird [probably the winter-wren of the Pacific coast, a variety of *Anorthura hiemalis*], which seems to frequent logs and the roots of trees.   Of other animals there is a great abundance. We see great quantities of snakes, lizards, worms, and spiders, as well as small bugs, flies, and other insects of different kinds.   The vegetable productions are also numerous.   The hills along the coast are high and steep ; the general covering is a growth of lofty pines of different species, some of which rise more than 200 feet, and are 10 or 12 feet in diameter near the root.   Besides these trees we observe on the point a species of ash, the alder, the laurel, one species of wild crab, and several kinds of underbrush, among which rosebushes are conspicuous.[8]

Sunday, December 1st, 1805.[9]   Again we had a cloudy day, and the wind so high from the east that, having ven-

[8] The plants here named are : ash, *Fraxinus oregana ;* alder, *Alnus rubra* or *A. rhombifolia ;* laurel, the Californian rhododendron, *Rhododendron californianum ;* crab-trees, *Pirus rivularis ;* the roses probably *Rosa pisocarpa*.

[9] Clark I 51 has another name for the Pacific—a grim witticism of the half-starved and half-drowned soldier : "24 days since we arrived at the *Great Western* (for I cannot say Pacific) Ocian as I have not seen one pacific day since my arrival in its vicinity, and its waters are forming [foaming] and petially [perpetually] breake with emence waves on the sands and rockey coasts, tempestous and horiable."   He was not a sea-dog, nor were his dug-outs sea-worthy.

tured in a boat with a view to hunt at some distance, we were obliged to return. We resumed our occupation of dressing leather and mending our old clothes, in which we passed the day. The hunters came in with a report of having seen two herds of elk; but they could kill nothing, and we therefore again fed upon dried fish. At sunset it began to rain violently, and continued all night.

December 2d. This disagreeable food, pounded fish, has occasioned so much sickness among the men that it is now absolutely necessary to vary it. Three hunters therefore started out, and three more were sent up Ke-(*p. 89*) kemahke creek in search of fish or birds. Toward evening one of them [J. Fields] returned; he had observed great appearances of elk and even seen two herds of them; but it rained so hard that he could with difficulty get a shot. He had, however, at last killed one, at the distance of six miles from camp, and a canoe was sent to bring it. The party from Kekemahke creek were less successful; they had seen no fish, and all the birds, in consequence probably of being much hunted by the Indians, were too shy to be approached.

December 3d. The wind was from the east and the morning fair; but, as if one whole day of fine weather were not permitted, toward night it began to rain. Even this transient glimpse of sunshine revived the spirits of the party, who were still more pleased when the elk killed yesterday was brought into camp. This was the first elk we had killed on the west side of the Rocky mountains, and condemned as we have been to the dried fish, it formed a most nourishing food. After eating the marrow of the shank-bones, the squaw chopped them fine, and by boiling extracted a pint of grease, superior to the tallow itself of the animal. A canoe of eight Indians, who were carrying down wappatoo-roots to trade with the Clatsops, stopped at our camp; we bought a few roots for small fish-hooks, and they then left us. Accustomed as we were to the sight, we could not but view with admiration the wonderful dexterity with which they guide their canoes over the most boisterous seas; for though the

waves were so high that before they had gone half a mile the
canoe was several times out of sight, they proceeded with the
greatest calmness and security.   Two of the hunters [Pryor
and Gibson] who set out yesterday had lost their way, and
did not return till this evening.   They had seen in their
ramble great signs of elk and had killed six, which they had
butchered and left at a great distance.   A party was sent in
the morning,

December 4th,[10] to carry the elk to a bay some distance
below, to which place, if the weather permitted, (*p. 90*) we
would move our camp this evening; but the rain, which had
continued during the night, lasted all next day, and was
accompanied by so high a wind from the southeast and
south that we dared not risk our canoes on the water.   It
was high water at eleven o'clock, when the spring-tide rose
two feet higher than the common flood-tides.   We passed
the day around our fires, and as we are so situated that the
smoke will not immediately leave the camp, we are very
much incommoded and our eyes injured by it.   No news
has yet been received from Captain Lewis, and we begin to
have much uneasiness for his safety.

December 5th.   It rained during the whole night, and this
morning the rain and high wind compelled us to remain at
our camp.   Besides the inconvenience of being thus stopped
on our route, we now found that all our stores and bedding
were again wet with rain.   The high water was at twelve
o'clock, and rose two inches beyond that of yesterday.   In
the afternoon we were rejoiced at the return of Captain
Lewis, who came in a canoe with three of his men, the other
two being left to guard six elk and five deer which they had
killed.   He had examined the coast, and found a river [the
Netul] a short distance below, on which we might camp
during the winter, with a sufficiency of elk for our subsist-

[10]Clark I 54: "I marked my name on a large pine tree imediately on the isthmus."

William Clark December 3rd 1805. By Land
from the U. States in 1804 & 5.

ence within reach. This information [11] was very satisfactory, and we decided on going thither as soon as we could move from this point. But all night and the following day, *December 6th,* it rained, and the wind blew hard from the southwest, so that the sea was still too rough for us to proceed. The high tide of to-day rose 13 inches higher than it did yesterday, and obliged us to move our camp to a high situation. Here we remained waiting for better weather, till about dark the wind shifted to the north and the sky cleared. We had now some prospect of being able to leave our situation, and indeed, though some rain fell in the course of the night, the next morning,

(*p. 91*) *December 7th,* was fair; we therefore loaded our canoes and proceeded. But the tide was against us and the waves were very high, so that we were obliged to proceed slowly and cautiously. We at length turned a point and found ourselves in a deep bay; here we landed for breakfast, and were joined by the [Sergeant Pryor's] party sent out three days ago to look for the six elk. In seeking for the elk they had missed their way for a day and a half, and when they reached the place, found the elk so much spoiled that they brought the skins only of four of them. After breakfast we coasted round the bay, which is about four miles across, and receives, besides several small creeks, two rivers called by the Indians, the one Kilhowanakel [12]

[11] Gass, p. 172, records the good news thus : "They have found a place about 15 miles from this camp, up a small river [Netul] which puts into a large bay [Meriwether's] on the south side of the Columbia, that will answer very well for winter quarters, as game is very plenty, which is the main object with us ; and we intend to move there as soon as circumstances will permit." I have before me five leaves of the notebook which was in Captain Lewis' pocket when he made this reconnoissance, and which now form Codex Ia. This is a mere fragment, of dates Nov. 29th–Dec. 1st ; to be complete it should extend to Dec. 5th. Slight as it is, this codex is significant, as the site for Fort Clatsop was discovered and determined upon during the trip recorded on its pages.

[12] Kil-how-â-nah-kle, Clark I 58; Kil-hou-a-nak-kle, Gass, p. 186 ; now the Klaskanine or Young's river, the larger one of the main two which fall into Meriwether's or Young's bay. The other, Netul, is usually charted as Lewis and Clark's river, because Fort Clatsop was built on it. To reach this bay, the

the other Netul. We called it Meriwether's bay, from the Christian name of Captain Lewis, who was no doubt the first white man to survey it. As we went along the wind was high from the northeast; in the middle of the day it' rained for two hours and then cleared off. On reaching the south side of the bay, we ascended the Netul for three miles, to the first point of highland on its western bank, and formed our camp in a thick grove of lofty pines, about 200 yards from the water, and 30 feet above the level of the high tides.

December 8th. This seemed the most eligible spot for our winter establishment. In order, therefore, to find a place for making salt, and to examine the country further, Captain Clark set out with five men, and pursuing a course S. 60° W., over a dividing ridge through thick pine timber, much of which had fallen, passed the heads of two small brooks. In the neighborhood of these the land was swampy and overflowed, and they waded knee-deep till they came to an open ridgy prairie, covered with the plant known on our frontier

Expedition rounded Smith's point, on which Astoria was founded ; town there now so called, and an Upper Astoria a little nearer Point Tongue or William. Ship " Tonquin," from N. Y. Sept. 8th, 1810, *via* Hawaii Feb. 12th, 1811, reached mouth of the Columbia Mar. 22d, 1811 ; eight men lost making land ; anchored in Baker's bay ; Apr. 5th, M'Dougal and David Stuart (latter founder of Okinagan, autumn of 1811), crossed to S. side, Point George ; Apr. 12th, 16 persons from the " Tonquin " camped " at bottom of a small bay within Point George," and named the place Astoria, which the overland party found ready for them on their arrival. Famous David Thompson, no doubt first white man to descend the Columbia to the Snake, got here July 15th, 1811, just in time to be too late, as he wished to preëmpt the place, but found the Astorians already in possession, and left for Montreal, July 23d. Oct. 16th, 1812, M'Dougal unwarrantably, and perhaps perfidiously, passed all Mr. Astor's property over to the Northwest (British) Company, at nominal figures. Dec. 12th, 1812, Fort Astoria formally taken possession of by Captain Black, of the British sloop-of-war " Racoon," 26 guns, 120 men ; name changed to Fort George (in honor of one of those peculiar persons we read of in Thackeray's " Four Georges "). Astoria reverted to the U. S. by the Treaty of Ghent ; was repossessed by Captain Biddle, of the sloop-of-war " Ontario " ; was abandoned in 1821 ; and in 1835 consisted of two log cabins, with a population of two persons. Lewis and Clark had less trouble with Fort Clatsop ; when they had done with it, they made a present of it to Comowool, king of the Clatsops, who had kept his eye on it all winter.

by the name of sacacommis [bearberry, *Arctostaphylos uva-ursi*]. Here is a creek about 60 yards wide and running toward Point Adams; they passed it on a small raft. At this place they discovered a large herd of elk, and after pursuing them for three miles over bad swamps [13] and small ponds, killed one of them. The (*p. 92*) agility with which the elk crossed the swamps and bogs seems almost incredible ; as we followed their track the ground for a whole acre would shake at our tread, and sometimes we sunk to our hips without finding any bottom." [14] Over the surface of these bogs is a species of moss, among which are great numbers of cranberries ; [15] and occasionally there rise from the swamp small steep knobs of earth, thickly covered with pine and laurel. On one of these we halted at night, but it was scarcely large enough to suffer us to lie clear of the water, and had very little dry wood. We succeeded, however, in collecting enough to make a fire ; and having stretched the elk-skin to keep off the rain, which still continued, slept till morning.

December 9th. We rose perfectly wet with rain during the night. Three [two—Drewyer and Shannon] men were then sent in pursuit of the elk, while with the other three Captain Clark proceeded westward toward the sea. He passed over three swamps, and then arrived at a creek which was too deep to ford, and there was no wood to make a raft. He therefore proceeded down it for a short distance, till he

[13] " Slashes," Clark I 58 and elsewhere—a perfectly good word, which perhaps Biddle had not heard, and which does not appear in this work. It means a swamp or marsh—a wet, dirty place, overgrown with bushes. So the adjective slashy, which Clark uses as " slashey." The noun is common speech in Maryland and Virginia, in the plural. What is now the most fashionable part of Washington, north of N street, west of 14th, and south of Florida avenue, on which I look out of the window in penning this note, was just such a place when I was a boy. It was always called " The Slashes " ; was the dumping-ground for dead horses and night-soil, and shitepokes bred there.

[14] " I prosued this gang of Elk through bogs which the wate of a man would shake for ½ an acre, and many places I sunk into the mud and water up to my hips without finding any bottom on the trale of those Elk," Clark I 59.

[15] The interesting *Vaccinium macrocarpon:* see No. 11, described in Chap. vii.

found that he was between the forks of a creek, one branch
of which he had passed yesterday; this turns round toward
the southwest to meet another of equal size from the south,
and together they form a small [Necanicum] river, about 70
yards wide. He returned to the place where he had left the
raft, and having crossed proceeded down about a mile, when
he met three Indians. They were loaded with fresh salmon
which they had taken with a gig, and were now returning
to their village on the seacoast, where they invited him to
accompany them. He agreed, and they brought out a
canoe hid along the banks of the creek. In this they passed
over the branch which he had just crossed on a raft, and
then carried the canoe a quarter of a mile to the other fork,
which they crossed and continued down to the mouth of the
river. At this place it makes a great bend, where the river
is 70 yards wide; just above, or to the south of which, is
the (*p. 93*) village.

We crossed over, and found that it consisted of three
houses, inhabited by twelve families of Clatsops. They
were on the south exposure of a hill, sunk about four feet
deep into the ground; the walls, roof, and gable-ends were
formed of split pine boards; the descent was through a small
door down a ladder. There were two fires in the middle of
the room, and the beds disposed round the walls two or three
feet from the fall,[16] so as to leave room under them for their
bags, baskets, and household articles. The floor itself was
covered with mats. Captain Clark was received with much
attention. As soon as he entered clean mats were spread,
and fish, berries, and roots set before him on small neat plat-
ters of rushes. After he had eaten the men of the other
houses came and smoked with him. They all appeared
much neater in their persons and diet than Indians generally are, and frequently wash their hands and faces, a cere-

[16] *Sic*—read floor. "Their beads [beds] ar all around raised about 2½ feet
from the bottom flore all covered with mats and under those beads was stored
their bags," etc., Clark I 61. The river above named Necanicum, from a
Clatsop county map, is joined by O'Hara creek near the coast.

mony by no means frequent elsewhere. While he was conversing with them a flock of brant alighted on the water, and with a small rifle he shot one of them at a great distance. They immediately jumped in and brought it on shore, very much astonished at the shot, which contributed to make them increase their attention. Toward evening it began to rain and blow very violently from the southwest; Captain Clark therefore determined to remain during the night. When they thought his appetite had returned, an old woman presented him, in a bowl made of light-colored horn, a kind of syrup, pleasant to the taste, made from a species of berry, common in this country, about the size of a cherry, called by the Indians shelwel;[17] of these berries a bread is also prepared, which, being boiled with roots, forms a soup, which was served in neat wooden trenchers; this, with some cockles,[18] was his repast.

The men of the village now collected and began to gamble. The most common game was one in which one of the company was banker, and played against all the rest. He had a piece of bone, about the (*p. 94*) size of a large bean, and having agreed with any individual as to the value of the stake, would pass the bone from one hand to the other with great dexterity, singing at the same time to divert the attention of his adversary; then holding it in his hands, his antagonist was challenged to guess in which of them the bone was, and lost or won as he pointed to the right or wrong hand. To this game of hazard they abandoned themselves with great ardor; sometimes everything they possess is sacrificed to it; and this evening several of the Indians lost all the

---

[17] Elsewhere "shellwell," etc.; preferably salal, the usual form of the word; fruit of *Gaultheria shallon*, a small evergreen ericaceous shrub of Oregon and California, congeneric with *G. procumbens*, our wintergreen or checkerberry, whose small red berries and green leaves have such an agreeably aromatic taste.

[18] Perhaps meaning mussels. Two species of salt-water mussels in this region are, one which has not been satisfactorily distinguished from the common edible mussel, *Mytilus edulis*, and another named *Mytilus californianus* by Conrad (Journ. Acad. Nat. Sci. Philada. VII. p. 242, pl. 18, fig. 15). The latter attains a length of nine inches or more. See pp. 896, 897.

beads which they had with them. This lasted for three
hours; when, Captain Clark appearing disposed to sleep, the
man who had been most attentive, and whose name was
Cuskalah, spread two new mats near the fire, ordered his
wife to retire to her own bed, and the rest of the company
dispersed at the same time. Captain Clark then lay down,
but the violence with which the fleas attacked him did not
leave his rest unbroken.[19]

December 10*th*. The morning was cloudy with some rain.
He walked out on the seashore, and observed the Indians
walking up and down the creek, examining the shore; he
was at a loss to understand their object, till one of them
came to him and explained that they were in search of fish
which had been thrown on shore and left by the tide, adding
in English, "sturgeon is very good." There is, indeed, every
reason to suppose that these Clatsops depend for their subsistence, during the winter, chiefly on the fish thus casually
thrown on the coast. After amusing himself for some time
on the beach, he returned toward the village, and shot on his
way two brant. As he came near the village, one of the
Indians asked him to shoot a duck about thirty steps distant; he did so, and having accidentally shot off its head,
the bird was brought to the village by the Indians, all of
whom came round in astonishment; they examined the duck,
the musket, and the very small bullets, which were a hundred
to the pound, and then exclaimed, (*p. 95*) " Clouch musquet,
wake, commatax musquet " (a good musket, do not understand this kind of musket). They now placed before him
their best roots, fish and syrup, after which he attempted to
purchase a sea-otter skin with some red beads which he happened to have about him; but they declined trading, as
they valued none except blue or white beads. He therefore
bought nothing but a little berry-bread and a few roots in
exchange for fish-hooks, and then set out to return by the
same route on which he came. He was accompanied by

[19] " I was attacked most violently by the flees, and they kept up a close siege
dureing the night," Clark I 63, with military precision.

Cuskalah and his brother as far as the third creek, and then proceeded to camp through a heavy rain. The whole party had been occupied during his absence in cutting down trees to make huts, and in hunting.

December 11*th.* The rain continued last night and the whole of this day. We were, however, all employed in putting up our winter-cabins, which we are anxious to finish, as several of the men are beginning to suffer from the excessive dampness ; four of them have very violent colds, one has a dysentery, a third has tumors on his legs, and two have been injured by dislocation and straining of their limbs.[20]

December 12*th.* We continued to work in the rain at our houses. In the evening there arrived two canoes of Clatsops, among whom was a principal chief, called Comowol. We gave him a medal and treated his companions with great attention ; after which we began to bargain for a small sea-otter skin, some wappatoo-roots, and another species of root called shanataque [*Cnicus edulis*]. We readily perceived that they were close dealers, stickled much for trifles, and never closed the bargain until they thought they had the advantage. The wappatoo is dear, as they themselves are obliged to give a high price for it to the Indians above. Blue beads are the articles most in request ; the white occupy the next place in their estimation ; but they do not value much those of any other color. We succeeded at last in purchasing their whole cargo for a few fish-hooks and a (*p. 96*) small sack of Indian tobacco, which we had received from the Shoshonees. The next morning,

---

[20] " Prior unwell from a dislocation of his sholder, Gibson with the disintary, Jo. Fields with biles on his legs, & Werner with a strained knee," Clark I 66. Sergeant Pryor's case is peculiar. I hardly see how he could have got into the way of slipping his humerus out of its socket so easily and so often as his shoulder is said to be " dislocated," in this work ; nor is this luxation so readily reduced as it seems to have been on several occasions. I imagine the sergeant displaced the tendon of the long head of the biceps from the bicipital groove in the first instance, by an unlucky wrench, and was afterward liable to a recurrence of this accident from slighter causes. It is a rare affection; but I have treated such cases.

December 13*th*, we treated them to a breakfast of elk-meat, of which they seemed very fond, and having purchased from them two skins of the lucervia [loup-cervier [21]], and two robes, made of the skin of an animal [*Haplodon rufus*] about the size of a cat, they left us. Two hunters [Drewyer and Shannon] returned with the pleasing intelligence of their having killed 18 elk about six miles off. Our huts begin to rise; for though it rains all day we continue our labors, and are rejoiced to find that the beautiful balsam-pine [*Pseudotsuga douglasi*] splits into excellent boards more than two feet in width. In the evening three Indians came in a canoe with provisions and skins for sale, and spent the night with us.

December 14*th*.[22] Again it rained all day; but by working constantly we finished the walls of our huts, and nearly completed a house for our provisions. The constant rains have completely spoiled our last supply of elk; but, notwithstanding that scarcely a man has been dry for many days, the sick are recovering. Four men were dispatched to guard the elk which were killed yesterday, till a larger party joined them. Accordingly,

December 15*th*, Captain Clark with 16 men set out in three canoes, and having rowed for three miles up the river turned up a large creek from the right, and after going three miles further landed about the height of the tide-water. The men were then dispatched in small parties to bring in the elk, each man returning with a quarter of the animal. In bringing the third and last load, nearly half the men missed their way, and did not return till after night; five [Ordway, Colter, Collins, Whitehouse, and M'Neal] of them indeed were not able to find their way at all. It had been cloudy all day, at

[21] Not the Canada lynx or true loup-cervier, as heretofore, but *Lynx rufus fasciatus*—that variety of the common bay lynx which is found in Oregon and Washington. See note [35], p. 211, and the natural history chapter beyond.

[22] "*Saturday* 14*th*. We completed the building of our huts, 7 in number, all but the covering, which I now find will not be so difficult as I expected ; as we have found a kind of timber in plenty, which splits freely and makes the finest puncheons I have ever seen. They can be split 10 feet long and 2 broad, not more than an inch and a half thick." Gass, p. 174.

night began to rain, and as we had no cover we were obliged to sit up the greater part of the night; for as soon as we lay down the rain would come under us and compel us to rise. It was indeed a most uncomfortable situation; but the five men who joined us in the morning,

(*p. 97*) *December* 16*th*, had been more unlucky; for, in addition to the rain which had poured down upon them all night, they had no fire; and drenched and cold as they were when they reached us, exhibited a most distressing sight. They had left their loads where they slept, and some men were sent after them, while others were dispatched after two more elk in another bend of the creek, who, after taking these last on board, proceeded to our camp. It rained and hailed during the day, and a high wind from the southeast not only threw down trees as they passed along, but made the river so rough that they proceeded with great risk.

We [*i. e.*, the main party at the fort] now had the meat-house covered, and all our game carefully hung up in small pieces.

December 17*th*. It rained all night, and this morning there was a high wind; hail as well as rain fell; and on the top of a [Saddle] mountain about ten miles to the southeast of us we observed some snow. The greater part of our stores is wet; our leathern tent is so rotten that the slightest touch makes a rent in it, and it will now scarcely shelter a spot large enough for our beds. We were all busy in finishing the inside of the huts. The after part of the day was cool and fair. But this respite was of very short duration; for all night it continued raining and snowing alternately, and in the morning,

December 18*th*, we had snow and hail till twelve o'clock, after which it changed to rain. The air now became cool and disagreeable, the wind high and unsettled; so that, being thinly dressed in leather, we were able to do very little on the houses.

December 19*th*. The rain continued all night with short intervals, but the morning was fair and the wind from the southwest. Situated as we are, our only occupation is to work as diligently as we can on our houses, and to watch the changes of the weather, on which so much of our comfort depends. We availed ourselves of this glimpse of sunshine to send [Sergeant Pryor with eight men in two canoes] across Meriwether's bay for the boards of an (*p. 98*) old Indian house; but before the party returned with them, the weather clouded, and we again had hail and rain during the rest of the day. Our only visitors were two Indians, who spent a short time with us.

December 20th. A succession of rain and hail during the night. At ten o'clock it cleared off for a short time, but the rain soon recommenced. We now covered in four of our huts. Three Indians came in a canoe with mats, roots, and the berries of the sacacommis. These people proceed with a dexterity and finesse in their bargains which, if they have not learned it from their foreign visitors, may show how nearly allied is the cunning of savages to the little arts of traffic. They begin by asking double or treble the value of what they have to sell, and lower their demand in proportion to the greater or less degree of ardor or knowledge of the purchaser, who, with all his management, is not able to pro-cure the article for less than its real value, which the Indians perfectly understand. Our chief medium of trade consists of blue and white beads, files,—with which they sharpen their tools,—fish-hooks, and tobacco; but of all these articles blue beads and tobacco are the most esteemed.

December 21st. As usual it rained all night, and continued without intermission during the day. One of our Indian visitors was detected in stealing a horn spoon and turned out of the camp. We find that the plant called sacacommis forms an agreeable mixture with tobacco; we therefore dis-patched two men to the open lands near the ocean, in order to collect some of it, while the rest continued their work.

December 22d. There was no interval in the rain last night and to-day; so that we cannot go on rapidly with our buildings. Some of the men are indeed quite sick, others have received bruises, and several complain of boils. We discover that part of our elk-meat is spoiling in consequence of the warmth of the weather, though we have kept a constant smoke under it.

(*p. 99*) *December* 23*d*.   It continued raining the whole day, with no variation except occasional thunder and hail.   Two canoes of Clatsops came to us with various articles for sale; we bought three mats and bags, neatly made of flags and rushes; and also the skin of a panther [*Felis concolor*], seven feet long, including the tail.   For all these we gave six small fish-hooks, a worn-out file, and some pounded fish, which had become so soft and moldy by exposure that we could not use it; it is, however, highly prized by the Indians of this neighborhood.   Although a very portable and convenient food, the mode of curing it seems known to, or at least practiced only by, the Indians near the Great Falls; and coming from such a distance it has an additional value in the eyes of these people, who are anxious to possess some food less precarious than their ordinary subsistence.   Among these Clatsops was a second chief, to whom we gave a medal, and sent some pounded fish to Cuscalah, who could not come to see us on account of sickness.   The next day,

December 24*th*, however, he came in a canoe with his young brother and two squaws.   Having treated Captain Clark so kindly at his village we were pleased to see him, and he gave us two mats and a parcel of roots.   These we accepted, as it would have been offensive to decline the offer, but afterward two files were demanded in return for the presents, and not being able to spare those articles, we restored the mats and roots.   Cuscalah was a little displeased; in the evening, however, he offered each of us one of the squaws, and even this being declined, Cuscalah as well as the whole party of Indians were highly offended; the females particularly seemed to be much incensed at our indifference about their favors.[23]   The whole stock of meat

---

[23] " He then offered a woman to each of us, which we also declined axcepting of, which displeased the wholl party verry much—the female part appeared to be highly disgusteded at our refuseing to axcept of their favours, &c.," Clark I 75.

being now completely spoiled, our pounded fish became again our chief dependence. It had rained constantly all day, but we still continued working, and at last moved into our huts.

December 25th. We were awaked at daylight by a discharge of firearms, which was followed by a song from the (*p. 100*) men, as a compliment to us on the return of Christmas, which we have always been accustomed to observe as a day of rejoicing. After breakfast we divided our remaining stock of tobacco, which amounted to twelve carrots, into two parts ; one of which we distributed among such of the party as make use of it, making a present of a handkerchief to the others.[24] The remainder of the day was passed in good spirits, though there was nothing in our situation to excite much gayety. The rain confined us to the house, and our only luxuries in honor of the season were some poor elk, so much spoiled that we ate it through sheer necessity, a few roots, and some spoiled pounded fish. The next day,

December 26th, brought a continuation of rain, accompanied with thunder, and a high wind from the southeast. We were therefore obliged to still remain in our huts, and endeavored to dry our wet articles before the fire. The fleas, which annoyed us near the portage of the Great Falls, have taken such possession of our clothes that we are obliged to have a regular search every day through our blankets as a

---

[24] Captain Clark's stocking would have been full, if he had had any stockings to hang up for Christmas. " I received a present of Capt. L. of a [illegible] Shirt, Draws and Socks, a pr. mockersons of Whitehouse, a small Indian basket of Gutherich [Goodrich], two Dozen white weazils tails of the Indian woman [Sacajawea] and some black root of the Indians before their departure," Clark I 76.

Christmas looked to Gass thus, p. 176 : " At daybreak all the men paraded and fired a round of small arms, wishing the Commanding Officers a merry Christmas. In the course of the day Capt. Lewis and Capt. Clarke collected what tobacco remained and divided it among those who used tobacco as a Christmas-gift ; to the others they gave handkerchiefs in lieu of it. We had no spirituous liquors to elevate our spirits this Christmas ; but of this we had but little need, as we were all in very good health. Our living is not very good ; meat is plenty, but of an ordinary quality, as the elk are poor in this part of the country. We have no kind of provisions but meat, and we are without salt to season that."

necessary preliminary to sleeping at night.[25]   These animals, indeed, are so numerous that they are almost a calamity to the Indians of this country.   When they have once obtained the mastery of any house it is impossible to expel them, and the Indians have frequently different houses, to which they resort occasionally when the fleas have rendered their permanent residence intolerable ; yet, in spite of these precautions, every Indian is constantly attended by multitudes of them, and no one comes into our house without leaving behind him swarms of these tormenting insects.

December 27th.   The rain did not cease last night or the greater part of to-day.   In the evening we were visited by Comowool, the chief, and four men of the Clatsop nation, who brought a very timely supply of roots and berries. Among these was one called culhomo,[26] resembling licorice in size and taste, and which they roast like a potato ; there was also the shanataque, a root of which they are very fond. (*p. 101*) It is of a black color, sweet to the taste, and is prepared for eating in a kiln, as the Indians up the Columbia dry the pasheco.   These, as well as the shellwell [salal (*Gaultheria shallon*)] berries, they value highly; but were perfectly satisfied with the return we made them, consisting of a small piece of sheepskin to wear round the chief's head, a pair of ear-bobs for his son, a small piece of brass, and a little ribbon.   In addition to our old enemies the fleas, we observed two mosquitoes, or insects so completely resembling them that we can perceive no difference.

December 28th.   Again it rained during the greater part of last night and continued all day.   Five [Drewyer, Shannon, Labiche, Collins, and R. Fields] men were sent out to hunt, and five [J. Fields, Bratton, Gibson, Willard, and Wiser] others dispatched to the seaside, each with a large kettle, in

---

[25] " We dry our wet articles before the fire and have our blankets *fleed*," *i. e.*, flead, Clark I 77,—" to flea " being a useful verb under the circumstances.

[26] Elsewhere culwhamo.   This is a true licorice, *Glycyrrhiza lepidota*, congeneric with the commercial article, *G. glabra*, of Eurasiatic countries, though of a distinct species.   Shanataque is root of *Cnicus edulis*.   See p. 821.

order to begin the manufacture of salt. The route to the seacoast is about seven miles in length, in a direction nearly west. Five miles of the distance is through thick woods varied with hills, ravines, and swamps, though the land in general possesses a rich black mold. The remaining two miles is formed of open waving prairies of sand [-dunes], with ridges running parallel to the river, and covered with green grass. The rest of the men were employed in making pickets and gates for our new fort. Although we had no sun, the weather was very warm.

Sunday, December 29th. It rained the whole night, but ceased this morning, and but little rain fell in the course of the day; still, the weather was cloudy and the wind high from the southeast. The Clatsop chief and his party left us, after begging for a great number of articles, which, as we could not spare them, we refused, except a razor. We were employed all day in picketing the fort. In the evening a young Wahkiacum chief, with four men and two women, arrived with some dressed elk-skin and wappatoo for sale. We purchased about a bushel and a half of those roots for some red beads and small pieces of brass wire and old check [cloth]. The chief made us a present of half a bushel more, for which we gave him a medal, and a piece of ribbon to tie around (*p. 102*) his hat. These roots are extremely grateful, since our meat has become spoiled, and we were desirous of purchasing the remainder; but the chief would not dispose of any more, as he was on his way to trade with the Clatsops. They remained with us, however, till the next day,

December 30th, when they were joined by four more of their countrymen from the Wahkiacum village. These last began by offering us some roots ; but as we had now learned that they always expect three or four times as much in return as the real value of the articles, and are even dissatisfied with that, we declined such dangerous presents. Toward evening the hunters brought in four elk [which Drewyer had killed], and after a long course of abstinence and miserable diet, we had a most sumptuous supper of elk's tongues and marrow. Besides this agreeable repast, the state of the weather was quite exhilarating. It had rained during the night, but in the morning, though the high wind continued, we enjoyed the fairest and most pleasant weather since our arrival; the sun having shone at intervals, and there being only three showers in the course of the day. By sunset we had completed the fortification [named Fort Clatsop], and now announced to the Indians that every day at that hour the gates would be closed, and they must leave the fort and not enter it till sunrise. The Wahkiacums who remained with us, and who were very forward in their deportment, complied very reluctantly with this order; but, being excluded from our houses, formed a camp near us.

December 31*st*. As if it were impossible to have 24 hours of pleasant weather, the sky last evening clouded and the rain began and continued through the day. In the morning there came down two canoes, one from the Wahkiacum village; the other contained three men and a squaw of the Skilloot nation. They brought wappatoo and shanataque roots, dried fish, mats made of flags and rushes, dressed elk-skins, and tobacco; for which, particularly the skins, they asked a very extravagant price. We purchased some (*p. 103*) wappatoo and a little tobacco, very much like that we had seen among the Shoshonees, put up in small neat bags made of rushes. These we obtained in exchange for a few articles, among which fish-hooks were the most esteemed. One of the Skilloots brought a gun which wanted some repair, and having put it in order, we received from him a present of about a peck of wappatoo; we then gave him a piece of sheep-skin and blue cloth, to cover the lock, and he very thankfully offered a further present of roots. There is, in fact, an obvious superiority in these Skilloots over the Wahkiacums, who are intrusive, thievish, and impertinent. Our new regulations, however, and the appearance of the sentinel, have improved the behavior of all our Indian visitors. They left the fort before sunset, even without being ordered.

Besides the fleas, we observe a number of insects in motion

to-day. Snakes are yet to be seen; snails, too, without covers [27] are common. On the rivers, and along the shores of Meriwether's bay, are many kinds of large water-fowl, but at this period they are excessively wild. The early part of the night was fair.

Wednesday, January 1st, 1806.[28] We were awaked at an early hour by the discharge of a volley of small-arms to salute the new year.[29] This is the only mode of doing honor to the day which our situation permits; for though we have reason to be gayer than we were at Christmas, our only dainties are the boiled elk and wappatoo, enlivened by draughts of pure water. We were visited by a few Clatsops, who came by water, bringing roots and berries for sale. Among this nation we have observed a man about 25 years old, of a much lighter complexion than the Indians generally; his face was even freckled, and his hair was long and of a color inclining to red.[30] He was in habits and manners perfectly Indian; but, though he did not speak a word of English, he seemed to understand more than the others of his party; and, as we could obtain no account of his origin, (*p. 104*) we concluded that one of his parents, at least, must

[27] "Snails without covers," *i. e.*, without shells, are slugs. We have no specification of the kind here meant. A large slug, attaining a length of six inches, abounds in the damp coniferous forests of the Pacific coast. This is *Limax columbianus* of Dr. A. A. Gould, in W. G. Binney's Terrest. Moll. U. S. II. p. 43, pl. lxvi, fig. 1, and U. S. Expl. Exped. p. 3, fig. 1, a, b, c. See also Wm. Cooper, in P. R. R. Rep. XII. pt. ii. 1860, p. 377.

[28] At this date begins Lewis J., running to Mar. 20th, 1806. Thus, during a considerable part of the stay of the Expedition at Fort Clatsop, we have two journals, not only parallel but practically duplicate—for the language is often identical for long passages. One is in Lewis' handwriting, the other in Clark's. I do not think that either was copied from the other, in the form in which we have them. More probably Lewis and Clark each made his own fair copy of an original joint journal which has not reached us.

[29] "The only mark of respect which we had it in our power to pay to the selibrated day. Our repast of this day, tho' better than that of Christmas consisted principally in the anticipation of the 1st. day of January, 1807," Clark I 85. So, in substance, Lewis J 3.

[30] Gass had noticed this fellow Nov. 23d, p. 169 : "One of these men had the reddest hair I ever saw, and a fair skin much freckled."

have been completely white. These Indians stayed with us during the night, and left the fort next morning,

January 2d, having disposed of their cargo for fishing-hooks, and other trifling articles. The hunters brought in two elk, and we obtained from the traps another [*sic* [31]]. This animal, as well as the beaver and the raccoon, is in plenty near the seacoast, and along the small creeks and rivers as high as the Grand Rapids, and in this country possesses an extremely good fur. The birds which most strike our attention are the large [*Cygnus buccinator*], as well as the small, or whistling swan [*C. columbianus*], the sand-hill crane [*Grus canadensis*], large and small geese, cormorants, brown and white brant, duckaulnmallard [*sic—Anas boscas*], canvass [-back, *Aristonetta vallisneria*], and several other species of ducks. There is also a small crow [*Corvus caurinus*], the blue crested corvus [*Cyanocitta stelleri*], the smaller corvus with a white breast [*Perisoreus obscurus*], the little brown wren [*Anorthura hiemalis pacificus*], a large brown sparrow [*Zonotrichia coronata*], the bald eagle [*Haliaëtus leucocephalus*], and the beautiful buzzard of the Columbia [the Californian condor, *Pseudogryphus californianus*]. All these wild-fowl continue with us, though they are not in such numbers as on our first arrival in this neighborhood.

January 3d. At 11 o'clock we were visited by our neighbor, the Fia [read Tia] or chief, Comowool, who is also called Cooné, and six Clatsops. Besides roots and berries, they brought for sale three dogs, and some fresh blubber. Having been so long accustomed to live on the flesh of dogs, the greater part of us have acquired a fondness for it, and our original aversion for it is overcome, by reflecting that while we subsisted on that food we were fatter, stronger, and in general enjoyed better health than at any period since leaving the buffalo country, eastward of the mountains. The blubber, which is esteemed by the Indians an excellent food, has been obtained, they tell us, from their neighbors, the

---

[31] Misprint for " an otter." They did not set traps for elk, and elk have no fur. " Drewyer visited his traps at [and] took out an otter," Clark I 86.

Killamucks,[32] a nation who live on the seacoast to the southeast, near one of whose villages a whale had recently been thrown and foundered. Three [R. Fields, Potts, Collins] of the hunters who had been (*p. 105*) dispatched on the 28th ult., returned about dark; they had been 15 miles up the [Kilhowanakel or Klaskanine] river to the east of us, which falls into Meriwether's bay, and had hunted a considerable distance to the east; but they had not been able to kill more than a single deer, and a few fowls, scarcely sufficient for their subsistence—an incident which teaches us the necessity of keeping out several parties of hunters, in order to procure a supply against any exigency.

January 4th. Comowool left us this morning with his party, highly pleased with a present of an old pair of satin breeches. The hunters were all sent in different directions, and we are now becoming more anxious for their success, since our store of wappatoo is all exhausted.

January 5th. Two [33] [Willard, Wiser] of the five men who had been dispatched to make salt returned [at 5 p. m.]. They had carefully examined the coast, but it was not till the fifth day after their departure that they discovered a convenient situation for their manufacture. At length they formed an establishment about 15 miles southwest of the fort, near some scattered houses of the Clatsop and Killamuck nation, where they erected a comfortable camp and killed a stock of provisions. The Indians treated them very kindly, and made them a present of the blubber of the whale, some of which the men brought home. It was white and not unlike the fat of pork, though of a coarser and more spongy

---

[32] Callamox, Clark I 87 ; Kilamox, Clark I 89 ; Callemex, Gass, p. 180 ; meant for Killamucks, which is the same word as Tillamook, name of a head, bay, town, and county on the coast of Oregon, a few miles south of the Columbia and north of Cape Lookout. The Tillamook was a large and powerful tribe of the Salishan family, which lived on the Oregon coast from 35 miles below Point Adams to below Tillamook Head. The tribe was also called Nsietshawus. There are or were recently five Tillamook Indians living at Grande Ronde Agency, Oregon.

[33] Colter also returned this evening, " unsecksessful from the chase, having been absent since the 1st. inst." Clark, I 90.

texture, and on being cooked was found to be tender and palatable, in flavor resembling the beaver.   The men also brought with them a gallon of salt, which was white, fine, and very good, but not so strong as the rock-salt common to the western parts of the United States.   It proves to be an agreeable addition to our food, and as the salt-makers [J. Fields, Bratton, Gibson] can manufacture three or four quarts a day, we have a prospect of a very plentiful supply.[34]

The appearance of the whale seemed to be a matter of importance to all the neighboring Indians, and as we might be able to procure some of it for ourselves, or at least purchase blubber from the (*p. 106*) Indians, a small parcel of merchandise was prepared, and a party of the men held in readiness to set out in the morning.   As soon as this resolution was known, Chaboneau and his wife requested that they might be permitted to accompany us.   The poor woman stated very earnestly that she had traveled a great way with us to see the great water, yet she had never been down to the coast, and now that this monstrous fish was also to be seen, it seemed hard that she should be permitted to see neither the ocean nor the whale.   So reasonable a request could not be denied ; they were therefore suffered to accompany Captain Clark, who,

January 6th,[35] after an early breakfast, set out with twelve men in two canoes.   He proceeded down the Netul into Meriwether bay, intending to go to the Clatsop town and

[34] " This salt was a great treat to many of the party, having not had any since the 20th. ulto.   As to myself I care but little whether I have any with my meat or not ; provided the meat [is] fat, haveing from habit become entirely cearless about my diat, and I have learned to think that if the cord be suffecently strong which binds the soul and boddy together, it does not so much matter about the materials which compose it," *ı. e.*, the " boddy," Clark I 90.   " My friend Capt. Clark declares it to be a mear matter of indifference with him whether he uses it or not ; for myself I must confess I feel a considerable inconvenience from the want of it ; the want of bread I consider as trivial," Lewis J 8.

[35] During this absence of Captain Clark, till Jan. 10th, Lewis J 8 continues his journal at the fort, with various matters of ethnology, natural history, etc., all of which are duly woven into the text by Biddle, and are noted by me in their respective connections.

there procure a guide through the creeks, which there was reason to believe communicated not only with the bay, but with a small [Clatsop] river running toward the sea, near where our salt-makers were camped. Before, however, he could reach the Clatsop village, the high wind from the northwest compelled him to put into a small creek. He therefore resolved to attempt the passage without a guide, and proceeded up this creek three miles to some high open land, where he found a road. He therefore left the canoes and followed the path over three deep marshes to a pond about a mile long and 200 yards wide. He kept on the left of this pond, and at length came to the creek which he had crossed on a raft when he had visited Cuscalah's village on the 9th of December. He proceeded down it till he found a small canoe, fit to hold three persons, in which the whole party crossed this creek. Here they saw a herd of elk; the men were divided into small parties, and hunted them till after dark, when they met again at the forks of the river. Three of the elk were wounded, but night prevented their taking more than one (*p. 107*), which was brought to the camp and cooked with some sticks of pine which had drifted down the creeks. The weather was beautiful, the sky clear, and the moon shone brightly, a circumstance the more agreeable as this is the first fair evening we have enjoyed for two months.[36]

[36] Gass, p. 178, says he set out to the salt-works with one man, on the 3d inst. They did not have a very pleasant trip, and one incident of it, on the 5th, was as follows, p. 179: "This was a very wet day. We killed a squirrel and eat it; made a raft to cross the creek; but when it was tried we found it would carry only one person at a time; the man with me was therefore sent over first, who thought he could shove the raft across again; but when he attempted, it only went half way; so there was one of us on each side and the raft in the middle. I, however, notwithstanding the cold, stript and swam to the raft, brought it over and then crossed on it in safety." On the 6th he notes that "the weather cleared up, after two months of rain, except 4 days."

CHAPTER XXII.

INDIAN TRIBES OF FORT CLATSOP AND VICINITY.

Captain Clark's party en route to see the whale—Clatsop river—Salt-makers camp—Indians returning with oil and blubber—Fine prospect from top of a mountain 30 miles below Cape Disappointment, named Clark's Point of View—The whale found skeletonized—Whale creek named Ecola—Killamuck Indians and river—M'Neal's life saved by a Chinnook squaw—Return of the party from the whale—A canoe lost—Hunters sent out—Account of the Chinnooks—" J. Bowman" tattooed on a squaw—A statistical view of the Indians on the coast north and south of the Columbia—Disposition of the dead—Religions—Implements and weapons—Fishing-gear—Houses—Hats—Domestic utensils—Bags and baskets—Canoes of four different models—Their marvelous management.

TUESDAY, January 7th, 1806. There was a frost this morning. We rose early, and taking eight pounds of flesh, which were all the remains of the elk, proceeded up the south fork of the creek. At the distance of two miles we found a pine-tree, which had been felled by one of our salt-makers, and on which we crossed the deepest part of the creek, and waded through the rest. We then went over an open ridgy prairie three-quarters of a mile to the sea-beach ; after following which for three miles, we came to the mouth of a beautiful river, with a bold rapid current, 85 yards wide, and three feet deep in its shallowest crossings. On its northeast side are the remains of an old village of Clatsops, inhabited by only a single family, who appeared miserably poor and dirty. We gave a man two fish-hooks to ferry the party over this river, which, from the tribe on its banks, we called Clatsop river.[1] The creek which we had passed on a tree approaches this river within 100 yards, and by means of a portage supplies a communication with the villages near Point Adams. After going on for two miles, we found the salt-makers camped near four houses of (*p. 109*) Clatsops and Killamucks [Tillamooks], who, though poor, dirty, and covered with fleas, seemed kind and well-disposed.

[1] Nehanan or Nekanican river, falling into the ocean in the bay above Tillamook Head. The creek they crossed on a log was a branch of the Skeppernawin.

We persuaded a young Indian, by a present of a file and a promise of some other articles, to guide us to the spot where the whale lay. He led us for 2½ miles over the round slippery stones at the foot of a high hill projecting into the sea; then suddenly stopping, and uttering the word "peshack" (bad), explained by signs that we could no longer follow the coast, but must cross the mountain. This promised to be a most laborious undertaking, for the side is nearly perpendicular and the top lost in clouds. He, however, followed an Indian path which wound along as much as possible; still the ascent was so steep that at one place we drew ourselves up for about 100 feet by means of bushes and roots. At length, after two hours' labor, we reached the top of the mountain, where we looked down with astonishment on the prodigious height of 1,000 or 1,200 feet which we had ascended. Immediately below us, on the face of this precipice, is a stratum of white earth, used, as our guide informed us, as a paint by the neighboring Indians. It obviously contains argile,[2] and resembles the earth of which French porcelain is made; though whether it contains silex or magnesia, or in what proportions, we could not observe. We were here met by 14 Indians, loaded with oil and blubber, the spoils of the whale, which they were carrying in very heavy burdens over this rough mountain. On leaving them, we proceeded over a bad road till night, when we camped on a small run [which falls into the sea, now Elk creek]. We were all much fatigued; but the weather was pleasant, and, for the first time since our arrival here, an entire day has passed without rain.

January 8th. We set out early and proceeded to the top of the mountain, the highest point of which is an open spot facing the ocean. It is situated about 30 miles southeast of Cape Disappointment, and projects nearly 2½ miles into the

---

[2] Alumina. Argile or argil was a name proposed for alumina when the nature of this substance was first discovered; its use has fluctuated; now it means technically clay fit for potters' use by reason of the amount of aluminium in its composition. So argillaceous, meaning clayey, and other derivatives.

sea. Here one of the most delightful (*p. 110*) views in nature presents itself. Immediately in front is the ocean, which breaks with fury on the coast, from the rocks of Cape Disappointment as far as the eye can discern to the northwest, and against the highlands and irregular piles of rock which diversify the shore to the southeast. To this boisterous scene the Columbia, with its tributary waters, widening into bays as it approaches the ocean, and studded on both sides with the Chinnook and Clatsop villages, forms a charming contrast ; while immediately beneath our feet are stretched rich prairies, enlivened by three beautiful streams, which conduct the eye to small lakes at the foot of the hills. We stopped to enjoy the romantic view from this place, which we distinguished by the name of Clark's Point of View,[3] and then followed our guide down the mountain. The descent was steep and dangerous ; in many places the hillsides, which are formed principally of yellow clay, have been washed by the late rains, and are now slipping into the sea in large masses of 50 and 100 acres. In other parts, the path crosses the rugged perpendicular rocks which overhang the sea, into which a false step would have precipitated us. The mountains are covered with a very thick growth of timber, chiefly pine and fir [*Abies grandis* or *Pseudotsuga douglasi*] ; some of which, near Clark's Point of View, perfectly sound and solid, rise to the height of 210 feet, and are from eight to twelve in diameter. Intermixed is the white cedar or arbor vitæ [*Thuja occidentalis*], and a small quantity of black alder [*Alnus rubra*], two or three feet thick and 60 or 70 in height.

At length we reached a single house, the remains of an old Killamuck village, situated among some rocks in a bay immediately on the coast. We then continued for two miles along the sand-beach ; and after crossing a creek 80 yards in width,

[3] First sighted Nov. 18th : see note, p. 714. Called by Gass " Clarke's view on the seashore," p. 179, Jan. 4th. The 1000-foot contour-line approaches nearest to the coast opposite Cape Falcon, or False Tillamook Head, Ore. Mt. Neahkahna or Necamey is a spur of this elevation immediately over Nehalem bay, into which latter empties the large river of the same name (Ecola or Whale creek of the text).

near which are five cabins, reached the place where the
waves had thrown the whale ashore.   The animal had been
stranded between two Killamuck villages, and such had been
their industry that there now remained nothing more than
the skeleton, which we (*p. 111*) found to be 105 feet in
length.⁴   Captain Clark then returned to the village of five
huts on the creek, to which he gave the name of Ecola or
Whale creek.⁵   The natives were all busied in boiling the
blubber in a large square trough of wood, by means of heated
stones, and preserving the oil thus extracted in bladders and
the entrails of the whale.   The refuse of the blubber, which
still contained a portion of oil, hung up in large flitches,
which, when wanted for use, are warmed on a wooden spit
before the fire and eaten either alone, or dipped in oil, or
with roots of the rush and shanataque.   These Killamucks,
though they had great quantities, parted with it reluctantly,
and at such high prices that our whole stock of merchandise
was exhausted in the purchase of about 300 pounds of blubber and a few gallons of oil.⁶   With these we set out to
return; and having recrossed Ecola creek, camped on its
[north] bank, where there was abundance of fine timber.

We were soon joined by the men of the village, with
whom we smoked, and who gave us all the information they
possessed   relative   to   their   country.   These Killamucks

---

⁴ This whale was probably *Rhachianectes glaucus*, the great gray whale of the
North Pacific ; perhaps the sulphur-bottomed rorqual, *Balænoptera sulphurea*.
But whatever the species may have been, the length as stated is exaggerated.
The largest whale of any known species does not exceed a length of about 80 feet,
which is attained by the great Atlantic rorqual, *Balænoptera sibbaldi*.   Clark I 99
erases " 105 " and gives no dimensions.   It is a psychological law that when one
thinks of " bigness," the object that excites the thought looks bigger than it
really is ; and conversely.   Few persons can guess the length of a mouse or
canary-bird within an inch.   The tendency is always to exaggerate " size," both
in bigness and littleness.

⁵ The Nehalem river, falling into the bay of the same name, under Mt.
Neahkahna or Necamey.   This is a very considerable stream, running in Washington, Columbia, and Clatsop counties, and then for some distance dividing
the latter from Tillamook Co., Ore.

⁶ " Small as this stock is I prize it highly ; and thank providence for directing

[note *anteà*, p. 744] are part of a much larger nation of the same name ; they now reside chiefly in four villages, each at the entrance of a creek, all of which fall into a bay on the southwest coast ; that at which we now are being the most northern, and at the distance of about 45 miles southeast of Point Adams. The rest of the nation are scattered along the coast, and on the banks of a river, which, as we found it in their delineations, we called Killamuck's [7] river, emptying itself in the same direction. During the salmon season they catch great quantities of that fish in the small creeks, and when these fail, their chief resource is the sturgeon and other fish stranded along the coast. The elk are very numerous in the mountains, but they cannot procure many of them with their arrows. Their principal communication with strangers is by means of the Killamuck river, up which they pass to the Shocatilcum [8] (or Colum- (*p. 112*) bia) to trade for wappatoo-roots. In their dress, appearance, and indeed every circumstance of life, they differ very little from the Chinnooks, Clatsops, and other nations in the neighborhood. The chief variation we have observed is in their manner of burying the dead ; the bodies being secured in an oblong box of plank, which is placed in an open canoe on the ground, with the paddle and other small articles of the deceased by his side.

the whale to us ; and think him much more kind to us than he was to jonah having sent this monster to be *swallowed by us*, in sted ot *swallowing of us* as jonah's did," Clark I 99. This same witticism is in Lewis J 18, and really Mr. Biddle should not have withheld from the world a brand-new and entirely serviceable Jonah joke. The old ones have been much overworked.

[7] " Which I call Kilamox," Clark I 100. Captain Clark is now speaking upon Indian information, and identifications are not easy. The bay upon which we " now are " is Nehalem bay. Next southward is Tillamook bay, bounded by Cape Meares. Next comes Nelart's or Netarts bay ; then Cape Lookout. Tillamook bay is large, and receives several streams, with which we may compare the four creeks of the text : Niami creek, with Garibaldi near its mouth ; a certain creek, with Kilchis at its mouth ; Wilson's river, large ; Trask's river, also large, with which unites one now called Tillamook river ; county town of Tillamook at the mouth. Compare text of Jan. 14th, p. 757. Clark charts four rivers below the Clatsop, nameless, except the third, marked " Killamoucks R."

[8] Spelled Chockalilum, beyond ; Shockalilcom, Clark I 100.

Whilst smoking with the Indians, Captain Clark was surprised, about ten o'clock, by a loud, shrill outcry from the
opposite village, on hearing which all the Indians immediately started up to cross the creek, and the guide informed
him that someone had been killed. On examination one of
the men [M'Neal] was discovered to be absent, and a guard
[Sergeant Pryor and four men] dispatched, who met him
crossing the creek in great haste. An Indian belonging to
another band, who happened to be with the Killamucks that
evening, had treated him with much kindness, and walked
arm in arm with him to a tent where our man found a
Chinnook squaw, who was an old acquaintance. From the
conversation and manner of the stranger, this woman discovered that his object was to murder the white man for the
sake of the few articles on his person ; when he rose and
pressed our man to go to another tent where they would
find something better to eat, she held M'Neal by the blanket ;
not knowing her object, he freed himself from her, and was
going on with his pretended friend, when she ran out and
gave the shriek which brought the men of the village over,
and the stranger ran off before M'Neal knew what had
occasioned the alarm.[9]

January 9th. The morning was fine, the wind from the
northeast. Having divided our stock of blubber, we began at
sunrise to retread our steps, in order to reach Fort Clatsop,
at the distance of 35 miles. Our route lay across the same
mountains we had already passed. We met several parties
of Indians on their way to trade for blubber and oil with
the Killamucks ; we also overtook a (*p. 113*) party returning
from the village, and could not but regard with astonishment
the heavy loads which the women carry over these fatiguing
and dangerous paths. As one of the women was descending

---

[9] Gass also notes this fracas, under date of Jan. 9th, p. 180. "The Indians who
live up there [where the whale was stranded] are of another nation, and call
themselves the Callemex [Tillamooks] nation. They are a ferocious nation:
one of them was going to kill one of our men, for his blanket ; but was prevented by a squaw of the Chinook nation, who lives among them, and who
raised an alarm." Clark I 101 is substantially the same, at greater length.

a steep part of the mountain, her load slipped from her back, and she stood holding it by a strap with one hand, with the other supporting herself by a bush. Captain Clark, being near her, undertook to replace the load, and found it almost as much as he could lift—above 100 pounds in weight. Loaded as they were, they kept pace with us till we reached the salt-makers' tents, where we passed the night, while they continued their route.

January 10*th.* We proceeded across Clatsop river to the place where we had left our canoes; and as the tide was coming in, immediately embarked for the fort, at which place we arrived about ten o'clock at night.

During their [10] absence, the men had been occupied in hunting and dressing skins; but in this they were not very successful, as the deer have become scarce, and are, indeed, seen chiefly near the prairies and open grounds along the coast.

This morning, however, there came to the fort twelve Indians, in a large canoe. They are of the Cathlamah nation, our nearest neighbors above, on the south side of the river. The tia or chief, whose name was Shahawacap, having been absent on a hunting-excursion as we passed his village [where we dined Nov. 26th], had never yet seen us; we therefore showed him the honors of our country, as well as our reduced finances would permit. We invested him with a small medal, and received a present of Indian tobacco and a basket of wappatoo in return, for which we gave him a small piece of our tobacco, and thread for a fishing-net. They had brought dried salmon, wappatoo, dogs, and mats made of rushes and flags ; but we bought only some dogs and wappatoo. These Cathlamahs speak the same language as the Chinnooks and Clatsops, whom they also resemble in dress and manners.

[10] " Their absence " is that of Captain Clark and party ; for here Biddle turns to Lewis I 17 for matters which had gone on at Fort Clatsop during the absence of the scouting party, and so the change from "our" to "their." To-day, Jan. 10th, Lewis notes the return of the party ; also the return of the hunters, Drewyer and Collins, and the visit of the tia (chief) with Cath'lâhmâhs.

(*p. 114*) *January* 11*th*. A party was sent out to bring in some elk killed yesterday, and several were dispatched after our Indian canoe, which had drifted away last night; but, though the whole neighborhood was diligently searched, we were unable to find her. This is a serious loss, as she is much superior to our own canoes, and so light that four men can carry her readily without fatigue, though she will carry from 1,000 to 1,200 pounds, besides a crew of four. In the evening the Cathlamahs left us, on their way to barter their wappatoo with the Clatsops for some blubber and oil, which these last have procured from the Killamucks in exchange for beads and other articles.

Sunday, January 12*th*. [Lewis J 21, Clark I 112.] Our meat is now becoming scarce; we therefore determined to jerk it, and issue it in small quantities, instead of dividing it among the four messes, and leaving to each the care of its own provisions; a plan by which much is lost, in consequence of the improvidence of the men. Two hunters had been dispatched in the morning, and one of them, Drewyer, had before evening killed seven elk. We should scarcely be able to subsist, were it not for the exertions of this most excellent hunter. The game is scarce, and nothing is now to be seen except elk, which for almost all the men are very difficult to be procured; but Drewyer, who is the offspring of a Canadian Frenchman and an Indian woman, has passed his life in the woods, and unites, in a wonderful degree, the dexterous aim of the frontier huntsman with the intuitive sagacity of the Indian, in pursuing the faintest tracks through the forest. All our men, however, have indeed become so expert with the rifle that we are never under apprehensions as to food; since, whenever there is game of any kind, we are almost certain of procuring it.

January 13*th*. Captain Lewis took all the men who could be spared and brought in the seven elk, which they found untouched by the wolves, of which there are few in the neighborhood. The last of the candles which we (*p. 115*) brought with us being exhausted, we now began to make others of elk-tallow.

From all that we have seen and learned of the Chinnooks, we have been induced to estimate the nation at about 28 houses and 400 souls [see note, p. 710]. They reside chiefly along the banks of the river to which we gave the same name; and which, running parallel with the seacoast, waters a low country with many stagnant ponds and then empties into Haley's bay. The wild fowl of these ponds, and the elk and deer of the neighborhood, furnish them with occasional luxuries; but their chief subsistence is derived from salmon and other fish, which are caught in the small streams by means of nets and gigs, or thrown on shore by the violence of the tide. To these are added some roots, such as the wild licorice, which is the most common, the shanataque, and the wappatoo brought down the river by the traders.

The men are low in stature, rather ugly and ill-made, their legs being small and crooked, their feet large, and their heads, like those of the women, flattened in a most disgusting manner. These deformities are in part concealed by robes made of sea-otter, deer, elk, beaver, or fox skins. They also employ in their dress robes of the skin of a cat [11] peculiar to this country, and of another animal of the same size, which skin is light and durable, and sold at a high price by the Indians who bring it from above. In addition to these are worn blankets, wrappers of red, blue, or spotted cloth, and some old sailors' clothes, which were very highly prized. The greater part of the men have guns, powder, and ball.

The women have, in general, handsome faces, but are low and disproportioned, with small feet and large legs and thighs, occasioned, probably, by strands of beads, or various strings, drawn so tight above the ankles as to prevent the circulation of the blood. Their dress, like that of the Wah-

[11] *Lynx rufus fasciatus*, a variety of the common wildcat or bay lynx. The " other animal," about to be mentioned, is the sewellel, *Haplodon rufus*. See note [27], p. 734, and the natural history chapter, beyond.

kiacums, consists of a short robe and a tissue of cedar-bark. Their hair hangs loosely down the shoulders and (*p. 116*) back ; their ears, neck, and wrists are ornamented with blue beads. Another decoration, which is very highly prized, consists of figures made by puncturing the arms or legs ; on the arm of one of the squaws we observed the name of J. Bowman, executed in the same way. In language, habits, and almost every other particular, they resemble the Clatsops, Cathlamahs, and indeed all the people near the mouth of the Columbia. They, however, seem to be inferior to their neighbors in honesty as well as in spirit. No ill-treatment or indignity, on our part, seems to excite any feeling except fear ; nor, although better provided than their neighbors with arms, have they enterprise enough to use them advantageously against the animals of the forest, or offensively against their neighbors, who owe their safety more to the timidity than the forbearance of the Chinnooks. We had heard of instances of pilfering whilst we were amongst them, and therefore had a general order, excluding them from our camp ; so that, whenever an Indian wished to visit us, he began by calling out " No Chinnook." It may be probable that this first impression left a prejudice against them, since when we were among the Clatsops and other tribes at the mouth of the Columbia, the Indians had less opportunity of stealing, if they were so disposed.

January 14*th*. We were employed in jerking the meat of the elk, and searching for one of the canoes which had been carried off by the tide last night. Having found it, we now had three of them drawn up out of reach of the water, and the other secured by a strong cord, so as to be ready for any emergency.

After many inquiries and much observation, we are at length enabled to obtain a connected view of the nations who reside along the coast, on both sides of the Columbia. To the south our personal observation has not extended beyond the Killamucks ; but we have obtained from those who were acquainted with the seacoast, a list of the Indian (*p. 117*) tribes in the order in which they succeed each other, to a considerable distance.

The first nation to the south are the Clatsops [see note, p. 710, Nov. 17th], who reside on the southern side of the bay, and along the seacoast on both sides of Point Adams. They are represented as the remains of a much larger nation; but about four years ago a disorder, to which till then they had been strangers, but which seems from their description to have been smallpox, destroyed four chiefs and several hundred of the nation. The dead are deposited in canoes, a few miles below us on the bay, and the survivors do not number more than 14 houses and about 200 souls.

Next to them, along the southeast coast, is a much larger nation, the Killamucks [see note, p. 744], who number 50 houses and 1,000 souls. Their first establishment is the four huts at the mouth of Ecola [or Whale] creek, 35 miles from Point Adams; two miles below are a few more huts; but the principal town is situated 20 miles lower, at the entrance of a creek called Nielee [Niami], into the bay which we designate by the name of Killamuck bay [Tillamook bay]. Into the same bay empties a second [not identified] creek, five miles further, where is a Killamuck village called Kilherhurst; at two miles is a third creek [Wilson's river], and a town called Kilherner; and at the same distance a town called Chishuck, at the mouth of Killamuck river [or Trask's]. Towerquotton and Chucktin are the names of two other towns situated on creeks which empty into the bottom of the bay, the last of which is 70 miles from Point Adams. The Killamuck river is about 100 yards wide, and very rapid; but, having no particular fall, is the great avenue for trade. There are two small villages of Killamucks settled above its mouth, and the whole trading part of the tribe ascend it [Trask's river?], till by a short portage they carry their canoes over to the Columbian valley, and descend the Multnomah to Wappatoo island. Here they purchase roots, which they carry down the Chockalilum [12] or Columbia, and, after trafficking with the tribes on its banks for the various articles which they require, either return (*p. 118*) up the Columbia, or cross over through the country of the Clatsops. This trade, however, is obviously little more than loose and irregular barter on a very small scale; for the materials for commerce are so extremely scanty and precarious that the stranding of the whale was an important commercial incident, which interested all the adjoining country. The Killamucks have little peculiar, either in character or manners, and resemble, in almost every particular, the Clatsops and Chinnooks [but are of Salishan, not Chinookan, stock].

Adjoining the Killamucks, in a direction S.S.E., are the Lucktons, [13] a small tribe inhabiting the seacoast. They speak the same language as the Killamucks, but do not belong to the same nation. The same observation applies to the Kahunkle nation, their immediate neighbors, who are supposed to consist of about 400 souls;

The Lickawis, [14] a still more numerous nation, who have a large town of 800 souls;

The Youkone [15] nation, who live in very large houses, and number 700 souls;

[12] Spelled Shocatilcum before. For other names in this paragraph, see note [7], p. 751, Jan. 8th.

[13] A tribe known only through this notice of Lewis and Clark. We may conjecture some connection between " Luckton," as a word, and *Nestocton*, present name of a town on Tillamook river.

[14] Elsewhere Lukawis ; more correctly Yik'-qaics. A Yakwina or Yaquina sub-tribe (of the Yakonan family), on the north side of the Yaquina river, opposite where is now Elk City, Ore. See next note.

[15] The Youkones, elsewhere called Youikcones by Lewis and Clark, are here wrongly classed with the " Killamucks," or Tillamooks. Their proper name is Yakwina (same word as Yaquina, name of the river on which they chiefly lived, and, according to Everette, meaning " spirit"). They were the principal tribe of the Yakonan nation, which once inhabited Western Oregon from the Yaquina south to the Umpqua river. This nation reckoned, besides the Yakwina tribe, three others whose names are now given as Alsea (on Alseya river), Kuitc, and Siuslaw. The few surviving Yakwinas are on the Siletz Reservation, Tillamook Co., Ore., with some Alseas and other remnants of many different tribes—altogether less than 600 persons. The Yakonan family

The Necketo[16] nation, of the same number of persons;

The Ulseah[17] nation, a small town of 150 souls;

The Youitts,[18] a tribe who live in small towns, containing 150 souls;

The Shiastuckle[19] nation, who have a large town of 900 souls ;

The Killawats[20] nation, of 500 souls, collected into one large town.

includes the tribes called Yakones, Iakons, and Lower or Southern Kil-lamucks, by Hale, U. S. Expl. Exped. VI. 1846, pp. 198, 218, 579 ; Jacon or Jakon, by Gallatin, Trans. Amer. Ethn. Soc. II. 1848 ; Yakon, Sainstskla, and Killiwashat, by Latham, Nat. Hist. Man. 1850, pp. 324, 325. Several of the Yakonan tribes are enumerated by Lewis and Clark among their " Killamucks," though under names not easy to recognize on sight.

[16] The Necketo Indians, in the Estimate printed Neeketoos, were a sub-tribe or gens of the Alsea tribe (Yakonan stock), who lived on the north side of the Alsea or Alseya river, at Seal Rock, on the Pacific coast of Oregon. They are now called Kû-taú-wa.

[17] A tribe of the Yakonan stock on Alseya or Alsea river in Oregon, and now called by this name. Some also inhabited the adjacent coast. Their remnants are on the Siletz Reservation, and it is supposed a few are on the Grande Ronde Reservation.

[18] A tribe of the Yakonan family, whose name is now spelled Kuitc. They are also known as Lower Umpqua Indians, from having their villages on that river for about 30 miles up from its mouth, though the Indians of the upper Umpqua were of a different (Athapascan) stock. A few of the Kuitc tribe still live on the Siletz Reservation.

[19] Also called by Lewis and Clark " Sheastuckles " ; one of the four principal tribes of the Yakonan family. These are the Sainstskla Indians of Latham, the Sayuskla of Gatschet (Mag. Amer. Hist. 1882, p. 257), who inhabited the lower Umpqua, Sayuskla, and Smith's rivers. They are mentioned by Drew, under his Katla-wot-sett bands (Rep. U. S. Indian Affairs, 1857, p. 359). The name is now spelled Siuslaw. " The Sayusklan language has usually been assumed to be distinct from all others, and the comments of Latham and others all tend in this direction. Mr. Gatschet, as above quoted, finally classed it as a distinct stock, at the same time finding certain strong coincidences with the Yakonan family. Recently, Mr. Dorsey has collected extensive vocabularies of the Yakonan, Sayuskla, and Lower Umpqua languages, and finds unquestioned evidence of relationship." (Powell, Ann. Rep. Bureau of Ethnol. for 1885–86, pub. 1891, p. 134.)

[20] Yet another tribe or band of the Yakonan family. These are the Killiwashat Indians of Latham, Nat. Hist. of Man. 1850, p. 325, whose habitat is given at the mouth of the Umkwa (Umpqua) river. The name is also spelled Katla-wotsett.

With this last nation ends the language of the Killamucks.[21] The coast, which then turns toward the southwest, is occupied by nations whose languages vary from
that of the Killamucks, and from each other. Of these,
the first in order are:

The Cookoooose,[22] a large nation of 1,500 souls, inhabiting the shore of the Pacific and the neighboring mountains. We have seen several of this (*p. 119*) nation who
were taken prisoners by the Clatsops and Killamucks.
Their complexion was much fairer than that of the Indians
near the mouth of the Columbia, and their heads were not
flattened. Next to these are:

[21] When Lewis and Clark state that the above tribes speak the same language
as the Killamucks (Tillamooks), we are to understand a certain degree of simi-
larity only. The Tillamooks are a tribe of the great Salishan linguistic family,
while the other tribes mentioned by Lewis and Clark are now classsd as Yakonan. But we must also remember that it is only recently that anything like the
classification which I follow in these notes was established. Our authors also
state explicitly that their personal observation extended to none of these tribes
beyond the Killamucks, so that what they have to say is entirely upon Indian
information. Under the circumstances, it is a remarkable piece of pioneering in
ethnography.

[22] The "Cookoooose," also spelled "Cookkoo-oose" by Lewis and Clark,
are the Indians mentioned by Hale (U. S. Expl. Exped. VI. 1846, p. 221),
under the name of the "Kaus or Kwokwoos" tribe, as living on a river of the
same name, between the Umpqua and the Clamet, and the "Kaus" of
Latham (Nat. Hist. Man. 1850, p. 325). No classification of these Indians
was then attempted. On the authority of a letter from Milhau to Gibbs, in
the U. S. Bureau of Ethnology, "Coos," in one of the Rogue river dialects,
is said to mean "lake, lagoon, or inland bay." Mr. A. S. Gatschet (Mag.
Amer. Hist. 1882, p. 257) makes the word "Kusa," and distinguishes the language as forming a distinct stock, spoken on the coast of middle Oregon, on
Coos river and bay, and at the mouth of Coquille river in Oregon. Major
J. W. Powell makes this linguistic distinction the basis of his Kusan family,
which he divides into four tribes, Anasitch, Melukitz, Mulluk (or Lower Coquille
Indians), and probably the Nacu. Most of the survivors of this family are
now on the Siletz Reservation in Oregon, but their number cannot be stated,
as the Agency returns are not given by tribes. (Report U. S. Bureau Ethnol.
for 1885–86, pub. 1891, p. 89.) Coos or Cookoooose is a collective name,
usually including two villages, viz., the Melukitz and Anasitch—names meaning,
respectively, "northern" and "southern." In 1884 Dorsey found two other
villages at the mouth of Coquille river—Ná′-cu-mi, or Anasitch, and Mûl-luk,
or Melukitz.

The Shalalahs,[23] of whom we know nothing except their numbers, which are computed at 1,200 souls.

Then follow:

The Luckasos,[24] of about the same number; and

The Hannakalals,[25] whom we estimate at 600 souls.

This is the extent of our Indian information, and judging, as we can do with considerable accuracy, from the number of " sleeps," or days' journey, the distance which these tribes occupy along the coast may be estimated at 360 miles.

On the north of the Columbia, we have already seen the Chinnooks, of 400 souls, along the shores of Haley's bay, and on the low grounds of Chinnook river. Their nearest neighbors to the northeast are :

The Killaxthokle,[26] a small nation on the coast, of not more than eight houses and 100 souls. To these succeed :

The Chilts,[27] who reside above Point Lewis, and who are estimated at 700 souls and 38 houses. Of this nation, we saw, transiently, a few among the Chinnooks, from whom they did not appear to differ. Beyond the Chilts we have seen none of the northwest Indians, and all that we learned consisted of an enumeration of their names and numbers.

The nations next to the Chilts are:

The Clamoitomish,[28] of 12 houses and 260 souls;

[23] " Shahala " or " Shalala " or " Shalalah " is a collective name by which Lewis and Clark cover four tribes of Chinookan stock, from the Cascades of the Columbia to the mouth of the Multnomah (or Willamette). In the Estimate at the end of the volume these four tribes are named as : 1. Ychuh. 2. Clahclellah. 3. Wahclellah. 4. Neerchokioon. Compare especially note [9], p. 1251.

[24] The Luckasos, elsewhere Luckkarsos, are known only through Lewis and Clark. The name is probably from Yu-qais', an Alsea village (Yakonan family).

[25] The Hannakalal or Hannakallal are doubtful ; probably a Salishan tribe. They are mentioned only by Lewis and Clark.

[26] Or Killaxthocle; properly Gatlakstχoke. These were a tribe of Chehalis, of Chinookan stock, who resided at the entrance of Shoalwater bay.

[27] Or Chiltz : see note [39], p. 717.

[28] The Clamoitomish are spelled in the Estimate Clamoctomichs. They are also called Klumaitumish, the name of an abandoned village on the south side of Gray's harbor. The name is derived from Tlemaitemc, an island near the entrance of this harbor. These Indians were a band who lived on Shoalwater bay, on or about Nasal river. They were of Chinookan stock.

The Potoashees,[29] of 10 houses and 200 souls ;
The Pailsk,[30] of 10 houses and 200 souls ;
The Quinults,[31] of 60 houses and 1,000 souls ;
The Chillates,[32] of 8 houses and 150 souls ;
(*p. 120*) The Calasthorte,[33] of 10 houses and 200 souls ;
The Quinnechant,[34] consisting of 2,000 souls.

A particular detail of the characters, manners, and habits of these tribes must be left to some future adventurers, who may have more leisure and a better opportunity than we had to accomplish this object. Those who first visit the ground can only be expected to furnish sketches, rude and imperfect.[35]

January 15*th*. Two hunting-parties intended setting out this morning ; but they were prevented by incessant rain, which confined us all to the fort.

The Chinnooks, Clatsops, and most of the adjoining nations dispose of the dead in canoes. For this purpose a scaffold is erected, by fixing perpendicularly in the ground four long pieces of split timber. These are placed two by two, just wide enough apart to admit the canoe, and sufficiently long to support its two extremities. The boards are connected by a bar of wood run through them at the height

[29] The Potoashees or Potoashes were a band of Salishan stock (not Chinookan), known only by the notice in this work.

[30] Pailsk, as here, Pailsh of the Estimate, is probably the same as Copalis, a Salishan village on the river of the same name, 18 miles north of Gray's harbor.

[31] For the name Quinults, printed Quiniilts in the Estimate, see note [8], p. 669. The tribe here named was of Salishan stock.

[32] The Chillates are not identifiable. We know nothing of them beyond this mention and the corresponding one in the Estimate. They were located on the coast of Washington. They are not the Chiltz or Chilts already mentioned.

[33] Calasthocle in the Estimate. A Salishan tribe ; no more known of them.

[34] Quinnechart in the Estimate. This appears to be for Quenaitsath, possibly a Salishan tribe. Nothing further is known of these Indians than Lewis and Clark give.

[35] The candid reader will doubtless agree with a sorely tried editor and proof-reader that Lewis and Clark's sketches are neither ruder nor more imperfect than their subjects. The Babylonian Tower of Babel was a Parsee Tower of Silence in comparison with the confusion of tongues that bombarded the explorers' ears on the Columbia river and the coasts of Oregon and Washington. The then

of six feet, on which is placed a small canoe containing the body of the deceased, carefully wrapped in a robe of dressed skins, with a paddle, and other articles belonging to him, by his side.   Over this canoe is placed one of a larger size, reversed, with its gunwale resting on the crossbars, so as to cover the body completely.   One or more large mats of rushes or flags are then rolled round the canoes, and the whole is secured by cords, usually made of the bark of the white cedar.   On these crossbars are hung different articles of clothing, or culinary utensils.   The method practiced by the Killamucks [Tillamooks] differs somewhat from this; the body being deposited in an oblong box of plank, which, with the paddle and other articles, is placed in a canoe resting on the ground.   With the religious opinions of these people we are but little acquainted, since we understand their language too imperfectly to converse on a subject so abstract; but it is obvious, from the different deposits which they (*p. 121*) place by their dead, that they believe in a future state of existence.*

January 16*th*.   To-day we finished curing our meat, and having now a plentiful supply of elk and salt, and our houses being dry and comfortable, we wait patiently for the moment of resuming our journey.[36]

" future adventurers," who have since then been the subsequent explorers of these linguistic fields, so yellow to the lexicographic scythe, have struggled with each " gugling kind of languaje spoken mostly thro' the throught," as Captain Clark says, till we are enabled to sort the tribes out with some confidence.   From this results that modern classification which I have attempted to supply, in its main features at least.   Nothing worse than this has happened since we began the book; and the reader may rest assured that nothing so bad will occur again. We will shed a sympathetic tear for the recording angel whose business obliged him to hear and write down all the *bad* words of the Chilluckittequaws, Weocksockwillicums, Killaxthokles, and Cookooooses, and pass on.

* This fact is much too equivocal to warrant an inference so important.   These deposits might have been intended for nothing more than the testimonials of surviving affection.   Amongst those savages, where the language was better understood, it does not appear that the Indians intended anything more by such sacrifices than to testify their reverence for the dead.—EDITOR.   (Original note.)

[36] Lewis J 27 and Clark I 121, both this date, have further reflections on the situation.   I cite the former; the language of the two is nearly identical: "Hav-

The implements used in hunting by the Clatsops, Chinnooks, and other neighboring nations, are the gun, bow and arrow, deadfall, pits, snares, and spears or gigs. The guns are generally old American or British muskets, repaired for this trade; and though there are some good pieces among them, they are constantly out of order, as the Indians have not been sufficiently accustomed to arms to understand the management of them. The powder is kept in small japanned tin flasks, in which the traders sell it; and when the ball or shot fails, they make use of gravel or pieces of metal from their pots, without being sensible of the injury done to their guns. These arms are reserved for hunting elk, and the few deer and bears in this neighborhood; but as they have no rifles, they are not very successful hunters. The most common weapon is the bow and arrow, with which every man is provided, even though he carries a gun, and which is used in every kind of hunting. The bow is extremely neat; and being very thin and flat, possesses great elasticity. It is made of the heart of the white cedar, about 2½ feet in length, and 2 inches wide at the center, whence it tapers to the width of half an inch at the extremities; the back is covered with the sinews of elk, fastened on by means of glue made from (*p. 122*) the sturgeon. The string is formed of the same sinews. The arrow generally consists of two parts; the first is about 20 inches long, and formed of light white pine, with the feather at one end, and at the other a circular hole, which receives the second part, formed of some harder wood,

ing made up our minds to remain untill the 1st of April, every one appears content with his situation and his fare. it is true that we could even travel now on our return as far as the timbered country reaches, or to the falls of the river, but further it would be madness for us to attempt to proceede until April, as the Indians inform us that the snows lye knee deep in the plains of Columbia during the winter, and on these plains we could scarcely get as much fuel as would cook our provisions as we descended the river ; and even were we happyly over these plains and again in the woody country at the foot of the Rocky mountains [Bitter-root ranges], we could not possibly pass that immence barrier of mountains on which the snows ly in winter to the debth in many places of 20 feet." This was sound; leaving Clatsop March 23d, as they did, they had to fall back from the Bitter-root mountains and wait for the snows to melt.

about five inches long, secured in its place by means of sinews. The barb is either of stone or else of iron or copper; in which latter case, the angle is more obtuse than any we have seen. If, as sometimes happens, the arrow is formed of a single piece, the whole is of a more durable wood; but the form just described is preferred, because much of the game consists of wild fowl on the ponds, and it is desirable that the arrows should be constructed so as to float if they fall into the water. These arrows are kept in a quiver of elk or young bear-skin, opening not at the ends, as the common quivers do, but at the sides; which, for those who hunt in canoes, is much more convenient. These weapons are not, however, very powerful, for many of the elk we kill have been wounded with them; and, though the barb with the small end of the arrow remains, yet the flesh closes and the animal suffers no permanent injury. The deadfalls and snares are used in taking the wolf, the raccoon, and the fox, of which there are, however, but few in this country. The spear or gig employed in pursuit of the sea-otter (which they call spuck), the common otter, and beaver, consists of two points of barbs, and is like that already described as common among the Indians on the upper part of the Columbia. The pits are chiefly for the elk, and are, therefore, usually large and deep cubes 12 or 14 feet in depth, and are made by the side of some fallen tree lying across the path frequented by the elk. They are covered with slender boughs and moss, and the elk either sinks into the hole as he approaches the tree, or, in leaping over the tree, falls into the pit on the other side.

January 17th. Comowool and seven other Clatsops spent the day with us. He made us a present of some roots and ber- (*p. 123*) ries, in return for which we gave him an awl and some thread, which he wanted for the purpose of making a net. We were not able to purchase any more of their provisions, the prices being too high for our exhausted stock of merchandise. One of the Indians was dressed in three very elegant skins of the sea-otter, for which we were very desirous of trafficking; but he refused every exchange except that of blue beads, of which he asked six fathoms for each skin, and as we had only four fathoms left, he would accept for the remaining two neither a knife nor any quantity of beads of another sort.

In fishing, the Clatsops, Chinnooks, and other nations near this place employ the common straight net, the scooping or dipping-net with a long handle, the gig, and the hook and line. The first is of different lengths and depths, and is used in taking salmon, carr [char], and trout, in the deep inlets among the marshy grounds, and at the mouths of deep creeks. The scooping-net is used for small fish in the spring and summer season ; in both kinds the net is formed of silk-grass or the bark of white cedar. The gig is used at all seasons, and for all kinds of fish they can procure with it ; so too is the hook and line, of which the line is made of the same material as the net, and the hook is generally brought by the traders, though before the whites came the Indians made hooks out of two small pieces of bone, resembling the European hook, but with a much more acute angle where the two pieces joined.[37]

January 18*th*. We were all occupied in dressing skins and preparing clothes for our journey homeward.

The houses in this neighborhood are large wooden buildings, varying in length from 20 to 60 feet, and from 14 to 20 in width. They are constructed in the following manner : Two posts of split timber or more, agreeably to the number of partitions, are sunk in the ground, above which they rise to the height of 14 to 18 feet. They are hollowed at the top, so as to receive the ends of a round beam or pole, stretching from one to the other, and forming (*p. 124*) the upper point of the roof for the whole extent of the building. On each side of this range is placed another, which forms the eaves of the house, and is about five feet high ; but as the building is often sunk to the depth of four or five feet, the eaves come

[37] Sketches of these hooks, Lewis J 28, Clark I 122.

very near the surface of the earth.   Smaller pieces of timber are now extended by pairs, in the form of rafters, from the lower to the upper beam, where they are attached at both ends with cords of cedar-bark.   On these rafters two or three ranges of small poles are placed horizontally, and secured in the same way with strings of cedar-bark.   The sides are now made with a range of wide boards, sunk a small distance into the ground, with the upper ends projecting above the poles at the eaves, to which they are secured by a beam passing outside, parallel with the eaves-poles, and tied by cords of cedar-bark passing through holes made in the boards at certain distances.   The gable-ends and partitions are formed in the same way, being fastened by beams on the outside, parallel with the rafters.   The roof is then covered with a double range of thin boards, except an aperture of two or three feet in the center for the smoke to pass through.   The entrance is by a small hole cut out of the boards, just large enough to admit the body.   The very largest houses only are divided by partitions ; for though three or four families reside in the same room, there is quite space enough for all of them.   In the center of each room is a space six or eight feet square, sunk to the depth of twelve inches below the rest of the floor, and inclosed by four pieces of square timber.   Here they make the fire, for which purpose pine-bark is generally preferred.   Around this fireplace mats are spread, which serve as seats during the day, and very frequently as beds at night ; there is, however, a more permanent bed, made by fixing, in two or sometimes three sides of the room, posts reaching from the roof down to the ground, at the distance of four feet from the wall.   From these posts to the wall itself one or two ranges of boards are placed so as to form shelves, on which they ei- (*p.125*) ther sleep, or where they stow away their various articles of merchandise.   The uncured fish is hung in the smoke of their fires, as is also the flesh of the elk, when they are fortunate enough to procure any, which is but rarely.

Sunday, January 20th [19th[38]]. This morning we sent out parties of hunters in different directions. Soon after, we two were visited by two Clatsop men and a woman, who brought several articles to trade ; we purchased a small quantity of train-oil for a pair of brass armbands, and succeeded in obtaining a sea-otter skin, for which we gave our only remaining four fathoms of blue beads, the same quantity of white ones, and a knife ; we gave a fish-hook also in exchange for one of their hats.

These hats are made of cedar-bark and bear-grass, interwoven together in the form of a European hat, with a small brim of about two inches, and a high crown widening upward. They are light, ornamented with various colors and figures, and being nearly water-proof, are much more durable than either chip or straw hats. These hats form a small article of traffic with the whites, and their manufacture is one of the best exertions of Indian industry. They are, however, very dexterous in making a variety of domestic utensils, among which are bowls, spoons, scewers [skewers], spits, and baskets. The bowl or trough is of different shapes —round, semicircular, in the form of a canoe, or cubic, and generally dug out of a single piece of wood ; the larger vessels have holes in the sides by way of handles, and all are executed with great neatness. In these vessels they boil their food, by throwing hot stones into the water, and extract oil from different animals in the same way. Spoons are not very abundant, nor is there anything remarkable in their shape, except that they are large and the bowl broad. Meat is roasted on one end of a sharp scewer, placed erect before the fire, with the other end fixed in the ground. The spit for fish is split at the top into two parts, between which the fish is placed, cut open, with its sides extended by

[38] Read 19th. In their long isolation, the captains have got mixed on the days of the week and month. Lewis J 33 has " Monday, January 19th," corrected to " Sunday." Clark I 123 has " Sunday, 17th January "; p. 126, " Monday, 18th January," etc., for many days, before he discovers and adjusts the error. The Biddle text has Sunday 20th, which was the 19th, and next Monday 20th, which is correct.

means of small splinters.   The usual plate is a small mat of rushes or flags, on which (*p. 126*) everything is served.   The instrument with which they dig up roots is a strong stick, about 3½ feet long, sharpened and a little curved at the lower end, while the upper is inserted into a handle, standing transversely, and made of part of an elk's or a buck's horn.   But the most curious workmanship is that of the basket.   It is formed of cedar-bark and bear-grass, so closely interwoven that it is water-tight, without the aid of either gum or resin.   The form is generally conic, or rather the segment [frustum] of a cone, of which the smaller end is the bottom of the basket ; and being made of all sizes, from that of the smallest cup to the capacity of five or six gallons, they answer the double purpose of a covering for the head or to contain water.   Some of them are highly ornamented with strands of bear-grass, woven into figures of various colors, which require great labor ; yet they are made very expeditiously and sold for a trifle.   It is for the construction of these baskets that the bear-grass forms an article of considerable traffic.   It grows only near the snowy region of the high mountains ; the blade, which is two feet long and about three-eighths of an inch wide, is smooth, strong, and pliant ; the young blades particularly, from their not being exposed to the sun and air, have an appearance of great neatness, and are generally preferred.   Other bags and baskets, not waterproof, arc made of cedar-bark, silk-grass, rushes, flags, and common coarse sedge, for the use of families.   In these manufactures, as in the ordinary work of the house, the instrument most in use is a knife, or rather a dagger.   The handle of it is small, and has a strong loop of twine for the thumb, to prevent its being wrested from the hand.   On each side is a blade, double-edged and pointed ; the longer from nine to ten inches, the shorter from four to five.   This knife is carried habitually in the hand, sometimes exposed, but mostly, when in company with strangers, is put under the robe.

Monday, January 20*th.*   We were visited by three Clat-

sops, who came merely for the purpose of smoking and conversing with (*p. 127*) us. We have now only three days'
provision; yet so accustomed have the men become to live
sparingly and fast occasionally, that such a circumstance
excites no concern, as we all calculate on our dexterity as
hunters.

The industry of the Indians is not confined to household
utensils; the great proof of their skill is the construction of
their canoes. In a country, indeed, where so much of the
intercourse between different tribes is carried on by water,
the ingenuity of the people would naturally direct itself to
the improvement of canoes, which would gradually become,
from a mere safe conveyance, an elegant ornament. We
have accordingly seen on the Columbia canoes of many
forms, from the simple boats near the mountains to those
more highly decorated, because more useful, near the mouth
of the Columbia. Below the grand cataract there are four
forms of canoes. The first and smallest is about 15 feet
long, and calculated for one or two persons; it is by no
means remarkable in its structure, and is chiefly employed
by the Cathlamahs and Wahkiacums, among the marshy
islands. The second is from 20 to 35 feet long, about 2½
or 3 feet in the beam, and 2 feet in the hold. It is chiefly
remarkable in having the bowsprit, which rises to some
height above the bow, formed by tapering gradually from
the sides into a sharp point. Canoes of this shape are
common to all the nations below the grand rapids [Cas-
cades].

But the [third kind, the] canoes most used by the Columbia Indians, from the Chillukittequaws inclusive, to the
ocean, are about 30 or 35 feet long. The bow, which looks
more like the stern of our boats, is higher than the other
end, and is ornamented with a sort of comb, an inch in thickness, cut out of the same log which forms the canoe, and
extending 9 or 11 inches from the bowsprit to the bottom of
the boat. The stern is nearly rounded off, and gradually
ascends to a point. This canoe is very light and convenient,

for though it will (*p. 128*) contain ten or twelve persons, it may be carried with great ease by four.

The fourth and largest species of canoes we did not meet till we reached tide-water, near the grand rapids below, in which place they are found among all the nations, especially the Killamucks and others residing on the seacoast.   They are upward of 50 feet long, and will carry from 8,000 to 10,000 pounds' weight, or from 20 to 30 persons.   Like all the canoes we have mentioned, they are cut out of a single trunk of a tree, which is generally white cedar, though the fir is sometimes used.   The sides are secured by crossbars, or round sticks, two or three inches in thickness, which are inserted through holes made just below the gunwale, and made fast with cords.   The upper edge of the gunwale itself is about five-eighths of an inch thick, and four or five in breadth, and folds outward so as to form a kind of rim, which prevents the water from beating into the boat.   The bow and stern are about the same height, and each is provided with a comb, reaching to the bottom of the boat.   At each end, also, are pedestals, formed of the same solid piece, on which are placed strange, grotesque figures of men or animals, rising sometimes to the height of five feet, and composed of small pieces of wood, firmly united with great ingenuity, by inlaying and mortising, without a spike of any kind.   The paddle is usually from 4½ to 5 feet in length, the handle being thick for one-third of its length, when it widens and is hollowed and thinned on each side of the center, which forms a sort of rib.   When they embark, one Indian sits in the stern and steers with a paddle; the others kneel in pairs in the bottom of the canoe, and, sitting on their heels, paddle over the gunwale next to them.   In this way they ride with perfect safety the highest waves, and venture without the least concern in seas where other boats or seamen could not live an instant.   They sit quietly and paddle, with no other movement, except when some large wave throws the boat (*p. 129*) on her side, and, to the eye of a spectator, she seems lost; the man to windward then steadies her by throwing his body toward the upper side, and sinking his paddle deep into the wave, appears to catch the water and force it under the boat, which the same stroke pushes on with great velocity. In the management of these canoes the women are equally expert with the men, for in the smaller boats, which contain four oarsmen, the helm is generally given to the female. As soon as they land, the canoe is generally hauled on shore, unless she be very heavily laden ; but at night the load is universally discharged, and the canoe brought on shore.

Our admiration of their skill in these curious constructions was increased by observing the very inadequate implements with which they are made. These Indians possess very few axes, and the only tool employed in their building, from felling of the tree to the delicate workmanship of the images, is a chisel made of an old file, about an inch or an inch and a half in width. Even of this too, they have not yet learned the management, for the chisel is sometimes fixed in a large block of wood, and being held in the right hand, the block is pushed with the left without the aid of a mallet. But under all these disadvantages, these canoes, which one would suppose to be the work of years, are made in a few weeks. A canoe, however, is very highly prized ; in traffic, it is an article of the greatest value, except a wife, which is of equal consideration ; so that a lover generally gives a canoe to the father in exchange for his daughter.

CHAPTER XXIII.

INDIANS OF THE VICINITY: CONTINUED.

Killamucks, Clatsops, Chinnooks, and Cathlamahs—Their personal appearance—Their flat heads, how produced—Dress and ornaments—Easy virtue of the females—Prevalence of venereal disease—Its obduracy and treatment—Loquacity and inquisitiveness of the Indians —Their good treatment of women and old persons—Their inoffensive but beggarly and thievish disposition—Tribal and domestic economy—No addiction to liquor—Vice of gambling—Sharp bargaining—Cunning calculation—Traffic with other Indians—Cured fish and wappatoo the staples—The white traders, English or American, who visit these Indians —No wars among the Indian tribes.

TUESDAY, January 21st, 1806. Two of the hunters [Shannon, Labiche] came back with three elk, which formed a timely addition to our stock of provisions. The Indian visitors left us at twelve o'clock.

The Killamucks, Clatsops, Chinnooks, and Cathlamahs, the four neighboring nations with whom we have had most intercourse, preserve a general resemblance in person, dress, and manners. They are commonly of a diminutive stature, badly shaped, and their appearance is by no means prepossessing. They have broad, thick, flat feet, thick ankles, and crooked legs; the last of which deformities is to be ascribed, in part, to the universal practice of squatting or sitting on the calves of their legs and heels, and also to the tight bandages of beads and strings worn round the ankles by the women, which prevent the circulation of the blood, and render the legs, of the females particularly, ill-shaped and swollen. The complexion is the usual copper-colored brown of the North American tribes, though rather lighter than that of the Indians of the Missouri and the frontier of the United States; the mouth is wide and (*p. 131*) the lips are thick; the nose is of a moderate size, fleshy, wide at the extremity, with large nostrils, and generally low between the eyes, though there are rare instances of high acqueline [*sic*—aquiline] noses; the eyes are generally black, though we occasionally see them of a dark yellowish-brown, with a black pupil.

But the most distinguishing part of their physiognomy is the peculiar flatness and width of the forehead, a peculiarity which they owe to one of these customs by which nature is sacrificed to fantastic ideas of beauty. The custom, indeed, of flattening the head by artificial pressure during infancy prevails among all the nations we have seen west of the Rocky mountains. To the east of that barrier, the fashion is so perfectly unknown that there the western Indians, with the exception of the Alliatan or Snake nation, are designated by the common name Flatheads.[1] This singular

---

[1] A significant remark. The name "Flathead" is used with scarcely less latitude by authors than by Indians themselves. In a comprehensive yet correct sense, the Flatheads are the great Salishan family, of which Powell names no fewer than 64 principal tribes. As originally employed by Gallatin (Trans. Amer. Antiq. Soc. II. 1836, pp. 134, 306), the name Salish included only the Flatheads in the strictest sense, being the single tribe (Ootlashoots) met with by Lewis and Clark on the headwaters of Clark's river (p. 583). The Salish or Flatheads of Keane (1878) is a composite group, inexactly synonymous with the Salishan family. The Salish of Bancroft (Nat. Races, III. 1882, pp. 565, 618) is the whole Salishan family of Powell. The Selish of Gatschet (Mag. Amer. Hist. 1877, p. 169) likewise corresponds to Powell's Salishan family. The Tsihaili-Selish of Hale (U. S. Expl. Exped. VI. 1846, pp. 205, 535, 569) includes eight tribes of Salishans. The Atnahs of Gallatin (Trans. Am. Antiq. Soc. II. 1836, pp. 134, 135, 306) are Salishans of Fraser's river, considered by him as distinct. The Atnas of Latham (Trans. Philol. Soc. London, 1856, p. 71) are the Tsihaili-Selish of Hale. The Tsihaili of Latham (Nat. Hist. Man. 1850, p. 310) includes ten tribes of Salishans, from lower parts of Fraser's river and thence to the Columbia. A tribe of Salishans from the mouth of Salmon river is given by Latham (Nat. Hist. Man. 1850, p. 300) as Billechula, a name also spelled by him Billechoola, and by others Bellacoola, Bilchula, and Bilhoola. The Nootka-Columbia group of Scouler (Journ. Roy. Geog. Soc. London, XI. 1841, p. 224) is a composite, exactly synonymous with no stock now recognized, but includes various Salishan tribes. The Nootka Indians of Bancroft (Nat. Races, III. 1882, p. 564) is to some extent heterogeneous, but contains 18 Salishan tribes. The Puget Sound group of Keane (1878), with the exception of one tribe (Chinakum), is entirely Salishan. The above are the leading names of this one much diversified linguistic stock, as recognized by Powell. Of their geographical distribution Major Powell writes (Rep. U. S. Bureau Ethnol. for 1885–86, pub. 1891, p. 104) :

" Since Gallatin's time, through the labors of Riggs, Hale, Tolmie, Dawson,

usage, which nature could scarcely seem to suggest to remote nations, might perhaps incline us to believe in the common and not very ancient origin of all the western nations.   Such an opinion might well accommodate itself with the fact that while on the lower parts of the Columbia both sexes are universally flat-headed, the custom diminishes in receding eastward, from the common center of the infection, till among the remoter tribes near the mountains nature recovers her rights, and the wasted folly is confined to a few females. Such opinions, however, are corrected or weakened by considering that the flattening of the head is not, in fact, peculiar to that part of the continent, since it was among the first objects which struck the attention of Columbus.[2]

Boas, and others, our knowledge of the territorial limits of this linguistic family has been greatly extended.   The most southern outposts of the family, the Tillamook and Nestucca, were established on the coast of Oregon, about 50 miles to the south of the Columbia, where they were separated from their kindred to the north by the Chinookan tribes.   Beginning on the north side of Shoalwater Bay, Salishan tribes held the entire northwestern part of Washington, including the whole of the Puget Sound region, except only the Macaw territory about Cape Flattery, and two insignificant spots, one near Port Townsend, the other on the Pacific coast to the south of Cape Flattery, which were occupied by Chimakuan tribes.   Eastern Vancouver Island to about midway of its length was also held by Salishan tribes, while the great bulk of their territory lay on the mainland opposite, and included much of the upper Columbia.   On the south they were hemmed in mainly by the Shahaptian tribes [Nez-percés, etc.].   Upon the east Salishan tribes dwelt to a little beyond the Arrow lakes and their feeder, one of the extreme north forks of the Columbia.   Upon the southeast Salishan tribes extended into Montana, including the upper drainage of the Columbia. They were met here in 1804 [read 1805] by Lewis and Clark.   On the northeast Salish territory extended to about the fifty-third parallel.   In the northwest it did not reach the Chilcat river.

" Within the territory thus indicated there is considerable diversity of customs and a greater diversity of language.   The language is split into a great number of dialects, many of which are doubtless mutually unintelligible."

The same authority gives the total Salish population in 1891 as 12,325 in British Columbia.   Most of the Salish in the United States are on reservations, to the number of about 5,500, including a dozen small tribes on the Yakama Reservation, amalgamated with the Clickatat (Shahaptian).   They are all distributed among the three Agencies, Colville, Puyallup, and Tulalip, in Washington, except a few Tillamooks at Grande Ronde Agency, in Oregon.

    [2] I have somewhere heard or read of the ingenious suggestion that the Indians

But wherever it may have begun, the practice is now universal among these nations. Soon after the birth of her child, the mother, anxious to procure for her infant the recommendation of a broad forehead, places it in the compressing-machine, where it is kept for ten or twelve months, though the females remain longer than the boys. The operation is so gradual that it is not attended with pain; but the impression is deep and permanent. The heads of the chil- (p. 132) dren, when they are released from the bandage, are not more than two inches thick about the upper edge of the forehead, and are still thinner above; nor with all her efforts can Nature ever restore the shape; the heads of grown persons being often in a straight line from the nose to the top of the forehead.

The hair of both sexes is parted at the top of the head, and thence falls loosely behind the ears, over the back and shoulders. They use combs, of which they are very fond, but contrive without the aid of them to keep their hair in very good order. The dress of the men consists in a small robe, reaching to the middle of the thigh, tied by a string across the breast, with its corners hanging loosely over their arms. These robes are generally composed of the skins of a small animal, which we have supposed to be the brown mungo.[3] They have, besides, those of the tiger-cat [lynx], deer, panther [cougar], bear, and elk, which last is principally used in war-parties. Sometimes they have a blanket woven with the fingers from the wool of their native sheep; occasionally a mat is thrown over them to keep off rain; but except this robe, they have no other article of clothing during winter or summer, so that every part of the body, but the back and shoulders, is exposed to view. They are very

flatten the head to facilitate labor in childbirth. But no Indian intellect would grasp the idea of heredity as a means of facilitating any future physiological processes.

[3] Meaning the mongos or mungoose, an old-world animal of the genus *Herpestes* and family *Viverridæ*, found in no part of America. The animal of whose skins these robes are made is the sewellel, *Haplodon rufus*, a rodent. See the natural history chapter.

fond of the dress of the whites, whom they call pashisheooks (cloth-men); whenever they can procure any clothes, they wear them in our manner; the only article, indeed, which we have not seen among them is the shoe.

The robe of the women is like that worn by the men, except that it does not reach below the waist. Those most esteemed are made of strips of sea-otter skin, which being twisted are interwoven with silk-grass, or the bark of the white cedar, in such a manner that the fur appears equally on both sides, so as to form a soft and warm covering. The skins of the raccoon or beaver are also employed in the same way, though on other occasions these skins are simply dressed in the hair and worn without further preparation. The garment which covers the body, from the waist as low as the (*p. 133*) knee before and the thigh behind, is the tissue already described, and is made either of bruised bark of white cedar, of twisted cords of silk-grass, or of flags and rushes. Neither leggings nor moccasins are ever used, the mildness of the climate not requiring them as a security from the weather, and their being so much in the water rendering them an incumbrance. The only covering for the head is a hat made of bear-grass and the bark of cedar, interwoven in a conic form, with a knob of the same shape at the top; it has no brim, but is held on the head by a string passing under the chin, and tied to a small rim inside of the hat. The colors are generally black and white only, and these are made into squares, triangles, and sometimes rude figures of canoes and seamen harpooning whales. This is all the usual dress of females; but if the weather be unusually severe, they add a vest formed of skins like the robe, tied behind, without any shoulder-straps to keep it up. As this vest covers the body from the armpits to the waist, it conceals the breasts, but on all other occasions these are suffered to remain loose and exposed, and present, in old women especially, a most disgusting appearance.

Sometimes, though not often, they mark their skins by puncturing and introducing some colored matter; this orna-

ment is chiefly confined to the women, who imprint on their
legs and arms circular or parallel dots.   On the arm of one
of the squaws we read the name of J. Bowman, apparently a
trader who visited the mouth of the Columbia.   The favorite decorations, however, of both sexes are common coarse
blue or white beads, which are folded very tightly round
their wrists and ankles, to the width of three or four inches,
and worn in large loose rolls round the neck, or in the shape
of ear-rings, or hanging from the nose; which last mode is
peculiar to the men.   There is also a species of wampum
very much in use, which seems to be worn in its natural
form without any preparation.   Its shape is a cone, somewhat curved, about the size of a raven's quill at the base,
and ta-(*p. 134*) pering to a point, its whole length being from
one to 2½ inches, and white, smooth, hard, and thin.[4]   A
small thread is passed through it, and the wampum is either
suspended from the nose, or passed through the cartilage
horizontally, thus forming a ring, from which other ornaments hang.   This wampum is employed in the same way as
the beads, but is the favorite decoration for the noses of the
men.   The men also use collars made of bears' claws, the
women and children those of elks' tusks, and both sexes are
adorned with bracelets of copper, iron, or brass, in various
forms.

Yet all these decorations are unavailing to conceal the
deformities of nature and the extravagance of fashion; nor
have we seen any more disgusting object than a Chinnook
or Clatsop beauty in full attire.   Their broad, flat foreheads,
their falling breasts, their ill-shaped limbs, the awkwardness
of their positions, and the filth which intrudes through their
finery—all these render a Chinnook or Clatsop beauty, in
full attire, one of the most disgusting objects in nature.
Fortunately this circumstance conspired with the low diet
and laborious exercise of our men to protect them from the
persevering gallantry of the fair sex, whose kindness always

---

[4] This wampum appears to be a species of tooth-shell, belonging to *Dentalium*
or a related genus.

exceeded the ordinary courtesies of hospitality. Among these people, as indeed among all Indians, the prostitution of unmarried women is so far from being considered criminal or improper, that the females themselves solicit the favors of the other sex, with the entire approbation of their friends and connections. Her person [5] is, in fact, often the only property of a young female, and is therefore the medium of trade, the return for presents, and the reward for services. In most cases, however, the female is so much at the disposal of her husband or parent that she is farmed out for hire. The Chinnook woman who brought her six female relations to our camp had regular prices, proportioned to the beauty of each female; and among all the tribes a man will lend his wife or daughter for a fish-hook or a strand of beads. To decline an offer of this sort is, indeed, to disparage the charms of the (*p. 135*) lady, and therefore gives such offense that, though we had occasionally to treat the Indians with rigor, nothing seemed to irritate both sexes more than our refusal to accept the favors of the females.   On one occasion we were amused by a Clatsop, who having been cured of some disorder by our medical skill, brought his sister as a reward for our kindness.   The young lady was quite anxious to join in this expression of her brother's gratitude, and mortified that we did not avail ourselves of it; she could not be prevailed on to leave the fort, but remained with Chaboneau's wife, in the next room to ours, for two or three days, declining all the solicitations of the men, till, finding at last that we did not relent, she went away, regretting that her brother's obligations were unpaid.

The little intercourse which the men have had with these women is, however, sufficient to apprise us of the prevalence of venereal disease, with which one or two of the party have

---

[5] A certain Parisian demimonder, summoned as witness in a suit at law, was harried by the opposing counsel, with the view of disconcerting her, and required to swear to her " state," *i.e.*, occupation or profession.   With charming innocence she replied : " L'état, c'est moi ! "   The Grand Monarch was less felicitous when he made that remark.

been so much afflicted as to render salivation necessary. The infection in these cases was communicated by the Chinnook women. The others do not appear to be afflicted with it to any extent; indeed, notwithstanding this disorder is certainly known to the Indians on the Columbia, the number of infected persons is very inconsiderable. The existence of such a disorder is very easily detected, particularly in the men, in their open style of dress; yet in the whole route down the Columbia, we have not seen more than two or three cases of gonorrhœa, and about double that number of lues venerea [syphilis]. There do not seem to be any simples which are used as specifics in this disorder, nor is any complete cure ever effected. When once a patient is seized, the disorder ends with life only; though from the simplicity of their diet and the use of certain vegetables, they support it for many years with but little inconvenience, and even enjoy tolerable health; yet their life is always abridged by decrepitude or premature old age. The Indians who are mostly successful in treating this (*p. 136*) disorder are the Chippeways. Their specifics are the root of the lobelia [*Lobelia inflata*], and that of a species of sumac [*Rhus*], common to the United States, the neighborhood of the Rocky mountains, and the countries westward, which is readily distinguished by being the smallest of its kind, and by its winged rib or common footstalk, supporting leaves oppositely pinnate. Decoctions of these roots are used very freely, without any limitation, and are said to soften the violence of the lues, and even to be sovereign in the cure of gonorrhea.

The Clatsops and other nations at the mouth of the Columbia have visited us with great freedom, and we have endeavored to cultivate their intimacy, as well for the purpose of acquiring information as to leave behind us impressions favorable to our country. Having acquired much of their language, we are enabled with the assistance of gestures to hold conversations with great ease. We find them inquisitive and loquacious, with understandings by no means deficient in acuteness, and with very retentive memories. Though fond of feasts, and generally cheerful, they are never gay. Everything they see excites their attention and inquiries; but having been accustomed to see whites, nothing appeared to give them more astonishment than the airgun. To all our inquiries they answer with great intelligence, and the conversation rarely slackens, since there is a constant discussion of events, trade, and politics, in the little but active circle of Killamucks, Clatsops, Cathlamahs, Wahkiacums, and Chinnooks. Among themselves the conversation generally turns on the subjects of trade, or smoking, or eating, or connection with females; before whom this last is spoken of with a familiarity which would be in the highest degree indecent, if custom had not rendered it inoffensive.

The treatment of women is often considered as the standard by which the moral qualities of savages are to be (*p. 137*) estimated. Our own observation, however, induces us to think that the importance of the female in savage life has no necessary relation to the virtues of the men, but is regulated wholly by their capacity to be useful. The Indians whose treatment of the females is mildest, and who pay most deference to their opinions, are by no means the most distinguished for their virtues ; nor is this deference attended by any increase of attachment, since they are equally willing with the most brutal husband to prostitute their wives to strangers. On the other hand, the tribes among whom the women are very much debased possess the loftiest sense of honor, the greatest liberality, and all the good qualities of which their situation demands the exercise. Where the women can aid in procuring subsistence for the tribe, they are treated with more equality, and their importance is proportioned to the share which they take in that labor; while, in countries where subsistence is chiefly procured by the exertions of the men, the women are considered and treated as burdens. Thus, among the Clatsops and Chinnooks, who live upon fish and roots, which the women are equally expert

with the men in procuring, the former have a rank and influence very rarely found among Indians. The females are
permitted to speak freely before the men, to whom indeed
they sometimes address themselves in a tone of authority.
On many subjects their judgments and opinions are respected,
and in matters of trade their advice is generally asked and
pursued. The labors of the family, too, are shared almost
equally. The men collect wood and make fires, assist in
cleansing the fish, and make houses, canoes, and wooden
utensils ; and whenever strangers are to be entertained, or a
great feast prepared, the meats are cooked and served up by
the men. The peculiar province of the female is to collect
roots, and to manufacture the various articles which are
formed of rushes, flags, cedar-bark, and bear-grass ; but the
management of the canoes, and many of (*p. 138*) the occupations which elsewhere devolve wholly on the female, are
here common to both sexes.

The observation with regard to the importance of females
applies with equal force to the treatment of old men.
Among tribes who subsist by hunting, the labors of the
chase, and the wandering existence to which that occupation
condemns them, necessarily throw the burden of procuring
provisions on the active young men. As soon, therefore, as
a man is unable to pursue the chase, he begins to withdraw
something from the precarious supplies of the tribe. Still,
however, his counsels may compensate his want of activity ;
but in the next stage of infirmity, when he can no longer
travel from camp to camp, as the tribe roams about for subsistence, he is then found to be a heavy burden. In this
situation he is abandoned among the Sioux, the Assiniboins,
and the hunting tribes on the Missouri. As they are setting
out for some new excursion, where the old man is unable to
follow, his children or nearest relations place before him a
piece of meat and some water ; tell him that he has lived
long enough ; that it is now time for him to go home to his
relations, who could take better care of him than his friends
on earth ; and leave him, without remorse, to perish when

his little supply is exhausted. The same custom is said to prevail among the Minnetarees, Ahnahawas, and Ricaras, when they are attended by old men on their hunting-excursions. Yet in their villages we saw no want of kindness to old men. On the contrary, probably because in villages the means of more abundant subsistence renders such cruelty unnecessary, the old people appeared to be treated with attention, and some of their feasts, particularly the buffalo-dances, were intended chiefly as a contribution for the old and infirm.

The dispositions of these people seem mild and inoffensive, and they have uniformly behaved to us with great friendship. They are addicted to begging and pilfering small articles, when it can be done without danger of detection, but do not (*p. 139*) rob wantonly, nor to any large amount. Some of them having purloined some of our meat, which the hunters had been obliged to leave in the woods, they voluntarily brought some dogs a few days after, by way of compensation. Our force and great superiority in the use of firearms enable us always to command; and such is the friendly deportment of these people, that the men have been accustomed to treat them with the greatest confidence. It is, therefore, with difficulty that we can impress on our men a conviction of the necessity of being always on guard, since we are perfectly acquainted with the treacherous character of Indians in general. We are always prepared for an attack, and uniformly exclude all large parties of Indians from the fort.

Their large houses usually contain several families, consisting of the parents, their sons and daughters-in-law, and grandchildren, among whom the provisions are common, and whose harmony is scarcely ever interrupted by disputes. Although polygamy is permitted by their customs, very few have more than a single wife; she is brought immediately after marriage into the husband's family, where she resides until increasing numbers oblige them to seek another house. In this state the old man is not considered as the head of

the family, since the active duties, as well as the respon-
sibility, fall on some of the younger members. As these
families gradually expand into bands or tribes or nations,
the paternal authority is represented by the chief of each
association. This chieftain, however, is not hereditary;
his ability to render service to his neighbors, with the
popularity which follows it, is at once the foundation
and the measure of his authority, the exercise of which
does not extend beyond a reprimand for some improper
action.

The harmony of their private life is secured by their igno-
rance of spirituous liquors, the earliest and most dreadful
present [except syphilis] which civilization has given to the
other natives of the continent. Although they have had so
much intercourse with whites, they do not appear to possess
any (*p. 140*) knowledge of those dangerous luxuries; at
least they have never inquired after them, which they probably would have done if once liquors had been introduced
among them. Indeed, we have not observed any liquor of
intoxicating quality among these or any Indians west of the
Rocky mountains, the universal beverage being pure water.
They, however, sometimes almost intoxicate themselves by
smoking tobacco, of which they are excessively fond, and
the pleasures of which they prolong as much as possible, by
retaining vast quantities at a time, till after circulating
through the lungs and stomach it issues in volumes from
the mouth and nostrils.

But the natural vice of all these people is an attachment
for games of hazard, which they pursue with a strange and
ruinous avidity. The games are of two kinds. In the first,
one of the company assumes the office of banker and plays
against the rest. He takes a small stone, about the size of
a bean, which he shifts from one hand to the other with
great dexterity, repeating at the same time a song adapted
to the game, and which serves to divert the attention of the
company ; till, having agreed on the stake, he holds out his
hands, and the antagonist wins or loses as he succeeds or

fails at guessing in which hand is the stone.[6] After the banker has lost his money, or whenever he is tired, the stone is transferred to another, who in turn challenges the rest of the company. The other game is something like the play of ninepins.[7] Two pins are placed on the floor, about the distance of a foot from each other, and a small hole is made behind them. The players then go about ten feet from the hole, into which they try to roll a small piece resembling the men used at draughts; if they succeed in putting it into the hole they win the stake; if the piece rolls between the pins, but does not go into the hole, nothing is won or lost; but the wager is wholly lost if the checker rolls outside of the pins. Entire days are wasted at these games, which are often continued through the night round the blaze of the fires, till the last article of clothing or even the last blue bead is won from the desperate adventurer.

(*p. 141*) In traffic they are keen, acute, and intelligent, and they employ in all their bargains a dexterity and finesse which, if it be not learnt from their foreign visitors, may show how nearly the cunning of savages is allied to the little arts of more civilized trade. They begin by asking double or treble the value of their merchandise, and lower the demand in proportion to the ardor or experience in trade of the purchaser; if he expresses any anxiety, the smallest article, perhaps a handful of roots, will furnish a whole morning's negotiation. Being naturally suspicious, they of course conceive that we are pursuing the same system. They, therefore, invariably refuse the first offer, however high, fearful that they or we have mistaken the value of the merchandise, and cautiously wait to draw us on to larger offers. In this way, after rejecting the most extravagant prices which we have offered merely for experiment, they

---

[6] A similar game of equal simplicity, a sort of odd-or-even, is of great antiquity, being figured on some classic monuments which have come down to us. The corresponding games of our own are thimble-rigging and three-card monte.

[7] Perhaps rather to be compared to our games of pool, the object being to put a rolling object into a certain hole, not to knock down pins.

have afterward importuned us for a tenth part of what they had before refused. In this respect, they differ from almost all Indians, who will generally exchange in a thoughtless moment the most valuable article they possess for any bauble which happens to please their fancy.

These habits of cunning, or prudence, have been formed or increased by their being engaged in a large part of the commerce of the Columbia ; of that trade, however, the great emporium is the falls, where all the neighboring nations assemble. The inhabitants of the Columbian plains,[8] after having passed the winter near the mountains, come down as soon as the snow has left the valleys, and are occupied in collecting and drying roots till about the month of May. They then crowd to the river, and fixing themselves on its north side, to avoid the incursions of the Snake Indians, continue fishing till about the first of September, when the salmon are no longer fit for use. They then bury their fish and return to the plains, where they remain to gather quamash till the snow obliges them to desist. They come back to the Columbia, and taking their store of fish, (*p. 142*) retire to the foot of the mountains and along the creeks, which supply timber for houses, passing the winter in hunting deer or elk which, with the aid of their fish, enables them to subsist till in the spring they resume the circle of their employments. During their residence on the river, from May to September, or rather before they begin the regular fishery, they go down to the falls, carrying with them skins, mats, silk-grass, rushes, and chappelell [*sic*] bread. They are here overtaken by the Chopunnish and other tribes of the Rocky mountains, who descend the Kooskooskee and Lewis' river for the purpose of selling bear-grass, horses, quamash, and a few skins which they have obtained by hunting, or in exchange for horses with the

---

[8] By this we are to understand the country along the Columbia east of the Cascade range, which, though flat, is higher than that between the Cascade and Coast ranges ; the latter being the Columbia *valley* of Lewis and Clark (otherwise Wappatoo valley, Clark H 110, and map).

Tushepaws. At the falls, they find the Chilluckittequaws, Eneeshurs, Echeloots, and Skilloots, which last serve as intermediate traders or carriers between the inhabitants above and below. These tribes prepare pounded fish for the market, and the nations below bring wappatoo-roots, the fish of the seacoast, berries, and a variety of trinkets and small articles which they have procured from the whites.

The trade then begins. The Chopunnish and Indians of the Rocky mountains exchange the articles which they have brought for wappatoo, pounded fish, and beads. The Indians of the plains, being their own fishermen, take only wappatoo, horses, beads, and other articles procured from Europeans. The Indians, however, from Lewis' river to the falls, consume as food or fuel all the fish which they take ; so that the whole stock for exportation is prepared by the nations between the Towahnahiooks and the falls, which amounts, as nearly as we could estimate, to about 30,000 [pounds'] weight, chiefly of salmon, above the quantity which they use themselves or barter with the more eastern Indians. This is now carried down the river by the Indians at the falls, and is consumed among the nations at the mouth of the Columbia, who in return give the fish of the seacoast, and the articles which they obtain from the whites. The neigh- (*p. 143*) boring people catch large quantities of salmon and dry them, but they do not understand or practice the art of drying and pounding fish in the manner used at the falls ; and being very fond of it, are forced to purchase it at high prices. This article, indeed, and the wappatoo, form the principal objects of trade with the people of our immediate vicinity. The traffic is wholly carried on by water; there are no roads or paths through the country, except across the portages which connect the creeks.

But the circumstance which forms the soul of this trade is the visit of the whites. These arrive generally about the month of April, and either remain until October, or return at that time ; during which time, having no establishment on shore, they anchor on the north side of the bay, at the

place already described, which is a spacious and commodi-
ous harbor, perfectly secure from all except the south and
southeast winds; and as they leave it before winter, they do
not suffer from these winds, which, during that season,
are the most usual and the most violent.   This situation is
recommended by its neighborhood to fresh water and wood,
as well as to excellent timber and repairs.   Here they are
immediately visited by the tribes along the seacoast, by the
Cathlamahs, and lastly by the Skilloots, that numerous and
active people who skirt the river between the marshy islands
and the grand rapids, as well as the Coweliskees, and who
carry down the fish prepared by their immediate neighbors
the Chilluckittequaws, Eneeshurs, and Echeeloots, residing
from the grand rapids to the falls, as well as all the other
articles which they have procured in barter at the market
in May.   The accumulated trade of the Columbia now consists of dressed and undressed skins of elk, sea-otter, common
otter, beaver, common fox, spuck, and tiger-cat.   The articles
of less importance are a small quantity of dried and pounded
salmon, biscuits made of chapelell [*sic*] roots, and some of
the manufactures of the neighborhood.   In return they
receive (*p. 144*) guns, principally old British or American
muskets, powder, ball, and shot, copper and brass kettles,
brass tea-kettles and coffee-pots, blankets of from two to
three points, coarse scarlet and blue cloth, plates and
strips of sheet copper and brass, large brass wire, knives,
tobacco, fish-hooks, buttons, and a considerable quantity of
sailors' hats, trousers, coats, and shirts.   But as we have had
occasion to remark more than once, the objects of foreign
trade most desired are common cheap blue or white beads,
of about 50 or 70 to the pennyweight, which are strung on
strands a fathom in length, and sold by the yard, or the
length of both arms; of these, blue beads, which are called
tia commashuck [chief beads], hold the first rank in their
ideas of relative value; the most inferior kinds are esteemed
beyond the finest wampum, and are temptations which can
always seduce them to part with their most valuable effects.

Indeed, if the example of civilized life did not completely vindicate their choice, we might wonder at their infatuated attachment to a bauble in itself so worthless. Yet these beads are, perhaps, quite as reasonable objects of research as the precious metals, since they are at once beautiful ornaments for the person, and the great circulating medium of trade with all the nations on the Columbia.

Those strangers who visit the Columbia for the purpose of trade or hunting, must be either English or American. The Indians inform us that they speak the same language as we do, and indeed the few words which the Indians have learned from the sailors, such as musket, powder, shot, knife, file, heave the lead, damned rascal, and other phrases [9] of that description, evidently show that the visitors speak the English language. But as the greater part of them annually arrive in April, and either remain till autumn, or revisit them at that time (which we could not clearly understand), the trade cannot be direct from either England or the United States, since the ships could not return thither during the remain- (*p. 145*) der of the year. When the Indians are asked where these traders go on leaving the Columbia, they always point to the southwest, whence we presume that they do not belong to any establishment on Nootka Sound. They do, however, mention a trader by the name of Moore, who sometimes touches at this place, who, last time he came, had on board three cows, and when he left them continued along the northwest coast; which renders it probable that there may be a settlement of whites in that direction. The names and description of all the persons who visit them in the spring and autumn are remembered with great accuracy, and we took down, exactly as they were pronounced, the following list: The favorite trader is Mr. Haley, who visits them in a vessel with three masts, and continues some time.

[9] The codices extend this choice vocabulary beyond the point where Mr. Biddle halted prudently, with consignments to perdition, aspersions on maternal ancestry, and "other phrases" which are happily or unhappily too familiar to require citation.

The others are : Youens, who comes also in a three-masted vessel, and is a trader; Tallamon, in a three-masted vessel, but is not a trader; Callalamet, in a ship of the same size; he is a trader and they say has a wooden leg; Swipton, three-masted vessel, trader; Moore, four-masted vessel, trader; Mackey, three-masted vessel, trader; Washington, three-masted vessel, trader; Mesship, three-masted vessel, trader; Davidson, three-masted vessel; does not trade, but hunts elk; Jackson, three-masted vessel, trader; Bolch, three-masted vessel, trader; Skelley, also a trader, in a vessel with three masts, but he has been gone for some years. He had only one eye.

It might be difficult to adjust the balance of the advantages or dangers of this trade to the nations of the Columbia, against the sale of their furs, and the acquisition of a few bad guns and household utensils.

The nations near the mouth of the Columbia enjoy great tranquillity, none of the tribes being engaged in war. Not (*p. 146*) long since, however, there was a war on the coast to the southwest, in which the Killamucks took several prisoners. These, as far as we could perceive, were treated very well, and though nominally slaves, yet were adopted into the families of their masters, and the young ones placed on the same footing with the children of the purchaser.

January 22d to March 22d, 1806. The month of February and the greater part of March were passed in the same manner. Every day parties, as large as we could spare them from our other occupations, were sent out to hunt, and we were thus enabled to command some days' provision in advance. It consisted chiefly of deer and elk; the first is very lean, and the flesh by no means as good as that of the elk, which, though poor, is getting better; it is, indeed, our chief dependence.[10] At this time of the year it is in much

---

[10] " I made a calculation of the number of elk and deer killed by the party from the 1st of Dec., 1805 to the 20th March, 1806, which gave 131 elk and 20 deer," Gass, p. 189, Mar. 20th.

better order on the prairies near the point [Adams], where
the elk feed on grass and rushes, considerable quantities of
which are yet green, than in the woody country up the
Netul. There they subsist on huckleberry bushes and ferns,
but chiefly on an evergreen called shallun [salal, *Gaultheria
shallon*], resembling the laurel, which abounds through all the
timbered lands, particularly along the broken sides of hills.
Toward the latter end of the month, however, they left the
prairies near Point Adams and retired back to the hills; but
fortunately, at the same time, sturgeons [*Acipenser transmontanus*] and anchovies [eulachon, *Thaleichthys pacificus*]
began to appear, and afforded us a delightful variety of food.
In the meantime the party on the seacoast supplied us with
salt; but though the kettles were kept boiling all day and
night, the salt was made slowly; nor was it till the middle
of this month [February], that we succeeded in procuring 20
gallons, of which 12 were put in kegs for our journey as far
as the deposits on the Missouri.

The neighboring tribes continued to visit us for the purpose of trading or merely to smoke with us. But on the
21st [of February] a Chinnook chief, whom we had never
seen, came over with 25 of his men. His name was Tahcum,
a man of about 50 years of age, with a larger figure and a
(*p. 147*) better carriage than most of his nation. We received
him with the usual ceremonies, gave the party something to
eat, smoked most copiously with them all, and presented the
chief with a small medal. They were all satisfied with their
treatment; and though we were willing to show the chief
every civility, could not dispense with our rule of not suffering so many strangers to sleep in the fort. They therefore
left us at sunset. On the 24th, Comowool, who is by far
the most friendly and decent savage we have seen in this
neighborhood, came with a large party of Clatsops, bringing,
among other articles, sturgeon and a small fish [the eulachon
or candle-fish, *Thaleichthys pacificus*] which has just begun,
within a day or two past, to make its appearance in the
Columbia.

From this time, as the elk became scarce and lean, we made use of these fish whenever we could catch them or purchase them from the Indians. But as we were too poor to indulge very largely in these luxuries, the diet was by no means pleasant, and to the sick, especially, was unwholesome. On the 15th of March we were visited by Delashilwilt, the Chinnook chief, and his wife, accompanied by the same six damsels, who in the autumn had camped near us, on the other side of the bay, and whose favors had been so troublesome to several of the men. They formed a camp close to the fort, and began to renew their addresses very assiduously; but we warned the men of the dangers of intercourse with this frail society, and they cautiously abstained from connection with them.

During the greater part of this month [March] five or six of the men were sick; indeed, we have not had so many complaining since we left Wood river. The general complaint is a bad cold and fever, something in the nature of an influenza, which, joined with a few cases of venereal, and accidental injuries, completes our invalid corps. These disorders may chiefly be imputed to the nature of the climate.

CHAPTER XXIV.

FORT CLATSOP IN FEBRUARY AND MARCH.

WEDNESDAY, Jan. 22d, 1806.[1] The party sent for the meat this morning returned with it in the evening. The elk were poor, and the meat was very inferior. R. Fields remained out with the other hunters, Shannon and Labiche. Our supply of salt is exhausted. We have no word from the other two hunting-parties, who are out below, in the direction of Point Adams and the prairies. Some rain fell at intervals.

Thursday, Jan. 23d. We dispatched Howard and Werner to the camp of the salt-makers for a supply of salt. The men of the garrison are busily employed in dressing elk-skins for clothing. They have great difficulty, from the want of brains with which to soften the skins. We have no soap to supply this deficiency, nor can we procure ashes to make lye. None of the pines we use for fuel affords ashes; singular as it may seem, the green wood is consumed without a residuum.

Friday, Jan. 24th. Drewyer and Lepage returned this morning with Comowool and six Clatsops, in a large canoe.

[1] Up to this point, the last formal entry in the Biddle text is of date Tuesday, Jan. 21st, 1806. This stands in Lewis J 34 as "Wednesday," interlined correctly "Tuesday." It stands in Clark I 131 as "Thursday, 21st," not corrected. Lewis was one day of the week ahead, and Clark two days, on the 21st of January. The Biddle text disposes of Jan. 22d–Mar. 22d in the foregoing two pages, then brings in the natural history chapter, and resumes the narrative with Mar. 23d, in the next chapter. I think it important, with the original manuscripts before me, to intercalate the regular diary for this period, even though certain incidents be consequently restated. Most of the journals of Lewis and of Clark, during the rest of their stay at Fort Clatsop, are occupied with natural history. All this of course I omit, merely giving a diary in brief. This I do, in language exactly of neither of the explorers, but digesting their text, as the original editor did. Of the two codices before me, Clark I and Lewis J, I follow the latter.

They brought two deer, the flesh of three elk, and one elk-skin, having given the flesh of another elk, and three elk-skins, to the Indians for their assistance in transporting the rest of the meat to the fort. The game had been killed near Point Adams, and the Indians carried it on their backs about six miles before they reached a place where the waves permitted it to be shipped on board the canoe. These Indians remained with us all day. They saw Drewyer shoot some of the elk, and formed an exalted though not exaggerated opinion of his skill as a marksman, as well as of the superiority of our rifles over their poor guns. This may be of service to us in preventing any acts of hostility they may have meditated. Our air-gun simply astonishes them; they cannot understand how it is discharged so often without reloading, and fancy it is great medicine—by which they mean anything that is incomprehensible to them.

Saturday, Jan. 25th. Comowool and the Clatsops departed early this morning. Colter returned and reported that Willard, with whom he had been, had continued to hunt from Point Adams toward the salt-makers, and that they had together killed only those two deer which were brought in yesterday. In the evening Collins came from the salt-works and reported that about a bushel of salt had been made; he also said that he, with two others, had hunted from the salt-camp for five days without killing anything, and had been obliged to subsist on some whale-flesh, procured from the natives.

Sunday, Jan. 26th. Werner and Howard, who were sent for salt on the 23d, have not yet returned, and we are apprehensive lest they have missed their way. Neither of them is a very good backwoodsman, and in this heavily timbered pine country, where the weather is constantly cloudy, it is difficult even for one skilled in woodcraft to keep his courses. We ordered Collins to rejoin the salt-workers early next morning, and gave him some small articles with which to purchase provisions from the Indians in the event of being unsuccessful in the chase.

Monday, Jan. 27th.   Collins set out for the salt-works. Shannon returned, and reported that his party had killed ten elk.   He had left Labiche and R. Fields with those elk, two of which he informed us were about nine miles distant, near the top of a mountain.   The route by which they would have to be brought in was at least five miles through a country almost inaccessible on account of windfalls and sink-holes, now hidden under the snow.   We therefore con-cluded to relinquish those two elk for the present, and ordered every man that could be spared from the fort to go early in the morning in search of the other eight, which lay at no great distance from the Netul river, on which we are. Goodrich has recovered from the lues veneris which he con-tracted from a Chinnook damsel ; he was cured by the use of mercury, as Gibson was last winter at Fort Mandan.

Tuesday, Jan. 28th.   Drewyer and Lepage set out this morning to hunt.   About noon Howard and Werner re-turned from the salt-works with a supply of salt ; the bad weather and worse road had caused their delay.   They informed us that the salt-makers were very short of provi-sions, having killed only two deer in the last six days, and that there were no elk in their vicinity.   The party that was sent this morning up the Netul for the eight elk returned in the evening, bringing three only.   They had all been killed just before a fall of snow, which so altered the face of the country that even the hunters who had killed them could not find their game again.

Wednesday, Jan. 29th.   Nothing notable occurred to-day.   Our fare is lean elk boiled, with very little salt.   The whale-blubber we have used sparingly, but that is now ex-hausted.   On such food we do not feel strong, but enjoy fair health—a keen appetite answers well instead of sauces and other luxuries, and meal-time is always interesting. Sometimes we find ourselves asking the cook when break-fast or dinner will be ready.

Thursday, Jan. 30th.   We are agreeably disappointed in the character of our fuel.   Being entirely green pine, we supposed it would burn badly; but we find that when split it burns very well.

Friday, Jan. 31st.   Sent a party of eight men up the Netul to renew the search for the lost elk, and to hunt for others to kill.   They had gone but few miles before they found the river so obstructed by ice that they were obliged to return.   Joseph Fields, who arrived this evening, said that he had been hunting with Gibson and Willard for the last five days, to procure some meat for themselves and for the other salt-makers.   He had, however, been unsuccessful until yesterday, when he was so fortunate as to kill two elk, about six miles from the fort and eight from the salt-works. He had left Gibson and Willard to dry the meat, and had come for help to carry it to the salt-works.   For this purpose we ordered four men to accompany him next morning. We discovered that M'Neal had the pox, and gave him mercury.   We also discovered that though the days of the month for January are right in our journal, the days of the week are wrong, Captain Lewis being one day out and Captain Clark two.   This error we now correct.

Saturday, February 1st, 1806.   The party of four men set out with J. Fields, as ordered yesterday.   Sergeant Gass, with a party of five, again went up the Netul in search of the elk killed several days ago, which had not been found in consequence of the snow.

We opened and examined all our ammunition, which had been sealed in leaden canisters.   We found that we had 27 of the best rifle-powder, four of common rifle, three of glazed, and one of musket, perfectly dry and in as good order as when first put in the canisters, though the whole of it, from various accidents, has been altogether some hours under water.   The canisters contain four pounds each of powder, and eight pounds of lead.   Had it not been for that happy expedient which we devised, of securing the powder by means of the lead, we should not now have a dry charge left.   Three of the canisters, which had been accidentally bruised and cracked, one which was carelessly stopped, and a fifth that had been penetrated by a nail, were damaged ; these we gave to the men to dry. But even exclusive of these five, we have a stock of powder amply sufficient to last us during our homeward journey. We are always careful to put a portion of ammunition in each canoe, so that, should one or more of these be lost, we should not be entirely out of ammunition. This is our only resource for subsistance and self-defense on a journey of over 3,000 miles we have to make through a country inhabited only by savages.

Sunday, February 2d. There is no occurrence to note to-day. All are pleased that one month of the dreary time that separates us from home and friends, and binds us to Fort Clatsop, has now elapsed.

Monday, February 3d. About three o'clock Drewyer and Lepage returned, the former having killed seven elk in the point below us, several miles distant, but approachable within less than a mile with canoes by means of a small creek² which discharges into the bay on this side of the Clatsop village. We ordered Sergeant Pryor to go in quest of the meat. The wind was so high that the party were unable to set out until a little before sunset. At ten o'clock they returned exceedingly cold, and reported that they could not make land on this side of the bay, or get into the creek, in consequence of an unusually low ebb-tide. We apprehend that the Clatsops, who know where the meat is, will rob us of some if not all of it. At half-past four Sergeant Gass returned with his party. They brought back with them the flesh of four other elk which the hunters had found, these being some of the ten which were killed up the Netul river the other day. Two of these having been recovered before, only four others are now missing. He had left R. Fields, Shannon, and Labiche to continue the hunt for those, making an appoint-

---

² Doubtless either Alder or Tansy creek, two small streams discharging into Meriwether bay, close together and near Tansy point, more than halfway from Fort Clatsop to Point Adams. The Skeppernawin is the much larger creek, which empties into the same bay, nearer the Fort, and would doubtless have been specified had it been meant.

ment to meet them next Friday. Late in the evening, the
four men who had been sent to assist the salt-makers in
transporting meat which the latter had killed, to their own
camp, also returned, and brought with them all the salt
which had been made—about a bushel. With only such
means as we have, we find it a tedious operation to boil the
sea-water, though we keep the fires going day and night.
We estimate that we shall require three bushels to supply us
on the journey hence to the deposit of the article which we
made on the Missouri.

Tuesday, February 4th. Observed meridian altitude of
the sun's upper limb with the sextant by direct observation.
The latitude deduced is 46° 10' 16" 3''' N. By means of several observations we found the error of the sextant to be
subtractive 0° 5' 45". [This observation is a very close one.]

Sergeant Pryor, with a party of five men, set out again in
quest of the elk which Drewyer had killed. Drewyer and
Lepage also went to continue their hunt in the same direction. The elk are in much better order in the point near the
prairies than they are in the woody country about us, or up
the Netul. In the prairies they feed on grass and rushes,
considerable quantities of which are still green and succu-
lent. In the woody country, their food is huckleberry
bushes, ferns, and an evergreen shrub [*Gaultheria shallon*]
which resembles the laurel in some measure. This last,
which constitutes the greater part of their food, grows abundantly all through the timbered country, particularly on the
hill-sides and other broken ground.

Wednesday, Feb. 5th. Late this evening one of the hunters whooped and fired his gun across the swamp of the
Netul opposite the fort, and we sent Sergeant Gass and a
party over there. The tide being in, they took advantage
of a little creek which makes up in that direction nearly to
the highlands, and on their way fortunately recovered our
Indian canoe, so long lost and lamented. The hunter
proved to be Reuben Fields, who reported that he had killed
six elk on the east side of the Netul, a little above us ; and

that yesterday he had heard Shannon and Labiche fire six
or seven shots after he had separated from them ; he therefore supposed that they had also secured some game.

Thursday, Feb. 6th. We sent Sergeants Gass and Ordway this morning with R. Fields and a party of men to
bring in the elk which Fields killed yesterday. Late in the
evening Sergeant Pryor returned with the flesh of only two
elk, and four skins, the Indians having purloined the balance
of the seven elk which Drewyer had killed the other day.

Friday, Feb. 7th. This evening Sergeant Ordway and
Wiser returned with a part of the meat which R. Fields had
killed. The balance of the party remained with Sergeant
Gass in order to bring the rest of the meat to the river at
the point agreed upon. There the canoe is to meet them
to-morrow morning. This evening we had what we called
an excellent supper. It consisted of a marrow-bone apiece
and a brisket of boiled elk that had an appearance of fat
about it. This, for Fort Clatsop, is living in high style.

Saturday, Feb. 8th. Sent Sergeant Ordway and two men
this morning to join the party with Sergeant Gass and bring
in the remainder of R. Fields' elk. In the evening they
returned with the flesh of five ; but one had become tainted
and unfit for use. Later Sergeant Pryor returned with Shannon and Labiche and his party down the Netul. They
brought with them the flesh of four elk which those two hunters had killed. We supped on tongues and marrow-bones.

Sunday, Feb. 9th. Collins and Wiser set out on a hunting-
excursion. They took our Indian canoe and passed the
Netul a little above us. In the evening Drewyer returned.
He had killed nothing but one beaver, though he saw a
black bear, the only individual of this species observed since
our arrival at this place. The Indians inform us that they
are abundant, but at this season hibernating in their dens.

Monday, Feb. 10th. Drewyer visited his traps to-day,
but caught no beaver. Collins and Wiser returned with no
elk. Willard arrived late from the salt-works ; he had cut his
knee badly with his tomahawk. He had killed four elk not

far from the salt-works, day before yesterday. These he had butchered, and taken a part of the meat to camp; but after the injury to his knee, being of no further use at the salt-works, he had returned. He informed us that Bratton was quite sick, and Gibson unable to sit up or walk without assistance; Willard had therefore come to the fort to request us to bring Gibson in. Colter returned this evening. We continue the operation of drying our meat.

Tuesday, Feb. 11th. This morning Sergeant Gass, R. Fields, and Thompson passed the Netul opposite us on a hunting-excursion. We sent Sergeant Pryor with a party of four men to bring Gibson to the fort. We also detailed Colter and Wiser to continue the business at the salt-works with J. Fields. As Bratton was sick we desired him to return to the fort if he thought proper; but in the event of his not doing so, Wiser was directed to return.

Wednesday, Feb. 12th. We were visited by a Clatsop who brought three dogs as remuneration for the elk which he and some of his people had stolen from us a few days ago, and we suffered him to remain in the fort all night.

Thursday, Feb. 13th. The Clatsops left us this morning at 11 a. m. Not anything happened to note. Yesterday we finished the operation of drying our meat, and think we now have enough to last us this month. The Indians inform us that we shall have a great abundance of a small fish [eulachon, *Thaleichthys pacificus*] in March, which from their description must be the herring. These people also tell us that one More [Moore?], who sometimes touches at this place and trades with the natives, had three cows aboard his vessel, and that when he left them he continued his course along the northwest coast. We think this strong circumstantial evidence that there is a settlement of white persons on Nootka Sound, or at some point to the N.W. of us on the coast.

Friday, Feb. 14th. We are very uneasy about our sick men at the salt-works. Sergeant Pryor and party have not returned, nor can we conceive what causes their delay.

Drewyer visited his traps, and caught a fine, fat beaver, on which we feasted.

On the 11th inst. Captain Clark completed a map of the country through which we have passed from Fort Mandan to this place. On this map, the Missouri, Jefferson's river, the S.E. branch of the Columbia, the Kooskooskee, and the Columbia from the entrance of the S.E. branch (Lewis' river), as well as a part of Flathead (Clark's) river and our track across the Rocky [and Bitter-root] mountains, are laid down by celestial observation and survey. The rivers are also connected (as we observed them at their sources) with other rivers agreeably to the information of the natives, and to the most probable conjecture arising from their respective capacities and the relative positions of their respective mouths, which last data have with few exceptions been established by celestial observations. We now find that we have discovered the most practicable and navigable passage across the continent of North America. It is that which we traveled, with the exception of that part of our route from the entrance of Dearborn's river into the Missouri to the entrance of Traveler's-rest creek into the Flathead (Clark's) river. The distance between these two points would be traversed more advantageously by land, as the navigation of the Missouri above Dearborn's river is laborious and 420 miles in length. No advantage is gained by this, as the route which we were compelled to travel by land from the source of Jefferson's river to the entrance of Traveler's-rest creek is 220 miles ; being further by 500 miles than the distance from the entrance of Dearborn's river to the last mentioned, and a much worse route, also, if Indian information is to be relied upon. According to the same information, the Flathead (Clark's) river, like the S.E. branch (Lewis') of the Columbia, which heads with Jefferson and Madison rivers, cannot be navigated through the Rocky mountains, in consequence of falls and rapids. In confirmation of this, we discovered that there were no salmon in Flathead river, the contrary being the case in the S.E. branch of the Columbia, although

this is not navigable.   The Indians inform us further that the
Flathead river runs in the direction of the Rocky mountains
for a great distance to the north before it discharges into
the Columbia river; which last, according to the same information, is obstructed, from the entrance of the S.E. fork to
that of Clark's river, by a great number of difficult and dangerous rapids.   Considering, therefore, the danger and difficulty attending the navigation of the Columbia in this part
of its course, as well as the circuitous and distant route
formed by itself and Clark's river, we conceive that, even
admitting Clark's river to be as navigable as the Columbia
river below the entrance of Clark's—which is contrary to our
information—the track by land over the Rocky mountains,
usually traveled by the natives from the entrance of Traveller's-rest creek to the forks of the Kooskooskee, is preferable ; this track being a distance of 184 miles.   The inference
therefore deduced from those premises is, that the best and
most practicable route across the continent is by way of the
Missouri to the entrance of Dearborn's river, or near that
point; thence to Flathead (Clark's) river at the entrance
of Traveler's-rest creek; thence up this creek to its forks ;
whence you pursue a range of mountains which divides the
waters of the two forks of this creek, and which range, still
pursuing its westerly course, divides the waters of two main
forks of the Kooskooskee river to their junction ; thence
you descend this river by water to the S.E. branch of the
Columbia, thence down this S.E. branch to the Columbia,
and down this last to the Pacific Ocean.[3]

Saturday, Feb. 15th.   Drewyer and Whitehouse set out

[3] A masterly and consummate piece of geography, under the circumstances—
one which the best modern geographer would find it hard to improve upon in its
main features.   In their dismal huts at Fort Clatsop, living like muskrats in a
hole, but unlike these animals, half-starved, the wonderful explorers conquered
the continent.   The land route indicated is the most direct.   Compared with that
by which they came, it is almost like passing from heel to heel of a horseshoe,
instead of around the curve of the toe.   The horseshoe turned southward is
Lewis' river and the Missouri above Dearborn's ; turned northward, Clark's river
and much of the Columbia.   They devised and accurately described a short cut

this morning to hunt toward the prairies of Point Adams. We have heard our hunters over the Netul fire several shots, but they have not yet returned. About 3 p. m. Bratton arrived from the salt-works, and informed us that Sergeant Pryor and party were coming with Gibson, who is so sick that he cannot stand, and whom they are bringing on a litter. Bratton himself is much reduced by his late illness, but is recovering fast. He reports that sergeant Pryor's delay was caused by the winds, which had been so violent that it was impossible to take a canoe up the creek to the point where they were to cross with Gibson. The sergeant's party arrived with Gibson after dark. We are pleased to find him not so sick as we had feared, and do not consider him in any danger, though he has still a fever and is much reduced. We believe his trouble originated in taking cold while hunting elk through the swamps. He is very languid, but nearly free from pain. We gave him broken doses of niter, made him drink freely of sage tea, put his feet in hot water, and at 9 p. m. administered 35 drops of laudanum.

Sunday, Feb. 16th. By several trials, made to adjust our octant and ascertain our error in direct observation, we found it to be 2° 1' 45" + or additive, beyond the fracture. This error was detected by comparison with the sextant, the error of which had already been determined. The octant error next to zero, or below 55° 20' inclusive, is only 2° additive.

We sent Shannon, Labiche, and Frazier this morning on a hunting excursion up the Kilhawanakle river, which discharges into the head of Meriwether's Bay. No tidings as

across from the mouth of Dearborn's river to the forks of the Kooskooskee—a route very nearly traversed by Lewis' party on the return trip, when he passed from Traveler's-rest creek along the "River of the Road to Buffalo" (Big Blackfoot) and so by Lewis and Clark's Pass of the Rockies to Medicine river. Had Lewis gone but ten miles south of this pass, he would have made the still shorter Cadotte's Pass, and gone down Dearborn's river to the Missouri. An unpublished sketch map before me, plotted by Clark from Lewis' notes, and now on pp. 149, 150 of Codex N, actually dots in the very shortest route from the mouth of Dearborn's river. It should have been published in 1814.

yet of Sergeant Gass and his party. Bratton is still weak
and complains of lumbago, which pains him to move ; we
gave him barks. Gibson's fever continues obstinate, though
not very high ; we gave him a dose of Dr. Rush's pills,
which have in many cases been found efficacious in fevers of
a bilious type. The niter produced a profuse perspiration
this evening, and the pills operated later ; after which the
fever abated and he had a good night's rest.

Monday, Feb. 17th. Collins and Windsor were sent to
hunt on the prairies of Point Adams, in the hope of procuring fresh meat for the sick. A little before noon Shannon, Labiche, and Frazier returned with the flesh and hide
of an elk which had been wounded by Sergeant Gass' party
and had taken to the water, where they pursued and killed
it. They saw neither the sergeant nor any of his party, nor
could they learn what success this party had had. We continued the bark treatment of Bratton, and commenced it
with Gibson, his fever being sufficiently reduced this morning to indicate a tonic. We think, therefore, there is no
further danger of his recovery [*sic !*]. At 2 p. m. J. Fields
arrived from the salt-makers and reported that they had
about two kegs of salt on hand ; this, with what we already
possess, will suffice, as we suppose, to last us till we reach
our deposit on the Missouri. We therefore directed a party
of six to go with Fields in the morning to bring the salt and
the kettles back to the fort.[4]

Tuesday, Feb. 18th. A party under Sergeant Ordway
left for the salt-works as directed yesterday, and another
under Sergeant Gass was sent over the Netul for the elk
killed there. In the evening Sergeant Ordway returned with
the information that the waves ran so high in the bay he
could not pass to the entrance of the creek we had directed
him to ascend with the canoe. Collins and Windsor returned
this evening with one deer they had killed. The deer are
now very poor, and the meat is by no means as good as that

[4] The codex continues with two pages descriptive of the Californian condor ;
a well-executed sketch of the head of which is drawn on p. 80.

of the elk. This is itself not prime, but has improved during the past few weeks. In the forenoon we were visited by eight Clatsops and Chinnooks, from whom we purchased a sea-otter's skin and two hats made of waytape [*sic*] and white cedar-bark. The Indians remained till late in the evening, when they departed for their village. They are people not easily hindered by waves from navigating their canoes.

Wednesday, Feb. 19th. Sergeant Ordway set out this morning with a party to proceed to the salt-works by land. In the evening Sergeant Gass returned with the flesh of eight elk, and seven of their skins, having left one skin with Shannon and Labiche, who remained to continue the chase over the Netul. We divided the hides among the several messes, in order that they might be dressed for covering our baggage when we set out in the spring. Our sick men appear to be improving, though they gain strength but slowly.

Thursday, Feb. 20th. We permitted Collins to hunt this morning, but in the evening he returned unsuccessful. He brought some cranberries [*Vaccinium macrocarpon*] for the sick. Gibson is recovering fast; but Bratton has an obstinate cough, besides the pain in his back, and seems to grow weaker. M'Neal is worse, from inattention to his disorder.

This forenoon we were visited by Tahcum, a principal chief of the Chinnooks, with 25 men of his nation. We had never seen this chief before. He is a good-looking man about 50 years of age, above the average stature of his tribe; as he came on a friendly visit, we gave him and his people something to eat, and plied them plentifully with tobacco-smoke. We also presented to the chief a small medal, with which he seemed much gratified. At sunset, we politely requested him to depart, as it is our custom to close the gates of the fort, and never permit a party of such numbers to remain inside all night. Notwithstanding their apparently friendly attitude, their greed and hope of plunder might lead to treachery; we have determined to be always on our guard, and never to place ourselves in a situation where we should be at the mercy of these or any other savages. We well know that the treachery of the American aborigines, and the undue confidence our countrymen have often placed in their professions of sincerity and friendliness, have cost many a life.[5] But so long have our men been accustomed to friendly intercourse with these natives, that we find it difficult to impress upon the minds of the garrison the necessity of eternal vigilance. Their confidence we can understand; but we know full well it is liable to be abused in an unguarded moment, and we must check its growth by reiterated warnings to our men. Our lives may depend upon being prepared for treachery at any moment, and in whatever form it may be encountered.

Friday, Feb. 21st. We were visited by three Clatsops, who remained all day. They are sad beggars. We gave them a few needles, with which they seemed pleased, and departed. Drewyer and Collins went in pursuit of some elk whose tracks Collins had discovered yesterday; but it rained so hard they could not follow the trail, and were obliged to return unsuccessful. Drewyer saw a black fox or fisher [the pekan, *Mustela pennanti*], which, however, escaped him in the fallen timber. Sergeant Ordway and his party returned from the salt-works, which are now abandoned, bringing the salt and the utensils. Our stock of salt is now about 20 gallons. Twelve of these we secured in two small iron-bound kegs and laid by for our voyage. We gave Willard and Bratton each a dose of Dr. Scott's pills; they operated on the former, but on the latter they did not. Gibson continues his tonic three times a day, and is recovering fast.

Saturday, Feb. 22d. We were visited by two Clatsop squaws and two boys. They brought a large lot of excellent hats, made of cedar-bark, ornamented with bear-grass. Two of these hats had been made to measures which we had given one of the women some time since, with a request to

[5] True, and almost prophetic in the light of events of July 27, 1806, when Captain Lewis nearly lost his life through the treachery of some Indians whom he could not keep out of his camp at night.

make each of us a hat. They fitted very well, and were of
the desired shape. We purchased the whole lot, and distributed them among our men. The woodwork and carving
of these people, as well as their hats and waterproof baskets, evince an ingenuity by no means common among the
aborigines of America. In the evening they departed,
accompanied in their canoes by Drewyer, who went to get
the dogs they had promised to give us to pay for the elk
they stole from us some weeks ago. These women informed
us that the small fish already mentioned have begun to run;
and also that their chief, Comowool, had gone up the Columbia to purchase wappatoo, a part of which he intended
to trade with us on his return. One of our canoes broke the
cord with which she was moored, and drifted off with the
tide; but she was recovered by Sergeant Pryor, whom we
sent for the purpose. The men on the sick-list—Ordway,
Gibson, Bratton, Willard, and M'Neal—are all recovering;
we have not before had so many on sick-report since we left
Wood river on the Mississippi.

Sunday, Feb. 23d. There is little to note to-day. Sergeant Ordway does not seem quite so well. The men are
now fully provided with leathern clothes and moccasins;
being better off in this respect, indeed, than at any previous
period of our journey.

Monday, Feb. 24th. The men on sick-report continue to
do well. Shannon and Labiche returned; they had killed
no elk, and said they believed the animals had returned from
their winter haunts back into the country to a considerable
distance. This is unwelcome intelligence; for, poor as it is,
elk-meat is our main dependence for subsistence. This evening we were visited by Comowool, the Clatsop chief, with
twelve men, women, and children of his nation. Drewyer
returned as a passenger in their canoe, bringing two dogs.
The party brought for sale the skin of a sea-otter, some hats,
sturgeon, and the species[6] of small fish [*Thaleichthys pacifi-*

---

[6] The codex has on p. 93 a full-length picture, diagonally from corner to corner, well executed and framed in an excellent description, from Clark R 80–84.

cus] which now begin to run. We purchased all the articles which the Indians brought. We suffered these people to remain all night, as it rained and blew violently and they had their women and children with them—a sure pledge of their pacific intentions. The sturgeon was good of its kind [*Acipenser transmontanus*]. We determined to send a party up the river to procure some of those fish, and another in same direction to hunt elk, as soon as the weather would permit.

Tuesday, Feb. 25th. It continued to rain and blow so hard that there was no movement of our party to-day. The Indians left us in the morning on their return to their village. Willard is somewhat worse; the other invalids are improving. We are mortified at our inability to make more celestial observations since we have been at Fort Clatsop; but the weather has been such as to render this impracticable.

Wednesday, Feb. 26th. We dispatched Drewyer and two men in the canoe up the Columbia to take sturgeon and anchovy; or, should they be unsuccessful in fishing, to purchase fish from the natives. For this purpose we furnished them with a few articles, such as please the Indians. We sent J. Fields, Shields, and Shannon up the Netul to hunt elk; R. Fields, and some others, to the prairies of Point Adams. We hope thus to shortly replenish our stock of provisions, now reduced to a minimum. We have only sufficient for three days in store, and that consists only of inferior dried elk, somewhat tainted—no very pleasant prospect for the commissary department.[7]

Thursday, Feb. 27th. R. Fields returned this evening empty-handed. He reports no elk toward Point Adams. Collins, who had hunted up the Netul, returned with one. Willard continues very sick. Goodrich and M'Neal, who have the pox, are improving; the others on the sick-list are nearly well.

Friday, Feb. 28th. R. Fields and Collins set out to hunt this morning. Kuskelar, a Clatsop, and his wife visited us.

---

[7] The codex continues with a three-page description of the sewellel, *Haplodon rufus*, fully treated in the next chapter.

They brought some anchovies, sturgeon, a beaver-robe, and some roots for sale; but they asked such prices for everything they had that we purchased nothing but part of a sturgeon, for which we gave a few fish-hooks. We allowed them to remain all night. J. Fields, Shields, and Shannon returned late, having killed five elk, two of which were left on a mountain at a considerable distance. We ordered these hunters to resume the chase early to-morrow morning, and Sergeant Gass to take a party in quest of the elk the other men had killed. Elk were reported to be tolerably plenty near the mountains, ten or twelve miles distant. Kuskelar brought a dog which Cruzatte had purchased.[8]

Saturday, March 1st. According to their orders Sergeant Gass and his party set out in quest of the elk killed by the hunters yesterday. Late in the evening they returned with the flesh of three of them. Thompson had been left with the hunters to jerk and take care of the meat of the remaining two elk. Kuskelar and his wife left us about noon. He had with him a good-looking boy about ten years old, who he told us was his slave. This boy had been taken prisoner by the Killamucks from some nation at a great distance on the southeast coast. Like other nations, the Clatsops adopt their slaves and treat them very much as if they were members of their own families. R. Fields and Collins, who had been absent since yesterday morning, returned without having killed any game.[9]

Sunday, March 2d. The diet of the sick is so poor that they gain strength but slowly. All are now convalescent, with keen appetites, but nothing to eat except poor elk-meat. Drewyer arrived with a most acceptable supply of fat sturgeon, fresh anchovies, and a bag of wappatoo holding about a bushel. We feasted on these fish and roots.[10]

[8] The codex continues with two pages descriptive of the hare, *Lepus campestris.*

[9] Codex continues with the beginning of the ornithology which is to occupy much of the next chapter.

[10] Codex continues with description of the cock-of-the-plains, *Centrocercus urophasianus,* and figure of the head on p. 107.

Monday, March 3d. Two of our canoes have been much injured lately by stranding on the shore at ebb tide; for when aground they split with their own weight. We had them drawn entirely out of the water for repairs. Lepage was taken sick. We gave him a dose of Scott's pills, which did not operate. There was no movement in the party; everything jogs on in the same old way; we count the days which separate us from April 1st, and still bind us fast to Fort Clatsop.

Tuesday, March 4th. Nothing happened to note; unless it be our better fare than usual, as the fresh fish and wappatoo are not yet all gone. The anchovies are so delicate that they soon spoil unless pickled or smoked; but there is no danger of their being kept too long in our case.[11]

Wednesday, March 5th. Visited by two parties of Clatsops, who brought some fish, some skins, and a hat for sale. We purchased most of their stock, and they departed. In the evening the hunters returned from Kilhawanackle [Young's] river, which discharges into the head of this bay. They had neither killed nor seen any elk, for these animals, as we had been before informed, were gone off toward the mountains. We made up a small assortment of articles to trade with the natives, and directed Sergeant Pryor to set out early in the morning in a canoe with two men, to ascend the Columbia as far as the resort of the native fishermen, and purchase some fish. We also directed a party of hunters to renew the chase to-morrow. If we satisfy ourselves that the elk are really gone away, we must make up our minds to start soon, ascend the river slowly, endeavoring to find subsistence on the way, and thus finishing all the rest of the month in the woody country.

Thursday, March 6th. The fishing and hunting parties set out according to yesterday's orders. During the forenoon we were visited by Comowool and two of his children. He presented us with some anchovies, which had been well cured in native fashion and were very acceptable; we gave

[11] Ornithology continues in the codex, two pages.

the old man some small articles in return. This we have found to be the most friendly and decent savage in the vicinity. Hall injured his foot and ankle seriously by the fall of a large stick of timber; fortunately no bones were broken, and he will soon be able to walk again. Bratton is still the weakest of our convalescents; he has had a particularly hard time of it, though all the sick suffer for want of proper food, which we have it not in our power to procure.

Friday, March 7th. The wind was so high that Comowool did not start till late to-day. Drewyer and Labiche returned at sunset, having killed one elk. They report some scattering bands of buck-elk near the place where this one was secured, about five miles up this side of the Netul. Bratton is much worse to-day, suffering great pain in his back. We gave him one of our flannel shirts and applied a flannel bandage to the parts, having rubbed him well with volatile liniment prepared from alcohol, camphor, and castile soap, with a little laudanum.[12]

Saturday, March 8th. Bratton is improving. Collins returned early and reported that he had killed three elk about five miles off, on the edge of the Point Adams prairie. One of them fell in a deep pool of water where he could not get at it; the other two he secured and butchered. He had seen two large herds. We therefore sent Drewyer and J. Fields to hunt for these, at the same time dispatching a party with Labiche up the Netul for the flesh of the elk which had been killed there, and with which they returned next evening. The party from the Kilhawanackle returned unsuccessful. M'Neal and Goodrich are so far recovered from the lues veneris that the use of mercury in their cases was discontinued.[13]

Sunday, March 9th. The men set out at daylight for the elk-meat, with which they returned in the course of the forenoon. Drewyer and J. Fields returned unsuccessful. Sergeant Pryor and the other fishermen did not arrive; we

[12] Ornithology continues, including a figure of the head of a fulmar petrel.

[13] Ornithology continues for several pages, at this and the next date.

suppose them detained by the wind.   Bratton is still complaining.   We were visited by three Clatsops with a dog, a
sea-otter-skin, and some fish for sale.   These Indians were
permitted to stay all night.   Shields was set to work making
sacks of elk-skin to contain various articles.

Monday, March 10th.   It became fair about one o'clock,
and we directed two parties of hunters to proceed along the
Netul, one up and the other down the river.   Another party
received orders to set out early to-morrow morning, cross the
bay, and hunt beyond the Kilhawanakle.   From the last
quarter we have much hope of game, as it has been as
yet but little hunted over.   It blew hard all day, and the
Indians did not leave till evening.[14]

Tuesday, March 11th.   Early this morning Sergeant Pryor
arrived with his party in a small canoe loaded with fish,
which he had obtained from the Cathlamahs for a very small
part of the articles he had taken to trade.   The wind had
prevented his going to the fishery across the Columbia, above
the Wahkiacums, and had also delayed his return.   Some
dogs at the Cathlamah fishery had chewed off the cord which
confined his canoe and set her adrift; so he borrowed from
the Indians the small one in which he returned.   But he
found his own canoe on the way and made her fast.   She
will therefore be secure until we return the Indians their
canoe and recover our own.   We sent Sergeant Gass and a
party to search for a canoe which was reported to have been
sunk in a small creek on the other side of the Netul, a
few miles below us, where she had been left by R. Fields,
Shields, and Frazier when they went to hunt over the river.
But they returned without finding the canoe, which no doubt
had parted her mooring and drifted away with the tide.
Drewyer, Frazier, and J. Fields set out by daylight this
morning to hunt, according to the orders previously issued.
Once more we live in clover, with wappatoo, fresh sturgeon,
and anchovies.[15]

[14] Botany and ornithology follow.
[15] Zoölogy continues, with various reptiles, mollusks, etc.

Wednesday, March 12*th.* We sent a party again to search for the sunk canoe, but they returned with no better than yesterday's result. A hunter who went along this side of the Netul remained out. On taking an inventory of some of our effects, we find that the party is provided with 358 pairs of moccasins, besides which we have a good stock of dressed elk-skins.

Thursday, March 13*th.* This morning Drewyer, Frazier, and J. Fields returned, having killed two elk and two deer. We were visited by two Cathlamahs, who remained all day. We sent Drewyer down to the Clatsop village to purchase, if possible, a couple of canoes. Sergeant Pryor and party made a search for the lost boat; but this also was unsuccessful. When engaged in that search Collins, one of the party, killed two elk near the Netul, below us. We sent Sergeant Ordway and a party for the flesh of one of the elk which had been killed beyond the bay, and with which they returned in the evening; the other one of those two elk, and both the deer, were farther off. R. Fields and Thompson have not yet returned. At present the old horns of some of the elk have not been shed, but of others the new ones have shotten out some six inches. The latter are in the best order; from which it would appear that poor elk longest retain their horns.[16]

Friday, March 14*th.* We sent a party after the two elk Collins killed last evening. They returned with the game about noon. Collins, Shannon, and J. Fields went in quest of the herd of elk of which the former had killed those two already mentioned. In the evening we heard upward of 20 shots, whence we supposed our hunters had fallen in with their game, and killed a goodly number. R. Fields and Thompson returned unsuccessful, bringing only a brant. Later on Drewyer came back with a party of Clatsops, who brought an indifferent canoe for sale, as well as some hats and roots. The latter we purchased, but could not make a satisfactory bargain for the boat,

[16] Celestial observations and ichthyology follow.

though Captain Lewis offered her owner a laced uniform coat.[17]

Saturday, March 15*th.* This morning the hunters returned, having killed four elk only. It seems that Labiche was the only one who fell in with the herd, and having lost the fore-sight of his gun, shot a great many times without effect. As the dead elk were lying some distance apart, we sent two details for them. Both returned in the evening, bringing the flesh of three and the skins of four, one carcass having become spoiled through the carelessness of the hunter, who had not removed the pluck and the liver. We were visited this afternoon by Delashelwilt and his wife, with six women of his tribe, whom the old Chinnook bawd, his wife, had brought to market. This was the same party who had last November infected so many of our men with venereal disease, from which not all are yet quite free. We therefore gave the men a particular charge, which they promised to keep. We were also visited by Catel, a Clatsop, with his family; he brought for sale a sea-otter-skin and a canoe, neither of which we purchased. The Clatsops who last evening brought the indifferent canoe to sell left us early this morning. Bratton is still on sick-report.[18]

Sunday, March 16*th.* Drewyer did not return with his party from the Cathlamahs, though we expected that he would be back by this evening. He has probably been prevented by the hard winds which have blown to-day. The Indians remained, but would not dispose of their canoe at any price which we could reasonably be expected to offer, considering how poor we have become. All the small merchandise we possess might be tied up in a couple of handkerchiefs. The rest of our stock in trade consists of six blue robes, one scarlet ditto, five robes which we made out of our large United States flag, a few old clothes trimmed with ribbons, and one artillerist's uniform coat and hat, which prob-

[17] Ichthyology continues.

[18] Celestial observations and ornithology follow, the latter including a characteristic figure of the head of the white-fronted goose, *Anser albifrons gambeli.*

ably Captain Clark will never wear again.   We have to depend entirely upon this meager outfit for the purchase of such horses and provisions as it will be in our power to obtain—a scant dependence, indeed, for such a journey as is before us.[19]

Monday, March 17*th.*   Catel and his family left us this morning.   Old Delashelwilt and his women remain.   They have camped close to the fort, and seem determined to besiege us; but we believe that, notwithstanding all their graces and winning ways, our men are keeping the vow of celibacy which they lately made.   We have prepared the canoes for our departure, and shall set out upon our voyage as soon as the weather will permit.   The weather is so precarious that we fear, should we wait till the 1st of April, we might then be detained several days longer before we could get as far as the Cathlamah village.   We cannot double Point William unless the weather is settled fair and calm.   Drewyer returned late this evening with our canoe— the one which Sergeant Pryor left some days ago with the Cathlamahs—and also brought another, which he had purchased from those people.   For this one he had given Captain Lewis' laced uniform coat, and nearly half a carrot of tobacco.   Nothing short of this coat would have induced them to part with the canoe.   In their scale of barter a canoe is the article of the greatest value, except a wife, with whom it is at par, being generally given to a father in exchange for his daughter.   Captain Lewis came to the conclusion that the United States owed him a coat, on the strength of Drewyer's trade.   We still need one more canoe; and as the Clatsops will not sell on any reasonable terms, we intend to " borrow " one from them by way of reprisal for the six elk they stole from us last winter.[20]

Tuesday, March 18*th.*   Drewyer was taken last night with

---

[19] Ichthyology continues, including a well-drawn figure of the white salmontrout, extending diagonally the length of p. 133, with a long description.

[20] Codex continues with the " pellucid jelly-like substance," etc., of Biddle's p. 199, and list of the traders who visit the Columbia, as already given, p. 790.

a violent pain in his side, like a pleurisy. Captain Clark bled him. Several of the men are complaining of being unwell, which is truly unfortunate on the eve of our intended departure. We directed Sergeant Pryor to prepare the two canoes which Drewyer brought last night for the use of his mess. They needed to be strengthened with several knees, and be calked in some seams which had opened. The sergeant put them in partial order, but was prevented from finishing the operation by frequent showers in the course of the day. Comowool and two Cathlamahs visited us to-day. We suffered them to remain all night. This morning we gave Delashelwilt a certificate of his own good deportment, and furnished him with a list of our names, after which we sent him home with all his female band. We have given such lists to several of the natives, and posted a copy in our own quarters. Our object in so doing we stated in the preamble of this muster-roll, as follows:[21]

" The object of this list is, that through the medium of some civilized person who may see the same, it may be made known to the informed world, that the party consisting of the persons whose names are hereunto annexed, and who were sent out by the govenment of the U'States in May 1804, to explore the interior of the Continent of North America, did penetrate the same by way of the Missouri and Columbia Rivers, to the discharge of the latter into the Pacific Ocean, where they arrived on the 14th of November 1805, and from whence they departed the [blank—supply 23d] day of March 1806 on their return to the United States by the same rout they had come out."

On the back of some of these lists we added a sketch of the connections of the upper branches of the Missouri with those of the Columbia, and particularly of its main south-

[21] Here I copy Lewis J 137 literally. One or more of these pieces of paper should be still in existence ; but if so, I have as yet no clew to what would be, considering the autograph signatures of the whole party, the most precious of all documents relating to the Expedition. See what Mr. Biddle says, p. 903, of that copy which reached Philadelphia by way of Canton, thus going nearly around the world.

east branch.   On the same lists we also delineated the track by which we had come, and that which we meant to pursue on our return, in so far as these were not the same.

There seemed to be so many chances that our Government would never obtain a regular report, through the medium of the traders and savages of this coast, that we did not think it worth while to leave any such in their hands. Our party is also too few in number for us to think of leaving any of them to return to the United States by sea, particularly as we shall necessarily be divided into three or four parties, at some stages of our return journey, in order to the best possible accomplishment of the important objects we have in view.[22]   And, at any rate, in all human probability, we shall reach the United States much sooner than any man who should be left here could be expected to do, as he would have to wait and take his chances of some trader upon whom he would have to depend for a passage to the United States. Such a trader might be long in arriving, would probably spend some months with the natives, and then might not return to the United States direct.

Wednesday, March 19*th.*   It continued to rain and hail, so that nothing further could be done to put the canoes in serviceable order.   A party was sent out for an elk which Drewyer killed yesterday, and with which they returned in a few hours.   We gave Comowool a certificate of good character, and witnessed the friendly intercourse he has maintained with us during our whole residence here. We also furnished him with the roster of our names.[23]

Thursday, March 20*th.*   Nothing could be done to expe-

---

[22] Briefly : 1st.   To try the shortest route from the mouth of Traveler's-rest creek to the Missouri, and then explore Maria's river, as was done by Captain Lewis and some of the men.   2d. To swing around from the same point by the shortest route to certain sources of Jefferson's river, down this, up the Gallatin, and thence over to explore the Yellowstone, as was done by Captain Clark and his men—the parties thus separated to unite at some point on the Missouri, below the mouth of the Yellowstone.   All of which was duly and truly carried into effect.

[23] The codex continues with ethnology and zoölogy, pp. 138–144.

dite our departure, in consequence of the violent wind and rain. We intended to dispatch Drewyer and J. and R. Fields to hunt along the bay on this side of the Cathlahmahs till we should join them hence; but the weather was so unsettled that we could not fix on a day for our departure, and we were unwilling to send them out in such uncertainty. We still have several days' provision on hand, which we hope will suffice for our subsistence during the time we may be weather-bound. Although we have not fared sumptuously the past winter and spring at Fort Clatsop, we have lived quite as comfortably as we had any reason to expect, and have accomplished every end we had in view in staying at this place, except that of meeting any of the traders who visit this coast and the mouth of the Columbia. Our salt will amply suffice to last us till we reach the Missouri, where we have cached a supply. It would have been very fortunate for us if some trader had arrived before our departure; for in that case we should have been able to add to our stock of merchandise, and made a much more comfortable homeward-bound journey.[24] Several of our men still complain of sickness; but we believe that this is mainly due to want of proper food, and we hope that as soon as we get under way we shall be much better off in this respect. The men have always been in better health when traveling than when stationary. Finding that the guns of both Drewyer and Sergeant Pryor were out of order, the first was fitted with a new lock, and the broken tumbler of the latter was replaced by a duplicate, which had been made at Harper's Ferry, where the gun itself had been manufactured. But for our precaution in bringing extra locks, and duplicate parts of the locks, most of our guns would

[24] The Expedition did not lack for means of purchasing anything that *money* could buy. When Lewis and Clark were projected into space, as it were, and essayed that mighty Missouri, coiled like a colossal interrogation-mark upon a continent, they were furnished by President Jefferson with probably the most comprehensive letter of credit ever handed to any individuals. It was addressed to the world, on faith in the credit of the United States; for neither Jefferson nor anyone else could have said whether, should the Expedition ever return, it

be now useless, in spite of the skill and ingenuity of John Shields in repairing them. Fortunately, as it is, we are able to record here that they are all in good order.[25]

Friday, March 21st. As we could not yet take our departure, we thought it best to send out some hunters, and accordingly detailed Shields and Collins to hunt on this side of the Netul, with orders to return this evening, or sooner if they were successful. They returned late, without game ; and now we have but one day's provision left. We therefore gave orders to Drewyer and J. and R. Fields to set out early to-morrow morning, and try to find us something to eat on the bay beyond Point William. We were visited by some Clatsops, who left us in the evening. Willard and Bratton do not seem to improve ; the former had a bad turn, and the latter is so much reduced by long continued ill-health that we are somewhat uneasy concerning his ultimate recovery. But in both cases it may be nothing more serious than rheumatism and lack of proper food.

Saturday, March 22d. Drewyer and J. and R. Fields left early this morning, agreeably to yesterday's orders. We also sent seven other hunters out in different directions on this side of the Netul. About ten o'clock we were visited by four Clatsops and a Killamuck ; they brought some dried anchovies and a dog for sale, all of which we purchased. The temperature is moderate, but it rained so hard that our canoes could not be put in readiness for our departure. At noon we were visited by Comowool and three Clatsops. To this chief we gave our house and furniture. He has been much more kind and hospitable to us than any other Indian in this vicinity. In the evening these Indians bade us farewell, and we never saw them again. All the hunters returned, unsuccessful, except Colter, who did not arrive. We

would be by the Horn or Good Hope. See this letter, as given in Jefferson's Memoir of Lewis, *anteà.* What was lacking at the mouth of the Columbia was simply a stock of kickshaws and trumpery for Clatsop barter.

[25] With the above date Lewis J ends, so far as the journal is concerned, though there are a few more pages, consisting of a meteorological register. The narrative passes directly to Codex K, March 21st.

have determined to move to-morrow in any event; we can stop the canoes with mud for a makeshift, and halt the first fair day to put them in better order.[26]

[26] This programme was carried out, and Fort Clatsop was evacuated at 1 p. m., on Sunday, March 23d, 1806.

Thus far in the Biddle edition of the History, the last formal entry by date is Tuesday, Jan. 21st, beginning Chap. vi. of Vol. II. This is merely *pro forma ;* for, after a few words of narrative, the chapter is occupied with ethnology to its last page, when a few more words resume the narrative, without date. Then Chapter vii. follows, entirely devoted to botany and zoölogy. Many have wondered why this matter happened to be interpolated just here, and the M'Vickar ed. of 1842 relegates it to the Appendix. Mr. Biddle was quite right. This natural history chapter is in its logical order and proper connection. It was prepared by Lewis and by Clark during their enforced residence at Fort Clatsop, as we have seen in studying Codices I and J, where usually a few words each day dispose of what little journalism the explorers had to indulge concerning their monotonous life, during which they had ample leisure to fill these codices with ethnology and natural history, on the basis of which were wrought Chaps. vi., vii.

After these, in the Biddle edition, Chap. viii. opens without date, but with a skillful *résumé* of the situation of the Expedition during the period from Jan. 21st to March 22d inclusive, and with an account of the way a copy of one of the muster-rolls left at the mouth of the Columbia reached Philadelphia from China. Whereupon, the regular narrative is resumed at date of March 23d. I think this was excellent editing of the Clatsop codices. If I have thought best now to do a little differently, and bring forward the dates seriatim from Jan. 21st to March 22d, it may be attributed to the change of historical perspective from 1814 to 1893. Neither Lewis nor Clark, nor Biddle himself, could fully realize at the beginning of this century the weight that their words would carry at its end.

" Probably no two men ever had a task given them of greater difficulty and magnitude, and involving the exercise of more skill, wisdom, intrepidity, discretion, and all manly attributes, and which after an ' experience epic in the grandeur of its unwitnessed valor,' was carried to a complete and successful termination." (Symons.)

END OF VOL. II.

A CATALOG OF SELECTED DOVER
BOOKS IN ALL FIELDS OF INTEREST

CONCERNING THE SPIRITUAL IN ART, Wassily Kandinsky. Pioneering work by father of abstract art. Thoughts on color theory, nature of art. Analysis of earlier masters. 12 illustrations. 80pp. of text. 5⅜ × 8½.　23411-8 Pa. $3.95

ANIMALS: 1,419 Copyright-Free Illustrations of Mammals, Birds, Fish, Insects, etc., Jim Harter (ed.). Clear wood engravings present, in extremely lifelike poses, over 1,000 species of animals. One of the most extensive pictorial sourcebooks of its kind. Captions. Index. 284pp. 9 × 12.　23766-4 Pa. $12.95

CELTIC ART: The Methods of Construction, George Bain. Simple geometric techniques for making Celtic interlacements, spirals, Kells-type initials, animals, humans, etc. Over 500 illustrations. 160pp. 9 × 12. (USO)　22923-8 Pa. $9.95

AN ATLAS OF ANATOMY FOR ARTISTS, Fritz Schider. Most thorough reference work on art anatomy in the world. Hundreds of illustrations, including selections from works by Vesalius, Leonardo, Goya, Ingres, Michelangelo, others. 593 illustrations. 192pp. 7⅛ × 10¼.　20241-0 Pa. $9.95

CELTIC HAND STROKE-BY-STROKE (Irish Half-Uncial from "The Book of Kells"): An Arthur Baker Calligraphy Manual, Arthur Baker. Complete guide to creating each letter of the alphabet in distinctive Celtic manner. Covers hand position, strokes, pens, inks, paper, more. Illustrated. 48pp. 8¼ × 11.
24336-2 Pa. $3.95

EASY ORIGAMI, John Montroll. Charming collection of 32 projects (hat, cup, pelican, piano, swan, many more) specially designed for the novice origami hobbyist. Clearly illustrated easy-to-follow instructions insure that even beginning papercrafters will achieve successful results. 48pp 8¼ × 11.　27298-2 Pa. $2.95

THE COMPLETE BOOK OF BIRDHOUSE CONSTRUCTION FOR WOOD-WORKERS, Scott D. Campbell. Detailed instructions, illustrations, tables. Also data on bird habitat and instinct patterns. Bibliography. 3 tables. 63 illustrations in 15 figures. 48pp. 5¼ × 8½.　24407-5 Pa. $1.95

BLOOMINGDALE'S ILLUSTRATED 1886 CATALOG: Fashions, Dry Goods and Housewares, Bloomingdale Brothers. Famed merchants' extremely rare catalog depicting about 1,700 products: clothing, housewares, firearms, dry goods, jewelry, more. Invaluable for dating, identifying vintage items. Also, copyright-free graphics for artists, designers. Co-published with Henry Ford Museum & Greenfield Village. 160pp. 8¼ × 11.　25780-0 Pa. $9.95

HISTORIC COSTUME IN PICTURES, Braun & Schneider. Over 1,450 costumed figures in clearly detailed engravings—from dawn of civilization to end of 19th century. Captions. Many folk costumes. 256pp. 8⅜ × 11¾.　23150-X Pa. $11.95

A CATALOG OF SELECTED
DOVER BOOKS
IN ALL FIELDS OF INTEREST

STICKLEY CRAFTSMAN FURNITURE CATALOGS, Gustav Stickley and L. & J. G. Stickley. Beautiful, functional furniture in two authentic catalogs from 1910. 594 illustrations, including 277 photos, show settles, rockers, armchairs, reclining chairs, bookcases, desks, tables. 183pp. 6½ × 9¼. 23838-5 Pa. $9.95

AMERICAN LOCOMOTIVES IN HISTORIC PHOTOGRAPHS: 1858 to 1949, Ron Ziel (ed.). A rare collection of 126 meticulously detailed official photographs, called "builder portraits," of American locomotives that majestically chronicle the rise of steam locomotive power in America. Introduction. Detailed captions. xi + 129pp. 9 × 12. 27393-8 Pa. $12.95

AMERICA'S LIGHTHOUSES: An Illustrated History, Francis Ross Holland, Jr. Delightfully written, profusely illustrated fact-filled survey of over 200 American lighthouses since 1716. History, anecdotes, technological advances, more. 240pp. 8 × 10¾. 25576-X Pa. $11.95

TOWARDS A NEW ARCHITECTURE, Le Corbusier. Pioneering manifesto by founder of "International School." Technical and aesthetic theories, views of industry, economics, relation of form to function, "mass-production split" and much more. Profusely illustrated. 320pp. 6⅛ × 9¼. (USO) 25023-7 Pa. $9.95

HOW THE OTHER HALF LIVES, Jacob Riis. Famous journalistic record, exposing poverty and degradation of New York slums around 1900, by major social reformer. 100 striking and influential photographs. 233pp. 10 × 7⅞. 22012-5 Pa $10.95

FRUIT KEY AND TWIG KEY TO TREES AND SHRUBS, William M. Harlow. One of the handiest and most widely used identification aids. Fruit key covers 120 deciduous and evergreen species; twig key 160 deciduous species. Easily used. Over 300 photographs. 126pp. 5⅜ × 8½. 20511-8 Pa. $3.95

COMMON BIRD SONGS, Dr. Donald J. Borror. Songs of 60 most common U.S. birds: robins, sparrows, cardinals, bluejays, finches, more—arranged in order of increasing complexity. Up to 9 variations of songs of each species. Cassette and manual 99911-4 $8.95

ORCHIDS AS HOUSE PLANTS, Rebecca Tyson Northen. Grow cattleyas and many other kinds of orchids—in a window, in a case, or under artificial light. 63 illustrations. 148pp. 5⅜ × 8½. 23261-1 Pa. $4.95

MONSTER MAZES, Dave Phillips. Masterful mazes at four levels of difficulty. Avoid deadly perils and evil creatures to find magical treasures. Solutions for all 32 exciting illustrated puzzles. 48pp. 8¼ × 11. 26005-4 Pa. $2.95

MOZART'S DON GIOVANNI (DOVER OPERA LIBRETTO SERIES), Wolfgang Amadeus Mozart. Introduced and translated by Ellen H. Bleiler. Standard Italian libretto, with complete English translation. Convenient and thoroughly portable—an ideal companion for reading along with a recording or the performance itself. Introduction. List of characters. Plot summary. 121pp. 5¼ × 8½. 24944-1 Pa. $2.95

TECHNICAL MANUAL AND DICTIONARY OF CLASSICAL BALLET, Gail Grant. Defines, explains, comments on steps, movements, poses and concepts. 15-page pictorial section. Basic book for student, viewer. 127pp. 5⅜ × 8½. 21843-0 Pa. $4.95

BRASS INSTRUMENTS: Their History and Development, Anthony Baines. Authoritative, updated survey of the evolution of trumpets, trombones, bugles, cornets, French horns, tubas and other brass wind instruments. Over 140 illustrations and 48 music examples. Corrected and updated by author. New preface. Bibliography. 320pp. 5⅜ × 8½. 27574-4 Pa. $9.95

HOLLYWOOD GLAMOR PORTRAITS, John Kobal (ed.). 145 photos from 1926–49. Harlow, Gable, Bogart, Bacall; 94 stars in all. Full background on photographers, technical aspects. 160pp. 8⅜ × 11¼. 23352-9 Pa. $11.95

MAX AND MORITZ, Wilhelm Busch. Great humor classic in both German and English. Also 10 other works: "Cat and Mouse," "Plisch and Plumm," etc. 216pp. 5⅜ × 8½. 20181-3 Pa. $5.95

THE RAVEN AND OTHER FAVORITE POEMS, Edgar Allan Poe. Over 40 of the author's most memorable poems: "The Bells," "Ulalume," "Israfel," "To Helen," "The Conqueror Worm," "Eldorado," "Annabel Lee," many more. Alphabetic lists of titles and first lines. 64pp. 5³⁄₁₆ × 8¼. 26685-0 Pa. $1.00

SEVEN SCIENCE FICTION NOVELS, H. G. Wells. The standard collection of the great novels. Complete, unabridged. First Men in the Moon, Island of Dr. Moreau, War of the Worlds, Food of the Gods, Invisible Man, Time Machine, In the Days of the Comet. Total of 1,015pp. 5⅜ × 8½. (USO) 20264-X Clothbd. $29.95

AMULETS AND SUPERSTITIONS, E. A. Wallis Budge. Comprehensive discourse on origin, powers of amulets in many ancient cultures: Arab, Persian, Babylonian, Assyrian, Egyptian, Gnostic, Hebrew, Phoenician, Syriac, etc. Covers cross, swastika, crucifix, seals, rings, stones, etc. 584pp. 5⅜ × 8½. 23573-4 Pa. $12.95

RUSSIAN STORIES/PYCCKNE PACCKA3bl: A Dual-Language Book, edited by Gleb Struve. Twelve tales by such masters as Chekhov, Tolstoy, Dostoevsky, Pushkin, others. Excellent word-for-word English translations on facing pages, plus teaching and study aids, Russian/English vocabulary, biographical/critical introductions, more. 416pp. 5⅜ × 8½. 26244-8 Pa. $8.95

PHILADELPHIA THEN AND NOW: 60 Sites Photographed in the Past and Present, Kenneth Finkel and Susan Oyama. Rare photographs of City Hall, Logan Square, Independence Hall, Betsy Ross House, other landmarks juxtaposed with contemporary views. Captures changing face of historic city. Introduction. Captions. 128pp. 8¼ × 11. 25790-8 Pa. $9.95

AIA ARCHITECTURAL GUIDE TO NASSAU AND SUFFOLK COUNTIES, LONG ISLAND, The American Institute of Architects, Long Island Chapter, and the Society for the Preservation of Long Island Antiquities. Comprehensive, well-researched and generously illustrated volume brings to life over three centuries of Long Island's great architectural heritage. More than 240 photographs with authoritative, extensively detailed captions. 176pp. 8¼ × 11. 26946-9 Pa. $14.95

NORTH AMERICAN INDIAN LIFE: Customs and Traditions of 23 Tribes, Elsie Clews Parsons (ed.). 27 fictionalized essays by noted anthropologists examine religion, customs, government, additional facets of life among the Winnebago, Crow, Zuni, Eskimo, other tribes. 480pp. 6⅛ × 9¼. 27377-6 Pa. $10.95

FRANK LLOYD WRIGHT'S HOLLYHOCK HOUSE, Donald Hoffmann. Lavishly illustrated, carefully documented study of one of Wright's most controversial residential designs. Over 120 photographs, floor plans, elevations, etc. Detailed perceptive text by noted Wright scholar. Index. 128pp. 9¼ × 10¾.
27133-1 Pa. $11.95

THE MALE AND FEMALE FIGURE IN MOTION: 60 Classic Photographic Sequences, Eadweard Muybridge. 60 true-action photographs of men and women walking, running, climbing, bending, turning, etc., reproduced from rare 19th-century masterpiece. vi + 121pp. 9 × 12. 24745-7 Pa. $10.95

1001 QUESTIONS ANSWERED ABOUT THE SEASHORE, N. J. Berrill and Jacquelyn Berrill. Queries answered about dolphins, sea snails, sponges, starfish, fishes, shore birds, many others. Covers appearance, breeding, growth, feeding, much more. 305pp. 5¼ × 8¼. 23366-9 Pa. $7.95

GUIDE TO OWL WATCHING IN NORTH AMERICA, Donald S. Heintzelman. Superb guide offers complete data and descriptions of 19 species: barn owl, screech owl, snowy owl, many more. Expert coverage of owl-watching equipment, conservation, migrations and invasions, etc. Guide to observing sites. 84 illustrations. xiii + 193pp. 5⅜ × 8½. 27344-X Pa. $8.95

MEDICINAL AND OTHER USES OF NORTH AMERICAN PLANTS: A Historical Survey with Special Reference to the Eastern Indian Tribes, Charlotte Erichsen-Brown. Chronological historical citations document 500 years of usage of plants, trees, shrubs native to eastern Canada, northeastern U.S. Also complete identifying information. 343 illustrations. 544pp. 6½ × 9¼. 25951-X Pa. $12.95

STORYBOOK MAZES, Dave Phillips. 23 stories and mazes on two-page spreads: Wizard of Oz, Treasure Island, Robin Hood, etc. Solutions. 64pp. 8¼ × 11.
23628-5 Pa. $2.95

NEGRO FOLK MUSIC, U.S.A., Harold Courlander. Noted folklorist's scholarly yet readable analysis of rich and varied musical tradition. Includes authentic versions of over 40 folk songs. Valuable bibliography and discography. xi + 324pp. 5⅜ × 8½. 27350-4 Pa. $7.95

MOVIE-STAR PORTRAITS OF THE FORTIES, John Kobal (ed.). 163 glamor, studio photos of 106 stars of the 1940s: Rita Hayworth, Ava Gardner, Marlon Brando, Clark Gable, many more. 176pp. 8⅜ × 11¼. 23546-7 Pa. $11.95

BENCHLEY LOST AND FOUND, Robert Benchley. Finest humor from early 30s, about pet peeves, child psychologists, post office and others. Mostly unavailable elsewhere. 73 illustrations by Peter Arno and others. 183pp. 5⅜ × 8½.
22410-4 Pa. $5.95

YEKL and THE IMPORTED BRIDEGROOM AND OTHER STORIES OF YIDDISH NEW YORK, Abraham Cahan. Film Hester Street based on Yekl (1896). Novel, other stories among first about Jewish immigrants on N.Y.'s East Side. 240pp. 5⅜ × 8½. 22427-9 Pa. $6.95

SELECTED POEMS, Walt Whitman. Generous sampling from *Leaves of Grass*. Twenty-four poems include "I Hear America Singing," "Song of the Open Road," "I Sing the Body Electric," "When Lilacs Last in the Dooryard Bloom'd," "O Captain! My Captain!"—all reprinted from an authoritative edition. Lists of titles and first lines. 128pp. 5³⁄₁₆ × 8¼. 26878-0 Pa. $1.00

THE BEST TALES OF HOFFMANN, E. T. A. Hoffmann. 10 of Hoffmann's most important stories: "Nutcracker and the King of Mice," "The Golden Flowerpot," etc. 458pp. 5⅜ × 8½. 21793-0 Pa. $8.95

FROM FETISH TO GOD IN ANCIENT EGYPT, E. A. Wallis Budge. Rich detailed survey of Egyptian conception of "God" and gods, magic, cult of animals, Osiris, more. Also, superb English translations of hymns and legends. 240 illustrations. 545pp. 5⅜ × 8½. 25803-3 Pa. $11.95

FRENCH STORIES/CONTES FRANÇAIS: A Dual-Language Book, Wallace Fowlie. Ten stories by French masters, Voltaire to Camus: "Micromegas" by Voltaire; "The Atheist's Mass" by Balzac; "Minuet" by de Maupassant; "The Guest" by Camus, six more. Excellent English translations on facing pages. Also French-English vocabulary list, exercises, more. 352pp. 5⅜ × 8½. 26443-2 Pa. $8.95

CHICAGO AT THE TURN OF THE CENTURY IN PHOTOGRAPHS: 122 Historic Views from the Collections of the Chicago Historical Society, Larry A. Viskochil. Rare large-format prints offer detailed views of City Hall, State Street, the Loop, Hull House, Union Station, many other landmarks, circa 1904–1913. Introduction. Captions. Maps. 144pp. 9⅜ × 12¼. 24656-6 Pa. $12.95

OLD BROOKLYN IN EARLY PHOTOGRAPHS, 1865–1929, William Lee Younger. Luna Park, Gravesend race track, construction of Grand Army Plaza, moving of Hotel Brighton, etc. 157 previously unpublished photographs. 165pp. 8⅞ × 11¾. 23587-4 Pa. $13.95

THE MYTHS OF THE NORTH AMERICAN INDIANS, Lewis Spence. Rich anthology of the myths and legends of the Algonquins, Iroquois, Pawnees and Sioux, prefaced by an extensive historical and ethnological commentary. 36 illustrations. 480pp. 5⅜ × 8½. 25967-6 Pa. $8.95

AN ENCYCLOPEDIA OF BATTLES: Accounts of Over 1,560 Battles from 1479 B.C. to the Present, David Eggenberger. Essential details of every major battle in recorded history from the first battle of Megiddo in 1479 B.C. to Grenada in 1984. List of Battle Maps. New Appendix covering the years 1967–1984. Index. 99 illustrations. 544pp. 6½ × 9¼. 24913-1 Pa. $14.95

SAILING ALONE AROUND THE WORLD, Captain Joshua Slocum. First man to sail around the world, alone, in small boat. One of great feats of seamanship told in delightful manner. 67 illustrations. 294pp. 5⅜ × 8½. 20326-3 Pa. $5.95

ANARCHISM AND OTHER ESSAYS, Emma Goldman. Powerful, penetrating, prophetic essays on direct action, role of minorities, prison reform, puritan hypocrisy, violence, etc. 271pp. 5⅜ × 8½. 22484-8 Pa. $5.95

MYTHS OF THE HINDUS AND BUDDHISTS, Ananda K. Coomaraswamy and Sister Nivedita. Great stories of the epics; deeds of Krishna, Shiva, taken from puranas, Vedas, folk tales; etc. 32 illustrations. 400pp. 5⅜ × 8½. 21759-0 Pa. $9.95

BEYOND PSYCHOLOGY, Otto Rank. Fear of death, desire of immortality, nature of sexuality, social organization, creativity, according to Rankian system. 291pp. 5⅜ × 8½. 20485-5 Pa. $8.95

A THEOLOGICO-POLITICAL TREATISE, Benedict Spinoza. Also contains unfinished Political Treatise. Great classic on religious liberty, theory of government on common consent. R. Elwes translation. Total of 421pp. 5⅜ × 8½. 20249-6 Pa. $8.95

MY BONDAGE AND MY FREEDOM, Frederick Douglass. Born a slave, Douglass became outspoken force in antislavery movement. The best of Douglass' autobiographies. Graphic description of slave life. 464pp. 5⅜ × 8½. 22457-0 Pa. $8.95

FOLLOWING THE EQUATOR: A Journey Around the World, Mark Twain. Fascinating humorous account of 1897 voyage to Hawaii, Australia, India, New Zealand, etc. Ironic, bemused reports on peoples, customs, climate, flora and fauna, politics, much more. 197 illustrations. 720pp. 5⅜ × 8½. 26113-1 Pa. $15.95

THE PEOPLE CALLED SHAKERS, Edward D. Andrews. Definitive study of Shakers: origins, beliefs, practices, dances, social organization, furniture and crafts, etc. 33 illustrations. 351pp. 5⅜ × 8½. 21081-2 Pa. $8.95

THE MYTHS OF GREECE AND ROME, H. A. Guerber. A classic of mythology, generously illustrated, long prized for its simple, graphic, accurate retelling of the principal myths of Greece and Rome, and for its commentary on their origins and significance. With 64 illustrations by Michelangelo, Raphael, Titian, Rubens, Canova, Bernini and others. 480pp. 5⅜ × 8½. 27584-1 Pa. $9.95

PSYCHOLOGY OF MUSIC, Carl E. Seashore. Classic work discusses music as a medium from psychological viewpoint. Clear treatment of physical acoustics, auditory apparatus, sound perception, development of musical skills, nature of musical feeling, host of other topics. 88 figures. 408pp. 5⅜ × 8½. 21851-1 Pa. $9.95

THE PHILOSOPHY OF HISTORY, Georg W. Hegel. Great classic of Western thought develops concept that history is not chance but rational process, the evolution of freedom. 457pp. 5⅜ × 8½. 20112-0 Pa. $9.95

THE BOOK OF TEA, Kakuzo Okakura. Minor classic of the Orient: entertaining, charming explanation, interpretation of traditional Japanese culture in terms of tea ceremony. 94pp. 5⅜ × 8½. 20070-1 Pa. $3.95

LIFE IN ANCIENT EGYPT, Adolf Erman. Fullest, most thorough, detailed older account with much not in more recent books, domestic life, religion, magic, medicine, commerce, much more. Many illustrations reproduce tomb paintings, carvings, hieroglyphs, etc. 597pp. 5⅜ × 8½. 22632-8 Pa. $10.95

SUNDIALS, Their Theory and Construction, Albert Waugh. Far and away the best, most thorough coverage of ideas, mathematics concerned, types, construction, adjusting anywhere. Simple, nontechnical treatment allows even children to build several of these dials. Over 100 illustrations. 230pp. 5⅜ × 8½. 22947-5 Pa. $7.95

DYNAMICS OF FLUIDS IN POROUS MEDIA, Jacob Bear. For advanced students of ground water hydrology, soil mechanics and physics, drainage and irrigation engineering, and more. 335 illustrations. Exercises, with answers. 784pp. 6⅛ × 9¼. 65675-6 Pa. $19.95

SONGS OF EXPERIENCE: Facsimile Reproduction with 26 Plates in Full Color, William Blake. 26 full-color plates from a rare 1826 edition. Includes "The Tyger," "London," "Holy Thursday," and other poems. Printed text of poems. 48pp. 5¼ × 7. 24636-1 Pa. $4.95

OLD-TIME VIGNETTES IN FULL COLOR, Carol Belanger Grafton (ed.). Over 390 charming, often sentimental illustrations, selected from archives of Victorian graphics—pretty women posing, children playing, food, flowers, kittens and puppies, smiling cherubs, birds and butterflies, much more. All copyright-free. 48pp. 9¼ × 12¼. 27269-9 Pa. $5.95

PERSPECTIVE FOR ARTISTS, Rex Vicat Cole. Depth, perspective of sky and sea, shadows, much more, not usually covered. 391 diagrams, 81 reproductions of drawings and paintings. 279pp. 5⅜ × 8½. 22487-2 Pa. $6.95

DRAWING THE LIVING FIGURE, Joseph Sheppard. Innovative approach to artistic anatomy focuses on specifics of surface anatomy, rather than muscles and bones. Over 170 drawings of live models in front, back and side views, and in widely varying poses. Accompanying diagrams. 177 illustrations. Introduction. Index. 144pp. 8⅜ × 11¼. 26723-7 Pa. $8.95

GOTHIC AND OLD ENGLISH ALPHABETS: 100 Complete Fonts, Dan X. Solo. Add power, elegance to posters, signs, other graphics with 100 stunning copyright-free alphabets: Blackstone, Dolbey, Germania, 97 more—including many lower-case, numerals, punctuation marks. 104pp. 8⅛ × 11. 24695-7 Pa. $8.95

HOW TO DO BEADWORK, Mary White. Fundamental book on craft from simple projects to five-bead chains and woven works. 106 illustrations. 142pp. 5⅜ × 8. 20697-1 Pa. $4.95

THE BOOK OF WOOD CARVING, Charles Marshall Sayers. Finest book for beginners discusses fundamentals and offers 34 designs. "Absolutely first rate . . . well thought out and well executed."—E. J. Tangerman. 118pp. 7¾ × 10⅝. 23654-4 Pa. $5.95

ILLUSTRATED CATALOG OF CIVIL WAR MILITARY GOODS: Union Army Weapons, Insignia, Uniform Accessories, and Other Equipment, Schuyler, Hartley, and Graham. Rare, profusely illustrated 1846 catalog includes Union Army uniform and dress regulations, arms and ammunition, coats, insignia, flags, swords, rifles, etc. 226 illustrations. 160pp. 9 × 12. 24939-5 Pa. $10.95

WOMEN'S FASHIONS OF THE EARLY 1900s: An Unabridged Republication of "New York Fashions, 1909," National Cloak & Suit Co. Rare catalog of mail-order fashions documents women's and children's clothing styles shortly after the turn of the century. Captions offer full descriptions, prices. Invaluable resource for fashion, costume historians. Approximately 725 illustrations. 128pp. 8⅜ × 11¼. 27276-1 Pa. $11.95

THE 1912 AND 1915 GUSTAV STICKLEY FURNITURE CATALOGS, Gustav Stickley. With over 200 detailed illustrations and descriptions, these two catalogs are essential reading and reference materials and identification guides for Stickley furniture. Captions cite materials, dimensions and prices. 112pp. 6½ × 9¼. 26676-1 Pa. $9.95

EARLY AMERICAN LOCOMOTIVES, John H. White, Jr. Finest locomotive engravings from early 19th century: historical (1804–74), main-line (after 1870), special, foreign, etc. 147 plates. 142pp. 11⅜ × 8¼. 22772-3 Pa. $10.95

THE TALL SHIPS OF TODAY IN PHOTOGRAPHS, Frank O. Braynard. Lavishly illustrated tribute to nearly 100 majestic contemporary sailing vessels: Amerigo Vespucci, Clearwater, Constitution, Eagle, Mayflower, Sea Cloud, Victory, many more. Authoritative captions provide statistics, background on each ship. 190 black-and-white photographs and illustrations. Introduction. 128pp. 8⅞ × 11¾. 27163-3 Pa. $13.95

EARLY NINETEENTH-CENTURY CRAFTS AND TRADES, Peter Stockham (ed.). Extremely rare 1807 volume describes to youngsters the crafts and trades of the day: brickmaker, weaver, dressmaker, bookbinder, ropemaker, saddler, many more. Quaint prose, charming illustrations for each craft. 20 black-and-white line illustrations. 192pp. 4⅝ × 6. 27293-1 Pa. $4.95

VICTORIAN FASHIONS AND COSTUMES FROM HARPER'S BAZAR, 1867–1898, Stella Blum (ed.). Day costumes, evening wear, sports clothes, shoes, hats, other accessories in over 1,000 detailed engravings. 320pp. 9⅜ × 12¼. 22990-4 Pa. $13.95

GUSTAV STICKLEY, THE CRAFTSMAN, Mary Ann Smith. Superb study surveys broad scope of Stickley's achievement, especially in architecture. Design philosophy, rise and fall of the Craftsman empire, descriptions and floor plans for many Craftsman houses, more. 86 black-and-white halftones. 31 line illustrations. Introduction. 208pp. 6½ × 9¼. 27210-9 Pa. $9.95

THE LONG ISLAND RAIL ROAD IN EARLY PHOTOGRAPHS, Ron Ziel. Over 220 rare photos, informative text document origin (1844) and development of rail service on Long Island. Vintage views of early trains, locomotives, stations, passengers, crews, much more. Captions. 8⅞ × 11¾. 26301-0 Pa. $13.95

THE BOOK OF OLD SHIPS: From Egyptian Galleys to Clipper Ships, Henry B. Culver. Superb, authoritative history of sailing vessels, with 80 magnificent line illustrations. Galley, bark, caravel, longship, whaler, many more. Detailed, informative text on each vessel by noted naval historian. Introduction. 256pp. 5⅜ × 8½. 27332-6 Pa. $6.95

TEN BOOKS ON ARCHITECTURE, Vitruvius. The most important book ever written on architecture. Early Roman aesthetics, technology, classical orders, site selection, all other aspects. Morgan translation. 331pp. 5⅜ × 8½. 20645-9 Pa. $8.95

THE HUMAN FIGURE IN MOTION, Eadweard Muybridge. More than 4,500 stopped-action photos, in action series, showing undraped men, women, children jumping, lying down, throwing, sitting, wrestling, carrying, etc. 390pp. 7⅞ × 10⅝. 20204-6 Clothbd. $24.95

TREES OF THE EASTERN AND CENTRAL UNITED STATES AND CANADA, William M. Harlow. Best one-volume guide to 140 trees. Full descriptions, woodlore, range, etc. Over 600 illustrations. Handy size. 288pp. 4½ × 6⅜. 20395-6 Pa. $5.95

SONGS OF WESTERN BIRDS, Dr. Donald J. Borror. Complete song and call repertoire of 60 western species, including flycatchers, juncoes, cactus wrens, many more—includes fully illustrated booklet. Cassette and manual 99913-0 $8.95

GROWING AND USING HERBS AND SPICES, Milo Miloradovich. Versatile handbook provides all the information needed for cultivation and use of all the herbs and spices available in North America. 4 illustrations. Index. Glossary. 236pp. 5⅜ × 8½. 25058-X Pa. $6.95

BIG BOOK OF MAZES AND LABYRINTHS, Walter Shepherd. 50 mazes and labyrinths in all—classical, solid, ripple, and more—in one great volume. Perfect inexpensive puzzler for clever youngsters. Full solutions. 112pp. 8⅛ × 11. 22951-3 Pa. $4.95

PIANO TUNING, J. Cree Fischer. Clearest, best book for beginner, amateur. Simple repairs, raising dropped notes, tuning by easy method of flattened fifths. No previous skills needed. 4 illustrations. 201pp. 5⅜ × 8½.   23267-0 Pa. $5.95

A SOURCE BOOK IN THEATRICAL HISTORY, A. M. Nagler. Contemporary observers on acting, directing, make-up, costuming, stage props, machinery, scene design, from Ancient Greece to Chekhov. 611pp. 5⅜ × 8½.   20515-0 Pa. $11.95

THE COMPLETE NONSENSE OF EDWARD LEAR, Edward Lear. All nonsense limericks, zany alphabets, Owl and Pussycat, songs, nonsense botany, etc., illustrated by Lear. Total of 320pp. 5⅜ × 8½. (USO)   20167-8 Pa. $6.95

VICTORIAN PARLOUR POETRY: An Annotated Anthology, Michael R. Turner. 117 gems by Longfellow, Tennyson, Browning, many lesser-known poets. "The Village Blacksmith," "Curfew Must Not Ring Tonight," "Only a Baby Small," dozens more, often difficult to find elsewhere. Index of poets, titles, first lines. xxiii + 325pp. 5⅜ × 8¼.   27044-0 Pa. $8.95

DUBLINERS, James Joyce. Fifteen stories offer vivid, tightly focused observations of the lives of Dublin's poorer classes. At least one, "The Dead," is considered a masterpiece. Reprinted complete and unabridged from standard edition. 160pp. 5³/₁₆ × 8¼.   26870-5 Pa. $1.00

THE HAUNTED MONASTERY and THE CHINESE MAZE MURDERS, Robert van Gulik. Two full novels by van Gulik, set in 7th-century China, continue adventures of Judge Dee and his companions. An evil Taoist monastery, seemingly supernatural events; overgrown topiary maze hides strange crimes. 27 illustrations. 328pp. 5⅜ × 8½.   23502-5 Pa. $7.95

THE BOOK OF THE SACRED MAGIC OF ABRAMELIN THE MAGE, translated by S. MacGregor Mathers. Medieval manuscript of ceremonial magic. Basic document in Aleister Crowley, Golden Dawn groups. 268pp. 5⅜ × 8½.   23211-5 Pa. $8.95

NEW RUSSIAN-ENGLISH AND ENGLISH-RUSSIAN DICTIONARY, M. A. O'Brien. This is a remarkably handy Russian dictionary, containing a surprising amount of information, including over 70,000 entries. 366pp. 4½ × 6⅛.   20208-9 Pa. $9.95

HISTORIC HOMES OF THE AMERICAN PRESIDENTS, Second, Revised Edition, Irvin Haas. A traveler's guide to American Presidential homes, most open to the public, depicting and describing homes occupied by every American President from George Washington to George Bush. With visiting hours, admission charges, travel routes. 175 photographs. Index. 160pp. 8¼ × 11. 26751-2 Pa. $10.95

NEW YORK IN THE FORTIES, Andreas Feininger. 162 brilliant photographs by the well-known photographer, formerly with *Life* magazine. Commuters, shoppers, Times Square at night, much else from city at its peak. Captions by John von Hartz. 181pp. 9¼ × 10¾.   23585-8 Pa. $12.95

INDIAN SIGN LANGUAGE, William Tomkins. Over 525 signs developed by Sioux and other tribes. Written instructions and diagrams. Also 290 pictographs. 111pp. 6⅛ × 9¼.   22029-X Pa. $3.50

ANATOMY: A Complete Guide for Artists, Joseph Sheppard. A master of figure drawing shows artists how to render human anatomy convincingly. Over 460 illustrations. 224pp. 8⅜ × 11¼. 27279-6 Pa. $10.95

MEDIEVAL CALLIGRAPHY: Its History and Technique, Marc Drogin. Spirited history, comprehensive instruction manual covers 13 styles (ca. 4th century thru 15th). Excellent photographs; directions for duplicating medieval techniques with modern tools. 224pp. 8⅜ × 11¼. 26142-5 Pa. $11.95

DRIED FLOWERS: How to Prepare Them, Sarah Whitlock and Martha Rankin. Complete instructions on how to use silica gel, meal and borax, perlite aggregate, sand and borax, glycerine and water to create attractive permanent flower arrangements. 12 illustrations. 32pp. 5⅜ × 8½. 21802-3 Pa. $1.00

EASY-TO-MAKE BIRD FEEDERS FOR WOODWORKERS, Scott D. Campbell. Detailed, simple-to-use guide for designing, constructing, caring for and using feeders. Text, illustrations for 12 classic and contemporary designs. 96pp. 5⅜ × 8½. 25847-5 Pa. $2.95

OLD TIME CRAFTS AND TRADES, Peter Stockham. An 1807 book created to teach children about crafts and trades open to them as future careers. It describes in detailed, nontechnical terms 24 different occupations, among them coachmaker, gardener, hairdresser, lacemaker, shoemaker, wheelwright, copper-plate printer, milliner, trunkmaker, merchant and brewer. Finely detailed engravings illustrate each occupation. 192pp. 4⅜ × 6. 27398-9 Pa. $4.95

THE HISTORY OF UNDERCLOTHES, C. Willett Cunnington and Phyllis Cunnington. Fascinating, well-documented survey covering six centuries of English undergarments, enhanced with over 100 illustrations: 12th-century laced-up bodice, footed long drawers (1795), 19th-century bustles, 19th-century corsets for men, Victorian "bust improvers," much more. 272pp. 5⅜ × 8¼. 27124-2 Pa. $9.95

ARTS AND CRAFTS FURNITURE: The Complete Brooks Catalog of 1912, Brooks Manufacturing Co. Photos and detailed descriptions of more than 150 now very collectible furniture designs from the Arts and Crafts movement depict davenports, settees, buffets, desks, tables, chairs, bedsteads, dressers and more, all built of solid, quarter-sawed oak. Invaluable for students and enthusiasts of antiques, Americana and the decorative arts. 80pp. 6½ × 9¼. 27471-3 Pa. $7.95

HOW WE INVENTED THE AIRPLANE: An Illustrated History, Orville Wright. Fascinating firsthand account covers early experiments, construction of planes and motors, first flights, much more. Introduction and commentary by Fred C. Kelly. 76 photographs. 96pp. 8¼ × 11. 25662-6 Pa. $8.95

THE ARTS OF THE SAILOR: Knotting, Splicing and Ropework, Hervey Garrett Smith. Indispensable shipboard reference covers tools, basic knots and useful hitches; handsewing and canvas work, more. Over 100 illustrations. Delightful reading for sea lovers. 256pp. 5⅜ × 8½. 26440-8 Pa. $7.95

FRANK LLOYD WRIGHT'S FALLINGWATER: The House and Its History, Second, Revised Edition, Donald Hoffmann. A total revision—both in text and illustrations—of the standard document on Fallingwater, the boldest, most personal architectural statement of Wright's mature years, updated with valuable new material from the recently opened Frank Lloyd Wright Archives. "Fascinating"—*The New York Times.* 116 illustrations. 128pp. 9¼ × 10¾. 27430-6 Pa. $10.95

PHOTOGRAPHIC SKETCHBOOK OF THE CIVIL WAR, Alexander Gardner. 100 photos taken on field during the Civil War. Famous shots of Manassas, Harper's Ferry, Lincoln, Richmond, slave pens, etc. 244pp. 10⅝ × 8¼.
22731-6 Pa. $9.95

FIVE ACRES AND INDEPENDENCE, Maurice G. Kains. Great back-to-the-land classic explains basics of self-sufficient farming. The one book to get. 95 illustrations. 397pp. 5⅜ × 8½.
20974-1 Pa. $7.95

SONGS OF EASTERN BIRDS, Dr. Donald J. Borror. Songs and calls of 60 species most common to eastern U.S.: warblers, woodpeckers, flycatchers, thrushes, larks, many more in high-quality recording.
Cassette and manual 99912-2 $8.95

A MODERN HERBAL, Margaret Grieve. Much the fullest, most exact, most useful compilation of herbal material. Gigantic alphabetical encyclopedia, from aconite to zedoary, gives botanical information, medical properties, folklore, economic uses, much else. Indispensable to serious reader. 161 illustrations. 888pp. 6½ × 9¼.
2-vol. set. (USO)
Vol. I: 22798-7 Pa. $9.95
Vol. II: 22799-5 Pa. $9.95

HIDDEN TREASURE MAZE BOOK, Dave Phillips. Solve 34 challenging mazes accompanied by heroic tales of adventure. Evil dragons, people-eating plants, bloodthirsty giants, many more dangerous adversaries lurk at every twist and turn. 34 mazes, stories, solutions. 48pp. 8¼ × 11.
24566-7 Pa. $2.95

LETTERS OF W. A. MOZART, Wolfgang A. Mozart. Remarkable letters show bawdy wit, humor, imagination, musical insights, contemporary musical world; includes some letters from Leopold Mozart. 276pp. 5⅜ × 8½.
22859-2 Pa. $7.95

BASIC PRINCIPLES OF CLASSICAL BALLET, Agrippina Vaganova. Great Russian theoretician, teacher explains methods for teaching classical ballet. 118 illustrations. 175pp. 5⅜ × 8½.
22036-2 Pa. $4.95

THE JUMPING FROG, Mark Twain. Revenge edition. The original story of The Celebrated Jumping Frog of Calaveras County, a hapless French translation, and Twain's hilarious "retranslation" from the French. 12 illustrations. 66pp. 5⅜ × 8½.
22686-7 Pa. $3.95

BEST REMEMBERED POEMS, Martin Gardner (ed.). The 126 poems in this superb collection of 19th- and 20th-century British and American verse range from Shelley's "To a Skylark" to the impassioned "Renascence" of Edna St. Vincent Millay and to Edward Lear's whimsical "The Owl and the Pussycat." 224pp. 5⅜ × 8½.
27165-X Pa. $1.95

COMPLETE SONNETS, William Shakespeare. Over 150 exquisite poems deal with love, friendship, the tyranny of time, beauty's evanescence, death and other themes in language of remarkable power, precision and beauty. Glossary of archaic terms. 80pp. 5³⁄₁₆ × 8¼.
26686-9 Pa. $1.00

BODIES IN A BOOKSHOP, R. T. Campbell. Challenging mystery of blackmail and murder with ingenious plot and superbly drawn characters. In the best tradition of British suspense fiction. 192pp. 5⅜ × 8½.
24720-1 Pa. $5.95

THE WIT AND HUMOR OF OSCAR WILDE, Alvin Redman (ed.). More than 1,000 ripostes, paradoxes, wisecracks: Work is the curse of the drinking classes; I can resist everything except temptation; etc. 258pp. 5⅜ × 8½. 20602-5 Pa. $5.95

SHAKESPEARE LEXICON AND QUOTATION DICTIONARY, Alexander Schmidt. Full definitions, locations, shades of meaning in every word in plays and poems. More than 50,000 exact quotations. 1,485pp. 6½ × 9¼. 2-vol. set.
Vol. I: 22726-X Pa. $16.95
Vol. 2: 22727-8 Pa. $15.95

SELECTED POEMS, Emily Dickinson. Over 100 best-known, best-loved poems by one of America's foremost poets, reprinted from authoritative early editions. No comparable edition at this price. Index of first lines. 64pp. 5³⁄₁₆ × 8¼. 26466-1 Pa. $1.00

CELEBRATED CASES OF JUDGE DEE (DEE GOONG AN), translated by Robert van Gulik. Authentic 18th-century Chinese detective novel; Dee and associates solve three interlocked cases. Led to van Gulik's own stories with same characters. Extensive introduction. 9 illustrations. 237pp. 5⅜ × 8½. 23337-5 Pa. $6.95

THE MALLEUS MALEFICARUM OF KRAMER AND SPRENGER, translated by Montague Summers. Full text of most important witchhunter's "bible," used by both Catholics and Protestants. 278pp. 6⅝ × 10. 22802-9 Pa. $11.95

SPANISH STORIES/CUENTOS ESPAÑOLES: A Dual-Language Book, Angel Flores (ed.). Unique format offers 13 great stories in Spanish by Cervantes, Borges, others. Faithful English translations on facing pages. 352pp. 5⅜ × 8½. 25399-6 Pa. $8.95

THE CHICAGO WORLD'S FAIR OF 1893: A Photographic Record, Stanley Appelbaum (ed.). 128 rare photos show 200 buildings, Beaux-Arts architecture, Midway, original Ferris Wheel, Edison's kinetoscope, more. Architectural emphasis; full text. 116pp. 8¼ × 11. 23990-X Pa. $9.95

OLD QUEENS, N.Y., IN EARLY PHOTOGRAPHS, Vincent F. Seyfried and William Asadorian. Over 160 rare photographs of Maspeth, Jamaica, Jackson Heights, and other areas. Vintage views of DeWitt Clinton mansion, 1939 World's Fair and more. Captions. 192pp. 8⅞ × 11. 26358-4 Pa. $12.95

CAPTURED BY THE INDIANS: 15 Firsthand Accounts, 1750-1870, Frederick Drimmer. Astounding true historical accounts of grisly torture, bloody conflicts, relentless pursuits, miraculous escapes and more, by people who lived to tell the tale. 384pp. 5⅜ × 8½. 24901-8 Pa. $8.95

THE WORLD'S GREAT SPEECHES, Lewis Copeland and Lawrence W. Lamm (eds.). Vast collection of 278 speeches of Greeks to 1970. Powerful and effective models; unique look at history. 842pp. 5⅜ × 8½. 20468-5 Pa. $14.95

THE BOOK OF THE SWORD, Sir Richard F. Burton. Great Victorian scholar/adventurer's eloquent, erudite history of the "queen of weapons"—from prehistory to early Roman Empire. Evolution and development of early swords, variations (sabre, broadsword, cutlass, scimitar, etc.), much more. 336pp. 6⅛ × 9¼. 25434-8 Pa. $8.95

AUTOBIOGRAPHY: The Story of My Experiments with Truth, Mohandas K. Gandhi. Boyhood, legal studies, purification, the growth of the Satyagraha (nonviolent protest) movement. Critical, inspiring work of the man responsible for the freedom of India. 480pp. 5⅜ × 8½. (USO) 24593-4 Pa. $8.95

CELTIC MYTHS AND LEGENDS, T. W. Rolleston. Masterful retelling of Irish and Welsh stories and tales. Cuchulain, King Arthur, Deirdre, the Grail, many more. First paperback edition. 58 full-page illustrations. 512pp. 5⅜ × 8½.
26507-2 Pa. $9.95

THE PRINCIPLES OF PSYCHOLOGY, William James. Famous long course complete, unabridged. Stream of thought, time perception, memory, experimental methods; great work decades ahead of its time. 94 figures. 1,391pp. 5⅜ × 8½. 2-vol. set.
Vol. I: 20381-6 Pa. $12.95
Vol. II: 20382-4 Pa. $12.95

THE WORLD AS WILL AND REPRESENTATION, Arthur Schopenhauer. Definitive English translation of Schopenhauer's life work, correcting more than 1,000 errors, omissions in earlier translations. Translated by E. F. J. Payne. Total of 1,269pp. 5⅜ × 8½. 2-vol. set. Vol. 1: 21761-2 Pa. $11.95
Vol. 2: 21762-0 Pa. $11.95

MAGIC AND MYSTERY IN TIBET, Madame Alexandra David-Neel. Experiences among lamas, magicians, sages, sorcerers, Bonpa wizards. A true psychic discovery. 32 illustrations. 321pp. 5⅜ × 8½. (USO) 22682-4 Pa. $8.95

THE EGYPTIAN BOOK OF THE DEAD, E. A. Wallis Budge. Complete reproduction of Ani's papyrus, finest ever found. Full hieroglyphic text, interlinear transliteration, word-for-word translation, smooth translation. 533pp. 6½ × 9¼.
21866-X Pa. $9.95

MATHEMATICS FOR THE NONMATHEMATICIAN, Morris Kline. Detailed, college-level treatment of mathematics in cultural and historical context, with numerous exercises. Recommended Reading Lists. Tables. Numerous figures. 641pp. 5⅜ × 8½. 24823-2 Pa. $11.95

THEORY OF WING SECTIONS: Including a Summary of Airfoil Data, Ira H. Abbott and A. E. von Doenhoff. Concise compilation of subsonic aerodynamic characteristics of NACA wing sections, plus description of theory. 350pp. of tables. 693pp. 5⅜ × 8½. 60586-8 Pa. $14.95

THE RIME OF THE ANCIENT MARINER, Gustave Doré, S. T. Coleridge. Doré's finest work; 34 plates capture moods, subtleties of poem. Flawless full-size reproductions printed on facing pages with authoritative text of poem. "Beautiful. Simply beautiful."—*Publisher's Weekly*. 77pp. 9¼ × 12. 22305-1 Pa. $6.95

NORTH AMERICAN INDIAN DESIGNS FOR ARTISTS AND CRAFTSPEOPLE, Eva Wilson. Over 360 authentic copyright-free designs adapted from Navajo blankets, Hopi pottery, Sioux buffalo hides, more. Geometrics, symbolic figures, plant and animal motifs, etc. 128pp. 8⅜ × 11. (EUK) 25341-4 Pa. $7.95

SCULPTURE: Principles and Practice, Louis Slobodkin. Step-by-step approach to clay, plaster, metals, stone; classical and modern. 253 drawings, photos. 255pp. 8⅛ × 11. 22960-2 Pa. $10.95

THE INFLUENCE OF SEA POWER UPON HISTORY, 1660-1783, A. T. Mahan. Influential classic of naval history and tactics still used as text in war colleges. First paperback edition. 4 maps. 24 battle plans. 640pp. 5⅜ × 8½.
25509-3 Pa. $12.95

THE STORY OF THE TITANIC AS TOLD BY ITS SURVIVORS, Jack Winocour (ed.). What it was really like. Panic, despair, shocking inefficiency, and a little heroism. More thrilling than any fictional account. 26 illustrations. 320pp. 5⅜ × 8½.
20610-6 Pa. $8.95

FAIRY AND FOLK TALES OF THE IRISH PEASANTRY, William Butler Yeats (ed.). Treasury of 64 tales from the twilight world of Celtic myth and legend: "The Soul Cages," "The Kildare Pooka," "King O'Toole and his Goose," many more. Introduction and Notes by W. B. Yeats. 352pp. 5⅜ × 8½.
26941-8 Pa. $8.95

BUDDHIST MAHAYANA TEXTS, E. B. Cowell and Others (eds.). Superb, accurate translations of basic documents in Mahayana Buddhism, highly important in history of religions. The Buddha-karita of Asvaghosha, Larger Sukhavativyuha, more. 448pp. 5⅜ × 8½.
25552-2 Pa. $9.95

ONE TWO THREE . . . INFINITY: Facts and Speculations of Science, George Gamow. Great physicist's fascinating, readable overview of contemporary science: number theory, relativity, fourth dimension, entropy, genes, atomic structure, much more. 128 illustrations. Index. 352pp. 5⅜ × 8½.
25664-2 Pa. $8.95

ENGINEERING IN HISTORY, Richard Shelton Kirby, et al. Broad, nontechnical survey of history's major technological advances: birth of Greek science, industrial revolution, electricity and applied science, 20th-century automation, much more. 181 illustrations. ". . . excellent . . ."—Isis. Bibliography. vii + 530pp. 5⅜ × 8¼.
26412-2 Pa. $14.95

Prices subject to change without notice.
Available at your book dealer or write for free catalog to Dept. GI, Dover Publications, Inc., 31 East 2nd St., Mineola, N.Y. 11501. Dover publishes more than 500 books each year on science, elementary and advanced mathematics, biology, music, art, literary history, social sciences and other areas.